POLITICS IN A CHANGING WORLD

A COMPARATIVE INTRODUCTION TO POLITICAL SCIENCE

SIXTH EDITION

MARCUS E. ETHRIDGE
University of Wisconsin-Milwaukee

HOWARD HANDELMAN
University of Wisconsin-Milwaukee

WADSWORTH
CENGAGE Learning·

Australia • Brazil • Japan • Korea • Mexico • Singapore • Spain • United Kingdom • United States

Politics in a Changing World: A Comparative Introduction to Political Science, Sixth Edition
Marcus E. Ethridge, Howard Handelman

Executive Editor: Carolyn Merrill

Acquisitions Editor: Anita Devine

Associate Development Editor: Katie Hayes

Assistant Editor: Laura Ross

Editorial Assistant: Scott Greenan

Program Manager: Caitlin Green

Marketing Communications Manger:
Heather Baxley

Senior Content Project Manager: Josh Allen

Art Director: Linda Helcher

Senior Rights Acquisition Account Manager:
Jennifer Meyer Dare

Manufacturing Planner: Fola Orekoya

Production Service: PreMediaGlobal

Cover Designer: Rokusek Design

Cover Credits: Seleznev Oleg/© Shutterstock,
James Steidl/© Shutterstock, Phecsone/
© Shutterstock, E Alisa/© Shutterstock,
Aleksejs Krivcuns/© Shutterstock, Fuyu liu/
© Shutterstock, Yu Lan/© Shutterstock

For product information and technology assistance, contact us at
Cengage Learning Customer & Sales Support, 1-800-354-9706.
For permission to use material from this text or product, submit all requests online at **www.cengage.com/permissions**.
Further permissions questions can be emailed to
permissionrequest@cengage.com.

Library of Congress Control Number: 2011942004

ISBN-13: 978-1-111-83253-7

ISBN-10: 1-111-83253-6

Wadsworth
20 Channel Center Street
Boston, MA 02210
USA

Cengage Learning is a leading provider of customized learning solutions with office locations around the globe, including Singapore, the United Kingdom, Australia, Mexico, Brazil, and Japan. Locate your local office at **international.cengage.com/region**.

Cengage Learning products are represented in Canada by Nelson Education, Ltd.

For your course and learning solutions, visit **www.cengage.com**.

Purchase any of our products at your local college store or at our preferred online store **www.cengagebrain.com**.

Instructors: Please visit **login.cengage.com** and log in to access instructor-specific resources.

Printed in the U.S.A.
1 2 3 4 5 6 7 15 14 13 12 11

CONTENTS

PREFACE

We designed the sixth edition of *Politics in a Changing World* to provide a foundation for understanding political life and the increasingly diverse field of political science.

Although we hope the book will be helpful for those who become political science majors, its primary purpose is to introduce students from a wide range of fields to the discipline. Citizens in every walk of life—not only politicians, government officials, and political analysts—need to understand the consequences of political choices and the processes through which those choices are made.

THE CHANGING WORLD IN THE TWENTY-FIRST CENTURY

Revising a political science textbook through six editions is a wonderfully compelling way to confront the reality of political change. When we wrote the first edition, neither the United States nor Europe had ever experienced a significant terrorist attack, partisan politics in the United States was far less polarized, the Institutional Revolutionary Party (PRI) still controlled Mexico, Saddam Hussein had a firm grip on power in Iraq as did Hosni Mubarak in Egypt, Western economies were still booming, India was struggling to achieve sustained economic growth, and the North American Free Trade Agreement was just about to take effect. Political scientists were only beginning to consider how international affairs would be changed by the end of the Cold War, and there was widespread optimism that genuine democracy was dawning in Russia.

Although political scientists correctly predicted few of these changes and events, the accumulated knowledge generated by the discipline helps us to make sense of them. Studies of voting behavior, the causes of war, the process of political development, and the impact of economics on politics help us understand what factors will be important as government and international relations evolve in the years to come. The increasing importance of international trade will figure in both foreign and domestic policy in nearly all countries, and the protracted state of cultural and ethnic conflict—particularly conflict involving radical Islamic fundamentalism—will influence many of the choices governments and citizens will make. The spread of democracy throughout the world has slowed, but the trend toward greater openness in both the political and the economic spheres is firmly entrenched in many areas. Technological advances and the spread of the Internet will shape a great deal of our lives, including commerce, our expectations of privacy, and national security. Political science sheds light on all of these factors.

Politics in a Changing World focuses on the ways in which accumulated knowledge in political science helps us account for the basic changes taking place in politics, and it explores the ways in which those changes have forced political scientists to revise their concepts, theories, and ideas.

POLITICS IN DIFFERENT NATIONS

Beginning with the first edition of *Politics in a Changing World*, we have been guided by the firm conviction that politics cannot be understood fully by considering only a single country. Just as a biologist cannot hope to understand the basic elements of life by studying one species, and just as a physicist cannot hope to understand the nature of combustion by studying only one chemical compound, we cannot understand politics if we restrict ourselves to analysis of a single political system.

Thus, as in the previous editions, a key feature of the sixth edition of *Politics in a Changing World* is its separate chapters on different countries—the United States, Great Britain, Russia (and its predecessor, the Soviet Union), China, and Mexico—along with a chapter on the special problems of developing nations. Although these chapters are not intended even to summarize what is known about those governments, they allow us to give meaningful contexts to our discussions of elections, parties, legislatures, chief executives, courts, and interest groups. They also provide useful historical grounding. For example, the story of Britain's gradual development of democracy is important if we are to understand its current party system, and we need to know something about the Mexican Revolution to appreciate modern political issues and institutions in that country.

Most readers of *Politics in a Changing World* are students born in the United States, and most of them have considerable knowledge about the U.S. system of government. But we believe that even a limited understanding of one's own political system is enhanced by coming to understand government and politics in other countries. Government in the United States is unique in many ways, and helping students to appreciate its special nature is one of our objectives in designing this comparative section of the book.

THE PLAN OF THE BOOK

When the discipline of political science reached its adolescence during the 1950s, leading political science departments were hotly divided between those who approached their work with advanced statistical tools and quasi-experimental research methods and those who used more traditional approaches. Over the years, that division between "empiricist-quantifiers" and "traditionalists" was largely replaced by an increasingly diverse array of distinct subfields. Some political scientists study institutions, others study individual behavior, some study ideology, and still others apply economic theories to politics. There is also a great division between those who study government in many nations and those who emphasize a single nation or area. As discussed in Chapter 1, there is now something of a backlash against quantitative analysis in the discipline, although statistics and mathematics continue to dominate political science research methods.

The divisions in contemporary political science present significant challenges for any introductory text. However, we are convinced that the diversity of perspectives, approaches, and methods in political science is beneficial. Specialists in one subfield often make good use of insights generated in other subfields. Indeed, the opportunity to bring together the diverse elements of the discipline has confirmed that impression for us, and we hope our positive feelings about political science as a discipline are communicated effectively to our readers.

We have organized the book into five parts: Fundamentals, Political Behavior, Political Institutions, Politics in Selected Nations, and International Relations. Each section contains chapters devoted to more specific topics. Part IV comprises the chapters on five countries and the developing world. These chapters can be read as a special unit after the more general chapters are covered, or they may be used as supplementary reading during discussions of political behavior, institutions, or international relations.

Each of the chapters devoted to specific country contains a map to help readers understand that country's geographical context. Key terms in each chapter are introduced in boldface and are defined in the Glossary. Although the material may be organized in different ways, we have arranged the chapters to correspond to the steps that citizens typically take in approaching politics: Culture and ideology affect us first, then various options for political activity present themselves, and then we consider the institutions we wish to influence. Special issues pertaining to gender transcend the study of ideology, behavior, institutions, and political development, and so appropriate sections devoted to those issues are included in many chapters. Similarly, political economy is relevant to virtually all areas of our discipline, and readers will find that topic addressed throughout the text.

NEW TO THIS EDITION

We have included several changes and numerous updates for the sixth edition of *Politics in a Changing World*. Some of these changes bring the text up to date, and others reflect helpful suggestions from students and instructors.

A Closer Look

New "A Closer Look" boxes provide additional information on examples of chapter topics.

New Organization

To better reflect the way you teach your course, the chapters on executive institutions and bureaucratic institutions have been combined into a new chapter called "Executive Institutions, Political Leadership, and Bureaucracy." The content has been streamlined and shortened while maintaining its breadth and depth of coverage.

Extensive Updates Throughout

The wars in Iraq and Afghanistan, and the broader tensions associated with international terrorism, profoundly affect both domestic and international politics in most parts of the world. While the death of al Qaeda chief Osama bin Laden was an important psychological and tactical victory for the war on terror, it is still uncertain whether his death will actually reduce the terrorist threat. Rapidly increasing prices for food in the less-developed nations (an increase tied, in part, to the shift of croplands to biofuels) have exacerbated conflicts and deepened divisions in many nations. Readers will encounter discussions of issues related to those events in several chapters.

Both the 2008 U.S. presidential election and the 2010 congressional elections were historic, and we include extensive coverage of their implications for the study of voting behavior, public opinion, and the future of U.S. government. China's astounding economic growth (perhaps now being replicated by India), the threat of Iran's and North Korea's nuclear weapons programs, and the still uncertain consequences of Osama bin Laden's death are but three of the important forces that will shape international relations for decades. We include significant coverage of these subjects.

As in earlier editions, we also include accessible, brief discussions of recent political science research. For example, Chapter 1 discusses the nature of the ongoing global financial crisis. Chapter 4 contains extensive new data on the gender gap, voter turnout, and the impact of proportional representation or single-member districts on parliamentary elections. In Chapter 5 we examine the rise of Europe's radical right parties, caused in large part by economic insecurity, joblessness, and fears of massive immigration from the developing world (particularly Islamic immigration). Chapter 6 contains a discussion of recent research on interest group strategies. Chapter 7 features a new box (A Closer Look) on how the size of a national legislature may influence how much it wastes tax revenue. Because chief executives increasingly influence policy through their control of bureaucracies, we now discuss executive and bureaucratic institutions in a single chapter (Chapter 8).

As in previous editions, Chapters 10 through 13 and 15 contain case studies of the politics in long-established democracies (the United States and Great Britain), former communist (Russia) and reformed communist (China) nations, and a struggling new democracy (Mexico). Chapter 14 offers a more comprehensive analysis of the special challenges facing the world's less politically and economically developed nations, including a new case study on Kenya. Throughout we apply and test many of the theories and ideas discussed in the previous chapters. Chapter 10 includes discussion of the 2010 congressional elections and the subsequent increase in political partisanship, the new Patient Protection and Affordable Care Act, and other recent developments. In Chapter 11 we discuss the transfer of political power in Britain from Labour to the Conservatives, and the highly unusual Conservative coalition with the Liberal Democrats. Chapter 13 examines China's dramatic economic gains along with the many problems that growth has created. In Chapter 14 we discuss the important implications of the ongoing prodemocracy, mass protests in the Arab world. In Chapter 15 we analyze Mexico's shaky democracy and the country's massive war on drugs. These new sections are, we hope, interesting in themselves, but we included them because they also help to clarify basic concepts.

Instructor and Student Supplements

Instructor's Manual/Test Bank and Book-Specific PowerPoints on SSO for Ethridge/Handelman's *Politics in a Changing World*, 6th Edition
ISBN-10: 1111945969 | ISBN-13: 9781111945961

A revised Instructor's Manual and Test Bank offer chapter key points, suggestions for class discussions, writing assignments, and exam questions to make course preparation easier. A set of book-specific PowerPoint® lectures makes it easy for you to assemble, edit, publish, and present custom lectures for your course. The slides provide outlines specific to every chapter of *Politics in a Changing World* and include tables, statistical charts, graphs, and photos from the book as well as outside sources. In addition, the slides are completely customizable for a powerful and personalized presentation. The Instructor's Manual/Test Bank and PowerPoint lectures have all been updated with new material to reflect changes in the new edition.

Companion Website for Ethridge/Handelman's Politics in a Changing World
ISBN-10: 1111826358 | ISBN-13: 9781111826352

Students will find open access to learning objectives, tutorial quizzes, chapter glossaries, flashcards, and crossword puzzles, all correlated by chapter. Instructors also have access to the Instructor's Manual and PowerPoints.

CourseReader: Introduction to Political Science
ISBN-10 1133232167 |9781133232162 CourseReader 0-30: Introduction to Political Science Printed Access Card

1133232159 | 9781133232155 CourseReader 0-30: Introduction to Political Science Instant Access Code

1133232124 | 9781133232124 CourseReader 0-60: Introduction to Political Science Printed Access Card

1133232132 | 9781133232131 CourseReader 0-60: Introduction to Political Science Instant Access Code

1133232183 | 9781133232186 CourseReader Unlimited: Introduction to Political Science Printed Access Card

1133232191 | 9781133232193 CourseReader Unlimited: Introduction to Political Science Instant Access Code

CourseReader: Introduction to Political Science is a fully customizable online reader which provides access to hundreds of readings and audio and video selections from multiple disciplines. This easy-to-use solution allows you to select exactly the content you need for your courses and is loaded with convenient pedagogical features like highlighting, printing, note taking, and audio downloads. You have the freedom to assign individualized content at an affordable price. CourseReader: Introduction to Political Science is the perfect complement to any class.

ACKNOWLEDGMENTS

One of the most rewarding aspects of writing this new edition was the opportunity for each of us to explore in detail subjects beyond our current specialized interests. Nevertheless, several colleagues have provided valuable assistance in correcting errors and omissions, pointing us to helpful examples, and sharpening our arguments. Shale Horowitz, Uk Heo, John Bohte, David Garnham, Steve Redd, and Don Pienkos generously gave their time to answer endless questions and to provide sources for us to explore. Sandee Enriquez and Kate Day helped Marc locate some highly interesting insights through their diligent research. In addition, the book reflects the suggestions of the following professors and specialists who participated in Wadsworth's rigorous review process: Finally, our editor helped to guide this new edition, gently keeping us on schedule and working with us to ensure that it will be stimulating and accessible to students.

About the Authors

Marcus E. Ethridge is emeritus professor of political science at the University of Wisconsin, Milwaukee. He is a specialist in the study of American government, focusing on interest group behavior, rational-choice theory, and administrative law. His publications include *The Political Research Experience, Legislative Participation in Implementation*, and numerous articles in the *American Journal of Political Science, Political Research Quarterly*, the *Journal of Politics*, and other journals. His latest book is *The Case for Gridlock: Democracy, Organized Power, and the Legal Foundations of American Government*.

Howard Handelman is emeritus professor of political science at the University of Wisconsin, Milwaukee. He specializes in Latin American politics and the politics of developing nations. His books include *The Challenge of Third World Development* (Seventh Edition), *Üçüncü Dünyanin: Meydan Okuryan Ilerles,i* (Turkish-language edition of *The Challenge of Third World Development*), and *Mexican Politics: The Dynamics of Change*. He has contributed journal articles to the *Latin American Research Review, Canadian Journal of Latin American Studies*, and *Studies in Comparative International Development*, among others.

PART I

FUNDAMENTALS

Like many other disciplines, political science addresses a wide range of problems, issues, and topics, employing a diverse assortment of research approaches. Nevertheless, there are some concepts that are important to everyone interested in the field. Chapter 1 includes basic information on definitions of politics and government, an exploration of the functions of government, approaches to classifying governments, a discussion of the stakes of politics, and a brief digression regarding the different ways in which political scientists conduct research.

Chapter 2 is devoted to an overview of the most commonly discussed ideologies that influence the way we think about politics and government. Conservatism, liberalism, Marxism, and other ideologies frame debates about specific political issues, and they also figure in the way we evaluate different countries, the causes of war, and efforts to understand political change. A basic understanding of these ways of thinking about politics and government is essential for all political scientists.

CHAPTER 1

Politics, Government, and Political Science

Rebels fought against forces loyal to the dictatorship of Muammar Gaddafi, who had held power in Libya since 1969. With the assistance of France, Britain, and the U.S., the rebels toppled Gaddafi's regime in September 2011.

- Politics and Government Defined
- Government Functions
- Kinds of Governments
- The Stakes of Politics

- Politics in a Changing World
- Conclusion: Why Study Political Science?

The worldwide economic crisis that began in 2007 has had devastating effects, leading some economists to label it the "Great Recession"* (see A Closer Look 1.1). The contraction in credit and consumer spending led to a major destruction of wealth, increasing unemployment in nearly all industrialized nations. Budget deficits exploded when governments attempted to stimulate their economies through increased spending, prompting fears of future runaway inflation.

Like all major economic events, the causes of this crisis are a matter of some dispute. But virtually every expert agrees that government is centrally involved in the explanation. Through a combination of ill-considered actions and inactions, decisions made in governments were important factors in creating the crisis. Moreover, changes in the stability of government budgets and in the role of government regulation of the economy will be its most important long-term legacies.

The financial crisis has created problems for citizens in countries that had recently enjoyed a substantial period of prosperity. So far, it has had less impact on the developing world. But many other difficulties—most of them unrelated to the financial meltdown—pre-dated this crisis and will certainly continue after it subsides. Many millions of people in Africa, Latin America, Asia, and elsewhere live in terrible poverty; the AIDS crisis still claims thousands each year throughout the world, particularly in parts

---

* Several commentators began using this term during 2009. Among them is Robert J. Samuelson, a syndicated columnist whose writings appear in the *Washington Post*. See his "The Great Recession's Stranglehold," *Washington Post*, July 12, 2010.

of Africa, India, and China; Russia is becoming less democratic and increasingly antagonistic to the West (and to some of its neighbors); tensions in the Middle East remain high; armed conflict continues in Afghanistan, Pakistan, the Darfur region of Sudan, and in many other places; a nuclear Iran appears to be inevitable; and many scientists believe that a radical restructuring of the world's industrial economies is essential if we are to avoid the catastrophic effects of global climate change.

Political decisions within and among nations will largely determine whether the future is one of expanding progress, prosperity, and an improved quality of life or one of escalating war, worsening economic conditions, and tyranny. The way governments work (or fail to work) has tremendous effects on all of us.

At the same time, we should not lose sight of the fact that politics does not explain or determine *everything*; many of the best things in life have little or nothing to do with politics. Personal relationships, the satisfaction of learning and working, artistic achievement and enjoyment, the challenges and deep fulfillment of raising a child—we can experience all of those things without doing anything "political." Most aspects of our day-to-day lives do not necessarily involve political institutions, issues, and movements. There is much more to life than politics.

Politics and government have to do with *public* policies and *public* decision making, concerns that most people think about only occasionally. Yet political decisions do have a huge impact beyond purely governmental matters. Political decisions frequently affect parenting, for example. In most countries, the government determines what material children must learn in school and when they will learn it. Often the government mandates what kinds of health-related precautions parents and teachers must take to protect students and what kinds of discipline and religious training children can be given in public schools. Most governments restrict artistic expression. Sometimes these limits restrict exhibitions seen as improper in their cultures, and sometimes they are intended to prevent the dissemination of ideas that may foster dissent and disloyalty.* Governments sometimes restrict political expressions that may undermine stability or that breed ethnic or religious intolerance, raising difficult questions about how to balance basic elements of democracy. Virtually everywhere, governments regulate membership in selected professions (including not only law and medicine but also plumbing, architecture, and many other fields), restricting career choices. Governments are the only organizations that may legally apply the death penalty to their citizens. And, of course, when nations decide to make war on one another, virtually all aspects of their citizens' personal lives are drastically changed.

Why politics has such pervasive effects is itself a controversial matter. Some contend that government is extensively involved in our lives because much of what people do as individuals affects the economic opportunities of others, the environment, or public safety, and citizens demand that government take action to control those

---

* In Egypt in 2010, a blogger named Ahmed Mustafa was prosecuted for "criticizing the army" in a blog post in which he accused Egypt's top military academy of favoritism. An Iranian court sentenced Hossein Derakhshan, a blogger credited with sparking the blogging boom in Iran, to 19 years in prison. Derakhshan was arrested in 2008 and was often denied access to a lawyer. Freedom House reported that declines in press freedom have recently outnumbered improvements by a 2-to-1 margin. (See www.FreedomHouse.org for more details.)

A CLOSER LOOK

(1.1

The "Great Recession" of 2008–2009

The financial crisis that began in 2007 quickly produced an economic crisis with worldwide repercussions. The impacts have been severe, and they will be felt for years to come. Global unemployment increased by 8.4 million as early as 2008. At the end of 2010, several European countries had unemployment rates well over 10 percent, and unemployment was nearly that high in many others. The shift to lower-productivity jobs resulted in over 200 million more working poor around the world, many of whom are in South Asia.*

In 2011, over 23 percent of U.S. homes financed with mortgages were "under water," a phrase used to indicate that the owner owes more on the mortgage than the home is worth. In normal times, only about 5 percent of mortgaged homes are in this situation. U.S. households experienced an *average* of nearly $100,000 in lost wealth and income, according to a study by former Treasury Department economist Phillip Swagel.[1] In reaction to the severe downturn, consumers reduced spending, credit became more difficult to obtain, and businesses became more reluctant to invest and hire new workers.

There is a great deal of debate regarding the causes of the crisis. Most economists conclude that a critical factor was the proliferation of "subprime" mortgages in the U.S. during the early part of the decade. With historically low interest rates, real estate prices were increasing rapidly, and lenders began approving mortgage applications from borrowers who were not good credit risks. Some members of Congress pressured the Federal Home Loan Mortgage Corporation ("Freddie Mac") and the Federal National Mortgage Association ("Fannie Mae") to make credit more easily available so that more Americans could afford homeownership.

* These figures are from www.worldbank.org and other sources.

This pressure accelerated the increase in home prices, eventually causing a housing "bubble." *

Many financial institutions—including many with global affiliations—had invested in mortgage-based securities built on "bundles" of good loans and bad loans. As long as the market value of real estate kept going up, there were few problems. But when borrowers began to default on their loans, real estate prices dropped quickly, and these securities lost a great deal of their value. A major liquidity crisis ensued. There was a sharp drop in investment capital, people stopped spending, employers stopped hiring, and banks sharply reduced their lending. And, because the economies of most of the world's nations are intricately connected, the U.S. financial crisis quickly became an international economic crisis.

The U.S. government began a series of measures to keep some financial institutions from collapsing, making billions of dollars in credit available. These controversial "bailouts" were initially for financial institutions, but the government used them to keep General Motors and Chrysler from going bankrupt. In addition, governments in nearly all the developed nations increased spending to stimulate the economy and generate jobs. The deficits created by this spending are huge. According to two

* In this context, a "bubble" refers to a period of "trade in high volumes at prices that are considerably at variance with intrinsic values." The idea is that a rapid increase in prices for something (stocks, real estate, etc.) takes place for some reason—perhaps in this case it was the unusually low interest rates set by the Federal Reserve during the years after the 9/11 attacks—and the rising prices draw speculators into the market. The increased demand means that prices rise even more rapidly. Eventually, the "bubble" bursts, and prices fall quickly, reducing the value of assets held by investors and banks. See Ronald King, Vernon Smith, and Mark V. van Boening, "The Robustness of Bubbles and Crashes in Experimental Stock Markets," in *Nonlinear Dynamics and Evolutionary Economics*, R. H. Day and P. Chen, eds. (New York: Oxford University Press, 1993).

effects. Government policies in many countries restrict industrial development because of problems with pollution. Private actions often have public consequences, and many governments regulate those consequences. The nature of modern life thus accounts for a growing governmental role as societies turn to government to safeguard widely shared interests in an increasingly complex, technological age.

1.1

A CLOSER LOOK

| FIGURE 1.1 | The Exploding Public Debt Among OECD Countries |

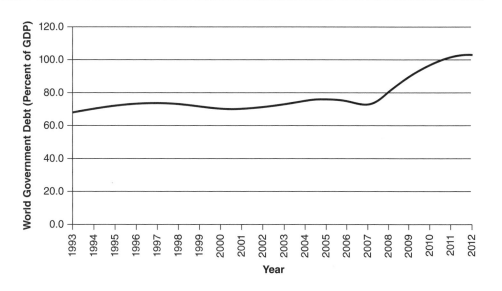

Source: Organization for Economic Cooperation and Development (OECD). There are currently 34 member nations in the OECD, including the United States, the United Kingdom, France, Germany, Australia, Chile, Mexico, Korea, and Poland. The information used to construct this table is contained in the OECD's "Economic Outlook" report, available at www.oecd.org/oecdEconomic Outlook.

British economists, "the scale of intervention to support the banks in the UK, US, and the euro-area during the current crisis … totals over $14 trillion or almost a quarter of global GDP. It dwarfs any previous state support of the banking system."[*]

[*] See Andrew G. Haldane and Piergiorgio Alessandri, "Banking on the State," a presentation delivered at the Federal Reserve Bank of Chicago Twelfth Annual International Banking Conference on "The International Financial Crisis: Have the Rules of Finance Changed?" Chicago, 25 September 2009. Available at www.bis.org/review/r091111e.pdf.

The recession in the U.S. officially ended in June 2009, but the unemployment remains high in nearly all developed nations, and the exploding budget deficits will have a long-term effect. (See Figure 1.1.) The extraordinary level of public debt may lead to serious inflation problems and sluggish growth in the years to come.

If nothing else, the "Great Recession" demonstrates the close connection between politics and economics. Government policy may or may not have been part of the cause of the crisis, but governments have taken dramatic steps to respond to it, and the effects of these measures—positive and negative—will be felt for decades.

There are other reasons for the growing role of government. Large numbers of citizens in many countries feel that government should be used as a tool to enforce and strengthen certain moral principles. In the United States, contending groups vigorously debate the morality (and legality) of abortion, while in some countries people argue for and against laws allowing husbands to beat their wives.* In these and many other instances, people demand government actions that reflect their moral or religious views, and many governments respond by enacting new restrictions and regulations.

Governments also apply power in pursuit of economic objectives. Sometimes this power is used to stimulate economic growth and opportunity or to reduce economic inequality, and in other cases government power is employed to increase the wealth of individuals or groups that have gained access to government officials. The British National Health Service, established shortly after World War II, is an example of the use of government power to reduce economic inequality; various laws passed under the Somoza regime (1937–1979) in prerevolutionary Nicaragua employed government power to maintain a privileged status for the ruling family and its allies, making inequality more severe.

In short, government can be beneficial or devastating, but its significance is growing almost everywhere. Given the potential impact of government on so much of our lives, it is important to understand how government works, how it changes, how it can be influenced, and why different forms or designs of government operate differently.

Political science is the effort to shed light on these questions through careful, systematic, and informed study.

Politics and Government Defined

The study of political science requires that we define *politics*, *political power*, *influence*, and *government*—terms about which most of us have definite opinions. Consequently, political scientists have crafted definitions designed to be objective and applicable to all cultures, which is why they may strike us as abstract and sterile. The scope of our concerns is broad—the terms we employ must apply to systems very different from our own if we are to discover and understand the basic elements of political life.

The definitions of two terms are particularly important: *politics* and *government*.

Politics

People commonly use the term *politics* in a negative or pejorative sense, as in "There's only one explanation for her being appointed to be the new ambassador—*politics*"; or, simply, "It's back to *politics* as usual." The idea behind this casual use of the term implies that a decision is "political" if influence or power is involved in making it. The negative connotation that often surrounds *politics* derives from the belief that decisions *should* be made objectively on the basis of merit, quality, achievement, or some other legitimate standard. When we find that influence and power has had an effect on an important decision in government or in large organizations, most people

* A German judge in 2007 rejected a woman's petition for a speedy divorce. Her legal basis for seeking the divorce was that her husband physically beat her. The judge argued that her reasons were insufficient, because "the couple came from a Moroccan cultural milieu, in which it is common for husbands to beat their wives" (*New York Times*, March 22, 2007).

develop a very cynical attitude, accepting the idea that "politics" is synonymous with cheating or underhanded dealing.

Here are some definitions coined by political scientists:

"Politics is the science of who gets what, when, and how."

Politics is "the authoritative allocation of values."

"Politics [is] ... the activity by which differing interests within a given unit of rule are conciliated by giving them a share in power in proportion to their importance to ... the whole community."

Politics is "the processes by which human efforts towards attaining social goals are steered and coordinated."

"Political science is the academic subject centering on the relations between governments and other governments, and between governments and peoples."[2]

The most basic idea contained in these definitions is that politics involves decision making among people in some large group. An isolated person on a desert island cannot meaningfully be said to act *politically*, although economists could model his or her decisions regarding the investment of time and resources and his or her consumption, historians could chronicle his or her activities, and psychologists could examine the individual's changing mental state. But a political scientist would find nothing to study in the behavior of a totally isolated person.

More important, the definitions also suggest that political decisions involve *influence* and *power*. We can thus contrast political decisions with decisions made through, say, scientific computation or religious revelation. Although some of us may wish that governments would make decisions with the same kind of precision and objectivity that a chemist uses to determine the atomic weight of an element, a key characteristic of political decisions is that they are made in less objective ways. That is what makes the study of politics so interesting, and, ironically, it is also what sometimes makes politics a "dirty" word. Political decision making involves divergent interests, ideas, and preferences, and it applies power and influence to resolve them.

Politics, then, is the process of making collective decisions in a community, society, or group through the application of influence and power.

Government

When U.S. citizens think of government, they normally think of the president, the Congress, governors and state legislatures, mayors, and the courts and agencies that implement programs. In primitive societies, "the government" may consist of a few individuals. Government can be a vast, multifaceted, and complex arrangement, or it can be as simple as one village chieftain or tribal council.

However, in order to qualify as a government, the system, institutions, or persons must *govern*, and to do this they must wield *authority*. Government decisions are normally more coercive than decisions made by other forces in society. For example, if the Japanese corporation that produces Lexus automobiles decides to make a different model, no one is compelled to buy it. However, if the British Parliament decides to purchase new aircraft for its navy, British citizens are compelled to purchase the new planes with their tax money.

A **government** is the people or organizations that make, enforce, and implement political decisions for a society.* Accomplishing these tasks involves the performance of certain basic *functions*, which we now explore in more detail.

GOVERNMENT FUNCTIONS

Because actual governments are so different in scale, complexity, and structure, many political scientists have found it useful to itemize the **government functions** performed, in one way or another, in all thriving political systems. Asserting that "all governments have a legislature, an executive branch, courts, and bureaucracies" would imply that a government has to operate and be organized along the lines of governments in the United States, France, Japan, and other developed democracies in order to qualify as a "government." This would be a limiting and culturally biased approach. Identifying universal government *functions* helps us to appreciate that even when a government does not have institutions that seem familiar to us, it is still a government. It simply performs the basic governmental functions in different ways.[3]

Rule Making

Perhaps the most fundamental function of government is **rule making**—that is, making what are normally called *laws* or *orders* or even *constitutions*. These rules define what is legal and illegal, what actions are required, and the rights and responsibilities of citizens. In the United States, Congress (with participation by the president and sometimes the bureaucracy and the Supreme Court) performs this function; in China, the People's Congress officially makes rules (although most legislative decisions are really made by top Communist Party leaders). Councils of elders often act in this capacity in traditional societies, and the king and his advisers establish rules in the monarchy in contemporary Saudi Arabia.

In some way, all governments perform the task of making rules for their citizens. Some rules apply to criminal behavior, others establish economic regulations, and still others create or change public services. A rule is simply an *authoritative act.*

Rule Execution

Rules must be enforced and carried out if they are to have impact; this is what we mean by **rule execution**. A government that proclaims laws and programs will not be very effective if it lacks the ability to put force behind its decision making. Some governments appear to have had the capacity to perform the former function without the latter. For example, many historians have noted that the French Fourth Republic (1875–1940) had the ability to make rules (it had an energetic legislature) but that it had a terribly weak executive, a combination that led to protracted periods of

---

* In the United States, *government* applies broadly to a vast array of national, state, and local institutions. In European parliamentary systems (for example, Great Britain, Italy, Norway), we may speak of "the Government" to apply specifically to the prime minister and cabinet serving at a particular point in time. Thus, when the Italians say that "the Government resigned today," they are using the term in this more restricted sense.

instability. Many Latin American governments have passed social legislation in the areas of health care or agrarian reform, but they lack executive establishments capable of enforcing the law. The failure of some systems to thrive can thus be attributed partly to an inability to perform the basic function of rule execution.*

Rule Adjudication

Governments normally apply their laws to specific cases and individuals. If there is a law against murder, for example, there will be situations in which it will be necessary to determine whether a particular killing was murder, manslaughter, self-defense, or even an accident. Laws are frequently ambiguous. As a result, virtually all governments have some way of performing **rule adjudication**. Legal systems, usually with courts and judges, are established to apply and interpret laws that are made in general terms but that must have an impact at the individual level. In most modern societies, institutions for rule adjudication (courts) are at least partly distinct from the bodies that make the rules. In a tribal society or a traditional monarchy, a single governmental group may perform both functions.

Other Functions

Making, executing, and applying rules are the most basic functions of government, but other tasks must be performed for the system to operate effectively. Governments must be able to *communicate* with their citizens. People must be aware of laws if they are to obey them, and they must know about new programs if they are to participate in them. The leaders must also have some way of determining what people want, what they will support, and what they will not tolerate. Governments need some way to *recruit leaders*, perhaps through a party system or through a well-established routine of succession to the throne. It is also necessary that governments have some means of *extracting resources* (such as taxes, military service, or labor in public works projects) from their citizens.

Finally, a healthy political system has some means through which citizens come to support the basic principles and values of their government. Creating this foundation of involvement and awareness is referred to as the process of **political socialization**. Stable political systems also have some established ways for people to present demands for change. Interests must be expressed so that the government is able to take them into account in its decision making. Political parties, interest groups, and voting systems are some familiar mechanisms through which this function of **interest articulation** is performed.

A good political theory directs us to helpful questions. **Functionalism**, or the notion that healthy governments must perform certain basic functions, tells us what to look for in our efforts to understand and evaluate actual governments. The concept also suggests that these functions can be performed in many ways and through many different governmental organizations or processes.

---

* Students of early twentieth-century France point out that the system was held together during periods of political instability in the executive branch during the Fourth Republic (1946–1958) by its strong, stable bureaucracy. See Michael Crozier, *The Bureaucratic Phenomenon* (Chicago: University of Chicago Press, 1964), for the classic discussion along these lines.

KINDS OF GOVERNMENTS

There are many ways to classify governments. The kind of classification most of us probably encountered as children simply divided governments into free and unfree, or maybe even good and evil. Those concepts can be interesting to discuss, but political scientists have found it valuable to devise somewhat more precise classifications. The Greek philosopher Aristotle (384–322 BCE) constructed one of the first classification schemes, one that focused on who was in charge and in whose interests the ruler ruled. (See A Closer Look 1.2.) Many other classification approaches have been devised, some emphasizing economic systems, others reflecting legal arrangements, and still others based on wealth, culture, or even size.

An often useful approach is to classify political systems on the basis of how *developed* they are. The United States, New Zealand, and Sweden have developed political systems, whereas those in Nigeria, Chad, and Peru are termed *developing* (or, alternatively, *underdeveloped* or *less developed*). Unfortunately, the criteria for making these distinctions are often unclear. What determines whether Nigeria or the People's Republic of China is a developed or a developing nation? Are *political* development and *economic* development the same thing? If not, does political development require

---

A CLOSER LOOK

1.2

Aristotle's Approach to Governments

Type of Ruler	Ruler Rules in Interest of	
	Ruler	**All Citizens**
One	Tyranny	Monarchy
Few	Oligarchy	Aristocracy
Many	Democracy	Polity

Aristotle's classification is remarkable for its combination of an empirically observable factor (is the ruler a single person, a small elite group, or the masses?) with a more value-laden factor (does the ruler rule in his or her own interest or in the interest of all?). Aristotle obviously felt that nations with any of these three governing systems could operate fairly or with great injustice. His categories have suggested questions for political research for centuries.

One of these questions has to do with the actual *purpose* of government. Aristotle felt that governments can, and should, help to promote "the good life," not simply provide basic security for private pursuits.* His preference for an enlightened polity reflects his belief that achieving virtue and justice requires that governments be motivated by something other than self-interest. A notable feature of Aristotle's classification is the assumption that democracy is a bad form of government; this concept was also on the minds of several of the framers of the U.S. Constitution, as we discuss in Chapter 10.

* See Kevin M. Cherry, "Aristotle and the Eleatic Stranger on the Nature and Purpose of Political Life," *American Journal of Political Science* 52 (2008): 1–15.

economic development? Was wealthy Kuwait on the eve of the 1990 Iraqi invasion a developed nation? (It was quite prosperous, but it had an ancient form of government.) Does Costa Rica's thriving democracy make it a developed nation (despite its poor economy)?

In their classic book, *Comparative Politics: A Developmental Approach*, Gabriel Almond and Bingham Powell offer one answer. Political systems are developed, they argue, *if they can effectively carry out the functions of government.* To the extent that they cannot, undeveloped governments are often prone to political instability, violence, and military takeovers.[4] We discuss the idea of **political development** in Chapter 14.

What Is Democracy?

Political scientists often compare governments on the basis of how democratic they are. In practice, **democracy**, like political development, is a matter of degree, and so we speak of governments being "more" or "less" democratic. The degree to which a government is democratic depends on several related factors.

First, democratic government requires adherence to the principle of *political equality*. If large segments of the population are denied political rights by virtue of their race, family heritage, economic status, or religious affiliation, then political influence is not in the hands of the people, and the government thus fails to meet a basic principle of democracy. Governments can be undemocratic with respect to this principle in many ways: by giving special political power to the upper echelons of an economic elite or a ruling family, as in El Salvador or Kuwait; by excluding significant parts of society from political life, as South Africa did until the end of *apartheid*; by concentrating power in the hands of the military, as in Nigeria and Burma; or by putting nearly all political power in the hands of a political elite, as in North Korea, Cuba, China, Nazi Germany, and the former Soviet Union.

Even if political equality is generally secure, a government is not really democratic unless there is some process or mechanism through which the people have an opportunity to express their opinions. **Popular consultation** is thus a key component of democracy. It means that the people have a real opportunity to be heard and that this opportunity takes place regularly. (A country would not be very democratic, for example, if its next general election were scheduled for a date 20 years in the future.)

Finally, democracy requires substantial adherence to the principle of **majority rule**. This principle is simple but often controversial. It means that when citizens disagree about a political decision or candidate, as they virtually always do, then the decision made or the candidate selected will be the one preferred by the larger group of people. If a minority (an elite group of landed aristocrats or an exclusive religious leadership, for example) makes political decisions over the objections of the majority of a country's people, the government would not be very democratic.

It is important to recognize, however, that majority rule can lead to the violation of other democratic norms. What if the majority votes to deny electoral rights to a religious or racial minority? Such an action would violate the principle of political equality and would be undemocratic despite the fact that it was adopted through popular consultation and majority rule. Hence, if democracy is to be preserved, the majority must not be allowed to erase fundamental minority rights; democracy implies at least some *limitation* on majority rule. The relationship between majority rule and minority rights is a sticky problem, and it is a central challenge encountered by all democratic governments. As we will see later, although the United States generally appears democratic with respect to the principles of political equality and popular consultation, several features of its Constitution limit majority rule.*

Nondemocratic governments also operate in many ways, but most political scientists recognize two well-established types. Both kinds effectively deny political equality, popular consultation, and majority rule, maintaining real political power in the hands of a ruling party, elite group, dictator, or family. The difference between the two types of nondemocratic regimes has to do with the government's long-term goals.

Authoritarian systems require only that citizens obey government edicts and limit their dissent. Africa, Asia, and Latin America have been replete with authoritarian governments in recent decades. Such governments may violently repress opposition groups and torture political prisoners, but ultimately the state simply insists that the people not challenge the orders of the ruling elite. The governments of Haiti and Indonesia are good current examples.

In contrast, **totalitarian systems** energetically seek to change the political thinking and the allegiance of their citizens. The governments of Nazi Germany and Stalinist Russia, for example, sought to indoctrinate their populations into the dominant ideology (fascism or communism), a phenomenon not found in authoritarian regimes. Political recruitment and indoctrination take place in totalitarian regimes largely through a ruling party that dominates public affairs and much of private life as well. Totalitarian systems attempt to politicize virtually all pursuits, including sports and art, that are less constrained in democratic and even in authoritarian societies. For example, under the leadership of Mao Zedong in the 1960s, China's "top ten" pop songs often dealt with such unexpected topics as surpassing Great Britain in steel production or resisting Western imperialism. Even as recently as 2006, the Chinese government told the Rolling Stones that they couldn't play "Brown Sugar," among several other classic Jagger/Richards tunes, when they performed in Singapore because the song was "inappropriate."[†]

Although citizens have little voice in the affairs of either type of nondemocratic system, authoritarian governments often permit churches, unions, and some interest groups to retain relative independence as long as they do not challenge state authority. Totalitarian governments generally dominate or dismantle existing organizational features of a society in their attempt to permeate the totality of their citizens' lives.[‡] In fact, we might think of democratic, authoritarian, and totalitarian governments as ranging along a continuum; they differ in the degree of independence from government control that they allow individual citizens and groups in society.

It is important to understand that both democratic and nondemocratic governments can perform the basic functions of government. Both kinds of governments make, enforce, and adjudicate rules; they communicate with their citizens; and they

---

* See Dahl, Robert A., *How Democratic Is the American Constitution?* 2nd ed. (New Haven, CT: Yale University Press, 2003).

† Surprisingly, the Chinese government did allow them to play "Bitch," which they chose to open the show.

‡ Totalitarianism is a twentieth-century political concept. Most analysts argue that totalitarianism is possible only in countries with the technology to support mass communications, rapid transportation, and the means to engage in active, comprehensive surveillance of their citizens. Thus, all nondemocratic governments before that century were simply authoritarian. For a classic discussion, see Hannah Arendt, *The Origins of Totalitarianism* (New York: Harcourt, Brace, and World, 1966).

establish some basis for political socialization. Interest articulation occurs in nondemocratic governments as well as in democracies (although smaller segments of citizens articulate a narrower range of demands in nondemocratic governments). Quite simply, whether it operates according to democratic principles or in violation of them, a government is still a government.

Politics and government constitute the scope of inquiry and analysis for political scientists. The preceding sections describe the kinds of things that political scientists study in their efforts to contribute to our understanding. Through the scientific study of politics we attempt to find out why some forms of government work better than others, how people influence government, how governments change over time, how economic systems influence politics, and many other related matters. Ultimately, however, questions about politics and government are important because of what is at stake when governments act (or fail to act).

THE STAKES OF POLITICS

Most of the important consequences that can be traced to governmental action or inaction fall into one of five categories:

1. The allocation of resources
2. Human rights
3. The physical environment
4. Public services
5. War and peace

These are the primary "stakes" of politics, the scope of concerns in which politics makes a difference. Although some specific issues may pertain to more than one of these categories, the categories identify distinct aspects of our lives in which government and politics are critical.

The Allocation of Resources

Although politics affects many other things, it is fair to say that the majority of political decisions have to do with the **allocation of resources**.

Government power often has a tremendous, authoritative impact on how wealth is distributed and on the purposes to which scarce resources are devoted. The word *authoritative* in this definition is crucial. In many countries, a considerable share of national resources is allocated through economic exchange (investing, buying, and selling). This is the normal domain of economic analysis. Some get rich, and others become poor, through the economic choices made by consumers, workers, producers, and investors. In contrast, when governmental acts allocate resources, we refer to the allocation as authoritative.

The distinction is important. When Henry Ford applied assembly-line manufacturing methods to his auto plant, manufacturing costs plummeted, prices fell, and a huge increase took place in the number of people who could afford cars. The labor of thousands of people was diverted from agricultural production and small craft activities to auto assembly. Through an economic process of exchange, a large share of national resources—both materials and labor—was allocated to the manufacture of automobiles. Yet this allocation was not *authoritative*, because the decisions creating it were made voluntarily—most importantly, by consumers.

New laws may also increase or decrease the proportion of taxes to be paid by the richest and the poorest citizens. These decisions involve allocations, whether they have to do with tax rates or expenditures. And such allocations are authoritative—citizens are required to make the contributions, and the expenditures are made as a matter of law.* Although resource allocation in *all* countries is affected by both economic exchange and authoritative governmental acts, the relative importance of economic and political allocations is very different in different countries. Most of the resource allocation that takes place in Taiwan, for example, is driven by economic exchange. The public sector is relatively small. In Cuba the government directly influences the bulk of resource allocation by making decisions regarding what is produced, at what prices, and with which raw materials. The forces of *both* economic exchange and government authority are important in the United States, Great Britain, Mexico, France, Italy, and most other countries. We use the term *mixed economies* to describe such societies.

Many things contribute to the differences among countries with respect to wealth and the equality with which wealth is distributed. Natural resources, climate, population, access to transportation, and other such factors are obviously important. However, the nature of government and the policies governments enact are profoundly important. In fact, according to Nobel laureate Douglass North, institutions "are the underlying determinant of the long-run performance of economies."[5] Table 1.1 indicates the differences among 13 selected countries with respect to per capita income, governmental corruption, infant mortality rates, corporate tax rates, and the number of days that it takes, on average, to obtain government approval to start a business.

A look at the figures quickly demonstrates that the quality of life and the workings of government vary tremendously across the world. There are dramatic differences among governments with respect to these factors. In countries where there is less governmental corruption, a more established rule of law, and more efficient approvals of business start-ups, there are lower infant mortality rates and more wealth. Culture, climate, natural resources, and other factors are extremely important, but the quality of government makes an even greater difference in the lives of citizens.

A great deal of the political conflict among people reflects different views regarding the extent to which government effort *should* be devoted to shifting the allocation of resources from one group of people to another. In developing nations, where gaps between rich and poor are often particularly sharp, conflicts between "haves" and "have nots" periodically unleash revolutionary forces (as in Nicaragua, the Philippines, and El Salvador). Extreme inequality in the distribution of income or land increases the likelihood of political instability in developing nations.

In industrial democracies, economic inequality is a less explosive issue but, nevertheless, the major parties in the United States, Great Britain, France, and Germany tend to define themselves primarily by their different positions on resource allocation. More generally, the distinction between "left" and "right" on the political

---

* To qualify as authoritative, however, the allocation must be made under *legitimate* public authority. Resources are involuntarily "allocated" from one person to another when a burglar carries off your big-screen television and MP3 player. It is coercion by *legitimate government power* that makes the allocation authoritative and thus distinctively political.

TABLE 1.1	Differences in Living Conditions in Selected Political Systems				
	GDP/ Capita (2010 U.S. dollars)	Infant Mortality	Corruption Score (*rank*)	Life Expectancy	Adoles- cent Fertility	# of Days to Start a Business
U.S.	$46,970	6.8	7.5 (19)	78.11	35.0	6
France	$41,051	3.2	6.9 (24)	80.98	6.8	7
Japan	$39,727	2.4	7.7 (17)	82.12	4.8	23
Russia	$ 8,676	11.1	2.2 (146)	66.03	24.8	30
Brazil	$ 8,114	17.3	3.7 (75)	71.99	75.1	120
Kazakhstan	$ 6,870	25.6	2.7 (120)	67.87	30.3	20
Colombia	$ 5,056	16.2	3.7 (85)	74.07	73.8	20
Thailand	$ 3,894	12.0	3.4 (84)	73.10	37.0	32
El Salvador	$ 3,598	14.6	3.4 (84)	72.33	82.2	17
Philippines	$ 1,745	26.2	2.4 (139)	71.09	44.4	52
Haiti	$ 667	63.7	1.8 (168)	60.78	45.9	195
Malawi	$ 326	71.4	3.3 (89)	50.03	133.0	39
Burundi	$ 160	101.3	1.8 (168)	57.80	18.5	32

NOTE: *Gross Domestic Product Per Capita* figures are based on 2009 data, using 2010 U.S. dollars. *Infant Mortality* is the number of deaths of persons under five years of age per 1,000 live births. The *Corruption Score* is Transparency International's "Corruption Perception Index," based on a series of surveys. Higher scores indicate less corruption, and the figures in parentheses indicate each country's ranking on corruption. *Adolescent Fertility* is the number of births per 1,000 females aged 15–19, using 2008 data. The *Number of Days to Start a Business* indicates how long, in days, it is estimated to take to obtain government licenses and other approvals.

SOURCES: Data on GDP per capita, adolescent fertility, and infant mortality were obtained from the World Bank, *World Development Indicators Database*, www.worldbank.org; data on life expectancy were obtained from the U.S. Central Intelligence Agency's *World Factbook*, www.cia.gov; data on the number of days needed to start a business were obtained from the World Bank, *Doing Business Project*, www.doingbusiness.org; and data on corruption were obtained from Transparency International, www.transparency.org. All websites were accessed October 2010.

spectrum is largely, although not entirely, a matter of differing positions on what government should do to alter the distribution of resources; those on the left favor more active efforts to redistribute income, whereas those on the right are either less supportive of, or hostile to, such efforts.

Governments are also heavily involved in resource allocations that, though involving large shares of wealth, do not alter the balance between rich and poor. These *intersector allocations* constitute a second set of concerns in the area of **political economy**. For example, import restrictions alter the allocation of resources. When a government restricts or severely taxes the importation of a particular good, the domestic manufacturers and workers who produce that good find that the demand for what they have to sell is greater (because consumers can no longer buy the imports). Domestic resources that would otherwise be devoted to the production of other goods are then devoted to manufacture of the previously imported good. The trade restriction thus changes the allocation of resources from the production of one good to another, and it increases the income of the manufacturers and workers producing the protected good.

Of course, other groups realize a net decrease in wealth. When the state restricts importation of a good, the total supply of that good is reduced, and the price charged by domestic producers goes up. People who had paid $18,000 for a car

A CLOSER LOOK

Government, Capitalism, and Democracy

1.3

The decline of communism at the end of the last century sparked increased interest in the connection between capitalism and democracy. Ardent advocates of capitalism have long argued that the economic freedoms of capitalism inevitably lead to political freedoms, and that a nation that enjoys genuine political freedom will always construct and maintain a market economy.[6] Although cases can be found to support this argument, the actual record is not so clear.

Historically, the rise of liberal democracy (competitive elections with guaranteed civil liberties) evolved first in Britain and then spread to other parts of Western Europe and the United States at the same time that capitalism was emerging as the new economic system. The tendency of these political and economic systems to develop simultaneously was far from coincidental. As scholars from Karl Marx onward have recognized, it was the rising class of capitalist entrepreneurs and businessmen—often known as the bourgeoisie—who mounted the first major challenges to the political and economic power of the feudal or semifeudal aristocracy that had previously dominated Europe. The bourgeoisie became the most powerful voice for parliamentary government, wider citizen participation in politics, and notions of guaranteed individual liberties.

In general, capitalism tends to produce democracy because the existence of an independent bourgeoisie in a capitalist society creates centers of economic power independent of the government and makes it easier for political pluralism to flourish. For example, the students who organized China's short-lived democracy movement in 1989 were partly financed by the country's new class of independent businessmen. In a classic study, a leading scholar of political and economic development nicely summed it up by exclaiming "no bourgeoisie, no democracy!"[7]

However, not all capitalist countries are democratic and not all democracies are purely capitalist. From the 1960s through the 1980s, a number of East and Southeast Asian countries became models of capitalist economic development, with very high levels of growth, while at the same time maintaining relatively repressive dictatorships. These countries included South Korea, Taiwan, Singapore, Indonesia, and Malaysia. From 1973 to 1990, Chile's president, General Augusto Pinochet, imposed one of Latin America's more brutal regimes. But at the same time, led by U.S.-trained economists, the country developed what Nobel Prize–winning economist (and champion of unfettered capitalism) Milton Friedman hailed as one of the world's purest capitalist systems. Moreover, China today seems to be developing an essentially capitalist economy within the confines of an authoritarian, communist political system.

Examples of democracies that are not capitalist are harder to find, and it probably is true that no modern democracy has existed without some elements of capitalism. It should be noted, however, that a number of Western European countries have thrived under highly developed democratic political systems and mixed economic systems that combine elements of capitalism and socialism. Norway, Sweden, Denmark, Finland, and Iceland have some of the highest standards of living in the world, socialist welfare systems, and highly

---

before import restrictions were in place may now have to pay $22,000 for the same car. These people have experienced a net wealth reduction of $4,000. The government has "allocated" thousands of dollars from consumers to workers and corporations involved in the auto industry by enacting the change in trade policy.

Governments also allocate resources in other ways—by adjusting interest rates, changing tax rates and exemptions, nationalizing private industries, and controlling prices and wages. Using these and many other kinds of powers, governments have a

1.3

A CLOSER LOOK

democratic politics. It could be argued that in the last years of the Soviet Union (see Chapter 12), President Mikhail Gorbachev's political reforms in the 1980s produced a country that was moderately democratic (competitive elections, multiple parties, a fairly free press, religious tolerance) with an economy that was still primarily state controlled (communist).

Many of these exceptional cases have proven to be transitory. Chile, Taiwan, and South Korea have all democratized. But change is rarely steady or uninterrupted. Russia's totalitarian political system first became authoritarian (after Stalin's death) and then, when the communist economic and political system collapsed, it moved toward capitalism and democracy in the 1990s. Today, capitalism in Russia seems more secure, although it is undermined by corruption and organized crime. But Vladimir Putin (first as president and then as prime minister) turned the country away from democracy. Similarly, although China has moved very effectively toward a largely capitalist economy, and although political controls and repression have diminished in many respects, the country remains quite authoritarian. Experts are still divided as to when, if at all, real democracy will emerge there. Still, although capitalist societies can be authoritarian, at least for a substantial number of years, and although Scandinavia's mixed economies coexist very smoothly with democracy, there is no question that in the long run capitalist economic systems and democratic political systems seem to reinforce each other.

Perhaps democratic systems produce a redistribution of resources that counteracts the disparities in wealth prompted by capitalist economics. A fascinating study by two young political scientists, David S.

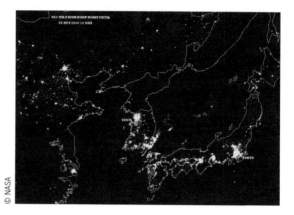

The Lights Are Out This nighttime satellite photo provides a striking visual indicator of how different forms of government can create very different living conditions. Although the cities of Seoul, South Korea, Beijing, China, and Tokyo, Japan are very obvious, North Korea is almost completely dark. It is estimated that 22 million people live there.

Brown and Ahmed Mobarak, found that democratic governments "increase the residential sector's share of electricity consumption relative to industry's share" of electricity consumption in poor countries.[8] Less democratic governments are apparently more likely to favor interests with substantial political influence.

In short, there is clearly an important connection between capitalism and democracy, but it is far too simple to claim that one always produces or requires the other.

tremendous capacity to change economic conditions. Governments can make societies richer or poorer; they can foster a more equal or a less equal distribution of wealth; they can hasten or retard the development of specific industries. Perhaps there is also a connection between government policies that encourage economic freedom and the emergence of democracy. (See A Closer Look 1.3.) In short, the widely varying economic conditions among contemporary nations reflect, in large measure, the political choices made by governments.

A CLOSER LOOK

1.4

Four Statements of Human Rights

I. THE MAGNA CARTA (THE GREAT CHARTER) [EXCERPTS]

Signed by King John of England in 1215.

–No bailiff for the future shall, upon his own unsupported complaint, put anyone to his "law," without credible witnesses brought for this purpose.

–No freemen shall be taken or imprisoned ... or exiled or in any way destroyed, nor will we go upon him nor send upon him, except by the lawful judgment of his peers or by the law of the land.

–We will appoint as justices, constables, sheriffs, or bailiffs only such as know the law of the realm and mean to observe it well.

–Wherefore we will and firmly order that the English Church be free, and that the men in our kingdom have and hold all the aforesaid liberties, rights, and concessions, well and peaceably, freely and quietly, fully and wholly, for themselves and their heirs, of us and our heirs, in all respects and in all places forever, as is aforesaid. An oath, moreover, has been taken, as well on our part as on the part of the barons, that all these conditions aforesaid shall be kept in good faith and without evil intent. Given under our hand—the above named and many others being witnesses—in the meadow which is called Runnymede, between Windsor and Staines, on the fifteenth day of June, in the seventeenth year of our reign.

II. THE UNITED STATES BILL OF RIGHTS [EXCERPTS]

Adopted in 1791.

Amendment 1. Congress shall make no law respecting an establishment of religion, or prohibiting the free exercise thereof; or abridging the freedom of speech, or of the press....

Amendment 2. A well-regulated militia being necessary to the security of a free State, the right of the people to keep and bear arms shall not be infringed.

Amendment 4. The right of the people to be secure in their persons, houses, papers, and effects, against unreasonable searches and seizures, shall not be violated....

Amendment 5. No person ... shall be compelled in any criminal case to be a witness against himself, nor be deprived of life, liberty, or property, without due process of law....

Amendment 8. Excessive bail shall not be required, nor excessive fines imposed, nor cruel and unusual punishment inflicted.

Human Rights

Although economic issues often seem to dominate politics, many of the political issues that most sharply divide us involve governmental policies in noneconomic areas. In the United States, heated debates have focused on prayers in public schools, the achievement of racial balance in public and private organizations, the right to have an abortion, and the rights of homosexuals. In India, Lebanon, Northern Ireland, and Canada, conflicts over religious or language policies have sometimes erupted in violence. Governments have a tremendous capacity both to protect and to trample on the liberties of their citizens.

1.4

III. THE UNITED NATIONS UNIVERSAL DECLARATION ON HUMAN RIGHTS [EXCERPTS]

Adopted and proclaimed by the General Assembly Resolution 217 A (III) of December 10, 1948.

> *Article 1:* All human beings are born free and equal in dignity and rights.
>
> *Article 2:* Everyone is entitled to all the rights and freedoms set forth in this Declaration, without distinction of any kind, such as race, color, sex, language, religion, political or other opinion, national or social origin, property, birth, or other status.
>
> *Article 3:* Everyone has the right to life, liberty, and the security of person.
>
> *Article 4:* No one shall be held in slavery....
>
> *Article 18:* Everyone has the right to freedom of thought, conscience, and religion....
>
> *Article 23:* Everyone has the right to work, ... to just and favorable conditions of work and to protection against unemployment.
>
> *Article 26:* Everyone has the right to education. Education shall be free....

IV. THE CHARTER OF FUNDAMENTAL RIGHTS OF THE EUROPEAN UNION [EXCERPTS]

Adopted on December 7, 2000.

> *Article 8, Section 1:* Everyone has the right to the protection of personal data concerning him or her.

> *Article 9:* The right to marry and the right to found a family shall be guaranteed in accordance with the national laws governing the exercise of these rights.
>
> *Article 11, Section 1:* Everyone has the right to freedom of expression. This right shall include freedom to hold opinions and to receive and impart information and ideas without interference by public authority....
>
> *Article 11, Section 2:* The freedom and pluralism of the media shall be respected.
>
> *Article 13:* The arts and scientific research shall be free of constraint. Academic freedom shall be respected.
>
> *Article 17, Section 1:* Everyone has the right to own, use, dispose of and bequeath his or her lawfully acquired possessions. No one may be deprived of his or her possessions, except in the public interest and in the cases and under the conditions provided for by law, subject to fair compensation being paid in good time for their loss. The use of property may be regulated by law in so far as is necessary for the general interest.
>
> *Article 21:* Any discrimination based on any ground such as sex, race, colour, ethnic or social origin, genetic features, language, religion or belief, political or any other opinion, membership of a national minority, property, birth, disability, age or sexual orientation shall be prohibited.

The homepage for the European Union's charter may be found at www.europarl.europa.eu/charter/default_en.htm.

Nearly everywhere, there is always great disagreement regarding the nature and extent of **human rights**, and even when people agree that a particular right should be respected, they often differ about when and under what conditions the right may be appropriately abridged. A great deal of political conflict thus involves disputes regarding human rights.

Although issues of human rights can be approached in many ways, two kinds of rights can be distinguished according to how they relate to government. Some rights correspond to limits on government power and are thus called *negative rights*. Examples include the right to free expression, to religious freedom, to a fair trial before punishment, to travel, and so on. They are called negative rights because we enjoy them when government is *prevented* from certain actions. We have freedom of the press, for example, to the extent that the government is *not* free to limit what can be written, printed, or broadcast. In contrast, *positive rights* require governmental action. For example, if we feel that every person has the right to a job or to health care, the government must take steps to provide them to people who are unable to obtain private employment or to pay their own medical bills.

Both negative and positive rights are contained in the United Nations Universal Declaration on Human Rights and in the U.S. Bill of Rights. (See A Closer Look 1.4.) We explore controversies about human rights in our discussions of ideology in the next chapter.

A special set of human rights issues involves the treatment of women. The rights of women are severely restricted in many political systems, most notably under the infamous Taliban regime in Afghanistan, which was quickly toppled in 2001 by a coalition of forces led by the United States. Taliban policies and laws provided for physical beatings if women failed to observe a wide range of clothing requirements, and these punishments were regularly carried out. Women face restrictions on reproductive choices in China, many Latin American countries, and much of Africa. Although most factors affecting gender equality stem from cultural influences, government policies play a major role in reinforcing or reforming them.

In short, people disagree about human rights on many levels, and government action is often demanded either to secure or to modify those rights. Human rights even figure in foreign policy issues. In the United States, the government has been criticized for its present or past affiliation with regimes that have poor records on human rights, for the fact that capital punishment is used in many states, and for the violent suppression of civil rights activists in the 1950s and 1960s. One of the justifications that the George W. Bush administration gave for military action against Iraq was that country's horrendous human rights abuses, including mass murder and the use of chemical weapons against its citizens. In 2011, a concern for human rights was central to U.S. President Obama's decision to give military assistance to the rebels attempting to overthrow the Libyan government. Especially when the protection of human rights conflicts with other national interests, such as international trade, political decision making becomes very difficult. How human rights should be defined and respected are issues that are very much at stake in political life.

The Physical Environment

Governments play a special role with respect to issues of environmental protection. Most goods and services can be produced entirely through private efforts because investors know that they can be paid for what they produce. But clean air and water, the elimination of toxic wastes, and protection of the natural beauty of the wilderness are "goods" that profit-seeking firms are not necessarily motivated to preserve. If we are to have environmental protection, most people feel that the government must act.

Protection of the environment thus depends almost entirely on governmental action. The continuing controversy over the "greenhouse" effect (the idea that Earth's climate is becoming warmer because of various pollutants entering the atmosphere and because of the destruction of rainforests) is only the most spectacular illustration of the stakes involved—and of the inability of any institution except government to do anything about it.

Although virtually everyone favors protection of the environment, people differ greatly about the priority that environmental protection should be given and about who should pay for it. Should Brazil limit farming in rainforest regions if it means that destitute people in that area will have less food? Should auto makers be forced to produce more electric and hybrid cars, even if it means that consumers will be denied some of the choices they would like to have? Does the use of ethanol as a supplement for gasoline drive up the cost of food in poor countries? In the long run, the quality of human life will be crucially affected by what governments do and fail to do concerning environmental protection.

Public Services

Governments do more than govern. People also look to government for important services—most notably, public education, public transportation, cultural amenities such as museums and libraries, and "infrastructure" support (road repair, street sweeping, and so forth). Although most people accept the need for government to play a role in providing these services, considerable controversy surrounds the scope and nature of this role.

For one thing, public services cost a great deal of money. Paying for them requires taxes, and some taxpayers are reluctant to support the provision of these services. Even the richest of nations can never afford to pay for all desirable services. In the United States, the problem has become increasingly severe, particularly in light of the current economic stresses. According to the American Society of Civil Engineers, an investment of $2.2 trillion will be needed over the next five years to improve bridges, dams, aviation facilities, solid waste disposal systems, and other essential elements of the nation's basic infrastructure. The Society's "2009 Infrastructure Report Card" gave the United States an average grade of "D."* Where will the money to fix these problems come from, and what other critical services (education, health care, defense) will be cut? In poor nations, with greater needs and far fewer resources, the choices are yet more difficult.

War and Peace

"War," according to Karl von Clausewitz, is "a real political instrument, a continuation of political commerce ... by other means."[9] Although a war might be started through some terrible accident, and although military leaders can start wars by taking sudden actions on their own, most wars begin as a result of deliberate policy choices made by political leaders. Those choices may be rational or irrational and well informed or grounded in miscalculation and distorted thinking. The monumental consequences of war make questions of war and peace a central reason for concluding that politics matters.

We discuss several approaches to understanding the causes of war in Chapter 16. For now, it is important simply to appreciate Clausewitz's notion that war is a "political instrument." Wars can erupt when governments are moved to pursue a moral

---

* American Society of Civil Engineers, *Report Card for America's Infrastructure*, 2009, available at www.infrastructurereportcard.org, accessed June 2011.

purpose, when they seek material gain, when they are anxious about their security, or when domestic pressures move them into conflict. In short, the same sets of conflicting passions, interests, and needs that influence political decision making in general are often involved, in one way or another, in the causes of war.

It is difficult to overstate the extent to which government action can make a difference in each of the five areas we have outlined. Governments can help provide a basis for economic growth and opportunity, and they can condemn the vast majority of their citizens to poverty and hopelessness. They can plunge their citizens into devastating military conflicts, and they can contribute to peace. Governments can secure or destroy basic rights, protect or savage the environment, and provide or not provide needed public services.

A disinterested extraterrestrial observer, looking at Earth for the first time, would probably be startled by the vast range of conditions in which humans live throughout the planet. Different political choices, made by various kinds of governments, account for much of the diversity in the quality of human life. Perhaps that is why Aristotle referred to politics as the "master science"—political choices have effects, direct and indirect, on virtually everything.

POLITICS IN A CHANGING WORLD

It is an obvious understatement to note that the first dozen years of the twenty-first century constituted a period of dramatic change. Terrorism and the economic crisis are simply the two most prominent reasons that this decade's events will affect political life for generations.

Before 2000, few Americans had heard of the Taliban or al-Qaeda, and fewer still were thinking about a crisis in home prices or credit markets. Ethnic conflicts had begun to replace the Cold War as the most common topic in international relations, as hundreds of thousands died in the Rwandan genocide and the Bosnian War. After these disastrous struggles subsided, violence in Pakistan, Afghanistan, and Sri Lanka worsened, and thousands died in the U.S.-led war in Iraq. The economic stresses that began in 2007 produced unprecedented deficit spending and a dramatic decline in trade, consumer confidence, and lending. Stable democracy remains threatened in a number of regions.

The long-term trend is difficult to deny. As recently as 1977, Freedom House classified only 43 countries as "free" and another 48 as "partly free," while 64 countries were "not free." In 2011, 87 countries were "free," and the number of "not free" countries had declined to 47.[10] Nevertheless, serious problems threaten the further spread of democracy. Some contemporary analysts fear that the U.S. actions in Iraq and Afghanistan only aggravated the tensions in the region, prompting an escalation of violence and instability that will become increasingly severe in years to come. At the time of this writing, the Iranians appear to be well on their way to developing nuclear weapons that can be deployed on missiles capable of reaching Israel, India, and parts of Europe. North Korea remains dangerous and unpredictable. The European Union, Japan, Korea, China, and the United States are still working through the uncertain waters of economic globalization, making it very difficult to predict even near-term developments in politics and economic policy. Given much of Africa's extremely low literacy rates, low gross national product (GNP) per capita, and lack of democratic traditions in national government, the prospects for democratization there seem limited. The futures of Cuba and China are far from clear, although many experts feel that democratic pressures will be hard to resist in the long run. Countries in East Asia, South America, and Eastern Europe (with some still authoritarian and others only marginally democratic) tend to offer better hopes for greater democracy. Even in those more developed countries, deeply rooted class tensions (as in Peru or Colombia) or ethnic hostilities (Bosnia, Sudan, Malaysia) undermine democratic forces.

The knowledge and understanding accumulated through generations of political science research suggest that the growth of democratic government is rooted in societal forces more fundamental than the actions or vision of particular leaders or the fallout from single events. Most political scientists conclude that economic growth creates greater social and political diversity as well as heightened political participation and awareness; that all governments need some degree of popular support; and that governments cut off from the pressures of competitive political influences are inherently unstable in the long run. Building on this understanding and related ideas, several leading political scientists and political economists anticipated the breakdown of communist rule as long ago as 1960.[11]

It is plain that we are living in an era in which political life is both extremely important and highly volatile. As economic growth spreads (unevenly) through the world and as nations become increasingly interdependent, we will find that the old conflict between communists and anticommunists has been replaced by a more complex pattern of economic, ethnic, and religious relations. The task of political science is to bring sound scientific inquiry to these problems.

Approaches to Political Understanding

The preceding sections present the scope of our concerns and explore why they are worth studying. It is important to understand, however, that political scientists approach their discipline in a variety of ways. More than most fields of study, political science is eclectic: it borrows from other fields to forge its own identity. Although political science enjoys a healthy diversity, it is also one of the most fragmented of academic disciplines.

The first effort to study political life was as a subtopic of *philosophy*. Those studying politics in this manner focus on questions pertaining to the origins of government, the problem of human rights and justice under law, the idea of a "just war," and other basic philosophical concerns. It is important to emphasize, however, that political philosophy includes several very different approaches. Most scholars claim that the field began in ancient Greece with Plato (427–347 BCE) and his student Aristotle. Essential elements of **classical political philosophy** include a distrust of democracy and an emphasis on the problem of designing a political community in accordance with principles of justice. **Modern political philosophy**—beginning with Machiavelli (1469–1527), Hobbes (1588–1679), Locke (1632–1704), and Rousseau (1712–1778)—is distinguished by its emphasis on individualism and its rejection of Plato's search for an ideal state order. Both classical and modern political philosophy include a wide range of more specific perspectives.

The study of *law* was a second major influence on political science. Legal scholars study different approaches to interpreting laws and principles pertaining to how courts operate. Legal analysis is also relevant to questions about the powers of governmental institutions and their procedures. Much of political science through the first quarter of the twentieth century was influenced by legal thinking, and the term **formal-legal analysis** was used to describe pre–World War II political science. During this period, political scientists devoted themselves to issues of constitutional design and formal governmental institutions.

At the beginning of the twentieth century, some political scientists began to criticize philosophical and legal approaches to understanding politics. They argued that we could not fully account for policy choices by considering ethical concerns or legal powers and rights alone. Instead, we should observe actual political *behavior*. The "behavioral revolution" took root and, by the 1960s, was firmly established as the mainstream of the discipline. Perhaps the first shot in this revolution was fired in 1908 by Arthur Bentley in *The Process of Government*, an important book that argued persuasively for the observation of behavior in political research.[12] In political science, this approach is known as **behavioralism**.

The behavioral approach to political science necessitates borrowing skills from other disciplines. When we observe behavior—in the form of voting, political demonstrations, voicing opinions, and so on—we usually need to quantify it. How many people voted in the last election, and what caused them to vote as they did? What kinds of people participated in the demonstrations? Analyzing data in a quantified form requires that political scientists have some familiarity with *statistics*. The emphasis on statistical analysis is readily apparent to students exploring political science journals for the first time. Political research often (although not always) involves the use of basic and even highly advanced statistical tools as scholars try to discover and identify patterns in the behavior they observe.

Particularly in the past 20 years or so, political scientists have increasingly drawn from *economics* in their work. (See A Closer Look 1.5.) Some have applied the economic concept of the rational, self-interested person in analyzing everything from voting to group membership. The rational choice school is controversial within the discipline because many political scientists believe that it oversimplifies human motivations. But there is general agreement on the relevance of economic concepts and tools in the study of political behavior.

Perhaps in reaction to the dominance of the behavioral method and the increasing influence of approaches using economic theory, a significant number of political scientists now argue that there is an important place for less-mathematical research methods. This way of thinking is sometimes termed "**postmodernism**" or "postbehavioralist interpretivism." Although it is not an approach given to clear definition, its adherents share a conviction that the behavioralists and the rational choice analysts have allowed mathematical rigor to displace the politics in political science. Numbers can tell us some things, but they cannot reveal the whole sense of what is critical about political issues and events, and methods steeped in mathematics may even obscure or distort the essential political nature of the things they do measure, according to postmodernists.

Political scientists thus attempt to understand politics and government by using a wide range of approaches to study. Sometimes, the differences among political scientists with respect to their research methods can become rather heated, and a number of essays have been published attacking and defending various approaches. We may hope that the decades-long debate over research methods in political science will

1.5

"Rational Choice" in Political Science

Political scientists are hotly divided over the role of "rational choice" theory in their discipline. Drawn largely from economic theory, the rational choice approach begins with the assumption that individuals seek to maximize "utility" with their choices and behaviors. This assumption is rarely controversial in economics, where it is used to construct models pertaining to producing, buying, and selling oranges, computers, and "widgets," but some political scientists apply it to politics and government. For example, using rational choice logic, one analyst argued that party leaders should be expected to shape their ideological positions in ways that appeal to voters in the center of the ideological spectrum, where the party can "maximize" its votes, just as a retailer shapes a marketing campaign to maximize customers.

Although this example is hardly controversial, other applications are much more contentious. For example, some have used rational choice to construct theories of bureaucratic behavior, predicting that bureaucrats will have a natural urge to expand their agencies in order to increase their personal wealth. We will explore one of the most famous rational

choice ideas in Chapter 6 (on interest groups). It holds that people will not willingly participate in collective political efforts because the rational person will realize that one person's contribution is inconsequential and because noncontributors will receive as much benefit from the group's success (if any) as contributors. Political scientists have also used rational choice logic in understanding the emergence of democracy in developing countries.[13]

Advocates of rational choice contend that the approach opens new avenues for understanding political institutions and individual behavior. Others insist that it oversimplifies motivations, that it contains a conservative ideological bias, and that it has not produced any meaningful predictions that could not be derived from other approaches.[14] In a book provocatively entitled *Pathologies of Rational Choice Theory*, two members of the Yale Political Science Department argue essentially that rational choice theory has been a failure.[15] This volume prompted the publication of *The Rational Choice Controversy*, by another Yale political scientist, which includes essays both criticizing and defending rational choice theory.[16]

prove to be useful in moving the discipline to refine and strengthen its ability to produce genuine understanding.

CONCLUSION: WHY STUDY POLITICAL SCIENCE?

Political science encompasses a wide variety of approaches. Sometimes the diversity is enriching and stimulating, but it must be acknowledged that political science is also a highly divided discipline. Some are quite vocal in disparaging the efforts of colleagues who use different tools or methods. Disagreements can be healthy, however, even when they are heated. The diversity and the energy that political scientists bring to their work reflect the deep interest they share in their subject. These are also reasons that political science is fascinating and so involving.

The primary answer to the question "Why study political science?" is simply that it helps us understand the problems and issues that define public affairs. Studying political science is also an excellent foundation for careers in law, government, public administration, and other areas, but the most fundamental justification is that it helps us to become more effective participants in the civic life that increasingly affects our future. The passion for political understanding, shared among professionals and amateurs alike, is nicely captured in the following statement by a pioneering political scientist:

> No one can deny that the idea is fascinating—the idea of subduing the phenomena of politics to the laws of causation, of penetrating to the mystery of its transformations, of symbolizing the trajectory of its future.... If nothing ever comes of it, its very existence will fertilize thought and enrich imagination.[17]

◆ ◆ ◆

Key Terms and Concepts _____

allocation of resources
authoritarian systems
behavioralism
classical political philosophy
democracy
formal-legal analysis
functionalism
government
government functions
human rights
interest articulation
majority rule

modern political philosophy
political development
political economy
political socialization
politics
popular consultation
postmodernism
rule adjudication
rule execution
rule making
totalitarian systems

DISCUSSION QUESTIONS

1. *What are the most basic functions of government? Explain why a political system cannot be stable and effective unless each of these functions is performed.*
2. *What is the difference between "positive" and "negative" human rights?*
3. *If politics means "the application of influence and power in making public decisions," does this mean that politics is underhanded?*
4. *How are free markets and democracy related to each other?*

Notes _____

1. See Rebecca Christie, "U.S. Household Losses from Financial Crisis Averaged $100,000, Study Says," April 27, 2010, available at www.bloomberg.com/news/2010-04-28/u-s-households-lost-100-000-on-average-in-financial-crisis-study-says.html (accessed May 25, 2011).
2. These definitions are adapted from Harold Lasswell, *Politics: Who Gets What, When, and How* (New York: McGraw-Hill, 1936); David Easton, *The Political System*, 2nd ed. (New York: Knopf, 1971); Bernard Crick, *In Defense of Politics*, 2nd ed. (Chicago: University of Chicago Press, 1972); Karl Deutsch, *The Nerves of Government* (New York: Free Press, 1963), and from the Glossary on the "About Economics" website, http://economics.about.com/od/economicsglossary/g/political.htm.

3. Much of this discussion is drawn from a basic, pioneering work that still influences contemporary political analysis. See Gabriel Almond and G. Bingham Powell, *Comparative Politics: A Developmental Approach* (Boston: Little, Brown, 1966).

4. Ibid.

5. North, Douglass C., *Institutions, Institutional Change and Economic Performance* (Cambridge: Cambridge University Press, 1990), p. 107.

6. One of the most widely read books making this argument is *Free to Choose*, by Milton and Rose Friedman (New York: Harcourt Brace Jovanovich, 1980).

7. Barrington Moore, Jr., *Social Origins of Dictatorship and Democracy: Lords and Peasants in the Making of the Modern World* (Boston: Beacon Press, 1967). For an important refinement of Moore's work, see Dietrich Rueschemeyer, Evelyn Huber Stephens, and John Stephens, *Capitalist Development and Democracy* (Chicago: University of Chicago Press, 1992).

8. David S. Brown and Ahmed Mushfiq Mobarak, "The Transforming Power of Democracy: Regime Type and the Distribution of Electricity," *American Political Science Review* 103 (2009): 193–213.

9. This famous quote is from *On War*, bk. 1, chap. 1, as translated by J. J. Graham (New York: Barnes & Noble, 1956), p. 23.

10. See "Freedom in the World, 2011: The Authoritarian Challenge to Democracy," Freedom House. Available at www.freedomhouse.org/images/File/fiw/FIW%202011%20Booklet_1_11_11.pdf

11. A famous statement of this idea can be found in W. W. Rostow, *The Stages of Economic Growth* (Cambridge: Harvard University Press, 1960).

12. Arthur Bentley, *The Process of Government* (Cambridge: Harvard University Press, 1906). Several decades later, David Truman wrote the similarly titled *Governmental Process* (New York: Knopf, 1958), a book that extended and applied Bentley's approach.

13. See Barbara Geddes, "The Uses and Limitations of Rational Choice," in *Latin America in Comparative Perspective*, ed. Peter H. Smith (Boulder, CO: Westview, 1995), pp. 81–108.

14. See Robert Abelson, "The Secret Existence of Expressive Behavior," in *The Rational Choice Controversy*, ed. Jeffrey Friedman (New Haven, CT: Yale University Press, 1996), pp. 25–36. The study Abelson refers to is Frank, Robert H., Thomas Gilovich, and Dennis T. Regan, "Does Studying Economics Inhibit Cooperation?" *Journal of Economic Perspectives*, 7 (1993), 159–171.

15. Donald P. Green and Ian Shapiro, *Pathologies of Rational Choice Theory* (New Haven, CT: Yale University Press, 1994).

16. Jeffrey Friedman, ed., *The Rational Choice Controversy* (New Haven, CT: Yale University Press, 1996).

17. Quoted in David Easton, *The Political System*, 2nd ed. (New York: Knopf, 1971), p. viii.

cartoonstock.com

The most influential political ideologies are often the target of ridicule by those who have a different point of view.

CHAPTER 2

Ideologies: Images of Political Life

- Liberalism and Conservatism
- Capitalism
- Marxism
- The Political Relevance of Marxist Ideology

- Socialism
- Other Ideologies
- Conclusion: Ideology Shapes Political Community and Political Conflict

Each of us thinks about politics in a unique way. Our views of political issues, controversies, and values are expressions of our personalities and backgrounds. Some of us want government to control more of the economy, while others feel that markets should be less regulated. Some of us think most about domestic social problems, others focus on ethical concerns, and still others think about foreign affairs or legal concepts. Some advocate radical change, and others seek to preserve traditions.

Nevertheless, despite the individualized nature of political orientations, we can identify certain well-established *ideologies* that describe patterns of political thinking among large numbers of people. An **ideology** is a more or less coherent system of political thinking. The most elaborate and complete ideologies, such as Marxism, contain a vision of justice, an identified adversary, a plan for attaining an ideal society, and a conception of good government. Less elaborate ideologies are simply approaches based on assumptions regarding the kinds of policies and that work best.

Understanding the most important ideologies is useful in two ways. First, the nature of the prevailing ideology that exists in a society affects the way its government works. It influences the way citizens participate in politics, how the government makes decisions, and what people expect from government. The articulation of interests; the making, adjudication, and execution of rules; the way that people are socialized into political life—the ideology that prevails among a nation's citizens affects all these things dramatically. The dominant ideology in

North Korea, for example, provides a foundation for widespread deference to state authority in social, economic, and even personal affairs, whereas the strong elements of individualism and capitalism in Australia produce a very different kind of politics.

Second, the degree of ideological *consensus* in a political system has an important influence on its stability. If a society experiences severe ideological conflict (as Nicaragua did in the 1980s), political life is often violent and unstable, whereas a general ideological consensus contributes to a relatively settled political order, as in Britain or Japan.

In addition to the usefulness of ideology as an aid in understanding the behavior of citizens and governments, studying ideologies helps us to decide for ourselves how we feel about political issues. Many of us have a fairly good idea about the differences between liberalism and conservatism, and we may know something about Marxism, socialism, or other ideologies. But even a brief analysis of the basic principles of these ideologies may help us understand our own political thinking. An individual may find that his or her positions on affirmative action, abortion, and arms control, for example, are manifestations of a political perspective that shapes the development of many other political opinions.

The following sections discuss ideologies that vary considerably with respect to their coherence and comprehensiveness. By some strict definitions, some of them do not fully qualify as "ideologies" at all. In keeping with familiar usage, however, and because of their great practical importance, we discuss each of them here.

LIBERALISM AND CONSERVATISM

Most Americans think of themselves, to some degree, as either liberal or conservative—even people who are generally uninterested in politics. Although being a "liberal" or a "conservative" does not require a consistent adherence to a comprehensive system of thought, there is a meaningful contrast between these ways of thinking about politics.

Liberalism

Liberalism has a long and complex history. Some analysts contend that the first important statement of liberalism was contained in the writings of the British political philosopher John Locke (1632–1704), whose ideas influenced the American Declaration of Independence. Perhaps the core idea of Lockean **liberalism** is simply the recognition that there is a sphere of individual rights that government should respect and leave untouched.

The widespread acceptance of this idea for generations in the United States makes it seem obvious to contemporary Americans. However, it is important to realize that other ways of thinking about politics—particularly the classical political philosophy of Plato and Aristotle—attributed no special status to individual rights.

John Locke (1632–1704), one of the foundational philosophers of liberalism.

Portrait of John Locke (1632–1704) (see also 1419), Kneller, Sir Godfrey (1646–1723) (after)/Private Collection, © Philip Mould Ltd, London/Bridgeman Art Library

An individual's place was to be defined with respect to the nature of the social order. Liberalism *begins* with the idea that individual rights come first. Government power is then built around them, so to speak.

Modern liberalism has evolved in ways that have transformed and extended Locke's ideas. Modern liberals oppose the application of state power to enforce conventional moral, religious, or traditional standards of behavior. In this respect, they carry forward a basic component of Lockean liberalism. When some politician or group proposes a law banning abortion or prohibiting flag burning, liberals unite in opposition. In such instances, liberalism advocates the security of individual choices over the state's (or the majority's) demands for the continuation of a single set of values. Liberalism thus emphasizes *tolerance*.

Yet modern liberals advocate the expansion of government authority to counteract corporate economic power and to create social conditions that improve the opportunities for people to engage in a full, satisfying life. This is not necessarily a contradiction, although conservatives often claim that it *is* inconsistent to be simultaneously opposed to state power and also supportive of expanding that power. The consistency is in the liberal's commitment to freeing the individual from forces that interfere with personal advancement and growth. Thus, liberals want to keep the state from enforcing moral conformity, but they support aggressive *government intervention* to provide disadvantaged individuals a way out of the economic and social conditions that condemn them to a bleak, limited future.

Modern liberals see many of society's problems as being rooted in negative social conditions. Again, we can see the common thread running back to the initial concerns of liberal thinking. If, as liberals believe, individuals need to be free both from the restrictions of antiquated traditions *and* from the restrictions created by poverty, it is logical to suppose that many people will fail to thrive when economic distress, racial discrimination, and religious intolerance frustrate their hopes. Poor people turn to crime, teenagers become pregnant and drop out of school, and rates of drug addiction reach epidemic proportions, say liberals, because social conditions deny those people real opportunities.

Although the range of identifiably "liberal" policy positions is quite wide—including everything from advocating gay rights to supporting labor unions to demanding national health plans—modern liberalism is not simply a patchwork quilt of ideas. Its precepts are held together by a faith in the ability of all people to prosper and grow. Liberal policies are thus designed to preserve the rights of individuals and to expand opportunities when social conditions dampen them.

Conservatism

Many capsule definitions begin with the conservative's preference for preserving society's political, social, and economic traditions, thus seeing conservatism as nothing more than support for the status quo. (One of contemporary American conservatism's elder statesmen, the late William F. Buckley, gave support to this view of conservatism when he famously stated that the role of the conservative is simply to "stand athwart history, yelling Stop!") A second often heard claim is that conservatism is based on the belief that human reason is limited and that it cannot solve social and political problems. Neither of these views gives us a complete view of conservatism.

The most fundamental element of **conservatism** is support for the idea that *traditional values strengthen society*. Most conservatives feel that humans have natural tendencies toward greed, promiscuity, aggressiveness, and sloth, and that the best way to inhibit those tendencies is through strong traditional values. Churches, schools, and even the state should act to preserve those values, according to conservative thinking, even at the expense of some freedoms.

Sir Edmund Burke (1729–1797) is often considered the father of conservative thinking, particularly in light of his 1790 essay, "Reflections on the Revolution in France."* While liberals applauded the revolution's goals of "Liberty, Equality, and Fraternity," Burke was appalled by the revolution's violent attacks against the aristocracy and the church. He argued that the "customs and traditions" that define the character of a society are essential in preserving stability, culture, and progress. Burke felt that the French revolutionaries were bent on the destruction of French culture and that their success in doing so would create disorder, injustice, and a lower quality of life for all.

A particularly controversial aspect of Burke's thinking was his acceptance of *class distinctions*. He argued that society is better off with its aristocratic heritage intact, even if it perpetuates vast differences between the rich and the poor. Thus, Burke felt that the trappings of class distinctions, including attendance at different churches

* The text of this classic essay may be found at the website of the Constitution Society: www.constitution.org/eb/rev_fran.htm.

for upper- and lower-class citizens, differences in clothing and accents, and deferential forms of address to one's "betters," among other things, are traditions that make society work. When people know and accept their places in society, order and stability are possible. Perhaps reflecting that kind of thinking, all Conservative British prime ministers until the 1970s had aristocratic roots.

In its modern form, conservatism has two identifiable branches. One focuses on the moral sphere. According to this aspect of conservative thinking, a good society is one in which people place greater value on "self-restraint" than self-expression and pleasure. Conservatives are thus more inclined than liberals to support, for example, restrictions on obscene artistic expressions, marijuana use, same-sex marriages, and strict discipline in schools.

Consequently, conservatives often look to *erosions* of traditional moral values as the primary cause of social ills, while modern liberals are apt to blame poverty or racism. "Bad conditions do not cause riots, bad men do" is a commonly heard conservative refrain. Similarly, many conservatives argue that unwanted teenage pregnancies do not occur as a result of poverty, racism, or inadequate sex education, but as a result of the erosion of traditional morality. In fact, conservatives often contend that public school sex education contributes to the perception that sexual behavior has nothing to do with values. In a wide variety of contexts, conservatism looks to moral standards as a guide to behavior and claims that liberals, in their emphasis on tolerance, erode the force of those moral standards, producing disorder, hopelessness, crime, and poverty.

A second identifiable branch of conservatism emphasizes economic concerns. Conservatives who focus exclusively on economics may become indistinguishable from capitalists in their policy positions (see the following section). Free-market economics is not supported wholly by all conservatives, but it is not a coincidence that many conservatives blend a traditional perspective on moral issues with support for the free market. A common thread linking "traditional values" conservatism and "economic" conservatism is support for the work ethic as a traditional value. Conservatives claim that they defend the work ethic by maintaining an economic system that rewards initiative, talent, and hard work while penalizing idleness. Conservatives feel liberals interfere with the market's ability to allocate resources by enacting policies that restrict initiative and allocate rewards on the basis of need or simply to produce a more equal distribution of wealth.

American and European conservatives tend to place differing amounts of emphasis on economic freedoms. A strong communitarian perspective is often present among European conservatives, whereas many American conservatives embrace individualism more firmly. William Bennett, a former Secretary of Education who gained national fame with his successful volume *The Book of Virtues*, is an exception among modern American conservatives, emphasizing social values much more than free-market liberties.*

---

* See Bennett, *The Book of Virtues* (New York: Simon and Schuster, 1993). Bennett's conservative themes are also apparent in *America: The Last Best Hope, Volumes I and II* (Nashville, TN: Thomas Nelson, 2007), and *A Century Turns: New Hopes, New Fears* (Nashville, TN: Thomas Nelson, 2010).

The Policy Relevance of Liberal and Conservative Ideologies

In most industrialized democracies, policies typically reflect a mixture of conservative and liberal thinking. Perhaps the best illustration of this is the changing size and scope of the welfare state. Liberal administrations often expand the welfare state, while conservatives restrain their growth. A comprehensive study of U.S. income distribution policies after World War II confirmed this general impression: "When the Democrats are at average or above-average congressional strength … transfer spending … tends to trend upward…."[1] The rate of growth in social programs in this country thus reflects the ever-changing competition between liberal and conservative political influence.

The policies that divide conservative and liberal ideologues make a real difference in citizens' lives. Figure 2.1 shows the impact of several important government programs on economic inequality in the U.S. Using census data and other information, political scientist Nathan J. Kelly estimated the impact of the federal income tax, Social Security, Medicare, Medicaid, and the food stamp program on inequality, as measured by the Gini Index (discussed later in this chapter). Each of these programs has reduced economic inequality. Perhaps surprisingly, Social Security and the progressive income tax have had the greatest impacts, reducing inequality much more than means-tested programs like Medicaid and food stamps. Taken together, economic inequality in the U.S. would be nearly 20 percent greater than it currently is without the government programs that liberal ideology has traditionally supported.

FIGURE 2.1   **The Effect of Government Programs on Inequality in the U.S.**

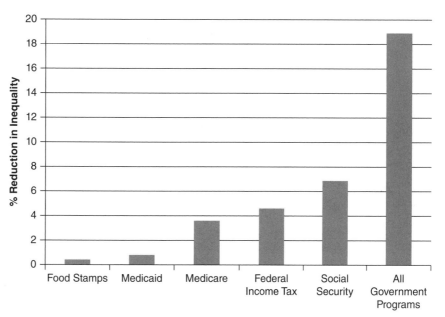

Source: Data from Nathan J. Kelly, *Political Choice and Income Inequality in the United States*, Ph.D. dissertation, University of North Carolina at Chapel Hill, 2004.

A CLOSER LOOK

2.1

Conservatives and Liberals: Has the World Wide Web Created a Nation of Isolated Ideological Extremists?

If the differences between conservatives and liberals seem greater than ever before, it is probably due to major changes in mass communication. The expansion of cable television, the growth of the World Wide Web, and the end of the "fairness doctrine" in the United States are three developments that have taken place in roughly the same time period, and, taken together, they have arguably created a more heated debate between liberals and conservatives throughout the world.

Sometimes, the vitriol can be almost comical in its harshness. Here are two colorful examples of contemporary political discourse:

Keith Olberman, referring to conservative columnist Michelle Malkin:

She received death threats and hate-filled voice mails all thanks to the total mindless, morally bankrupt, knee-jerk, fascistic hatred—without which Michelle Malkin would just be a big mashed-up bag of meat with lipstick on it.*

Ann Coulter, discussing Senator Patty Murray, a Democrat from Washington State:

After Murray was elected to the U.S. Senate, the Democrats tried to keep her locked in her office to prevent her from saying anything that might end up in a newspaper. But in the confusion after the

9/11 attack, the leadership must have lost the keys and Murray escaped to say this about Osama bin Laden: *"He's been out in these countries for decades, building schools, building roads, building infrastructure, building day-care facilities, building health-care facilities, and the people are extremely grateful. He's made their lives better.'*

I defy anyone to produce something stupider ever uttered by a homo sapiens. Not Barbara Boxer, Joe Biden or even John Edwards can hold their dimly lit candles to her."*

Until the mid-1980s, citizens read newspapers and magazines, and they watched three or four television networks. There was very little political content on radio stations, and, at least in the United States, all broadcasters dampened their coverage of controversial political issues so that they would not run afoul of the "fairness doctrine."† Liberals and conservatives got

* Keith Olbermann, speaking on MSNBC's *Countdown with Keith Olbermann*, October 13, 2009.

* Ann Coulter, "Patty Murray: The Stupidest Person in America," September 29, 2010, available at www.anncoulter.com.

† The Federal Communications Commission established the "fairness doctrine" in 1949. Under the doctrine, the FCC could conclude that a licensed broadcaster had not been serving the public interest if the content of its programming did not present "balanced coverage of various and conflicting views on issues of public importance." In 1986, the Commission repealed the fairness doctrine, making it possible for broadcasters to air programs that were clearly conservative or liberal in nature. It is often argued that the fairness doctrine was an unconstitutional infringement on freedom of the press, but some Americans and some members of Congress have recently expressed interest in reinstating it.

However, conservatives often argue that efforts to reduce inequality have led to an unfair burden on wealthier citizens. According to data available from the Internal Revenue Service, while the richest 1 percent of U.S. households earned nearly 17 percent of the nation's income, they supplied 36.7 percent of all federal income taxes, and paid an average tax rate of 24 percent on their incomes. The bottom 50 percent earned over 13 percent of the nation's income, but paid only 2.3 percent of all federal income taxes, paying an average tax rate of just 1.85 percent. Conservatives and liberals employ very different approaches, and take note of very different

2.1

A CLOSER LOOK

most of their information from the same sources. Today, we can choose to watch Ann Coulter or Chris Matthews on television and to read dailykos.com or rushlimbaugh.com on the Web. What has been the effect of having so many decidedly conservative and decidedly liberal news and opinion sources on the nature of modern democracy?

If stable, healthy democracy requires that citizens share exposure to some unifying ideas and that people read, hear, and see ideas presented from perspectives other than their own, the explosion of divisive Internet, radio, and cable television outlets may be a cause for concern. Today, anyone with an ideological identification can seek news and opinion outlets that confirm and strengthen his or her views, and few of these outlets present the "other" side.

Cass Sunstein, currently administrator of the White House Office of Information and Regulatory Affairs, expressed his concerns in a book entitled *Republic.com*. He argued that the new system of mass communications has given citizens the power to "filter" the information they receive, a power that may not be a positive thing for democracy:

> [Democracy] requires something other than free, or publicly unrestricted, individual choices. First, people should be exposed to materials that they would not have chosen in advance. Unanticipated encounters, involving topics and points of view that people have not sought out and perhaps find irritating, are central to democracy and even to freedom itself. Second, many or most citizens should have a range of common experiences. Without shared experiences, a heterogeneous society will have a more difficult time

addressing social problems and understanding one another."*

Most of us can point to plenty of recent examples of divisive political rhetoric that generate more heat than light. However, a 2008 study explored changes over time with respect to "cross-ideological" discussions on the Internet, and while the researchers found that people tend to communicate most often with persons sharing their political views, they found that this pattern had not become more pronounced over time: "Over the ten-month span included in our data set, we find no evidence that conservative or liberal bloggers are addressing each other less at the end of our time period than at the beginning."† Most of the discussions between conservatives and liberals were classified by the researchers as "straw-man" arguments that do not contribute to substantive debates, but even these discussions increase awareness of opposing points of view.

Passionate arguments between conservatives and liberals (and among proponents of other ideologies) have been going on since Aristotle's time, and they will doubtlessly continue. It is probably too early to conclude that the Internet, cable television, and talk radio have transformed political discourse in modern countries, but there is no denying that it is far easier to find heated, "over-the-top" ideological material than it once was.

* See Sunstein, Cass R. *Republic.com* (Princeton, N.J.: Princeton University Press, 2001). This excerpt was published in the *Boston Review* at www.bostonreview.net.

† Eszter Hargittai, Jason Gallo, and Matthew Kane, "Cross-ideological Discussions among Conservative and Liberal Bloggers," *Public Choice* 134 (2008): 67–86.

facts, in evaluating the existing level of inequality. This debate will probably never be settled, but the policies that conservatives and liberals argue about have important consequences.

Of course, when policy disputes emphasize moral concerns, it is difficult to make decisions that reflect some measure of both liberal and conservative ideology. Opposing perspectives on abortion severely divide several societies, including the United States. Many proponents of abortion rights tend to view any restriction, even laws requiring parental notification or limits on public funding of abortions, as invasions of a fundamental right. Some of those opposing abortion argue that virtually any abortion, even an abortion to save the woman's life or one to serve the victim of rape or incest, constitutes murder. The U.S. Supreme Court essentially removed this issue from the legislative process with its 1973 **Roe v. Wade** decision, and it is fair to say that many state legislators were glad that they were spared the necessity of taking an official stand.* Following the 2008 decision by the California Supreme Court striking down state laws prohibiting same-sex marriages, an especially heated fight between liberals and conservatives continues to rage over this issue as well.

CAPITALISM

Capitalism refers both to an economic system and to an ideology. As an economic system, **capitalism** may be defined by its reliance on economic exchange and private ownership to allocate society's resources. A capitalist system is one in which profit-seeking behavior, not governmental decision making, determines what happens in the economy. Capitalist ideology provides philosophical and analytical support for such a system.†

The Elements of Capitalist Ideology

There are two identifiable elements in capitalist ideology. First, capitalism places a heavy emphasis on **individualism**. Whereas socialists focus on communal values and needs, those drawn to capitalism tend to emphasize individual accomplishments and talents and the private sphere of life. Advocates of capitalist ideology typically believe that the general good is best served when each individual seeks his or her economic self-interest. Adam Smith stated this idea in 1776 in his landmark treatise *An Inquiry into the Nature and Causes of the Wealth of Nations*: "[An individual who] intends only his own gain [is] led by an invisible hand to promote an end which was no part of his intention.... By pursuing his own interest he frequently promotes that of the society more effectually than when he really intends to promote it."[2] Factories are built, jobs are provided, and wealth is generated—all as the result of free individuals seeking profits in a free marketplace.

Second, capitalist thinking is often associated with *distrust of government control* of social resources. The capitalist sees central bureaucracies as inherently wasteful and inefficient, whereas the market, with its multitude of individual decisions driven by self-interest, is rational and productive. Government decisions are driven by the vague, ill-informed, and misguided motivations of leaders, not by the precise incentives of profit seeking. Thus, those favoring a capitalist economy point with great satisfaction to the vast differences between what used to be East Germany and West Germany. Two states with essentially similar people, a similar culture, and the same climate had very different economic growth rates and conditions between 1947 and

---

* On April 18, 2007, the U.S. Supreme Court held that the federal "Partial Birth Abortion Ban Act of 2003" was constitutional (see *Gonzales v. Carhart*). Many observers, along with the four dissenters on the Court, noted that the decision reflected a change in the ideological composition of the Court following the appointment of Justice Samuel Alito to replace retired Justice Sandra Day O'Connor.

† The French phrase *laissez faire*, meaning "leave alone," is commonly employed to designate the essence of what we here term *capitalist* ideology. In fact, some economists say that capitalism is not a "system" at all, but simply a description of what happens when no system is imposed on free individuals, as long as basic property rights and freedoms are protected.

1990. In 1988, before German unification, the gross domestic product (GDP) per capita was $18,480 in West Germany and only $11,860 in East Germany. An even starker contrast exists today between North and South Korea. The GDP per capita is over $30,200 in South Korea but only $1,900 in North Korea. Differences of this magnitude reflect the tremendous impact of ideology on the lives of people.[3] (See the nighttime photo of North and South Korea in Chapter 1.)

Policy Implications of Capitalist Ideology

Believing in individualism and free-market economics does not require one to favor the elimination of government's role in society. If it did, capitalist ideology would have little practical relevance to real-world politics. Capitalist ideas can find their way into policy making in less radical ways.

For example, political leaders who support capitalist ideology often advocate tax policies that deemphasize the goal of economic equality. Proportional tax rates take the same percentage of income from each citizen, regardless of income, whereas progressive systems take an increasing percentage from wealthier citizens. The rich pay more taxes than the poor under both approaches, but progressive taxes are slanted more toward the advantage of the poor. Capitalists claim that steeply progressive taxes stifle the initiative of talented people (since economic success is "penalized" by placing high earners in a higher tax bracket).

Capitalist thinking similarly supports policy choices that emphasize or strengthen private production of goods and services and that give consumers a wider range of choices. (See A Closer Look 2.2.) During the Reagan administration (1981–1989), some significant changes along those lines were made in the United States, resulting in a considerable increase in what is called *contracting out* for public services. The current trend in many Latin American societies is also toward greater privatization of state enterprises. In this arrangement, private contractors submitting the lowest qualified bid provide services previously provided by public employees. Capitalist ideology welcomes this approach as a way to harness the power of competition.

2.2

A C L O S E R   L O O K

Ideology and the Controversy over
Health Care Reform in the United States

Most citizens, elected leaders, and policy analysts agree that the health care system in the United States provides high-quality services but that it costs too much. The fact that health insurance is usually obtained as a benefit through the workplace makes many workers feel trapped because they may not be able to obtain health coverage if they leave their current jobs. Employers are increasingly reluctant to hire new employees.

Politically, the matter is complicated by the fact that most Americans are pleased with their existing health care coverage. These citizens want the system to become more efficient, and most of them are concerned about fellow citizens without health care

(Continued)

Ideology and the Controversy over Health Care Reform in the United States (*Continued*)

insurance, but they oppose changes that would undermine their access to health care and their range of choices. The issue is further complicated by the fact that policy analysts have produced widely varying cost projections and estimations of savings from alternative reform proposals. Virtually everyone agrees that changes are needed, but the issue remains divisive and unsettled, even after the passage of the Patient Protection and Affordable Care Act of 2010.

The debate over health care reform in the United States also highlights a deep ideological divide. Setting aside disputes regarding the practical impact of specific reforms and arguments over cost projections, the health care problem is controversial because it highlights the fundamental tension between liberal and conservative principles.

It should not be surprising that liberals have long been drawn to the idea of a governmental entitlement to health care services. Citizens without access to health care are not able to enjoy the freedoms necessary to a fulfilling life, and thus, most liberals see health care as a basic right, not a privilege. Drawing on their natural discomfort with the profit motive, liberals also claim that a stronger government role in health care will create a more efficient and more equitable system.

Michael Walzer, a leading contemporary philosopher, articulates a position that many modern liberals take when they approach the health care issue. He argues that the possession of great wealth creates an unjust society because wealth enables some people to dominate others and because it is wrong for one's share of wealth to determine his or her access to all kinds of goods and services. For example, it may be acceptable that only those with great wealth can get elegant villas in Monte Carlo, but it is *not* acceptable that this same wealth enables such persons to consume more MRIs and prescription drugs and to receive more services from health care professionals than less wealthy citizens.* The nature and degree of the individual's

need, not the individual's financial holdings, should determine access to health care, according to Walzer.

The conservative's emphasis on individualism, the work ethic, and the free market leads to a very different perspective on health care reform. A major conservative argument voiced during debates over the Patient Protection and Affordable Care Act has to do with *government rationing* of health care. When the government creates an entitlement to a scarce resource (hospital beds, services by doctors and nurses, pharmaceuticals, etc.), shortages are inevitable, say conservatives. These critics look to the experiences of Canada and Great Britain to support the claim that government management of health care leads to long delays in service and outright denials of certain treatments.

For example, the British National Health Service recently adopted a policy of denying treatment for macular degeneration, the leading cause of blindness in the elderly, until the individual becomes fully blind in one eye. According to the (London) *Daily Mail*, "Thousands of patients will be condemned to blindness because of a decision to ration the NHS treatment which could save their sight.... [They will] effectively have to lose the use of an eye before qualifying for therapy to save their remaining vision."[4] Conservatives argue that this kind of restriction is inevitable when the government provides health care services. Unlike most liberals, conservatives are deeply opposed to the idea that government will decide who has access to scarce medical treatments.

The ideological divide guarantees that health care reform will remain controversial during the next several years. Policy experts and planners will argue over specific features of the new law and other laws that refine or replace it, and they may devise compromises and innovative solutions. But the fundamental tensions between conservatism and liberalism ensure a protracted period of energetic dissent.

---

* See Walzer's *Spheres of Justice: A Defense of Pluralism and Equality* (New York: Basic Books, 1982).

MARXISM

Strictly speaking, Marxism is the set of ideas derived from the German philosopher Karl Marx (1818–1883). In contrast to liberalism and conservatism, Marxism is an elaborate, detailed system of thought. It is therefore arguably the most complete example of an ideology. Marxism incorporates an interpretation of history, the identification of an adversary, a plan for the future, and a conception of the just society. Marx was convinced that everything important in society, even the way people *think*, could be accounted for through the impact of class struggles: "It is not the consciousness of men that determines their existence, but, on the contrary, their social existence determines their consciousness."[5] Marxism still exerts a strong political influence in today's changing world.

The essence of **Marxism** is *the belief that economic conflict between a ruling class and an exploited lower class is unavoidable and that it is the driving force in social and political life.* Unlike conventional modern liberals, most of whom believe that better policies and leaders can produce social justice, Marx argued that economic forces essentially *determine* ideas and political movements. In Marx's view, poor people are exploited not because some people are greedy or because people do not fully appreciate the social costs of poverty but because *the economic structure of capitalist society makes exploitation of the poor inevitable.* According to his concept of **economic determinism**, human history is the process of economic forces pushing society from one stage of development to another until the inevitable end point (**communism**) is reached.

How do economic forces shape history? Marx provided a remarkably influential set of answers. According to Marx, the first "stage" of "prehistory," **primitive communism** (or communalism), was the economic system that existed before the evolution of private property, slavery, or classes. Small bands of humans lived together in joint control over the land, wildlife, and food supplies. Marx's distinctive idea was that the communal nature of such societies was created by an economic fact: people lived communally *because the primitive level of agricultural productivity made land ownership and slavery* economically *impossible.*

Why would this be true? Since each person could produce only enough to stay alive, a slave would have had to consume everything that he or she produced, leaving nothing for a master to save or consume. Because nearly all one's time was spent gathering food, it was also impractical to devote resources to defending a territory. Ownership of land and exploitation of others simply did not make *economic* sense. Humans shared resources in primitive society entirely because the low state of productivity made any other arrangement impractical.

Feudalism arose when agricultural productivity advanced. As some people happened upon fertile land and discovered ways to cultivate it, they found that they could produce more food than they and their families consumed. Wanting to secure their produce, some of them hired soldiers (fed with food not needed by the owners) to defend estates. Land ownership then produced power, since large acreages could support armed strength. Feudalism thereby created the first *class* divisions: in one group were those who owned the land, and in the other were those who worked on it.

Capitalism emerged as a consequence of further economic development. Greater farm productivity made resources available for enterprises other than agriculture, and people acquired power through their ownership of *capital*. They invested that capital in factories, hiring workers to trade their labor for wages. The "surplus value" created by the workers was then taken by the capitalists, who used it to add to their wealth and power.

However, Marx argued that capitalism would inevitably fall. Capitalists would eventually have to compete aggressively with one another, forcing them to exploit workers ever more severely. Wages would drop, work hours would increase, and work conditions would deteriorate. And, unlike the exploited serfs under feudalism who lived in isolation across huge farms, the increasingly exploited workers under capitalism (the "proletariat") lived and worked together in large numbers in factory settings. This was a fatal "contradiction" of capitalism. The downtrodden workers would achieve a sense of class consciousness, realizing their common bond and their common capitalist class enemies. Capitalism would have to fall.

The resulting system, *socialism*, would be the fourth and final stage of "prehistory." Under this system, workers would be paid fairly, industrial production would be driven by the real needs of the vast majority of people, and, most important, there would no longer be a ruling class. Eventually, productivity would increase to the point at which all the real needs of society could be satisfied without government help. "True" history would begin as *communism* emerged from human prehistory, and the state would "wither away" with no class conflict to resolve.

THE POLITICAL RELEVANCE OF MARXIST IDEOLOGY

In discussing how Marxism has affected government and politics, it is essential to remember that Marx himself was primarily an economic philosopher and his main contribution was the development of a theory. The real "founding father" of communism—and of the first communist system, the Soviet Union—was Vladimir Ilyich Ulyanov, better known as Lenin (1870–1924). Hence, we usually speak of the guiding ideology of communist systems as "Marxism-Leninism.[*]

Following Lenin's contributions, communist systems share at least two characteristics that are a result of Marxist-Leninist ideology. First, the premise that political conflict is essentially a conflict between workers and those who exploit them leads to restrictions on political diversity. Competitive political party systems are illegitimate in Marxist-Leninist thinking because only the Communist Party is believed to have the true interests of the people (that is, the working class) at heart. Second, communist governments have frequently used the idea of class conflict as the intellectual justification for repressing political, religious, and artistic expression. Drawing on Marx's contention that "religion is the opium of the people," Marxist governments in Europe and elsewhere have restricted religious freedom, viewing the Orthodox and Catholic churches as distracting the working class from its true political interests. In

---

[*] Similarly, Chinese communism is sometimes termed "Marxism-Leninism-Maoism" because of the importance of Mao Zedong's influence on that version of the ideology. In addition to Lenin and Mao, Fidel Castro, Ché Guevara, and others adapted and altered Marxist concepts in the course of revolutionary movements. We outline the most crucial of the extensions of Marxism in discussing Russia and China (Chapters 12 and 13).

2010, Freedom House included Cuba and North Korea, both Marxist nations, among the 17 most repressive regimes on earth.*

SOCIALISM

Socialism is a much more generalized ideology that actually predates Marxism. Although many socialists, particularly in years past, have shared many Marxist beliefs, others have not. Socialism shares with Marxism a deep concern about the divisive effects of private property, and it too is driven by a hope that greater social and economic equality can be achieved. Some socialists would even agree that the best way to make progress is to work toward a revolution, although socialist ideology does not require such a position. Once we get beyond the basic problem of social inequality, it becomes clear that *socialism* is a term applied to a rather diverse range of approaches to politics.

Fundamental Elements of Socialism

The core idea of **socialism** is the assumption that a just society requires purposeful social action, or, to put it negatively, that actions based on *private interests* prevent the achievement of a fair society. Socialists focus on the potential for *community* and *public interest*, opposing what they see as an excessive emphasis on profit seeking and self-interest in other approaches to political life. Clearly, the most important fault socialists find in capitalist systems is social and economic inequality, but the creation of greater equality is not their only goal. Socialists also want to establish a greater public role to counter the forces dividing society and the selfishness unleashed by private interests.

Nowhere is this sentiment more wonderfully captured than in the following statement by French philosopher Jean-Jacques Rousseau (1712–1778):

> The first man, who after enclosing a piece of ground, took it into his head to say, *this is mine*, and found people simple enough to believe him, was the real founder of civil society. How many crimes, how many wars, how many murders, how many misfortunes and horrors, would that man have saved the human species, who … should have cried to his fellows: Beware of listening to this impostor; you are lost, if you forget that the fruits of the earth belong equally to us all, and the earth itself to nobody![6]

Socialists are a diverse lot. The person generally regarded as the first to use the term *socialism* was a British industrialist named Robert Owen (1771–1858). He supported the free-market system in most respects, although he advocated the establishment of state schools and supported the idea, radical for its time, that children under 12 years of age should not be permitted to work a full (13-hour) day. Although one does not have to be a socialist to agree wholeheartedly with those reforms, they do embody the essence of socialism: the force of the public interest must be brought to bear as a restraint on the forces of private interest.[7]

---

* See the full ranking of nations with respect to several measures of freedom at www.freedomhouse.org.

For most socialists, profit-motivated behavior is less fair and even less efficient than public decision making, and thus socialists favor public ownership of much industrial production. Democratic socialist governments in Western Europe have taken control only of certain key industries, such as steel, electric power, or railroads. Public ownership means, for a socialist, that prices and wages will be set equitably, the environment will be protected, work conditions will be safe, and consumers will obtain reliable products and services. It should be noted, however, that in practice European socialist parties in countries such as France and Spain have recently become far more skeptical about the value of state ownership in the economy. Still, they continue to believe that the state should be able to allocate scarce resources to where they are most needed, not simply to where the market demands them.

Democratic Socialism and Marxism

Democratic socialism and Marxism share a common view of social injustice, but they diverge with respect to what should be done about it. Marxists (especially those who accept Lenin's ideas) typically advocate revolution, whereas democratic socialists believe in working for change through democratic political channels. Although some people who consider themselves Marxists would not agree, most Marxists assume that political decision making in a capitalist societies is inevitably driven by the interests of an elite ruling class.

Most Marxists reject the idea that capitalists can be "voted out" of power, and they therefore distrust elections.* (An important exception to this generalization was the Marxist-Leninist Sandinista Party in Nicaragua, which allowed elections in which opposition parties voted it out of power in 1984.) In contrast, democratic socialists work for progressive policies and programs in hopes of creating greater equality of economic conditions and opportunities and bringing communal interests to bear on social choices.

Perhaps the most important aspect of this divergence has to do with the problem of democracy itself. Democratic socialists accept the idea of democracy as a *process*. When people are able to express their views and choose among competitive parties, socialists expect to be able to achieve their objectives. Many Marxists define democracy as an *outcome*—namely, a just distribution of wealth. Democracy, for a Marxist, thus requires the elimination of class divisions; as long as class differences exist, the democratic process is empty, misleading, and doomed to fail.

The Political Relevance of Socialist Ideology

Despite the diversity among those who support socialism, there is an identifiable pattern of policy choices associated with this ideology. First, as noted earlier, socialist systems usually have adopted some degree of *public ownership* of banking, communications, transportation, and steel production, among other industries, to ensure that allocations are in the public interest.

---

* Many contemporary Marxist political thinkers and intellectuals, particularly in Europe, strongly support democratic principles, arguing that there is no necessary contradiction between Marxist theory and democracy. However, the record of Marxist regimes in practice has not been tolerant of opposing points of view.

Second, socialist governments usually *regulate private industries* extensively. A distrust of profit-driven decision making leads to government requirements regarding worker safety, equity in compensation of employees, consumer safety, and environmental protection. Although all modern governments have adopted at least some regulatory initiatives, socialist ideology is associated with more extensive and more comprehensive regulation of private industry.

Third, socialist countries have *large, expensive welfare systems*. The government sector of the economy employs a large proportion of the workforce in implementing programs for social security, education, income maintenance, and health care. Many socialists contend that a basic income and adequate medical care are fundamental human rights, not simply advantages that those with good fortune can enjoy. Along with a large **welfare state** (an extensive array of government programs in housing, health care, and education), socialist ideology generally leads to higher public spending relative to the size of the economy. For example, socialist thinking has long influenced politics in Sweden, and government spending there is quite high, but it is much lower in less-socialist Paraguay.

The high taxes and extensive welfare state associated with socialist ideology are also linked to a fourth policy implication of socialism: *redistribution of income*. Socialists, as discussed earlier, are often drawn to their ideology by a concern for the plight of the poor and by a corresponding discomfort at the opulence of the rich. Socialists contend that taking from the rich does not rob them of anything they genuinely need (since they have enough left to provide for themselves), but that it does make the difference between stark poverty and a minimally acceptable standard of living for the poor. Hence, not only do socialist systems have high taxes, but their tax systems also take a larger proportion of taxes from those with high incomes.

Despite the socialist emphasis on income equality, it is not always true that socialist systems as a whole are strikingly more egalitarian than other systems. Some comparisons suggest that socialism leads to greater equality—for example, largely socialist Sweden has greater income equality than France. Yet capitalist South Korea and Taiwan both have very high income equality, approaching a distribution of wealth similar to that in China.

In a controversial empirical study, two prominent political scientists attempted to determine the effect of socialism on economic equality. Although individual comparisons can be found to support the idea that socialist ideology promotes greater equality, the results of this study supported the idea that *higher levels of economic development are, in general, associated with greater equality* and that the degree to which the country adopts socialist policies makes little difference.[8] For example, on the "Gini Index" measure of **income inequality** (in which a score of zero indicates perfect equality and a score of 100 indicates perfect inequality), China's score of 41.5 is higher (indicating less equality) than the U.S. score of 40.8, and South Korea's 31.6 score indicates greater equality than Mexico's 51.6.[9] Obviously, there is no simple explanation for differences among nations with respect to income inequality.

Fifth, socialist ideology usually favors *public service delivery* over private services. Support for public education is actually widespread in most industrialized countries, but public education is especially central to socialist thinking. Reliance on private institutions to provide educational services would be contrary to socialist principles both because, according to socialists, it would foster elitism and because a public educational institution is the most effective way to instill communal, shared ideals in the citizenry. Socialists favor public over private service delivery in other areas, of course, including most municipal services (public safety, road building and repair, garbage collection, prison administration, and many others). The public role in these areas allows the government to make policy choices in accordance with community purposes, and, as an additional socialist benefit, it enables government to provide employment opportunities to those who may not be able to obtain private jobs.

OTHER IDEOLOGIES

Most contemporary political systems make policies that, in varying degrees and mixtures, reflect the ideologies already discussed. Still other ideological strains can be identified, however, and although they have not been as pervasive, these other ideologies have exerted considerable influence on policy decisions, important political movements, or both.

Feminism

Feminism actually applies to two rather different sets of ideas. On one hand, feminism is the demand that females should enjoy the same rights and responsibilities enjoyed by males, and that laws and practices placing females in a lower status are unfair, foolish, and wasteful. This type of feminism is largely a statement of basic liberal principles specifically applied to the rights of women. On the other hand, feminism also refers to an approach that attempts to identify special feminine (and masculine) qualities, usually arguing that feminine qualities have not been fully appreciated and that masculine qualities have dominated and distorted social and cultural development.

The first variety of feminism is a widespread, sustained movement that focuses on opening opportunities for women with respect to voting and other civil rights and the removal of gender restrictions in various occupations and in the armed services. For example, a woman may not legally drive a car in contemporary Saudi Arabia, and the former Taliban government of Afghanistan prevented women from obtaining education and mandated severe beatings for women who appeared in public without the *burkas* that covered them literally from head to toe.*

Although the Taliban regime in Afghanistan was perhaps the most extreme form of widespread restrictions on women's rights, it is important to note that women were denied the vote in virtually all democracies until the early 1900s. In its simplest forms, feminism is a demand that these kinds of inequities be removed. Often, feminists argue that removing legal or even constitutional restrictions is not enough; there must be representation of women where traditions and "old boy" networks effectively exclude them, even when laws officially open the doors to all applicants. Hence,

---

* In May, 2011, Katya Koren, 19, a Ukrainian teenager who had participated in a beauty pageant, was stoned to death for violating Sharia law. One of her attackers, a 16-year-old boy, reported that he had no regrets about her death.

feminists have fought for the appointment of more women to leadership positions in government, universities, and professions historically considered beyond their reach (firefighting, science teaching, space programs).

Feminism also embraces noneconomic policies. The abortion issue occupies a central place among feminist policy demands in the United States, and it is related to the status of women in several ways. Most feminists argue that laws restricting abortion lead women to obtain dangerous illegal abortions, and they note that men are not subject to any parallel restriction. More fundamentally, they see abortion restrictions as a violation of privacy. In Africa, many feminists battle against forced female circumcision, a painful procedure designed to minimize women's enjoyment of sex.

Senator Hillary Clinton's historic campaign to become the Democratic Party's 2008 nominee for the U.S. presidency was a very conspicuous indicator of how successful this first type of feminism has been. Although she did not win, data from the primaries revealed that millions of Democrats voted for her, including people of both genders, all ethnicities, and in different socioeconomic circumstances. She won important primaries in Ohio, Texas, and California, among many others, and, while female voters preferred her virtually everywhere, nearly half of all males in many Democratic primaries voted for her as well. (A majority of men voting in the Ohio, Kentucky, and West Virginia Democratic primaries voted for Clinton, for example.) This level of success for a female candidate demonstrates that the mainstream feminists' demands for equality have produced important changes, even if full gender equality remains a challenge.

The second variant of feminism (sometimes termed "radical" or "gender" feminism) generally supports those and other efforts to achieve social and economic equality, but it focuses more on the *differences* between the sexes. Some of these feminists contend that females have greater humanism, are more pacifist, and have a broader ability to nurture than males do, and that these characteristics stem from fundamental biological differences.[10] According to these feminists, the fact that men continue to hold dominant positions in corporations, government, and education suggests that the nature of private and public life is driven by the "male" traits of competition and individualism. Identifying essential feminine characteristics helps us to see that society would become more peaceful, more humane, and more community-oriented if females achieve equal status.

Both strands of feminist thinking will likely grow in importance in the years ahead. At least in the industrial democracies, women have become influential players in national leadership positions, and feminists have acquired a strong voice in academic and policy-making circles. Although it is important to note that feminism embodies a very diverse set of ideas, this ideology will have considerable impact on virtually all areas of public policy in future decades.

Libertarianism

The basic feature of libertarian ideology is its insistence on *liberty* from government control. The movement thus shares some of the views of both liberalism and capitalism. Libertarians oppose laws restricting abortion or the freedoms of religion and expression. They also oppose the military draft, restrictions on drug use, occupational-safety legislation, and most pollution-control laws. They support an isolationist foreign policy, primarily because an active foreign policy usually requires extensive preparations for war, which interfere with personal freedom on many levels.

However, libertarians sharply oppose the modern liberals' advocacy of government as a force to create or maintain better conditions for the poor and disadvantaged. For example, most libertarians oppose the minimum wage law. If a person wants to sell his or her labor for $6 per hour, and if an employer wants to buy it at that price, libertarians believe that government has no right to interfere. Moreover, they contend the government has no right to force people to use seat belts in a car or to wear helmets while riding motorcycles. Libertarians disagree with conservatives regarding laws that criminalize marijuana, prostitution, or obscenity.

Thus, both left and right are attracted and repelled by **libertarianism**. Both liberals and conservatives support the ideal of privacy in different ways, but each also advocates principles regarding the public interest, and each contains some idea of "civic virtue." Liberals suggest that the public interest requires certain activist social policies, and conservatives argue that the public interest demands the support of traditional values that nurture and preserve culture. In very different ways, then, both liberalism and conservatism advocate an activist government. In contrast, libertarianism will probably always be a limited movement because its ideas cannot incorporate any positive idea of the public interest.

Environmentalism

A great number of people, primarily in developed societies, are deeply concerned about the physical environment, and some of them approach politics and government largely through those concerns. There are many interest groups and at least one well-known political party, the Green Party, for which environmental issues are central. At the beginning of the twenty-first century, **environmentalism** has become large and influential enough to be considered an ideology.

For most people, environmental issues are simply one important issue to be considered and debated alongside other issues, such as poverty, national defense, economic security, and education. But quite a few citizens in the United States, Western Europe, Japan, and elsewhere are convinced that current threats to the environment are so critical that virtually every policy decision should be made on the basis of its potential impact on the environment. These people are interested not only in specific pollution control plans but also in the globalization of the economy, public transportation, public management of housing patterns, and foreign aid programs, among many other kinds of policies.

The environmental movement focused on fairly specific policy objectives a few decades ago. The publication of Rachel Carson's *Silent Spring* was a landmark event, depicting how pesticides such as DDT had devastated several endangered bird species.[11] Serialized in 1962 in *The New Yorker*, Carson's book eventually led to restrictions on pesticide use. Environmentalists were also key players in the development of regulations on automobile emissions. However, the more recent issue of "global warming" has produced an even more contentious debate, largely because the actions proposed to address the issue would arguably shake the foundations of industrial society.

There is a worldwide movement focused on the issue of global climate change.* In 2008, former Vice President Al Gore, Jr., received an Academy Award for his documentary, "An Inconvenient Truth," which makes the case for the idea that human activity significantly contributes to global warming and that the world's oceans will rise to catastrophic levels in several decades. The film—along with the book it was based on, many other books, speeches, Internet sites, and essays—has helped to make climate change one of the leading issues of the new century. Many scientists and laypersons believe that storms of all kinds will become more severe, droughts will kill millions, and coastal cities will be flooded, and that these tragedies can be averted by controlling industrialization.

With the demise of communism, a great deal of political energy that was previously expended on class-based revolutionary struggle and other such issues is now being devoted to environmental problems. Left-leaning parties in industrialized countries have incorporated environmental concerns into their platforms, but it is fair to say that environmentalism transcends traditional party lines. In the United States, for example, a substantial number of upper-class voters, many of whom support the Republican Party, have become ardent advocates for environmental preservation, especially wilderness protection. The environmental debate will doubtlessly grow in importance in the years to come.

Fascism

As an ideology, **fascism** is short on intellectual content and long on emotion. All ideologies have an element of emotional appeal, of course; people have been known to wax sentimental over socialism, Marxism, and even capitalism. But fascist thinking seems to thrive on emotion. Fascism is aimed more at the heart than at the mind.

The components of fascism vary with culture and the particular historical context in which it takes root. However, all fascist thinking includes an extreme belief in *political obedience*, a pathological *distrust of foreigners*, and the conviction that *progress is possible only through conquest and war*. The following "Commandments of the Fascist Fighter" capture the essence of fascist ideology: "Whoever is not ready to give himself body and soul for his country and to serve … without discussion, is not worthy…. Discipline is not only a virtue of the soldiers in the ranks, it must also be the practice of every day. And thank God every day for having made you Fascist and Italian!"[12] Although those statements were written to inspire Benito Mussolini's Fascist movement in Italy in the 1930s, they reflect the general character of fascism: slavish obedience, an appetite for war, and extreme nationalism.

The policy content of fascist ideology is vague, except that it always supports a large military establishment and a sense of "supernationalism." In addition, fascist distrust of foreigners typically promotes racist or ethnic divisions, as when Hitler targeted the Jews as enemies of German culture, when ultrarightists in South Africa attacked blacks, or when Iraq's Saddam Hussein effectively designated the Kurds as a group to be eliminated. In Europe, where the ideology originated, fascism was

---

* The U.S. Environmental Protection Agency maintains a website with a wealth of resources on climate change: www.epa.gov/climatechange/.

historically associated with anti-Semitism and has retained that feature in almost all settings. Fascism clearly rejects the liberal's notion that all people have equal rights that should be protected and enhanced. But fascism does not speak directly to questions regarding economic systems or many specific problems of social policy.

Some have argued that fascism is simply an extreme form of conservatism, since it is primarily driven by a fanatical attraction to the traditions of the dominant culture. Historically, extreme conservatives in Europe and Latin America have on occasion joined forces with fascist movements. Fascism, however, usually destroys the institutions from which the customs and traditions of a society derive. Whereas conservatives often support traditional religious values, fascists usually permit only a state-approved version of religion (or no religion at all) to exist as a source of influence. Fascists also dominate business and economic enterprise, subordinating those private affairs to the needs of the state. Even extreme conservatism thus breaks with fascism; the elimination of all pillars of traditional society is necessary for fascists but abhorrent to conservatives.*

Given their emphasis on supernationalism and military might, it is not surprising that fascist governments have often brought their countries to disastrous wars. Although people may quibble over which countries may fairly be considered fascist, Hitler's Germany, Mussolini's Italy, and Saddam Hussein's Iraq were arguably fascist states, and all were thoroughly defeated in war.

Islamic Fundamentalism

We normally don't think of religions as political ideologies, and Western religions generally have restricted themselves to the spiritual realm, at least in modern times. But it should be noted that the Catholic Church has been closely linked to important Christian Democratic political parties in Europe and Latin America and those parties have, in turn, based their ideologies substantially on church teaching. And the so-called "Christian Right" of American Protestantism has been closely linked to the conservative wing of the Republican Party and other conservative movements. Similarly, leftist politicians such as Jesse Jackson and Al Sharpton have used their religious backgrounds as a base of political support in the Democratic Party.

In the Islamic world there has always been a far closer link between politics and religion. For example, in the Turkish Empire that dominated the Middle East for several centuries, the Caliph was both the temporal ruler of the empire and the top official of the Muslim religion. Today in the Muslim world (stretching from Indonesia to Turkey), there are some countries in which there is a very close linkage between the political and the religious systems (Saudi Arabia and Iran, for example) and others in which there is more of a separation of church and state (Egypt and Turkey). Adherents of Islam themselves vary from very secular Muslims to fundamentalists who believe that the Koran, the Muslim holy book, must be interpreted literally and that

---

* In a highly controversial book, *Liberal Fascism: The Secret History of the American Left, From Mussolini to the Politics of Meaning* (New York: Doubleday, 2008), author Jonah Goldberg argues that fascism arose not from conservative thinking but from socialist concepts.

government laws and policies should reflect traditional Islamic values in all aspects of human life.

Just as fundamentalists are a minority of Christian believers in the Western world, Islamic fundamentalists are a minority in the Middle East and other parts of the Muslim world. Moreover, even within the fundamentalist minority, most reject violence and some (including the Saudi royal family) are strongly pro-Western.

Despite their minority status, adherents of fundamentalist beliefs and militant (violent) fundamentalist Islam have multiplied recently in the Middle East and other parts of the Islamic world (most notably in Afghanistan and Pakistan). Militant **Islamic fundamentalism** has the qualities both of a political ideology and of a religious theology. It envisions an ideal political system in which political leaders are inspired by the Koran, in which Western and other non-Islamic values are largely purged from society and in which citizens are required to live according to traditional Islamic codes. In February 2006, Abdul Rahman, a citizen of Afghanistan who had converted to Christianity, was on trial for his life for his religious beliefs. U.S. Secretary of State Condoleezza Rice and others put considerable pressure on the government of Afghanistan, and Rahman was finally released. This incident illustrates the conflict between Islamic fundamentalism and the most basic freedoms associated with democracy.

IDEOLOGY AND LEADERSHIP Iranian President Mahmoud Ahmadinejad speaks during a conference on Wednesday October 26, 2005 in Tehran entitled "The World without Zionism." He has said that Israel should be "wiped off the map."

The influence of Islamic fundamentalism is apparent in both the domestic and the foreign policies of several nations, and it motivates important political movements that challenge the governments of countries not officially run by fundamentalists. Some contend that this way of thinking is on the wrong side of history, with its antimodern, antidemocratic features, but others see it as a force that will grow for decades to come. At least for the present, Islamic fundamentalism is an ideology that demands our attention.[13]

Anarchism

The idea of a society without government, or **anarchism**, appears in many different contexts. Some religious traditions contain elements of anarchism in their belief that secular influences (such as government) should be limited or are unnecessary. Some early socialists believed that once private property was eliminated, a common bond would develop among all people, making government obsolete. Serious anarchists consistently paint an idealized picture of human society, one in which community and sharing replace individual interests and competition. In such a world, government becomes a useless relic and is soon discarded.*

More radical anarchists work to destroy government by force and violence. Although usually motivated by some particular concern, violent anarchists put their energy more into destruction than into creating a new order or demanding innovative policies. As an ideology, anarchism is thus profoundly limited, both in practical and in philosophical terms.

Conclusion: Ideology Shapes Political Community and Political Conflict

Any overview of ideology will necessarily omit some perspectives or movements that some people consider important. The New Left, certain racially based movements, extreme religious sects, and other approaches to politics also could have been discussed here as examples of ideologies. But the ideologies included in this chapter are arguably those with the greatest political significance.

Although only a small percentage of citizens are ideologically inclined, appreciating the elements of existing ideologies is a necessary part of learning the language of political life. The conflicting values that undergird most of what is at stake in political struggles are based in ideologies.

◆ ◆ ◆

---

* Some of the counterculture leaders of the 1960s in the United States and Western Europe articulated heartfelt notions along these lines. In a highly euphoric state, many interpreted the famous Woodstock festival, in which 300,000 people lived together for three days of "peace, love, and music," as confirmation that people could live together without government if they only had the right frame of mind.

Key Terms and Concepts _____

anarchism
capitalism
communism
conservatism
economic determinism
environmentalism
fascism
feminism
feudalism
ideology

income inequality
individualism
Islamic fundamentalism
liberalism
libertarianism
Marxism
primitive communism
socialism
Roe v. Wade
welfare state

DISCUSSION QUESTIONS

1. *Give two examples of policy choices or positions associated with liberal and conservative ideology.*
2. *What is the role of economic analysis in Marxist ideology?*
3. *Is feminism one ideology or two?*
4. *What do you think makes some people more rigid than others in their adherence to an ideology?*

Notes _____

1. See Douglas A. Hibbs, Jr., and Christopher Dennis, "Income Distribution in the United States," *American Political Science Review* 82 (June 1988): 482, 485. A more recent study confirms the pattern, particularly with respect to taxation policy. See Carla Inclan, Dennis P. Quinn, and Robert Y. Shapiro, "Origins and Consequences of Changes in U.S. Corporate Taxation: 1981–1998," *American Journal of Political Science* 45 (January 2001): 179–201.
2. Adam Smith, quoted in Milton Friedman and Rose Friedman, *Free to Choose* (New York: Harcourt Brace Jovanovich, 1980), p. 2.
3. Figures for Germany are taken from Michael J. Sullivan, ed., *Measuring Global Values* (New York: Praeger, 1991), p. 102; and figures for North and South Korea from the *CIA World Factbook*, www.cia.gov/library/publications/the-world-factbook/.
4. See "You Must Go Blind in One Eye before NHS Will Treat You," Daily Mail, January 24, 2011, accessed at www.dailymail.co.uk/health/article-122995/You-blind-eye-NHS-treat-you.html
5. Karl Marx, "A Contribution to the Critique of Political Economy, Preface," in *Marx and Engels: Collected Works*, vol. 29, *Marx: 1858–1861* (New York: International Publishers, 1987), p. 263.
6. Jean-Jacques Rousseau, *The Social Contract and Discourse on the Origins of Inequality*, bk. 1 [1762] (Harmondsworth, England: Penguin, 1968).
7. See Robert Owen's collection of essays titled *A New View of Society* (London: Cadell and Davies, 1813).
8. Thomas R. Dye and Harmon Zeigler, "Socialism and Equality in Cross-National Perspective," *PS: Political Science and Politics* 21 (Winter 1988): 45–56.
9. Data from *The Real Wealth of Nations: Pathways to Human Development*, Human Development Report 2010, United Nations, available at http://hdr.undp.org/en/
10. See, for example, Lynne Segal, *Is the Future Female?* (New York: Peter Bedrick, 1988); Adrienne Rich, *Of Woman Born* (London: Virago, 1977); Susan Griffin, *Rape, the Power of Consciousness* (San Francisco: Harper and Row, 1986); Andrea Dworkin, *Pornography: Men Possessing Women* (New York: Putnam, 1981); Nancy J. Hirschmann, "Freedom, Recognition, and Obligation: A Feminist Approach to

Political Theory," *American Political Science Review* 83 (1989): 1227–1244; and Mary L. Shanley and Carole Pateman, *Feminist Interpretations and Political Theory* (College Park, PA: Penn State Press, 1991). For a controversial and very different view, see Christina Hoff Sommers, *Who Stole Feminism? How Women Have Betrayed Women* (New York: Simon & Schuster, 1994).

11. Rachel Carson, *Silent Spring* (New York: Mariner Press, 1994; originally published 1962).

12. Cited in Roy C. Macridis, *Contemporary Political Ideologies*, 2nd ed. (Boston: Little, Brown, 1983), p. 204.

13. A recent book on Islamic fundamentalism provides excellent historical background and informed analysis. See Mansoor Moaddel, *Islamic Modernism, Nationalism, and Fundamentalism* (Chicago: University of Chicago Press, 2005).

PART II

POLITICAL BEHAVIOR

A society's beliefs, values, and resulting behaviors shape the way its political system works and affect its prospects for the future. Nearly all political systems have an identifiable political culture—sometimes several *conflicting* political cultures, as explored in Chapter 3. Political culture influences what people expect from politics, what kind of role they feel they should have in government decisions, and the rights they demand. Chapter 4 focuses on elections and public opinion. Elections are increasingly common in political life everywhere, but the behavior of voters in different countries varies dramatically. Some people choose not to vote, and those who do are influenced by a number of important factors that help us predict voter choices. Finally, Chapters 5 and 6 address political parties and interest groups. Parties and interest groups provide the population with additional opportunities for political participation, and understanding their impact on political systems is a central problem in political science.

© John McConnico/AP Photo

CHAPTER 3

Political Culture and Socialization

Spreading Fundamentalist Culture

A boy awaits classes in front of a *madrasa*, or Islamic school, outside of Peshawar, Pakistan, a city largely populated by Afghan refugees at that time (2001). Many of the fundamentalist *madrasas* for refugees were funded by the Saudi government. Subsequently, many of their graduates became Taliban activists.

- **Political Culture: Origins of the Concept**
- **Agents of Political Socialization**
- **Classifying Political Cultures**

- **The Evolution of Political Cultures**
- **Conclusion: The Utility of Political Culture**

For many people, one of the most exciting and interesting aspects of foreign travel is the opportunity to observe and interact with cultures that are very different from their own. For example, they may find that it is impolite to shake somebody's hand in Bangkok, where people are accustomed to greeting others by holding their own palms together at chest or face level (with that exchange initiated by the person of inferior social status). A visitor to Saudi Arabia or Pakistan soon notes that these cultures allow women more restricted behavior, employment, and dress than in the West. Other cultural values are less immediately obvious. Indians and Colombians are more likely than Canadians are to judge people based on their caste or class origins. Survey research has revealed that the percentage of the population that believes that "most people can be trusted" is much higher in the United States and Britain than in Chile or Romania, but substantially lower than in Sweden or Finland.[1]

People coming from different cultures may hold dissimilar views regarding the value of voting in national elections, their willingness to live near people of different races or ethnicities, the level of free speech they would allow political dissidents, and a host of other politically relevant issues. Nations or regions also vary in the extent to which their populations follow politics or are informed about key political leaders and institutions.

A **political culture** is defined as "a people's predominant beliefs, attitudes, values, ideals, sentiments, and evaluations about the political system of its country, and the role of the self in that system."[2] It includes a society's level of political knowledge as well as its evaluations of the political system and its institutions. But it also encompasses attitudes toward family, neighbors and religion, as well as many other values, beliefs, and feelings that shape and influence people's political outlook.

Political cultures vary both between and within individual nations. For example, Russians are more skeptical than Australians about the advantages of democracy. The French are more inclined to follow politics than are the citizens of Bhutan. Southern Italians tend to be more suspicious of elected officials than northerners are. While these differences are surely important, political scientists disagree about how well we can actually measure differences between political cultures, what the relationship is between political culture and political behavior, and what limits a nation's political culture imposes on its political system. In short, for many years scholars have debated the question, "Does political culture matter?" Or, perhaps more precisely, "How much does political culture matter?"

Those who believe in the importance of political culture argue that cultural values affect vital issues, such as the likelihood of a specific country or region keeping political disagreements peaceful or whether a nation establishes and maintains democracy. Thus, for example, many political scientists argue that the reason so few Muslim nations are democratic is that a number of Islamic values violate democratic standards. Specifically, they point to Islam's merger of church and state and the limits many Islamic nations put on women's political and social participation. However, as we will see, the rise of powerful, prodemocratic mass movements in Tunisia, Egypt, Libya, and elsewhere in the Arab world in 2011 may indicate that Islamic political culture needs not impede democratic change.

Gabriel Almond, one of the first scholars to study political culture cross-nationally, noted that "political culture affects governmental structure and performance—constrains it, but surely does not determine it."[3] But scholars still debate the degree of influence culture has over political behavior. Similarly, they disagree about how extensively a nation may change its own or some other political culture in a relatively short period of time. "Culturalists" point to elements of German and Japanese political culture that they feel contributed to the rise of militarism and authoritarianism in the years leading up to World War II. Critics, pointing to the great cultural shift in those two countries *after* the war, argue that political culture is more malleable than culturalists admit, and insist that new political institutions (such as competitive elections) can change popular attitudes and values relatively quickly. The success of the United States' effort to democratize Iraq will depend heavily on the extent to which Iraqis can develop a democratic political culture.

In discussing a political culture or subculture, the unit we analyze may be a country, a portion of a country, a continent, or a religion. Thus, we may speak about European political culture (assuming that the region has important common values that are distinguishable from those of other continents or regions), Irish political culture (presumably different from, say, Italian political culture), and Irish *Catholic* political culture (whose beliefs are distinct from Irish *Protestant* political values). Similarly, there may be values in American political culture—including a belief in equality of opportunity and a pragmatic (rather than ideologically determined) approach to solving political problems—that distinguish it from Guatemalan or Thai culture.

At the same time, although Americans share many common values, the country also encompasses distinct Southern, Midwestern, Evangelical, and Chicano **political subcultures**, each with its own distinguishing characteristics.

We study political culture because it helps us understand political life. For example, why do different ethnic groups cooperate reasonably well in Switzerland but have more problems in South Africa? Why are Iraqis more inclined than Swedes to support an all-powerful political leader? Why has political corruption been a serious and long-standing problem in Mexico but not in Chile? Political culture may provide at least partial answers.

Although ideology (Chapter 2), political culture, and public opinion (Chapter 4) all explain how people feel about politics, they are distinct concepts. Ideologies reflect *intellectual efforts*—often identified with political philosophers, such as Locke or Marx—to achieve an ideal society. In contrast, political culture encompasses the actual *values, attitudes, and beliefs* that most people hold in a society. Thus, although many Americans lack a well-defined ideology, their political knowledge (or lack of interest), attitudes, and values contribute to their society's political culture.

Even though political culture and public opinion both measure people's feelings, they also are distinct concepts. Public opinion reflects short-term outlooks, such as how French citizens rate their president or what Americans want government to do about high gas prices. Such opinions normally vary considerably within a country and may change from month to month. For example, in 2008, American voters tended to be unhappy with the Bush administration, in part because of the economic recession. Hence, the majority voted for Barack Obama and many liberal, Democratic congressional candidates. Two years later, dispirited by the country's slow progress in ending the recession, public opinion (and voting) swung toward conservative Republicans. Political culture, on the other hand, measures a society's more deepseated values, such as what role people feel organized religion should play in politics or how tolerant citizens are of people holding very different political views—attitudes that are more deeply held and slower to change than public opinion. But as we will see, political cultures are not entirely static. They often change over time, and sometimes that change can be accelerated.

POLITICAL CULTURE: ORIGINS OF THE CONCEPT

Decades ago, as political scientists expanded their understanding of other political systems, they realized that institutions such as political parties or national legislatures operate differently from one society to the next, even when they are structured in similar ways. Moreover, they observed that particular forms of political behavior, such as voting, often have different meanings for, say, Mexicans or Russians than for Icelanders or Costa Ricans. So merely studying political parties, the bureaucracy, or interest-group membership does not afford a full understanding of a nation's political processes. We also need to consider the cultural foundations upon which political systems operate.

Just as anthropologists and psychologists once analyzed the "national character" of countries such as India or Japan, political scientists today analyze political cultures, asking questions such as these: Do Chinese citizens value a free press as much as the Swiss do? Do South Africans trust their fellow citizens? Do Kenyans feel that they can influence their own political system? Answers to such questions offer important insights into the nature of various political systems and help us predict change.

It is also important to recognize, however, that *within a single nation there is usually a degree of cultural diversity*. When we describe the Nigerian and Indian political cultures in a certain way, we are not claiming that *all* Nigerians and *all* Indians have the same beliefs. We are merely identifying certain distinctive national patterns while acknowledging substantial variation within each country's borders.

Moreover, not only do *individuals* in any society vary in their political values, but *groups* within a society also often have distinctive political orientations. As we have seen, any political culture may include a number of political subcultures. In the United States, for example, there is a national political culture encompassing our society's general political value system. There are, however, also distinctive political subcultures in different regions of the country, and among African Americans, Hispanics, Whites, Catholics, Jews, Muslims, and Southern Baptists. A healthy political system, which both respects diversity and imposes broad guidelines on everyone, can accommodate such differences. If, however, regional, religious, ethnic, or other subcultures become so different that no discernible "national" culture seems to exist—as still seems true in Iraq among its Shi'ite, Sunni, and Kurd populations— political stability is likely to be threatened.

In studying various groups in society, political scientists need to ascertain which attitudinal or behavioral differences grow out of diverse cultural patterns and which simply reflect different realities. For example, survey research reveals that poor Mexicans have less confidence in their country's legal system than do their middle- or upper-class counterparts, and they are also less likely to sign political petitions.[4] Are these attitudes a reflection of a distinct working-class political culture? In other words, do poor Mexicans have less trust in the courts and less confidence in their ability to influence politics because of the values they learned as children? Or do their attitudes simply mirror the harsh reality that Mexican government officials (including judges) are less likely to give poor citizens a fair hearing?

Of course, changes in objective conditions can produce changes in political culture, which in turn lead to changes in the way the government works. As South Korea's and Mexico's educational levels rose in the last decades of the twentieth century, and as more people entered the middle class, their political values changed. As citizens of these countries became more educated, affluent, and urban, they began to demand a more open political system, forcing their authoritarian governments to democratize.

Historical factors—particularly dramatic events such as wars, revolutions, and economic depressions—can also alter a nation's political culture. For example, the Great Depression of the 1920s and 1930s convinced many Americans and Europeans of the need for greater government intervention in the economy (guaranteeing bank savings, for example, and providing social security). Such historical events often continue to influence political behavior and the political system long after they are over. From World War II through the 1970s, the role of government (as measured by its percentage of the GNP) grew substantially in Europe and the United States as citizens, many of whom grew up in the Depression, sought the protective blanket of government social welfare programs. Since the 1970s, however, new generations of voters have emerged who were raised in the growing prosperity of the 1950s through the 1970s and who are less concerned about having a government safety net.

Even more profoundly, the Nazi era had an enduring impact on German political culture. In their landmark 1960s study of political culture, Almond and Verba discovered that in the decades after World War II, even though West Germans were more likely than Mexicans to expect fair treatment from local government officials, they were less proud of their political institutions. Moreover, despite their higher educational level, Germans felt less obligated than did Mexicans to participate in local politics. The Germans' more negative view of government probably reflected a wariness stemming from their country's Nazi past. Mexicans, in contrast, although critical of specific government behavior, expressed general pride in their political system, reflecting the stability and nationalism that emerged from their 1910 revolution.[5] Since that study was completed, further historical changes have made Germans far more confident of their democracy. But even today, Germany's political culture remains influenced by events that occurred more than 60 years ago. For example, most Germans oppose foreign military involvement because of their country's suffering in World War II and the international notoriety that Nazi military conquests brought them. Thus, Germany refused to join U.S. and British troops in Iraq and strictly limited its commitment of troops in Afghanistan.

Political culture is a simple concept, but it can easily be misunderstood. The fact that we may characterize a given nation's culture in some manner should not lead us to underestimate the importance of diverse subcultures within it. Similarly, the fact that political culture may be an explanatory factor should not lead us to overlook the possibility that objective conditions within a country may be responsible for behavior often attributed to culture.

AGENTS OF POLITICAL SOCIALIZATION

How do individual citizens in any country acquire the values and feelings that constitute their political culture? **Political socialization** is the process of shaping and transmitting a political culture. It involves the transfer of political values from one generation to another and usually entails changes over time that lead to a gradual transformation of the culture.

Agents of political socialization are individuals, groups, or institutions that transmit political values to each generation. Obviously, the importance of specific socialization agents differs from culture to culture and from individual to individual. Nevertheless, the following agents are important in virtually every society.

The Family

As in so many other aspects of life, the family is the first, and frequently the most important, source of political values. Youngsters who often hear their parents at the dinner table expressing their opinions of the country's political parties or the police often absorb those judgments as they grow up. Because the family exerts its influence from such an early age, when people are most impressionable, many political scientists view the family as the most critical agent for transmitting broad moral and political values during a person's formative years. "Other individuals may have profound influence on a person's political outlook, but none of them is typically credited with as much influence as the child's parents."[6]

Education

From their kindergarten days making Thanksgiving decorations through high school civics and college political science courses, most American students acquire important political values from the educational system: patriotism, the importance of voting, and the value of constitutional rights, for example. In communist nations such as Cuba, schools have been an important agent for socializing youth into the values of Marxism-Leninism. And in Afghanistan and Pakistan, many young boys have been enrolled in fundamentalist *madrassas*, or religious schools, some of which promote a militant brand of Islam.

Peer Groups

Although family and school are the most influential early influences on political values, the socialization process continues into our adult years. As people grow older, their political values are influenced by their friends and coworkers. During adolescence, peers compete with parents and teachers as the most important source of values. The impact of friends and coworkers seems to be especially strong in Western societies, where the influence of family elders, kinship groups, and religion is weaker than in developing countries. In fact, even membership in social clubs and bowling leagues may influence the political culture.

The Media

In advanced industrialized societies, people receive much of their political information and many of their political values from the mass media. Newspapers, news magazines, radio, and television play an important role in transmitting political culture. In recent years, U.S. radio talk shows (mostly with a conservative orientation) have become a potent influence on adults' political values. The Internet is now also a major source of political ideas and values, particularly among young adults (see A Closer Look 3.2). Even in developing nations radios are fairly universal, and in many Third World countries increasing numbers of people have access to television. Well aware of television's potential for shaping political values, the Cuban government has supplied a free television set to most recipients of public housing.

A CLOSER LOOK

3.1

Social Capital, Trust, and Bowling Alone

Robert Putnam's extensive research on Italy indicated that there were marked differences in the quality of performance of the country's regional governments and linked those disparities to cultural and historical factors. Regional governments were more effective when their citizens were more civically engaged and wished to further the good of the community, not just the welfare of their family and friends. People in more civic-minded regions were more likely to belong to local associations, ranging from sports clubs to bird-watching groups, causing them to interact with others in their community and to work cooperatively. A region's **social capital** was a measure of the density of associational involvement in a town, region, or country, and the norms and social trust that these group activities produced.[7]

Regions or communities with high levels of social capital, according to Putnam's research, produced citizens who were more law abiding and more trustful of their neighbors, including those whom they did not know very well. These attitudes, in turn, were conducive to effective democratic government. But not all involvement in clubs, associations, or groups produces social capital, argues Putnam. Relationships between members must be "horizontal"—between relative equals. If, however, relationships are "vertical"—with a top-down, hierarchical structure like the Mafia in Sicily—that kind of group membership does not build social capital.

In his bestselling book, *Bowling Alone*, Putnam notes that the United States has always enjoyed a dense network of groups, clubs, and associations. But while it still compares well with many other nations, "the vibrancy of American civil society has notably declined over the past few decades."[8] For example, more and more Americans have preferred to "bowl alone" or with a small number of friends and family members, while they have been less inclined to bowl in leagues, where they could network with people whom they know less well. Thus, between 1980 and 1993, the number of bowlers in the United States increased by 10 percent, but the number of people in bowling leagues *decreased* by 40 percent (and that decline continued into the twenty-first century). There

have been similarly sharp declines in the past 30 to 50 years in the number of Americans belonging to parent–teacher associations (PTAs), the League of Women Voters, and the Red Cross. Putnam maintains that all of these changes reflect a broader decline in social engagement.

It is true that some organizations have increased their membership greatly during this period, including the American Association of Retired Persons (AARP) and the National Organization for Women (NOW). But unlike the associations just mentioned with sharply declining memberships, these expanding organizations involve little or no face-to-face contacts between members. And despite gains by some groups, total membership in associations declined by almost 30 percent from 1967 to 1993, a trend that has continued since.

The reasons for the decline in groups such as the PTA and bowling leagues are complex and varied: Many people are busier with their careers; playing video games, surfing the Web, and other relatively solitary activities have become more prevalent; and traditional families, which are often the hubs of associational activity (Boy Scouts, PTA) have been weakened by rising divorce rates and the increased numbers of people who postpone or avoid marriage.

Whatever the reasons (and there are many others), Putnam argues that America's stock of social capital has eroded, a decline that has significant social and political consequences. During the past 40 years or so, as fewer people have joined associations that bring them into contact with new people, as people are less likely to invite neighbors to their homes for dinner, and as the percentage of Americans attending church has declined, the percentage of people who give to charity and the share of total national income contributed to charity has also declined. It is equally disconcerting that during the last decades of the twentieth century, the percentage of people who had worked for a political party fell 42 percent, the proportion of those who had attended a political rally or speech declined by 34 percent, and the percentage

3.1

who had written to their congressperson or senator fell by 23 percent. At the same time Americans have become less trustful of each other. Moreover, states with the highest social capital (such as South Dakota, Minnesota, and Vermont) have higher levels of tolerance for racial and gender equality and fewer prosecutions for violation of federal income tax laws than do states with the lowest levels of social capital (Nevada, Mississippi, and Georgia). They also have school systems that are more effective. These findings suggest to Putnam and others that the growing tendency of Americans to "bowl alone" and reduce social contacts with coworkers or neighbors is troublesome for American democracy and civil society.

A more recent book by Russell J. Dalton discusses a somewhat related phenomenon in 18 advanced **industrial democracies**. Data from the World Values Survey and the Eurobarometer shows that in 16 of those 18 nations there has been a clear decline in citizen support for and trust in their country's political institutions (such as the courts). Such declines were frequently not related to government performance or contemporary events. For example, in the United States,

> In … 1966, with the war in Vietnam raging and race riots in Cleveland, Chicago, and Atlanta, 66 percent of Americans *rejected* the view that "the people running the country don't really care what happens to you." In … 1997, after America's cold war victory and in the midst of the longest period of peace and prosperity in more than two generations, 57 per cent of Americans *endorsed* the same view.[9]

Similar declines in support for government, the courts, and other political institutions took place in almost all advanced democracies during those three decades (and continued into the twenty-first century). For example, the percentage of Swedes who expressed confidence in their parliament declined from 51 percent in 1986 to 19 percent in 1996. Despite growing

public distrust of government, the level of support for democracy as the best form of government has remained high (or even risen) in all 18 nations, ranging from a high of 97 to 99 percent support in Denmark, Iceland, and Austria to a low (within this group) of 78 percent in Britain and 86 to 87 percent in the Netherlands and the United States.[10] Still, Dalton and others argue that if distrust of government and negative evaluations of government institutions continues to grow, this trend could well undermine democracy.

Thus, for example, because growing cynicism about government is associated with reduced participation in politics, a vicious cycle can develop whereby politicians, who are less closely scrutinized by a "turned-off" citizenry, become less responsible to the voters and generate further political apathy. Furthermore, survey research across these nations indicates that citizens who express lower trust in and support for the political system reveal a somewhat greater willingness to cheat on their tax payments and to break the law more generally. They are also less willing to fulfill civic duties such as sitting on juries. All of these data suggest that growing alienation from the political system should be a cause for concern.

Survey data also indicate that dramatic events such as corruption scandals in Italy and Japan, or Watergate and the Vietnam War in the United States, do not fully account for this increased political distrust. Although there are multiple causes of greater political dissatisfaction, ironically it appears that two important reasons are increased educational levels and growing concern for "postmaterial" issues such as protecting the environment and promoting gender equality. The evidence suggests that more-educated citizens as well as postmaterialists (those more concerned about issues like those just named and less concerned about their own material interests) are more likely to have higher expectations of government. Consequently, they are more disappointed with the political system if it fails to meet those standards. At the same time, however, postmaterialists (who are generally more educated) express the highest level of support for civil liberties such as free speech.

A CLOSER LOOK

3.2

Is The Spread of Information Technology Helping or Hurting Political Participation?—Generation Y

Over the past few decades in the United States, Great Britain, France, Italy, and a number of other Western democracies, interest and participation in national politics seem to have declined. The most dramatic evidence is the fall in voter turnout (the percentage of eligible voters who actually vote) over the past 50 years. Many political scientists have suggested that broad voter apathy or even antipathy toward politics plays a role. Numerous opinion surveys indicate that voters in Western democracies have become more negative about the political process, more cynical about government, and more suspicious of political leaders.

That raises a problem. If many people are tuning out politics and voter turnout is declining, then election results might only be reflecting the views of portions of the population who vote more regularly (such as older voters and more affluent voters), while inadequately representing others who don't (younger voters, minority groups, and the poor). Furthermore, if the public is disinterested in politics, elected officials are likely to be less accountable to their constituents. These concerns are most acute regarding younger citizens (aged 18–25), the group that has been least likely to vote, join a political party, or follow politics.

These issues point to the importance of political socialization and the creation of a participant political culture. The evidence suggests that in the United States and countries such as the United Kingdom, Italy, and Ireland, as newspaper circulation and television news audiences decline, the influence of **information and communications technology (ICT)** has surged.[11]

ICT—particularly the Internet, but also texting and podcasting—has been of particular importance to younger citizens. These technologies provide young adults with an enormous and growing portion of their political information and values. In fact, Barack Obama first announced who his running mate would be in text and e-mail messages. Furthermore, the share of the population in developed democracies who participate in the digital revolution will only grow over the years.

Some scholars argue that ICT offers tremendous opportunities for mobilizing political participation and overcoming voter apathy. Others question how much these new technologies will contribute to a more participatory political culture and even see potential dangers in digital forms of political socialization. The first group argues that if political leaders and commentators wish to reach **Generation Y**, also known as "Echo Boomers" or "the Millennium Generation" (those born in the years of 1978 through 2000, roughly) who are coming of age in the early decades of the twenty-first century, they need to communicate with them through their media of choice—the Web, text messages, podcasts, and the like. At the same time, these so-called **techno-enthusiasts** insist, ICT has substantial advantages as an agent of political socialization. Unlike television, radio, and the press, which only allow one-way (top-down) communications between politicians and the public, the Internet and text messaging allow young citizens to communicate with their political leaders and with each other. ICT supporters argue that this allows Generation Y and future generations to develop a more participatory

Business and Professional Associations, the Military, Labor Unions, and Religious Groups

Unlike schools, these organizations are all examples of "secondary groups"—organizations that people join for a common goal. Like the family, schools, and the media, their main role is not to influence political values. Yet each of these groups

3.2

view of democracy. Furthermore, these analysts maintain that it will raise levels of participation eventually. Studies have also found that members of Generation Y are more receptive than their elders were to opinions and information from friends and peers and are less likely to follow the views of "experts." All of these factors, the techno-enthusiasts argue, are producing higher levels of political involvement among young adults.

Critics of that perspective have marshaled a number of arguments. They point out that during the first decade or so after the explosion of Web usage in the United States, voter turnout among those aged 18 to 24 continued to fall and continued to lag far behind participation by older voters. Thus, in the 2000 presidential election (Bush vs. Gore), turnout among citizens aged 25 and older was 63 percent (itself a low figure for an industrialized democracy), while among people aged 18 to 24 a mere 36 percent managed to vote, close to a record low.[12] Looking at the data somewhat differently, in the 1972 presidential election, young voters cast 14.2 percent of the total vote. By the 2000 election (the first presidential election for Generation Y), after nearly three decades of steady decline, that age group contributed 7.8 percent. This seems to suggest that expanded use of the Internet in the 1990s did not increase political participation by young citizens. Small wonder that critics argue that "the Internet [merely] reinforces existing trends. It may be more than a blip, but it falls far short of being a revolution."[13]

It is possible, however, that these critics have spoken too quickly. More recent evidence indicates that Generation Y's political participation and civic involvement are now on the rise. For example, surveys revealed that volunteerism by college students increased by 20 percent between 2002 and 2005. Similarly, between the 2000 and 2004 presidential

elections, turnout among young adults (18–24) jumped sharply—from 36 percent to 47 percent— reaching one of the highest rates since 1952. Young voter turnout in 2006 (including congressional elections) was also up from recent midterm (nonpresidential) elections and was among the highest in recent decades. Finally, in 2008 the rate of young voter participation in state primaries and caucuses increased phenomenally, roughly doubling the 2004 turnout.[14] Supporters of Barack Obama have provided the lion's share of that increase. They not only have voted in huge numbers but have been key participants in his grassroots organization. The Internet, particularly You-Tube, has played an important role in that mobilization (though youthful participation and enthusiasm declined in the 2010 congressional election).

In short, there is considerable recent evidence to support the techno-enthusiasts' belief that ICT has been a positive socializing agent in promoting political participation among younger voters. Skeptics worry that, while political communication through such social networks as Facebook has its value, young citizens may be overly prone to accept their peers' opinions at the expense of input from older experts. They believe that expert analyses of the candidates in outlets such as PBS's *News Hour* are far more informative than opinions expressed on Facebook. Others fear that Web-based political socialization puts greater stress on personality and charm than on issues. For example, some maintain that Barack Obama's meteoric rise to national prominence in 2007 and 2008 had more to do with his charisma and oratory skills than with his initially ill-defined policy prescriptions. His ICT outreach was symbolized by people such as at Chris Hughes, the 24-year-old cofounder of Facebook, who left that company in 2007 to play a crucial role in Obama's online campaign.

may exert substantial political influence over its members. That influence may be direct, as when business groups distribute material to their members criticizing government intervention in the economy. Or it may be indirect, as when the leaders of a religious group promote patriarchal (male-dominant) family values. In Israel, which has nearly universal military service for young men and women, the armed forces have effectively integrated generations of young immigrants into the nation's political culture. The military often plays a similar role in the Third World, socializing recruits into national values.

In both Chile and Italy, men are more likely than women to work in factories or other sites that are unionized. Since unions in those countries have often been associated with the socialist or communist parties, men are more likely than women to vote for leftist political parties. Conversely, since women are more likely than men to attend Catholic Church services, they are also more likely to vote for the Christian Democrats or their successor parties.

CLASSIFYING POLITICAL CULTURES

Survey research on culture (including political culture) has produced a gold mine of information that can be invaluable at cocktail parties or in trivia games. We know, for example, that among western and southern Europeans, the Irish are most prone to feel that divorce can *never* be justified, whereas the Danes and the French are most likely to accept it. The Netherlands and Denmark have the highest percentage of respondents who said that they were "very happy," while Portugal and Greece have the lowest.[15] Although such facts are interesting, what do they tell us about the political process? How do different cultures cause their governments to behave differently?

When Almond and Verba wrote their landmark study of political culture, *The Civic Culture*, they did more than merely describe the political knowledge, values, and beliefs of the five countries that they had studied (the United States, Great Britain, West Germany, Italy, and Mexico). Beyond that, they examined which political values are most compatible with democracy. As many Third World nations have found, simply copying political institutions from the West is not enough to produce stable democracy. "A democratic form of participatory political system requires as well a political culture consistent with it."[16]

Much of the subsequent research on political culture has examined the compatibility of a nation's values with desired political goals. For example, this textbook's discussions of politics in selected nations (Chapters 10 to 15) note that political values in the United States and Great Britain support democratic practices and institutions better than the political cultures in Russia and China do. Indeed, both of the latter countries have held authoritarian values that long preceded the rise of communism.

Similarly, political scientists have often examined the relationship between political culture and political stability. If people distrust one another or if they are sharply divided along class, racial, religious, or ethnic lines, the prospects for political stability in that society diminish. Northern Ireland, Lebanon, Rwanda, Bosnia, and Iraq come to mind. In turn, a nation clearly needs some level of stability in order for democracy to take hold. On the other hand, China's and Mexico's political cultures until recently may have placed so high a value on stability that many citizens rejected democratic protests (such as Tiananmen Square) because they feared that they would create disorder.

As we have noted, the core values of a political culture change more slowly than public opinion does. For example, American support for the war in Iraq declined sharply in only two years after the invasion. Similarly, candidates for office may start their campaigns with wide public support only to see that support evaporate by Election Day. Basic cultural values, however, normally take years or even generations to change. More than half a century ago, European sociologist Gunnar Myrdal noted "an American dilemma," a disconnect in U.S. political culture between its commitment to the fundamental equality of all citizens and its persistent racial prejudices.[17] Even though American racial attitudes have changed significantly since that time and institutionalized racism has been greatly reduced, racial prejudice continues to linger in our culture. Barack Obama's presidential victory strongly demonstrated how significantly racial prejudice has declined in the United State in recent decades. But the considerable minority of White voters in states such as Mississippi, Pennsylvania, and West Virginia who admitted to pollsters that they would not vote for a Black presidential candidate (or, more tellingly, the higher percentage of respondents who said that their friends would not) indicated that some degree of racism persists in the political culture.

Sometimes cultural differences also explain differences in economic or political policies in comparable countries. For example, American political culture has historically valued individuality and the protection of individual citizens from government intervention more than European culture does. On the other hand, Western Europeans—such as the French, Germans, and Swedes—are more insistent than Americans are on government's obligation to help society's disadvantaged citizens, such as the poor. Those cultural differences have remained fairly constant for at least 70 years. Consequently, Western Europeans have been more likely than Americans to support extensive social welfare programs and to accept the tax burden that those programs require. Conversely, American culture's insistence on individual rights and its wariness of government restrictions help explain why U.S. gun laws are much less restrictive than European regulations are.

Still, over time, *political cultures do change!* Sometimes those changes are the result of conscious government or societal planning as, for example, the concerted efforts after World War II by the schools, mass media, labor unions, and other agents of political socialization in both Germany and Japan to erase fascist and ultranationalistic sentiments and to create more democratic political cultures. (See the discussion of political resocialization later in this chapter.) At other times, more gradual social and economic changes alter the political culture. In Mexico during the last half of the twentieth century, the spread of education and literacy, expansion of the broadcast media, and rapid urbanization created a better-informed and more participatory political culture. More recently, the surge of prodemocracy demonstrations in the Arab World (often referred to as the **Arab Spring**) and the willingness of many protesters to risk death for democracy show the capacity of political cultures to change. In the decades since a worldwide wave of democratic transitions began in the early 1970s, the Arab nations of the Middle East and North Africa have been the most resistant to change of any region and the least open to democracy. This led many scholars to believe that Arab political culture (more so that non-Arab Islamic culture) was authoritarian. However, the rapid succession of broadly based democratic uprisings in Tunisia, Egypt, Libya, Syria, and other Arab nations suggests that economic modernization, the expansion of the middle class, more widespread education, and growing exposure to the outside world through the Internet, Twitter, and the like have transformed Arab political culture and made it more democratic.

Political scientists have categorized various kinds of political cultures. We define some of them next and briefly refer to others. These are not necessarily mutually exclusive categories.

Democratic Political Culture

Although the cultural prerequisites for democracy are quite varied and not always fully understood, certain attitudes clearly are helpful. Democracy is most likely to emerge and endure in societies that tolerate diverse points of view, including unpopular or dissenting opinions. When the U.S. Supreme Court ruled that individuals have the right to burn the American flag as an expression of free speech, it took this principle beyond the point that many Americans thought reasonable. Despite some initial outrage, however, Congress chose not to introduce a constitutional amendment to ban flag burning. On the other hand, in Iranian or Sudanese political cultures there is no such tolerance for somebody who criticizes or mocks the Koran.

As democratic values become more firmly entrenched in a country's political culture, a nation can more easily tolerate antidemocratic political actors. Nations struggling to establish or stabilize democracy in a formerly authoritarian setting, however, sometimes believe that it is necessary to initially exclude political parties and groups that do not accept democratic principles. For that reason, postwar West Germany barred the Nazi Party from political participation in elections. In 1992, following a series of neo-Nazi attacks on immigrants, the German parliament, mindful of the country's history, restricted the speech rights of hate groups.

Other important components of a democratic political culture include "moderation, accommodation, restrained partisanship, system loyalty, and trust."[18] Survey research indicates that levels of trust (in one's fellow citizens and in government) are very low in Russia and many other former communist nations in Eastern Europe. When that happens, people are more likely to support repression of fellow citizens with unpopular points of view, more likely to evade taxes, and less likely to extend business credit, thereby inhibiting both democracy and economic growth.

Authoritarian Political Culture

Despite the growing strength of democratic values worldwide, most political cultures have some authoritarian strains. In the developing world, only a few nations—such as Costa Rica and India—have long-established democratic traditions. And even in India, where competitive elections and parliamentary government have been the norm, most of the population live in villages where the caste system, domination by powerful landlords, and local political machines create undemocratic conditions.

What do we mean when we say that Malaysia, Russia, and Iran have authoritarian political cultures or subcultures? The phrase suggests that both the leaders of the country and much of the population reject either majority rule or minority rights. In particular, authoritarian political cultures are less tolerant of dissenters and of ethnic or religious minorities. In Iran, for example, fundamentalist Islam denies the legitimacy of other religions (such as Baha'i) or of opposing political viewpoints. In both communist North Korea and capitalist South Korea, many citizens believe that journalists have no right to publish material that contradicts the country's prevailing political ideology or that potentially destabilizes society. Similarly, Guatemalan political culture features *caudillaje*, a set of values that makes the pursuit of power the "referent for life's activities." These values support political leaders with "manipulative, exploitative, and opportunistic" personalities.[19]

Authoritarian political cultures stress the importance of stability and order. The rough-and-tumble of democratic competition may seem threatening to that order. In Russia, many citizens felt threatened by the crime and economic disarray that followed the collapse of communism, leading voters to overwhelmingly support President (now Prime Minister) Putin in spite of his repeated assaults on democratic institutions. When asked if they approved or disapproved of strong authoritarian leaders, respondents in countries such as Denmark, the Netherlands, Spain, and Iceland overwhelmingly disapproved, while Tanzanians, Jordanians, Nigerians, and Romanians were far more likely to approve.[20] Many authoritarian cultures support traditional authority structures and hierarchy. For example, women may be socialized to unquestioningly obey their husbands. Similarly, authoritarian political cultures believe that the nation's leaders know what is best for society and should be obeyed. Some Mexican anthropologists have argued that their country's children have been raised to unquestioningly accept their fathers' authority. Consequently, when they grow up, they have often transferred that obedience to the nation's president and to other authority figures, at least until recently.[21] In the Soviet Union many people had a paternalistic view of the ruling, communist party, which claimed to know with scientific certainty what was good for the people (see Chapter 12). That acceptance of government authority also prevails in the authoritarian cultures of Confucian (and capitalist) Singapore and Muslim Saudi Arabia.

In recent years, a debate has raged among scholars (and some political leaders) as to whether democratic values can readily flourish in Islamic or East Asian cultures. Some have argued that there are aspects of Islamic and Confucian values that are incompatible with democratic norms. In some cases political leaders, such as Lee Kuan Yew, the founding father and long-time prime minister of Singapore (1959–1990), have used such arguments to justify nondemocratic practices in their own countries. Others, however, see these arguments as ethnic stereotyping. They object strenuously to the idea that Muslims in, say, Malaysia, or Confucians in Singapore, are somehow culturally predisposed to reject democracy.[22] As we have seen, the recent prodemocracy protests in the Arab World also challenge that notion.

In fact, countries with certain dominant religions are more likely than others to be democratic *even when we statistically control for educational or income differences that are known to affect the likelihood of democracy.* In other words, when we compare countries of comparable educational and income levels with one another, Protestant nations have been most likely to be democratic and Islamic nations have been least likely. Some scholars have argued that Protestantism emphasizes individuality, which contributes to democratic government, whereas Islam believes in a merger of church and state that retards democratic development.

Although there is likely some truth to these assertions, and although the statistical correlations cannot be denied, it is important to keep in mind our previous assertion that *though cultures are generally slow to change, they can and do change!* Historically, Catholic countries in the West have been less hospitable to democracy than Protestant nations were. Not long ago, Spain, Portugal, Brazil, Mexico, and a large percentage of other Catholic nations had authoritarian regimes. Some analysts attributed this to the hierarchical nature of the Catholic Church and its belief in papal infallibility in matters of faith. But in the Third Wave of democratization, starting in the early 1970s, Catholic countries in Europe and Latin America were among the most important players. Indeed, the Third Wave started in the Catholic nations of Portugal and Spain. Similarly, culture and religion allegedly explained why, at one time, Confucian South Korea and Taiwan remained authoritarian despite their relatively high income and educational levels. Today, however, both have become democracies. And, as we have seen, this year's Arab Spring challenges the notion that Islamic culture, particularly in the Middle East, is a major barrier to democratic change. Indeed, these examples suggest that some religious and cultural traditions may inhibit democratization for a period of time, but they do not make democratic change *impossible.*

Thus, when some political scientists say that countries such as Russia or Iraq lack key elements of a democratic political culture, they are talking about important cultural hurdles impeding those countries' transitions to democracy. However, that does not mean that those hurdles are permanent or that authoritarian cultural values cannot be changed. Surveys in contemporary Russia, for example, have indicated that younger citizens—partly or wholly socialized since *glasnost* (the Soviet Union's political opening in the late 1980s) and the fall of communism—are more inclined to support democratic values than older Russians are. On the other hand, it is certainly possible that countries that have endured long periods of ineffective or corrupt rule by a democratic government may see democratic values weaken.

Consensual and Conflictual Cultures

We can also classify political cultures according to their degree of consensus or conflict over crucial political issues. In **consensual political cultures**—such as Great Britain, Japan, and Costa Rica—citizens tend to agree on basic political procedures (for example, the legitimacy of free elections) and on the general goals of the political system. **Conflictual political cultures**—found in nations such as Rwanda, Bosnia, and Guatemala—are highly polarized by fundamental differences over those issues. In Central America during the 1980s, deep ideological divisions between left-wing and right-wing political subcultures brought El Salvador, Guatemala, and Nicaragua to civil war.

Ethnic, religious, or racial divisions may also polarize countries. The people of Bosnia have been violently divided by ethnic nationalism pitting Bosnian Muslims, Serbs, and Croats against one another. Similarly, in Lebanon, militias representing various Christian and Islamic denominations have decimated one another for years. In 1994, Hutus in Rwanda massacred perhaps 800,000 of their Tutsi countrymen. Obviously, relatively homogeneous cultures (which share a common language, religion, and ethnicity)—such as Denmark or Japan—are more likely to achieve a consensual political culture than are multiracial or multicultural nations (Lebanon or South Africa). Nevertheless, Canada, Switzerland, and the United States demonstrate that some heterogeneous societies have developed consensual cultures despite the obstacles.

Other Cultural Classifications

Along with the categories that we have mentioned, political scientists have a host of other classifications of political cultures. Observers of Cuban and Vietnamese politics have often spoken of those countries' revolutionary or Marxist political cultures. Some analysts characterize countries as having a capitalist political culture, indicating that the values are congruent with a free-market ideology. And, as we have seen, still others have focused on religion as a critical determinant of political values in a specific region or nation. They point to a Confucian political culture in China, Taiwan, Korea, and Singapore; a Catholic culture in Latin America; and an Islamic political culture in Iran and Algeria. Finally, a number of political scientists have argued that certain geographic regions have distinct values and orientations that define, for example, a Latin American, African, or Mediterranean political culture.

All these classifications are reasonable if they capture a distinctive set of political values and attitudes that characterize a society or region and distinguish it from other political cultures. Thus, the label "Islamic political culture" is scientifically meaningful only if it describes important political values that are common to most Muslims and are distinct from non-Muslim values. If the classification does not do both things (identify common values and attitudes of one culture *and* distinguish those from other cultures), then it is not useful.

THE EVOLUTION OF POLITICAL CULTURES

Political cultures reflect a balance of *stable* values that have endured for centuries, *gradual changes* in beliefs that transpire over many years, more *rapid value changes* resulting from socioeconomic or political development (such as greater education), and *dramatic events* (such as war or revolution). Thus, although all cultures change (some more rapidly than others), the cultural foundations of political systems are not transformed overnight. Like all value systems, traditional beliefs may serve as anchors of stability in an otherwise confusing world or may be impediments to progress. Hindu political culture has supported the caste system, limiting the opportunities available to many Indian citizens and contributing to hierarchical political values. On the other hand, some experts argue that Hinduism's separation of church and state and the absence of an organized religious hierarchy help explain why India, despite its poverty and relatively low literacy rate, has been such a stable democracy.

Because all political cultures change, our understanding of individual societies needs to be constantly reexamined. Clearly, neither Nigerians nor Spaniards nor Americans believe the same things today that they did 20 or 30 years ago. Sometimes, substantial cultural changes are the unintended consequence of rapid urbanization, economic modernization, or increased education. At other times, however, cultural change occurs through **political resocialization**, a conscious effort by government leaders to transform their society's political culture. And sometimes, cultural change is a byproduct of both conscious and unconscious factors.

Of course, in recent decades some aspects of American political culture also have undergone change. In 1959, Almond and Verba found that Americans had more confidence in their political institutions than did citizens in any of the other four countries they had studied. However, that confidence eroded during the late 1960s and the 1970s as a result of the assassinations of President Kennedy and Martin Luther King, an unpopular war in Vietnam, and the Watergate scandal, which almost led to the impeachment of President Richard Nixon. Although the Reagan presidency, the Gulf War, and even the September 11 terrorist attacks all rekindled national pride, public opinion polls indicate that Americans currently have less faith than they once did in political institutions, such as Congress.

More dramatic changes sometimes occur in countries where the government deliberately tries to transform the political culture. Such efforts are always difficult and are sometimes disastrous. Just as it is hard to teach an old dog new tricks, it is difficult to change long-standing cultural traditions rapidly. These attempts are most likely to take place when a war, a revolution, or other upheaval has radically altered the political system or the government's political ideology. In our analysis of Chinese politics in Chapter 13, we discuss how Mao Zedong's government conducted political campaigns to create mass commitment to volunteer labor, social equality, and other revolutionary values.

Following the Cuban Revolution, the government introduced a massive adult literacy campaign and created neighborhood political units, called Committees for the Defense of the Revolution (CDRs), throughout the nation. The literacy campaign used reading primers with overtly political messages about the benefits that Fidel Castro had brought to the island. CDRs stressed the value of hard work and individual sacrifice for the good of society, while advocating racial, class, and sexual equality. School curricula stressed similar values. Richard Fagen's study of Cuban revolutionary culture suggested a number of impressive results. Surveys of high school students indicated that boys were developing less sexist attitudes toward females. Violent crime rates diminished, and poor Cubans became more confident that they could get ahead through study and hard work.[23] In short, the Cuban government had seemingly used education and mass mobilization to reduce prejudice, fatalism, and other prerevolutionary values. Yet the radical transformation of any political culture has its costs. Although Cuban crime rates declined, visits to psychiatrists rose as many Cubans were told at CDR meetings that their prerevolutionary values were wrong. The introduction of feminist concerns into a *macho* political culture improved sexual equality (husbands, for example, were pressured to do housework, and women were encouraged to enter the labor force) but likely also contributed to a sharp rise in the country's divorce rate.

Other studies have suggested that rapid, government-directed cultural transformations sometimes have been more apparent than real. Although revolutionary activists in Cuba readily mouthed the "correct" political slogans, some of them privately felt or acted differently. For example, one study of a Havana slum found that CDR leaders in that neighborhood were using the organization as a front for gambling and prostitution operations.[24] Other evidence from Cuba, Nicaragua, and Eastern Europe suggests that although many people accepted at least some revolutionary values, others just went through the motions or feigned a cultural transformation for the sake of personal advancement (see A Closer Look 3.3).

3.3

A CLOSER LOOK

Transforming Eastern European Political Culture after the Fall of Communism

Between 1989 and 1991, much to the world's surprise, communist regimes collapsed, first in Eastern and Central Europe (including East Germany, Poland, Hungary, and Bulgaria), and subsequently in the USSR. An obvious concern was whether or not these countries' political cultures would accept democratic values after 45 to 75 years of communist-directed political socialization. Lucian Pye, one of the pioneers of political culture research, argued that this change represented the greatest transformation of political cultures since the nations of Africa, Asia, and the Middle East shed colonialism from the 1940s through the 1960s.[25] Would Eastern and Central Europeans readily adopt democratic values? Would some countries have an easier time than others developing a democratic political culture?

In 1996 a multinational survey of political attitudes revealed some important differences and a few surprising similarities between the political cultures of mature, Western democracies and those of postcommunist societies. Drawing on data from that survey, one study examined three mature democracies—the United States, Britain, and the former West Germany (now the western part of a united Germany)—and eight Eastern and Central European postcommunist countries (including the former Soviet republics of Russia and Latvia).

Respondents were asked to evaluate how well democracy had been working in their own country. Column 1 of Table 3.1 shows the combined percent of the population who felt democracy was working either perfectly well or pretty well and who saw little or no need for change. In the three Western

TABLE 3.1	Support for Democratic Political Values		
Country	**Satisfied with Democracy (Percent)**	**Support Free Speech Even by Extremists (Percent)**	**Resistance to Democracy Index (RTDI)**
United States	72	67	0.641
(former) West Germany	83	64	0.721
Britain	70	59	0.763
Czech Republic	48	64	1.114
(former) East Germany	60	64	1.144
Bulgaria	45	54	1.145
Slovenia	49	64	1.231
Poland	57	47	1.316
Latvia	42	31	1.329
Hungary	23	42	1.436
Russia	18	43	1.705

SOURCE: Jurgen Jacobs, Olaf Muller, and Gert Pickel, "Persistence of the Democracies in Central and Eastern Europe," in *Political Culture in Post-Communist Europe*, eds. Detlef Pollack et al. (Burlington, VT: Ashgate Publishing, 2003), pp. 96, 99.

(*Continued*)

Transforming Eastern European Political Culture after the Fall of Communism
(*Continued*)

democracies, the number desiring little or no change ranged from 70 percent (Britain) to 83 percent (Western Germany). Of the postcommunist nations, only Eastern Germany (60 percent) and Poland (57 percent) were at all close to those levels. Among the other postcommunist countries, there was much less satisfaction with democracy, ranging from only 18 percent in Russia to 49 percent in Slovenia.

A second question asked whether respondents felt that their government should deny the right of free speech to people with "extremist" political views. This measured their willingness to tolerate unpopular political opinions, a key component of a democratic political culture. Column 2 shows the percentage of people in each country who fully supported free speech, even for those with extreme views. As expected, citizens of mature democracies supported free speech (even for extremists) more broadly than did postcommunist respondents. Americans were most committed to free speech even for extremists (67 percent). West Germans and the British (both at 64 percent) were almost as tolerant. Respondents in several postcommunist countries were much less willing to extend free speech that far—Latvia, Hungary, Russia, and Poland. On the other hand, three postcommunist societies—East Germans, Czechs, and Slovenians—supported full free speech as strongly as the three Western democracies did.

Finally, the third column in the table presents the most comprehensive indicator of support for democratic values and attitudes. Each country was rated on a "Resistance to Democracy Index" (RTDI), an index that combined 16 variables measuring how *opposed* respondents were to democratic values. A *lower* RTDI score in column 3 indicates that that people in that country were less wary of democracy. As anticipated, the three mature Western democracies had the lowest RTDI scores (i.e., the strongest democratic political culture), well ahead of any postcommunist nation. Of the postcommunist countries, Czechs, East Germans, Bulgarians, and Slovenians had the most democratic

political cultures. Poland and Latvia came next, while Hungary and especially Russia fell behind.

Some of these results conformed to existing theories about political culture and political socialization, but other findings were unanticipated. Not surprisingly, two of the three countries with the highest resistance to democracy—Latvia and Russia—had previously been part of the Soviet Union and had little historical experience with democracy. At the other end of the spectrum, however, Eastern Germans and Czechs had some of the strongest democratic values even though they had endured intense political socialization and indoctrination from two of Central Europe's most repressive communist regimes. In the East German case, the explanation seems to be that after the fall of its communist government, the country was quickly reunited with West Germany, one of the world's wealthiest nations, with a strong commitment to democratic values developed in the post-Nazi era. West Germany was able to subsidize the former East Germany's economy and soften the painful transition to capitalism that other postcommunist countries endured. In the Czech case, the explanation may lie in its precommunist past. The country had been the more modern part of Czechoslovakia (before it split into the Czech Republic and Slovakia), a nation that had enjoyed Central Europe's strongest democratic tradition prior to its occupation by Nazi Germany and the subsequent Soviet takeover (1948). In 1968, a reformist communist government, with considerable public support, broadened civil liberties until Soviet troops invaded the country and crushed Czechoslovakia's modest attempts at democratization. Thus, as of the mid-to-late 1990s, postcommunist political cultures in both countries seem to have been shaped more by events before the advent of communism (the Czech Republic) or after the collapse of communism (East Germany) than by the decades of communist political socialization.

Perhaps the most surprising finding in this survey was Hungary's very negative attitude toward democracy and democratic values. That country had enjoyed one of Central Europe's highest levels of economic

3.3

development and had the region's least repressive communist regime. So Hungary's unexpectedly high Resistance to Democracy Index score may have less to do with its political culture under the communists than with events preceding and following the fall of communism. Perhaps Hungary's reformist government in the last years of communism and the relatively smooth transition to democracy had raised unrealistic hopes among Hungarians, hopes that were confounded by the country's very difficult economic transition to capitalism in the 1990s.

All of this suggests that political culture may have a less enduring and significant impact than many of its champions have suggested, at least in the European postcommunist experience. With the apparent exception of Russia and Latvia (and the perplexing case of Hungary), decades of communist political socialization did not seem to impede those countries' rapid absorption of democratic or semidemocratic political values in less than a decade. In many—perhaps most—countries, mass attitudes toward democracy seemed to be influenced primarily by how painful their economic transition to capitalism was.* In Germany and the Czech Republic that economic transition went relatively smoothly, while Russians endured a decade of terrible economic suffering (see Chapter 12).

Finally, we ask how well the different levels of support for democracy (as shown in Table 3.1) predicted each nation's subsequent political development. Did postcommunist countries with more democratic political cultures (as of the mid-1990s) more effectively achieve and maintain democratic government than did those with seemingly less democratic commitment? Clearly Russia's high RTDI helps explain why most citizens accepted President Putin's authoritarian measures (2000–2008) as long as he presided over an economic recovery. On the other hand, other postcommunist nations with weak democratic cultures (Hungary, Latvia, and Poland) were subsequently able to consolidate democracy as effectively as the countries with stronger democratic values did. So in this case, at least, political culture did not predict well a country's chances of consolidating democracy.

---

* During that economic transition there was a gap between the end of the communist-era benefits and the beginning of the capitalist gains. Prices soared as postcommunist governments stopped subsidies for food, rent, and other consumer goods. They also terminated free health care and guaranteed employment. For more details, see the discussion of Russia's economic transformation in Chapter 12.

Postmaterialism and Cultural Change

We have seen that earth-shattering events such as Germany's defeat in World War II, the collapse of Soviet communism, or the Cuban revolution may dramatically change that society's political culture. But other cultural transformations may occur more gradually as the result of broad social and economic developments. The phenomenon of **postmaterialism** is one of the most significant examples of such a cultural transformation. During the quarter century following World War II, North American and Western European living standards improved at a historically unparalleled rate. Drawing on data from Western Europe and other economically advanced areas, Ronald Inglehart argued that extensive modernization and economic growth substantially altered the political culture of advanced industrial democracies.[26]

He noted that most people who grew up during the expanding prosperity of the postwar period (1945 through the early 1970s) felt more economically secure than their parents and grandparents, who had suffered through the Great Depression and the ravages of World War II. Having enjoyed greater economic security during their formative years, they were often less concerned than their elders were about economic stability and growth and more concerned than their parents about issues such as civil liberties and protecting the environment. Based on their answers to survey questions, Inglehart classified respondents in advanced industrial democracies as materialists, postmaterialists, or a combination of the two subcultures. Materialists, still the largest portion of the population, tend to make political decisions based on economic self-interest. Thus, most middle-class materialists oppose higher taxes, while poorer materialists tend to favor expansion of social welfare programs. In addition, materialists tend to be especially concerned about domestic law and order, a strong national defense, maintaining a stable economy, and controlling inflation.

In the decades since Inglehart developed his theory, the number of postmaterialists has gradually increased in many of the world's industrialized democracies, including Norway, Britain, and Germany. But the pattern is neither universal nor unilinear. Between 1973 and 1999, the proportion of postmaterialists in Germany jumped from 13 to 43 percent. But by 2007 their number had fallen to 30 percent. Similarly, during the 1990s, the number of postmaterialists in Spain and the United States dropped significantly.[27] It remains to be seen whether the economic crisis of 2008–2010 (or beyond) brings a resurgence of materialist concerns. Although they are sympathetic to many of the materialists' concerns (few people, after all, like street crime, inflation, or economic instability), postmaterialists put those goals lower on their political agenda

Joe Raedle/Staff/Getty Images

Florida's then-Governor, Charlie Christ, meets with middle-class postmaterialist environmentalists.

than materialists did. At the same time, they are more concerned than materialists are about "moving toward a society where ideas count more than money," as well as "moving toward a friendlier, less impersonal society," protecting the environment, increasing grassroots participation in politics and at the workplace, and defending free speech and other civil liberties. Postmaterialists tend to be more liberal on social issues such as divorce, abortion, and homosexual marriage. They are also more sympathetic to feminist concerns, more committed to disarmament, and less religiously conservative.[28]

As the number of postmaterialist voters in economically advanced countries grew, Inglehart argued, pocketbook issues played a declining role in elections, and social class diminished as a determinant of voting. We will see in Chapters 4 and 5 that working-class voters have been historically more likely to support left-of-center parties in Europe and the United States, whereas the middle and upper classes have tended to vote for more conservative candidates. That relationship endures, but in recent decades the correlation between class and party ideology has weakened. Today, many middle-class postmaterialists vote for the Democrats in the United States, the Liberal Party in Canada, or the various Socialist parties in Western Europe, attracted by their position on issues such as the environment or civil liberties. On the other hand, increasing numbers of workers vote for conservative candidates, often based on their conservative religious and social values.

Using extensive European survey data over the past few decades, Inglehart and Russell Dalton noted that the number of people in the postmaterialist political culture has grown as young people raised in postwar affluence have entered the political system and as older materialists have died or retired from politics. That trend helps explain the growth of ecologically oriented Green parties in Western Europe and suggests that issues such as the environment will become increasingly important. At the same time, as Western Europeans became more economically secure and postmaterialist culture expanded, class divisions diminished and voters became less attracted to the welfare-state programs once endorsed by the Continent's leftist political parties. As a result, a traditional Marxist party, the French Communist Party—unable to adapt to changing public attitudes—saw its proportion of the vote decline from more than 25 percent in the late 1940s to less than 5 percent today. Conversely, the French and German Socialist Parties moved to the ideological center and dropped their prior belief in class conflict in order to stay electorally competitive.

Inglehart's theories have greatly influenced the study of political culture in advanced industrial democracies. However, chronic joblessness in Europe and persistently high unemployment rates in the United States in recent years may slow or even reverse the growth of postmaterialism. In Europe, especially, high unemployment rates over an extended period have increased support for France's neofascist National Front Party and for neo-Nazi skinhead activity in Austria and Germany (though these groups remain on the fringe, for the most part). These groups express views that are quite the opposite of postmaterialist beliefs. More broadly, in recent years many voters in the Western democracies have become suspicious of "big government" and have turned to conservative political parties in countries such as France, Germany, and the United States (at least as evidenced in the large Republican gains in the 2010 congressional election). All of this suggests that the growth and influence of postmaterialist values may not be as great or inevitable as Inglehart and Dalton predicted.

CONCLUSION: THE UTILITY OF POLITICAL CULTURE

Some years ago, Harry Eckstein, a pioneer in the study of political culture, argued that political culture theory had been one of the two most important developments in political theory during the previous 40 years. (We discuss the other development, rational choice theory, in Chapters 1 and 6).[29] Culturalist theories have enabled us to progress beyond the study of government institutions in order to understand more fully how politics differs in nations throughout the world. After a period of some disuse, cultural approaches to understanding politics have experienced a revival in recent years, examining such subjects as the prospects for democracy in Eastern Europe and the Middle East and the relationship of religious values to political beliefs.

Like any important theory, however, cultural explanations of politics have not been without their critics. One significant criticism is that survey research on political values and beliefs sometimes uses questions that are not meaningful in other cultures or are translated into terms that have different meanings in different languages. To some extent, that problem can be addressed by more careful translation and greater concern for cultural differences.

A more subtle criticism of much of the political culture research is that it has implicit cultural and ideological biases. Carole Pateman has argued that *The Civic Culture* was based on the erroneous assumption that British- and American-style democracy is the ideal form of government and consequently that political cultures throughout the world should be judged by the degree to which they support that form of democracy.[30] Richard Wilson goes a step further by arguing that all political cultures consist of widely held (or inculcated) values that justify their political system.[31] Thus, both British and Chinese schoolchildren are politically socialized to support their own system.

Perhaps the most telling criticism of political culture theory is that too often it is imprecise and often fails to explain or predict important political changes. For example, we noted earlier the assertion that Latin America has an authoritarian political culture. Yet that claim fails to explain why Costa Rica has been able to establish a stable democratic order or how Venezuela—historically one of the least democratic nations in South America—was able to transform itself in the late 1950s into one of the region's most stable democracies and later regressed to authoritarianism in the 1990s. Similarly, there do not appear to be any identifiable cultural traits that explain why India has been democratic for almost all of the 60 years since its independence, yet none of its neighbors in South Asia have enjoyed a comparable record. And, as we have noted, culturalist theories totally failed to anticipate the recent democratic uprisings in the Arab world, a region with an allegedly authoritarian culture.

Too often, analysts use culture as a "second-order" or residual explanation.[32] In other words, if scholars cannot explain why Indian and Pakistani politics are so different or why Canada has less political violence than the United States, they simply chalk it up to culture. Thus, political culture frequently becomes a fallback explanation. In other words, when analysts are unable to explain differences between two political systems, they often simply assume that the explanation lies in their political cultures.

These criticisms indicate that some culturalist research and some culturalist explanations are weak. Surely, analysts must be careful not to overstretch these theories or to use their own political values as measuring sticks for evaluating other cultures. These criticisms notwithstanding, most political scientists recognize the substantial value of political culture theory when it is carefully and prudently applied.

◆ ◆ ◆

Key Terms and Concepts _____

agents of political socialization
Arab Spring
conflictual political cultures
consensual political cultures
Generation Y
industrial democracies
information and communications
    technology (ICT)

political culture
political resocialization
political socialization
political subcultures
postmaterialism
social capital
techno-enthusiasts

DISCUSSION QUESTIONS

1. *Discuss the ways in which a society transmits its political values to its members, particularly to new generations. What are the principal agents of political socialization in the United States, and how might their role in the United States differ from their role in socioeconomically underdeveloped nations?*

2. *Compare the primary characteristics of a democratic political culture with those of an authoritarian political culture. When analysts characterize countries such as Russia or Egypt as having an authoritarian or semi-authoritarian political culture, what does that say about those countries' chances of ever becoming democratic?*

3. *How do information and communication technologies (ICT) such as the Internet or text messaging affect political socialization in developed democracies? What are the advantages and disadvantages of ICT as a socializing agent?*

4. *Some political scientists believe that the 2011 surge of democratic protest movements in North Africa and the Middle East raises fundamental challenges to the notion of authoritarian political culture. What questions do you think the Arab Spring poses regarding the nature and endurance of Arab political culture?*

5. *How enduring was the influence of communist political culture in Eastern and Central Europe? Which countries in those regions have embraced democratic values more extensively and quickly, and which have lagged behind? Explain some of these differences between postcommunist countries.*

6. *What evidence is there to support the claim that Islamic political cultures are less receptive to democracy? What evidence suggests that this argument is untrue?*

Notes _____

1. World Values Survey data in Ronald Inglehart, *Modernization and Postmodernization: Cultural, Economic, and Political Change in 43 Societies* (Princeton, NJ: Princeton University Press, 1997), p. 174.
2. Larry Diamond, "Introduction: Political Culture and Democracy," in *Political Culture and Democracy in Developing Countries*, ed. Larry Diamond (Boulder, CO: Lynne Rienner, 1993), pp. 7–8.
3. Gabriel Almond, "The Study of Political Culture," in *A Divided Discipline: Schools and Sects in Political Science*, ed. Gabriel Almond (Newbury Park, CA: Sage, 1990), p. 144.
4. Data from the World Values Survey cited in Frederick C. Turner, "Reassessing Political Culture," in *Latin America in Comparative Perspective*, ed. Peter H. Smith (Boulder, CO: Westview, 1995), p. 202.
5. Gabriel Almond and Sidney Verba, *The Civic Culture* (Boston: Little, Brown, 1965).
6. Paul Allen Beck and M. Kent Jennings, "Family Traditions, Political Periods, and the Development of Partisan Orientations," *Journal of Politics* 53, no. 3 (August 1991): 743.
7. Robert Putnam with Robert Leonardi and Raffaella Nanetti, *Making Democracy Work: Civic Traditions in Modern Italy* (Princeton, NJ: Princeton University Press, 1993).
8. Robert Putnam, "Bowling Alone: America's Declining Social Capital," *Journal of Democracy* 6, no. 1 (1995): 65; Robert Putnam, *Bowling Alone* (New York: Simon and Schuster, 2000).
9. Russell J. Dalton, *Democratic Challenges, Democratic Choices* (New York: Oxford University Press, 2004), p. 191.
10. Ibid, p. 42.
11. Brian D. Loader, ed. *Young Citizens in the Digital Age: Political Engagement, Young People, and the New Media* (London and New York: Rutledge, 2007).
12. Mark Hugo Lopez, Emily Kirby, and Jared Sagoff, "The Youth Vote 2004," www.civicyouth.org/PopUps/FactSheets/FS_Youth_Voting_72-04.pdf.
13. Doris Graber, "Mediated Politics and Citizenship in the Twenty-First Century," Vol. 55 (2004), 568, quoted in Loader, *Young Citizens*, p. 31.
14. The Pew Charitable Trust, "Young Voter Turnout Up for the Second Election in a Row," www.pewtrusts.org/news_room_detail.aspx?id=20306; Rock the Vote, "Young Voter Turnout, 2008 Primaries and Caucuses," www.blog.rockthevote.com/; Lopez, Kirby and Sagoff, op. cit.
15. Ronald Inglehart, *Culture Shift in Advanced Industrial Society* (Princeton, NJ: Princeton University Press, 1990), pp. 197, 449.
16. Almond and Verba, *Civic Culture*, p. 3.
17. Gunnar Myrdal, *An American Dilemma* (New York: McGraw-Hill, 1962; Twentieth Anniversary Edition).
18. Diamond, "Introduction: Political Culture and Democracy," in *Political Culture and Democracy*, p. 5.
19. Glen C. Dealy, *The Public Man: An Interpretation of Latin America and Other Catholic Countries* (Amherst: University of Massachusetts Press, 1977), pp. 34–35.
20. World Values and European Values Surveys 1995–2001 as cited in Pippa Norris and Ronald Inglehart, *Sacred and Secular: Religion and Politics Worldwide* (New York: Cambridge University Press, 2004), p. 147.
21. Turner, "Reassessing Political Culture," p. 209.
22. For arguments on both sides of this issue, see Samuel P. Huntington, "The Clash of Civilizations," *Foreign Affairs* 72, no. 3 (Summer 1993): 22–49; Donald Emerson, "Singapore and the Asian Values Debate," *Journal of Democracy* (October 1995): 95–105.
23. Richard Fagen, *The Transformation of Cuban Political Culture* (Stanford, CA: Stanford University Press, 1969).
24. Douglas Butterworth, "Grass Roots Political Organization in Cuba: The Case of the Committees for the Defense of the Revolution," in *Latin American Urban Research*, vol. 4, eds. Wayne Cornelius and Felicity Trueblood (Beverly Hills, CA: Sage, 1974).
25. Lucian W. Pye, "Culture as Destiny," in *Political Culture in Post-Communist Europe*, eds. Detlef Pollack et al. (Burlington, VT: Ashgate Publishing, 2003), pp. 3–16.
26. Ronald Inglehart, *Culture Shift*; Inglehart, *Modernization and Postmodernization*.
27. Russell J. Dalton, *Citizen Politics*, 5th ed. (Washington, D.C.: CQ Press, 2008), p. 86.
28. Inglehart, *Modernization and Postmodernization*, pp. 276–292.
29. Harry Eckstein, "A Culturalist Theory of Political Change," *American Political Science Review* 82, no. 3 (September 1988): 789–804.
30. Carole Pateman, "The Civic Culture: A Philosophical Critique," in Almond and Verba, *Civic Culture Revisited* (Boston: Little, Brown, 1980).
31. Richard W. Wilson, *Compliance Ideologies: Rethinking Political Culture* (New York: Cambridge University Press, 1992).
32. David Elkins and Richard Simeon, "A Cause in Search of Its Effect, or What Does Political Culture Explain?" *Comparative Politics* (January 1979): 127–145.

CHAPTER 4

Public Opinion and Elections

© Getty Images

Birmingham, England—April 29
Conservative Party leader David Cameron speaks as Liberal Democrat leader Nick Clegg looks on during the third and final debate of the 2010 general election in Great Britain. After the election produced a parliament in which no party had a clear majority, Britain's first coalition government in over 70 years was formed, and Cameron became Prime Minister.

- Influences on Public Opinion and Voting Choice
- Voter Turnout
- The Electoral Process and Campaign Money
- Electoral Systems

- Public Opinion Polling
- Conclusion: Elections and Public Opinion—The People's Voice?

People participate in politics in many ways. They write to government officials, join political parties and interest groups, take part in demonstrations (violent and nonviolent), and discuss politics with relatives and friends. When governments attempt to suppress political involvement, creative people participate in politics in more subtle ways, perhaps through literature, music, or films containing political messages. In some countries, most notably in the Middle East, Latin America, and parts of Eastern Europe, religious activities constitute an important setting for political involvement.

Nevertheless, the act of *voting* occupies a central place in political behavior. Elections are a direct and generally accepted approach to popular consultation, and they remain a basic component of democratic government. By selecting one candidate or party over another, citizens express preferences regarding who should govern them and which government policies should be adopted or changed. Apart from voting choices, *public opinion* itself is an important aspect of political behavior. By studying voting and public opinion, we are able to understand a great deal about politics, at least in democracies.

Of course, nondemocratic political systems hold elections as well, with the voters often given a "choice" of a single slate of candidates. Such single-party elections are held in China, Vietnam, North Korea, and most African nations. They were the norm, until recently, in the former Soviet Union and Eastern Europe. Other nations have held elections in which weak opposition parties have been permitted to nominate candidates but have not been given an opportunity to win.

Because of the obvious predictability of rigged elections, they tell us little about public opinion or electoral behavior. Hence, this chapter focuses on public opinion and elections in democratic systems.

The study of public opinion and voting focuses primarily on factors that influence how citizens vote and why people hold different views on policies and candidates. Researchers are also interested in the strength and distribution of opinions. Analysts want to know what kinds of people support each political party, how the rich and poor or people of different religions differ with respect to opinions and voting choices, how economic conditions and foreign policy crises affect elections, and how a candidate's personality or character amplifies or restricts his or her support. As a practical matter, the study of voting and public opinion is crucial to strategists who manage campaigns and allocate scarce campaign funds.

In this chapter, we discuss five important problems: factors influencing the direction of public opinion and voting choices, factors affecting voter turnout, campaign financing, electoral laws and procedure, and public opinion polling.

INFLUENCES ON PUBLIC OPINION AND VOTING CHOICE

In our discussion of political culture (Chapter 3), we noted the major agents of political socialization—family, education, friends, religious and social groups, and the media—and analyzed their impact on political culture. In this section, we shift our focus to consider the determinants of *specific* political opinions and voting choices: What led some Californians to support Barbara Boxer while others supported Carly Fiorina in the 2010 Senate election? How can we explain the choices of some British citizens to support the Cameron government's dramatic increase in college tuition rates while others opposed them?

Orientations to Politics: How Citizens "Filter" Political Information

In a modern industrial democracy, citizens are flooded with complex and detailed information about political issues, national events, and candidates. People must interpret that information before it will affect their opinions or votes. Political scientists have identified two important ways in which people "filter" political information, helping them to develop their preferences and their votes: party identification and ideology.

Party Identification   Imagine that your instructor asks you to guess which way a randomly selected fellow student (with whom you are not acquainted) will vote in the 2012 presidential election. If you guess correctly, you will win an all-expenses-paid spring break in Cancun. Before guessing, the instructor tells you that you can ask the student *one* question to help you guess. What question should you ask?

Political scientists would not hesitate—if they had to guess which way a given citizen will vote in a democratic country's national election, and if they could only have *one* piece of information to help them guess correctly, they would want to know the person's **party identification**. A citizen who clearly identifies with a particular political party will nearly always develop opinions consistent with that party's policy goals and vote for that party's candidates. Even when it is relatively weak, party identification affects people's political opinions.

In 2008, approximately 53 percent of the voters voted for Barack Obama and 47 percent voted for John McCain. If a student had to guess which way a randomly chosen citizen voted in that election, the student would logically guess that he or she voted for Barack Obama. This guess would be wrong, of course, 47 percent of the time. The student's chance of getting the free trip to Cancun would increase substantially if he or she had information about the randomly chosen voter's party identification. Exit polls show that 89 percent of Republicans voted for John McCain and 89 percent of Democrats voted for Barack Obama. In the U.S. congressional elections of 2010, 92 percent of Democrats voted for Democratic candidates for the House, and 95 percent of Republicans voted for GOP candidates.[1] With knowledge of a voter's party identification, we have an excellent chance of predicting who he or she will vote for. If the student knows the party identification of the randomly chosen voter, some of his or her guesses would still be wrong, but nearly all would be correct.

A renowned American political scientist, V. O. Key, Jr. (1908–1963), observed in 1952 that "the time of casting a ballot is not a time of decision for many voters; it is merely an occasion for the reaffirmation of a partisan faith of long standing."[2] The typical voter rarely evaluates candidates objectively. A person may not immediately know anything about, say, Thomas Carper (Democratic senator from Delaware) or Ron Johnson (Republican senator from Wisconsin), but upon discovering each politician's party affiliation, most people will quickly develop a strong opinion. If a voter identifies with the candidate's party, he or she almost always concludes that the candidate is the best choice.

Party identification even influences the way people evaluate a politician's character. Bill Clinton's second term (1997–2001) was marked by the scandal surrounding his testimony about his relationship with intern Monica Lewinsky in a sexual-harassment lawsuit brought by former Arkansas state employee Paula Jones. Although polls regularly indicated that nearly all Americans disapproved of his behavior, most of those identifying with the Democratic Party concluded that Clinton's behavior was a personal issue, whereas Republicans argued that he was guilty of multiple felonies, particularly perjury and obstruction of justice. Party identification also influences how people interpret news about the economy. Comparing those with college degrees, only 17 percent of Democrats approved of the way President George W. Bush handled the economy, but over 82 percent of Republicans approved. Party identification had a somewhat smaller impact on the perceptions of less educated citizens, but the effect was still dramatic.[3]

Why does party identification play such a role? For one thing, people get much of their political information from parties or from advertisements paid for by parties, and information is always presented in ways that show the party's position to full advantage. Few of us have the time or the inclination to unearth detailed information independently; parties collect and digest the raw data regarding government and politics, presenting it to their supporters (and potential supporters) in an intelligible way.

Beginning in the 1970s, political scientists noted a decline in partisan attachment, both in the United States and in Western Europe. A study of 21 Western nations concluded that party identification steadily declined in 19 of them, including the United States, Britain, France, Germany, Sweden, Austria, and Italy. The authors found that there was still a great deal of political activity, but parties had become less central to it.[4]

At least in the United States, however, partisan attachment has become considerably stronger in the last decade, following a period of decline. One important indicator of the changing strength of partisan affiliation is the extent to which voters "split" their tickets, voting for one party's candidate for president and the other party's candidate for the House of Representatives. In the early part of the twentieth century, majorities of voters in over 90 percent of the voting districts chose candidates from the same party for both presidential and congressional races. By the 1980s, majorities of voters in more than one-third of the districts selected a presidential candidate from one party and a congressional candidate from another.[5] Many observers decried the rise of "ticket-splitting," arguing that parties were losing their influence over voters.

However, ticket-splitting in the United States has returned to the low levels observed before World War II. As we will discuss in Chapter 10, the two major parties in the United States have become more polarized and thus more clearly associated with liberal (Democrats) and conservative (Republicans) ideologies. Before the last two decades, many conservatives in the South were Democrats, while that party was more liberal at the national level. Many of these citizens split their tickets, voting for a conservative Democrat to represent them in Congress and a Republican for president. Now that party affiliation is more closely aligned with ideology, a major source of ticket-splitting has been removed.

Ideology   The most significant influence on political opinions after party identification is *ideological orientation*. As discussed in Chapter 2, we often speak of a person's being liberal or conservative, suggesting a predisposition to interpret political issues from a particular viewpoint. As with party identification, ideological orientations shape voters' opinions. Conservatives tend to discount allegations of impropriety on the part of conservative politicians, and liberals tend to do the same with liberal politicians. Moreover, someone may hear of a specific issue or policy question on which he or she is initially undecided. If this person considers himself or herself a "liberal," and then finds out which side is the "liberal" side, he or she will tend to support that position (unless other influences operate in the opposite direction). Of course, conservatives act this way as well.

Thus, liberals vote for liberal candidates and conservatives vote for conservative candidates. In 2004, conservatives rated George W. Bush nearly twice as highly as liberals did. Liberal and conservative votes followed the same pattern in 2008, as 88 percent of liberals voted for Barack Obama and 78 percent of conservatives voted for John McCain.

In short, if we want to understand how to account for the public's opinions on candidates or issues, it is useful to begin with party identification and ideological orientation. These general frameworks often determine how citizens make their specific political choices. Although most voters occasionally disagree with their party or with ideologically similar friends about some issue or candidate, predictions about a person's vote are likely to be much more accurate if we have firm data about that person's partisan and ideological orientations.

Sources of Party Identification and Ideological Orientation

Where do these important influences on vote choice and public opinion come from? (Almost no one thinks they are determined by our DNA.) People develop their party identification and ideological orientation through the influence of family, education, work groups, religious affiliation, the media, unions and professional associations, and other important relationships. Despite the individualized nature of this process, however, some general patterns can be identified.

Socioeconomic Status (SES)   For some time, social scientists have discussed the importance of **socioeconomic status**, or SES. A person's SES is determined by income, education, and job status. (Successful neurosurgeons and certified public accountants with leading firms have "high" SES; the typical migrant farm laborer has "low" SES.) Political scientists, sociologists, and campaign strategists have noted a strong relationship between SES and partisan and ideological orientations, at least among people in industrialized democracies.

Simply put, people with high SES tend to support conservative parties and ideology, and low-SES people tend to support leftist parties and ideology. This relationship has been observed in many countries and over a long period of time. A classic study of U.S. public opinion found that in 1964 nearly 50 percent of self-identified "working-class" respondents identified themselves as "completely liberal," compared with only 20 percent of respondents from higher classes.[6] The same pattern was evident in recent presidential elections. In both 1992 and 1996, Democrat Bill Clinton received 59 percent of the votes cast by citizens with annual incomes under $15,000. Wealthier voters found him and his party far less appealing. Clinton received only 35 percent of the votes cast by people with household incomes over $75,000 in 1992, and only about 40 percent of the votes from this group in 1996. In 2004, Democrat Kerry beat Republican Bush 63 percent to 36 percent among the lowest income group, while Bush won handily among those making $200,000 or more, 63 percent to 35 percent. And, in 2008, Democrat Barack Obama only received 49 percent of the vote from those with incomes above $100,000, but he received 55 percent from those with incomes below $100,000. The tendency for SES to influence partisan and ideological orientation is also regularly found in Great Britain, France, Germany, Sweden, and many other democratic political systems.

Two important facts must be noted about this relationship. First, the relationship between SES on the one hand and ideology or party identification on the other is valid only in the *aggregate*. A thousand randomly selected wealthy Britons will include more Conservatives than will a thousand randomly selected blue-collar workers. One will also find more Democratic Party supporters among a thousand randomly selected Americans living under the poverty line than among a thousand wealthy Americans. There will obviously be many exceptions.

Second, the impact of SES has been declining in the United States and Europe over the past five decades. In the United States and Great Britain, as working-class voters have become more economically comfortable (particularly as they have become home-owners), many have become less attached to the economic policies of the Democratic and Labour parties. Substantial numbers of them voted for Ronald Reagan and George Bush in the United States and for the Conservative Party in Great Britain. At the same time, increasing numbers of high-SES citizens are drawn to leftist parties and candidates who advocate more vigorous environmental regulation. Both trends run counter to the traditional relationship between SES and opinion or voting choice.

In the previous chapter, we discussed Ronald Inglehart's evidence of a "culture shift" associated with the rise of what he terms postmaterialist values in the industrial democracies of Europe and North America.[7] As societies move beyond struggles over industrial and economic policy, political issues become immersed in other matters, and the impact of SES on party and ideology is less straightforward.

Figure 4.1 shows how the political effect of SES changed in four democracies during the second half of the twentieth century. The vertical axis is the "Alford Class Voting Index," which is simply the "difference between the percentage of the *working class* voting for the left and the percentage of the *middle class* voting left."[8] Thus, where the curves are in the upper part of the graph, it indicates that the influence of SES on vote

| FIGURE 4.1 | The Decline of "Class-Based" Voting |

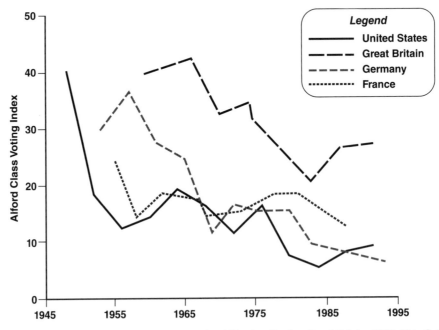

Sources: United States, 1948–92, American National Election Studies. Great Britain, 1959, Civic Culture Study; 1964–92, British Election Studies. Germany, 1953–94, German Election Studies. France, 1955, MacRae (1967, 257); 1958, Converse and Dupeux study; 1962, IFOP survey; 1967, Converse and Pierce study; 1968, Inglehart study; 1973–88, Eurobarometer studies. Reprinted from Russell J. Dalton, *Citizen Politics* (Chatham, NJ: Chatham House, 1996) p. 172. Reprinted by permission.

choice was very strong—that the percentage of *working-class voters* who voted for leftist parties was much higher than the percentage of *middle-class voters* who chose such parties. Where the curves are in the lower part of the graph, there was little difference between lower and middle classes with respect to their support for leftist parties. In 1948, 75 percent of Swedish working-class voters favored the Socialist Party, whereas only 25 percent of middle-class Swedes did the same (producing a difference score of 50 points). The 1948 presidential election in the United States between Harry Truman and Thomas Dewey produced almost as big a gap, with working-class voters 45 points more favorable to Truman than middle-class voters were.

However, the figure reveals a fairly sharp drop in the relationship between class and vote during the second half of the twentieth century in the United States and in three countries in Western Europe. In the 1972 U.S. presidential race (Democrat George McGovern versus Republican Richard Nixon), for example, there was virtually no difference in the percentages of working-class and middle-class voters favoring the liberal candidate. Among the countries in Figure 4.1, Britain retains the strongest relationship between class and voting preference, whereas in the United States and Germany that linkage is quite low. A recent study of public opinion in Russia presents further evidence suggesting that the traditional relationship between SES and political attitudes is not as simple or as strong as it once was. According to Ada Finifter, the belief that the individual—not the state—is primarily responsible for a person's well-being (a basic axiom of conservatism) is not strongly related to the respondent's level of education in Russia.* Contemporary Russian public opinion thus does not confirm the traditional pattern of high-SES conservatism.

A recent study by three European political scientists concluded that "the decline of the relationship between class and voting behavior has been caused by a … decrease in the tendency of the well educated to vote for parties on the right and a decrease in the poorly educated to vote for parties on the left."[9] Their analysis of the data attributes this change to the rise of "cultural" issues, and the authors argue that, apart from the voting choices influenced by these factors, there is still an underlying tendency for SES to play its established role (i.e., high-SES citizens vote for conservatives, low-SES citizens vote for liberals). "Class voting" still exists, they argue, but its effects are often obscured by "cultural voting."

As discussed in Chapter 3, the reasons for the declining importance of SES are complex, but they have to do with the increasing economic security and accumulated property on the part of lower-income voters and the increasing concern for noneconomic values (for example, environmental protection) among the more affluent. Thus, more low-SES voters are drawn to conservative parties than in earlier decades, and more high-SES voters support liberal parties. The traditional pattern—high-SES conservatives and low-SES liberals—becomes weaker.

Despite the contemporary erosion of the relationship between SES and party or ideological orientations, this basic feature of modern politics is far from obsolete. Liberal candidates generally do not spend a major share of their time or money

---

* See Ada W. Finifter, "Attitudes toward Individual Responsibility and Political Reform in the Former Soviet Union," *American Political Science Review* 90 (1996): 138–152. The study also reported results from 39 other countries, suggesting that educational level is only weakly related to conservative views on this issue.

campaigning in the wealthier suburbs of British or Australian cities, for example, and conservative Republicans rarely hold rallies in low-income urban neighborhoods in the United States. These strategies (and many others) are based on the widely recognized relationship between SES and partisan and ideological orientations. SES remains the best single predictor of a person's party and ideology, even though such predictions are less secure than they used to be.

Gender Beginning the 1980s, political scientists and journalists noted that the distribution of opinion among women and men was conspicuously different in many industrialized democracies. Polls show that women are likely to be somewhat more liberal than men on foreign policy, domestic spending priorities, and several other policy issues. Hence, analysts now often speak of a **gender gap**, suggesting that gender is an increasingly important influence on opinion formation and voting choices.

Figure 4.2 shows the influence of gender on political attitudes in a large array of countries, including both industrial and developing nations. The data are from a survey in which respondents were asked if they think that the government or private industry should be given increased influence in society. Those favoring private industry were judged to be "right wing," and those favoring a stronger government role were judged to be "left wing." When the bar on the figure corresponding to a given country is on the left side, it indicates the degree to which women in that country are more liberal than men.[10] When it is on the right side, it indicates the degree to which women are more conservative than men. The data show that the tendency for women to be more liberal than men is almost universal, at least since the 1990s.

The idea that men and women approach politics differently is not new. In the early years of the twentieth century, in both the United States and Great Britain, supporters of voting rights for women argued that the political impact of such a reform would be dramatic. Wars would be avoided, there would be less corruption, and family values would be strengthened if women were allowed to vote. Early empirical work suggested that those predictions were wrong. In the 1960s, Almond and Verba's *The Civic Culture* concluded that "women differ from men ... only in being somewhat more ... apathetic, parochial, conservative, and sensitive to the personality, emotional, and aesthetic aspects of political life and electoral campaigns."[11]

Things have certainly changed since *The Civic Culture* was published. In the United States, women are clearly more supportive of the Democratic Party than are men, and they adopt somewhat more liberal positions on policy. Women are less sympathetic to large defense expenditures than men are, and, in general, women are less "hawkish." As a group, women were more hesitant about entering the 1991 Gulf War and the 2003 invasion of Iraq and are also more likely than men to see a need for state intervention in the economy for health care and education.

Nevertheless, the extent to which the sexes hold different opinions is often exaggerated. For example, although female voters in the United States have been more sympathetic than males to Democratic presidential candidates in recent years, women as a group still favored Ronald Reagan over Jimmy Carter in 1980 and over Walter Mondale in 1984, and they were evenly split between George Bush and Michael Dukakis in 1988. Table 4.1 also shows that both men and women preferred Clinton to Bush in 1992, although the margin among women was considerably larger. Beginning in 1996, majorities of U.S. men and majorities of U.S. women

| FIGURE 4.2 | The Political Gender Gap Around the World |

The lengths of the bars indicate the gender gap for each country. When the bar is to the left of the zero line, it indicates that women are more supportive of left-wing ideologies than men are; for the few countries in which the bar is to the right, it indicates that women are more supportive of right-wing ideologies than men are.

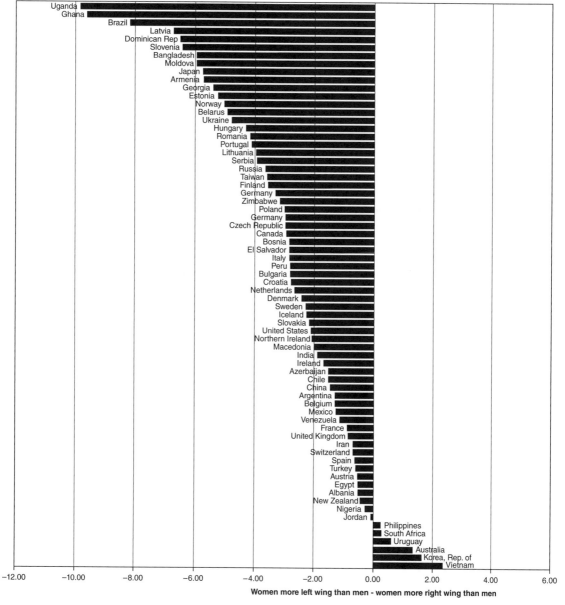

Women more left wing than men - women more right wing than men

Source: Ronald Inglehart and Pippa Norris, *The Rising Tide: Gender Equality and Cultural Change Around the World* (Cambridge, UK: Cambridge University Press, 2003), p. 82.

TABLE 4.1		Electoral Results from Recent U.S. Presidential Elections, by Gender (percent)										
	1988		**1992**			**1996**		**2000**		**2004**		**2008**
	Bush	Dukakis	Clinton	Bush	Perot	Clinton	Dole	Bush	Gore	Bush	Kerry	McCain	Obama
Men	57	41	41	38	10	43	44	53	42	55	44	48	49
Women	50	49	48	37	7	54	38	43	52	48	51	43	56

Source: Exit poll data. *New York Times* on the Web at www.nyt.com. Results for the 2000, 2004, and 2008 elections are from the CNN exit polls, available at www.cnn.com/POLITICS/

preferred different candidates. In 1996, men slightly favored Dole (44 to 43 percent), whereas women clearly favored Clinton (54 to 38 percent); in 2000, men favored Bush (53 to 42 percent), whereas women favored Gore (54 to 43 percent); and in 2004, men favored Bush (55 to 44 percent), whereas women favored Kerry (51 to 48 percent). In 2008, men were almost evenly split between the candidates, 49 percent for Obama and 48 percent for McCain, but women favored Obama by a strong margin of 56 percent to 43 percent.

What has caused this conspicuous difference in political opinions? Many observers (and nearly all journalists) attribute the gender gap in the United States to the success of the feminist movement. By raising women's "consciousness," feminist organizations have made women see that their interests demand leftist policies, according to this view. Moreover, as women have entered the workforce in greater proportions, their traditional roles have all but vanished. Many women thus have acquired a pronounced feminist perspective regarding such issues as child care, nuclear disarmament, and abortion. Perhaps the modern gender gap has been created by the fact that the remaining vestiges of traditional gender roles seem increasingly antiquated and unfair in modern life.

However, an important study in the *American Journal of Political Science* evaluated data on U.S. elections beginning in the 1950s and concluded that the "gender gap is the product of the changing partisanship of *men.*"[12] In other words, the observed differences between male and female voters have grown not because women have deserted the Republican Party *but because many men have deserted the Democratic Party.* In the 1950s, majorities of both men and women identified with the Democratic Party. Beginning in the 1980s, however, women remained generally unchanged in their party allegiance, while men substantially drifted to the Republicans. It is the Democratic Party that has been damaged by the gender gap: The last time a majority of nonminority males voted for a Democratic presidential candidate was 1964, and the Republican "revolution" of 1994 was often attributed to the fact that many male voters had left the Democratic Party. The pattern has continued. In 2008, a Rasmussen Report found that 47 percent of U.S. women identified with the Democratic Party, compared to just 36 percent of U.S. men, and in 2010, 52 percent of females voted for Democratic House candidates while only 40 percent of males did.[13]

A recent study suggests that men and women also differ with respect to how readily their opinions change in response to the drift of public policy. In the aggregate, both men and women become more conservative during periods in which public policy moves to the left, and they become more liberal during periods of conservative policy adoption. However, the evidence indicates that men are more responsive to changes in public policy. "[When] policy moves in a liberal direction,

... men move in a conservative direction at a faster rate than women. In contrast, when policy moves to the right, the opinions of both men and women will respond by moving to the left, but the greater responsiveness among men will decrease the gap, bringing male preferences closer to the preferences of women."[14]

As political scientists have worked to understand the influence of gender on vote choice and public opinion, they have recently focused on the importance of *marital status*. In several recent U.S. elections, the gap between married and nonmarried voters has actually been greater than the gap between men and women. For example, in the 2004 election, married voters were considerably more supportive of the Republican George W. Bush over Democrat John Kerry (57 percent to 42 percent), while nonmarried voters preferred the Democrats (58 percent to 40 percent). Married women support the Republican Party almost as strongly as married men do, but nonmarried women are nearly twice as supportive of the Democrats as they are of the Republicans.[15]

Other Influences on Party Identification and Ideological Orientation Several other factors influence partisan and ideological orientation. In many countries, *race* continues to be critical, often overriding the effects of party or ideology. Most observers of U.S. politics are aware, for example, that fewer than 8 percent of African Americans have voted for Republican presidential candidates in recent elections. Race and ethnicity are also profoundly important factors in elections in Israel, where Sephardic Jews (those descended from Jews in Spain, Portugal, the Middle East, and North Africa) are traditionally more supportive of the conservative Likud Party, while Ashkenazi Jews (Jews of European origin) are more likely to vote for leftist parties.

Religion remains a major political influence in some countries. French and Italian citizens who regularly attend church have more conservative beliefs than those who do not.[16] Voters in different *regions* of some countries approach politics in distinctive ways, revealing modern echoes of ancient conflicts.

Psychological factors constitute a rather different (and often questioned) influence on partisan and ideological orientations. A famous U.S. study in the 1950s concluded that people who held conservative beliefs tended to have psychological traits that were different from liberals. People suffering from significant anxiety, for example, supposedly developed an aversion to change and thus chose to support conservative leaders and parties.[17]

Recent research suggests a more complete picture. Many psychologists are convinced that an individual's disposition is largely determined by what they call the "Big Five" traits: Extraversion, Agreeableness, Conscientiousness, Emotional Stability, and Openness to Experience. A group of political scientists wanted to know if a tendency toward conservative or liberal ideology is associated with these fundamental building blocks of personality. In a series of studies, they found that "Openness to Experience is associated with liberalism and Conscientiousness is associated with conservatism." Also, "Extraversion and Emotional Stability are associated with conservatism, while Agreeableness does not appear to be related to self-reported ideology."[18]

The idea that each individual's personality traits influence his or her political ideology is fascinating but highly controversial. Nearly all analysts agree that other factors, especially socioeconomic status, are more important influences. Nevertheless, the linkage between personality and political views is becoming an important subject for political research.

Candidate Evaluation: A Confounding Element in Public Opinion

Citizens do not always form opinions or make their voting choices on the basis of party identification and ideological orientation. It is well established that people often react strongly to the personality, style, or "charisma" of a particular candidate. Such reactions, positive or negative, can influence not only a person's vote but also his or her opinions regarding policies and political controversies.

This simple, obvious fact often makes public opinion and voting behavior unpredictable. The influence of **candidate evaluation** was extensively discussed in the United States in the 1980s when Ronald Reagan persuaded large numbers of Democratic Party identifiers to vote for him. Democratic Party leaders claimed that most of those voters *really* supported their policies but were deluded into voting for Reagan by his winning personality and his professional actor's gifts for communication. Similarly, many political analysts argued that Robert Dole lost in 1996 in part because his dour personality (at least on television) made him less appealing than Bill Clinton. In Britain, Labour Party leader Tony Blair used his John Kennedyesque appeal to become the longest-serving British Prime Minister (1997–2007). On the other hand, Stephen Harper, whose Conservative Party won a 2006 election in Canada, is generally considered rather introverted and has a reputation for stiffness in public appearances. Many consider Barack Obama to be the most charismatic U.S. politician in decades, and his ability to inspire citizens was a factor in 2008, as were some nagging questions about the persons he was associated with early in his career. While candidate personality and appeal may matter, other things obviously can overwhelm their effects.

Generally speaking, candidate evaluation can be especially important in elections in which the mass media figure prominently and when highly paid consultants successfully manipulate a candidate's "image." Candidate evaluation presents a problem for political analysis, however, because it is so unpredictable. Since citizens can be influenced by factors as changeable as the prevailing image of a candidate's personality, predictions of electoral results on the basis of partisan identification and ideological orientation will often be wrong.

The Impact of Mass Media

In most countries, the mass media, especially newspapers and television, influence voters significantly. The media can amplify or undercut support for a specific candidate; over time, they may even influence deep-seated ideological and partisan attachments. Questions pertaining to the actual workings and effects of the media in these matters are thus critical to the study of public opinion and electoral behavior.

At the outset, it is vital to recognize that not all countries have the same mass media influences. Americans (as well as French and British citizens) rely heavily on television for their political information. According to BBC Tokyo Bureau Chief William Horsley writing in the 1980s, Japanese voters avidly read newspapers, which "play the role of the constructive critic of the government."[19] In rural areas of the developing world, radio has a great influence. In virtually all societies, however, mass media of some form exert an influence on public opinion.

Gauging the impact of the media on opinions and voting choices is difficult because it is so hard to separate the influence of the media from the influence of party affiliation, family and peer groups, and other organizational relationships. The most difficult questions have to do with the bias allegedly created by broadcasters and newspapers in democratic societies. There is an intriguing symmetry to the charges of bias; nearly always, activists and politicians on *both* the right and the left present charges that the media slant the news. Richard Nixon was strident in his repeated attacks against media bias. He often claimed that the media "kicked him around," and revelations during the Watergate period indicated how much he resented the media. (Nixon had an "enemies" list that included correspondent Daniel Schorr and other journalists.)

Although not as aroused as Nixon was by the media, virtually every president has argued that journalists are unfair. Bill Clinton's scandals were thoroughly covered in both broadcast and print media, and the subject matter involved enabled reporters and news anchors to keep their readers and audiences continually interested. Mere weeks prior to the 2004 election, former CBS News Director Dan Rather presented a very critical report about George W. Bush's National Guard Service, although the documents that figured prominently in the story were almost certainly forged. In 2008, Bill Clinton complained bitterly about the media's treatment of Senator Hillary Clinton's campaign to become the Democratic Party's presidential nominee, claiming that the press was sexist and profoundly biased toward Senator Barack Obama.

Beyond bias, the most troubling political problem associated with the media has to do with the tendency to oversimplify and distort serious political issues, thereby degrading political discourse. (See A Closer Look 4.1.) Television seems particularly susceptible to damaging manipulation, but sophisticated campaign managers are often creative in achieving the same effects in other contexts. One famous example of an oversimplifying, emotional political advertisement occurred during the 1964 U.S. presidential race, when Democrat Lyndon Johnson's campaign ran a television spot— designed to discredit Republican candidate Barry Goldwater—showing a little girl playing with a flower. A narrator spoke in ominous tones about Goldwater's allegedly "warmongering" policy proposals, and then the girl looked up as a mushroom cloud rose from an atomic bomb. Although the commercial aired only once, it demonstrated the power of television to use emotion in influencing voters. In 2004, perhaps the most controversial ads on television were those run by the Swiftboat Veterans for Truth, a group claiming that Democrat John Kerry had misrepresented his combat record in Vietnam. The 2008 U.S. presidential race was memorable for television (and YouTube) coverage of fiery sermons by Reverend Jeremiah Wright, a former pastor and friend of Senator Barack Obama. In all these cases, the mass media treated important and complex issues in ways that were arguably emotional and manipulative while making little contribution to rational analysis.

It is thus ironic that a recent study concluded that "political advertising [in the United States] contributes to a well-informed electorate."* Researchers found that U.S. respondents who paid attention to paid political advertisements had more

---

* See Craig Leonard Brians and Martin P. Wattenberg, "Campaign Issue Knowledge and Salience: Comparing Reception from TV Commercials, TV News, and Newspapers," *American Journal of Political Science* 40 (1996): 172–193.

A CLOSER LOOK

4.1

The Effect of the Media on Political Tolerance

"Do we really believe that ALL red-state residents are ignorant fascist knuckle-dragging NASCAR-obsessed cousin-marrying road-kill-eating tobacco-juice-dribbling gun-fondling religious fanatic rednecks; or that ALL blue state residents are godless unpatriotic pierced-nose Volvo-driving France-loving left-wing Communist latte-sucking tofu-chomping holistic-wacko neurotic vegan weenie perverts?" This question, posed by humorist Dave Barry in December 2004, is perhaps less of an exaggeration of the way Americans view their ideological opposites than we would like to think.*

In an important recent article in the *American Political Science Review*, Diana Mutz examined findings from a series of experimental studies, concluding that contemporary television news coverage in the United States tends to make people less tolerant of candidates and issue positions they oppose: "The 'in-your-face'

---

* Dave Barry's rhetorical question was quoted in Diana C. Mutz, "Effects of 'In-Your-Face' Television Discourse on Perceptions of a Legitimate Opposition," *American Political Science Review 101* (November 2007): 621.

intimacy of uncivil political discourse on television discourages the kind of mutual respect that might sustain perceptions of a legitimate opposition." Vehement and even violent disagreements are nothing new in political life, but there are indications that television coverage of politics on 24-hour news channels during the last two decades has intensified "citizens' negativity toward those people and ideas that they dislike."[20]

Tolerance for dissenting opinions is a fundamental component of stable democracy. If television coverage of politics leads a large share of the population to become less tolerant of political opposition, it could lead to some real problems in the future. On the other hand, a highly mobilized public can be a healthy characteristic of democratic society, even when debate is heated and passionate. Despite Dave Barry's very funny caricature, there are few signs of a basic breakdown of democratic political culture in the United States (or in other countries with access to our news channels), but the rhetoric is sometimes striking.

---

information about the candidates' issue positions than those who only read newspapers and watched television news. Apparently, campaign commercials transmit at least some real information along with the "sound bites."

Contemporary democracies vary with respect to regulation of political advertising. Paid political advertisements are permitted in Australia, Canada, and Japan but have been prohibited in Great Britain, Sweden, Italy, India, France, and Germany, among other countries. The Bipartisan Campaign Reform Act of 2002, signed into law by President Bush on March 27, 2002, regulates contributions and some issue ads in the United States, and we will discuss this legislation in detail in Chapter 10. Most of the countries that prohibit paid ads reserve free broadcast time for parties, typically allocated to each in proportion to its voting strength. The objective is to ensure that broadcast media will bring information to voters while minimizing the chances that money and clever tactics will manipulate the voters. However, in many Third World countries, one party often has much more money for media advertising than others, giving it a distinct advantage.

Perhaps the most critical factor is the *diversity* of mass media; if no single voice controls newspapers and broadcasting, it is much more difficult to produce significant shifts in support and opposition through the media. A state-controlled or censored press—such as has existed in Chile, Vietnam, China, and elsewhere—is clearly an influential tool. Television, radio, and newspapers in these countries are used to generate support, direct citizens, and retain power. Yet the demise of repressive regimes in Eastern Europe, Chile, and elsewhere suggests that the power of state-owned media to control public opinion has its limits. Where the press is free and open, some alternative spokesperson will find an outlet to criticize the government or the ruling party, and some people will listen. The impact of the media is substantially blunted when real media diversity exists, and it is greatly multiplied when all media are in the hands of one ruling party or group.

A particularly controversial news source was added to the international mix of media outlets in 2006. In that year, Al Jazeera launched "Al Jazeera International," a 24-hour English language news and current affairs channel. (There is also a Web version of Al Jazeera, at http://english.aljazeera.net/English.) With little competition in the Middle East, the question of Al Jazeera's political influence in these unsettled countries is profoundly important. U.S. government officials have argued that Al Jazeera's news coverage is anti-American and anti-Israeli and that it gives implicit support to al-Qaeda and other terrorist organizations.

Dr. Walid Phares, a professor of Middle East Studies and comparative politics at Florida Atlantic University, stated that Al Jazeera misrepresented a prodemocracy demonstration in central Baghdad. In December of 2003, some 20,000 men and women marched through the streets shouting *"La' la' lil irhab. Na'am, na'am lil dimurcratiya."* ("No, no to terrorism. Yes, yes to democracy!"). Instead of reporting that a significant demonstration had taken place that supported the United States and coalition activities, the Al Jazeera coverage stated that about half that many people marched and that they "were 'expressing views against *what they call* terrorism.'"[*] James Morris, of the Institute of Arab and Islamic Studies at the University of Exeter in Britain, concluded that the network is simply "Osama bin Laden's loudspeaker."

The network's defenders claim that it is often criticized by radical Islamic fundamentalists as serving as a mouthpiece for the West, and that it simply presents both sides of all issues. They also point out that errors in translating their stories into English have been responsible for some of the apparent bias in the stories Al Jazeera broadcasts. In any case, this controversial news outlet will probably have a significant degree of influence as conflict within the Islamic world continues.

Perceptions of the Government's Economic Performance

Significant evidence shows that the state of the economy sometimes overrides the effects of other influences on voting choices, even the effects of party and ideology. Many citizens vote for or against the incumbent party on the basis of their perceptions regarding the government's economic performance. If economic growth and employment are high and inflation is low, the incumbent party will generally do well with voters, regardless of party and ideology.

---

* The Phares essay is available at http://frontpagemag.com/Articles/Read.aspx?GUID=B8515BAE-52A2-4B96-A6B8-B2CD4161D804.

A study from the 1980s concluded that, in British elections, "economic variables [exceeded] the impact of partisan identification," and those variables were generally as important as party identification in Germany.[21] Using data from presidential elections between 1956 and 1988, a prominent U.S. political scientist concluded that "each 1 percent increase in real disposable per capita income is estimated to result in a 2 percent direct increase in the incumbent's vote share, other factors held constant."[22] A recent study of British elections found that "evaluations of national economic performance are of greater importance than are personal measures," although voter perceptions of their personal economic conditions is also associated with the extent to which voters support the incumbent party.[23]

A 2006 book found that the pattern even holds in former communist countries. Political scientist Joshua Tucker examined voting patterns in Russia, Poland, Hungary, Slovakia, and the Czech Republic and found that parties identified with "liberal-capitalist" reforms received more support from regions in each country in which economic conditions had improved.[24]

A general appraisal of data from several sources led to the following conclusion about economic conditions and voter choices:

> The powerful relationship between the economy and the electorate in democracies the world over comes from the economic responsiveness of the electors, the individual voters. Among the issues on the typical voter's agenda, none is more consistently present, nor generally has a stronger impact, than the economy. Citizen dissatisfaction with economic performance substantially increases the probability of a vote against the incumbent. In a sense, the volatility of short term economic performance makes this factor a particularly interesting influence on voter choices—it has its greatest effect on those with low levels of partisan attachment, and can therefore change the outcomes of elections where the parties are of relatively equal strength. Thus, in these situations, the fall of a government is more likely to come from a shift in economic evaluations than from a shift in party attachments.[25]

Given that voters in many countries appear increasingly willing to stray from their party loyalties, contemporary economic conditions will probably become even more important in future elections.

However, it is important not to overstate the importance of this factor. The relatively poor state of the U.S. economy during the months preceding the 1992 election clearly hurt George H. W. Bush, just as a strong economy obviously helped Bill Clinton in 1996. Although the U.S. economy and the stock market had started to stall during the two quarters of 2000, the economy had been quite strong for several years, and traditional indicators suggested that the incumbent party (the Democrats) would do extremely well. Vice President Al Gore did receive slightly more of the popular vote than Republican George W. Bush, but he received far less than models based on economic performance variables had predicted. The predictive models were far more accurate in 2004, suggesting a slight advantage for the incumbent Republican.[26]

In 2008, most voters felt that the U.S. economy was failing, and the voters who were most negative were far more likely to vote for Barack Obama than for John McCain. Among the few voters who judged the economy to be "excellent" or "good," McCain received 72 percent of the vote, but Obama won 54 percent of those who felt that the economy was "not so good" or "poor." With a Democrat in the White House and with Democratic majorities in the House and Senate, voter perceptions of the economy helped the Republicans in 2010. In that election, 68 percent of those who were "very worried" about the economy voted for Republican candidates for the House of Representatives. But 81 percent of voters who were "not too worried" voted for Democratic candidates, according to a CNN exit poll.

Summary: Voting Choices and Opinion Formation

As the preceding sections show, the influences that shape voting choices and public opinions are diverse, complex, and changing. The most critical point to remember is that research has demonstrated that voting and opinion are not random behaviors but can often be predicted and understood as the results of a complex set of known influences.

SES normally works on opinion formation and voting choice indirectly, by determining party identification and ideological orientation. Gender, race, religion, regional identifications, and psychology, in contrast, often determine both partisan and ideological attachments and specific opinions and voting choices. The impact of candidate evaluation and economic conditions vary with each election. Each of these factors has greater or lesser importance in different political systems, at different times, and when different candidates are involved, but most of them are involved in our best efforts to predict and explain electoral behavior.

VOTER TURNOUT

Although research on public opinion and voting often focuses on the nature of the respondents' opinions or their vote preferences, it also deals with the question of **voter turnout**. The percentage of citizens who actually vote varies considerably across countries. (See Table 4.2.) The reasons for variations in turnout are many, including factors related to voters themselves (such as economic position, psychological orientation to politics, education, and access to transportation), the competitiveness of candidates and parties, and the nature of political system (legal requirements pertaining to voting, the activities of parties and other organizations to encourage turnout, and the expected closeness of elections).

Cultural norms are often important in determining voter turnout—in some countries, citizens consider voting a moral duty, and people vote for that reason even when they are unconcerned about the outcome of the election. Public opinion surveys in Venezuela and Mexico, for example, show that most voters feel that elections make little difference in determining government policy. Yet respondents in both countries stated that it was very important to vote.

A decline in partisan loyalty can also reduce turnout. People vote less often when they lose a sense of partisan loyalty, voting only when the few special issues they care about are at stake. In contrast, strong partisans vote regularly because of their commitment to the party itself.

TABLE 4.2	Turnout Rates for Selected Democracies

Percent of registered voters voting in all national elections from 1945 through 2007 (number of elections held during the period is shown in parentheses)

Italy (14)	92.5
New Zealand (18)	86.2
Australia (21)	84.4
Sweden (17)	83.3
Germany (13)	80.6
Greece (17)	80.3
Israel (14)	80.0
Norway (14)	79.5
Palestinian Authority (1)	75.4
United Kingdom (15)	74.9
Ireland (16)	74.9
Uruguay (10)	70.3
Nicaragua (10)	62.0
India (12)	60.7
Honduras (12)	55.3
Switzerland (13)	49.3
United States (26)	48.3
Colombia (20)	36.2
Guatemala (15)	29.8
Mali (2)	21.7

NOTE: Turnout percentages are for national elections to the lower house of the national legislature, except for Chile, Mali, and the United States, where turnout percentages are for presidential elections.

SOURCE: Institute for Democracy and Electoral Assistance (Stockholm, Sweden) at www.idea.int.

Legal considerations significantly affect voting turnout. Voter registration is still relatively cumbersome in many states in the United States, often requiring a special visit to city hall; easier voter registration in some other industrial democracies thus helps to explain why U.S. turnout is lower. Other legal factors can increase or decrease turnout. In a number of Latin American countries, parents cannot register their children in school unless they have a stamped identification card proving they voted in the last election (although such requirements can be overcome by paying fines or bribes). Large numbers of Italian citizens working in other parts of Europe return home to vote. Although some of these Italians may be motivated by a sense of civic duty, their behavior is also influenced by the fact that the government pays their passage home on such occasions. Moreover, many nations schedule national elections on Sunday, when people are not at their weekday jobs.

Voting is compulsory in some nations, and it is strictly enforced in Australia, Switzerland, Singapore, and Uruguay, among a few others, all of which have very high turnout rates. Part of the drop in the U.S. turnout rate since the 1960s is related to the lowering of the voting age from 21 to 18, since turnout among younger voters is usually low. Another systemic factor affecting turnout is the type of electoral system each country has: countries with **proportional representation** (PR) generally have higher turnout rates than countries with *single-member districts*. As discussed below, voters have a wider range of parties to choose from in PR systems, thus increasing the chances that each voter will have an appealing choice).

Rational Choice Theory and Voter Turnout   The rational choice approach to political analysis has had some real difficulties with the empirical fact of substantial voter turnout. Regardless of the electoral laws, other legal factors, and party loyalty and cultural norms, the purely rational individual should find it difficult to justify any expenditure of time or resources to vote. The tiny probability that a single vote will determine the election's outcome makes it, strictly speaking, irrational to vote, even when the voter cares deeply about the outcome. Nevertheless, millions of people do vote. Some rational choice scholars have attempted to reconcile their assumptions about self-interest and rationality with the fact that significant voting occurs by arguing that there are some "side benefits" to voting, such as obtaining a feeling of self-respect by going to the polls, or a social status benefit when others see the voter doing his or her civic duty.

Instead of trying to find out why any voting takes place at all, a recent theoretical analysis uses rational choice ideas to explore the circumstances in which voter turnout should be somewhat higher or lower. Two political scientists considered the "size effect," which suggests that voting turnout percentages should be lower when the electorate is larger (because a single vote is less likely to make a difference than it does in smaller electorates). They also studied the "competition" and "underdog" effects, which suggest that voting turnout should be higher when an election is expected to be close, and that it should be higher among those who support an unpopular candidate.[27]

The researchers found that there is support for the rational choice ideas that citizens do take the competitiveness of elections into account when they decide to vote, and that their behavior is also affected by the size of the electorate and the "underdog" effect. Thus, even though more people vote than a strictly rational calculus would suggest, factors affecting the costs and projected benefits of voting apparently do have an effect on turnout.

The Causes of Low Voter Turnout   Considering the reasons for different levels of voting turnout across countries may help us understand how well, or how poorly, democracy works in practice. For example, turnout may be very low in less developed regions because of poor transportation, literacy requirements, or even intimidation. According to International IDEA (the International Institute for Democracy and Electoral Assistance, based in Sweden), literacy has a substantial influence on turnout: the 52 countries with 95 percent or better literacy rates have an average turnout of 71 percent, while the 104 less literate countries have an average turnout rate of only 61 percent. In Guatemala, where large portions of the nation's population are Indians who speak no Spanish, literacy requirements particularly suppress the vote. Violence and the threat of violence also keep citizens away from the polls.

National voter turnout figures typically obscure great disparities in voting among different segments of society. Perhaps the most consistent research finding regarding turnout is that people of different economic conditions have different turnout rates. Before careful statistical analysis was applied to the question, many observers speculated that poorer people would probably vote more regularly than the rich because the poor were more dependent on government. This "mobilization" hypothesis suggested that the effect of economic distress on turnout would be to mobilize the poor to participate in politics more that the rich. Others argued for the opposite view (termed the "withdrawal" hypothesis), which is the idea that economic distress destroys a voter's sense of self-worth and hope for the future, diminishing interest in elections and leading to lower turnout among the poor.

It is well established that the mobilization hypothesis is completely wrong. Although some poor people doubtlessly respond to their economic distress by voting, a disproportionate number of them withdraw from such activities. In 2000, middle-class voters (those with family incomes between $50,000 and $75,000) made up only 21.6 percent of the population, but they accounted for 25 percent of the votes cast. In contrast, those with incomes lower than $15,000 made up 9.6 percent of the population, but accounted for only 7 percent of the votes cast. In 2008, more than 78 percent of citizens with incomes above $150,000 reported that they voted, but fewer than 45 percent of those making less than $20,000 did so.[28]

The Comparative Study of Electoral Systems, an extensive international research consortium based at the University of Michigan, reported the results of a recent study of income and voting across 25 countries. In three countries (New Zealand, Ireland, and Taiwan), wealthier citizens were somewhat less likely to have voted than poorer citizens (see Figure 4.3). But in all the other countries, there is a substantial gap in the other direction: the income of *voters* is much higher than the income of *nonvoters*.

A 2005 study of 18 democracies added further support to this conclusion.[29] Table 4.3 reports the bias in turnout created by income and education differences for eight democracies. The table entries indicate the degree to which the turnout rate is higher among citizens in the highest income or education category compared to the turnout rate among citizens in the lowest income or education category. (For example, the 10.8 percent income bias for France means that voter turnout by wealthy French citizens is 10.8 percent higher than it is for poorer French citizens.)

In all these democracies, citizens with wealth and education vote at considerably higher rates than other citizens. To the extent that these citizens have different political interests or preferences than poorer, less educated citizens, the fact that they vote in greater numbers means that electoral outcomes will disproportionately favor their interests. This creates a significant challenge for virtually all modern democracies—the ballot box is not, in practice, the "voice of all the people."

Why do the poor vote less often? Wealthier citizens are more likely than the poor to be literate, to read newspapers and books, and to be members of civic associations. These activities and associations help them develop a strong interest in politics. The rich vote more because they are more involved and more informed, and because they are more likely than the poor to have developed a sense of political efficacy. Yet another problem depresses voter turnout among the poor: Complicated voter registration requirements constitute obstacles to voting that are particularly difficult for the poor and uneducated. Sometimes these obstacles are intentionally designed to have this effect.

Before the Civil Rights Act of 1964, it was extremely difficult for many African Americans, particularly if they were poor, to register to vote in rural areas of the South. In many Third World countries, candidates may be so closely identified with

| FIGURE 4.3 | Income Level of Voters and Nonvoters in 25 Political Systems |

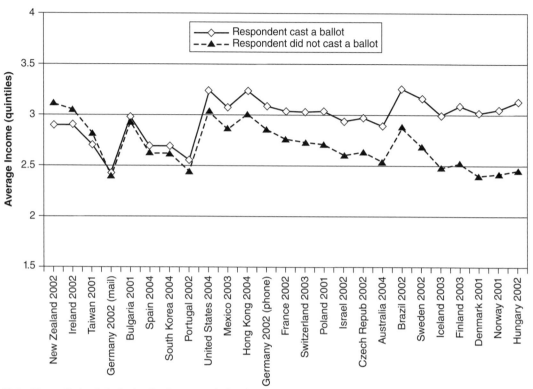

Note: The vertical axis indicates the income *quintile* of voters and nonvoters. For example, in Iceland, the average voter is in the third quintile, meaning that the average citizen in this group has an income that is higher than 60 percent of Icelanders. However, the average income of nonvoters is just below the 2.5 quintile, meaning that nonvoters, as a group, have incomes at the national average.

Source: Comparative Study of Electoral Systems, *Income and Current Election Participation*, available at www.cses.org/resources/results/CSESresults_IncomeParticipation.htm, accessed February 22, 2011.

economic elites that the poor see no purpose in voting. In Colombia and Mexico, for example, long-term declines in voting are often attributed to the perception among poor voters that the political system offers them little.

Changes in Turnout over Time

It is difficult to interpret the meaning of changes over time in voting turnout. In the United States, turnout has fallen in recent years: 62.8 percent of the voting-age population voted in the presidential election in 1960, only 52.8 percent in 1980, 53.3 percent in 1984, and only 50.3 percent in 1988. Then, after rising to 55.2 percent in 1992, turnout fell in 1996 and was only 50.3 percent in 2000. In 2004, it rose to 55.5 percent, and in 2008, well over 60 percent of eligible voters cast a ballot, the strongest turnout figure in nearly half a century.

TABLE 4.3	Voter Turnout Is Higher for the Wealthy and Better Educated		
Country	Income Bias	Education Bias	Year of Election
Australia	5.1	4.4	2004
Britain	6.8	2.2	1997
France	10.8	7.9	2002
Germany	3.8	6.3	2002
Israel	5.9	4.4	2003
Sweden	12.3	6.8	2002
U.S.	30.0	32.9	2004

Source: Data from the Comparative Study of Electoral Systems (www.cses.org), as compiled in Miki Caul Kittilson, "Rising Political Inequality in Established Democracies: Mobilization, Socio-Economic Status, and Voter Turnout, 1960s to 2000," paper presented at the 2005 Annual Meeting of the American Political Science Association.

Some are quick to suggest that low turnout is a sign of alienation. Large segments of the population, say such analysts, are disgusted by scandal or hopeless about the future. Others argue that the decline in American voter turnout reflects the fact that, compared with the period before the 1960s, Americans discuss politics less often with others. Since that time, there has been a "decline in peer interaction itself, caused by a decline of the traditional family, suburbanization, and increased television watching." On the other hand, the Internet appears to have a positive impact on voting participation.[30]

Research on the causes of variations in voter turnout is an important area of political inquiry. A particularly interesting line of research has explored the impact of compulsory voting on government policy. In 2005, two researchers analyzed data on several countries, and their findings make a strong case for the importance of turnout: countries with enforced compulsory voting not only had higher turnout rates, but they also had *more equal distributions of national income.*[31] Because of the central place of voting in democratic government, understanding variations in voting across classes or across different time periods helps us to see who the "people" are in "government by the people," and it helps explain the policies governments adopt and the resulting conditions in their citizens' lives.

The Electoral Process and Campaign Money

One of the most controversial aspects of modern elections is the impact of campaign contributions. In some countries, publicly owned broadcasting systems provide free television and radio time for candidates to present their views to voters, but candidates and their parties usually must pay for printing and dissemination of literature, for staff support, and for travel expenses. Candidates in major U.S. elections pay for most of their media time, making campaign dollars an extremely important resource.

Campaign expenditures vary widely across nations. In some nations, campaign spending is as low as $0.20 per voter, but it can be much higher than that, especially where there are no spending limits. Where most of these expenditures are covered by public funding, candidates and parties do not have to raise the funding themselves, but fund-raising becomes a vitally important task where there is less public funding. For example, the typical Senate campaign in the United States costs the candidate over $2 million, requiring that an incumbent raise an average of nearly $7,000 *per week* during the six years he or she is in office in order to run for reelection.

Table 4.4 provides information on the differences among modern nations with respect to the laws governing campaign finance. There is considerable variation among the countries in this table, reflecting different cultural and political attitudes about elections and campaigns. Consider this summary statement comparing Canada and the United States:

> Canada pursues a more egalitarian approach, providing public financing of about two-thirds of candidate and party costs, while seeking to achieve a "level playing field" by imposing expenditure ceilings on candidate, party, and even "third party" or interest group spending. On the other hand, the United States follows more of a libertarian or free-speech approach, with more dependence upon private financing through more generous contribution limits from individual, political action committee and political party sources.[32]

It is difficult to determine precisely the degree to which campaign spending affects electoral outcomes. In Great Britain, analysts have typically assumed that the

TABLE 4.4	Political Finance Laws in Selected Nations					
Country	Must Contributions to Parties Be Disclosed?	Is There a Maximum on Contributions to Parties?	Is There a Ban on Foreign Contributions to Parties?	Are Contributions from Corporations or Unions Banned?		Do Parties Receive Public Funding?
				Corps.	Unions	
Australia	yes	no	no	no	no	yes
Austria	no	no	no	no	no	yes
Denmark	yes	no	no	no	no	yes
El Salvador	no	no	no	no	no	yes
France	yes	yes	yes	yes	yes	yes
Germany	yes	no	no	no	no	yes
India	yes	no	no	no	no	no
Mexico	yes	yes	yes	yes	no	yes
Nicaragua	yes	no	no	no	no	yes
Norway	yes	no	no	no	no	yes
Peru	yes	no	no	no	no	no
Poland	yes	yes	yes	yes	yes	yes
Russia	yes	yes	yes	no	no	yes
Switzerland	no	no	no	no	no	yes
Ukraine	yes	yes	yes	no	no	no
United Kingdom	yes	no	yes	no	no	yes
United States	yes	yes	yes	yes	yes	no

SOURCE: Reginald Austin and Maja Tjernström, eds., *Funding of Political Parties and Election Campaigns*, International IDEA Handbook Series (Stockholm, Sweden: International Institute for Democracy and Electoral Assistance, 2003), pp. 181–238.

national campaign—largely driven by publicly funded broadcasts—is the primary factor in determining the results of parliamentary elections, although a study from the 1990s suggested that local spending may have an impact in constituencies where neither party is dominant.[33]

Recent U.S. elections suggest that campaign spending can be a major factor not only in Senate races but also in presidential contests. Most observers believe that the very close victory of Republican Richard Nixon over Democrat Hubert Humphrey in 1968 would have been reversed if the Democratic Party had not exhausted its funds during the last weeks of the campaign. More recently, President Clinton's 1996 reelection bid was certainly made easier by the fact that his opponent, Senator Robert Dole, had to spend millions during a difficult primary contest, exhausting the spending limits that applied until after the August conventions. During the long months between April and August, the Dole campaign was relatively silent, while Clinton maintained a consistent presence on the airwaves. In 2000 and 2004, both parties had large war chests, and both elections were close.

In 2008, Democrat Barack Obama became the first presidential candidate to reject public financing in a general election since the system was created in the early 1970s. As a result, he had many millions more to spend than his opponent, Republican John McCain. There were many factors making a McCain victory very unlikely, but the fact that Obama outspent him by nearly 3 to 1 in the final weeks put McCain at a distinct disadvantage.

Because candidates and parties may be expected to make promises and commitments to groups and individuals in exchange for contributions, most countries have strict limits on such contributions, and many limit the amount that can be spent, regardless of the source of the funds. There have been troubling reports of campaign finance problems in the United States for decades, and the problems have involved both major parties. In 1996, the Democratic Party allegedly accepted donations funneled through a Buddhist monastery and an Indian tribe, and there were indications that the government of China had directed campaign funds to both parties in an effort to influence U.S. policy in the Far East. Similar concerns arose regarding both parties again in 2000, and a great deal of controversy surrounded campaign contributions from the failed Enron Corporation. Contributions from oil and tobacco interests to Republican candidates have been examined for many years. Concerns about these contribution patterns, coupled with the persistent efforts of Senators McCain and Feingold and others, led to the passage of the Bipartisan Campaign Reform Act of 2002, as noted above.

ELECTORAL SYSTEMS

The "people" can be said to have a real voice in any electoral system in which the right to vote is secure, the votes are counted honestly, the choices are meaningful, and the elections are regularly scheduled. Even when those conditions are met, however, the nature of the electoral system can have an important impact on electoral outcomes. In the following sections, we consider the most important kind of variation among election systems, as well as the issues of malapportionment and redistricting.

Single-Member Districts versus Proportional Representation

Electoral systems based on **single-member districts** divide the nation into a relatively large number of legislative districts with one legislative seat for each. For example, for its general elections, Britain is divided into 659 districts of roughly equal population, and each elects one Member of Parliament. Elections for the U.S. House of Representatives also follow this model. The system is sometimes called "winner take all," because the candidate who receives the most votes in a given district wins "all" the legislative power from that district. No seats are awarded to the losers, even if the election is very close. Approximately half of the democracies around the world use some form of the single-member-district system.

Proportional representation divides the nation into a smaller number of larger electoral districts and assigns several seats to each district. (In Israel, the whole country is a single district.) Rather than vote for an individual candidate, voters normally choose among "party slates" of candidates.* When the votes are tallied, each party receives seats in the legislature in proportion to the share of the popular vote its slate received. Thus, if Party A receives 40 percent of the vote, and there are five seats in that district, two seats will go to candidates on Party A's slate. The other seats will be awarded to the other parties in proportion to the votes they receive.† About one-third of the countries around the world use a PR system. A few countries—New Zealand and Germany, for example—use some combination of the two systems. (See A Closer Look 4.2 and Table 4.5.)

Some readers may assume that the choice between these two electoral arrangements makes no difference—as long as the principles of majority rule and universal suffrage are followed, *both* systems are democratic. However, the choice of electoral system can have tremendous political effects, influencing the decisions of both parties and citizens.

In a single-member-district system, party leaders realize that they will get zero representation for their party in any given district if any opposing candidate receives one more vote than their candidate receives. Candidates and party leaders in such systems tend to take moderate positions likely to attract a winning majority or plurality of voters in many districts. Thus, all other factors being equal, systems using single-member-district electoral arrangements tend to have a small number of centrist parties, as shown in Table 4.5.

The big losers in a single-member district are smaller parties trying to establish a base of support. It can be done, as the U.S. Republican Party proved in the nineteenth century and the British Labour Party showed in the twentieth century. But doing so is quite difficult. If an up-and-coming third party succeeds in attracting 20 or 30 percent of the national vote, it will still receive virtually no seats because it will fail to come in first in many districts.

For example, as we discuss in Chapter 11, that was precisely the experience of the British Alliance and its successor, the Liberal Democrats. The Alliance (1983 and 1987) and the Liberal Democrats (1992 to the present) received 17 to 25 percent of the popular votes in the last five national elections, but they never received more than 9.6

---

* In some countries, voters choose a party slate and indicate their top choices of individuals on the slate.

† Actual PR systems have detailed rules regarding, among other things, a "threshold" of votes that a party must receive to win any seats.

A CLOSER LOOK

4.2

New Zealand's Hybrid Electoral System

New Zealand adopted a new system for electing its parliament in a 1993 referendum. The new system, called *mixed-member proportional* (or MMP), includes elements of both a single-member district and a PR system.

Under an MMP system, each citizen has *two votes*: an "electorate vote" and a "party vote." Half the 120 Members of Parliament (MPs) are chosen by voters under the single-member-district system, using their "electorate votes" to select named candidates running for election in each electorate (or district). The other 60 winners are "list MPs," selected from lists of candidates nominated by the political parties. Among these 60 MPs, the total number of MPs from each party corresponds to each party's share of the party votes. New Zealand's new MMP system stipulates, however, that a party must win at least 5 percent of the party votes or win at least one electorate seat to receive a proportional allocation of the seats for list MPs.

The sample ballot shown here is based on the one distributed to voters by the government of New Zealand for educational purposes.

The MMP system in New Zealand is an effort to secure some of the advantages of both PR and single-member-district systems. Any party that can command even 5 percent of the nation's party vote will have at least one of its members in Parliament. Such parties would never win a seat in single-member-district systems.

However the electorate votes, the system should ensure that large, established parties will continue to be dominant, since half the seats in Parliament will be awarded to candidates who have received the highest vote totals in their respective electorates. Thus, candidates receiving small percentages of the votes in each electorate will always lose. The hybrid system will produce a more diverse range of partisan voices than would a pure single-member-district system, but it will have more built-in stability than a pure PR system (since the single-member-district system for the electorate votes will ensure that large, established parties continue to dominate).

Sample Ballot—New Zealand National Parliamentary Election

You Have Two Votes

Party Vote	Electorate Vote
(This vote decides the share of seats that each of the parties listed below will have in Parliament.)	(This vote decides the candidate who will be elected Member of Parliament of the _____ electorate.)
Vote for One Party	*Vote for One Candidate*

Party Vote		Electorate Vote	
Carrot Party	_____	Allenby, Fred	_____
Peach Party	_____	Barnardo, Mary	_____
Squash Party	_____	Dummlop, Alice	_____
Banana Party	_____	Edlinton, Tony	_____
Broccoli Party	_____	Nectar, Lizzy	_____
Pear Party	_____	Omega, Richard	_____

TABLE 4.5	Electoral Systems for Selected Nations (Lower House of Parliament or General Assembly of Representatives)

	Threshold % of Vote Needed for Seat	Effective Number of Parliamentary Parties*
Majoritarian (Single-Member District)		
Australia	n/a	2.61
Canada	n/a	2.98
United Kingdom	n/a	2.11
United States	n/a	1.99
Combined Systems		
Germany	5	3.30
Mexico	2	2.86
Rep. of Korea	5	2.36
Russia	5	5.40
Taiwan	5	2.46
Ukraine	4	5.98
Proportional Representation		
Czech Rep.	5	4.15
Denmark	2	4.92
Israel	1.5	5.63
Netherlands	0.67	4.81
Norway	4	4.36
Peru	0	3.81
Poland	7	2.95
Romania	3	3.37
Slovenia	3	5.52
Spain	3	2.73
Sweden	4	4.29
Switzerland	0	5.08

*The *effective number of parliamentary parties* is a measure that estimates the number of political parties that have enough strength to constitute a meaningful influence in parliamentary activity.

SOURCE: Pippa Norris, *Electoral Engineering: Voting Rules and Political Behavior*, Cambridge University Press, 2004, pp. 66–67.

percent of the seats in the House of Commons. Proportional representation would have resulted in a stronger British Alliance or Liberal Democratic presence in the House.

Party leaders are well aware of the effects of electoral systems, and sometimes parties with a majority in the legislature enact new electoral laws to benefit their own electoral chances. In a 1959 national referendum, for example, the conservative majority in France introduced a new constitution that moved the country from proportional representation to single-member districts. A major objective was to weaken the Communist Party in the parliament. Of course, sometimes the strategy fails. In 1986, the Socialist parliamentary majority reinstituted PR in an effort to dilute the conservative opposition (they hoped PR would produce several new parties, taking voters from the conservatives). The conservatives won anyway and reinstituted single-member districts.

A comprehensive study of comparative electoral systems by Pippa Norris led her to conclude that the basic character of the political system is substantially determined by its electoral laws.[34] Single-member-district systems produce **adversarial democracy**, where the losing side is excluded from power until the next election, whereas proportional representation systems produce **consensual democracy**, because these systems require a wide range of parties (including those with relatively small shares of the nation's votes) to cooperate in forming governments. There are arguments to be made for both arrangements:

> For advocates of *adversarial* democracy, the most important considerations for electoral systems are that the votes cast in elections should decisively determine the party or parties in government.... At periodic intervals the electorate should be allowed to judge the government's record.... Minor parties in third or fourth place are discriminated against by majority elections for the sake of governability ... [and] proportional systems are [seen as] ineffective since they can produce indecisive outcomes, unstable regimes, ... and a lack of clear-cut accountability....
>
> By contrast, proponents of *consensual* democracy argue that majoritarian systems place too much faith in the winning party.... For the vision of consensual democracy, the electoral system should promote a process of conciliation, consultation, and coalition-building within parliaments. [According to this view], majoritarian systems over-reward the winner, producing 'an elected dictatorship' where a government based on a plurality can steamroller its policies, and implement its programs, without the need for consultation and compromise with other parties in parliament or other groups in society.[35]

In short, proportional representation increases the electoral opportunities of new or narrow-based parties, often producing a situation in which a wider range of parties are involved in making government policy. A party able to obtain only a small share of the popular vote would still win a proportional number of seats in the legislature. Supporters of small parties would not feel that they are wasting their votes by voting for them, and potential donors would not feel that they are wasting their money by contributing. Not surprisingly, countries such as Israel and the Netherlands, which use PR electoral systems, are more likely to have multiparty systems with a number of small parties represented in the parliament.

As noted earlier, single-member-district systems usually hurt extreme leftist and rightist parties. The French experience shows how both the far-left Communist Party and the far-right National Front gained more electoral seats when the country used PR. But the single-member-district system tends to hurt *moderate* third parties as well (parties that are not in the top two). In Great Britain, the party that would gain most in a switch to PR—the Liberal Democrats (successors to the Alliance)— is more moderate than either the Labour Party or the Conservative Party. Similarly, in Germany, if PR were eliminated, the biggest loser would be the centrist Free Democrats. It is therefore more accurate to say that the single-member-district system creates an obstacle for *less established* parties, regardless of whether they are extreme or centrist.

However, the electoral system affects the political system in other ways, particularly with respect to stability, voter turnout, and the quality of representation. As we discuss in Chapter 5, the nature of the existing political divisions in society is a key factor in determining whether a country has two or three large moderate parties instead of a large number of smaller, more ideologically distinct parties, but it should be noted that most of the countries of Western Europe use some variant of PR and that most of them have maintained very moderate and stable political systems. If a country has a consensual political culture, a generally centrist electorate, and an established two-party system, as in the United States, switching to PR may have little impact. However, if a society is more conflictual and ideologically diverse, such as Israel or Italy, PR tends to produce larger numbers of parties with more polarized ideologies. Although this encourages active input from a wide range of diverse political interests, PR systems can lead to political instability, since elections will often produce a result in which no single party has enough support to govern. To minimize the problem, most PR systems have a "threshold" provision, requiring that parties receive at least a certain percentage of the vote to be represented in the parliament. (See Table 4.5.)

Instability is often a serious problem for PR systems: During the past 50 years, Italian elections have never produced governments (that is, prime ministers and cabinets) backed by stable parliamentary majorities. Italian governments have been forced to resign, on average, every 15 months.* Italy's 1993 reform created a system in which three-fourths of the legislators are elected in single-member districts. This change may increase cabinet stability in the long run. However, as noted above, PR systems generally have higher voter turnout, most likely as a consequence of the wider range of choices that citizens have. According to recent data compiled by International IDEA, countries with PR systems had an average turnout rate of nearly 70 percent, while countries with single-member-district systems had an average turnout rate of only 58 percent.

Malapportionment and District Boundaries

Whatever electoral system is chosen, **malapportionment** (having electoral districts with vastly different numbers of citizens) can also affect electoral results. In severely malapportioned systems, a rural district may be so sparsely populated that its one representative represents only 15,000 citizens. An adjacent urban district may also have only one representative for its 600,000 citizens. The political result can be easily anticipated: A legislature made up of representatives elected through such a malapportioned system would give much greater weight to rural political concerns than would be warranted on the basis of population. Put another way, each citizen in the rural district has 40 times more political power than a citizen in the urban district.

Malapportionment was held unconstitutional in the United States in the landmark decision *Baker v. Carr* (369 U.S. 186, 1962). The Court argued that severe malapportionment effectively violated the Constitution's grant of equal voting power to all citizens. Because of continuing population shifts, this decision requires that the allocation of representatives to each state be reviewed every decade and that states use **redistricting** to correct imbalances among districts. Even when the *number* of citizens in each district is roughly the same, districts can be drawn in ways that affect the ability of the electoral system to represent all voters.

As mentioned previously, when there is widespread knowledge of which parts of a metropolitan area or region support which parties, a party with a majority in the

---

* As we see in our discussion of British politics (Chapter 11), under a parliamentary system, the government (the prime minister and cabinet) needs to be supported by a majority of Parliament. If the prime minister and cabinet lose that support, they must resign.

state legislature (which redraws the congressional district lines) and control of the governor's office (who must sign the redistricting) is often able to take this knowledge into account in drawing district boundaries. The requirement that electoral districts be roughly equal in population does not prevent some creative redistricting in ways that diminish the chances of one's opponents.[*] The areas in which the opposing party is strong are simply divided, and the portions are then included in districts where the favored party has a clear majority.[†] Strategic redistricting thus creates another way to distort the vote.[‡]

The most controversial issue surrounding the drawing of district boundaries in the United States has to do with the issue of race. The Voting Rights Act of 1965 made it illegal to draw district lines in ways that reduce the ability of racial minorities to elect a candidate to represent them. In 1986, the Supreme Court held that districts could be found illegal if minority voting power is diluted, even if there is no specific intent on anyone's part to create such a dilution.[§] The Voting Rights Act required that Southern states obtain Justice Department approval of their congressional districts, and, in many cases, boundaries were drawn that created "majority-minority" districts (in which racial minorities made up the majority of citizens). In several cases—*Shaw v. Reno* (509 U.S. 630, 1993); *Miller v. Johnson* (132 L.Ed.2d 762, 1995); and *Bush v. Vera* (135 L.Ed.2d 248, 1996)—the Supreme Court has held that districts which are drawn *primarily* on the basis of race are unconstitutional. The controversy rages on, with one side arguing that the government should not assume that members of minority groups are unrepresented unless a person of the same race is elected from their district, and the other side arguing that district boundaries drawn without regard to race will effectively preclude the election of minority representatives.

PUBLIC OPINION POLLING

Much of what we know about public opinion depends on the familiar **public opinion polls** we hear about so frequently during presidential campaigns. Candidates have their own polls, but in most industrialized democracies private organizations have

---

[*] In 1812, Governor Elbridge Gerry of Massachusetts helped engineer a particularly creative example of this practice. When it was remarked that the district drawn to his party's advantage looked like a salamander on the map, someone pointed out that it wasn't a salamander; it was a *Gerrymander*. The term has stuck as a description of partisan redistricting.

[†] William E. Brock, chairman of the Republican National Committee from 1977 to 1981, claimed that the Democrats used their control of state legislatures to draw district boundaries so that the Republicans routinely won far fewer congressional seats in the 1970s than their vote totals would have predicted. See John Aldrich et al., *American Government* (Boston: Houghton Mifflin, 1986), p. 238.

[‡] A controversial example of strategic redistricting in the United States was applied in Texas in 2003. The new district lines in that state were drawn so that Republicans would gain several seats in Congress, and the strategy bore fruit in the 2004 election. The League of United Latin American Citizens in Texas went to federal court to present its claim that the redistricting plan was unconstitutional. When the Supreme Court ruled in 2006, it held that the plan did not violate the Constitution, but that it did violate the Voting Rights Act of 1965 because it effectively denied the right of Latino voters as a group to elect a favored candidate, because the plan diluted their political influence. (See *League of United Latin American Citizens v. Perry*, 548 U.S. 399, 2006).

[§] See *Thornburg v. Gingles*, 478 U.S. 30 (1986).

been established to provide independent polling services. (In the United States, the Gallup, Harris, NBC/*Wall Street Journal*, CBS/*New York Times*, and ABC/*Washington Post* polls are the best known.) Opinion polls are essential to those running campaigns since they help strategists identify where scarce funds should be spent and how messages should be crafted. Polls are important in other respects, too, raising questions of real significance for the health of modern democracy.

First, the accuracy of polls is often questioned. Since it is obviously impossible to determine every citizen's views, modern opinion polling works through *sampling*. In the United States, national polls usually are based on responses from no more than two thousand people. If the sample is chosen carefully, the poll will be accurate enough to be useful.* For example, the Gallup, Harris, and CBS/*New York Times* polls were off by no more than 4 percentage points during recent elections and generally predicted the results within 1 or 2 points.[36]

The second issue raised by opinion polls has to do with their possible effects on elections. The argument is often made that undecided voters may make their final choice on the basis of which candidate is ahead in the polls. This possibility is particularly disturbing when we realize that so many news items, in both broadcast and print media, are devoted to poll results. It is not well established that polls have a predictable or significant effect along those lines, but the potential for such influences was enough to prompt the French government to adopt restrictions on poll coverage during the weeks preceding elections.

An analysis of public opinion polling by the Brookings Institution nicely captured the promise and the difficulties involved in interpreting and using the results of polls:

> Polling results can be exceptionally powerful, largely because of their seeming legitimacy as neutral evidence. Even though many people report being skeptical of public opinion polls, these surveys do, however crudely, appear to reflect some kind of underlying reality. After all, aren't they "scientifically" conducted and accurate within a specific margin of error? Don't presidential election surveys ordinarily get the results roughly right? Besides, polling results are reported in numerical formats. If we can quantify something, that ordinarily means that we can measure it with reasonable accuracy.[37]

CONCLUSION: ELECTIONS AND PUBLIC OPINION—THE PEOPLE'S VOICE?

The study of public opinion and voting increasingly reveals the complexity of individual political choices. Because of ample data and sophisticated analytical tools, political scientists have developed a large body of knowledge regarding public opinion and voting behavior, making predictions in these areas more useful than in any

---

* Perhaps you have heard a national commentator report of poll results with a statement like this: "The results have a margin of error of plus or minus 3 points." This is not precisely correct. The logic of sampling means that if 44 percent of those polls support a given candidate, for example, and if we have a margin of error of plus or minus 3 points, we can be very sure (usually 95 percent sure) that the candidate's support in the whole population is between 41 and 47 percent. This level of certainty requires that the citizens polled constituted a random sample, meaning that every person in the whole population had an equal chance of being included in the sample.

other set of subjects in the discipline. Nevertheless, our knowledge tells us that useful predictions cannot be based on simple models and that results are often surprising. The most practical bit of knowledge derived from voting and opinion studies is the critical realization that opinions and votes are often influenced by organized entities, particularly political parties, the subject of our next chapter.

◆ ◆ ◆

Key Terms and Concepts _____

adversarial democracy	proportional representation (PR)
candidate evaluation	public opinion polls
consensual democracy	redistricting
gender gap	single-member districts
malapportionment	socioeconomic status (SES)
party identification	voter turnout

DISCUSSION QUESTIONS

1. *Compare the mobilization and withdrawal hypotheses as explanations for differences between economic classes with respect to voter turnout.*
2. *Why is proportional representation (PR) thought to create consensual democracy?*
3. *Why do single-member-district systems create adversarial democracy?*
4. *How does the rise of postmaterialism affect the impact of socioeconomic status (SES) on the voting preferences of upper- and lower-class voters?*
5. *Given that newspapers, television, and radio can influence public opinion and even vote choices, should these media outlets be restricted by the government? Why or why not?*

Notes _____

1. CBS Exit Poll results, cited in *The American: The Journal of the American Enterprise Institute*, November 16, 2010, available at www.american.com/archive/2010/november/what-the-voters-actually-said-on-election-day (accessed February 3, 2011).
2. V. O. Key, Jr., *Politics, Parties, and Pressure Groups* (New York: Crowell, 1952), chap. 20.
3. See Gregory E. McAvoy and Peter K. Enns, "Using Approval of the President's Handling of the Economy to Understand Who Polarizes and Why," *Presidential Studies Quarterly* 40, no. 3 (2010), p. 549.
4. Russell J. Dalton and Martin Wattenberg, eds., *Parties without Partisans: Political Change in Advanced Industrial Democracies* (Oxford, UK: Oxford University Press, 2000), chap. 2.
5. Morris Fiorina, "The Electorate in the Voting Booth," in *The Parties Respond*, ed. L. Sandy Maisel (Boulder, CO: Westview, 1990), p. 119. See also Fiorina's discussion in *Divided Government* (New York: Macmillan, 1992), in which he notes that party identification for many Americans has been weakened by the perception that the two major parties have become increasingly more ideological and extreme.
6. Lloyd A. Free and Hadley Cantril, *The Political Beliefs of Americans: A Study of Public Opinion* (New York: Simon & Schuster, 1968), p. 216.

7. Ronald Inglehart, *Culture Shift in Advanced Industrial Society* (Princeton, NJ: Princeton University Press, 1990).
8. See Russell J. Dalton, *Citizen Politics: Public Opinion and Political Parties in Advanced Western Democracies*, 2nd ed. (Chatham, NJ: Chatham House, 1996), pp. 167–176.
9. "Class is Not Dead—It Has Been Buried Alive: Class Voting and Cultural Voting in Postwar Western Societies (1956–1990)," *World Political Science Review* 3 (2007), available online from the Berkeley Electronic Press.
10. Ronald Inglehart and Pippa Norris, *The Rising Tide: Gender Equality and Cultural Change around the World* (Cambridge, UK: Cambridge University Press, 2003).
11. Gabriel Almond and Sidney Verba, *The Civic Culture* (Boston: Little, Brown, 1965), p. 325.
12. Karen M. Kaufmann and John R. Petrocik, "The Changing Politics of American Men: Understanding the Sources of the Gender Gap," *American Journal of Political Science* 43 (1999): 864, 887.
13. Rasmussen Report, June 3, 2008, available at www.rasmussenreports.com. For the 2010 voting for the House of Representatives, see data provided by Edison Research, www.edisonresearch.com/home/archives/2010/11/increasingly_its_the_daddy_party_vs_the_mommy_party.php.
14. See Paul M. Kellstedt, David A. M. Peterson, and Mark D. Ramierz, "The Macro Politics of a Gender Gap," *Public Opinion Quarterly* 74 (2010): pp. 477–498.
15. Data available from the Pew Research Center for the People and the Press, http://people-press.org/reports/display.php3?PageID=750.
16. See Ivor Crewe and David Denver, *Electoral Change in Western Democracies* (London: Croom Helm, 1985), pp. 218–219.
17. See Herbert McClosky, "Conservatism and Personality," *American Political Science Review* 52 (1958): 27–45.
18. Alan S. Gerber, Gregory A. Huber, David Doherty, Conor M. Dowling, and Shang E. Ha, "Personality and Political Attitudes: Relationships across Issue Domains and Political Contexts," *American Political Science Review* 104 (2010): 111–133; and Mondak, Jeffery J. , and Karen D. Halperin, "A Framework for the Study of Personality and Political Behaviour," *British Journal of Political Science* 38 (2008): 335–362.
19. William Horsley, "The Press as Loyal Opposition in Japan," *Newspapers and Democracy: International Essays on a Changing Medium*, ed. Anthony Smith (Cambridge: MIT Press, 1980), p. 212.
20. Diana C. Mutz, "Effects of 'In-Your-Face' Television Discourse on Perceptions of a Legitimate Opposition," *American Political Science Review* 101 (November 2007): 521–635.
21. Michael S. Lewis-Beck, "Comparative Economic Voting: Britain, France, Germany, Italy," *American Journal of Political Science* 30 (1986): 315–346.
22. Gregory B. Markus, "The Impact of Personal and National Economic Conditions on Presidential Voting, 1956–1988," *American Journal of Political Science* 36 (August 1992): 830.
23. Sean Carey and Matthew J. Lebo, "Election Cycles and the Economic Voter," *Political Research Quarterly* 59 (2006): 543–556.
24. See Joshua A. Tucker, *Regional Economic Voting: Russia, Poland, Hungary, Slovakia, and the Czech Republic, 1990-1999.* (Cambridge, UK: Cambridge University Press, 2006).
25. Michael S. Lewis-Beck and Mary Stegmaier, "Economic Determinants of Electoral Outcomes," *Annual Review of Political Science* 3 (2000): 211.
26. See Robert S. Erikson, Joseph Batumi, and Brett Wilson, "Was the 2000 Presidential Election Predictable?" *PS: Political Science and Politics* 34 (2001): 815–819; and Alfred G. Cuzan and Charles M. Bundrick, "Deconstructing the 2004 Presidential Election Forecasts: The Fiscal Model and the Campbell Collection Compared," *PS: Political Science and Politics* 38 (April 2005): 255–262.
27. David K. Levine and Thomas R. Palfrey, "The Paradox of Voter Participation: A Laboratory Study," *American Political Science Review* 101 (February 2007): 143–158.
28. U.S. Census Bureau, Current Population Survey, November 2004.
29. Miki Caul Kittilson, "Rising Political Inequality in Established Democracies: Mobilization, Socio-Economic Status, and Voter Turnout, 1960s to 2000," paper presented at the 2005 Annual Meeting of the American Political Science Association.
30. Carol A. Cassell and David B. Hill, "Explanations of Turnout Decline," *American Politics Quarterly* 9 (1981): 193. See also Caroline J. Tolbert and Ramona S. McNeal, "Unraveling the Effects of the Internet on Political Participation," *Political Research Quarterly* 56 (June 2003): 175–185.
31. Alberto Chong and Mauricio Olivera. 2005. "On Compulsory Voting and Income Inequality in a Cross Section of Countries," Inter-American Development Bank Working Paper #533, available at www.iadb.org.
32. Herbert E. Alexander, "Comparative Analysis of Political Party and Campaign Financing in the United States and Canada," in *The Delicate Balance between Political Equality and Freedom of Expression:*

Political Party and Campaign Financing in Canada and the United States, eds. Steven Griner and Daniel Zovatto (Washington, DC: Organization of American States, 2005).

33. Charles J. Pattie, Ronald J. Johnston, and Edward A. Fieldhouse, "Winning the Local Vote: The Effectiveness of Constituency Campaign Spending in Great Britain, 1983–1992," *American Political Science Review* 89 (1995): 969–983.

34. Pippa Norris, *Institutions Matter* (Cambridge, UK: Cambridge University Press, 2003).

35. Norris, *Institutions Matter*, Ch. 2.

36. See the compilation of figures in James MacGregor Burns and Jack Peltason, *Government by the People: The Dynamics of American National, State, and Local Government*, 11th ed. (Englewood Cliffs, NJ: Prentice Hall, 1989), p. 217. Also see Philip E. Converse, "The Advent of Polling and Political Representation," *PS: Political Science and Politics* 29 (December 1996): 649–657.

37. Brookings Institution, "From Hootie to Harry (and Louise): Polling and Interest Groups" (2003), available at www.brookings.edu/articles/2003/summer_elections_loomis.aspx

CHAPTER 5

Political Parties

**French Socialist Party
Presidential Candidate,
Segolene Royal (right)**

- What Are Political Parties?
- The Functions of Political Parties
- The Origins of Political Parties
- Party Systems
- Types of Political Parties
- Conclusion: Parties in a Changing World

> However [political parties] may now and then answer popular ends, they are likely, in the course of time and things, to become potent engines, by which cunning, ambitious, and unprincipled men will be enabled to subvert the power of the people, and to usurp for themselves the reins of government.
>
> *—George Washington's Farewell Address*

Since the time of the founders, many Americans have shared Washington's suspicion of political parties. They have regarded parties as divisive and self-serving, more interested in winning elections or representing narrow constituencies than in furthering the national good. In recent decades, growing numbers of Americans and Europeans have viewed political parties and partisanship negatively. Indeed, growing numbers of Americans have identified themselves as "independents," loyal to no party.[1] Similarly, news analysts sometimes accuse some certain political officials of playing partisan politics, just as they praise others for "rising above party politics."

Political scientists, on the other hand, have a more positive view of political parties as institutions, even though they may be critical of how parties perform in contemporary democracies. Rather than viewing parties as inherently divisive or unscrupulous (although some are), they consider them indispensable vehicles for organizing the broad citizen participation that is essential to the maintenance of democracy and political stability. In fact, while having parties does not guarantee that a country will be democratic, it is impossible to have democracy without them. To best appreciate the positive impact of parties, we need only consider examples of contemporary governments that have none. For example, Saudi Arabia has no parties; the royal family and its advisers make critical political decisions. Under the absolute rule of President Yoweri Museveni, Uganda outlawed political parties until 2005. Elsewhere, authoritarian military governments in Latin America and Africa have often banned political party activity after they seized power.

So it is obviously *possible* for governments to function without parties—but only in societies with very limited socioeconomic development (and, hence, little pressure for mass political participation) or countries ruled by monarchs or military dictators, where political participation is repressed. On the other hand, some dictatorships, especially in countries with moderate socioeconomic development, do have a dominant political party. That is, all **totalitarian** regimes and many **authoritarian** governments have a ruling political party in order to mobilize and control mass participation. Some of these parties penetrate virtually all aspects of public life. For example, the Chinese Communist Party (CCP) offers its members prestige and various material privileges. Consequently, its ranks now include not only politicians and civil servants but millions of factory workers, doctors, teachers, farmers, and even businessmen. The Soviet Communist Party had a similar structure. In all, some 80 million people currently belong to the CCP, while the Soviet Communist Party had 19 million members at its peak. Similarly, tens of thousands joined the Italian Fascist Party or Germany's Nazi Party in the 1930s, motivated either by conviction or by opportunism.

PASSING THE TORCH South Africa's legendary president, Nelson Mandela, right, raises the hand of the next African National Congress (ANC) President Thabo Mbeki, who was elected national president soon after. As the force behind the liberation of South Africa's black majority population, the ANC has been the country's dominant political party.

In some dictatorships, the government encourages widespread political participation, but only under the tight control of the ruling party. That party promotes mass support for the government, while state security forces suppress antigovernment groups. For example, the CCP, with close to 80 million members, has greatly expanded political participation in that country but has repressed any opposition. To appreciate how parties affect government and society, we must first define what distinguishes them from related political organizations and then identify their basic functions.

WHAT ARE POLITICAL PARTIES?

The enormous variation among political parties makes it difficult to devise a definition that fits all of them, but they all share a few characteristics. A **political party** is an organization that unites people in an effort to place its representatives in government offices so as to influence government activities and policies. Many parties, perhaps most, explicitly or implicitly espouse an ideology or at least a set of principles and beliefs, although these vary greatly in their coherence and consistency. The British Conservative and French Socialist parties proclaim the ideologies given in their names. America's major political parties do not, but those who follow U.S. politics know that the Republican Party is the more conservative of the two and the Democratic Party the more liberal. In democratic political systems, parties compete to elect their leaders to public office, and voters use party labels to identify and classify candidates. Although many authoritarian and totalitarian regimes hold elections as well, their real purpose is to *legitimize* the leaders in power rather than to allow meaningful opposition.

Political parties differ from interest groups—the subject of our next chapter—in that they usually seek to control the reins of government, whereas interest groups merely seek to influence government decisions affecting that group's special concerns. Thus, American interest groups try to influence government policy in areas such as environmental preservation (the Wilderness Society), manufacturing regulations (the National Chamber of Commerce), and firearms regulation (the National Rifle Association).

THE FUNCTIONS OF POLITICAL PARTIES

The fact that parties have become such a pervasive and central component of modern political systems suggests that they perform vital functions. An examination of those functions allows us to appreciate how parties contribute to the political process.

Recruitment of Political Leadership

Every political system must have some means of recruiting its leaders. In premodern systems, leaders inherited their positions as kings, feudal lords, or tribal chieftains. As mass political participation grew—first in the United States and Western Europe and then in other parts of the world—an *institutionalized* process of **leadership recruitment** through political parties became a key feature of their political systems. Conversely, governments operating *without* an established arrangement for selecting new leaders often face a crisis when the existing leaders die, resign, or are removed from office. In most countries, the political leadership inadequately represents segments of the population such as women or racial minorities. But frequently they have been vehicles for broadening representation as they look for additional votes. One example of this is the efforts made by many parties—especially in Western Europe, Latin America, and Africa—to increase parliamentary representation for women (see A Closer Look 5.1).

By spelling out their ideologies and programs over time, political parties give the population signals about what candidates from their ranks will do if elected. While elected leaders such German Chancellor Angela Merkel and French President Nicolas Sarkozy cannot expect to fulfill *all* of their campaign pledges, voters had a general idea about where they were heading when they elected them. In contrast, voters in some developing countries have had fewer election cues since prominent political figures have created ad hoc, **personalistic parties** designed solely to get them elected. Because these parties have no track record and have revealed few objectives other than electing their leader, voters have little idea of what to expect if they are elected. In Peru, for example, Alberto Fujimori came out of obscurity (he had never run for office previously) to form his own personalistic party and won the presidential election. While running on a very vaguely defined platform, Fujimori rejected the unpopular, but necessary, economic stabilization program proposed by his leading opponent. Once he took office, however, he implemented that very program.

Unlike such personalistic parties, which generally collapse after their leader leaves politics, aspiring national leaders in mainstream political parties must first complete a de facto apprenticeship (including running for lesser offices), work with the party organization, and identify with the party's program and ideology. Indeed, in countries with modern party systems, anyone aspiring to become president or prime minister normally must first become active in a major party and then attain its nomination. General Dwight Eisenhower was a partial exception to this rule, as he was a career military officer who had not belonged to any party and had not participated in politics prior to being chosen as the Republican presidential nominee in 1952. Previously, his party preference, if he had one, had been such a mystery that leaders of both the Republican and Democratic parties had tried to convince him to be their candidate. Yet even Eisenhower, an enormously popular World War II hero, still needed to get a major-party nomination in order to win the presidency. In 1992 and 1996, Ross Perot, a Texas billionaire, tried to break the major parties' dominance by running for the presidency as an independent. But, despite his enormous financial resources and initial popular support, Perot failed to win a single state in either election or a single electoral college vote.

Political parties also provide voters with "scorecards" for evaluating what might otherwise be a bewildering array of individuals seeking office. By knowing the candidates' party labels, voters have important clues about their positions on major

5.1

Parties as Ladders (or Obstacles) to Women's Representation in Parliament

Over the past decade or so, the number of women representatives in national parliaments throughout the world has increased from under 12 percent in 1995 to nearly 20 percent in 2011.* Still women remain grossly underrepresented. In fact, only in seven countries (Rwanda, Sweden, South Africa, Cuba, Iceland, Finland, and Norway) do women hold 40 percent or more of the parliamentary seats and only in Rwanda do female MPs outnumber the men.[2] Western Europe, Latin America, and Sub-Saharan Africa have made the most impressive gains, while there has been slower progress in Asia, the Muslim world, and in several developed democracies (including the United States and Ireland). Currently, Northern Europe's Nordic nations (Denmark, Finland, Iceland, Norway, and Sweden) have the highest percentage of women members of parliament (MPs) of any world region (42 percent), while Arab nations had the lowest, with only 11 percent. Political parties have often been the most effective vehicles for recruiting more female MPs. Some of them, however, have been uninterested in that goal or have actually tried to subvert it.

There are a number of reasons why female representation has grown so rapidly since 1995 and why there continues to be so much variation between countries and regions. Changes in political cultures, the expansion of the feminist movement, and the growing number of women in the workplace have all raised the number of female elected officials. But none of those societal changes explains why women's representation in parliament scarcely grew from 1975 (11 percent) to 1995 (12 percent)—when these cultural and economic trends were already at work—but then increased far more rapidly, reaching nearly 20 percent by 2011.

In some countries the level of female representation reflects that nation's (or region's) culture and history. It is not surprising that the Nordic countries were among the first to institute procedures to raise the number of women in parliament and that they currently have a substantially higher percentage of women MPs than any

other region of the world. These achievements mirror their political culture's strong commitment to gender and class equality. Conversely, the relatively sheltered life of women in most Arab nations helps explain the scarcity of female MPs in those countries.*

But in other cases, the proportion of female political leaders does not correspond to the country's or region's political cultural and history. For example, as of 2011, Latin America—known for its allegedly *macho* (male chauvinist) culture—had the second highest proportion of women MPs among all world regions (behind the Nordic countries, but slightly ahead of Europe as a whole). Conversely, the United States—a very modern country with a dynamic feminist movement—has fewer women MPs (i.e., Congresswomen) than the averages for either Sub-Saharan Africa, Latin America, or Asia. As a matter of fact, when 188 countries are ranked according to their percentage of women MPs, we find that a number of advanced democracies—with modern cultures, high proportions of women in the workforce, high female educational levels, and strong feminist movements—have lower-than-expected female representation in parliament. Thus, the percentage of women in the United States Congress ranks only 85th in the world. Similarly, Canada (53rd), Britain (55th), Italy (60th), and France (75th) all badly trail less developed countries such as Angola (11th) and Ecuador (22nd).[3] The proportion of women in the U.S. House of Representatives (17 percent) is lower than the percentages in 10 Latin American parliaments.

How do we account for the fact that the percent of women MPs frequently does not seem to correlate with that country's cultural values, educational level, or degree of modernity? It appears that the most effective means of raising female representation rapidly is either for political parties to voluntarily introduce gender quotas or for the government to require all parties to meet a quota. In her study of female representation

---

* We use the generic term *parliament* here to refer to all national legislatures, including those, primarily in the Americas, that call themselves "Congress."

* Contrary to stereotype, women are not as excluded from political power in non-Arab Muslim nations. For example, Bangladesh, Indonesia, Pakistan, and Turkey—all Muslim—have had women prime ministers or presidents.

(Continued)

A CLOSER LOOK

5.1

Parties as Ladders (or Obstacles) to Women's Representation in Parliament
(Continued)

in parliament, Miki Caul Kittilson notes that political parties have often played a critical role in increasing female representation by establishing gender quotas for their slate of parliamentary candidates.[4] Today 87 nations worldwide employ some form of gender quota.

Legal quotas are mandated by the government either in the constitution or through election laws. They are binding on all political parties and, in turn, include two subtypes. One subtype reserves a certain percentage of all parliamentary seats for women (i.e., only women may run for or be appointed to those seats). About 40 countries throughout the world (mostly less developed nations) have reserved some parliamentary seats for women. Some of them reserve a substantial share. For example, the African nations of Eritrea and Rwanda both reserve 30 percent of their parliamentary seats for women. At the other side of the spectrum, Jordan reserves only 5 percent, not nearly enough to influence government policy. Ironically, a higher percentage of seats (8 percent) are reserved for Jordanian Christians, who only constitute 4 percent of the country's population. To be sure, women can also run for nonreserved parliamentary seats. But in Jordan and many other countries, the reserved seats represent a glass ceiling since women virtually never get elected to the other seats.

The second subtype of legally enforced quota does not guarantee women any percentage of the seats but instead requires every party to nominate a certain percentage of women candidates on their parliamentary tickets. Most commonly, these quotas oblige parties to nominate women in about 30 percent of the parliamentary contests, the minimum number of female MPs that appears to be needed to influence government policy on issues of particular concern to women.[5]

Voluntary quotas, on the other hand, are not legally required but rather are introduced voluntarily by individual political parties. Today, one or more parties in 59 countries have such quotas—including major parties such as South Africa's African National Congress (ANC) and the British Labour Party.

Sometimes legal quota systems fail to substantially increase the number of female MPs because political parties can evade their intent. For example, French law requires all parties to run women candidates for half of all parliamentary seats (the highest gender quota in the world) or face stiff fines. Yet in the last two elections for the National Assembly women won fewer that 20 percent of the seats. While that figure is almost double the percentage of female MPs elected in the election immediately before the 2001 quota law, it is well below 50 percent. What happened? Some parties filled most of their required quota by nominating women in districts where any candidate from their party—male or female—has little chance of winning. Why didn't those parties give women more of a chance to win? It is not necessarily because (mostly male) party leaders object to having more female colleagues. Rather it is more likely because they were unwilling to pressure senior, male MPs representing party strongholds to step down in favor of new women candidates. Consequently women often end up running in districts that are far less winnable.[*]

Unlike France or Britain, most European democracies elect their parliaments through proportional representation (PR), with each party presenting a list of candidates, usually ranked from first to last. Many countries have legal gender quotas that require all parties to nominate women for at least some mandated percentage—say 30 percent—of candidates on their party list. As with single-member districts (SMDs), some parties have also violated the spirit of the law, in this case by ranking most of their quota of female candidates at the bottom of their lists, where they have little chance of winning.[†] In order to

---

[*] In the United States, the primary system gives a woman or any other challenger the ability to run and win in winnable districts by defeating the incumbent in their own party primary. However, few other countries in the world have primaries. Instead, party leaders pick the candidates.

[†] For example, let us say that all parties are legally required to name women to one-third of the places on their party list of candidates for the 100-seat parliament. In the election, party X finishes first with 40 percent of the vote and the same percentage of parliamentary seats. By law, 33 of that party's 100 candidates on the list were women. But if those women were all ranked in the bottom half of the party list, none of them won a seat.

5.1

prevent such evasions of the quotas' intent, some countries with PR have imposed **zipper-style gender quotas** that not only apply to the percentage of female candidates but guarantee that they have an equal chance of winning. For example, if a party wins 50 percent of the vote in the election, they would win half the seats in parliament. In countries with zipper-style gender quotas, not only must each party field women candidates for, say, 25 percent of the party list, but they are also required to place women in every fourth spot on the list, ranked from top to bottom. So, the 4th, 8th, 12th, and 16th-ranked party list candidates would be women, and so forth. Therefore, no matter how many seats a party wins, about one-fourth of their candidates *taking office* would be women. Since it is nearly impossible to enforce tough gender quotas in SMD elections, the most effective quotas exist in nations with PR.

Argentina illustrates how effective zipper-style quotas can be in PR elections. In the three congressional elections preceding passage of a zipper-style quota law, an average of only 4 percent of all congressional representatives were women. After the quotas were introduced, however, that number jumped to 21 percent in 1993 and 39 percent today.

Ultimately, then, political parties can either contribute to or impede greater female representation in parliament. In South Africa, soon after the advent of majority rule (1994), the ANC, the country's dominant political party, voluntarily adopted a zipper-style quota mandating that every third candidate—ranked from the top—be a woman. As a consequence, the percentage of female MPs elected rose from 4 percent (141st in the world) before the ANC adopted the voluntary quota system to 25 percent (11th) in the election following the change. Today, as other South African parties have also raised their share of women candidates, women hold 45 percent of all seats (the third highest percentage in the world). On the other hand, as we have seen, some French parties have undermined the nation's gender quotas.

What causes some parties to embrace gender quotas and others to reject voluntary quotas or evade legal ones? In her study of contemporary European political parties, Kittilson identified several factors—most importantly, party ideology. She placed European parties into one of these categories: "Old Left," "New Left," centrist, conservative, religious, and ultraright (neofascist). How did some of those groups perform?

- Old Left parties, mostly Socialist, were founded in the late nineteenth or early twentieth centuries, with close links to labor unions. Eventually they came to dominate Scandinavian politics and to periodically win national elections in Britain, France, Germany, Greece, Spain, and elsewhere. The Nordic Socialist parties were the first parties to voluntarily adopt gender quotas and, as a group, Old Left parties elsewhere in Europe varied, but now have higher proportions of women MPs than their conservative rivals do.

- New Left parties first emerged in the 1970s and, unlike the Old Left, have focused primarily on postmaterialist concerns (see Chapter 3) such as the environment, nuclear proliferation, and women's rights more than on class-based economic issues. The most successful of the New Left parties have been the Green parties built around environmental issues. While their share of parliamentary seats has been small (rarely have they won more than 6 to 7 percent), they have been part of several governing coalitions. New Left parties have the highest proportion of female MPs of any group.

- Conservative parties are less likely to introduce voluntary gender quotas and frequently hold a more traditional view of the role of women in society. Yet as of the early 1970s they actually had a higher percentage of women MPs, on average, than the Socialists did. Since that time, however, the proportion of Socialist female MPs has grown more rapidly, and by the 1990s they had passed the conservatives.

- Religious and ultrarightist parties have had far lower proportions of women MPs than the New Left, Old Left, or the conservatives.

issues—whether the candidate is liberal or conservative, for example. While many independents in the United States base their presidential vote on the candidates' personal views and qualities (charisma, debating skills, intelligence, and the like), they are less likely to know much about individual candidates for offices such as the House of Representatives or the state legislature. Using that party label as a clue, a majority of Americans, including independents, still vote repeatedly for the candidates of one party.

Because most major European parties are more tightly organized and, until recently, more ideologically unified than American parties, and because their parliamentary representatives are more likely to vote as a bloc, European voters are usually less interested than Americans in the candidate's personal characteristics and comparatively more interested in his or her party label. In fact, since most Western European countries use PR, their voters can only choose a party list, not an individual parliamentary candidate.

Even in many nondemocratic political systems, parties play an important role in recruiting government officials. In China, for example, aspiring leaders must first rise through the ranks of the Communist Party. As they work their way up, those with more powerful political patrons, greater commitment, and greater talent are selected for party and government leadership positions. A similar process took place within Mexico's PRI during the 70 years it ran that country. Beyond that, in countries governed by communist parties—such as China, Cuba, and North Korea—the ruling party promotes its ideology as it seeks to unite and mobilize the population behind the party's goals. In the past, ruling fascist parties in countries such as Italy (under Mussolini) and Spain (under Franco) played a similar ideological role.

As we have noted, many military regimes and monarchies in the developing world govern without parties. But military governments generally do not hold power for extended periods, falling victim to their lack of popular support, internal struggles for power, or both. Thus, General Pervez Musharraf's military government had prohibited opposition political party activity in Pakistan, but a national protest movement forced him to restore party participation in the 2008 parliamentary elections. Soon afterwards, he was forced to resign from office. In recent decades the number of military **no-party regimes** has declined rapidly, as democratic or semidemocratic governments have replaced them in many developing nations (see Chapter 14). Most of the remaining countries with long-lived, no-party rule are either absolute or near-absolute monarchies, including Saudi Arabia and Qatar. While the number of military governments has declined sharply, a few no-party military regimes remain in countries such as Burma (Myanmar).

Formulating Government Policies and Programs

Parties do more than merely select candidates and identify government leaders. They also help formulate government programs. All societies, particularly democratic ones, have countless interest groups trying to influence government policy. A major function of parties is **political aggregation**—that is, reducing the multitude of conflicting political demands from civil society to a manageable number of alternatives.

Every four years, the Democratic and Republican national conventions devote considerable energy to the construction of a **party platform**, a long document outlining in detail the party's position on issues. Hardly any voters actually read the platforms. In fact, shortly after the 1996 Republican convention, even the party's nominee, Bob Dole, indicated that he hadn't. Nevertheless, a platform reflects a party's efforts to turn the raw demands of citizens and pressure groups into policy proposals. Therefore, parts of the platform may become the subject of heated debate.

For example, at the 1948 Democratic convention, a number of segregationist, southern delegates ("Dixiecrats")—led by South Carolina's Senator Strom Thurmond—left the party after it inserted a pro-integration plank into the platform. In the 55 years since that split, the Democrats have remained identified with civil rights for minorities. The South, once solidly Democratic, has turned Republican. More recently, the lead-up to the 1996 Republican convention featured a bitter internal conflict over the party's stance on abortion. For party nominee Bob Dole, that created a difficult dilemma. If the platform moderated the party's "prolife" position, it would alienate some of its most important party activists within the Christian Right. If it took a hard line on the issue, he risked losing the votes of moderate, middle-class, Republican women as well as independents. When the party took a strong stance against abortion, it cost Dole support within that moderate group once known as "soccer moms." In the 2000 and 2004 Republican conventions (with George W. Bush heading the ticket) and again in 2008 (with John McCain), on the other hand, the Republican nominees more strongly committed themselves to an antiabortion position and subsequently benefited (especially Bush) from grassroots campaigning and a strong turnout by conservative Christians.

In communist nations, the party has had a still more fundamental role in formulating government policy. In China, Cuba, and Vietnam, for example, it is the Communist Party leaders, rather than the national parliaments or any other government body, who make the most important policy decisions. Similarly, many of Africa's single-party systems concentrated policy making in the ruling party. During the late 1980s, Soviet President Mikhail Gorbachev shifted policy making from the Communist Party Politburo to the government, specifically the president and his cabinet. That transfer of power was a key factor leading party hard-liners to attempt a coup against him in 1991.

Organizing Government

After national elections in democracies, either a single party or a coalition of parties commands a majority in the national legislature. In parliamentary systems, that winning party or coalition chooses the prime minister. Their party label ties governing-party MPs together and enables their leaders to present a coherent program. Even though the major American political parties have become more ideologically uniform in recent years, congressional Democrats are still less likely to vote as a cohesive bloc than are their European counterparts.

THE ORIGINS OF POLITICAL PARTIES

Throughout the world, the growth of parties has been linked to the spread of mass political participation. As long as a hereditary elite ruled most nations, there was no need for broadly based political organizations. That situation changed during Europe's transition from a **hierarchical**, agricultural economy to an industrial, capitalist one. Urbanization and industrialization created important new political actors—the middle class and then the industrial working class. In many Third World countries, a similar process began in the twentieth century.

The first European and Latin American parties in the nineteenth century were merely competing aristocratic or upper-middle-class, male parliamentary factions. As the right to vote was gradually extended to a larger portion of the population, however, these elite-led parties reached out to the middle class, then to workers, farmers, women, and the poor. In Great Britain, for example, the Conservative Party represented the interests of the landed aristocracy while the rising business class led the Whigs (later to become the Liberal Party). As the franchise expanded in the nineteenth and early twentieth centuries, however, both parties broadened their support. Similarly, in Colombia, the Conservative and Liberal parties—one headed by wealthy, rural landowners and the other by powerful merchants—eventually established strong ties to the peasants through **patron–client relations**.

With the advent of universal male suffrage in Europe by the early twentieth century, new types of political parties emerged, known as **mass parties**. Unlike their predecessors, which were led by elites seeking popular support, these were led by political outsiders wishing to challenge the established order. Most were socialist parties closely tied to the labor movement, including the French Socialist Party (SFIO) and the British Labour Party. So, unlike their conservative predecessors, they were interested in more than winning votes. They also wished to introduce their followers to socialism and thereby create a new political culture.

During the mid-twentieth century, Western Europe's conservative and centrist parties also adopted aspects of mass-party structure, including grassroots organizations. Later in that century mass-party organizations and strategies became the models for many of the contemporary parties in Africa, Asia, and Latin America.

PARTY SYSTEMS

The term *party system* refers to the characteristics of the set of parties operating in a particular country. It indicates the number of parties that have a serious chance of winning major elections and the degree of competition between them. The number of competitive parties operating in a particular country fundamentally influences that nation's entire political system. Obviously, countries governed continuously by a single party—even if opposition parties are legal—are less than fully democratic. Conversely, countries that have multiple parties, with none able to garner a majority in the national parliament, are frequently less politically stable. Because of the great importance of the number of competitive political parties, descriptions of, for example, the Chinese, American, British, and Italian political systems typically label them, respectively, as one-party, two-party, two-and-one-half-party, and multiparty systems.

Americans often think of a two-party system as "natural," since we are accustomed to it. If by that we mean that a two-party system is *preferable* to, say, a multiparty system, that is debatable. And if we believe that having two dominant parties is the most *common* arrangement, that is simply incorrect. For example, until recently, single-party systems were predominant in Africa, the Middle East, parts of Asia, and the old communist bloc, and there are still many of them. At the same time, many European and Latin American countries have multiparty systems. In short, two-party systems are the exception, not the rule, and they predominate primarily in English-speaking democracies.

Of course, even the United States has more than two political parties. Besides the Democrats and the Republicans, American parties include, among many others, the Green Party, the Libertarian Party, and the United States Marijuana Party (founded in 2002). The "Tea Party" has been the subject of much news coverage in the United States. However, it is not really a party (since it doesn't field candidates under its label in the general election) but rather a movement that endorses candidates in Republican Party primaries. Although so-called third parties in the United States occasionally win local elections, they do not attract a large share of votes in national races. Sometimes, however, they have played the role of spoilers. Had Ralph Nader not run in the 2000 presidential election as the Green Party candidate, it is likely that most of his votes (including those he won in Florida) would have gone to Al Gore, the Democratic nominee, and that Gore, rather than George Bush, would have won the presidency.

Two parties, Conservative and Labour, have dominated British politics for almost 90 years. But unlike the United States, other parties have attracted a substantial share of the vote in recent years. In the 2010 election, although the Conservative Party had the largest number of MPs, it failed to attain a majority of parliamentary seats. Consequently, it had to form a coalition government with the Liberal Democratic Party, which had captured 9 percent of the seats in the House of Commons (with 23 percent of the vote). Consequently, some political scientists argue that the British currently have a **two-and-one-half-party system**, defined as a party system in which two parties predominate, but a third party presents a significant challenge.

Because they sometimes use different definitions, analysts may differ as to whether a country such as Japan or Mexico in the second half of the twentieth century—when many parties competed but one party always won—had a single-party or a multiparty system. Building on a classification system originally created by Jean Blondel, we offer the following party-system categories and yardsticks for identifying them.[6]

1. *No-party system*: Either political parties have never developed or an authoritarian government has outlawed them.

2. *Single-party system*: One party regularly receives more than 65 percent of the vote in national elections.

3. *Two-party system* (including a two-and-one-half-party system such as Britain's): Two major parties regularly divide more than 75 percent of the national vote (but no single party receives as much as 65 percent).

4. *Multiparty system*: The two largest parties have a combined total of less than 75 percent of the vote.

No-Party Systems

Although political parties are hallmarks of modern political systems, there remain a number of countries that have never formed political parties with any significant following or that have proscribed previously active political parties. The first group, very limited in number, consists principally of countries with premodern social structures and low levels of political participation. In countries such as Saudi Arabia, relatively small, elite bodies (sheikhs, princes, and tribal chiefs) have made political decisions with no need for parties. In many less-developed countries (LDCs), active, sometimes vibrant, political parties have been repressed. However, with the spread of democracy in the developing world since the 1970s, military governments and their no-party systems are now less common (see Chapter 14).

Single-Party Systems

Many authoritarian regimes, once so common in the developing world, and all totalitarian governments have single-party systems. As we have seen, totalitarian parties, most notably fascist and Marxist–Leninist parties, are mass-membership organizations that seek to exercise total control over society and to inculcate the ruling party's ideological values into the population. Following revolutions in Russia, China, North Korea, Vietnam, and Cuba, each country's Communist Party launched an extensive resocialization campaign to restructure their political cultures (see Chapters 3). At least initially, many party activists seemed strongly committed to their party's vision of a new social order.

Because of their capacity to penetrate and control other social institutions, totalitarian political parties were once considered nearly impossible to dislodge once they had taken power.[7] In Eastern Europe and Central Europe, Communist Party functionaries controlled the military, police, factories, state farms, and schools. Yet ultimately their grip on power weakened and those regimes collapsed, from the Soviet Union to Hungary. Currently, communist parties retain power in only a handful of nations.

A second group of single-party states emerged throughout Africa, Asia, and the Middle East following World War II and the disintegration of Europe's colonial empires. Their leaders argued that developing nations needed the unifying influence and direction of a single-party system. Often these ruling parties were organized along **Leninist** lines, like communist parties, with highly centralized control. They usually espoused a nationalistic ideology and wished to resocialize the population into a new, postcolonial political culture. Subsequently, however, many of them governed ineffectively and became too self-serving and corrupt to attract a loyal mass following. Consequently, ruling parties in countries such as Libya and Syria maintained power more through intimidation than through mass mobilization.

Until the 1980s, few African or Middle Eastern countries permitted viable opposition parties. However, with the wave of democracy that has swept across the world in the past 30 to 40 years (see Chapter 14), many African and Asian nations have introduced relatively free and fair elections, with opposition parties sometimes winning.

To be sure, not all entrenched ruling parties are self-serving or incompetent. When headed by well-intentioned leaders, they sometimes have served their nations well. During the late 1930s, Mexican President Lázaro Cárdenas used the ruling party to integrate previously excluded peasants and workers into the political system. More recently, Tanzanian President Julius Nyerere's Tanganyika African National Union (TANU) channeled the demands of the country's villagers to the national government. In time, however, the absence of party competition and the passing of idealistic leaders such as Cárdenas and Nyerere have perverted even well-intentioned dominant parties. In fact, most Third World single-party systems have fallen victim to corruption and the pursuit of special interests.

Two-Party Systems

Two-party and two-and-one-half-party systems are most prevalent in Anglo-American societies, including Great Britain, the United States, Canada, New Zealand, and Australia.* However, other countries, such as Austria, Germany, Colombia, Costa Rica, and Uruguay, have had two dominant parties as well.

Why do these countries have two dominant parties while most democracies have multiparty systems? One important factor influencing the number of parties that compete effectively is the country's electoral arrangements. We have seen (Chapter 4) that PR more easily facilitates (but does not guarantee) the development of several competitive political parties, whereas SMD systems are more likely to produce two dominant parties.

Among advanced parliamentary democracies, two-party systems tend to be more stable than multiparty systems because one of the parties is likely to achieve a legislative majority. But in a number of Latin American countries with two-party systems, stability has been elusive. For example, Colombia has had a turbulent history of political violence. Just as they are not universally stable, neither are two-party systems always democratic. During its years of minority (White) rule, South Africa had competitive elections, pitting the two leading parties against each other. But since

---

* Political scientists often cited Britain as an archetypal example of a two-party system. Since the 1980s, however, the two largest parties (Labour and Conservative) have often failed to receive a combined total of 75 percent of the parliamentary vote, Blondel's threshold for a two-party system. Thus, Britain has moved to a two-and-one-half party system with the Social Democrats getting over 20 percent of the vote. Still, because Britain has SMD, one of the two major parties (Conservatives or Labour) continued to win over half the seats in parliament until the 2010 election (see Chapter 11).

only the White minority could vote for important posts, the two-party system was hardly democratic. Similarly, before Nicaragua's 1979 revolution, the ruling Somoza dictatorship regularly sponsored elections between its own Liberal Party and the Conservatives, a puppet opposition party. The government, however, predetermined the outcomes of those elections.

Multiparty Systems

Multiparty systems predominate in Western Europe but also exist in a number of developing nations. Sometimes these parties mirror multiple societal divisions—class, religious, linguistic, racial, and ethnic—that translate into multiple political cleavages. So, it is not surprising that a country such as Switzerland—with religious divisions between Catholics and Protestants, class and ideological divisions, and several spoken languages—has a multiparty system. Yet even some fairly homogeneous nations, such as Sweden and Iceland, also have multiple parties.

Indeed, social divisions are neither the only factor that determines the number of competitive parties nor even the most important one. Electoral procedures are tremendously important. We have noted that countries that elect their parliament or congress through PR are more likely to have multiparty legislatures than those using SMD (Chapter 4). This is because SMD elections—for example, those that select the U.S. House of Representatives and the British House of Commons—discriminate against small parties by denying them legislative representation proportional to their voting strength (see A Closer Look 11.2). Moreover, as it becomes evident how difficult it is for third-party candidates to win in SMD elections, their initial supporters may eventually conclude that continuing to vote for them is a wasted effort.

Proponents of PR point out that it is a fairer electoral system because it makes it easier for smaller parties to win some seats in the national legislature, with their number of seats proportional to their support among the voters. At the same time, however, it makes it harder for any single party to achieve a legislative majority. Consequently, in parliamentary systems—where the government needs to command a legislative majority to stay in power—the prime minister often must secure the backing of a multiparty coalition. If there are many policy and strategic divisions among the coalition partners, the government's life is precarious because coalition members may withdraw their support at any time. For example, in Italy a succession of unstable parliamentary coalitions produced more than 50 governments during the second half of the twentieth century (although recently government coalitions have been more durable).* And in 2010–2011, Belgium shattered Iraq's world record for the longest stretch without achieving a ruling parliamentary coalition. That resulted in more than a year of ineffective "acting governments."

---

* In parliamentary parlance, each time a prime minister and his cabinet lose their parliamentary majority, an aspiring new prime minister (or even the one just voted out) must form a governing coalition (including a new cabinet), which is called a new government.

Students and others protest over the failure of Belgium's political parties to break a prolonged parliamentary stalemate and form a coalition government.

Wu Wei/Xinhua/Photoshot/Newscom

How stable multiparty parliamentary systems are depends on how cooperative the political parties are. Although postwar Italy and Fourth Republic France had to live with ruling coalitions that fell apart every year or so, other countries with more cooperative political parties manage to maintain stability. These include Finland, Israel, the Netherlands, Norway, and Switzerland. Indeed, Finland and Switzerland have two of the most fractionalized party systems in the democratic world (that is, a very large number of parties hold some parliamentary seats and none predominates). Yet they are models of political stability. Clearly, they have benefited from political cultures that stress parliamentary cooperation between parties rather than conflict.

TYPES OF POLITICAL PARTIES

Let us now turn our attention from party systems to the characteristics of individual political parties. Among the many possible ways of classifying these parties, we focus here on two important characteristics: internal organization and ideological message.

Party Organization

Although all major parties have similar goals—fielding candidates for elected office, winning elections and, hopefully, controlling the government, and implementing their programs—their internal organizations differ greatly. Some are highly centralized with top-down command structures, and others are loose federations of regional or local organizations. In the United States, the combined effects of a federal structure (a division of power between the national and state governments), the separation of powers within the federal government itself, and historical and cultural preferences have created highly decentralized parties. As John Bibby has noted, "It is hard to overstate the extent to which American political parties are characterized by decentralized power structures…. Within the party organization, the national institutions of the party … rarely meddle in nominations and organizational affairs of state parties."[8]

Even at the national level, Democrats and Republicans are organizationally weaker than are most major parties in other advanced democracies. Whereas Western European and Canadian party leaders select their party's parliamentary candidates, the United States is one of the few democracies to select candidates through primary elections. Because American congressmen are less beholden to their party for their nomination, until recently they have also been less prone to vote cohesively than Western European parliamentary delegations generally were.

Which model is more desirable? Many Americans prefer having senators and congressional representatives who vote their own minds and do not automatically vote with their fellow Democrats or Republicans. But critics contend that the absence of party discipline (voting as a unified bloc) makes it difficult to develop coherent governmental programs or to hold either party accountable for its performance in office. In recent years, however, party discipline in Congress has increased. As the number of conservative Democrats and progressive Republicans in Congress has declined, party unity in both parties (but especially the Republicans) has increased.

Communist parties represent the other end of the organizational spectrum. Following the Leninist principle of democratic centralism, they concentrate policy making and candidate selection power at the top, particularly in countries that they have governed. This extreme centralization has often led to paralysis at lower party levels, whereby officials have hesitated to make even the most mundane decisions on their own. (See A Closer Look 5.2)

Party Ideologies: Right Wing through Left Wing

A political party's ideology defines its most fundamental message and the government policies that it proposes. Some parties—such as the French Socialists, the British Conservatives, and the Chinese Communists—hold well-delineated ideological positions and bear names that clearly identify them. Others, such as the Mexican PRI, are more ideologically ambiguous, often housing different political factions with conflicting outlooks. Still others have no explicit ideology at all. But most parties, especially in advanced democracies, can be classified according to their ideological orientation.

In Chapter 2 we defined the beliefs and aspirations of the major political ideologies. Here, we classify major political parties according to their ideological leanings and discuss where and when parties in each ideological camp have been successful at the ballot box. We list the party ideologies from right (ultraconservative) to left (radical).

Radical Right Parties These ultra-right-wing parties generally stress militant nationalism and the preservation of alleged ethnic purity, usually mixed with explicit

5.2

Varieties of Party Organization

Many years ago, the legendary American humorist Will Rogers used to tell his audiences, "I am not a member of any organized political party—I am a Democrat." Although his joke specifically poked fun at the long-standing Democratic propensity for internal quarreling, it could also have referred to the organizational weaknesses of *both* American parties. In Europe and other democracies outside of the United States, candidates for parliament are selected at party meetings or conventions. In contrast, because their candidates are chosen in party primary elections, the leaders of U.S. political parties have limited control over their party's choice of nominee. Periodically, primary voters will elect fringe candidates with views that are unacceptable to the national or state party leadership. In Louisiana, for example, David Duke, a former Grand Wizard of the Ku Klux Klan, won Republican nomination for a state legislative seat despite the opposition of the Chairman of the Republican National Committee and then-President George H. W. Bush. To be sure, Marjorie Randon Hershey notes that both national parties, but especially the Republicans, have strengthened their national organizations since the 1980s and that each national committee now plays a stronger role in supporting its party's congressional and state campaigns.[9] Still, major American parties remain decentralized and weak compared to parties elsewhere.

It is instructive to contrast this looseness of structure with Communist Party organization in the former Soviet Union. Consider the following reaction of a local party official to the failed 1991 coup attempt by Communist hard-liners against Soviet President Mikhail Gorbachev (Chapter 12). In the Russian city of Klin, only 50 miles outside Moscow, the Communist Party held a previously scheduled lecture on the day that the coup was beginning to unravel. Asked by party members to explain what was happening, local officials waffled: "We had no instructions from Moscow," Igor Muratov, the Klin party leader, later explained. "We could not give our assessment of what was happening."[10]

Most Western European parties fall between those two organizational extremes. Those parties are far more centrally controlled and cohesive than American political parties but not nearly as centralized as ruling Communist parties.

and implicit racism, anti-Semitism, or other forms of bigotry. As such, many of them, especially **neofascists**, bear some resemblance to the Nazis and Fascists during World War II, though today's ultrarightists are generally less extreme and are likely to deny such links. Radical right parties have been active in both Western and Eastern Europe and have experienced a revival in recent decades. They have been most destructive in several multiethnic Central European countries—such as Serbia and Bosnia—where they have aroused hatred against minority ethnic groups and engaged in "ethnic cleansing."

Over the past 20 to 30 years, two factors, which the far right sees as linked, have particularly contributed to the growth of the far right in Western Europe: the arrival of large numbers of illegal and legal immigrants (from North Africa, Asia, Turkey, and Eastern Europe) and chronic unemployment (often over 10 percent). Far rightists have also capitalized on substantial public resentment against the European Union (EU), which they see as a violation of national sovereignty, and globalization, which they blame for Europe's unemployment problems. Finally, extreme-right-wing parties support tough, law-and-order policies as they seek to capitalize on public concern over rising levels of crime (though European crime rates are still far below America's).

A CLOSER LOOK

5.3

The Growth of Europe's Radical Right Parties

Because World War II and its worst horrors had been authored by extreme right-wing political movements in Germany (the Nazi Party) and Italy (the Fascist Party), radical right parties and ideologies were shunned or even banned (the Nazis in Germany) in postwar Western Europe. Since the 1980s, however, a number of far-right political parties have gained strength in Western Europe and, to a lesser extent, in Eastern Europe.* These include France's National Front, the Danish People's Party, the Freedom Party in Austria, the Progress Party of Norway, and Russia's Liberal Democratic Party.

To be sure, few of the radical right parties have attained as much as 10 percent of the vote in parliamentary elections, and few are likely to soon play a substantial role in a **coalition government**, much less head one. But, in a few countries—including Austria, Denmark, Italy, and the Netherlands—conservative parties have been forced to accept far-right partners into the ruling coalition in order to achieve a parliamentary majority. The Progress Party has been the second-place finisher in three of Norway's last four parliamentary elections, and National Front leader Jean-Marie Le Pen finished second in the first round of France's 2002 presidential election. Furthermore, even if a far-right party only wins some 10 percent

of the vote and fails to win a substantial bloc of seats in parliament, it can still influence public policy and political discourse. Because ascendant radical right parties often draw many of their new electoral supporters from mainstream conservative parties, those parties may feel the need to adopt more radical campaign positions or policies in an attempt to head off defections from their ranks. Thus, for example, in France, when the National Front's extremist, anti-immigration stance threatened to draw voters away from President Nicolas Sarkozy's conservative UMP party, the president ordered the expulsion of many Roma (Gypsy) immigrants from Eastern Europe in order to shore up support in his right flank. While that move may have won the support of some right-wing voters, it was criticized by human rights groups and condemned by the EU.

Radical right parties have diverse objectives, policies, and tactics in different countries. Many work within accepted legal boundaries while others resort to violence and intimidation. For example, in Serbia, Italy, and Britain, organized gangs of "football [soccer] hooligans" associated with local neofascist parties frequently riot and attack other spectators at soccer stadiums and their surrounding areas.* But all radical-right parties have all or most of the following ideological features[11]:

Super Nationalism: They aggressively oppose any perceived threat to national sovereignty. Before the

---

* Different authors and analysts have given these parties a large number of labels, including *radical right, populist radical right, far right, extreme right, fascist,* and *neofascist.*

* Outside of North America, the sport of soccer is called "football."

Conservative Parties   Conservative parties are among the oldest parties in Western Europe and Latin America. Although their programs and styles differ from region to region and country to country, they usually share certain common beliefs (described below) regarding tradition, stability, religion, family, and country.

At the same time, however, there are also important distinctions between conservative parties in different parts of the world. Latin America's conservative parties have long represented elite economic interests and, historically, have opposed the full incorporation of workers and peasants into the political system. In politically polarized Latin American and Southern European nations, with strong leftist unions and political parties, many conservative parties have supported repressive measures to

5.3

collapse of Soviet communism, Western European far-right parties viewed the USSR as the major *external* threat. Today, the radical right in both Western and Eastern Europe tend to view American "cultural and economic imperialism" as the primary outside menace. The targets of super-nationalist anger vary from country to country. In Serbia, for example, radical right parties have focused on the secession of Kosovo (an Albanian-speaking, Muslim region, formerly part of Serbia) and on the West, whose military and diplomatic intervention facilitated that secession.

Nativism: Today, most radical right parties believe that the *internal* threat posed by ethnic, racial, or religious (allegedly "nonnative") minorities is even more menacing than any external threat. Originally, European Nazis and fascists attacked the Jews as the most dangerous minority, and today some far-right parties —especially in Eastern Europe—remain overtly anti-Semitic. In the past several decades, however, as huge numbers of legal and illegal immigrants from North Africa, Asia, Turkey, Eastern Europe, and elsewhere have entered Western Europe, they have become primary targets of nativists who believe these groups are an economic and cultural threat—taking jobs from "natives," lowering the wage scale, and bringing in undesirable, foreign cultural values and habits.* Nativists frequently focus their attacks on Muslim and non-White immigrants, appealing to racism.

* Southwestern vigilante groups in the United States often share this view of Mexican undocumented workers (illegal aliens).

In Eastern Europe, where there has not been a wave of recent immigrants, far-right-wing parties direct their animosity against indigenous ethnic minorities who may have lived in the country for centuries. These include the Roma (Gypsies) in Hungary and Romania, ethnic Hungarians in Slovakia and Romania, and Turks in Bulgaria.

Authoritarianism: Unlike mainstream conservative parties, most radical right parties are authoritarian—that is, most favor a strong government that takes a hard line on crime and favors order even at the expense of civil liberties. More often than not, their electoral appeal is tied to a strong, charismatic authoritarian leader (such as Italy's Mussolini, Spain's Franco, or France's Le Pen).

Populism: Historically, conservative and far-right political parties were allied with powerful rural landowners or urban big business and drew a disproportionate share of their support from middle- and upper-class voters. Today's radical right parties are usually distrustful or even hostile to big business interests and seek support primarily from lower-income and lower-middle-class voters. Indeed, they frequently blame economic and cultural elites for a range of injustices. Thus, they may charge big business with facilitating illegal immigration (to provide cheap labor) or with promoting globalization (which populists believe allows companies to use cheap labor abroad and causes unemployment at home). Also, they accuse institutions representing "cultural elites"—including universities, liberal newspapers, progressive church leaders, and filmmakers (the "Hollywood establishment")—with coddling criminals and illegal aliens, supporting multiculturalism, and the like.

---

crush a perceived threat from the radical left.[12] For example, when faced with radical leftist challenges at the ballot box, labor unrest, or guerrilla insurgencies, a number of conservative parties in Brazil, Chile, Greece, and Uruguay supported coups by right-wing militaries.

In contrast, conservative parties in stable democracies with moderate left-wing parties and a relatively consensual political culture—such as the United States, New Zealand, Britain, and Germany—are firmly committed to democracy. As the perceived threat from communist or other leftist movements has receded in Latin America and southern Europe, conservative parties in those regions have also embraced democracy.

All conservative parties are strongly committed to the free enterprise system and, in varying degrees, want to limit government involvement in the economy. Some parties—including the Republicans in the United States and, more recently, the British Conservatives—have stressed economic issues, strongly defending the free markets and other elements of capitalism. On the other hand, many European conservatives have accepted or even initiated extensive government economic planning and comprehensive welfare programs. In some cases, upper-class conservative leaders have expressed a sense of *noblesse oblige*—a responsibility of the "well born" to help those of lesser standing. Others have endorsed government welfare programs as a means of limiting working-class support for leftist parties. Consequently, Western European conservative parties such as France's "neo-Gaullists" and Germany's Christian Democrats have often supported economic policies similar to those supported by the Democratic Party in the United States. But despite their economic policy differences, European and American conservatives share a commitment to traditional social principles, including: family values, nationalism, patriotism, religion, social stability, and a commitment to law and order.

In the aftermath of World War II, the most prominent European conservative parties accepted or even endorsed a major role for government in society. By the 1980s, however, as Europe strained to stay competitive in the world and as inflation and unemployment rose, a new generation of conservatives, led by Britain's Prime Minister Margaret Thatcher, concluded that the state had become too intrusive in the economy, taxes were too high, and benefits for workers and the poor, which far exceeded their magnitude in the United States, had become too expensive. Thatcher and American President Ronald Reagan became symbols of a conservative resurgence. Today, conservative parties govern a number of countries worldwide, including Britain, France, Germany, Italy, Chile, Colombia, and Mexico. Resentful of growing budget deficits and higher inflation, the electorate began to demand a lid on taxes. As a result, many Western European governments, even leftist ones (socialists), have been forced to cut back on welfare measures and other spending programs. In Greece, where citizens were unwilling to reduce the welfare state or to pay sufficient taxes to pay for it, a severe government debt crisis forced sharp spending cuts in 2011, which provoked protests and rioting.

Liberal Parties Even more than conservatism, liberalism has meant different things in different countries and time periods. The first liberal parties in Europe and Latin America ("classical liberals") advocated the separation of church and state, greater equality of opportunity, and the defense of personal freedom. In Western Europe, liberal parties often still defend small-business interests and oppose "excessive" state economic intervention. Indeed, many of them—including Germany's Free Democrats and Italy's Liberal Party—have represented middle-class and small-business interests and have frequently joined conservative parties in government coalitions. Normally, European and Latin American liberal parties occupy the political center between conservatives on the right and socialists or populists on the left.

But liberalism has developed a somewhat different meaning in the United States. From the time of President Franklin Roosevelt's New Deal, the Democratic Party has supported government activism to solve social and economic problems, including the social security program, student loans, food stamps, bank deposit insurance, and, most recently, President Obama's health care reform. Because the United States, unlike Western Europe or Latin America, has no significant socialist or **populist** parties, and since American labor unions support the Democratic Party (not the socialists, as in Europe), the Democrats occupy the left side of the American political spectrum, although their policies would be considered middle-of-the-road in Western Europe.

But despite these differences on economic matters, liberals in both Europe and the United States share a number of important social and political concerns, including their defense of civil liberties and individual rights. Similarly, liberal interest groups such as the American Civil Liberties Union use the judicial system to protect the rights of criminal defendants, minority groups, and political dissidents against government intrusion. In short, whereas conservative parties (especially in the United States) have been most concerned about government intrusion in the economic sphere (trying to limit taxes and government regulation), liberal parties have focused on government intrusions in areas such as civil liberties and a pregnant woman's "right to choose."

Western European liberal parties have not done well in the past half century. They have been squeezed from the left by socialist parties and from the right by conservatives. Hence, they no longer can attract a significant portion of the vote except when they have allied with other parties, as Britain's Liberal Party did when it merged with the Social Democratic Party in the 1980s to form the Liberal Democratic Party. Recently, the Liberal Democrats have joined the British Conservatives in a coalition government.

In the United States, the Democratic Party was the leading force in national politics from the 1930s (after the Great Depression) until 1980. Since then, however, far fewer American voters have identified themselves as liberals, and Democratic candidates have generally tried to escape that label. While the party has often won control of one or both houses of Congress, it lost 7 of the 11 presidential elections between 1968 and 2008 and lost control of the House of Representatives in 2010.

Socialist Parties   As we noted in Chapter 2, the label *socialist* is sometimes confusing, since it has been used to refer to democratic parties in Western Europe, to the communist government of the Soviet Union, and to some of the ruling communist parties in Eastern Europe before their fall.* We will reserve the terms *socialist* and *social democratic* for parties, particularly in Western Europe, which are committed to democracy and wish to modify, but not end, capitalism. Usually, we use the party labels **socialist** and **social democrat** interchangeably, though they sometimes denote certain ideological differences. France's Socialist Party and Germany's Social Democratic Party are both major electoral contenders that have periodically led the national government. Sweden's Social Democratic Workers' Party and Norway's Labor Party (Social Democratic) have governed their respective countries most of the time since the early 1930s. In the past 20 years, socialists or social democrats have also led governments for some period of time in many other European nations, including Austria, Denmark, Finland, France, Germany, Greece, Portugal, and Spain. In Latin America they have played major roles in Chile, Costa Rica, and Venezuela.

---

* The Soviet Union's official name was the Union of Soviet *Socialist* Republics (USSR).

Historically, many European socialist parties were split between more radical (Marxist) and more moderate factions. In the decades after World War II, however, most shed their Marxist factions, siding with the West against the Soviet Union in the Cold War and adopting more moderate domestic policies. Faced with a strong conservative challenge since the late 1970s, including popular disenchantment in many countries with "big government," parties such as Britain's Labour Party, the Spanish Socialists, and the German Social Democrats moved cautiously toward the political center as they reduced their commitment to government intervention and became more sympathetic to free markets. In Chapter 11, we will see how former British Prime Minister Tony Blair unofficially relabeled his party "New Labour" and accepted many of the free market policies of former Conservative Prime Minister Margaret Thatcher. Chile's governing Socialist Party made similar modifications to its program and ideology. Hence, many socialist parties, in Europe and elsewhere, now favor economic policies only somewhat different than their centrist or conservative opponents.[13]

That does not mean that there is no longer a significant difference between socialists and their conservative (or centrist) competition. For one thing, socialists are still far more likely to support welfare programs and other government safety nets. Furthermore, they differ substantially on social issues. For example, Spain's current Socialist Party government has legalized same-sex marriages, eased restrictions on abortion, and facilitated fast-track divorce in a country once known as among the most socially conservative in Europe.

Communist Parties After the fall of the Soviet Union and its allied communist governments in Eastern Europe, the number of nations governed by communist parties has been reduced to a handful, mostly in Asia. China, with some 1.3 billion people and the world's second largest economy, is obviously the most important of these (see Chapter 13). Other single-party communist regimes include Cuba, Laos, North Korea, and Vietnam.

Outside of that much-reduced communist bloc, communist parties remain competitive at the ballot box in several European democracies, though their support has declined substantially since the 1970s. At one time, communist parties throughout the world faithfully followed policy directives from the Soviet Union. That began to change in the 1960s and 1970s, when different strains of communism emerged. For example, several Western European communist parties, led by the Italians, followed a new path known as "Eurocommunism." They rejected Soviet-style authoritarianism and embraced (or in some cases, claimed to embrace) Western democratic values. The Italian Communists, the most democratically oriented of that group, was that country's second-largest party (with up to one-third of the national parliamentary vote) and governed many of Italy's major cities. It broke openly with the Soviet Union after it condemned the Soviet invasion of Afghanistan in 1979. Since the 1990s, the party has changed its name twice. First, most of the party abandoned communism and transformed itself into the Democratic Party of the Left, a socialist party. It later joined with a number of other center-left parties to form the Democrats of the Left. From 1996 to 1998 and again in 2006 to 2008, that party joined governing coalitions.

Elsewhere in Western Europe, communist parties that were once influential—most notably in France, Greece, Finland, Portugal, and Spain—have lost considerable support in recent decades. The French Communist Party regularly attracted 15 to 20 percent of the vote into the 1980s but now receives perhaps one-third of that total. Even before the demise of Soviet communism, several demographic factors weakened Western Europe's communist parties. Although those parties received some white-collar and middle-class support, their core constituency has always been blue-collar workers. As European workers bought homes and acquired more middle-class lifestyles during the postwar economic boom, many of them switched allegiance to more moderate political parties, abandoning the communists and their doctrine of class conflict. In addition, as economic changes since the 1970s have reduced the proportion of blue-collar jobs in the workforce, and as the size and influence of leftist labor unions has diminished, communist parties have lost an important part of their base.

After the collapse of Eastern European communism in 1989, most of the former ruling parties changed their names and policies, though many analysts still refer to them as "former communist parties." Because they continue to support the welfare state and because they promise full employment, these parties have received considerable support from workers whose jobs or pensions have been threatened by the transition to capitalism. Reformed communist parties have occasionally led governments in Albania, Bulgaria, Hungary, Lithuania, Moldova, Poland, Romania, Serbia, and Slovakia. They have governed more effectively in countries such as Hungary and Poland than in nations such as Bulgaria and Moldova, where reformed communists governments were associated with corruption and incompetence.

Religious Parties   In many Catholic and Muslim countries (and a few with diverse Christian populations) religiously affiliated parties have been important political players. **Christian Democratic** parties have often governed Germany, Italy, Chile, El Salvador, and a number of other European and Latin American countries. Usually, they are linked to the Catholic Church or at least to Catholic theological doctrine. But in Germany, the party has a Protestant wing as well, and the small Christian Democratic movement emerging in Russia is associated with the Russian Orthodox Church. Religious parties are also influential in Asia and the Middle East. Violence between Muslims and Hindus in India has sometimes been stirred up by groups aligned with the BJP (Indian People's Party), a predominantly Hindu party that moderated its policies when it led governing coalitions from 1998 to 2004. In Israel, several orthodox Jewish parties have won a combined total of 10 to 15 percent of the parliamentary seats in recent elections. Because that country's parliament is highly factionalized and no single party has won a majority of the seats, the major parties need some support from the religious parties if they are to form a majority coalition. That gives religious parties leverage to push their agenda. In the Muslim world, the ties between some parties and Islamic institutions are very strong and explicit, with clerics holding key party positions. For example, the Shi'ite Hezbollah is both an armed militia and one of Lebanon's major political parties. Elsewhere, links are only theological or philosophical, as with Europe and Latin America's Christian Democratic parties. Although most religiously affiliated parties are conservative, some Christian Democratic parties, most notably in Latin America, have been at the center or even the left of the ideological spectrum.

For the most part, the influence of religious parties in Europe has declined over the years. For example, whereas the Christian Democrats in France, and especially Italy, were once an important political force, they have since largely collapsed. The United States, with a constitutional and cultural separation of church and state, has no significant religious parties. But religious groups and institutions such as evangelical Christians and the Catholic Church continue to exert a strong influence. In Muslim nations such as Iraq, Pakistan, and Turkey, religious parties have grown in influence as the result of an Islamic religious resurgence. In Egypt, the previously repressed Muslim Brotherhood may emerge as the country's largest political party following the democratic revolution.

Conclusion: Parties in a Changing World

This chapter has highlighted several important trends in the current role of political parties. In many Western European countries and the United States, voter preferences and the political dialogue have often swung toward the right of the ideological spectrum in recent decades. As we have noted, in these countries the public has become more skeptical of government economic intervention, be it welfare programs in the United States or government control of key productive enterprises in Western Europe.* At the same time, the relative size of the working class (a major voting bloc for left and left-center parties) has diminished in these postindustrial societies, and many of the remaining blue-collar workers have acquired middle-class living standards and political attitudes.

These changes have presented substantial challenges to leftist parties in Western Europe and, to a lesser extent, to the Democrats in the United States. Changes in public opinion and the weakening of the left's electoral base (including organized labor) have hurt them at the polls. Thus, Scandinavia has long been the stronghold of Europe's Social Democrats. For example, that party governed Sweden for 65 of the past 78 years. It has lost the last two elections to opposition coalitions, and Social Democratic or Socialist parties elsewhere in Europe have generally lost ground in recent years.

In response to this challenge, many left-of-center parties now accept a more modest role for government and profess a more middle-of-the-road ideology in an effort to win back disaffected working-class voters and attract greater support from the middle class. Chastened by the Republican congressional triumph of 1994, Bill Clinton set aside his hopes for government-guaranteed health insurance and concentrated instead on such issues as safe streets, education, and welfare reform. And following the broad Republican gains in the 2010 congressional elections, Barack Obama has also moved toward the political center. Similarly, in the face of troubling

---

* France illustrates the extent of government ownership that once existed in many European economies. During the early 1980s, the French government, which had already owned 12 percent of the nation's economy under the conservative governments of the previous decade, increased its share to 16 percent of GNP under the Socialists. In the 1990s, however, that proportion dropped as conservative governments reprivatized parts of the economy.

budgetary deficits, most European socialist and labor parties have reduced or abandoned their previous support for government ownership of strategic sectors of the economy and have accepted reductions in the welfare state. By moving the Labour Party toward the center, Britain's Tony Blair led that party to three consecutive victories in national elections after a long period in the political wilderness, though his party was defeated in 2010.

The movement of most major parties in the Western **industrial democracies** toward the political center has generally reduced ideological and programmatic differences between them. Thus, there are few major economic policy differences between the French Socialists and the conservative UMP or between the Labour and Conservative parties in Great Britain. Increasingly, elections in the developed world are being decided by voters' perceptions of party competence—deciding which party will be able to govern most effectively—rather than by differences in party ideology (this is not true in the United States, where differences on social issues such as abortion and same-sex marriage often polarize the electorate and where the ideological gap between the two major parties has widened in recent decades).

The biggest losers in this move toward less ideological, centrist politics have been Western Europe's communist parties. As we have seen, they once received as much as 34 percent of the national vote in Italy and close to 25 percent in France, where they were both the principal voices of working-class discontent. As Europe became more prosperous and many workers achieved middle-class lifestyles, class tensions decreased. At the same time, more centrist white-collar workers replaced once-radical blue-collar workers in the workforce, and the strength of unions declined. All these factors diminished support for the region's communist parties. Their authoritarian and stodgy leadership hurt them as well. Thus, even before the collapse of Soviet communism, Western European communist parties were in decline. The notable exception had been the Italian Communist Party and its successor, the Democrats of the Left. That party has abandoned its communist beliefs in favor of social democracy, but still receives far fewer votes than the communists once did.

Latin America has experienced a number of dramatic political and economic changes since the 1980s that have left a deep imprint on the region's political parties. First, after almost two decades of military dictatorships and severe political repression in many countries, almost all of the region is now governed democratically. The collapse of the Soviet bloc and the resulting decline of the Cuban economy (because of the cut-off of Soviet aid) deeply unsettled Latin America's leftist parties, many of whom had subscribed to the Cuban revolutionary model. Finally, much like Western Europe and parts of Asia, most Latin American governments in the last decades of the twentieth century reduced the economic role of the state— privatizing state enterprises and, in some cases, even privatizing social security systems. Faced with this new political landscape, a number of formerly radical leftist parties moderated their political and economic positions and embraced democracy.[14]

The most notable example, perhaps, was El Salvador's FMLN, which had waged a revolutionary struggle for over a decade against the Salvadorian armed forces. Faced with a stand-off, the two sides signed a peace agreement in 1992.

The FMLN renounced armed struggle, moderated its policies, and transformed itself into a political party. In 2009 its candidate was elected national president. Moderate leftist parties now govern Argentina, Brazil, Peru, and Uruguay. At the same, however, the region's economic stagnation for much of the past 40 years, the negative impact of many IMF-mandated economic reforms on low-income voters, and the persistence of the world's widest economic inequalities have contributed to the rise of more radical leftist governments in Venezuela, Bolivia, Ecuador, and Nicaragua.

While the fortunes of parties representing various ideologies in Western democracies have ebbed and flowed during the past half century, one trend has hung over all of them—declining public support for political parties in general.[15] Thus, a growing portion of the European and American public identifies itself as independent and does not support any party. Commenting on this apparent decline of party strength, Kay Lawson and Peter Merkl had difficulty identifying a cause: "We don't know if major parties are failing because they are ideologically out of touch with their electorates, poorly organized, underfinanced, badly led, unaccountable, corrupt, overwhelmed by unethical or fanatical competition, unable to run effectively, or some combination of those factors."[16]

Russell Dalton maintains that, rather than looking for the causes of decreased *political party* support, we should look at the origins of a broader phenomenon. He notes that for many years citizens of most Western democracies have felt declining confidence not just in parties but in almost all political institutions including the legal system and national legislatures.[17] Thus, he argues, declining interest in political parties is not the core problem; diminishing interest in *politics* is.

Despite these developments, however, many other political scientists insist on the continuing importance of parties in democratic societies. For example, some have argued that, if anything, parties in the United States play an increasingly important role in attracting voters to the polls and in governing the country.[18] And reports of the decline of party affiliations in the United States may be exaggerated. It is true that the percentage of Americans who categorize themselves as independents (as opposed to Republicans or Democrats) increased from about 22 percent in 1952 to more than 35 percent in the late 1970s.[19] But that percentage has held fairly steady since the 1990s, and by late 2010 was about 37 percent— still a larger proportion than those who self-identify as Democrats (35 percent) or Republicans (28 percent).[20] Yet other indicators suggest that the importance of independent voting in the United States has been overstated. First of all, while it is true that nearly 40 percent of all Americans identify themselves as independents, more than two-thirds of them are "leaners," people who call themselves independent but lean toward one of the major parties most of the times that they vote. Second, if we divide respondents who identify themselves with a political party into two groups—strong partisans (those who are devoted to one party) and weak partisans—we find that the percentage of people in the first group has risen significantly since 1972. So, in fact, the major change in American political identification since the 1970s is that the percentage of weak party partisans has dropped and the number of independent leaners has grown. But there is not a huge difference in the politics of those two groups. The number of "true" independents—people who are not influenced by party labels at all—has actually declined since the 1970s.[21] In short, "we should not underestimate the persistence of party ID [identification] … almost all Americans, if leaners are included … still report some degree of attachment to either the Democratic or the Republican Party."[22] Similarly, Pippa Norris's examination of party membership over time in the United States and other democracies indicates that the decline in party membership has been less uniform, less sharp, and indeed, less certain than many political scientists had maintained.[23]

It is even more difficult to assess or predict trends elsewhere in the world. In much of Africa, Asia, and the Middle East, parties are in their infancy and often represent the narrow interests of powerful economic and political actors. Similarly, it is too early to say what kinds of party systems or party loyalties may emerge in Russia and Eastern Europe. The first free elections for the Polish parliament (in 1991) featured more than 50 competing parties, including the Polish Beer Drinkers Party. Russia had a similar multiplicity of parties, but Vladimir Putin's United Russia now totally dominates the political scene.

Although new institutions (such as neighborhood associations and social movements) have emerged in many countries to carry out functions previously reserved for political parties, and although many voters are cynical about parties, political scientists are still impressed by their enduring strength. A number of leading political scientists have concluded that, while support for political parties has eroded in the West (often for reasons that can't be blamed on the parties themselves), parties continue to play a critical function in democratic political systems.[24] Similarly, Thomas Carothers, a leading scholar on contemporary democratization, has noted that democracies cannot exist without political parties and that the most productive assistance that Western nations can offer in order to buttress democratic transitions in the developing world and in former communist nations is to help them develop and strengthen parties.[25] Wherever national elections have been held on a continuing basis, political parties have played a fundamental role.

◆ ◆ ◆

Key Terms and Concepts _____

authoritarian	patron–client relations
Christian Democratic	personalistic parties
coalition government	political aggregation
hierarchical	political party
industrial democracies	populist
leadership recruitment	socialist
legal quotas	social democrat
Leninist	totalitarian
mass parties	two-and-one-half-party system
neofascists	voluntary quotas
no-party regimes	zipper-style gender quotas
party platform	

DISCUSSION QUESTIONS

1. *What are the major functions of political parties in a democracy? What are the major arguments for and against political parties?*
2. *How have political parties contributed to the growth of women's representation in Western European parliaments? Discuss the reasons why some types of parties have more aggressively tried to raise their number of women MPs than have other parties. Discuss how a country's electoral system (PR or SMD) influences its parties' ability to increase female representation in parliament.*
3. *What factors have contributed to increased support for radical right-wing parties in Western Europe in recent decades? Why do you suppose that these factors have not contributed similarly to increased support for radical left-wing parties?*
4. *What are some factors that explain why the United States and Britain have two-party systems whereas France, Germany, and most of Western Europe have multiparty systems?*
5. *Are political parties becoming less popular and less important in the United States and other Western democracies? What is the evidence on both sides of that question?*

Notes _____

1. Marjorie Randon Hershey, *Party Politics in America*, 12th ed. (New York: Pearson Longman, 2007), pp. 106–107.
2. Data in this box are drawn from Inter-Parliamentary Union (IPU), "Women in National Parliaments" (situation as of April 30, 2011), www.ipu.org/wmn-e/classif.htm. Actually, the tiny European principality of Andorra also has a parliament that is half female. But, because the nation's entire population is less than 85,000, it is too small to be included in this list.
3. The IPU data incorrectly fails to adjust rankings for countries that follow ties. Thus, for example, if two countries are tied for third place, the IPU ranks the next country as fourth, when it should be fifth. I have corrected for that error, so the rankings presented here differ somewhat from the IPU listing.
4. Miki Caul Kittilson, *Challenging Parties, Changing Parliaments: Women and Elected Office in Contemporary Western Europe* (Columbus: Ohio State University Press, 2006).
5. Analysts agree that normally, in order for women MPs to change government policies on "women's issues" such as child care, elementary education, affirmative action, or divorce, they need to attain a "critical mass" of 30 percent of all parliamentary seats.
6. Jean Blondel, "Types of Party Systems," in *The West European Party System*, ed. Peter Mair (New York: Oxford University Press, 1990).
7. Jeane J. Kirkpatrick, *Dictatorships and Double Standards* (New York: Simon & Schuster, 1982).
8. John Bibby, *Politics, Parties and Elections in America* (Chicago: Nelson Hall, 1987), p. 58.
9. Hershey, *Party Politics in America*, pp. 77–83.
10. *New York Times*, August 29, 1991
11. Cas Mudde, *Populist Radical Right Parties in Europe* (New York: Cambridge University Press, 2007), pp. 11–59. See also "Europe's Far Right," *The Guardian* (2010), http://guardian.co.uk/gall/0,,711990,00.htm.
12. David Collier, ed., *The New Authoritarianism in Latin America* (Princeton, NJ: Princeton University Press, 1979).
13. See, for example, Donald Share, "Dilemmas of Social Democracy in the 1980s: The Spanish Socialist Workers Party in Comparative Perspective," *Comparative Political Studies* 21 (October 1988): 429.

14. Salvador Martí I Puig and Salvador Santiuste Cué, "The Parliamentary Left," in *Politicians and Politics in Latin America*, ed. Manuel Alcántara Sáez (Boulder, CO: Lynne Rienner Publishers, 2008), pp. 195–218.

15. For evidence that support for political parties is falling in most Western democracies, see Russell J. Dalton, *Citizen Politics*, 3rd ed. (Chatham, NJ: Chatham House, 2002).

16. Kay Lawson and Peter Merkl, "Alternative Organizations: Environmental, Supplementary, Communitarian and Authoritarian," in *When Parties Fail*, eds. Kay Lawson and Peter Merkl (Princeton, NJ: Princeton University Press, 1988), p. 3.

17. Dalton, *Citizen Politics*, pp. 240–246.

18. L. Sandy Maisel, ed., *The Parties Respond: Changes in the American Party System* (Boulder, CO: Westview, 1990); see also Paul Herrnson, *Party Campaigning in the 1980s* (Cambridge: Harvard University Press, 1988).

19. Donald Green, Bradley Palmquist, and Eric Schickler, *Partisan Hearts and Minds: Political Parties and the Social Identities of Voters* (New Haven, CT: Yale University Press, 2002), p. 15.

20. Chris Kirk, "Independent Voters Are Not Rising," *Dailynorthwestern.com* (November 11, 2010). An analysis of a poll released by the Pew Research Center.

21. Hershey, *Party Politics in America*, pp. 106–107.

22. Ibid, p. 116.

23. Pippa Norris, *Democratic Phoenix* (New York: Cambridge University Press, 2002), pp. 218–219.

24. Richard Gunther, José Ramón Montero, and Juan Linz, eds., *Political Parties: Old Concepts and New Challenges* (New York: Oxford University Press, 2002).

25. Thomas Carothers, *Confronting the Weakest Link: Aiding Political Parties in New Democracies* (Washington, D.C.: Carnegie Endowment for International Peace, 2006).

CHAPTER 6

Interest Groups

- **Interest Groups: What They Are and How They Work**
- **The Power of Interest Groups**
- **The Growth of Interest Groups**
- **How Interest Groups Are Formed**
- **Conclusion: Interest Groups—A Challenge for Democracy?**

In February, 2011, Greek workers and students clashed with police during a demonstration in protest of the government's austerity measures. GSEE, the private sector union, and ADEDY, the public sector union, which together represent about half of the Greek workforce, were key players in the demonstration.

ARGYROPOULOS/SIPA/Newscom

Most Americans are vaguely aware that their government has had a system of farm subsidies for decades, but very few hold strong opinions about them, and even fewer citizens base their voting choices on this issue. The major parties rarely mention farm subsidies in their platforms, and candidates for national office do not prominently feature the issue in their stump speeches.

How is it that such a costly program persists without pressure from voters or parties? One of the world's leading economists, Richard Posner, offers the following explanation:

> [Farm subsidies in the U.S.] lack any economic justification and at the same time are regressive. They should offend liberals on the latter score and conservatives on the former; their firm entrenchment in American public policy illustrates the limitations of the American democratic system. A million farmers receive subsidies in a variety of forms (direct crop subsidies, R&D, crop insurance, federal loans, ethanol tariffs, export subsidies, emergency relief, the food-stamp program, and more)....
>
> Farm subsidies account for about a sixth of total farm revenues. So, not surprisingly, the income of the average farmer is actually above the average of all American incomes, and anyway 74 percent of the subsidies go to the largest 10 percent of farm enterprises.
>
> There is no justification for the Farm Bill in terms of social welfare.
>
> All the subsidies should be repealed.
>
> This of course will not happen, and that is a lesson in the limitations of democracy, at least as practiced in the United States at this time, though I doubt that it is peculiarities of American democracy that explain the farm programs, for their European counterparts are far more generous.
>
> The small number of American farmers is, paradoxically, a factor that facilitates their obtaining transfer payments from taxpayers. They are so few that they can organize

effectively, and being few the average benefit they derive ($50,000 a year) creates a strong incentive to contribute time and money to securing the subsidies.[1]

In 1996, Congress passed the "Freedom to Farm Act," which was to phase out crop subsidies over seven years. But in 2002, Congress passed the "Farm Security and Rural Investment Act," reenacting many farm subsidies. The current farm program will cost $288 billion over five years and billions more in higher prices for consumers.

Posner, along with virtually every other economist who has studied farm subsidies, attributes their existence to the power of interest groups. Each and every person living in the United States is a consumer of agricultural products, and nearly 99 percent are *not* farmers. One would think that consumers would easily prevail in a clash of political interests between consumers and producers of agricultural products. But the producers win, and the programs they demand transfer millions of dollars to them from consumers. Whatever the merits of current farm subsidy programs, it is obvious that the political power of *interest groups* is a key reason that they are very difficult to reform.

When political scientists emerged from law libraries and shifted their emphasis from the analysis of documents to the observation of behavior, they immediately discovered something very important: *Organized* political activity—not the outcome of elections—is often the critical factor in explaining what government does (and does not do). If we want to understand why some policies are changed and others are not, we rarely find the answers by examining the words of the Constitution or even the preferences of voters. At least some of the answers have to do with which interests are organized and which interests are not. The interest group thus became a basic subject of political study many decades ago.

The influence of interest groups raises some troubling questions: If some, but not all, people are represented by effectively organized groups, is a system that responds to group influence really democratic? Is such a system fair? Why do some people join groups while others do not? Does the growing power of interest groups threaten the position of political parties? Does it make voting less important? How do interest groups function in nondemocratic systems such as those in China and Egypt, or in democracies such as India's with social systems far different from our own? These and many related questions help us see that the study of interest groups has become one of the most important, and most controversial, research problems in contemporary political science.

INTEREST GROUPS: WHAT THEY ARE AND HOW THEY WORK

An **interest group** is *an organization that attempts to influence public policy in a specific area of importance to its members.* In contrast to political parties, interest groups do not usually try to achieve their political objectives by electing their leaders to government office.

Instead, they attempt to persuade elected leaders, administrative officials, judges, and others to make and implement laws and policies in line with their positions. They may be well organized, with strong institutional foundations and professional staffs, or they may be looser arrangements of part-time participants. People establish some organizations to be explicitly political, whereas others are created to achieve religious, economic, or other goals and only occasionally work in the political arena. The term *interest group* thus applies to a diverse array of organizations.*

For example, interest groups in the United States include the Tobacco Institute, the National Rifle Association, the Sierra Club, and the National Association for the Advancement of Colored People (NAACP). The British Medical Association, the Mexican Confederation of Labor, and France's National Union Federation of Agriculturalists (FNSEA) are often in the news in those countries. Although each group is unique, all seek to promote government decisions that advance their interests. (See A Closer Look 6.1.)

Kinds of Interest Groups

Interest groups can be classified in several ways. Perhaps the most useful approach is simply to classify them descriptively, on the basis of the interests they pursue. Most fall into one of the following categories.

Labor Unions   Unions such as the Teamsters and the United Automobile Workers (UAW) in the United States, the General Confederation of Labor (CGT) in France, and the Australian Nursing Federation are primarily collective-bargaining units that negotiate contracts for their members with employers. From time to time, however, these organizations apply their energies to the political arena, becoming interest groups by our definition.

In Britain, the British Trades Union Congress (TUC) is directly involved in politics through its powerful role in the Labour Party. In the United States, the Teamsters, the American Federation of State, County, and Municipal Employees (AFSCME), and other unions are always an active presence in elections. In some countries, the impact of unions is less influential. For example, the governments and ruling parties of many African countries have dominated the leadership of most unions, using them as a means of controlling working-class political participation and robbing them of their status as independent interest groups.

Business Organizations   Many kinds of business organizations attempt to influence government. A few business organizations pursue the interests of business itself (the National Association of Manufacturers, the Chamber of Commerce), although most focus on the special problems of a particular economic sector (such as the Used Car Dealers Association). Business groups sometimes oppose labor-group demands and often pursue changes in tax codes or regulations that affect the

---

* Some prefer other terms, such as *factions, organized interests, pressure groups,* and *special interests.* (See the introductory chapter in Allan J. Cigler and Burdett A. Loomis, *Interest Group Politics,* 6th ed. (Washington, DC: CQ Press, 2002.)

6.1

The National Rifle Association in the United States

The National Rifle Association is one of the most powerful and familiar interest groups currently working in the U.S. NRA members receive a publication (*American Rifleman*) and other benefits, including gun insurance and "shooter's liability insurance," but a key NRA activity is participation in electoral campaigns. The NRA regularly takes part in thousands of federal, state, and local campaigns, and it raises millions of dollars for candidates committed to NRA goals.

Founded in 1871 to promote the "shooting sports," marksmanship, and gun safety, the NRA has become one of the most effective and most controversial U.S. interest groups. The organization promotes gun ownership, shares information about collectible guns, and has a vigorous program regarding gun safety, but it is also prominent in its opposition to virtually any legislation limiting gun ownership. According to the NRA's Political Victory Fund, "of the 282 candidates endorsed by the NRA-PVF for the U.S. House in the 2010 elections, 227 were victorious, for an 85% winning percentage. In every case but one where an NRA-PVF–endorsed candidate lost, a pro-gun challenger replaced him.* Even in 2006, when the less gun-friendly Democratic Party took over the U.S. Congress, the NRA still found that it had been successful in its election efforts:

> on a day that saw an electorate expressing dissatisfaction over such things as conduct of the war, political corruption and competency to govern, Americans cast their votes for pro-gun candidates from both parties. Candidates who

* See the NRA's report on the 2010 elections, "Election 2010 Recap," at http://www.nraila.org/GrassrootsAlerts/Read.aspx?ID=578.

championed gun control in contested races were nearly non-existent.[2]

The growth of the NRA tells us a great deal about interest groups in general. For one thing, NRA membership has grown tremendously as the U.S. economy grew. When more people have discretionary income, more citizens can afford the "luxury" of contributing to an organization. However, increases in membership dues created at least a temporary decline in membership, demonstrating that people do take costs into account when they decide to join interest groups.

But the overall pattern of growth shows something else. During the 1990s, gun owners in the United States felt that the Clinton White House was a potential threat to their interests. Many citizens apparently responded to that threat by joining the NRA. In fact, viewed in a longer historical perspective, the overall growth of the NRA, showing a 400-percent increase in membership since the late 1970s, corresponds well to the increased momentum in the United States for stricter gun control. Congress passed the Gun Control Act of 1968 following the assassinations of Robert Kennedy and Dr. Martin Luther King, Jr., and opinion polls have shown substantial support for stricter gun laws, especially after incidents such as the assassination attempt on President Reagan in 1981 and the Columbine High School shootings in Colorado in 1999. Although those events may temporarily dampen NRA membership (it dropped to 2.8 million following the Columbine shootings), the general perception that new gun restrictions are likely has made the NRA a larger and possibly more influential organization. In 2010, the organization had nearly 4 million dues-paying members.

---

profitability of their operations. In some Third World nations with powerful economic elites, business groups are linked so closely to government through family ties and friendships that they exercise a dominant role in policy making. In El Salvador, for example, the "14 families," a group of landowners known by this name since colonial times, controlled much of the country's coffee production and export and thus held veto power over government policy for many years. In other nations, however, with Marxist-oriented regimes, business groups either do not exist or have been on the fringes of the policy process.

Gender, Religious, Ethnic, and Age Groups   The feminist movement in the United States led to the creation of groups such as the National Organization for Women (NOW), which seeks to influence government policies of special concern to women. Similarly, a host of civil rights groups—the NAACP, the Urban League, La Raza Unida—serve as advocates for racial and ethnic minorities. In India, religious and caste groups work closely with the political parties to advocate for their political demands. Interest groups based on age are less common, but the Gray Panthers and the American Association of Retired Persons (AARP) forcefully advocate for the interests of the elderly in the United States. Similarly, the Children's Defense Fund promotes children's interests.

Communist governments often organize women's or youth organizations that profess to act as interest groups but more frequently are designed to mobilize support for the government. However, the Federation of Cuban Women, which was founded in 1960 and now has over 3 million members, helped persuade the Cuban government to implement a family code that not only called for the legal equality of the

© Harley Schwadron/www.cartoonstock.com

sexes but also required both spouses to share housework equally. The federation's clout was undoubtedly enhanced by the fact that its leader was Fidel Castro's sister-in-law.

Public Interest Groups   Although labor unions and business organizations would have us believe that they are selfless crusaders for the general good, they normally pursue government decisions that specifically benefit their members. A rather different type of interest group is concerned primarily with a vision of fairness and justice for some kind of general public interest. Although it is sometimes difficult to draw the line precisely between private and public interests, public interest groups are distinctive political organizations.

This kind of group is centrally featured in what is probably the most divisive public issue in contemporary U.S. politics: abortion. Organizations favoring or opposing abortion rights—each of which is very committed to strongly held principles—have become important factors in lawmaking and elections at all levels of government.

Other reform groups are formed to fight a particular social problem, such as alcohol-related traffic accidents, in the case of Mothers Against Drunk Driving (MADD). The Sierra Club works to influence government to preserve the environment by supporting such varied steps as recycling, preservation of endangered species, and restrictions on public use of wilderness areas. The Americans for Tax Reform supports a general policy of lower taxes at all levels of government. These organizations are "public interest" groups because they seek the actions and decisions that they feel are justified for the benefit of *all* citizens.

Public interest groups are most prevalent in economically developed countries, where higher levels of education, political awareness, leisure time, and disposable income facilitate their proliferation. But they also exist on a more limited basis in some Third World nations. Citizens in developing nations have begun to organize around environmental issues such as the preservation of rain forests. In Thailand, for example, a Buddhist monk organized farmers to promote environmentally sound use of the land and to work with the government for the preservation of shrinking forest preserves.

Professional Associations and Occupational Groups   Literally hundreds of professions and occupations in industrialized nations are represented by organizations. In the United States, the American Bar Association and the American Medical Association are probably the best known, but other organizations represent electrologists, plumbers, nursing home administrators, hairdressers, podiatrists, and people in many other professions. Farmers have powerful lobbies in the United States as well as in France, Japan, and Argentina. These groups are distinguished by their focus on the special interests of members of an identifiable profession or occupation.

Professional associations work actively to share information—hence the constant parade of conventions in virtually all major cities. Members attending these meetings can go to panel discussions and workshop sessions at which they learn about new techniques or materials relevant to their profession. Professional associations also attempt to influence government, however, particularly with respect to licensing laws and regulations.

These groups are concerned about licensing both because they are naturally interested in maintaining the public's confidence in their respective professions and because they want to keep unqualified people from taking business away from them.* Since effective licensing requirements can be enforced only through governmental action, professional associations exert much of their energy by acting as interest groups.

How Interest Groups Work

Interest groups exploit a wide range of methods in their efforts to influence government. The following approaches are the main ways in which interest groups attempt to get what they want.

Lobbying Whenever interest groups communicate with governmental officials, they are **lobbying**.[†] Contact is sometimes informal, as when a legislator or an agency head discusses a policy issue over the phone, through correspondence, or at lunch.

Interest groups also testify before congressional committee hearings, file *amicus curiae*[‡] briefs (documents arguing for or against a particular interpretation of the law) with state and federal courts, submit written reports to administrative agencies, and participate in public hearings of all kinds. All of these activities are important *access opportunities*, providing settings in which interest groups can directly contact decision makers.

Contacts between lobbyists and governmental officials in the United States and other established democracies are generally honest, legitimate meetings, despite popular impressions to the contrary. Interest groups lobby primarily by providing information to decision makers, not by purchasing votes. In fact, political scientists specializing in the study of the U.S. Congress often tell of the newly elected representative who, after a year in office, asked, "Where are the lobbyists? I haven't seen one yet." Of course, he had seen and heard dozens of them, but none had tried to *bribe* him. All the people he met with were simply giving him useful facts and introducing him to their points of view—innocent contacts that the freshman representative could not possibly interpret as lobbying.

Legislators, agency officials, and even judges listen to lobbyists because the information they have is often valuable, even though the group providing the information has an axe to grind. For example, when new legislation is considered

---

* Some analysts argue that the public would be much better off with unfettered access to these "unqualified" professionals and that, in the name of protecting us against "charlatans," professional associations merely seek to keep competition out and prices up. See Milton Friedman, *Capitalism and Freedom* (Chicago: University of Chicago Press, 1962), for the classic argument along these lines.

† This term derives from the widely observed practice among legislators of discussing major decisions with interested parties in the cloakrooms and lobbies outside the official legislative chamber. Persons meeting with legislators in such settings are commonly called lobbyists.

‡ Literally translated, this means "friend of the court."

regarding auto emission standards, one of the groups that Congress and the Environmental Protection Agency (EPA) will turn to for data is the auto industry. Although the interest groups representing the automakers obviously have a stake in the outcome, they also have a great deal of knowledge and experience relevant to the matter at hand. Ultimately, government officials have to decide what weight or credibility they will give that information. Even when the group has a financial stake in the outcome (as with the automakers), the information may still be useful.

Interest groups can exert considerable influence by lobbying. Being in a position to provide critical information is itself a source of power. Good lobbyists are always ready to answer questions and explain the importance of their views. Decision makers often respond to lobbyists' suggestions, incorporating them in compromise solutions that take the groups' positions into account.

In countries where public agencies are not as capable of evaluating private-sector data, interest groups often exercise even more influence than in the United States. In a classic study from the 1960s, a leading expert argued that many Italian regulatory agencies relied so heavily on information from the very industrial groups they were supposed to be monitoring that they had become their virtual clients.[3] The same observation is commonly made today about interest groups in most developed and developing countries. However, in some countries, interest groups and government agencies are mutually dependent: A French study from the 1990s concluded that interest groups in that country, particularly "public" interest groups, are dependent upon the powerful central French state bureaucracy, although they are frequently able to get government elites to adopt their goals.[4]

Influencing Public Opinion   In democratic systems, it is much easier for an interest group to persuade a legislator or an agency official if public opinion is on its side. Interest groups thus often spend a great deal of time and money attempting to generate support among the public. When they succeed, legislators are less likely to introduce or support legislation opposed by the group. Interest groups in good standing with the public are more effective in influencing government officials.

Interest groups most often adopt the "influencing public opinion" strategy when governments are considering policy changes that would hurt group interests. Such a strategy often helps them block actions they oppose. Interest groups are less likely to mobilize public opinion when they seek something new from government; in these cases, groups prefer to work with legislative committees or with administrative agencies.

For example, you may recall seeing television commercials showing people voicing opinions about what should be done to produce alternative forms of energy. The statements were followed by messages from the oil company sponsoring the ads that it has already taken these very steps. A number of recent advertisements from pharmaceutical companies emphasize their programs that provide free or low-priced prescription drugs to people who cannot afford them. These commercials are certainly aired in hopes of generating increased sales, but the corporations producing them also hope to persuade voters to stop pressuring Congress for even stricter environmental regulations or for price controls. To the extent that a group is successful in creating a favorable image, it reduces public demands on the government to take action against it.

Clearly, influencing public attitudes is a useful strategy used most often in developed democracies, with their high degree of political participation and awareness. It is a far less relevant strategy in authoritarian or less-developed systems. Modern technology, such as computer-controlled telephoning, is exploited effectively by interest groups in the United States, Great Britain, and other advanced nations. Yet, even in a semiauthoritarian society such as Mexico was before the 1990s one could find newspaper advertisements by business or labor groups making their cases to the public.

Influencing Group Members   Interest groups with large memberships can wield additional power by enlisting the active support of their members. Most interest groups publish some sort of newsletter to communicate with their members, and those publications give them a chance to promote the group's official positions and political preferences. On June 19, 2008, the American Federation of State, County, and Municipal Employees announced that it had endorsed Senator Barack Obama after having endorsed Senator Hillary Clinton several months earlier. Through its website and its newsletters, AFSCME ensured that its 1.4 million members read dozens of articles making the case for Obama over the Republican candidate, Senator John McCain, and poll results revealed that the vast majority of them voted for the Democratic candidate.

An organization's efforts to persuade its members often lead to real payoffs because individuals who are members of organizations are more likely to vote than are unaffiliated people. Government officials realize that the outcomes in close elections are frequently determined by interest group endorsements that influence the voting choices of members.

Making Campaign Contributions   Usually within strict legal limits, interest groups can influence government by contributing to electoral campaigns.* Money is the most typical contribution, but interest groups often supply volunteers and in-kind services to help a candidate in an election.

There are two ways of seeing a connection between campaign contributions and legislative decisions. First, the model of *legislative influence* assumes that a *quid pro quo* (literally, "something for something") develops between legislators and groups: The legislator promises, explicitly or implicitly, to support or oppose certain bills in exchange for campaign contributions. Contributions can also make a difference as described in the model of *electoral influence*. In this second scenario, interest groups steer their contributions to the candidates whose expressed views would advance group interests. When the campaign money produces electoral success, groups benefit because politicians supporting policies beneficial to the group are in a position to make law.†

---

* In the United States, the law on campaign financing and spending is in flux. The Bipartisan Campaign Reform Act of 2002, signed into law by President George W. Bush, was significantly undermined by the Supreme Court in 2010. We will discuss the law and the controversial *Citizens United* case in Chapter 10.

† For a helpful discussion of these two complementary models, see John R. Wright, *Interest Groups and Congress* (New York: Longman, 2003), pp. 146–148.

It is easy to see why campaign contributions from interest groups are a cause of concern in a democracy. If politicians need huge sums of money to buy television time, and if they obtain much of that money from interest groups, they obviously come to depend on interest groups. Such dependence is a source of considerable political power. In a democracy, elected officials are expected to serve their constituents, and yet they are encouraged (some would say "forced") to serve the organized interests they depend on for contributions. As discussed in Chapter 4, many democratic systems have thus made efforts to eliminate the problem by limiting how much money can be spent in campaigns, by requiring that candidates and parties disclose the sources of their funding, and by limiting the amount of money that a single person or organization can contribute.

In other political systems, there may be a much more intimate relationship among parties, candidates, and interest group campaign contributions. For example, for many years in Great Britain, unions automatically checked off a small contribution from the paychecks of their members, which went to support the Labour Party. Workers could prevent the deduction only if they told their union that they wished to "opt out," a rather uncomfortable request to make. Subsequently, a Conservative-controlled Parliament passed legislation that stipulated that contributions would be deducted only if the union member "opted in." In the Philippines and many Latin American countries, candidates or parties are sometimes so heavily financed by powerful business interests that they become virtual spokespeople for those groups.

Litigation   Court systems are normally designed to try cases involving crimes and disputes between individuals. But interest groups are sometimes able to sue a governmental official or agency on the grounds that they were harmed by a governmental action (or inaction).* Once in court, the interest group may be able to delay a governmental action it opposes or to obtain more forceful implementation of something it favors. In order to use the courts to influence policy, the group must somehow demonstrate that a law or constitutional provision requires that a governmental official or agency stop or start doing something. Important public policy questions are often addressed when the court hands down a decision. (See A Closer Look 6.2.)

Demonstrations and Strikes   Sometimes an interest group can advance its cause or interests by bringing attention to a problem that most people would otherwise overlook. The visual impact of demonstrations, and the fact that they can be covered in brief television news reports, make such events particularly popular in developed

---

* In the United States, Britain, and other countries using the Anglo-American system of jurisprudence, the extent to which a group can do this depends on the law of standing. The familiar phrase "standing to sue" simply means that the party wishing to litigate has a real stake in the matter, not merely an ideological position. Thus, when the Sierra Club sues the U.S. Department of the Interior, it must be able to show that at least one of its members was personally harmed by that agency (or that he or she would be harmed if the challenged agency action were allowed to go forward). The standing doctrine thus limits interest groups' access to the courts because their concerns will not be heard if they only have an ideological position on the issue.

nations. Media events are also relatively inexpensive to organize. Virtually any demonstrating group can get exposure that would otherwise cost many thousands of dollars. In addition to getting exposure, the demonstration will often "fire up" the group's members, generating internal support that may be lagging.

Strikes are also sometimes used as a political statement instead of merely a means of demanding higher wages or better working conditions. Workers in Italy and Peru,

A CLOSER LOOK   6.2

The "Disadvantage Theory" of Interest Group Litigation

Achieving an interest group's policy goals through litigation is very different from achieving such goals by lobbying legislators or chief executives. Legislation requires that a majority of the parliament or assembly support the group's position, and both legislators and executives usually have to balance interest group demands against voter preferences and party demands. In most systems, judges enjoy some political independence, although their influence over public policy is usually limited. Still, in some circumstances an interest group may be able to convince a court that a particular governmental action must be changed or preserved, and the resulting decision of the court may produce policy changes the group wants. If a group is politically weak, it may have a greater chance of achieving its goals through litigation than through the legislative and executive branches, where the group is outspent and outvoted by larger, more powerful interests.

The **disadvantage theory** of interest groups and courts is based on these observations. Initially associated with Richard Courtner, the idea holds that the interest groups that turn to litigation as a strategy for achieving their goals are those groups that "are temporarily, or even permanently, disadvantaged in terms of their abilities to attain successfully their goals in the electoral process.... Politically 'disadvantaged' groups, [i]f they are to succeed at all in the pursuit of their goals ... are almost compelled to resort to litigation."[5] Perhaps the best example of interest group behavior illustrating this theory involved the NAACP: During the 1940s and 1950s, this group's efforts to end public school segregation by lobbying state legislatures failed completely, but a litigation strategy successfully produced dramatic public policy changes. The courts provided access that was denied in other quarters.

However important that example is, researchers are beginning to doubt that the "disadvantage theory" tells the whole story. Recent studies analyzing data on group wealth, goals, and strategies suggest that it is not only "politically disadvantaged" interest groups that use the courts. In fact, profit-seeking groups use litigation *more* than public interest groups do, and groups with better staffs and more financial resources use litigation more than groups with fewer resources.[6] Any interest group with the required financial resources can use litigation to change public policy, sometimes to enforce and secure policy objectives initially won in elected institutions. In such cases, litigation strategies actually reinforce the successes that group power brings through lobbying.

Because the empirical work on interest group litigation undermines the most common understanding of the disadvantage theory, some political scientists have started to think about the problem in different ways. Cary Coglianese concludes that groups suffering a disadvantage are, in fact, the ones most likely to pursue litigation, but the disadvantage that drives them to seek their goals through the courts is not a lack of financial or organizational strength. Instead, the groups that file lawsuits to change policy, almost always a long-shot approach, are *those groups whose goals are widely unsupported in society and who therefore face an unreceptive political system.*[7] So, it is not the "disadvantage" of poor resources that leads groups to turn to litigation as an influence strategy but the absence of widespread societal support.

for example, have often carried out one- or two-day general strikes in which transportation services, electrical power, and much of the nation's commerce grind to a halt. French farmers' associations use strikes and other aggressive actions—such as blocking highways or dumping produce on the roads—to influence agricultural and trade policies.

Demonstrations are most prevalent in political systems that are neither fully democratic (that is, where sectors of society do not have equal access to the political system) nor totalitarian. As long as the Communist Party controlled the mass media in the former Soviet Union and harshly repressed dissent, demonstrations were rare and quickly (often brutally) put down. Although Russia has become more authoritarian under Putin and his hand-picked successor, President Medvedev, there are still many more political demonstrations and protests than in the Soviet years.

These newer demonstrations in Russia range from the more serious and sometimes violent expressions of ethnic politics to less threatening demonstrations such as smokers protesting the shortage of cigarettes. Of course, in Hungary, Poland, and other Eastern European nations, demonstrations that started as a form of interest group activity by human rights organizations turned into peaceful revolutions that startled the world by toppling totalitarian regimes. In contrast, the massacre of student demonstrators in Beijing's Tiananmen Square in June 1989 revealed the limits of such demonstrations in the most repressive countries.

Demonstrations and other "confrontational" tactics are usually the choice of groups with little confidence that they will succeed through more conventional lobbying efforts. For example, in the American South, African Americans—often disenfranchised and lacking access to the local media—resorted to sit-ins and marches, particularly in the 1950s and 1960s. Similarly, Blacks in the townships of South Africa used demonstrations throughout the 1980s and early 1990s to express their opposition to apartheid legislation before the political process was opened to them. Mexican slum dwellers or peasants, who have been unable to satisfy their demands otherwise, may encamp themselves in front of government agencies either to influence public opinion or to show their resolve to government policy makers. In India, where hunger strikes and sit-ins were used by the legendary leader Mohandas Gandhi to achieve national independence, farmers—as well as language, religious, and caste groups—constantly resort to such tactics.

Although demonstrations can be a useful tool for otherwise weak or powerless groups, they also can be counterproductive. Demonstrations may become violent, producing fights and rock throwing. Even demonstrations that remain nonviolent may generate significant opposition to the group. Individuals who would otherwise be sympathetic to the group's cause may begin to see it as lawless or radical. Even though the vast majority of demonstrations are nonviolent, the distinction between demonstration and riot may be lost on much of the general public.

Corruption   We have suggested that, for the most part, the relationship between interest groups and public officials in industrial democracies is honest. In less-developed political systems, however, the roles of bribery and corruption are much more firmly entrenched.

A CLOSER LOOK

6.3

Interest Group Strategies: Evidence from Denmark

In a classic of political science, *Politics, Pressure, and the Tariff*, E. E. Schattschneider classified interest groups as "insiders" or "outsiders," and this distinction has remained a familiar concept in the literature on interest groups. Direct contacts with legislators or bureaucrats are "inside" strategies, while mobilizing citizens, grassroots memberships, and using mass media are "outside" strategies. The generally accepted idea is that interest groups use one strategy or the other in their efforts to influence policy.

In a recent study, a Danish political scientist surveyed interest group representatives in that country to gather data on the strategies groups employ.

The following table lists the most important "inside" and "outside" strategies she observed.

Interest Group Strategies

	Percentage of Groups Employing Each Strategy "Very" or "Fairly Often"
Inside Strategies	
Contacting Parliamentary Committees	19.5
Contacting Party Organizations	6.0
Contacting Party Spokespersons	20.6
Contacting National Public Servants	37.7
Responding to Requests for Comments	40.4
Outside Strategies	
Contacting Reporters	35.1
Arranging Debate Meetings and Conferences	42.5
Conducting Petitions	2.3
Strikes, Civil Disobedience, and Illegal Direct Action	0.7
Writing Letters to the Editor and Columns	28.0

Not surprisingly, the data show that some strategies are far more popular than others. However, the Danish study also suggests that the conventional wisdom overstates the extent to which interest groups actually choose inside or outside strategies to the exclusion of the other. Using data on all major interest groups politically active in Denmark, the researcher found that "there is no contradiction between pursuing strategies associated with insider access to decision-making and strategies where pressure is put on decision makers through media contacts and mobilization."[8] Thus, those with "privileged" access do not neglect outside strategies.

However, some groups (the author of this study terms them "cause" groups) primarily use mobilization and mass media to exert pressure. These groups may find that administrative agencies and key legislators are not inclined to meet with them, or perhaps they simply conclude that generating widespread public awareness and activism is the most fruitful approach to achieving their goals. In the United States, we would thus expect a group like ACT-UP, a controversial gay rights organization, to use outside strategies, while the National Association of Realtors will make use of its contacts in government while also placing ads on television and radio. In practice, interest groups choose strategies that seem most promising, and this will depend on the nature of the issue at stake and the public's perception of the interest itself.

It was widely understood that during Ferdinand Marcos' reign in the Philippines (1965–1986) business groups would not receive favorable government treatment without paying substantial contributions to the president. In Nigeria and the Central African Republic, the massive scale of government corruption has enabled these nations' leaders to become multimillionaires despite the fact that their populations are among the poorest in the world.

As we have seen, interest groups can select one or more of several strategies for influencing the political process. Their choices reflect their character, the degree to which their goals are considered "mainstream," and the kind and amount of resources they command. Interest group behavior is also affected by the nature of the system in which groups operate. Where political power is decentralized in both government structure and party organization (as in the United States), there are many "access points" for interest group influence. One group may find success lobbying Congress, whereas another may work for opposing policies by attempting to influence an executive department. Although the wide range of opportunities for influence makes it possible for many groups to work in the political arena, however, opposing groups can also find access.

A more centralized political system such as Great Britain's offers fewer points of access, but the groups that are fortunate enough to "get inside" can expect to have great influence. Thus, decentralized political systems tend to have more numerous and more visible interest groups, whereas centralized systems afford great power to those few interest groups that secure effective linkages.

THE POWER OF INTEREST GROUPS

Why Are Some Groups More Powerful than Others?

Interest groups operating in the same society are usually subject to the same laws and have access to the same media for communicating with citizens and officials. But it becomes clear on a moment's reflection that some groups are much more powerful than others. Most U.S. politicians safely ignore the Women's Christian Temperance Union, for example, but few British leaders ignore the British Trades Union Congress, and no U.S. senator or representative takes the National Rifle Association or the American Association of Retired Persons lightly. Several factors determine how much power and influence a given interest group enjoys.

Size   All other things being equal, groups with large memberships are more influential than groups with small memberships. A group that officially speaks for a large number of people can influence close elections, and elected officials will therefore listen to the leaders of such groups. A large membership also suggests broad public acceptance of the group's ideas since there are usually several nonjoining supporters for every supportive person who actually belongs to the group. Moreover, a large size means that the group has a huge supply of "soldiers" for its work. Letter-writing campaigns, contributions to candidates running for office, and even demonstrations are all more powerful forms of influence when the group can call on many members.

While size is an important factor, other characteristics may more than offset the advantages or disadvantages of large or small memberships.

Unity   Even large groups can lose much of their effectiveness if their members are divided. A governmental official who wants to be sympathetic to a particular cause or interest may find that a decision demanded by one segment of the group is opposed by another. The safe response is to do nothing. Hence, division within an interest group (or among organizations representing similar interests) leads to a reduction in effective influence.

Groups that can present a united front when pressing their claims are in a much better position. This point was made by a scholar of British politics in a comparison of the power of teachers and doctors. British teachers are represented by a divided array of bickering organizations, whereas doctors have the well-established, cohesive British Medical Association. Although there are more teachers than doctors, government officials regularly consult the BMA, whereas teachers' organizations are largely ignored.

Leadership   Effective leaders make a difference. Good leaders persuade the public, communicate effectively with elected officials, generate membership, and hold an organization together. Given the same resources, a group will have less success with a poor leader. This point is frequently made in discussions of the civil rights movement in the United States. During the 1960s, when Dr. Martin Luther King, Jr. (1929–1968) led the most important civil rights interest groups, the movement was remarkably successful. But after his death, even with more members and more money, these groups had less success. Many suggest that without King's leadership, civil rights groups lost both their unity and some of their capacity to generate support among the general public.

Social Status   A general perception of integrity, professionalism, or prestige is helpful to an interest group. In the United States, the American Bar Association (ABA) is only moderately large (nearly 400,000 members in 2011) but it has a substantial reservoir of support by virtue of the prestige of the legal profession (despite all of those lawyer jokes).

Hence, when a president nominates a person to a federal judgeship or to fill a vacancy on the Supreme Court, the ABA's rating of that individual is a prominent factor in evaluating him or her. The ABA is also consulted on many legislative proposals, indicating that elected officials care about the group's opinions and that they are willing to let the public know it. In many Latin American nations, the government has given professional associations of architects, lawyers, and the like the authority to determine who may legally practice the profession. In contrast, the Association of National Advertisers does not have a particularly compelling social status, and it has less power as a result (although it often has significant power with respect to some policy decisions).

A 2003 study compared several important U.S. interest groups with respect to their standing with the public. The researchers calculated a "net likeability" score by subtracting the percentage of respondents saying the group is the *least* liked from the percentage saying that the group is the *most liked*. For example, 24.3 percent of the respondents reported that environmental interest groups were the groups they liked the most, and 4.4 percent reported liking these groups the least, giving a net likeability score of 19.9. The National Rifle Association had a net likeability score of –.08, the tobacco lobby came in at –16.4, and gay rights groups had a very low score of –21.8. Differences in likeability can make a big difference in how influential an interest group can be, sometimes offsetting advantages in membership and even wealth.

Wealth   Wealth can contribute to a group's influence in several ways. An interest group with a large treasury, such as the AFL-CIO, can purchase airtime to broadcast "educational" statements and influence public opinion. Wealth can also facilitate access. A wealthy organization can purchase expensive legal services that enhance its participation in government decision making. Wealth does not always produce power for interest groups, but it helps.

Strategic Economic Location   A business group or a labor union may also gain political influence through its control over an important economic resource or its ability to disrupt a vital economic activity. In economies heavily dependent on the export of a small number of crops or minerals, business groups that control those resources (Salvadoran coffee growers or South African diamond-mining corporations, for example) carry considerable political weight in many aspects of a nation's political life. In South Korea, many observers argue that the *chaebols* (giant business conglomerates) control much of the country's economic policy. In most countries, unions have substantial influence, especially when they can threaten to disrupt important segments of the economy. Some years ago, the British coal miners' union wielded great power because of its ability to shut down a vital source of energy. In Peru, the bank workers exercised power far in excess of their numbers by demonstrating their ability to cripple the nation's economy with an extended bank strike.

Geographic Concentration   Some interest groups—such as medical and teacher associations—have members located throughout a political system, whereas others have memberships largely concentrated in a particular area or areas. Geographic dispersion often makes a significant difference with respect to political strength and influence. Groups with members in virtually all areas of the country can work effectively at the national level because they are able to make claims on representatives from virtually all legislative or parliamentary districts. Their influence may be small in any given district, but it is difficult for government to ignore an interest that can generate votes in every area of the country.

In contrast, some interests are geographically concentrated. French wine growers, for example, are primarily found in a few regions. Consumers in the United States are poorly organized compared with the strong union representing the interests of autoworkers, but consumers are obviously spread throughout the country. Thus, when a proposal to protect autoworkers' jobs by restricting imports is considered, the workers often lose. Members of Congress from a few states (including Michigan, Ohio, and Missouri) press for such proposals, but most representatives are likely to consider the damage they would do to consumers since consumers' concerns are present in all districts.

Do Interest Groups Control the System?

One of the most widely recognized images in political science is the "**iron triangle**." The term is an effort to depict a close relationship among a legislative committee, an administrative agency, and an interest group in a particular policy area (e.g., agriculture, defense procurement).* According to this idea, a group, a committee, and an agency working together develop a powerful and mutually beneficial relationship. Administrators want budget increases from the legislative committees; representatives on those committees want electoral and campaign finance support from the interest groups; and the interest groups want policies favorable to them. Each part of the triangle has a strong interest in pleasing the others. Since virtually all important areas of public policy will have their own "**iron triangles**," and since each one wants to have as much independent power as possible, legislators and administrators in a given triangle tend to leave other triangles alone to make their own decisions, a favor that they expect will be repaid in kind.[9]

The iron triangle concept implies that *policy decisions in each policy area are dominated by relatively autonomous sets of governmental officials and interest groups, leaving very little role for broader public interests in shaping what government does.* This perspective is therefore usually part of a rather negative view of the impact and role of interest groups in the policy process.

A U.S. Supreme Court decision from the 1980s provided a striking illustration of how strong, and how exclusive, the relationships in an iron triangle can be. In *Block v. Community Nutrition Institute* (464 U.S. 340, 1984), a group representing the interests of low-income consumers of dairy products tried to get the U.S. Agriculture Department to reconsider one of its rulings, one that would raise the cost of milk. The Court referred to the original arrangement set in place by Congress during the 1930s and denied standing to the community group. Justice Sandra Day O'Connor's statement in the majority opinion was remarkable in its frankness:

> [The intent of Congress was to] limit the classes entitled to participate in the development of [milk] market orders. The Act contemplates a cooperative venture among the Secretary, handlers, and producers the principal purposes of which are to raise the price of agricultural products.... Nowhere in the Act, however, is there an express provision for participation by consumers in any proceeding (at p. 346).

Advocates of the iron triangle concept could never hope to find a more perfect example to make their point. Agricultural policy clearly affects every citizen in one way or another, but Congress had established a "cooperative venture" among dairy producers and the Agriculture Department (overseen by congressional committees) to make decisions. Consumer interests were not only disregarded—they were authoritatively *excluded* from the process.

---

* Other names for iron triangles include *policy whirlpools*, *subgovernments*, and *triple alliances*. Perhaps the first work to use the idea was Ernest Griffith's *Impasse of Democracy* (New York: Harrison-Hilton, 1939). Another often-cited work is J. Leiper Freeman, The *Political Process* (New York: Random House, 1965).

Although the idea of the iron triangle was a leading political science concept for many years, analysts have recently argued that it is too simple or perhaps outdated in most policy areas. As discussed in the next section, there has been an explosion in the growth of interest groups, especially "public interest" groups advocating broader interests. As these groups have expanded their power, they have increasingly sought to influence the government officials who previously worked only with the longtime members of the various triangles. These new groups are not always successful, of course (as in the Agriculture Department case), but they have often succeeded in breaking down the exclusive control enjoyed by some groups in earlier decades.

As a result, some political scientists began discussing "issue networks" instead of "iron triangles." The idea is that, though there still may be some relatively stable relationships among interest groups, legislative committees, and administrative agencies in some policy areas, influence is much more fluid, open, and unpredictable than is implied by the iron triangle concept. As new groups enter the system, it becomes difficult for any group to dominate public policy in its area of interest, and thus the iron triangle image is less prominent among political scientists than it was in the 1950s.[10]

Moreover, some political scientists argue that a close relationship between interest groups and government agencies is not a negative thing at all. In 2004, two researchers studied the impact of interest group influence in 18 developed nations, focusing on the extent to which each country adopted "active labor market policies." These policies are an array of government efforts to help unemployed workers find secure jobs by providing training, subsidized jobs, and unemployment benefits. Although virtually all countries have programs to help the unemployed, there is substantial variation in their quality and effectiveness. According to this study, such policies are more comprehensive in countries in which employer interests are more coordinated in strong interest organizations and where those organizations are closely integrated into the public policy-making process.[11]

The question of whether interest groups "control" the political system is thus particularly difficult to resolve. Interest group influence sometimes produces policies opposed by a majority of a nation's citizens, but sometimes that influence is closely allied with the demands of popular movements. In some cases, interest groups form highly exclusive relationships with government bureaus and legislative committees, working to advance their interests in effective iron triangles, while in other cases they follow an open strategy of mobilizing public opinion. Perhaps the best answer is that the extent to which interest groups control the policy process depends on many factors, including the nature of the system, the visibility of the issue at hand, and the activities of other interest groups.

THE GROWTH OF INTEREST GROUPS

Why have interest groups proliferated in industrial democracies? First, forming an effective organization with dues-paying members and political effectiveness simply takes time. The American labor movement, for example, failed to establish viable organizations for decades, finally succeeding on a grand scale many years after the worst industrial abuses had ended. So we should expect a steady increase in the number of a nation's interest groups simply because, over time, more of them will overcome the barriers to organization. Second, a wealthier society can support a larger number of interest groups. When a society becomes affluent, more people have discretionary income, and some people use it to support organizations that pursue causes they care about. The organizations established to protect animal rights, for example, could only have been established in an affluent period; in poorer times, such concerns were secondary for nearly all citizens. Third, people in many countries are increasingly dissatisfied with political parties. As noted in Chapters 4 and 5, political parties have lost support in several nations. When political support and energy are directed away from political parties, interest groups often become the focal point for political concerns.

The growth of interest groups has worried political scientists for generations.[12] When government decisions are increasingly influenced by organized interests, the ballot box arguably becomes less important. Moreover, as interest groups sap power away from parties, the political system is subject to more difficult demands and controversies. Whereas parties tend to aggregate interests and then moderate the demands of their supporters in an effort to broaden their appeal, interest groups usually have no such concern for moderation. In fact, taking extreme positions is often a good way to generate more members. But it is more difficult for the system to respond to an array of divisive, single-minded groups than to a few moderate parties.

Nevertheless, it is also possible to view the growth in the number of interest groups favorably. The proliferation of groups may indicate that more people find political activity and involvement useful and that they have a reasonable expectation that, if they organize properly, the system will listen to them. Without interest groups, many demands go unheard and unheeded, producing unrest that will eventually threaten political order.

HOW INTEREST GROUPS ARE FORMED

Ironically, to evaluate the ultimate effect of the proliferation of interest groups, we must take a step backward and consider how interest groups *form*. The representativeness of the interest group system is largely a matter of which groups become effectively organized and which ones do not, so understanding the formation of interest organizations is essential if we are to appreciate the effects of interest groups in the political system.

The Pluralist View

Pluralism is one of the most widely discussed concepts in the study of modern democracies. Its core idea is simple: Pluralists believe that society has not one or two but *many* centers of power. In contrast to Marxism, which sees all political conflict as a struggle between capitalists and workers, pluralists argue that many interests exert influence in a political system and that public policy decisions thus incorporate most of those interests' demands and concerns. David Truman's classic, *The Governmental Process*, remains a foundational work stating the case for pluralism.[13]

Although pluralism is primarily a perspective on how group power is *distributed*, it also contains an argument regarding interest group *formation*. If political power is divided among a diverse array of interest groups, it must be true that interests naturally and easily become organized. Pluralists argue that virtually any interest can become an effective organized force. Thus, *pluralists claim that whenever a significant number of persons share an important objective, they will inevitably organize themselves.* This is the pluralists' answer to the question of how groups form.

The pluralists' straightforward and convincing perspective on interest group formation suggests an optimistic view. If virtually every interest in society is represented by effective organizations, then we can be confident that the *array of political organizations* operating in politics at any given time is reasonably representative of the *array of interests in society.* Even if organized groups influence governmental decisions, the system is still fair because virtually all interests are effectively represented by organizations and the largest interests produce the most powerful organizations.

The Elitist View

A very different interpretation has been offered by those who embrace **elite theory**. Instead of an open competition among a wide range of interests, elite theorists see a closed system controlled by a few. They assert that if pluralists were correct about the ability of people with shared interests to form effective organizations, the interests of the poor and racial minorities would have been more effectively advanced than they have been in virtually all developed democracies. Persistent social inequality confirms the weakness of the pluralist vision. *Real* political power is almost entirely in the hands of a **power elite** that represents the interests of only its members, leaving the rest of society and especially the poor relatively powerless.[14]

Elite theory is primarily about how political power is distributed throughout society, but, like pluralism, it derives many of its conclusions from a view of how groups form. Elite theorists accept the premise that everyone has a *legal right* to form organizations, but they insist that a relatively small range of groups actually succeed in getting a stranglehold on the primary centers of political power. In order for an interest to form an organization that will have any real impact, it must adapt itself to be compatible with the elite establishment.

Proponents of elite theory point out that the most powerful political organizations form through the frequent interactions of influential persons who have shared experiences and connections because they went to the same schools, belong to the same country clubs, and associate in the same social circles. Thus, the leaders of the largest corporations, the most powerful political officials, and the critically important masters of military institutions represent a narrow, elite segment of society. Far from representing a plurality of interests and perspectives, they are "peas in a pod," supporting essentially the same policies and programs. Consequently, they support governmental decisions that preserve the power of the dominant "corporate culture." Groups that exist outside the sphere of the power elite may exert influence over relatively unimportant issues, but the basic direction of social policy is firmly under the control of a narrow range of rather homogeneous interests.

Thus, elite theory leads to a profoundly pessimistic interpretation of interest group power in society. As long as the power elite exerts power, society is not very democratic. Elite theorists claim that having the right to vote makes little difference when government action is largely determined by an unrepresentative, essentially closed set of interests. Taken to its logical conclusion, elite theory usually leads to recommendations for radical changes in the nature of society itself, usually by limiting the power of private property.

The Rational Choice View

Until the mid-1960s, virtually all political scientists adopted either the pluralist or the power elite perspective on interest groups. In 1965, however, a radically different idea was advanced by an economist. In *The Logic of Collective Action*, the late Mancur Olson, Jr. reached a startling conclusion: "Rational, self-interested individuals will not act to achieve their common or group interests."[15] This idea rejected *both* pluralism and elitism. It undermined the pluralist faith that people sharing a common interest would automatically form interest groups to pursue common goals, and it undermined the elitist assumption that members of the power elite would work for *their* common interests in ruling society. Olson's idea of **rational choice** infuriated everyone and seemed totally illogical. How could such a claim be made?

Olson's logic is best set out by way of a concrete example. Imagine that a person comes to your door to solicit funds for an interest group called the Citizens' Utility Board (CUB). He explains that CUB will lobby the state Public Service Commission to reduce rates for electricity and natural gas—rates that you agree are too high. He further explains that CUB is working to support a new pricing policy that, if adopted, will save all households $350 per year in utility bills. He asks you for a $25 contribution. What do you do?

Pluralists would predict that CUB will succeed in getting new members and contributions if many people are strongly concerned about utility bills. People will see that they have a common interest and will band together to pursue it. That is why the pluralists can be so optimistic about interest groups in general: If an interest is shared by a significant number of citizens, a political organization will pop up somewhere to pursue it. As a result, all important interests will be effectively represented, and the system is therefore healthy and fair.

Elitists would say that the CUB would fail because powerful elite forces will obstruct its formation and exclude it from effective access to the political system.

Olson claimed that both pluralists and elitists miss the fundamental point. Drawing from microeconomics, Olson began by considering what a rational, self-interested person would do when asked to join the group. The man at the door is asking for $25 to help CUB achieve an objective that, if successful, will save each household $350 per year. Before contributing, the economically rational individual would ask two questions. First, "Will I get the lower utility rates that CUB is working for if you are successful, even if I don't contribute?" The man at the door will reluctantly admit that noncontributing consumers will pay the same low rates as group supporters.

That leads the rational person to ask a second question: "What difference will *my* $25 make in the successfulness of the lobbying effort?" In response, the man would probably get a bit emotional and claim that "every little bit makes a difference," or words to that effect. But a moment's reflection convinces the rational decision maker that the chances are vanishingly small that a *single* $25 contribution will somehow make the critical difference between success and failure in lobbying the Public Service Commission.

The rational person will thus refuse to help the CUB. If the individual makes the contribution, his or her money is certainly gone; yet there is virtually no chance that giving the money will change utility rates. Since everyone sees the same dismal facts, the solicitor will have a very long day.

Olson emphasizes that this result will occur *even when every person contacted by the man would desperately like the group to achieve its goal.* Even when citizens want the group to succeed, it is in the *individual* interests of potential contributors to keep their money. The rational person thus becomes a **free-rider** on the efforts (if any) of others, and we reach the conclusion that groups cannot form by simply leading people to see their shared interests.[16]

Real-world examples support the rational choice idea. Consider the payment of union dues. If the pluralists were right, we would expect that unions could thrive on voluntary contributions. But unions have to force members to pay dues. Most union members strongly support the benefits, working conditions, and wages sought by the union, but each member's individual interest is in getting those advantages *while still keeping their money.* Hence, unions must get legislatures to enact closed-shop laws and provisions for forced, automatic deductions from paychecks in order to obtain contributions.

As a result, virtually all the auto workers in unionized auto plants contribute to the collective efforts of the United Auto Workers Union. In contrast, organizations such as the Sierra Club—lacking any way to force supporters of wilderness preservation to contribute funds—exist with contributions from less than 1 percent of environmentally concerned American citizens. Even while acknowledging the importance of the Sierra Club's work, most people who are concerned about wilderness preservation (at least 99 percent of them) have refused to contribute to any environmental group, just as Olson would have predicted.

Olson's idea carries important implications. If interest groups do not form naturally whenever a common interest is shared, and if the size (and strength) of the groups that do exist is not proportional to the magnitude of the interests in society, we cannot reach the happy pluralist conclusion that the array of interest groups working in the system is balanced and representative. Some interests have special advantages, such as labor unions with the ability to deny a union card to anyone refusing to contribute to collective efforts. Other groups have the power to deny contracts and licenses to those who would "let George do it." Those interests form highly influential organizations *because they have ways to force their supporters to contribute,* even though they may speak for a relatively small number of citizens. However, other interests are not so easily organized. The rational choice idea thus suggests a very pessimistic conclusion: Many important interests will not be represented by effective political organizations, and those that are will unbalance the political system in their favor.*

---

* Columnist David Brooks wrote an essay in 2008 interpreting contemporary U.S. politics from an Olsonian perspective. See "Talking vs. Doing," *New York Times,* May 20, 2008.

Social Movement Theory

Largely in response to Olson's idea, some social scientists developed *social movement theory*, which argues that the rational choice perspective is too limited and too narrow in its view of human motivations. Instead of seeing people as soulless "maximizers of utility," advocates of social movement theory emphasize that people may decide to join a political organization because they identify with the social movement it represents. For example, a low-income citizen may be drawn to interest groups that speak for a movement to help the poor; instead of calculating the costs and benefits to himself or herself, the individual will be moved by an emotional identification with the larger movement, and that will often generate contributions. Thus, social movement theory leads to conclusions much closer to those of pluralism than to those drawn from the rational choice perspective; it contends that like-minded people will act collectively even when a purely *individual* assessment of interests would suggest that one should be a free-rider.[17]

An important illustration of the potential power of social movements is the transnational movement to force governments and international organizations to address the problem of gender violence. One researcher examined this movement, exploring the organizational power unleashed when people who were otherwise divided by race, social status, education, and other factors found themselves sharing the same perspective. When such factors divide activists, the power of their movement declines, but when an issue emerges that highlights their shared identity, solidarity and policy influence increases.[18]

A remarkable study of collective behavior in a slum neighborhood in a Ugandan town supports the fundamental tenets of social movement theory. The researchers found that there was greater cooperative behavior to obtain public goods among people with shared ethnic identities than among people of different ethnic backgrounds. This is not particularly surprising, but the researchers determined that the greater cooperation among co-ethnics occurred "because they adhere to in-group reciprocity norms—norms that are plausibly supported by expectations that non-contribution will be sanctioned," and by the fact that the social connections among them make noncontribution uncomfortable.

The study of social movements reveals that, at least in some situations, interest group activity is not entirely a matter of rational choices by self-interested individuals. Social networks and identities shape behavior in ways that cannot be explained by examining economic logic.

A Mixed View

Many contemporary political scientists see validity in all four perspectives on the role of interest groups in industrial democracies. Jack Walker, for example, published the results of an extensive study of U.S. interest groups, concluding that there are many different paths to group formation and power. Some form as pluralists would expect, although they are often helped by wealthy benefactors who make major contributions to get groups started.[19] Most political scientists would admit, however, that traditional pluralists are overly optimistic in their expectation that virtually all interests will be represented by effective organizations. Following the elite theorists, it is widely accepted that some groups are more powerful than others and that the most powerful are typically groups pursuing the interests of the large corporations and other members of elite parts of society.[20] Social movement theorists claim that their idea is supported by the numerous and often influential political organizations that gain members by drawing on the power of identification with social movements. Finally, advocates of rational choice thinking point to the fact that groups with the ability to force members to contribute are much more powerful than are interests of the same size that lack this ability.

CONCLUSION: INTEREST GROUPS—A CHALLENGE FOR DEMOCRACY?

However interest groups are ultimately evaluated, it is clear that we cannot begin to understand how government works unless we appreciate their power. The growth of a modern society unleashes a wide range of competing interests as new industries are developed and as people increasingly begin to affect the lives of others. One way or another, interest groups will form to advance many of these competing interests.

How well the society manages those interests while maintaining some degree of democracy and fairness is one measure of the health of a modern political system. For those reasons, many political scientists feel that the best way to secure a healthy democratic government in the age of interest groups is with strong political parties, as discussed in Chapter 5.

◆ ◆ ◆

Key Terms and Concepts _____

disadvantage theory
elite theory
free-rider
interest group
iron triangles

lobbying
pluralism
power elite
rational choice

DISCUSSION QUESTIONS

1. *How do political parties and interest groups compare as methods for representing and articulating citizens' interests?*
2. *Compare the different approaches to understanding how interest groups form. Which is the most valid, and why?*
3. *The most dramatic change in the politics of interest groups during the last 30 years or so has been the rise of so-called citizen groups or public interest groups. Is the emergence of these groups a good or a bad thing?*
4. *Compare elitism and pluralism as perspectives on the distribution of organized power. Which theory is more persuasive?*

Notes _____

1. See Posner's comments in full at the "Becker/Posner Blog," www.becker-posner-blog.com/2008/05/the-outlandish-farm-subsidies–posner.html, accessed June 14, 2011.

2. "Election Day 2006," NRA Political Victory Fund News Release, available at www.nraila.org/Issues/Articles/Read.aspx?id=227&issue=047, accessed June 14, 2011. Also see "Election 2010 Recap," www.nraila.org/GrassrootsAlerts/Read.aspx?ID=578, accessed June 14, 2011.

3. Joseph LaPalombara, *Interest Groups in Italian Politics* (Princeton, NJ: Princeton University Press, 1964).

4. See Frank Baumgartner, "Public Interest Groups in France and the United States," *Governance* 9 (January) 1996: 1–22.

5. Richard C. Cortner, "Strategies and Tactics of Litigants in Constitutional Cases," *Journal of Public Law* 17 (1968): 287–307.

6. See Susan M. Olson, "Interest Group Litigation in Federal District Court: Beyond the Political Disadvantage Theory," *Journal of Politics* 52 (August 1990): 854–882; and Kim Scheppele and Jack L. Walker, Jr., "The Litigation Strategies of Interest Groups," in *Mobilizing Interest Groups in America: Patrons, Professions, and Social Movements*, ed. Jack L. Walker (Ann Arbor: University of Michigan Press, 1991), pp. 157–183.

7. Cary Coglianese, "Legal Change at the Crossroads: Revisiting the Political Disadvantage Theory," John F. Kennedy School of Government, Harvard University, Working Paper, n.d.

8. Anne Binderkrantz. "Interest Group Strategies: Navigating between Privileged Access and Strategies of Pressure," *Political Studies* 53 (December 2005): 694–715.

9. See Jeffrey Berry and Clyde Wilcox, *The Interest Group Society*, 4th ed. (New York: Longman, 2007), chap. 9, for a good overview.

10. The first use of the term *issue networks* is attributed to Hugh Heclo, "Issue Networks and the Executive Establishment," in *The New American Political System*, ed. Anthony S. King (Washington, DC: American Enterprise Institute, 1978), pp. 87–124. Also see John P. Heinz, Edward Laumann, Robert Nelson, and Robert Salisbury, *The Hollow Core* (Cambridge, MA: Harvard University Press, 1993).

11. Cathie Jo Martin and Duane Swank, "Does the Organization of Capital Matter? Employers and Active Labor Market Policy at the National and Firm Levels," *American Political Science Review* 98 (November 2004): 593–611.

12. For example, see E. E. Schattschneider, *The Semi-Sovereign People* (New York: Holt, Rinehart, and Winston, 1960).

13. David Truman, *The Governmental Process* (New York: Knopf, 1956).

14. The most often-cited classic statement of elite theory is C. Wright Mills, *The Power Elite* (New York: Oxford University Press, 1956).

15. See Robert A. Dahl, *Who Governs?* (New Haven, CT: Yale University Press, 1961).

16. Olson, *The Logic of Collective Action*, chap. 1.

17. For a good survey of this perspective, see Jeff Goodwin and James M. Jasper, eds., *The Social Movement Reader: Cases and Concepts* (Malden, MA: Blackwell, 2003).

18. A recent article applies the social movement concept to efforts to curb violence against women; see L. Laurel Weldon, "Inclusion, Solidarity, and Social Movements: The Global Movement against Gender Violence," *Perspectives on Politics* 4 (2006): 55–74.

19. Jack L. Walker, Jr., "The Origins and Maintenance of Interest Groups in America," in *Mobilizing Interest Groups in America: Patrons, Professions, and Social Movements*, ed. Jack L. Walker (Ann Arbor: University of Michigan Press, 1991), pp. 19–40. Walker and David C. King presented the results of a survey attempting to determine the benefits provided by different kinds of groups in "The Provision of Benefits by Interest Groups in the United States," *Journal of Politics* 54 (May 1992): 394–426. This later study helped to demonstrate that no single theory applies to all important organized interests.

20. See the remarkable and accessible empirical analysis contained a recent book by Dara Strolovitch, *Affirmative Advocacy: Race, Class, and Gender in Interest Group Politics* (Chicago: University of Chicago Press, 2007).

PART III

POLITICAL INSTITUTIONS

The primary institutions of government—parliaments, presidencies, courts—are perhaps the first things we think about when we attempt to describe or compare governments around the world. Although the design and workings of these institutions vary dramatically, virtually all political systems have some kind of legislative assembly, an executive institution, a system of courts, and an assortment of bureaucratic agencies. The chapters in Part III describe the essential functions that each of these institutions performs. Although their functions are almost universal, we explore the importance of differences in the *design* of governmental institutions: the impact of having a presidential system (like the United States and Chile) instead of a parliamentary system (like Great Britain or Israel); the different roles that courts play in making policy; the problems of controlling state bureaucracies; and the issue of limiting executive power. The structure of a political system's institutions has a tremendous influence on the way its government works and on its prospects for stability and democracy.

© Filippo Monteforte/AFP/Getty Images

CHAPTER 7

Legislative Institutions

The Italian Senate Removes a Prime Minister
On January 24, 2008, the Italian senate voted against a motion of confidence in the government of Prime Minister Romano Prodi, by a close vote of 161 to 156, with one abstention. Following the vote, Mr. Prodi resigned.

- Lawmaking
- Legislatures: Features, Functions, and Structure
- Representation

- Party Responsibility and Legislative Behavior
- The Changing Role of Modern Legislatures

Folks, there's going to be a leetle mite of trouble back in town. Between me and that legislature-ful of hyena-headed, feist-faced, belly-dragging sons of slackgutted she-wolves. If you know what I mean. Well, I been looking at them and their kind so long, I just figured I'd take me a little trip and see what human folks looked like in the face before I clean forgot.[1]

> —Governor Willie Stark's description of the state legislature in
> Robert Penn Warren's novel All the King's Men

On May 12, 1780, when the British siege of Charleston, South Carolina, succeeded and the town surrendered, American officers were at first permitted to keep their swords. However, the swords were soon demanded by British commanders who were annoyed by the Americans' defiant shouts of "Long Live Congress!"[2]

> —George Will

It could probably be shown by facts and figures that there is no distinctly American criminal class except Congress.

> —Mark Twain

Citizens in most democracies have mixed and often heated opinions about their national legislatures. That is probably inevitable, given the contradictory pressures and expectations that these institutions are subject to. They are burdened with the responsibility to make collective decisions, and yet their membership mirrors divisions in society that often seem impossible to resolve. We want legislators to respond to the preferences of citizens in each district or state, but we also want them to act on the basis of all the pertinent scientific information available, even information that ordinary citizens cannot understand. We want them to help the chief executive make good public policy, but we also expect the legislature to obstruct executives who abuse their power.

Much of the study of legislative institutions is devoted to evaluating their behavior and determining the impact of various reforms and structural changes. In some legislatures, particularly the U.S. Congress, fear of excessive lawmaking power led to severe limits ("checks and balances") on the efficiency of the legislative process. Other legislatures are set up in ways that make them highly responsive to the winning party's platform. In **parliamentary systems** such as Germany's or Japan's, for example, the winning party or party coalition controls both the parliament (the legislature) and the executive branch and can more readily enact its campaign platform.

The design and the operation of legislative institutions often involve basic political questions. Are legislators supposed to make decisions in accordance with the wishes of others or as their own judgment dictates? What is the connection between legislative and executive institutions and powers? How are legislatures organized? As we will see, the manner in which these and other issues are resolved tells us a great deal about the workings and the nature of a political system.

LAWMAKING

Societies have been subject to law for millennia, but the establishment of specialized institutions to make law is a fairly recent phenomenon. There are at least two premodern methods of creating laws. First, in many traditional societies, the people believed that laws were given by a supreme being to a prophet, who then brought them to the political system. Second, some leaders identified elements of law emanating from nature itself. This notion of "natural law" is based on the assumption that "Nature endowed all beings with the faculty for preserving themselves, seeking good, and avoiding evil."[3] Thomas Jefferson's memorable opening to the American Declaration of Independence is an explicit statement of natural law: All citizens are "created equal" with "unalienable rights" that no persons or legislative institutions created or can take away. The essential elements of both divine and natural law are that certain fundamental laws exist independent of *human* lawmaking (which is often termed *positive law* to distinguish it from divine or natural law) and that these more fundamental laws prevail when laws made by people conflict with them.

A body of law that originates in "discoveries" of divine or natural law may be workable in societies that do not change very much. But even relatively underdeveloped nations are subject to enormous forces of change created by technology, international trade, and political movements. Governments in modern nations must manage complex economic relationships, provide for the expansion and maintenance of essential infrastructure, and respond to an active array of political demands. Thus, virtually all political systems have established legislative institutions.

LEGISLATURES: FEATURES, FUNCTIONS, AND STRUCTURE

What Are Legislatures?

Legislative institutions share three basic features. First, legislatures are *multimembered*. Individual legislators may represent provinces, districts, or even ethnic groups, but a legislature is made up of some (usually large) number of them. Second, the members are *formally equal* (although the members of one house may be more powerful than the members of another in cases where a legislature is divided into different houses). Third, legislatures make their decisions by *counting votes*.[4]

Legislative Functions

The primary function of legislatures is to legislate—that is, to *make laws*.* These laws create new restrictions, new rights, new programs, and new tax provisions, and they can repeal or amend existing laws.

Legislative involvement in lawmaking varies across different systems. In some countries (particularly those with parliamentary systems, discussed below), legislative lawmaking usually *legitimizes* policy choices made by a prime minister, a central committee, a chancellor, or some other chief executive. The U.S. Congress operates in a **presidential system** and has substantial influence over basic policy decisions. In parliamentary systems, the legislature often simply affirms decisions made by the executive. That act of affirmation, even when the legislature has little realistic opportunity to affect the choice of alternatives, can be very important to the public's general acceptance of the government's laws.

In addition to lawmaking, most legislative institutions perform four other functions. First, most legislatures *elect* or *appoint* at least some governmental officers. (This is arguably the most important legislative function in some parliamentary systems.) Second, legislatures often act in a *judicial capacity*, hearing charges brought against presidents, judges, and individual legislators.

Third, most legislatures also have the authority to *investigate* governmental operations. The information gathered may be taken into account in new lawmaking, but

---

* In the United States and other countries following Anglo-American patterns of jurisprudence, laws made by a legislature are called statutes, to distinguish them from the laws made by administrative agencies, court decisions, and executive orders. Laws passed by legislatures designate the purposes for which public monies are to be expended and therefore establish the parameters of public policy. Although laws can be made by people or institutions that do not have the basic features of legislatures—as when a tyrant issues edicts or a bureaucrat promulgates rules and regulations—lawmaking is central to the behavior of most legislatures.

sometimes the investigative process itself puts pressure on government officials to change their activities, to alter the way a law has been interpreted, or simply to become more efficient. In the United States, legislative investigations have brought important information to the public (for example, by publishing the results of important studies of consumer product safety).

Finally, in many systems, legislators perform **constituent service**. Constituents contact their representatives with questions about grant applications, the meaning of unclear regulations, and complaints about the actions (or inactions) of certain government officials. Consequently, legislators often act as **ombudsmen**,* helping their constituents with specific problems and concerns.

Legislative Structure

Every legislature has several specific structural features designed by constitutions or shaped by age-old traditions. In this section, we discuss three basic structural issues pertinent to virtually all contemporary legislative institutions.

Parliamentary Systems versus Presidential Systems   Although a few political systems operate without a legislative institution, it is fair to say that all have some kind of executive. The executive is responsible for carrying out and managing the government's programs and laws, as discussed in Chapter 8. How the legislature and the executive work together is one of the most basic issues related to legislative structure and process.

Most political systems can be classified as either parliamentary systems or presidential systems. In parliamentary systems, the legislature chooses the "head of government"—most often known as the prime minister—and this person must be an elected member of parliament. To stay in office, he or she must retain the support of the party in parliament that won a majority of seats (or the support of a parliamentary majority created by a *coalition* of parties that agree to work together to support the same prime minister). Using the conventional terminology, when the parliament elects a prime minister and when the key members of the cabinet are selected, a new *government* is created. Thus, when people speak of "the Cameron government" in Britain, they are referring to the prime minister and his cabinet.

Parliamentary systems typically have a separate "head of state," a monarch or some other person with largely symbolic powers. By contrast, in presidential systems, the chief executive is *both* head of state and head of government. He or she is selected independently by the voters and therefore is not accountable to the legislature. (See Figure 7.1.)

Which is the better system? According to supporters of presidential systems, the main advantage of their systems is that they provide greater "checks" on unwise legislatures. They point out that, in a parliamentary system, a simple legislative majority

---

* The position of ombudsman was first developed in Scandinavian countries. The person in this position investigates complaints brought by individual citizens regarding government programs, agencies, and policies.

FIGURE 7.1	Parliamentary and Presidential Systems

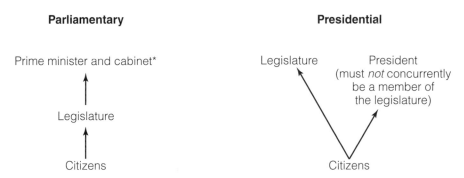

* Together, the prime minister and his or her cabinet are typically called "the government" in a parliamentary system. In many parliamentary systems, including Great Britain, the prime minister and his or her cabinet must also be current members of Parliament.

Note: Arrows indicate paths of political accountability.

can make any law it wants. There is no executive elected directly by the citizens to check the legislature. Parliamentary system advocates respond that this is the way it *should* be; the only thing that should ever "check" the decisions of the parliament is the possibility that the people will vote the other party into power if members of parliament make decisions that the people oppose. That is what democracy is all about! The choice between a parliamentary and a presidential system is thus among the most basic factors in determining how a democratic political system operates. (See A Closer Look 7.1.)

In short, presidential systems are normally thought to be slower to act with stronger checks on legislative or executive excesses, along with a greater possibility of gridlock. Parliamentary systems are thought to be more responsive to the party that wins the majority of public support. Which system produces greater stability? Some analysts contend that parliamentary systems may be more stable because they are not plagued by **dual democratic legitimacy**. This is a situation created in presidential systems as a result of the fact that both the separately elected executives *and* the legislature can claim to be the true representative of the public will. When the institutions disagree over policy, the result can be gridlock and political frustration.[8]

But the most important argument against presidential systems is that they can produce profound instability *when a president—for whatever reason—loses popular support.* The chief executive in presidential systems is elected for a fixed term and will normally complete that term (unless a constitutional crisis takes place). As a result, presidential systems sometimes encounter situations in which the government is led for years by a president with no real political clout and hence no power to lead effectively. In contrast, in parliamentary systems, prime ministers are forced to resign if

7.1

A CLOSER LOOK

Israel: A Failed Experiment with a Hybrid System

Underlying the two methods used to select the chief executive in almost all democracies are two distinct approaches to the allocation of power. Most nations of the Western Hemisphere have presidential systems that separate executive and legislative powers. The president is elected directly by the electorate and, at least theoretically, enjoys a national mandate. The legislature cannot remove the executive except through a relatively rare process of impeachment and conviction—not simply as a result of disagreeing with him or her on policy matters.

On the other hand, in a parliamentary form of government—used throughout most of Europe (with the important exception of France)—the powers of the executive and legislative branches are merged rather than separated. The prime minister is elected by the parliament and can be removed by parliament at any time.

Israel adopted a hybrid system in 1992, with a prime minister elected directly by the voters. Supporters of this system argued that a separately elected prime minister would command broad public support and have the necessary power to lead the country during times of crisis. However, in March 2001, the Knesset amended the Basic Law to return to a more conventional parliamentary system. The factors that led Israel to abandon its hybrid system reveal a great deal about the differences between parliamentary and presidential democracy.

The rationale for the short-lived system of a directly elected prime minister had to do with what many perceived to be the inappropriately large influence of small parties. When the main parties had virtually equal shares of seats in the Knesset, small parties—often Orthodox religious parties—could determine which of the major parties could form a coalition government and appoint its leader as prime minister. Some reformers believed that a directly elected prime minister system "would 'free' the prime minister from [the] constraining or 'blackmailing' influence of smaller parties."[5]

Ironically, the main impact of the hybrid system was an *increase* in the power of small parties. Why would this be the case? The system allowed voters to "split" their tickets, voting for one party's candidate for the Knesset and for another party's candidate for chief executive. Referring to the 1996 election, one observer reported the impact of the new system on voting choices:

Probably the single biggest surprise in the election was the *significant increase in representation of the smaller parties in the Knesset*, and the corresponding decrease in representation for the larger parties. The split-ballot system was in a sense "liberating" for Israeli voters. Many voters who traditionally supported Labor or Likud did so because they saw it as a way to influence the selection of the prime minister, since the leader of the party with the most seats would become prime minister.

Under the new system, a voter's choice for Knesset and prime minister can be from different parties. Many voters did this in the May election....[6]

Why did voters take advantage of the opportunity to split their tickets in such large numbers? Giving voters two ballots (one to elect the prime minister and one to elect a member of the Knesset) allowed voters to select a "mainstream" candidate when voting for prime minister and then cast a vote for a fringe candidate for the Knesset, thinking that such a vote would do little harm since a more moderate prime minister would be in place.

A British political scientist summed up the reasons that the semipresidential system in Israel was abandoned:

Israel turned to direct election [of the prime minister] to counteract ... fragmentation, instability, and immobilism.... Yet, the very effort to secure the passage of reform introduced distortions that caused it to fall short and even backfire. Much to the chagrin of reform's supporters, the 1996 and 1999 elections each led to a troubled time of coalition building. Small parties, far from being sidelined, vied to play kingmaker. And each time the result was an awkwardly patched-together coalition government with little coherence or staying power.[7]

As a result of these and other concerns, in 2001 Israel returned to a more conventional parliamentary system, used for the first time in January 2003. Voters select the members of the Knesset, and that body then selects the prime minister, who must be one of its members. Israel's short-lived experiment with a hybrid system reflects the conflicting values inherent in the choice between parliamentary and presidential democracies.

parliamentary support substantially weakens, thereby avoiding this destabilizing condition.[9]

Supporters of presidential systems argue that since the voters directly elect the president, he or she can become a stronger leader than prime ministers in parliamentary systems can be, serving as an effective focal point to hold a nation together during times of great difficulty. Presidential systems are also less likely to have rapid and frequent changes in government as a result of abrupt changes in the balance of power among parties.

The question of which system is superior is not easily answered. The fact that the chief executive in parliamentary systems depends on legislative support more than presidents do in presidential systems presents a difficult question for political scientists. On one hand, presidential systems can enjoy greater stability during shifts in the strength of competing parties since the president knows he or she can stay in office during a given term regardless of what happens in the legislature.

On the other hand, this independence from the legislature can tempt presidents to disregard growing legislative resistance to their policies. If a president overestimates his or her popular support, he or she can take actions that eventually produce disruptive or even violent opposition. In contrast, the legislature in a parliamentary system can remove a prime minister who has strayed significantly from popular demands by passing a "vote of no confidence" simply on the grounds that his or her policies have become seriously unpopular (see the opening photo and caption for this chapter). Knowing this, prime ministers are less likely to govern in ways that invite rebellious movements. Presidents, in contrast, may be removed only by impeachment, by resignation, or by a constitutional crisis of some kind, remaining in office even when they no longer enjoy political support.[10]

What about nondemocratic countries—does it matter whether they have presidential or parliamentary systems? A recent study suggested that parliamentary systems may provide for a somewhat more open government in nondemocratic regimes. When autocratic governments have a presidential system, elite factions work in private to manipulate the system so that the presidential candidate preferred by the elite "wins" the election. However, if the same country has a parliamentary system, "bargaining among the elites in selection of the head of state would occur *after* the elections" because "the elites would have to first secure parliamentary seats to be able to vote for the head of state…. [T]he balance of power among the elites in parliament would be decided by the people, giving them a voice in the process."[11]

Simply put, it is usually easier for elite factions to collude and manipulate a presidential election than it is to manipulate elections for hundreds of parliamentary seats. Once the general election is over, the prime minister will be chosen by bargaining among elites in nondemocratic systems, but there is a somewhat greater chance that their choices will be influenced by the voters' input in selecting the members of the parliament. When a nondemocratic government operates through a presidential system, everything is rigged before the people vote.

In the final analysis, the nature of a country's *party* system largely determines which arrangement is better. In both parliamentary and presidential systems, the existence of two strong parties usually produces considerable stability in the legislature, with one party in control for extended periods of time. Two-party systems may be ideal settings for presidential systems since the separately elected president can learn to work with the relatively stable group controlling the legislature. However, when a country has a large number of parties, none of which dominates the system, presidential systems may encounter serious political problems. The shifting coalitions of small parties in the legislature will often undermine the president's support. As noted above, when this occurs in a parliamentary system, the legislature may issue of vote of no confidence, and the prime minister resigns. But a president will try to complete his or her term regardless of growing opposition from a multiparty legislature. A deep chasm can arise between the two elected branches of government.

As one analyst put it, "Even though multi-partyism in itself is not troublesome for democratic stability, the combination of presidentialism and multi-partyism *is* problematic. In world history, only one *multi-party* presidential democracy—Chile—has survived for more than twenty-five years."[12] In short, a presidential system can work well when there are two strong parties, but the same arrangement becomes fragile when the legislature is run by shifting coalitions of many small parties.*

A large number of parties can also lead to problems in parliamentary systems. When no single party wins a majority of the parliament's seats, a coalition of parties must come together and agree to select a prime minister and form a government. Under the French Fourth Republic (1946–1958), for example, the legislature dominated the chief executive. Prime ministers had great difficulty getting bills passed and were regularly removed from office by the parliament.†

It is important to note that presidential systems vary considerably. The U.S. Constitution provides for a balance of power between the executive and the legislative branches, with the president being able to veto legislation while the Congress enacts laws and sometimes overrides vetoes. In Mexico and most of Latin America, both constitutional design and historical practice have produced dominant presidents and very weak legislatures. Mexican presidents can enact many programs through executive decree and generally can dominate the legislature. A recent study of Argentina found that because legislative candidates are largely

---

* However, a recent study suggests that many Latin American governments have adapted, creating arrangements in which political crises are often defused before they become destabilizing. In some cases, these "presidential regimes can work like parliamentary regimes and resort to early elections or votes of no-confidence in order to defuse a crisis, or the people and social movements may have the power to force a presidential resignation.... Latin American *presidentialism* is becoming more flexible and more like *parliamentarism*. See Leiv Marsteintredet and Einar Berntzen, "Latin American Presidentialism: Reducing the Perils of Presidentialism through Presidential Interruptions." Paper prepared for the Workshop "Parliamentary Practices in Presidential Systems: (European) Perspectives on Parliamentary Power in Latin America," European Consortium for Political Research Joint Sessions of Workshops, Nicosia, Cyprus, April 25–30, 2006.

† The fractured party system in Belgium made it impossible to form a government for more than a year. Beginning in June 2010 and continuing through the summer of 2011, Belgium had only a "caretaker" government because the parliament could not form a coalition to select a prime minister. One leader came up with an unusual plan to break the impasse. Belgian Senator Marleen Temmerman demanded that the spouses and partners of Belgian MPs "have no more sex until the new administration is posing on the steps of the Palace." It is not clear whether her urgings were heeded.

selected by provincial governors and "party bosses," legislators cannot develop professional careers or specialized expertise, making the legislature very weak relative to the executive.[13] In general, legislatures in the developing world are weak and generally do the bidding of the executive, regardless of whether there is a parliamentary or presidential system.

The Constitution of the French Fifth Republic (1958–present) was designed expressly to strengthen the presidency and weaken the parliament, which had been so dominant in the Fourth Republic. The French Constitution features a dual executive, combining elements of both presidential and parliamentary systems: It has a president (directly elected by the voters) and a prime minister (selected by the president). Both officers have considerable power and dominate a relatively weak legislature.

One or Two Houses   The division of legislative power into two chambers, or **bicameralism**, is the most common arrangement among the world's legislatures. However, the balance of power between the two chambers varies considerably. The U.S. Congress divides power roughly equally between its two branches. On the other hand, the French Assembly and the Japanese House of Representatives have considerably more authority than their upper houses. And in Great Britain, the House of Lords, once equal in power with the House of Commons, now can generally do little more than recommend changes to legislation passed by the Commons.*

Bicameral legislatures are popular for two main reasons. First, a second chamber makes it possible for subnational units (states, provinces) to be formally represented. Whenever seats in the legislature are apportioned on the basis of population (as in the U.S. House of Representatives), states, provinces, or other units with smaller populations will have a smaller number of representatives. The citizens of these smaller units may fear that their interests will be ignored in a legislative institution in which seats are allocated to states or provinces on the basis of population. They will be regularly outvoted on policy issues in which their citizens have preferences different from those of citizens in the more populous areas. Thus, seats in the "upper" house are often apportioned in such a way as to moderate those concerns. For example, the U.S. Senate is made up of two senators from each state, regardless of the state's population. A similar allocation of senate seats by state prevails in Mexico.

Second, some political thinkers advocate bicameralism to make it more difficult to enact ill-considered, dangerous, or unwise legislation. James Madison and his colleagues explicitly feared "mob rule," which they felt would be encouraged by the popularly elected House of Representatives, and they saw the more patrician and

---

* The House of Lords can delay the passage of nonmoney bills (those not involving expenditures of government funds) passed by the House of Commons for one session. Lords can suggest changes to a bill involving expenditures, but Commons is free to reject it. In practice, Lords rarely rejects a bill proposed by the cabinet and never rejects a bill fundamental to the prime minister's program.

politically independent Senate as an essential check needed to maintain stability and order.

Even where there is less fear of democracy itself, however, some people favor bicameralism as a kind of quality control. A genuinely bicameral arrangement means that legislation has two hurdles to clear before becoming law. Requiring passage in the additional house means that bad programs and policy decisions are more likely to be corrected or defeated. But the passage of *any* legislation (even good legislation) is more difficult in a bicameral legislature than in a unicameral arrangement. It is not at all uncommon for a bill to pass the U.S. Senate, for example, only to fail in the House.* For those reasons, many leaders and citizens have argued that bicameralism is an undemocratic feature: If the "people" are fairly represented in the lower house, how can a system be democratic if it permits the lower house's political choices to be overturned? Some systems (New Zealand, the U.S. State of Nebraska) have unicameral legislatures largely in response to that concern.

Legislative Committees   The large number of members in most legislatures prevents detailed consideration of legislative proposals when the assembly meets as a whole. To work out the "fine print" of a major proposal, virtually all legislative institutions have established committees, each made up of a workable number of legislators who are usually aided by specialized staffs. Although committees were created for these obvious practical reasons, they can have a profound *political* impact.

A key consideration is whether basic policy decisions are made *before* a proposal is assigned to a committee. In the U.S. Congress, bills are usually given to committees as soon as they are introduced. Hearings, discussions, and efforts by interest groups and government agencies to exert political influence take place while the bill is in committee, helping to explain why congressional committees are often called "little legislatures."[14] If a bill fares badly in committee deliberations, its fate can be sealed by negative action or even by inaction. Normally, the whole House (or Senate) acts only on bills recommended for passage by committee vote. Parliamentary committees in Japan are also quite influential and give opposition parties additional leverage in altering legislation proposed by the government.

In contrast, committees in the British Parliament are authorized to analyze proposed legislation, but they receive bills only after the whole body has made the basic policy decisions. Consequently, British committees are comparably much weaker than their American counterparts. French committees fall somewhere in between.

The strong **committee systems** in the U.S. Congress and the Japanese Diet (Japan's bicameral legislature), among others, are also characterized by member

---

* However, in Japan and Western Europe, in the event of a split between the two chambers of the parliament, the more powerful lower house can usually override the other—sometimes with a simple majority vote.

specialization. It is possible for a particular senator or representative to spend many years on a committee that reflects a special interest or expertise or that is of special importance to his or her district or state. The specialized nature of committees makes it more likely that the whole body will accept a committee's recommendations. Where members do not develop committee specialties—again as in the British Parliament—the committee's role as a policy-making unit is reduced correspondingly.

The political importance of legislative committees is generally greater when the legislature *decentralizes* political power. Again, the American Congress provides an extreme illustration: The majority party is often unable to enact bills that reflect its platform because committee chairs may not share the party leadership's perspectives (even though the chairs are members of the majority party). For years a majority of Democratic members of Congress favored reducing the oil-depletion allowance (a tax deduction applying to petroleum extraction), but their efforts were blocked by powerful Democratic committee chairs from Texas and Louisiana (major oil-producing states). The fact that committee power is independent of the majority party's power makes it more difficult to pass legislation, and it expands the range of interests and points of view that must be accommodated.

Gender Quotas   There are fewer women than men in virtually all elected legislatures, regardless of the nature of the political system. However, substantial evidence indicates that legislatures contain a higher percentage of women where proportional representation electoral systems are used than where single-member-district systems are used. As discussed in Chapter 4, PR systems make it possible for a party receiving less than a majority or plurality of votes in a given district to place some of its candidates in the legislature. In several countries, newer and often smaller parties nominate women more often than established parties do, and thus PR systems can increase the number of women serving in a nation's legislature. Countries with proportional representation nearly always have a higher proportion of women in their legislative assemblies.[18]

However, as discussed in Chapter 5, gender quotas have been established in nearly 90 countries, most of which (but not all) are democracies. Some of these quotas are mandated by government, but more than half are voluntary quotas instituted by political parties. The policy implications of gender quotas are unclear, but evidence suggests that the chances for legislation supporting education, health care, maternity benefits, and reproductive rights improve when legislatures contain at least 30 percent women.

Customs and Norms   Legislatures are an intriguing mixture of conflict and cooperation. Their members normally are drawn from diverse political parties and distinctive regions, and thus the political disagreements of the country are mirrored in the legislature itself. At the same time, at least some large segments of a legislature's membership must work together to produce legislation.

7.2

The Effect of the Legislature's Size on Government Spending

In 1981, a group of noted political theorists proposed the **law of 1/n**. The idea is that legislatures made up of a large number of representatives will enact larger, more inefficient spending programs than smaller legislatures.[15] Employing the often controversial logic of rational choice theory (discussed in Chapter 1), the law of 1/n is based on the idea that representatives in large legislatures have an incentive to propose projects that benefit their districts even when the total costs for the whole society drastically outweigh the project's benefits.

The incentive to be wasteful is a consequence of the fact that while the legislator's district gets all or most of the *benefits* of a given project, his or her constituents only pay 1/n of the cost, where n is the number of legislative districts in the legislature. For example, imagine a project that costs $100 million but produces benefits worth only $12 million. A rational person would see the project as a very bad deal. But imagine that the policy's benefits are concentrated in a single legislator's home district. If there are 500 legislative districts, each district will pay only 1/n, or 1/500th of the total cost of the project, about $200,000. But that district gets virtually *all* of the $12,000,000 benefit. The project is a wonderful value for his or her constituents! Since this logic applies to all districts, all legislators have an incentive to favor policies that waste the nation's resources. And

1/n—the proportion of the total cost borne by a given legislator's constituents—becomes smaller when the legislature has more members, so the incentive to waste should be strongest in large legislatures.

Do the facts support this logic? There is some evidence that they do. In a 2001 study, two economists found that countries with larger legislatures tend to have higher levels of government spending, although having a bicameral legislature reduces the impact of legislative size on spending levels.[16] The evidence is more mixed when comparing U.S. state governments, however. States with larger upper chambers tend to have higher levels of government spending than other states, but when the lower chamber is much larger than the upper chamber, the effect is reversed. More precisely, the ratio of lower-to-upper chamber seats is associated with lower spending levels.[17]

As with many theoretical concepts, the law of 1/n simplifies a great deal of complexity in order to identify a factor that can influence government spending levels. Its impact, if any, may be erased by other factors, such as the nation's level of development, political culture, economic conditions, and party competition, among many others. However, the law of 1/n is an interesting example of how an idea can progress from theory to hypothesis, and finally, to empirical testing.

Customs and norms are extremely helpful in maintaining cooperation in legislatures in which individual members have considerable independence. Where decisions are largely made by a central majority party leadership, an individual legislator's behavior is not as critical as it is where each member is given freer rein. In the latter case, the ability to get anything done requires that there be some basis for cooperation, some "rules of the game." In a classic study of the U.S. Senate,

Donald R. Matthews identified several **folkways** that, in the 1950s, firmly controlled each senator's behavior:

> *Apprenticeship*—new members are expected to be "seen and not heard"; *Legislative Work*—one must attend to the often tedious and politically unrewarding details of committee work instead of seeking publicity; *Specialization*—members should focus their attention on matters in a particular field; *Courtesy*—personal attacks are to be avoided, and members should be lavish in praise of other members,...; *Reciprocity*—members should give assistance and political support to colleagues; and *Institutional Patriotism*—members should hold the Senate in high esteem, maintain loyalty to it, and seek to preserve its status.[19]

Students of the U.S. Congress are fond of recounting anecdotes that show how strong those folkways have been. One often-cited instance had to do with a freshman senator who ignored the apprenticeship norm. After several senior senators made brief speeches honoring an elderly senator on his birthday, the freshman made a similar speech. At every mention of his name, the senator being honored grumbled to a colleague, "That son-of-a-bitch, that son-of-a-bitch."[20] It was considered horribly improper for such a junior member to presume to take the floor in this manner.

Legislative norms can change over time. A study of norms in the U.S. Senate completed a quarter-century after Matthews wrote his widely read analysis concluded that the apprenticeship and specialization norms had nearly disappeared, but norms that help to manage destructive conflict were still in force.[21]

Legislative customs also reflect the culture and the traditions of the society at large. (See A Closer Look 7.3.) Discussions in the British Parliament are supposedly still influenced by the style of debate (including controlled heckling of the speaker) that evolved at Oxford University hundreds of years ago. Making sense of the behavior in a particular legislature thus often requires an understanding of the unwritten rules that constitute legislative customs.

Electoral System　As discussed in Chapter 4, democracies using the proportional representation system are often very different from those employing the single-member-district system familiar to U.S. voters. Proportional representation makes it possible for a party with a small base of support to get a foothold in the national legislature (since the system grants legislative seats in proportion to each party's share of the popular vote in multimembered legislative districts). Winning a legislative seat in the single-member-district system requires that the candidate receive more votes than any other candidate. Thus, a system using proportional representation would be expected to have a greater diversity of parties than would a single-member-district electoral arrangement.

Evidence suggests that the choice between these two electoral systems affects legislatures. A study of one U.S. state (Illinois) compared the state legislature's ideological diversity before and after Illinois discarded its proportional representation system in 1970. The study is unusual because it is based on a comparison across time rather than on a comparison of different countries. (It is difficult to draw conclusions about the effect of such factors as electoral laws when making cross-country comparisons because cultural, economic, and other differences may be responsible for observed differences that *appear* to be caused by differences in the electoral systems.)

7.3

Legislative Violence

Anyone listening to heated debates in the U.S. Senate is struck by certain rules of etiquette that lead senators to preface a stinging attack on an opponent's position with an extremely polite opening. For example, "I believe that my distinguished friend from [New York, Mississippi] is dead wrong." If he or she opens with "my *very* distinguished colleague," it probably means that the disagreement is more intense.

It was thus very controversial when Representative Joe Wilson, a Republican from South Carolina, shouted "You lie!" during President Obama's address to Congress on September 9, 2009. The president had stated that his health care reform plan would not extend benefits to illegal aliens, and the representative disagreed. He was officially reprimanded by the House for his outburst.

In other national legislatures, the standards for debate are far less restrained, and in some nations legislative disagreement can get totally out of hand. In 1991, a Conservative Canadian MP expressed his opposition to the arguments of Sheila Copps, a New Democratic Party leader, by calling her a "slut." In

December 2010, members of the South Korean parliament became remarkably violent during a debate over a trade agreement with the United States. Chairs were thrown, fistfights broke out, and one legislator was hospitalized after a colleague hit him with a hammer. (See the photo below.)

Chung Sung-Jun/Getty Images

Photo of fight in South Korean legislature

The researcher concluded that the ideological diversity of the legislature diminished considerably after the introduction of the single-member-district system.*

A more recent study of the German *Bundestag* suggested that electoral-system factors affect how important constituency service is to legislators. In Germany, some members of the *Bundestag* (the lower house) are elected through proportional representation, and the others are elected in single-member districts. Once elected, members seek committee appointments that they expect will help them win reelection. The study found that members elected on the basis of voters' choices among *party lists* (the PR system) seek appointments to legislative committees that allow them to serve the party platform, whereas members elected under the single-member-district system gravitate to committees that allow them to work for their geographically based constituencies.[22] Thus, when members get their seats in parliament as a result of voters choosing their *party*, they are less interested in constituent service activities, but those activities become vital for members chosen directly by the voters.

* See Greg D. Adams, "Legislative Effects of Single-Member vs. Multi-Member Districts," *American Journal of Political Science* 40, no. 1 (February 1996): 129–144.

REPRESENTATION

Most of us naturally think of legislators as *representing* the citizens who elected them; most legislators are even given the title of "representative." But legislatures can make laws and perform other basic legislative functions while acting in ways that have little to do with representation. Even when legislators purport to act as representatives, they may "represent" in very different ways.

Three Models of Representation

The Delegate Model   Perhaps the simplest approach to representation is described by the **delegate model**. A legislator acting in this manner will make decisions largely on the basis of the expressed wishes of constituents, acting as their spokesperson. If a clear majority of a legislator's district favors (or opposes) a particular proposal, the legislator's decision is made. Thus, we would expect a senator from a U.S. farm state or a member of the Canadian Parliament from rural Saskatchewan to favor subsidies for farmers.

Nevertheless, it is difficult for a legislator to act as a delegate when constituents are equally divided (about abortion, for example) or when few voters have expressed views about the issue at hand. Many national issues today, such as international trade policy, are often technical or complex, and voters rarely have clear positions. Acting as a delegate is also difficult when the legislator's own views differ from those of his or her constituents.

The Trustee Model   Should legislators who deeply believe that abortion or capital punishment is morally unacceptable vote against their own principles when their constituents feel differently? In these or other situations, a legislator may make decisions as his or her own judgment dictates, with little regard for the opinions of constituents. Such a legislator acts as a trustee.

Following the **trustee model**, legislators may reason that the voters selected them not only for their specific campaign promises but also for their wisdom and reasoning ability. To make decisions entirely on the basis of what the constituents say, disregarding one's own judgment would be cheating the constituents out of the best job of representing that the legislator could do. Hence, the trustee acts in accordance with his or her own views of the issues faced in legislative decisions.*

---

* An important contemporary political theorist has suggested that a legislative representative in a democracy has a special obligation to be *honest*. Mark Warren recently wrote that "the representative's role is, in part, to provide citizens with the information they need to judge when they should trust and when they should more actively participate in political decision making. The representative can fill this role only if he is worthy of ... trust in the veracity of his words and deeds. A representative who is not trustworthy in this sense also denies citizens their rightful participation in public judgments." Thus, the ideal representative is honest in revealing his or her stands on policies, and the influences that affect his or her decisions, enabling citizens to judge whether or not the representative is acting in their interests. See Mark Warren, "Democracy and Deceit: Regulating Appearances of Corruption," *American Journal of Political Science* 50 (January 2006): 160–174.

The Politico Model   Many legislators follow a mixed approach, sometimes called the **politico model**. On some issues and at some times, these legislators will act as delegates; in other situations, they will choose the trustee approach. In both cases they are representing, by some definition, but their behavior is rather different.

Choices among Roles

A legislator's choice of exactly *how* to represent may reflect his or her philosophical position, the political culture of the society, and, of course, the legislator's judgment about the impact that adopting different roles would have on electoral success. For example, if a legislator feels that—by virtue of education, intelligence, or wisdom—he or she is better suited to make public policy choices than is the average citizen, the legislator will naturally tend toward a trustee role. Legislators who see everyone as equally qualified to make judgments will have more sympathy with the delegate model. Different views regarding the basis for government decisions also come into play. Some argue that decisions are largely a matter of scientific study and research, and others emphasize the role of different preferences. The first approach suggests a trustee role, whereas the latter is consistent with the role of delegate.

A study of members of the U.S. House of Representatives who pursued a Senate seat suggests that those who were successful in winning elections adopted more of a delegate role than those who were not. Using an innovative research strategy, Wayne Francis and Lawrence Kenny compared the ideological positions of House members' districts with the ideological positions in the whole state; they found that House members who ran successful statewide campaigns for the Senate usually changed their own ideologies to match the ideological position of the state. Those House members seeking Senate seats who maintained the ideological positions common in their home districts more often failed in the statewide election. This evidence argues that successful U.S. legislators frequently act as delegates, strategically adopting their constituents' policy positions.[23]

PARTY RESPONSIBILITY AND LEGISLATIVE BEHAVIOR

Political parties are critically important in the legislatures of virtually all democracies. Each legislator is usually a member of a party, and all the members from each party form a *caucus*, or *conference*, meeting together from time to time. The relationships among legislators who are members of the same party often have a great impact on what happens in the legislature.

As we discussed in Chapter 5, political parties vary greatly according to their internal cohesion and central control. Not surprisingly, then, there are corresponding differences in the amount of power that different parties wield over their national legislators. In Germany and Great Britain, for example, members of the legislature are quite constrained by party discipline; that is to say, each legislator usually votes on important legislation in accordance with the wishes of his or her party's

DEBATE IN THE BRITISH HOUSE OF COMMONS In this image made from television, Members of Parliament attend to a session in the House of Commons, in London, Friday, March 11, 2005, during a debate over the government's controversial anti-terrorism powers.

leadership. In other countries, such as the United States and Italy, party leaders have limited influence on the decisions of their members.

The German and British systems are thus said to have **responsible parties**, meaning that the voters can hold the major parties accountable for their performance because the party position is generally supported by all or most of the legislators from that party. Party discipline and responsible parties are highly valued by many political analysts who contrast that arrangement with the relatively undisciplined parties of the United States.

On first impression, the idea of legislators being dominated by their parties' leaders may be unappealing. Most of us disagree with some positions taken by the parties we support, and we often admire legislators who act contrary to the "party line." However, it is well established among most political scientists that the *absence* of party responsibility leads to very negative consequences.

Where party leaders have only limited influence over the policy choices of their members in the legislature, legislators are more easily drawn to represent narrow special interests. In contrast, if voters and interest groups realize that party responsibility is strong and that therefore most legislators will vote in accordance with the party leadership's wishes, there is less incentive to try to influence individual members. They will simply vote the party line, regardless of the influence exerted by lobbyists and contributors.

A recent study of several Latin American countries makes a strong case for party discipline in terms of its effect on national budget management. Two political scientists examined the differences among these countries with respect to the extent to which the "personal vote" was important in determining citizens' choices of legislators. Where the party leadership has the power to control nominations, the "personal vote" is low, and it is high where the leadership is weaker. The researchers predicted that where citizens made voting choices on the basis of *candidates* instead of *parties*, the politicians elected to the legislature had less incentive to concern themselves about the national interest in budget stability, instead demanding policies that helped their districts even if they were wasteful in terms of the impact on national economic conditions. The findings confirmed their prediction: countries in which the "personal vote" is a major factor tended to have more severe budget deficits than those in which party responsibility was stronger.[24]

Moreover, the proponents of strong party influence contend that such distractions as a legislator's personality, appearance, or personal habits are less important when voters know that the party effectively controls each legislator's votes. Instead, voters will focus on meaningful policy differences that define the competing parties, making their voting choices on the basis of the policies they prefer. When this happens, most political scientists argue that democracy is on stronger ground because the citizens' votes communicate what they want government to do, not simply how they feel about candidates' personalities and misadventures.

Three kinds of factors affect the extent to which party responsibility is achieved. First, the cohesion of the "party-in-the-electorate" will affect the degree of party discipline in the legislature. The American Democratic Party through most of the twentieth century is perhaps the most often cited example of a party whose divisions among its supporters often translated into divisions among its members elected to Congress. For decades, the Democrats had great electoral success in the American South (partly because of the legacy of the Republican-led Civil War) while maintaining support among most American liberals in other parts of the country. They were often severely divided as a result, and Democratic members of Congress from Southern states usually voted *against* the wishes of their party's leadership. Many French and Italian parties are also divided for similar reasons. On the other hand, voters supporting the British Labour Party or the Swedish Socialists are, relatively speaking, much less divided on issues, and the party's members in the Parliament thus vote with much greater unity and discipline.

Second, legislative rules and practices and national laws regarding political parties may be instituted to increase (or decrease) party control. If party leaders are to enforce discipline, they need to be able to apply sanctions that affect the political success of individual legislators. Whenever party organizations can grant or withdraw committee assignments, campaign funds, and national party support for a member's campaign, party discipline is likely to be high. British parties are able to use those and other sanctions, whereas American parties have much less leverage. Particularly since most U.S. legislators know that they must raise large sums of money *on their own* to compete in a close race, they have little reason to abide by the wishes of party leaders on policy questions. Where a legislator's political success depends more on pleasing a few important constituents or interest groups than on following the party platform, party discipline is diminished.

In the United States, the existence of *primaries* is the greatest factor detracting from party responsibility. A primary election is simply an election in which citizens vote to determine which candidate will be the nominee of their party in the *general election*, which usually takes place some months later. Before primaries were instituted (over a century ago), party leaders themselves selected the nominees, and they took each potential nominee's loyalty to the party platform into account when selecting him or her as a candidate. After primaries became the main method of selecting nominees, individuals could simply label themselves "Democrats" or "Republicans" and then get the nomination by winning in the primary. If he or she then wins the general election, the new legislator will owe very little to the party leadership. (Outside the United States, this approach to selecting candidates is very rare.)

Finally, party discipline is often self-imposed since legislators perceive the propriety of voting in accordance with their parties. The strength of tradition supporting party discipline in Great Britain leads many MPs to place great weight on party loyalty, and it affects their behavior even when the specific sanctions enforcing party discipline may not be so critical.

THE CHANGING ROLE OF MODERN LEGISLATURES

The role of legislative institutions changed considerably in most industrial democracies during the twentieth century. Legislatures were initially seen as the predominant power center in many democratic governments—as suggested, for example, by the fact that the framers of the U.S. Constitution devoted Article I to the Congress (not the presidency). Before the modern era, ideas for government policy often originated in legislatures themselves, and the executive role was correspondingly much less powerful.

Three related factors have diminished the prominence of legislatures in modern government. First, the growth of bureaucracies—one of the most universal developments of contemporary politics—inevitably displaces some of the influence that legislators would otherwise have in initiating policies. Proposals for new programs and changes in existing programs most often originate in the hundreds of agencies set up to administer the modern state. The size of the bureaucracy in most developed nations makes it unavoidable that **policy initiation** shifts to administrators. This tendency is most pronounced in Japan, France, and other countries in which a highly trained and knowledgeable bureaucracy dominates decisions made by the legislature and the executive. Second, modern government is often complicated by the technological nature of many public policy decisions and programs. Legislators are confronted with a dizzying level of detail and with subject matter about which they, as generalists, necessarily know very little. Legislators must allocate their scarce time and energy to matters of high visibility or high concern to their constituents, and thus most policy decisions are made without the knowledge or the direct participation of elected legislators.

Finally, the growing importance of international cooperation, the global economy, and the increasingly complicated nature of international relations in the modern world inevitably amplify the chief executive's importance in most political systems. Chief executives are necessarily the focal points of foreign policy in most countries, and the importance of international events and relationships thus makes legislatures less dominant than in earlier eras. Nevertheless, legislatures remain the most straightforward institutional embodiment of democratic principles.

◆ ◆ ◆

Key Terms and Concepts _____

bicameralism
committee systems
constituent service
delegate model
dual democratic legitimacy
folkways
law of $1/n$

ombudsmen
parliamentary systems
policy initiation
politico model
presidential system
responsible parties
trustee model

DISCUSSION QUESTIONS

1. *What makes legislative institutions distinctive?*
2. *What are the arguments for and against bicameralism?*
3. *Under what circumstances can a presidential system be politically less stable than a parliamentary system?*
4. *What is party responsibility, and why is it important in legislative behavior?*
5. *What are some different ways that legislators can claim to represent their constituents?*

Notes _____

1. This monumental American political novel was written in 1946 by Robert Penn Warren (New York: Harcourt Brace Jovanovich). The quotation appears on pp. 145–146. A film based on the book won best picture in 1950 and was remade in 2006 starring Jude Law, Kate Winslet, and Sean Penn.
2. George Will, *Restoration: Congress, Term Limits, and the Recovery of Deliberative Democracy* (New York: Free Press, 1992), p. 1.
3. Gilman Ostrander, *The Rights of Man in America* (Columbia: University of Missouri Press, 1960), p. 88. For more recent discussions of natural law, see Mark Graham, *Joseph Fuchs on Natural Law* (Washington, DC: Georgetown University Press, 2002), and Jean Porter, *Nature as Reason: A Thomistic Theory of the Natural Law* (Grand Rapids, MI: Wm. B. Erdmans Publishing, 2005).
4. See Nelson W. Polsby, "Legislatures," in *Handbook of Political Science*, eds. Fred I. Greenstein and Nelson Polsby (Reading, MA: Addison-Wesley, 1975), pp. 257–319; and the entry for "legislatures" in *The Blackwell Encyclopedia of Legislative Institutions* (Oxford, UK: Blackwell, 1987), pp. 329–333.
5. Gregory Mahler, "Israel's New Electoral System: Effects on Politics and Policy," *Middle East Review of International Affairs* 1 (July 1997).
6. Ibid., emphasis added.
7. Emanuele Ottolenghi, "Why Direct Election Failed in Israel," *Journal of Democracy* 12 (2001): 108–109.
8. Juan J. Linz, "Presidential or Parliamentary Democracy: Does It Make a Difference?" in *The Failure of Presidential Democracy: The Case of Latin America*, eds. Juan Linz and Arturo Valenzuela (Baltimore: Johns Hopkins University Press, 1994), pp. 3–90.
9. Ibid.
10. Arturo Valenzuela, "Party Politics and the Crisis of Presidentialism in Chile: A Proposal for a Parliamentary Form of Government," in *The Failure of Presidential Democracy: The Case of Latin America*, eds. Juan Linz and Arturo Valenzuela (Baltimore: Johns Hopkins University Press, 1994), p. 141.
11. See Sherzod Abdukadirov. "The Impact of Institutional Design on Non-Democratic Regimes: A Case for Parliamentary System in Central Asia?" Paper presented at the annual meeting of the Midwest Political Science Association, Palmer House Hotel, Chicago, April 12, 2007.
12. Scott Mainwaring, "Brazil: Weak Parties, Feckless Democracy," in *Building Democratic Institutions: Party Systems in Latin America*, eds. Scott Mainwaring and Timothy R. Scully (Stanford, CA: Stanford University Press, 1994), p. 392. See also Tsebelis, G. , "Decision Making in Political Systems: Veto

Players in Presidentialism, Parliamentarism, Multicameralism, and Multipartyism," *British Journal of Political Science* 25 (1995): 289–325.

13. See Mark P. Jones, Sebastian Saiegh, Pablo T. Spiller, and Mariano Tommasi, "Amateur Legislators—Professional Politicians: The Consequences of Party-Centered Electoral Rules in a Federal System," *American Journal of Political Science* 46 (July 2002): 656–669.

14. Woodrow Wilson, *Congressional Government* (Boston: Houghton Mifflin, 1885), p. 57.

15. The idea was formalized by Weingast, Barry R. , Kenneth A. Shepsle, and Christopher Johnsen, "The Political Economy of Benefits and Costs: A Neoclassical Approach to Distributive Politics," *Journal of Political Economy* 89 (August 1981): 642–664.

16. Bradbury, John C. , and William M. Crain, "Legislative Organization and Government Spending: Cross-Country Evidence," *Journal of Public Economics* 82 (December 2001): 309–325.

17. Chen, Jowei , and Neil Malhotra, "The Law of k/n: The Effect of Chamber Size on Government Spending in Bicameral Legislatures," *American Political Science Review* 101 (November 2007): 657–676. See David M. Primo and James M. Snyder, Jr. "Distributive Politics and the Law of 1/n." *Journal of Politics* 70 (2008): 477–486.

18. See Andrew Reynolds, "Women in the Legislatures and Executives of the World: Knocking at the Highest Glass Ceiling," *World Politics* 51 (1999): 547–572; Lane Kenworthy and Melissa Malami, "Gender Inequality in Political Representation: A Worldwide Comparative Analysis," *Social Forces* 78 (1999): 235–269; and Alan Siaroff, "Women's Representation in Legislatures and Cabinets in Industrial Democracies," *International Political Science Review* 21 (2000): 197–215.

19. Donald R. Matthews, *U.S. Senators and Their World* (New York: Random House, 1960).

20. Ibid., pp. 93–94.

21. David W. Rohde, Norman J. Ornstein, and Robert L. Peabody, "Political Change and Legislative Norms in the U.S. Senate, 1957–1974," in *Studies of Congress*, ed. Glenn R. Parker (Washington, DC: CQ Press, 1985), p. 150.

22. Thomas Stratmann and Martin Baur, "Plurality Rule, Proportional Representation, and the German *Bundestag*: How Incentives to Pork-Barrel Differ across Electoral Systems," *American Journal of Political Science* 46 (July 2002): 506–514.

23. See Wayne L. Francis and Lawrence W. Kenny, "Position Shifting in Pursuit of Higher Office," *American Journal of Political Science* 40 (August 1996): 768–786.

24. Mark Hallerberg and Patrik Marier, "Executive Authority, the Personal Vote, and Budget Discipline in Latin American and Caribbean Countries," *American Journal of Political Science* 48 (July 2004): 571–587.

In August, 2010, Chilean President Sebastian Pinera waved a note, written by one of the miners trapped deep inside a collapsed mine: "All 33 of us are fine in the shelter." The miners were rescued four months later.

CHAPTER 8

Executive Institutions, Political Leadership, and Bureaucracy

- The Functions of Executive Institutions
- Kinds of Executive Institutions
- Limits on Executive Power
- Approaches to Executive Leadership
- Bureaucratic Institutions
- What Is Bureaucracy?

- Bureaucratic Functions
- The Growth of Bureaucracy
- Bureaucracy Evaluated
- Bureaucracy and Democracy
- Can Bureaucracy Be Improved?
- Executives and Bureaucracies —From Policy Leadership to Policy Implementation

Although legislative institutions make the law (in most systems), their decisions would have little impact in the absence of executive leadership and without the activities of bureaucratic institutions. In nearly all political systems, developed and developing, the chief executive officer is the most widely recognized and most powerful governmental figure. He or she is the focus of media attention, the villain when economies and foreign relations go sour, and the hero when the country experiences success. And virtually everything depends on how well the bureaucracy works.

This chapter is divided into three parts. First, we will examine the nature and functions of the executive *institution* in modern political systems. Second, we will discuss the important concept of *leadership*. Finally, we will explore the nature of bureaucracy and how it can be controlled and improved.

The Functions of Executive Institutions

Deliberation and action are naturally contrasting processes. Legislative institutions are well designed for the former. They provide a setting in which opposing points of view may be expressed and debated, and they usually facilitate detailed consideration of major policy decisions through committee and staff discussions. Yet the same feature that makes them ideally suited to deliberate—the sharing of power among a large number of representatives with diverse perspectives—weakens their ability to carry out programs and policies. The nearly universal establishment of executive institutions reflects the need to place responsibility for deliberation and policy execution in different institutions. At the same time, there is often considerable tension and competition between a government's executive and legislative branches because each tends to involve itself in functions that the other considers to be its own.

Certain functions of government are nearly always performed by executive institutions. These tasks have one aspect in common: *They are best accomplished under the authority of a coherent, unified institution empowered to act quickly and decisively.*

Diplomacy

Even most legislators agree that **diplomacy** must be primarily under executive control. Although the German *Bundestag* may hold debates on trade policy and issues raised at the United Nations, the day-to-day implementation of foreign policy is the responsibility of the German Chancellor and her advisers. For one thing, diplomacy often involves negotiation, and it is all but impossible for a multimember legislature to negotiate with another country. The give-and-take of effective negotiation requires that the decision maker be able to respond quickly and decisively to new demands and concessions from the other side, and legislatures simply cannot work with sufficient coherence or quickness.

Secrecy is a more controversial rationale for the central executive role in diplomacy, but most observers accept it in some measure. The delicate maneuvering of Secretary of State Hillary Clinton during the creation of a no-fly zone in Libya in 2011 was necessarily done behind closed doors as she worked to build a multinational coalition. There have been several instances in which American, French, and British executive branch officials, among others, have worked to win the release of hostages, and secrecy was critical in each case. In such situations, the other side could never be allowed to know what concessions the executive may or may not have been ready to make. Even the idea that negotiations are underway can produce a public reaction that destroys the proceedings. Although executive control of diplomacy does not prevent all "leaks," virtually all observers feel that diplomacy would be severely hampered if a multimember legislature were in charge.

Even when secrecy is not an issue, diplomatic communication is simpler when only executive officials are involved. Summit meetings provide an opportunity for political leaders to explore mutual concerns, and these events often lay the foundation for more formal treaty negotiations. The flexible, personal communication that makes summits productive can take place only among executives and their staffs. Moreover, in case of an international crisis, some single official must be clearly designated as the person to contact.

Emergency Leadership

All countries need **emergency leadership** from time to time, and it is almost always the responsibility of the chief executive to coordinate and manage the governmental response. Why do we rely on chief executives in national emergencies?

First, the executive can act quickly, and he or she is in a position to coordinate governmental activities. Second, national security sometimes requires extraordinary actions, some of which might not be acceptable or even legal under normal conditions. Most well-known, perhaps, was U.S. President Abraham Lincoln's suspension of some basic constitutional rights during the Civil War. When that kind of emergency action is necessary, only the executive has the legitimacy needed to make critical decisions. In the aftermath of September 11, actions taken to strengthen domestic security by President George W. Bush's first attorney general, John Ashcroft, were controversial as well, with many citizens claiming that constitutional protections were weakened.

In the developing world, chief executives often cite real or perceived dangers and emergencies to justify their power. Third World leaders often defend tyrannical powers by pointing to the challenges of economic development and the threat of political instability. The same holds when developing countries are involved in war (Iran and Iraq, for example) or are threatened by outside intervention (Nicaragua).

Budget Formulation

A government budget has been called a set of "goals with price tags attached."[1] In most countries **budget formulation**, or at least a budget proposal, is an executive responsibility, and for very good reasons. Legislators represent specific states, provinces, or constituencies and often develop close ties with a few groups or interests. Strictly speaking, it would not be *rational* for a legislator to consider the benefits and the costs of a spending decision from a national perspective.* When a particular expenditure is targeted for his or her state or district, that legislator's judgment will be driven by a key fact: *His or her constituents will receive virtually all of the benefit created by the expenditure while paying only a small portion of the costs* (since those are divided among the whole nation's taxpayers). Because all legislators face these same facts, it is not realistic to expect them to pursue fiscal responsibility in budget decisions.

The need for executive responsibility for the budget proposal became all too clear in the United States during the early years of the twentieth century. Before

---

* See A Closer Look 7.2 in Chapter 7 for a discussion of the "law of 1/n."

The Dilemmas of Executive Branch Secrecy in Wartime: A Tragic Incident in World War II

Early in World War II, British intelligence officials successfully developed the capacity to decipher coded communications from German military sources. A Polish mathematician, Marian Rejewski, had employed advanced mathematics as early as 1932 to break code from Enigma, the name the Allies gave to the early German code machine, and he shared this information with the British in the years leading up to the war's outbreak in 1939. The British thus had access to German communications, obtaining information about where U-boats were deployed, German invasion plans, and, eventually, Luftwaffe bombing targets.

Prime Minister Winston Churchill was keenly interested in the information obtained from the German code system. However, he was also aware that he could never permit the Germans to learn that the British had succeeded in breaking it. If German officials realized that the British had succeeded in gaining access to top secret German military communications, they would change their code, and it would then be worthless to the British. The dilemma was stark: Churchill desperately wanted continued access to the intelligence, and he could not take actions that revealed to the Germans that he had broken their code.

The British worked out methods to conceal that they had broken the code while still acting on the secrets they had obtained. For example, when they learned where some German submarines or supply ships were headed, they were careful not to use air strikes against them unless they could do something to make the Germans believe that the British had learned about the location of the German ships through some method other than intercepting coded messages. Sometimes Churchill ordered British scout planes to fly in areas where German observers would see them, creating the impression that it was a lucky sighting by one of these planes that led to the sinking of German ships by British air strikes.

The most controversial decision that Churchill made regarding the German codes had to do with the German bombing of the town of Coventry in November 1940. Frederick Winterbotham, in a 1974 book entitled *The Ultra Secret*, reported that Churchill had knowledge of the German bombing raid on Coventry some 48 hours before the attack occurred. There was certainly time to evacuate much of the city and to take measures to avert the bombing. However, doing so would have alerted the

© AP Photo

Coventry Cathedral lies in ruins November 16, 1940, after the Nazi bombing attack of November 14 on Coventry, England. The entire roof was brought down in heaps of debris, foreground, by the high explosive.

Germans that their codes had been broken. According to Winterbotham's account, Churchill refused to alert the city. The bombings took place, killing more than 1,200 people and destroying over 4,000 homes.

Some historians (see the books by Peter Calvocoressi and Ronald Lewin, noted below) argue that the German communication that the British had intercepted was not as clear as has been often claimed. There may have been some doubt in Churchill's mind about whether Coventry was really the target, and thus it may have been this doubt that prevented him from ordering an evacuation. However, it is clear that Churchill placed a very high priority on preventing the Germans from learning that his intelligence service had broken their codes, and it is quite possible that he withheld information that could have minimized the loss of life from some attacks. Most historians agree that the British success in keeping Germany from learning about their success in code breaking may have shortened the war by as much as a year. But the dilemma created by the need for secrecy has rarely been as excruciating as it was in this case.

See Frederick Winterbotham, *The Ultra Secret* (New York: HarperCollins, 1974); Peter Calvocoressi, *Top Secret Ultra* (New York: Pantheon Books, 1980); and Ronald Lewin, *Ultra Goes to War* (New York: McGraw-Hill, 1978), for more about this famous example of military secrecy.

1921, the budget of the United States was simply a patchwork quilt of unrelated acts of Congress that authorized expenditures and established tax rates. The budget process was uncoordinated and ultimately irresponsible. It was as though a family decided to let the husband buy the car, the wife buy the house, and the children buy the food and the furniture—all working with no information about what the others were spending. Even members of the U.S. Congress agreed that the central control of budget preparation was needed, and the Budget Act of 1921 was passed, creating a new executive power.*

Control of Military Forces

Almost everywhere, the chief executive is the person primarily in charge of the nation's armed forces. It is also true, at least in democratic systems, that chief executives must usually consult with the national legislature (for example, the 1973 War Powers Act authorizes the U.S. Congress to cut off funding for military activities that extend beyond a 60-day period). Nevertheless, virtually all chief executives have a central role in control of military forces. There can be no ambiguity regarding the authority to act if a situation demands a military response or even if the threat of a response is important.

Investing the chief executive with supreme authority over the military is important for domestic reasons as well. In less politically developed nations, military leaders have frequently seized government power through **coups d'état**. When the troops' first loyalty is to their officers, military leaders can often displace the civilian government on the grounds that national security demands it. In some cases, a chief executive's very attempt to assert control over the military leads to his or her overthrow by a military coup.

Chief Administrator

Most chief executives also are **chief administrators**; they have primary responsibility for managing the agencies that implement government programs and laws. A centralized decision maker must be in charge of staffing, accounting, planning, and coordinating the activities of government agencies. Legislatures are ill suited to those tasks for the same reasons that they cannot effectively direct diplomacy or overall budget formulation: Sound management requires a comprehensive, coherent, authoritative voice that multimember legislatures do not have.

Moreover, their managerial duties inevitably give chief executives opportunities to change policies. When appointing officials to leadership posts in departments and agencies, a chief executive selects individuals who share his or her policy preferences and who can act on those preferences in setting priorities. Every new American president, for example, appoints hundreds of high-ranking federal officials. Even when the powers and duties of executive-branch agencies are established by legislation, there are usually numerous opportunities for

---

* It should be noted, however, that the U.S. president's budget proposal still must be enacted by Congress; the president simply proposes a comprehensive budget.

interpretation, prioritizing, and setting new initiatives within the framework of that legislation. The executive can therefore shape policy by making key appointments to the bureaucracy.

In Great Britain and in several other European nations, the chief executive has greater control of appointment power than in the United States, where the independently elected Congress must approve many important appointments. In part, this is because executive and legislative power is merged in most other democracies (the prime minister is elected or confirmed by the parliament) and the notions of separation of powers and checks and balances are not well developed. Also, in Third World nations, with typically weak legislatures, the executive has a fairly free hand in making appointments.

Although the specific features of executive powers to manage administrative agencies vary across different systems, the main point is that those powers inevitably give the executive opportunities to shape policy. The strongest executives exploit those opportunities to the fullest, applying their powers to advance their political preferences and to secure their continued support. It is simply not possible for a chief executive to have comprehensive administrative authority without also having substantial power to affect policy itself.

Policy Initiation

Although legislative action establishes government policy in most systems, the chief executive plays a prominent role in *initiating* policy.

In Great Britain, all important policies are initiated by the prime minister and the cabinet. A similar relationship exists in other parliamentary democracies, such as Germany and Canada. In Third World countries, legislatures tend to be thoroughly dominated by the executive branch. Even the U.S. president, who often faces a Congress dominated by the opposing party, is called the *chief legislator* since most bills that become law begin as presidential proposals.

Symbolic Leadership

Chief executives also act as **symbolic leaders** of their countries, a role that transcends their specific powers and functions. In times of crisis, it is easier to look to a specific human being as leader than to look to a committee or an assembly.

Charles de Gaulle galvanized the French and forestalled national disintegration in 1958 when France was rocked by a constitutional crisis and unrest in Algeria, and Winston Churchill effectively motivated and unified the British during World War II, as did Franklin D. Roosevelt in the United States during the Great Depression and through all but the last months of the same war. In each instance, those countries needed strong leaders to rally the loyalty and energy of their citizens, and their chief executives led them as no other public figures could have. More recently, some Third World leaders have become symbols to their people of the struggle for democracy. Two noteworthy examples are South Africa's Nelson Mandela and Myanmar's Daw Aung San Suu Kyi (a Nobel Peace Prize winner whom the military arrested and prevented from becoming prime minister after her party won a parliamentary majority in 1990; she was finally released in November 2010).

Kinds of Executive Institutions

Although each country's chief executive is unique in some respects, all can be usefully classified on the basis of two characteristics: (1) the way in which they are selected and (2) their relationship to the legislature. These two factors have a great bearing on how powerful the executive is and on how he or she performs executive functions.

Hereditary Monarchies

There are only some three dozen countries that currently have hereditary monarchs, and in many of those the monarchy has only a ceremonial or a symbolic role. Because they are selected on the basis of their parents' identities, there is usually little doubt about which person succeeds the current monarch. This is one of the benefits of the hereditary monarch system: The clear line of succession means that violent clashes over leadership can be avoided when a reigning monarch dies.

Although the hereditary monarch was the most typical chief executive in premodern times, monarchy has largely been eclipsed by more democratic types of executives. Modern political life involves widespread public involvement and participation, and—although modernity does not always make democracy inevitable—the chief executive must increasingly be seen as legitimate in ways that hereditary monarchs cannot be. Political history is thus filled with rejections of monarchy, including not only the American, French, and Russian revolutions but also the fall of the German kaiser and the shah of Iran.

Most surviving hereditary monarchies share power with legislative assemblies. Classic monarchies assumed power over all government functions, including lawmaking and even judging, but that simple arrangement has all but vanished. The monarch's powers in Great Britain, Belgium, the Netherlands, Sweden, and Norway have been lost, making them largely ceremonial. Monarchs have maintained substantial political authority in only a few countries, most notably in Morocco, Jordan, Saudi Arabia, and Kuwait.

Directly Elected Chief Executives

The presidents of Mexico, Colombia, the Philippines, the United States, and France are examples of directly elected chief executives. This method of selection creates a potentially powerful institution because the executive is then normally the only official chosen by the entire nation's electorate. (In fact, the French president is sometimes referred to as an "elected monarch" to underscore the tremendous powers he enjoys.) No individual legislator or judge can claim the legitimacy accorded to a directly elected chief executive.

Chief Executives in Parliamentary Systems

As noted in the previous chapter, the parliamentary system is the most common form of democratic government. The chief executive in such a system is elected not by the citizens but by the members of the legislature. Since the same parliamentary majority that selects its leader as prime minister is also able (by definition) to enact legislative proposals, parliamentary chief executives may be far less constrained by legislative preferences. However, a parliamentary chief executive sitting atop a shifting and uncertain multiparty coalition in the parliament can be less secure than an independently elected chief executive who has to enact policy through a separate legislative branch.*

Nondemocratic Executive Institutions

Executives tend to be strong in industrialized democracies because the executive office in such systems is at the center of a tremendous array of public programs and institutions and because these executives are highly visible in the mass media. Executive power is also dominant in developing societies, but for different reasons. Sometimes an executive is the national leader of an all-powerful ruling party, while in other cases he or she secures power by controlling the country's military forces. As we have seen, chief executives may be former heroes of wars for independence or revolution (Vietnam's Ho Chi Minh or China's Mao Zedong) or may have power and prestige by virtue of a religious position. In many of these cases, the individual is more of a national leader than a true executive, perhaps performing the function of symbolic leadership but otherwise having little to do with essential executive functions, which may be performed by other, less visible members of the executive establishment.

Moreover, legislative and judicial institutions are often less influential in nondemocratic and developing nations. They generally have less legitimacy, and many of them have been changed so often that they have not become an established part of the government. The executive, by contrast, is able to apply force and to personify the traditions and values of the dominant culture. Some 20 nations have no legislative assemblies at all, and many others have notoriously weak legislatures. The executive is thus dominant in these systems because the other institutions of government are weak and undeveloped. In the Third World, government power is primarily *executive* power.

---

* Of course, other factors—such as culture, a candidate's personality, and foreign policy events—are involved in determining how often the executive office changes hands. Israel has one of the most fractionalized party systems in the democratic world, for example, but it has had only 12 prime ministers since the system's founding in 1948. Many observers speculate that Israeli coalitions tend to stay together longer partly because of the perceived threat from the country's neighbors.

LIMITS ON EXECUTIVE POWER

Despite the substantial authority that they hold, executives in most countries—particularly executives in democratic systems—face limits on their power. In a classic study of the U.S. presidency, Richard Neustadt concluded that, even with all the president's legal and political powers, presidential power is simply the "power to persuade."[2] President Harry Truman certainly understood this when he chuckled over the likely experiences of his successor, General Dwight Eisenhower: "He'll sit here," Truman would remark (tapping his desk for emphasis), "and he'll say, 'Do this! Do that!' *And nothing will happen.* Poor Ike—It won't be a bit like the Army. He'll find it very frustrating."[3] Chief executives in other nations have doubtless had the same experience. Having achieved the most sought-after position in their countries, they often conclude that their powers are nothing like what they imagined.

Of course, some executives are more powerful than others, but the phenomenon of limited executive power is nearly universal. Why do modern executives so often find that their power is more limited than they expected?

Term Limits

The length and number of terms for many chief executives are restricted by constitutions or basic laws. The Twenty-Second Amendment to the U.S. Constitution (ratified on March 1, 1951) limits the president to two four-year terms. Many Latin American nations—including Mexico, Venezuela, El Salvador, Uruguay, and Chile—limit their presidents to one term. Near the end of that term limit, the incumbent often sees his or her influence diminish somewhat since the power to reward and punish supporters is coming to an end. (This is often termed the "lame duck" period.) The French president may serve two long (seven-year) terms, making that position potentially more powerful.

How Sources of Executive Power Create Limits on the Exercise of Executive Power

Paradoxically, the source from which an executive gains his or her power often constrains what he or she can do with it. An executive whose power is based on personal charisma, for example, finds it necessary to spend precious time and energy reinforcing the public's favorable perceptions. Such an executive cannot make decisions that could undermine his or her charisma. An executive whose authority is based primarily on citizens' respect for the law must avoid even the *appearance* of acting illegally. He or she will often find that those very laws restrict policy choices. (An executive whose power comes from charisma would not face this restriction.) The same point could be made about executives who draw their power from tradition or a sense of representativeness; they must continuously monitor the extent to which their actions erode the favorable perceptions that made their positions possible. Even a dictator holding power exclusively through military coercion avoids making choices that disturb the armed forces.

Examples abound of executives who lost power by exceeding these limits. While much of the world is familiar with controversies about U.S. presidents being accused of abusing their powers (Richard Nixon, Ronald Reagan, Bill Clinton, and George W. Bush can all be placed in this category), it is not only or even primarily an American phenomenon. In 2006, Thailand's Prime Minister Thaksin Shinawatra was in serious trouble despite having won a landslide election in 2005. He was accused of corruption, abuse of power, tax evasion, censoring the media, and other crimes. President Hosni Mubarak of Egypt left that country's presidency in 2011 after decades of widely reported abuses in office. In the last decade, top executive officials have been in serious legal and political trouble in Kuwait, South Korea, Spain, Haiti, Italy, South Africa, and Mexico.

Thus, although most executives have several sources of authority, maintaining power requires that they act in a prescribed manner. Their powers come with strings attached, and the most successful executives recognize that fact.

Governmental Institutions as Limits

A key characteristic of developed political systems is *institutional complexity*. Although most chief executives have formal authority over an array of institutions, the impression that one gets from looking at the "organizational chart"—that the executive's command is extensive and profound—is often misleading. Legislatures, agencies, courts, and commissions make modern, effective government possible, but they also check and constrain executive power.

For one thing, many government institutions have their own missions and often their own clientele interests. Legislators represent constituents or subnational units, and agencies are often associated with distinct groups (such as farmers, labor unions, or business organizations). Executives encounter resistance when they make policy choices that undermine the interests represented by those institutions.

In short, the institutions that a chief executive supervises are only partly controllable, and they must sometimes be accommodated to make and implement policy. They are in place—with their established ways of operating and their associated interests—long before a particular executive assumes office. He or she cannot treat those institutions as "blank slates" on which new programs and policy changes can be written. Even authoritarian political leaders usually have to pay heed to powerful institutions such as the military, organized business groups, established party leaders, and the clergy.

In developing political systems, the chief executive typically deals with a smaller number of weaker institutions. Legislatures, courts, and bureaucratic agencies usually exist, but they are normally much less influential, and citizens accord them much less respect as institutions. In a sense, chief executives in developing systems enjoy a greater latitude and freedom of decision than do their counterparts in the developed world. At the same time, the absence of effective governmental institutions limits the range and effect of what executives can accomplish. In short, when compared with their counterparts in developed nations, Third World executives are frequently stronger figures in weaker governments.

The Mass Media and Executive Power

Newspapers, radio, and television can serve as tools of executive power, and they can also severely limit it. As noted in Chapter 4, when the mass media are under the control of the government, they can be used to shape public sentiments and set the political agenda in ways helpful to those in power. Lenin, always an astute organizer and motivator of people, realized that a national newspaper could be a central tool in creating and maintaining support. The name of the paper he established for Soviet citizens, *Pravda*, means "truth," although *Pravda* was always far more concerned with ideological instruction than with accuracy. The Nazis in Germany—along with Marxist governments in China, North Korea, Cuba, and elsewhere—similarly used the mass media to strengthen the power of the political leadership.

In contrast, when the mass media are controlled by a diverse range of voices, "press reaction" can affect a chief executive's power position in a significant way. In 2003, British Prime Minister Tony Blair felt the impact of the media when a government expert on weapons, David Kelly, apparently killed himself after he was named as the source of a BBC story reporting that British analysis of weapons of mass destruction in Iraq had been distorted. The story, and the resulting suicide, considerably undermined Blair's authority.

Blair's experience with British newspapers and television coverage of his government led him to make some remarkably bitter statements. As he was leaving office in 2007, he gave a speech on the media. The following excerpts reveal that he developed strong views on the media during his time in 10 Downing Street:

> I am going to say something that few people in public life will say, but most know is absolutely true: a vast aspect of our jobs today—outside of the really major decisions, as big as anything else—is coping with the media, its sheer scale, weight and constant hyperactivity. At points, it literally overwhelms. Talk to senior people in virtually any walk of life today—business, military, public services, sport, even charities and voluntary organisations and they will tell you the same. People don't speak about it because, in the main, they are afraid to. But it is true, nonetheless, and those who have been around long enough, will also say it has changed significantly in the past years.

> … the fear of missing out means today's media, more than ever before, hunts in a pack. In these modes it is like a feral beast, just tearing people and reputations to bits. But no-one dares miss out.

> I do believe this relationship between public life and media is now damaged in a manner that requires repair. The damage saps the country's confidence and self-belief; it undermines its assessment of itself, its institutions; and above all, it reduces our capacity to take the right decisions, in the right spirit for our future.[4]

The explosion of Internet technology makes it increasingly difficult for any monopoly control of information to be secure. Chief executives cannot assume that their secrets will remain undercover when so many people have the ability to share information with millions of citizens almost instantly. As a result, media management has become a critically important skill for modern chief executives.

© Eddie Adams/AP Photo

THE SHOT SEEN ROUND THE WORLD Nguyen Ngoc Loan, then National Police Chief in South Vietnam, is shown executing a prisoner suspected of being a Viet Cong collaborator in 1968. The visual impact of this photo, among many others, reduced U.S. popular support for the war effort.

APPROACHES TO EXECUTIVE LEADERSHIP

The basic executive functions can be performed in widely different ways. Adolf Hitler, Franklin Roosevelt, Margaret Thatcher, Charles de Gaulle, and Saddam Hussein all performed most of the tasks of political executives, and all left a mark on history. Yet as leaders, they had little in common. Every chief executive is unique, and each faces distinctive problems and challenges, making it difficult to generalize. Nevertheless, we can identify some important factors that affect the ways in which executives operate; understanding these factors may help us make sense of the differences among executive leadership.

The *political culture* of the country, the *personality* of the individual, and *the way in which the executive attained power* are central influences on the nature of executive leadership. The prevailing ideology also may be critical in determining how a chief executive performs. The following categories describe approaches to leadership, but it should be noted that actual executives often exhibit aspects of several approaches or change from one to another during their tenure in office.

Sociologist Max Weber (1864–1920) discussed three kinds of authority in his classic work translated and published in English in 1947.[5] Although he focused primarily on leadership in organizations, the first three types of authority we discuss here—charismatic, rational-legal, and traditional—are drawn from his pioneering analysis of leadership, and they fully apply to chief executives in political systems.

8.2

A CLOSER LOOK

Huey Long

In his biography of Huey Long, the noted historian T. Harry Williams gives us this picture of Long's ability to generate and use charisma, even though he had to gain support among both the Protestants of northern Louisiana and the Catholics in the south:

> Throughout the day in every small town Long would begin by saying: "When I was a boy, I would get up at six o'clock in the morning on Sunday, and I would hitch our old horse up to the buggy and I would take my Catholic grandparents

to Mass. I would bring them home, and at ten o'clock I would hitch the old horse up again, and I would take my Baptist grandparents to church." The effect of the anecdote on the audiences was obvious, and on the way back to Baton Rouge that night the local leader said admiringly, "Why, Huey, you've been holding out on us. I didn't know you had any Catholic grandparents." "Don't be a damn fool," replied Huey. "We didn't even have a horse."[6]

Charismatic Authority

Historians, sociologists, psychologists, and others have long recognized that some people are able to exert considerable influence over others by virtue of their personal magnetism. In popular parlance, we refer to such people as *charismatic*. They command respect, and even adulation, sometimes moving followers to make great sacrifices. The key point is that **charismatic authority** flows not from the legal basis of one's power but from an individual's personal "gifts."*

Some charismatic leaders come to power as a result of heroism in revolution or through an ability to inspire citizens in war or during some other crisis. Some were among history's most brutal and repressive tyrants; others earned worldwide admiration for their pursuit of noble ideals; still others remain both admired *and* condemned. Adolf Hitler and Benito Mussolini were charismatic figures, as were Franklin D. Roosevelt, Winston Churchill, Juan Perón (Argentina), and Gamal Abdel Nasser (Egypt). Each of those leaders persuaded large numbers of downtrodden people to believe in a better future.

Charismatic leaders require more than an opportunity created by depression or war; they must also have a special personal appeal. For example, Huey Long, the infamous governor and senator from Louisiana in the 1920s and 1930s, was the object of unprecedented praise and affection on the part of many poor, uneducated residents of that state (as well as many wealthier citizens), in part because his style and personality were so appealing to them. (See A Closer Look 8.2.)

The problems of charismatic leadership stem from its foundation in the personal qualities of the leader. When one's authority derives from the personal regard in which he or she is held and not from law or the limits of established institutions,

* The term *charisma* comes from the Greek word for "divine gift."

the person's power may become dangerous. Indeed, part of the attractiveness of many charismatic leaders comes from their image as fighters—they are seen as being in combat with a selfish upper class, a hated ethnic group, or a hostile foreign power. Such leaders may even increase their personal appeal by creating new powers to wield against opposing forces.

Leaders whose claim to power is based primarily on their charismatic leadership often produce unstable conditions, particularly in nations with weak political institutions and little or no democratic traditions. The leader may be able to manipulate the adoration of the masses, who are often convinced that their support is justified by the executive's great wisdom or even supernatural talents. Replacing the executive in these situations is often very challenging. Term limits or constitutional restraints may be only limp impediments when a charismatic leader wants to stay in power.

Thus, the historical record of chief executives who rely primarily on charismatic leadership is mixed. As one would expect, when they are successful, charismatic leaders are extremely effective in performing the symbolic leadership function, and, in some instances, the unifying force of such leaders is precisely what a country needs. For example, Charles de Gaulle helped unify the French Resistance in World War II and brought the country together during the late 1950s when France was on the brink of civil war. And John Kennedy influenced the attitudes of many Americans toward race, laying the foundation for civil rights legislation after his assassination. Charismatic leaders are often less successful in handling other executive functions. For example, Kennedy was far less successful as chief legislator than was his decidedly *un*charismatic successor, Lyndon Johnson. Many charismatic leaders have performed poorly in financial management, in diplomacy, or in controlling the armed forces. Their failures occur because the personal quality that got them power—their ability to inspire the masses—was not accompanied by other leadership skills.

Traditional Leadership

In his discussion of different kinds of authority, Weber identified another distinctive kind of authority: **traditional authority**. People often give allegiance to leaders because the institutional positions they occupy are established in the traditions of the culture. The most common illustrations are the British monarchy and the Japanese emperorship. Great Britain's monarchy is the world's oldest continuous line of succession and is imbued with a tremendous sense of tradition. In many Third World peasant communities, councils of village elders may enjoy similar authority passed on from generation to generation.

Tradition is also a source of power for elected executives. Although the British monarch has virtually no power today, the prime minister claims authority and status by virtue of the long traditions associated with that office. A widely accepted perception that some power or prerogative is an established tradition adds to the executive's ability to lead. The force of tradition in this sense is apparent when executives attempt to wield power in nontraditional ways—they quickly find out that the executive's position is much more secure when operating within traditions than when trying to establish new ones.

For example, in the 1930s, U.S. President Franklin Roosevelt defied tradition when he proposed to "pack" the Supreme Court with justices who would be favorable to his economic wishes. Although the Constitution clearly does not specify the number of justices on the Court, the resulting public furor made it evident that *tradition* was a powerful force:

> The Court-packing plan was defeated despite the President's landslide victory at the polls only a few months earlier and despite the overwhelming popular support for New Deal legislation.... Although much of the opposition was partisan, the resistance to the Court-packing plan ran much deeper. At its source lay the American people's well-nigh religious attachment to constitutionalism and the Supreme Court, including their intuitive realization that packing the Court in order to reverse the course of its decisions would not only destroy its independence but erode the essence of constitutionalism in the United States.[7]

Nevertheless, it is fair to conclude that the importance of traditional authority diminished in the turbulent twentieth century, and most executive leaders must draw on other sources of power.

Rational-Legal Authority

Weber identified another kind of authority, which is based on the acceptance of established law. Executives make use of legal authority by making decisions and taking actions within the scope of authority granted to their positions under law. Where this kind of authority exists, people obey the executive because they accept his or her power under law.

Rational-legal authority can be a significant component of executive leadership where the people see the legal foundations of the government as legitimate and established. Leaders who come to power through a revolution or coup must rely on something else—charismatic authority, perhaps, or military force—since there is no widely recognized legal framework to lend legitimacy to their executive actions. The problem with legal authority is the opposite of the problem with charisma.

Sometimes executives must "bend" the law to maintain national security or lead the country through a crisis. If an executive's authority is based on nothing other than the people's acceptance of law, he or she may lack support when leadership requires steps of questionable legality. Thus, even in systems in which the force of law is strong, the most effective executives are able to draw on some other source of authority.

Representative Authority

The authority for some instances of executive leadership derives from the perception that the incumbent is representative of some legitimate power, usually the "people" or the "majority." This authority is distinct from the authority of a charismatic personality, tradition, or even law. In democratic systems, executives justify certain policy choices on the basis of **representative authority**, asserting that the majority elected them to make those choices. The presidents of France and the United States, for example, can make such a claim. In contrast, many analysts felt that Mikhail Gorbachev, former president of the then Soviet Union, made a critical error when he asked the constitutional assembly, established in March 1989, to elect him president rather than choosing to run for the post in a genuinely national election. Winning a popular election would have given Gorbachev greater legitimacy when making difficult decisions about the decaying economy.* The need to establish representative authority is even more essential in countries with strong democratic principles. In those nations, representative authority is a key ingredient in making executive actions legitimate.

Coercive Authority

The power to use force is an inescapable part of executive leadership. Effective executives generate support for their actions by staying within the law, through the attractiveness of their personalities, by embodying their countries' traditions, or by emphasizing how they are representing the people; but the possibility of force is always present. The significance of that possibility varies tremendously, of course. When charismatic leaders lose their charisma, they may use police or military force to demand the obedience that their personalities previously earned them.

In deeply divided countries, large segments of the population often reject the legal foundations and traditions that are held in high esteem by other parts of society. Both of these problems are common to the developing world. For example, General Augusto Pinochet (former president of Chile), President Bashar al-Assad (Syria), and the emir of Kuwait were not elected in competitive elections and have represented only a part of the population. Executives in such countries are thus unable to lead effectively by appealing to traditional, representative, or legal authority, and even their charismatic qualities may not be recognized in many quarters. In such cases, **coercive authority** becomes essential to executive leadership.

In modern political life, a single foundation for executive leadership is normally too limited and too vulnerable to change to enable an executive to operate effectively. Most successful executives thus combine several kinds of authority. The actual mix will depend on the leader's personal qualities, the nature and homogeneity of the country's political culture, and the legal and institutional setting.

BUREAUCRATIC INSTITUTIONS

We often think that government is all about policy *making*; that is why we focus so much attention on elections and on executive and legislative institutions. But policies must be *implemented*, and the workings of the **bureaucracy** often make the difference between success and failure, efficiency and waste, and even life and death.

Some democratic governments have delegated far greater authority to their bureaucracies than does the United States. The power of high-ranking bureaucrats in Great Britain is so widely recognized that a late 1980s television sitcom titled *Yes, Prime Minister* spoofed a fictitious prime minister who was repeatedly manipulated by senior civil servants. France's very centralized and powerful national bureaucracy predates the French Revolution and provided efficiency and stability during a period (1945–1958) when the nation's prime minister and cabinet changed on the average

---

* In fact, when Gorbachev eventually did run for the presidency in a popular election in 1996, he received only 1 percent of the vote.

of once every six months. The French Fifth Republic (1958–present) brought far greater political stability. Many of the most critical policy decisions are made by the president or the prime minister in concert with high-ranking technocrats, particularly those in the planning commissions.

In short, bureaucratic power exerts great influence in virtually all political systems. In the United States, bureaucrats make more than 80 laws (in the form of administrative regulations) for each law passed by Congress.[8] Those rules establish the level of emissions that will be tolerated from coal-burning power plants, a wide range of safety requirements, and other matters that involve basic policy choices. They decide where and how roads will be built, they approve and deny requests for public welfare, and they write and evaluate environmental impact statements. Regardless of culture or form of government, bureaucracy is a fact of modern political life.

WHAT IS BUREAUCRACY?

Although we often use the term *bureaucracy* as a pejorative ("He's just a mindless bureaucrat" or "She's going to give us some bureaucratic resistance"), the term actually refers to a distinctive form of organization.

Sociologist Max Weber (we discussed his typology of leadership styles above) outlined the concept of the bureaucracy in 1922. He argued that bureaucracy was a new and special kind of organization, and that no society could become modern without it. Weber identified several core principles of this new form of organization:[9]

1. Bureaucratic workers operate within **fixed jurisdictions** and are responsible for specific tasks. This enables bureaucrats to develop expertise in particular areas, and it also makes bureaucracy accountable by establishing which individuals are responsible for which concerns.
2. Bureaucrats exercise authority within a firm system of **hierarchy**. Subordinates are clearly under the control of their superiors, a fact known by subordinate and superior alike. In a well-ordered bureaucracy, this strengthens accountability because each bureaucrat knows which person he or she is expected to obey.
3. Bureaucracy operates on the basis of *written rules.* Consistency of treatment and efficiency are improved when bureaucrats are required to keep detailed official records of their actions and when specific rules apply to specific cases. Without a system of written rules, two welfare claimants with identical circumstances would receive different treatment, for example. Written rules ensure that the workings of bureaucracy do not depend on the personality or opinions of individual bureaucrats.
4. Bureaucrats assume their positions through *expert training.* Thus, bureaucrats should not normally be appointed on the basis of political **patronage** or through nepotism.

Weber's model is an ideal that the bureaucracies of even the most modern nations fail to achieve fully. In virtually all countries, including the United States, patronage and personal connections play a role in some bureaucratic appointments. Thus, in both Chicago and Mexico City, membership or active participation in the political party in power may be necessary to hold certain bureaucratic posts.

A 2006 study of bureaucracy in Ethiopia concluded that it is particularly difficult for a political system to maintain Weber's bureaucratic neutrality when ethnic or religious conflict is severe.[10] Where there is no shared national identity or uniform political culture, it is virtually impossible for a nation's bureaucracy to embody the traditional bureaucratic values of objectivity and consistency or professionalism. In such settings, the political leadership uses the bureaucracy to its own ends, ignoring the disenfranchised and creating a spoils system that undermines bureaucratic efficiency.

Yet Weber's model is worth considering for three reasons. First, even though bureaucratic principles are not perfectly realized anywhere, they are achieved to some degree everywhere. Second, Weber's model helps us understand why government effectiveness is impossible without some features of bureaucratic organization. Finally, we suggest that the very characteristics that Weber enumerated may have both negative and positive consequences. Indeed, scholars, bureaucrats, and politicians alike in various countries differ about how fully governmental bureaucracies *should* match the Weberian ideal.

Who Are the Bureaucrats?

In defining which people are bureaucrats, it is necessary to distinguish between theory and practice. We usually refer to all government officials who are not elected to a legislature or to a chief executive's post, and who are not judges or soldiers, as bureaucrats. For our purposes in this text, we define the term more narrowly in accordance with Weber's usage:

> **Bureaucrats** *are public officials who acquire their positions on the basis of their qualifications and skills and who are primarily responsible for the implementation of public policy.**

The degree of professionalization within actual bureaucracies varies greatly. Perhaps the most decidedly professional national bureaucracy is the French civil service. In France, most senior civil servants are recruited from the Ecole Nationale d'Administration (ENA), a highly competitive and prestigious institution of higher learning. In general, recruitment and promotion in the French civil service are closely tied to professional skills.[11] Although the U.S. bureaucracy is not as highly professionalized as the French—largely because of the absence of a national training institution dedicated to producing a corps of career bureaucrats—the use of entrance and promotional examinations ensures some level of professional skill.

British bureaucrats have a somewhat different reputation. Although they are also highly respected for their integrity and dedication, they are often criticized for elitism and lack of technical expertise. Senior civil servants often come from upper-class backgrounds and may benefit from having the proper connections in the "old boys'" network. Many have been educated at Oxford or Cambridge, but they tend to be generalists with a nontechnical education and are consequently less qualified than

---

* A number of political appointees are usually named to top posts in the bureaucracy when a new chief executive assumes office in most developed democracies, but this group is normally a small percentage of all bureaucrats. It should be noted, however, that in some local and state governments in the United States, a far higher proportion of positions are allocated through patronage. Nevertheless, an important Supreme Court case (*Rutan et al. v. Republican Party of Illinois*, 110 S. Ct. 2729, 1990) made it unconstitutional to require partisan affiliation as a condition for obtaining a state job.

their French or German counterparts to deal with the economic and technical problems of a modern, complex society.

In communist political systems, government bureaucrats are often recruited and promoted on the basis of their commitment to the regime's ideology rather than on the basis of their technical expertise. Following the Cuban Revolution, for example, agricultural production suffered because managers of state farms (officials in the Ministry of Agriculture and bureaucrats in the agrarian reform agency) were often selected on the basis of their commitment to the revolution, even if they knew nothing about farming. In both the Chinese and the Mexican bureaucracies, young administrators wishing to advance up the organizational ladder must attach themselves to a more powerful patron within their ministry or agency. As that patron advances up the bureaucratic ladder, he or she will bring lower-ranking "clients" up as well.

Thus, in everyday parlance, the term *bureaucrat* applies to a rather wide variety of people in different systems. But using Weber's approach, the most "bureaucratic" bureaucrat is one who fits the ideal of being appointed on the basis of expertise and training despite the fact that, in practice, many bureaucrats are selected on other grounds.

BUREAUCRATIC FUNCTIONS

Although the tasks assigned to bureaucrats vary widely, even among developed democratic nations, there are certain universal bureaucratic functions. The distinguishing features of those tasks are their technical nature and the level of detail they involve.

Revenue Collection

No viable political system can govern without tax revenues, and a regular, established process for collecting taxes is a key element of effective government. A specialized agency for tax collection is found in all developed systems, democratic or otherwise.

National Defense

In most countries, a significant proportion of modern government spending is devoted to national defense. In addition to the members of the armed forces, this function requires a considerable "army" of bureaucrats. Civilians employed by the U.S. Department of Defense currently number nearly 800,000, for example, and those employees are essential to the procurement of supplies and weapons systems and general management.

Service Delivery

Many services cannot be provided effectively by private means. Public health services, road construction, national park and forest management—among many other services—would not be performed as well, or would not be as widely available, if government agencies did not provide them. The magnitude of bureaucratic service delivery varies considerably, however, across systems.

Income Maintenance and Redistribution

Governments in modern industrial societies, capitalist and socialist alike, have established agencies to administer a wide variety of "safety net" programs designed to help people in financial difficulty. Bureaucrats are essential in this area because the policies require that each applicant's eligibility be determined case by case and because most programs attempt to provide follow-up help to the recipients of government assistance.

Regulation

Most societies seek to regulate individuals and businesses to ensure the safety of consumer products and the workplace, to restrict the use of public lands, to protect the environment, and to maintain the fairness of competition in the marketplace, among many other purposes. Although some people believe that regulation is excessive in modern societies, almost everyone believes that some level of regulation is needed, and regulatory agencies are established for that purpose.

Research

The market provides only things that people will buy, and basic research is not easily packaged as a consumer product. When societies want to engage in large-scale scientific work, bureaucrats often play important roles. Private universities and even corporations also make contributions to scientific knowledge, but much of the most important basic research—such as space exploration and advanced work in nuclear physics—is managed by government bureaucrats.

Specialized Governmental Functions

Nearly all governments also provide a national currency and postal services, with specialized bureaucratic agencies for each.

Management of State Enterprises

In most countries, even capitalist ones, some economic activities are publicly owned. These include the Tennessee Valley Authority (TVA) and most municipal bus systems in the United States; the computer, steel, and chemical industries in France; the petroleum industry in Mexico; the railroads and electric power in most of the world's nations; and the majority of industrial and commercial enterprises in China. Administration of those enterprises is an important part of bureaucratic activity.

THE GROWTH OF BUREAUCRACY

Bureaucracies expand as modern societies develop. Legislatures generally remain at a given size (although their staffs usually constitute growing bureaucracies in their own right), and societies usually do not increase the number of their chief executives.

Bureaucratic agencies multiply and expand, however, suggesting that growth itself is possibly a universal characteristic of bureaucracy.

Why Does Bureaucracy Grow?

There are several reasons given for the nearly universal phenomenon of bureaucratic growth. The first is our growing *need* for bureaucracy: We need more bureaucrats and agencies as scientific and technological advances make government activity increasingly necessary. As societies become industrialized, the tasks of monitoring and controlling pollution, regulating the safety of the workplace, and ensuring that consumer products are not harmful become more important and more difficult. Advances in science and industrial development eventually require government involvement as research expenses outstrip the resources of private organizations.

Second, advanced societies demand a broader range of government activities. When most of a society's people are concerned about their next meals, they have limited interest in issues such as animal rights or environmental protection. As people become more affluent, however, they often find that they care a great deal about these things. It is no coincidence that Americans and Europeans began to demand the protection of endangered species, the safety of workers and consumers, and wilderness preservation only after their societies became generally affluent.* Bureaucracies grow in response as policies are made to address these concerns and agencies are established to implement them.

Political pressures are a third reason for the growth of bureaucracies. In industrial democracies, interest groups demand regulations and services that require the creation of new agencies. In the United States, organized labor was largely responsible for the establishment of the National Labor Relations Board and the laws it implements, and environmental interest groups successfully demanded the establishment of the Environmental Protection Agency. Indeed, in the United States almost all government agencies enjoy the support of at least a few influential interest groups.

In developing nations, bureaucracies sometimes emerge as the result of international as well as domestic political pressures. In Latin America, where farmland is generally concentrated in the hands of a small percentage of the rural population, pressures developed in the 1960s for reforms that would redistribute some land from large estates or uncultivated public property to poor farmers. In Peru, Colombia, Venezuela, Chile, and elsewhere, peasants organized federations, invaded large estates, and sometimes joined revolutionary movements to protest rural conditions. President John Kennedy, worried by the specter of the Cuban Revolution, launched a major foreign aid program for Latin America, called the Alliance for Progress. Under its terms, the United States promised economic assistance to nations that implemented land redistribution and other reforms. In time, only a few of those nations actually redistributed much land, but the reform bureaucracies remained.

Political pressures of a different nature have also contributed to the expansion of Third World bureaucracies. (See A Closer Look 8.3.) Often, educational systems in developing nations have expanded more rapidly than employment opportunities in the modern sector of the economy. Hence, these nations are often faced with a

---

* See the discussion of postmaterialism in Chapter 3.

A CLOSER LOOK

8.3

Third-World Bureaucracies

Although bureaucracies are necessary components of any political system, they can become burdensome if they do not maintain proper professional standards. The governments of many developing countries overstaff their bureaucracies in order to reward political supporters and create employment for university and high school graduates facing a difficult job market. During the 1980s, Africa's public sector employed half the region's nonagricultural wage earners (many of whom worked in the bureaucracy). But a World Bank study of one West African country concluded that 6,000 of the 6,800 headquarters staff at two government ministries were redundant.*

While doing research at Ecuador's Ministry of Agriculture, one of this book's authors observed a ministry employee (whom we shall call "Mr. Sandoval") spending most of the day staring out the window or reading a book. Toward the end of the day, the office receptionist brought in a small group of peasants who wanted the ministry's help in a land dispute. When the nervous group leader had trouble getting his words out, the receptionist snapped at him, "Hurry up! Mr. Sandoval is a very busy man!" Not only do bloated bureaucracies create a drain on government expenditures, they also often justify their existence by turning out a vast array of regulations that stymie private businesses, large and small, and periodically force citizens of all kinds to spend hours on end getting unnecessary documents or permissions.

* Similar observations were made during the Great Depression in the United States about the Works Progress Administration (WPA), created by the Roosevelt administration to build public works and hire the unemployed. In both cases, however, it is possible that the social or political benefits to society of reducing unemployment may have outweighed the costs of inefficiencies.

large number of high school or university graduates who have no prospect for employment in the private sector. Left unattended, this group of skilled people might become a source of political unrest. Consequently, many governments prefer to hire them into the government bureaucracy, even if useful work cannot be found for them in the private sector. The visitor to a ministry of education or agriculture in Latin America will often see three bureaucrats doing the work of one.[12]

BUREAUCRACY EVALUATED

As noted earlier, the term *bureaucracy* often carries a negative connotation. Fortunately, real bureaucracies are not necessarily ineffective, unresponsive, or evil. Even in the United States, where bureaucracy regularly serves as a target of criticism during political campaigns, most people have fairly positive feelings about government agencies.* In a now-classic study, one researcher found that strong majorities of

* A study of "bureaucracy bashing" in U.S. elections found that the negative comments made by politicians have actually harmed bureaucratic effectiveness by creating low morale, hampering the recruitment of talented personnel, and "fostering an environment of distrust." See R. Sam Garrett, James A. Thurber, A. Lee Fritschler, and David H. Rosenbloom, "Assessing the Impact of Bureaucracy Bashing by Electoral Campaigns," *Public Administration Review* 66 (March/April 2006): 228–241.

respondents considered government workers to be competent, efficient, and even friendly.[13] More systematic evaluations suggest a more balanced view: Bureaucracies have a great positive potential for *efficiency*, but they are almost universally plagued by *rigidity* and *resistance to innovation*.

Positive Qualities of Bureaucracy: Efficiency and Responsibility

It may seem odd to speak of bureaucracy as efficient and responsible, but for many important functions of government, bureaucratic organization is the only way to approach acceptable levels of efficiency and responsibility. Before governments instituted bureaucracies, tasks were randomly assigned to amateurs who held positions on the basis of their friendship with a monarch or a politician. It was impossible to determine which person was responsible for which decision, and there was little specialized training. In contrast, core bureaucratic principles—clear lines of specialization and the strict application of written rules—enable the modern Internal Revenue Service, for example, to process millions of tax returns quickly and, generally, with considerable accuracy. A less bureaucratic arrangement would simply not work.

A Persistent Bureaucratic Problem: Rigidity and Resistance to Change

The most discussed, and probably most common, problem of bureaucracy has to do with rigidity. Bureaucracy is slow to adapt to new programs, conditions, or special concerns. It is not usually known for its encouragement of innovation. The problem of bureaucratic rigidity does *not*, however, stem from the personal characteristics of individual bureaucrats. According to Charles Goodsell's popular book on U.S. bureaucracy, "bureaucrats are no less flexible, tolerant, and creative than other people—perhaps they are a little more so."[14] If individuals do not create the problem, there must be something in the nature of bureaucracy itself that causes rigidity and resistance to change.

Observers of bureaucracy have identified three reasons that bureaucracies tend to resist change:

Rules and Routines   First, the **routines**—written rules and procedures—that make possible the efficient processing of typical cases and decisions also make it difficult for bureaucracy to make adjustments or modifications when an *atypical* case arises. The mere existence of bureaucratic rules often tempts officials to try to fit unique cases into established categories when an innovative response would better serve the public. Although these rules and routines make bureaucracy more efficient *when they are appropriate*, some cases require unique solutions, and bureaucrats often try to solve them by applying established routines.

Communication Problems   A second reason for bureaucratic inflexibility has to do with the fixed jurisdictions in which bureaucrats work. Communication is made difficult when each person's responsibilities are rigidly set. Bureaucrats have fixed jur- isdictions and specialized responsibilities so that they can become experts in a nar- row range of tasks and so that it will be clear who is responsible for which jobs, as discussed earlier. Those are important advantages to a bureaucracy. Nevertheless, some problems require discussion and cooperation among subordinates in different units. If bureaucrats feel that they can work only on problems assigned to them by their departmental supervisors, new solutions requiring joint operations with subordi- nates in other departments may be slow in coming.

Bureaucratic Power   Bureaucracy also inhibits innovation because major changes in policies and operations often threaten the power position of specific managers. If a particular bureaucrat is in charge of, say, a snow-removal unit, he or she enjoys cer- tain personal advantages (such as power, prestige, and control of a large budget). Those advantages would lead the bureaucrat to resist innovations that change his or her position. An innovative move to provide snow-removal service through contract work by private businesses may be a good idea, but it will be resisted if it leads to changes in the power positions of important bureaucrats.*

Bureaucracy and Democracy

Nothing in Weber's list of bureaucratic principles mentions "government by the people." Instead, bureaucracy is "government by experts obeying their superiors." Decisions are made on the basis of training, analysis, and authority, not on the basis of opinion polls or votes. The realization that an establishment of bureaucrats makes most laws and decides most legal cases makes many people wonder whether a system with a large bureaucracy can really be democratic.

There is evidence that bureaucrats themselves are aware of the inconsistency between the guiding principles of bureaucratic activity and the ideals of democ- racy. According to a recent study of bureaucrats in Seoul, South Korea, many gov- ernment officials regard basic elements of democracy as incompatible with bureaucracy.[15]

---

* Citizens in developing countries face tremendous problems with bureaucratic rigidity. One of the authors of this text recalls receiving a notice in the mail, while he was living in Ecuador, telling him that a package had arrived from a family friend in the United States. Knowing that the parcel contained about $30 worth of English-language paperbacks and other items hard to come by in Quito, he headed for the post office naively believing that all he needed to do to retrieve his package was to show his slip of paper and perhaps pay a small fee. Two days later—after having passed through five government offices scattered around town, paid three minor taxes totaling $12, secured the requisite importer's license for $7, and had at least nine documents stamped—he returned to the post office to claim his package. He left feeling far more fortunate than the Ecuadoran woman in front of him on "the last line." She was solemnly informed by the postal clerk that she had underpaid one of her tax payments by 3 sucres (worth $.02 in U.S. currency) and would have to go back across town to straighten out that tax. The postal clerk was unswayed by the woman's explanation that she had merely paid what the bureaucrat at one of the tax windows had told her to pay.

Why Bureaucracy Resists Democratic Control

The Bureaucrat's Information Advantage   Many administrative actions, decisions, and policies are based on scientific data, careful and elaborate studies, and highly technical issues. When a political leader questions a bureaucratic decision, he or she is usually in a poor position to evaluate whether or not the answer given by the bureaucrat is sound. The politician is a generalist; he or she knows a little about a great many issues. In contrast, the bureaucrat is usually a specialist with detailed knowledge of subject matter that may be highly technical. It is often difficult for the politician to make sense of the answers given by bureaucrats. One researcher found that there is a basic trade-off between the extent to which a bureaucracy develops useful expertise and the extent to which it remains politically dependent on elected legislators.[16] When legislators need an agency to acquire a broad range of expertise, they generally grant it a great deal of administrative independence, thus making political control more difficult.

Iron Triangles, Sloppy Hexagons, and Issue Networks   Even more important than their information advantage is the power that bureaucrats may enjoy as a result of their relationship with influential interest groups and legislative committees. The significance of this relationship is suggested by the "iron triangles" idea, as discussed in Chapter 6. Essentially, the term was coined to describe a close connection among bureaucratic agencies, interest groups, and legislative committees in specific policy areas. Interests outside the triangle are, according to the theory, typically powerless to force policy actions opposed by those inside it and are powerless to resist what the insiders want.

Where the iron triangle concept is an accurate picture of how policy decisions are made, it raises serious questions about bureaucratic power. *Reciprocity* is a common norm in democratic legislatures, suggesting that legislators often find it useful to support one member's proposals in return for that member's support on another matter. Legislative reciprocity can thus heighten the autonomy of iron triangles because the whole legislature may be willing to permit one committee to act in accordance with its fellow triangle participants (so that the members of that committee will be tolerant in return). Taken to its logical conclusion, the iron triangle concept implies that by allying themselves carefully with influential interests, bureaucratic agencies can insulate themselves from all but the friendliest control by the legislature.

Can Bureaucracy Be Made Compatible with Democracy?

The reality of bureaucratic power can arguably be accommodated within democratic principles in several ways. Considering them helps us appreciate the long-standing tension that has existed between bureaucracy and democracy.

The Politics/Administration Dichotomy   One approach is simply to deny the existence of the problem by invoking the *politics/administration dichotomy*. This is the

A CLOSER LOOK

The Politics of Bureaucratic "Optimism"

Nearly all administrative agencies engage in some kind of forecasting. Bureaucrats estimate the growing (or declining) demand for the programs they implement, future cost changes, and the number of people who will need or want certain programs in the years ahead. Given that bureaucratic organization is supposed to be driven by specialized experience and expertise, we might expect that agencies would make objective forecasts relating to the programs they manage.

However, bureaucrats do not operate in the world of objective precision that Weber's famous model of bureaucracy described. In 2007, two political scientists compared the accuracy of economic forecasts by the U.S. Social Security Administration to those by the Office of Management and Budget.[17] They wanted to determine if one of these agencies produced more "optimistic" budget and economic growth predictions than the other.

Both the Social Security Administration and the Office of Management and Budget produce forecasts regarding inflation, unemployment, tax revenues, budget deficits, and the composition of the workforce, among other factors. Each of these factors is critical to decisions that the president and congress must make about tax reform, entitlement reform, and general spending choices. While being optimistic may be a part of a healthy human nature, governments need accurate predictions, but political considerations can apparently get in the way.

George A. Krause and J. Kevin Corder began their study by considering the incentives that bureaucrat leaders face. On one hand, they want to maintain a good relationship with the president because he may be able to affect the agency's budget and because he can make decisions regarding the persons appointed

(and dismissed) from important administrative positions. On the other hand, bureaucrats are naturally concerned with the reputation of their agencies. Pressure from the White House may lead the agency to make rosy forecasts, but a concern for the agency's public standing will make most bureaucrats resist this influence.

Following simple rational choice assumptions, the researchers produced the following hypothesis: *The OMB's predictions about economic conditions would be more optimistic than those of the SSA.* Why the difference? There are more political appointees leading the Office of Management and Budget than is the case with the Social Security Administration, which is therefore more stable in its staffing and more independent of partisan influence. Consequently, while both agencies are tasked to make predictions, the top leaders of the OMB are not going to remain in power very long, thus giving these officials less of an incentive to safeguard the long-term reputation of their agency. The SSA should be more concerned about its reputation and less influenced by partisanship.

The empirical analysis generally confirmed the researchers' expectations. They found that the OMB forecasts were far more optimistic than those of the SSA. This conclusion will astonish few observers of bureaucracy. However, Krause and Corder demonstrated that the degree to which "politics" undermines the "neutral competence" of bureaucrats is, to some extent, predictable. When bureaucrats work in an agency that is closely tied to the influences of partisan strife, their objectivity is compromised more than when they are in organizations with the stability and independence to place greater weight on their long-term reputations.

notion that policies are made by politicians and that bureaucrats merely carry out, or administer, those policies. If bureaucratic power is applied only to the mundane tasks of implementing the policy choices made by political leaders, then we can be made to feel much more comfortable about the existence of bureaucratic power. Perhaps you have heard that "there is no Democratic or Republican way to pick up the garbage"; that sentiment is an expression of the politics/administration dichotomy. It suggests that bureaucrats make decisions on the basis of objective managerial considerations while steering clear of political matters. To the extent that this is true, the reality of bureaucratic power need not threaten democracy.

Nevertheless, this dichotomy cannot resolve our concerns about bureaucratic power in a democracy. As mentioned earlier, the vast majority of decisions—even many decisions involving basic policy choices—are actually made by bureaucrats. It is not enough, therefore, simply to assert the principle of the politics/administration dichotomy.

Technical Responsibility   Carl Friedrich, an important figure in political science from the first half of the twentieth century, suggested a second approach to the problem of bureaucratic power in a famous 1946 essay.[18] He began by admitting that bureaucrats make basic policy choices and, moreover, that they make so many of them, involving so much technical knowledge, that it is impossible for politicians to oversee bureaucrats effectively. But instead of concluding that democratic values are therefore hopelessly lost, Friedrich suggested that bureaucrats are effectively controlled and that they act responsibly because *their own standards and sense of professionalism force them to*. He called that force **technical responsibility**.

The idea is simple. An environmental engineer considering a new pollution standard may not be effectively controlled by public opinion (since the public is not able to evaluate the decision independently), but the bureaucrat's desire to maintain his or her professional standing leads him or her to make to generally sound and responsible decisions.

Friedrich's argument has merit. On a day-to-day basis, bureaucrats make more decisions on the basis of what sound professional practice demands than on the basis of public preferences. Yet it takes little imagination to think of cases in which bureaucrats make decisions opposed by the public but nonetheless sound in technical terms. As one of Friedrich's critics pointed out, "Many a burglar has been positively hated for his technical skill."[19] Professional standards and technical responsibility may make bureaucrats skillful, but if they are doing things that the people do not want, their professionalism in doing them does not make their actions democratic.

An Expanded Role for Citizens   Other approaches emphasize changing bureaucratic procedures, especially those having to do with **citizen participation**. It is often suggested that bureaucrats will be more innovative, flexible, and responsive to public needs if they are forced to listen to the public as they make decisions. Many governments therefore require that public hearings be held before new bureaucratic rules and regulations are passed into law. The bureaucrats are not normally required to abide by the wishes expressed at those hearings, but at least they are exposed to the complaints and ideas presented. Evidence suggests that public hearings lead bureaucrats to consider problems from different perspectives as they encounter factors that had not occurred to them before such hearings, and that the hearings thereby affect actual decisions.[20]

In Cuba, elected representatives to local, regional, and even national legislative bodies (called organs of *Poder Popular*, or "popular power") meet periodically with their constituents to hear complaints about the performance of the state bureaucracy. Indeed, in a society where opposition to governmental policy is not tolerated, these sessions are not only aimed at discovering instances of bureaucratic incompetence or malfeasance—they also serve as a pressure valve because they constitute the only way citizens can publicly lodge complaints.

Unfortunately, most public hearings required by law in developed or developing countries have little effect. The general public is normally not able to explore the highly technical issues involved in most bureaucratic decisions, and people's concerns are often met with such statements as, "Oh, we have considered that, and your idea cannot be adopted because of...." Moreover, many ideas at public hearings are contradictory (as when hunters and animal rights advocates press for opposite changes in a compromise about hunting regulations). Thus, although it is difficult to be against the idea of citizen participation, the ability of participation to remove concerns about bureaucracy in a democracy is limited.

Strengthened Political Supervision   This last approach has been used since bureaucracy was first established: Adopt reforms that enable elected officials to oversee bureaucracy more effectively. As mentioned earlier, the technical nature of many bureaucratic decisions, coupled with the vast number of bureaucrats and programs, normally makes it impossible for politicians to exert rigorous control. Nevertheless, steps can be taken to strengthen political supervision, thus improving the surveillance and monitoring of bureaucratic activity by both legislatures and chief executives.

Reorganizing the bureaucracy may also strengthen the hand of politicians in dealing with bureaucrats. Usually, reorganizing (that is, taking programs and officials from one agency and giving them to another or to a new agency) is advocated as an efficiency measure. Much duplication and waste are eliminated through effective reorganization. Nevertheless, reorganization can also help to disrupt the "iron triangles" that inevitably develop and that make bureaucrats so difficult to control. During the final years of the Soviet Union, Mikhail Gorbachev made great efforts at reorganization, largely in an attempt to counter the tremendous power of the Soviet bureaucracy. Richard Nixon initiated a failing attempt at a fundamental reorganization in the early 1970s for much the same reason.

In conclusion, none of the methods of reconciling bureaucracy with democracy seems entirely satisfying. Even with technical responsibility, citizen participation, and strengthened political supervision, bureaucrats will inevitably have tremendous power in all modern societies. Dealing with this problem is an enduring challenge for all modern political leaders, democratic or otherwise.

Can Bureaucracy Be Improved?

Almost everyone agrees that governments must have bureaucracies, and yet almost everyone also feels that bureaucracies cause serious problems. Since bureaucracies cannot be eliminated, two sets of ideas have been advanced to improve them, to make them more adaptable and more easily controlled.

Make Bureaucracy Less "Bureaucratic"

Studies of business administration since the 1950s suggest that organizations can become more adaptable if certain bureaucratic features are changed. For example, instead of maintaining the rigid lines of authority that lock people in fixed jurisdictions, many businesses have found it useful to give employees wider, more flexible job assignments. These arrangements allow workers to develop working relationships with many different people in the organization, not simply with people in the same official unit. Workers acquire a deeper interest in their tasks since they are given a greater range of responsibility and more room for creativity. These organizations find that they become more innovative and adaptable as a result.

The public sectors in many industrial democracies have also moved toward less "bureaucratic" bureaucracies. Although the basic bureaucratic rules are still observed to a large extent, the value of flexible organizational structure has made many public organizations more adaptable. Workers who are given broader and more flexible jurisdictions are likely to bring more creative energy to their jobs.

Make Bureaucracy Smaller

Many people are becoming convinced that the best way to avoid the problems created by bureaucracy is to make it smaller, removing powers previously entrusted to bureaucrats and giving them to the private sector. In China, Deng Xiaoping called for sharp reductions in the bureaucracy during the 1980s. Although some of the reduction was associated with the transfer of economic activities (most notably farming) to the private sector, bureaucratic cutbacks were an end in themselves. Clearly, Gorbachev had similar objectives in the former Soviet Union, although bureaucratic resistance stifled most of his efforts. In all communist societies, when state policy determines the prices and production of virtually all goods and services, bureaucratic shortcomings resonate throughout society. Taking some powers away from bureaucrats (and giving them to individuals making self-interested decisions in the marketplace) is one way to avoid bureaucratic problems.

Reducing the size of the vast state bureaucracies has become a high priority for many Latin American nations as well. Here, governments may be motivated as much by economic necessity as by the search for greater efficiency. Argentina, Mexico, and Brazil, for example, are saddled with huge budget deficits and vast external debts. To reduce those deficits and to secure refinancing of their debt from the International Monetary Fund (IMF) and from foreign banks, their recently elected governments have been forced to reduce the size of their bureaucracies.

In the United States, for similar reasons, some states, counties, and cities have "contracted out" for many public services previously handled by bureaucrats. When public officials manage garbage collection and street cleaning, for example, it is argued that they have no incentive to be innovative or particularly efficient. Critics of *public* service delivery thus charge that this approach is inherently wasteful.[21] Greater efficiency would be attained if governments opened bidding among private firms for contracts to perform those services. Fewer bureaucrats would be employed, and fewer dollars would be spent.

However, the contracting approach remains controversial. Government loses some measure of control when public services are not provided directly by public servants. Some people question how diligent private contractors can be in seeing that services are provided *equitably* when they have such an incentive to maintain *efficiency*. (For example, private garbage crews working on a city contract may not serve hard-to-reach or poor sections of town as often as they serve well-to-do areas.) Attempts to privatize prisons have been particularly controversial. In any event, even if contracting out proves to be workable, it is not applicable to many bureaucratic functions.

EXECUTIVES AND BUREAUCRACIES—FROM POLICY LEADERSHIP TO POLICY IMPLEMENTATION

Unlike the decisions made by legislators and judges, most actions by chief executives and bureaucrats have immediate effects, some of which are hugely significant (i.e., a U.S. president sending troops into battle), and some of which escape virtually all public notice (i.e., a decision by an official at the National Institutes of Health regarding which applicants deserve a scholarship for graduate studies). The common feature of executive and bureaucratic institutions is that they are both expected to *make things happen*, not simply to scrutinize partisan differences through extensive debate or to play the role of judges interpreting the law.

Implementing policy requires a considerable centralization of authority. Thus, executive institutions are characterized by a unity of command and (often) secrecy, and bureaucrats are organized in accordance with a hierarchy and specialization. In principle—and quite often in reality—these characteristics make it possible for policies to be implemented with both consistency and efficiency. But these characteristics also create the potential for abuses of power, resistance to change, and insufficient attention to contrasting points of view.

Consequently, a fundamental challenge for all political systems is to preserve the effective command, coordination, and access to specialized expertise that can only be achieved in executive and bureaucratic institutions while limiting their powers. Understanding the benefits and the dangers of executive and bureaucratic institutions is vital if we are to understand the promise and perils of modern government.

◆ ◆ ◆

Key Terms and Concepts _____

budget formulation	coups d'état
bureaucracy	diplomacy
charismatic authority	emergency leadership
chief administrators	fixed jurisdictions
citizen participation	hierarchy
coercive authority	iron triangles

patronage
Rational-legal authority
representative authority
routines

symbolic leader
technical responsibility
traditional authority

DISCUSSION QUESTIONS

1. *What are the features that make bureaucratic institutions distinctive?*
2. *What accounts for the tendency of bureaucracies to become rigid and resistant to innovation?*
3. *Why do governments need bureaucracy?*
4. *Can you think of an example in which a bureaucrat or agency resisted directions from an elected leader? Was the resistance proper? Why or why not?*
5. *Which governmental functions are most closely associated with executive institutions? Why are they normally seen as within the executive's domain?*
6. *Discuss some of the limits on the power of chief executives.*
7. *What are the differences among charismatic, rational-legal, and traditional authority?*
8. *What kind of executive leadership is best suited to democracy, and why?*

Notes _____

1. Aaron Wildavsky, *The Politics of the Budgetary Process*, 4th ed. (Boston: Little, Brown, 1984), p. 2.
2. Richard E. Neustadt, *Presidential Power: The Politics of Leadership from FDR to Carter* (New York: Wiley, 1980).
3. Ibid., p. 9.
4. Prime Minister Tony Blair, "Lecture on Public Life," London, June 12, 2007. Available at http://image.guardian.co.uk/sys-files/Politics/documents/2007/06/12/BlairReustersSpeech.pdf.
5. See Max Weber, *The Theory of Social and Economic Organization*, trans. A. M. Parsons and Talcott Parsons (New York: Free Press, 1947).
6. T. Harry Williams, *Huey Long* (New York: Bantam, 1970), p. 1.
7. See Archibald Cox, *The Court and the Constitution*. (Boston: Houghton-Mifflin, 1987), pp. 149–150.
8. Quoted from a statement by U.S. Representative S. Levitas of Georgia, in John Sheridan, "Can Congress Control the Regulators?" *Industry Week* (March 29, 1976): 25–26.
9. This discussion is drawn from *Max Weber: Essays in Sociology*, ed. H. Gerth and C. Wright Mills (New York: Oxford University Press, 1946).
10. See Berhanu Mengistu and Elizabeth Vogel, "Bureaucratic Neutrality among Competing Bureaucratic Values in an Ethnic Federalism: The Case of Ethiopia," *Public Administration Review* 66 (March/April 2006): 205–217.
11. Ezra N. Suleiman, *Politics, Power and Bureaucracy in France* (Princeton, NJ: Princeton University Press, 1974).
12. Richard Sandbrook, *The Politics of Africa's Economic Recovery* (New York: Cambridge University Press, 1993), p. 43.
13. Charles Goodsell. *The Case for Bureaucracy*. 4th ed. (Washington, D.C.: CQ Press, 2003).
14. Ibid.
15. Sung-Don Hwang, *Bureaucracy v. Democracy in the Minds of Bureaucrats* (New York: Peter Lang, 2000).
16. Kathleen Bawn, "Political Control versus Expertise: Congressional Choices about Administrative Procedures," *American Political Science Review* 89 (March 1995): 62–73.
17. George A. Krause and J. Kevin Corder, "Explaining Bureaucratic Optimism: Theory and Evidence from U.S. Executive Agency Macroeconomic Forecasts," *American Political Science Review* 101 (February 2007): 129–142.
18. Carl Friedrich, "Public Policy and the Nature of Administrative Responsibility," *Public Policy* 1 (1940): 3–24.

19. See the essay written in response to Friedrich's (note 22): Herman Finer, "Administrative Responsibility in Democratic Government," *Public Administration Review* 1 (Summer 1941): 335–350.
20. See William T. Gormley, Jr., "The Representation Revolution: Reforming State Regulation through Public Representation," *Administration and Society* 18 (1986): 179–196. For a negative view, see Amy McKay and Susan Webb Yackee, "Interest Group Competition on Federal Agency Rules," *American Politics Research* 35 (2007): 336–357.
21. See E. S. Savas, *Privatizing the Public Sector* (Chatham, NJ: Chatham House, 1982), for the most well-known statement supporting this movement. For a more recent statement see his 2005 book, *Privatization in the City* (Washington, DC: CQ Press).

CHAPTER 9

Judicial Institutions

This poster advertised a film that became the focal point of one of the most important Supreme Court cases in recent years, *Citizens United v. Federal Election Commission*, 130 S. Ct. 876 (2010). The 5-4 decision held that Congress had violated the U.S. Constitution by enacting limits on organizations' ability to fund electioneering communications.

- Judicial Functions
- Justice and the Political System
- Kinds of Law
- Judicial Institutions: Structure and Design

- Judicial Decisions and Public Policy
- Perspectives on Judicial Policy Making

The judiciary is perhaps the most controversial and most confusing of the major branches of modern governments. Legislatures and executives are expected to make and enforce policies; to authorize public expenditures for roads, schools, and social programs; to enact standards for worker and consumer safety; and to maintain national security, among many other things. The judiciary's functions are fundamentally different. Its decisions are, at least to a significant degree, based on judgments regarding *justice* and the *meaning of law*, not simply conclusions about which of several alternative policies is most cost effective or most desirable.

JUDICIAL FUNCTIONS

As noted in Chapter 1, rule adjudication is a basic function of government. Narrowly speaking, it involves the application of rules to individual cases. Nevertheless, the functions of courts in modern governments go far beyond the resolution of private conflicts between individuals or the application of law to particular individuals accused of crimes. Judicial decisions have an effect on the whole society, not only on those in the courtroom.

Of course, the primary function of judicial institutions is to *resolve conflict*. In a comprehensive, cross-national study, a noted scholar found that the practice of locating a disinterested third party to broker the resolution of a conflict between two people is so basic that "we can discover almost no society that fails to employ it."* Sometimes courts resolve conflict between two people regarding an alleged injury or contractual obligation. Courts also resolve conflicts of a higher order, as when they interpret constitutional provisions. Where they are perceived as trusted, nonpartisan institutions, courts typically have considerable power to resolve conflicts that citizens would not resolve on their own. (See A Closer Look 9.1.)

For that reason, judicial institutions can also help to *maintain social control*. To the extent that judicial authority is well established and stable, most citizens feel an obligation to comply with judicial decisions. Judicial institutions thus also perform the function of *legitimizing the regime*. When a court rules that a disputed legislative or executive action is in accordance with law, or constitutional, most citizens accept the result, giving greater support to the government. For example, the court system in Germany has been particularly important in legitimizing the profound governmental transitions that occurred in the process of integrating East and West. The dramatic changes in South Africa's political system brought about by the end of apartheid and the introduction of genuine universal suffrage were also legitimized with the aid of that country's court system.

Judicial institutions also frequently perform the function of *protecting minority rights*. Particularly in democracies, where legislatures and executives are responsive to majority will, courts may have a unique ability to hear and respond to the interests of those who, by virtue of their small numbers, cannot succeed in lobbying other branches of government. Finally, judicial institutions are often involved in *making public policy* since some judicial decisions shape policy choices made by executives and legislatures.

This list of functions emphasizes that judicial institutions often affect the functions and activities of other branches of the government, and yet judicial decisions involve a distinctive process that sets them apart. We evaluate legislative and executive decisions by the degree to which they promote the public interest, but we evaluate judicial decisions by whether or not they are *just*. Judicial decisions involve different standards, and judges operate in distinctive institutions that have a very different claim to legitimacy. The fact that courts are so different from electoral institutions while making their own contributions to policy is the main reason that questions about the proper role of courts in the political process remain confusing and divisive.

---

* The functions of judicial institutions are discussed in detail in Martin Shapiro, *Courts: A Comparative and Political Analysis* (Chicago: University of Chicago Press, 1981). Some of the following discussion is adapted from this source.

9.1

The Courts, Schools, Drugs, and Student Privacy

One of the most controversial aspects of the "war on drugs" in the United States is the increasingly common practice of drug testing. A number of private corporations routinely test their employees and applicants for present and past drug use, and some public school systems have initiated policies of drug testing for some students.

The issue of illegal drugs highlights a conflict between two important social goals: the elimination of damaging controlled substances and the preservation of privacy. It was perhaps inevitable that the issue of drug testing would reach the agenda of judicial institutions in the United States. In Tecumseh, Oklahoma, the local school district adopted a policy of requiring all students engaged in extracurricular activities to take a urinalysis drug test before participating in such activities and to submit to random drug testing thereafter. Two students, Lindsay Earls and Daniel James, were told that they must submit to the tests before they could participate in the show choir, the marching band, the Academic Team, and the National Honor Society, and they objected to

the drug testing as an unconstitutional violation of their privacy.

A previous decision by the Supreme Court held that schools could insist on random drug testing for students participating in *athletic* activities, largely because rigorous physical activity could create special problems for students engaging in drug use. However, in June 2002, the Court extended that idea to *all* extracurricular activities.* Although the Constitution does not *require* drug testing in schools, the majority concluded that it does not prohibit it and that a school can require any student electing to participate in extracurricular activities to undergo drug testing without obtaining a warrant and without any basis for suspecting the student of drug use.

Four justices dissented, arguing that student privacy requires that there be some individualized suspicion that a student is using illegal drugs before he or she can be forced to submit to urinalysis.

* The case was *Board of Education of Independent School District No. 92 v. Earls et al.,* 536 U.S. 822 (2002).

JUSTICE AND THE POLITICAL SYSTEM

The Concept of Justice

Nearly everything we can say about **justice** is culturally bound. Cultures vary tremendously with respect to concepts of "just" punishment, for instance. As discussed in Chapter 1, there is no universally accepted list of human rights. Consequently, it is difficult to say exactly what justice means in the abstract, although there is nearly universal agreement that it includes three things.

Perhaps the most widely accepted element of justice is the notion that *law must be fairly applied.* If the law states that a person should lose his or her hand as punishment for stealing (as it does in Saudi Arabia and some other Islamic nations), it would be unjust for that penalty to be applied only to people from a particular region or ethnic group. If the law states that all property will be taxed at the same rate, it would be unjust for an influential citizen to pay at a lower rate. If the law grants voting rights only to those who own land, it would be unjust for a person who owns the necessary land to be denied the right to vote because, for example, the individual is a member of a hated ethnic group. And if the law states that all young men and women must perform military service (as in Israel), it is unjust for those with connections to escape the draft.

Of course, few of us would find that simple principle of justice (equal application of the law) adequate. It describes only a part of what justice means. If justice is nothing more than consistent application of the law, what do we do about the possibility that the law *itself* is unjust? The example about voting and land ownership illustrates such a case. Even if judges apply that law in a just manner (that is, with consistency), most people would find it unjust to grant voting rights on the basis of land ownership. Similarly, many of us would question the justice of laws that deny certain legal rights to *all* females or to *all* members of a racial minority, regardless of how consistently they are applied. The problem is that cultural and historical differences across societies make it impossible to identify many universally accepted concepts of justice. Considerable agreement exists, however, about the more basic principle that—whatever the substance of the law—*justice demands that the law be consistently applied.*

A second widely accepted principle is the idea that *the severity of punishment should correspond to the severity of the crime.* Although cultures vary radically with respect to the kinds of punishment they find acceptable, nearly all have a range of punishments that vary in severity. Thus, although a number of nations deem capital punishment an appropriate penalty for murder, none find it just to apply that penalty to traffic violations or to underage drinking.

Third, it is almost universally accepted that justice demands *an accurate application of punishment.* Whatever the law, and whatever the punishment, the innocent should not be penalized. Thus, nearly all cultures have created some kind of fact-finding process, or trial, to determine whether a person who is accused of a crime is guilty. Widely accepted judicial values preclude punishing a person for something he or she did not do.

The essential nature of justice accounts for the distinctiveness of judicial institutions in most political systems.* It takes specialized institutions to produce fair and accurate decisions about individual guilt. The legitimacy of the political system itself is enhanced when citizens perceive judicial institutions as operating in accordance with standards of justice; the regime becomes illegitimate in the eyes of most citizens when judicial institutions appear unfair, "rigged," or helpful only to a certain part of the population.

Two Systems of Justice

The actual workings of judicial institutions are significantly affected by the system of justice under which they operate. Although each country has its own special features,

---

* Of course, we often use the terms *just* and *unjust* in a different way. We may say, for example, that it is unjust for a poor family to go without medical care or that it is unjust for wealthy people to be taxed at a higher rate than poorer ones. Such statements reflect views of what is in the public interest rather than legal norms, and they are therefore usually discussed in the explicitly political institutions of government.

most have either an *adversarial* or an *inquisitorial* system. The systems vary with regard to the role of judges, the importance of lawyers, and the approach to fact finding, although both systems are designed to evaluate evidence and apply the law fairly and accurately.

The Adversarial System Anglo-American law operates under the **adversarial system**. The judge is supposed to be impartial, representing neither party but standing for the interests of the justice system. He or she is relatively passive as the **plaintiff** and the **defendant** present evidence, examine witnesses, and make legal arguments.

The adversarial process typically includes provision for a **grand jury** to make preliminary decisions in criminal cases since the judge is essentially neutral. The prosecutor, who is formally distinct from the judge, first presents evidence to a grand jury in an effort to establish that a person should be formally charged (indicted) for a crime. If the grand jury issues an indictment (a formal accusation) and the case goes before the court, the judge's role is limited. Although he or she retains the power to decide which laws are applicable and how they should be understood by the jury, the judge has little power to introduce evidence or to question witnesses. The judicial decision itself thus critically depends on the positions articulated by contending prosecution and defense attorneys.

The Inquisitorial System Among industrial democracies, France has the best-known **inquisitorial system**, the most striking feature of which is the active role played by the judge. French magistrates fully examine the evidence in a criminal case, discussing the allegations with the defendant and the witnesses. Judges can also supervise the gathering of additional information.

Thus, cases normally come to the trial stage only when the judge is convinced that the accused is guilty. The trial provides an opportunity for the accused to dispute facts publicly, but new evidence or arguments are not usually presented. The conclusion reached many years ago by a leading scholar remains accurate today: It is rare for a criminal case brought to trial in an inquisitorial system to end in anything other than conviction.*

The Systems Compared No consensus exists regarding which of these two systems is superior. In democratic societies, both systems usually are acceptably fair and accurate, although serious miscarriages of justice have occurred in both systems. There are some important practical differences between the systems, however.

The adversarial system depends critically on the skill and experience of lawyers. If defendants are unable to obtain effective legal representation, their positions will not be articulated well. Since the judge assumes a largely passive role, facts and arguments that should be presented will probably not become part of the record. This problem is especially significant for poorer citizens, although most systems now provide for publicly funded legal assistance for the poor. But before 1963 in the United States, the state's experienced prosecuting attorney was often opposed by an unrepresented defendant. The unfairness of that situation led to the famous

---

* See Henry J. Abraham, *The Judicial Process*, 4th ed. (New York: Oxford University Press, 1980), pp. 105–107; and Shapiro, *Courts*, pp. 133ff.

Gideon v. Wainwright decision requiring the provision, at state expense, of a public defender so that the poor could receive legal representation.* Even so, poor criminal defendants are frequently represented today by overworked and underprepared public defenders, whereas Mafia dons, former professional athletes, or corrupt officials hire the best attorneys available.

The inquisitorial system is far less affected by differences in skill and experience among the lawyers representing defendants. Nevertheless, it requires the existence of highly skilled and scrupulously independent judges. If French judges were widely perceived as politically motivated or ignorant of the law, the system would certainly not have the legitimacy that it has. The established tradition of selecting judges through a special training academy is thus a basic adjunct to the French inquisitorial system of justice.

Kinds of Law

Law is one of the most widely used terms in political analysis. Understanding the law requires first that we appreciate the different kinds of law that exist. Laws vary with respect to origin, status, and subject matter.

Natural and Positive Law

Philosophers, judges, and politicians have argued about the existence and content of natural law for millennia, and such arguments will doubtless continue as long as people discuss justice and government. In simple terms, **natural law** is a moral or ethical standard grounded either in nature itself (how things *should* be according to some view of a natural order) or in theology (what the Divine has dictated). Natural law exists apart from **positive law**, the body of laws devised by humans. Some legal and moral philosophers have devoted great energies to discovering principles of natural law. Among the most important are Aristotle, Cicero, Thomas Aquinas, the Stoics, Locke, and Rousseau.

Aside from the realm of philosophy, natural law emerges most often in rhetoric as people debate political movements or issues. For example, following John Locke's writings, the American revolutionaries contended that several British laws governing them were invalid because they violated *rights under natural law*. Thomas Jefferson invoked natural law in the Declaration of Independence so that the radical action the colonists were taking would not appear to be simply arbitrary or selfish. Essentially, he argued that the laws enacted by the British king and parliament were unjust when held against the standard created by the view of natural law that he advocated.

Today, many people argue similarly that natural law demands the rejection of positive laws authorizing prison terms for political dissidents or members of particular religions. People on both sides of the abortion debate in the United States claim that natural law requires changes in positive law; some of those opposing abortion rights

---

* See *Gideon v. Wainwright*, 373 U.S. 335 (1963).

argue that natural law protects the right of the unborn, whereas many supporters of abortion rights assert the existence of a natural-law right of privacy that prohibits legislators from enacting restrictions on abortions. The idea of natural law is enormously important in political philosophy, but its most common role is as an argument in political debate.

Basic Law

The idea that some body of law is supreme exists in many political systems. **Basic law** may be found in a written constitution, in a religious document, or even in time-honored traditions. The key feature of basic law is that when other laws contradict it, basic law is assumed to be controlling. Basic law thus serves as a set of standards that limit which laws legislatures, agencies, or executives can enact.

The U.S. Constitution is perhaps the most well-known example of basic law, primarily because questions about the *constitutionality* of other laws are so often raised in disputes brought to court (see Chapter 10). Its first 10 amendments itemize specific actions that Congress and the president cannot take, thereby establishing important civil rights. Although the British constitution is unwritten, the strong traditions in that system limit the kinds of laws Parliament can pass, and thus those traditions serve as a kind of basic law. (See A Closer Look 9.2.) In Iran, all legislation must conform to Islamic law as expressed in the Koran.

An inevitable problem arises when basic law appears to conflict with other laws: Someone or some institution must decide whether a conflict actually exists. For example, when a U.S. community passes an ordinance prohibiting flag burning, a sharp debate erupts between proponents of the restriction and those who feel it violates the First Amendment. Courts generally resolve the dispute, creating a potential threat to democratic accountability, as we discuss later in this chapter and in Chapter 10. But if no judicial body is capable of overriding the legislative institution that makes regular law, basic law may lose most of its importance. In such instances, the parliament simply passes the law it wants, along with a resolution stating that the law does not violate basic law. The impact of basic law thus varies from one political system to another.*

Statutory Law

Laws passed by the legislature or a parliament make up a nation's **statutory law**. These laws include proscriptions of criminal acts, the establishment of tax obligations, the creation of regulatory powers, and many other matters. In addition to the texts of statutes themselves, statutory law exists in **statutory interpretation**. The application of statutes, even specific ones, is often unclear. In deciding cases, courts often issue interpretations of the provisions contained in statutes, and those interpretations become part of the law. Following the concept of *stare decisis* (Latin for "let the decision stand"), as most legal systems around the world do, the interpretations are written down and serve as guides for subsequent applications. In a very real sense,

---

* In Canada, interpreting basic law was previously a legislative task, although since 1982 the judiciary has assumed this role under the Canadian Charter of Rights and Freedoms.

A CLOSER LOOK

(**9.2**

Do Bills of Rights Matter?

The idea of a "bill of rights" is perhaps the most commonly discussed example of basic law, but it is arguable that its existence makes little difference in the actual workings of a political system. A 1996 study in the *American Political Science Review* evaluated the actual effects of bills of rights on the political process. The author, Charles Epp of the University of Kansas, noted that "nearly every new constitution or constitutional revision adopted since 1945 (almost 60 by rough count) contains a bill of rights."[1] To address the question of whether the adoption of a bill of rights has any impact, Epp studied the Canadian system, which adopted the Canadian Charter of Rights and Freedoms in 1982. He was therefore able to compare the system before and after the adoption of its bill of rights.

What difference are bills of rights *supposed* to make? Epp points out that supporters of such charters argue that they increase the emphasis on rights in the political culture and thus increase the tendency of courts to intervene in policy actions by the legislative and executive branches. Evidence does indicate that the Canadian Supreme Court has placed greater emphasis on civil liberties and rights cases in recent years, that it has been more likely to support rights claims, and that a greater proportion of its cases involves disputes between individuals and government. However, Epp found that most of these changes in judicial behavior have been a function of the development of a more complete "support structure" for legal mobilization, including steady growth in the size of the legal community and expanded government programs to finance rights litigation and advocacy.

The Canadian experience thus suggests that, at most, the adoption of a bill of rights is but one among many factors that can lead to greater limits on government power in the area of individual rights and freedoms.

Nevertheless, the idea of a bill of rights has considerable support in most democracies. In a May 1995 poll, over three-fourths of British citizens supported the idea of a written constitution and a bill of rights. After the signing of the European Charter of Fundamental Rights, a comprehensive bill of rights covering the European Union, they finally have one. However, a special protocol clarifies the limits of the Charter's impact on British law:

> The Charter does not extend the ability of the Court of Justice, or any court or tribunal of the United Kingdom, to find that the laws, regulations or administrative provisions, practices or action of the United Kingdom are inconsistent with the fundamental rights, freedoms and principles that it reaffirms.
>
> In particular, ... nothing in the Charter creates justifiable rights applicable to the United Kingdom except in so far as the United Kingdom has provided for such rights in its national law.*

* From the European Union's *Charter of Fundamental Rights*, Annex II, Protocol (No. 7), "On the Application of the Charter of Fundamental Rights to Poland and to the United Kingdom," available at www.publications.parliament.uk/pa/cm200708/cmselect/cmfaff/120/7101009.htm.

---

the meaning of statutes is derived *both* from their original texts *and* from judges' interpretations of them.

For example, in 2006, a case presented to the U.S. Supreme Court required the justices to decide what Congress had in mind when it enacted the Controlled Substances Act in 1970. Did the words of this statute make it a federal crime for doctors to prescribe drugs to be used in physician-assisted suicide, or did the statute only apply to illegal sales and possession of drugs? In 1994, the citizens of Oregon passed the Oregon Death with Dignity Act (through a state referendum), which permitted licensed physicians to dispense a lethal dose of drugs on request by a terminally ill patient.

The Bush Administration argued that, despite the Oregon law, physicians dispensing drugs for suicide could be prosecuted in federal court under the Controlled Substances Act because that act limited the use of controlled substances to "legitimate medical purposes." The state of Oregon argued that the Controlled Substances Act did not give the federal government power to interfere with a state's power to legalize physician-assisted suicide because Congress never intended for the federal Act to apply to such practices (only to the problem of illegal sales and possession of controlled substances).

The Court, in a 6–3 decision, interpreted the scope of the Controlled Substances Act in the way that the state of Oregon did: "we conclude the CSA's prescription requirement does not … bar [the] dispensing [of] controlled substances for assisted suicide in the face of a state medical regime permitting such conduct." Hence, to understand whether or not physician-assisted suicide violates federal drug law, it is necessary to read both the relevant statute (the Controlled Substances Act) *and* the majority opinion in *Gonzales v. Oregon*.[*]

Common Law

Even with their accumulated interpretations, basic and statutory law cannot cover all situations that confront courts. **Common law** is a distinct kind of law that also guides judicial decisions. Specifically, the term derives from the evolution of the British legal system. When Henry II became king in 1154, many disputes were settled by local courts using different standards and principles. He took steps that eventually produced a system of laws "common" throughout his kingdom.[2]

In the U.S. and British systems, perhaps the best illustration of common law is the law governing *torts*: "What limits a person's freedom to hurt another person? When does law say I cannot threaten someone with a blow? When can't I strike the blow? When may I not publicly insult another (libel and slander)? When may I not do careless things that injure other people (negligence)?"[3] Those and similar questions have been answered throughout much of British and American history by the precedents of common law. Traditional practices and concepts of fairness, as applied by generations of judges, delineated what constituted wrongful acts in those and many other contexts.

As a practical matter, when lawyers want to find out for their clients whether a particular activity is legal under common law, they consult the decisions in previous court cases that indicate the meaning of the common law. Instead of looking only at the laws made by legislatures (statutes), the lawyer must consider the "judge-made" common law to find the answer. The concept of *stare decisis* applies to matters of common law just as it applies to questions of statutory interpretation, and thus a lawyer can argue that a previous decision involving facts similar to those faced by his or her client should guide the judge's ruling. The opposing lawyer will search for precedents that suggest a different conclusion, and the judge (or jury) has to decide which precedent applies.

Of course, statutory law can displace common law by specifying certain interpretations. For example, the common law on nuisance behavior is, in many U.S. states, supplemented by statutory definitions. Statutory law often incorporates principles that first appeared as precepts of common law.

---

[*] See *Gonzales, Attorney General, et al. v. Oregon et al.*, 546 U.S. 243 (2006).

Civil and Criminal Law

A distinction between civil and criminal law is found in nearly all political systems. When two individuals have a dispute, the state may or may not be concerned. If the dispute is primarily between the private parties, it is a matter for **civil law**. Examples include disputes regarding slander, the location of property lines, and liability for accident damage. One party sues another for compensation, and the court is asked to decide which party has the valid claim.

Criminal law has to do with actions that the state has defined as offenses against the state. If a person robs a bank, for example, it is not up to the bank to sue the thief. The state will prosecute the violator under criminal statutes. The rationale is that the thief not only injured the bank but also threatened the security of the society at large. In some cases, the same action can result in *both* civil and criminal litigation. In what was one of the most widely publicized trials in decades, O.J. Simpson had to defend himself in criminal court against allegations that he murdered his wife and her friend. He was found not guilty in 1995, but a jury in a *civil* trial nevertheless found him liable for the victims' deaths a year later. Some people felt that it was unfair for Simpson to have to defend himself twice from the same accusation, but the state only prosecuted him once (the criminal trial). The civil action involved private parties attempting to gain compensation.

Most societies have broadened the range of conduct regulated by criminal statutes, creating the possibility of criminal convictions for actions previously settled as civil disputes under common law. This trend has great practical import since the victim does not have to take legal action for punishment to occur when the act in question is criminal. (The victim will still have to seek damages in civil court to receive compensation, however.) Civil rights laws, for example, made certain acts of discrimination or harassment criminal offenses, whereas previously the injured party would have needed to institute a civil suit in order for the guilty party to be penalized.

JUDICIAL INSTITUTIONS: STRUCTURE AND DESIGN

The best way to appreciate why judicial institutions are so different from legislatures is by looking at the special nature of the decisions they make. Consider the difference between a *legislative* question about taxation (Should we raise the property tax rate?) and a *judicial* question about taxation (Did Jane Doe submit a false tax return?). The answer to the first question is a matter of public policy: the need for more revenue, the predicted impact of higher taxes on economic growth or on different income groups, and so forth. The answer to the second question has to do with facts pertaining to an *individual's* behavior.

In most systems, citizens believe that these two kinds of decisions must be made in different kinds of institutions using different procedures. For example, bias is a very different matter in legislative and judicial decisions. It is perfectly appropriate for a Canadian member of Parliament to announce that she has reached a firm decision about a national farm bill before debating the issue in the legislative chambers. Nobody expects an Irish, Italian, American, or German legislator to be impartial when he or she participates in deliberations; in fact, the legislator would not be a very good representative if he or she had *no* preannounced positions. It is fine for a legislator to enter parliamentary session on a bill with a publicly stated point of view.

However, we would find it profoundly unjust for a judge to enter the courtroom after having publicly declared his or her view about the honesty of Jane Doe's tax return. We would also consider it unfair if the judge's decision had been affected by Doe's partisan affiliation or the judge's party's attitude toward her. Preannounced positions and external influences are fine when officials make legislative or policy decisions, but they constitute a miscarriage of justice when purely judicial decisions are at stake.

The difference between the standards applying to legislative and judicial decisions is the reason that judges and courts are given different powers and separate institutions and the reason that they are (usually) selected through a different process. Judges are even made to appear distinctive. In Western cultures, for example, judges frequently wear robes, elaborate wigs, and other striking apparel, and we often address them in ways that underscore their unique position. In some African tribal societies, judges may sit on a distinctive throne when rendering decisions. Judicial decision making is a special kind of governmental action, and most political systems make great efforts to establish and preserve its legitimacy. The way judges are selected, the structure of the judiciary, and the power of the judiciary over the other parts of government are three central questions about judicial institutions that we examine here.

Selection and Tenure of Judges

Judges can be chosen by appointment or by election and can serve fixed or indefinite (life) terms. Whereas U.S. Supreme Court judges serve for life (or until voluntary retirement), members of the French Constitutional Council serve fixed nine-year terms. Judges in some countries may be removed only after a finding of illegal conduct in office; in other systems, judges may be removed as easily as cabinet officers.

Judicial behavior is significantly affected by the choices made among these alternatives. Rules governing the selection and tenure of judges usually represent a compromise between two incompatible values: *political accountability* and *judicial independence*. Democratic values require accountability to the people, but, as noted earlier, judicial decisions are usually supposed to follow standards of fairness and objectivity. Thus, democratic systems typically expect their judges to be politically accountable *and* politically detached—responsive to public will and yet insulated from it. Systems for selecting judges are shaped by those often irreconcilable goals.

In some countries, judges are selected through a process that begins with their formal education. For example, French judges are selected only from among those who choose to enter the National Center for Judicial Studies for four years after completing their legal training. In the United States, judges may be elected (most states) or appointed (federal courts), but there are no strict guidelines regarding their education (although, in practice, a law degree is required). In contrast, Japanese judges must first pass a National Bar Examination to enter the Legal Training and Research Institute (*Shihou Kenshuu Sho*), and only about 1,000 of the more than 20,000 candidates who take the exam each year actually pass it. After two years of training, graduates of the institute must choose among three career options: attorney, prosecutor, or judge. There is virtually no movement between these career paths in

Japan.[4] Employing yet another approach to selecting judges, those who serve on Swiss courts are elected by the two chambers of the National Assembly.[5]

Most processes for selecting judges contain features that try to minimize the extent to which either independence or accountability is compromised. Perhaps the most explicit attempt to achieve both accountability and independence in the United States is the **Missouri Plan**, an arrangement adopted by that state in 1940. Under this system, the state governor selects a judge from a set of nominees submitted by an independent nominating commission. The commission is made up of lawyers, former judges, and citizens. Supporters contend that the Missouri Plan ensures that only qualified, competent judges will be nominated since the nominating commission has the time and the expertise to select the best candidates. At the same time, accountability is secured because the commission is designed to be somewhat representative and because the plan usually provides for the rejection of nominees (or the recall of appointed judges) by popular referendum. Since the governor is an elected official, further accountability is introduced into the process through his or her participation.

Where judges are elected by citizens, as in 31 U.S. states, the elections are usually officially nonpartisan (that is, the candidates cannot run as members of a political party). Candidates must also satisfy certain qualifications. The election system thus is expected to establish some responsiveness to the public, but safeguards are in place to minimize explicitly partisan political influence.

However, a recent study of U.S. state judges suggests that even nonpartisan elections affect the decisions that judges make. Using data on criminal sentences from over 22,000 cases in Pennsylvania, two political scientists found that "elected judges will become more punitive" as their reelection time approaches. Voters generally are more concerned about cases in which convicted criminals receive light sentences than cases in which judges hand down overly severe sentences. Because most judges are motivated to win reelection, they apparently make sentencing decisions that reflect voters' demands. The data from this 2004 study indicate that, due to their perception that voters prefer judges that are "tough on crime," Pennsylvania judges handed down an additional 1,800 to 2,700 years of incarceration in 22,000 cases.[6]

Similarly, a 2002 study found that, despite the existence of laws designed to protect judicial independence, political pressures in Argentina led judges to refrain from issuing rulings against government actions until the last months of a weakening regime. The courts there are reluctant to rule contrary to the wishes of the government while the administration is still strong. Finally, a 2001 study of Japan found that judges who support the government on sensitive policy questions tend to do better in their careers.[7]

In short, while appointed judgeships may seem completely removed from popular control, the voters have an important indirect influence. Presidents, prime ministers, and others who appoint judges make appointments that reflect their ideological positions, and they often influence the activities of those already serving.

The independence of judges depends on the extent to which removal is possible and the manner in which they are selected. Since both prosecutors and politicians may want to influence a judge's decisions, effective judicial independence requires that judges must be protected from these improper influences. The simplest way to achieve this protection is by granting judges permanent tenure and by limiting the extent to which their salaries can be reduced (as in the case of federal judges in the United States). French prosecutors and judges are lodged in the same ministry,

9.3

An Extreme Case of Judicial Independence

It is possible that judicial independence can get out of hand. In most Western nations, citizens cannot sue judges or hold them personally liable for making incorrect or even illegal decisions. The rationale for that is simple: Judges are supposed to make their decisions on the basis of the facts and the law pertaining to a case, not on the basis of a concern for their own financial interests. A 1978 U.S. Supreme Court case tested that principle.

The mother of a 15-year-old girl petitioned an Indiana federal judge to have her daughter surgically sterilized. Although the girl had been making adequate progress in school, she had allegedly become sexually active. Apparently fearing the consequences, her mother told the judge that the girl was "somewhat retarded" and asked him to order her sterilization.

Without any hearing, and acting without any legal power, the judge issued a court order.

Under the order, the hospital officials told the girl that she was being taken to the hospital for an appendectomy, where the sterilization procedure was performed. When she subsequently found out why she could not bear children, she sued the judge, and her case ultimately was brought before the U.S. Supreme Court. Three justices felt that the judge's decision was so far beyond his legal authority that it should be considered outside the limits of his role and thus that he should be liable for damages. Nevertheless, the Court's majority ruled that the judge was "immune from damages liability even if his approval of the petition was in error." See *Stump v. Sparkman*, 435 U.S. 349 (1978).

---

although the separateness of their positions is recognized. In other cases, special commissions are established to supervise judges. The purpose of all these provisions is to minimize the likelihood that judges will feel the necessity to make certain decisions to preserve their jobs or salaries. (See A Closer Look 9.3.)

Hierarchy in Judicial Institutions

Hierarchy is a nearly universal feature of judicial institutions. Virtually all political systems have multiple units of the judiciary, and some courts are explicitly subordinate to others. In the U.S. federal court system, for example, 94 district courts constitute the first level, 13 circuit courts of appeal represent the second level, and the Supreme Court stands at the top. That basic three-layer judicial system has been widely adopted, although the relative sizes of the layers vary widely across countries.*

The most important difference among levels is between the lowest court and all others. **Trial courts** are where cases are heard for the first time, and in adversarial systems they are where facts are introduced and discussed. Higher courts, known as **appellate courts**, normally do not consider new factual evidence bearing on cases but reserve their time to evaluate the application of the law in the lower court (or courts). Appellate courts attempt to determine whether the trial court applied appropriate law

---

* In France, the lower courts are the *Tribunaux de Premiere Instance;* in Germany, they are the *Landsgerichte;* and in Great Britain, the corresponding units are the county and the crown courts. The national supreme court of Germany is the *Bundesgerichtshof;* in Switzerland it is the *Swiss Federal Tribunal;* and in France it is the *Court of Cassation.*

and whether its interpretations were correct. Appellate courts are far less numerous than trial courts since most trials are not appealed. The hierarchy of judicial institutions has two important benefits. First, it provides for an effective check on incompetent, irresponsible, arbitrary, or corrupt judicial decisions. If a trial court improperly considers or excludes evidence, or if a judge or a prosecutor fails to follow legally required procedures, the appeals court may reverse the decision or call for a new trial. Even when errors are made in good faith, an appeal can lead to their correction. Second, a system of appellate courts creates the possibility of *uniform* interpretation of the law. Without a system of superior appellate courts, new interpretations of law would apply only in the districts in which trial courts devised them. When the highest appellate court interprets the law, the law has the same meaning throughout the system.

Judicial Review

The concept of basic law, discussed earlier, implies that ordinary or statutory law must not abridge certain basic principles. However, citizens, politicians, and scholars almost never agree about claims regarding a conflict between statutory law and basic law. Whether or not a given law (or executive action) actually violates basic law can be a matter of great controversy, and therefore some institutional power must be available to issue an authoritative judgment.

In some systems, the courts have that power. In a classic text by a leading scholar of judicial institutions, **Judicial review** was defined as "the power ... to hold unconstitutional and hence unenforceable any law that [is deemed] ... to be in conflict with the Basic Law."[8] Courts have the power of judicial review in the United States, Italy, Canada, Germany, Japan, India, the Republic of Ireland, Australia, and Norway, among some two dozen other countries. In France, the nine-member Constitutional Council can overturn parliamentary legislation as well as decrees made by the prime minister or the president, but its powers are somewhat limited and sometimes subject to presidential pressures.[9]

Although one often speaks of the "Anglo-American legal system" to indicate an approach to courts and law that has been partially adopted in a number of countries, the United States and Britain follow very different approaches to judicial review. The concept of **parliamentary supremacy** is firmly established in Britain. Where there are disagreements regarding whether or not a given Act of Parliament violates basic rights or well-established practices, Parliament itself has the power to decide the issue. The British parliament is thus legally free to enact any statute it wants.

Many U.S. citizens would be uncomfortable with such a system. For example, the Bill of Rights is a set of statements prohibiting Congress from taking certain actions—if Congress itself could decide whether or not a law it wants to enact is forbidden by the Constitution, most Americans would say that the Constitution would have no real impact. Congress would do what it wants and then pass a law saying it was constitutional. On the other hand, advocates of parliamentary supremacy argue that the U.S. system frustrates democratic government and that, even without a court system with powers to overturn Acts of Parliament, the British parliament is effectively held in check by the electoral system and competition among political parties.

Judicial review in Germany and India leads to less court involvement in public policy than in the United States but constrains the legislature more than in Britain. As one analyst put it, although courts in these systems rarely issue rulings that overturn major policy decisions, they do insist that legislative actions be "reasonable" and "nonarbitrary."[10]

JUDICIAL DECISIONS AND PUBLIC POLICY

As we stressed at the start of this chapter, the types of decisions they make is what distinguishes judicial institutions from executive and legislative institutions. Whereas democratic values require that policy makers be influenced by citizens, vote totals, parties, and interest groups, our concept of justice requires that judges be insulated from political influence so that their actions will be free from prejudice or partisanship.

In most political systems, citizens agree on the need for an independent judiciary. The winds of public opinion should not influence an appellate court's decision about whether or not to uphold a murder conviction. But when judicial decisions involve policy—school integration, pollution, or abortion, for example—the question of judicial independence becomes far more controversial.

How Judicial Policy Making Occurs

Many judicial decisions involve more than a determination of the facts; they also raise questions of legal interpretation. The precise meaning of the law is often uncertain, either because circumstances arise that were not foreseen when the constitutional provision or law was written or because policy makers deliberately avoided the politically painful process of spelling out particular applications of the law. When judges "fill in the details," they make their own interpretations, and those interpretations often include important policy choices.

Consider the following example: Before 1970, U.S. states could terminate benefits to welfare recipients as soon as the state welfare department decided that the recipient no longer satisfied the eligibility requirements. State law simply required that the agency send a letter to the recipient explaining that benefits had been terminated and that the recipient could request a hearing to dispute the agency's decision. No benefits were paid while these hearings were pending.

In accordance with applicable state law, New York welfare officials concluded that some welfare recipients had income levels that made them ineligible for continued assistance, and they terminated their benefits. The recipients appealed to federal court, claiming that the State of New York had violated the due process clause of the U.S. Constitution by terminating their benefits without an opportunity for an oral hearing to dispute the decision. The Due Process Clause, included in the Fourteenth Amendment, states that no person may be deprived of "life, liberty, or property" without due process of law. Claiming that welfare benefits were property, the plaintiffs argued that their benefits could not be terminated unless the state gave recipients an opportunity for a hearing *before* the termination of benefits.

The state interpreted the due process clause differently. It argued that the clause did not require the state to give the welfare recipient a hearing whenever the state concluded that he or she was no longer eligible for benefits. After all, the recipient was not being put in jail or being subjected to a fine.

The Supreme Court agreed with the welfare recipients, overturning the New York law.*

The Supreme Court's decision fundamentally altered the day-to-day administration of welfare policy throughout the country. A dissenting justice (Hugo Black) contended that the decision would require states to hire more lawyers and to devote more of the money allocated for public welfare to litigation expenses. Moreover, he suggested, the new arrangement could make welfare caseworkers reluctant to approve borderline welfare applications since it would now be more costly and time-consuming to terminate benefits awarded in error. Whether for good or ill, the way in which welfare policy is implemented in a number of states was significantly affected by the Supreme Court's interpretation of fewer than a dozen words of the Constitution.

Judicial decisions can also change or make policy when no constitutional or basic law issues are at stake. For example, beginning in the 1930s, U.S. federal law established that employees have the right to bargain collectively with their employers and that employers are guilty of an unfair labor practice when they refuse to bargain with a legally constituted union. In the 1940s, a group of "newsboys" (that rather old-fashioned term was used in the case) sought to bargain collectively with the Hearst Corporation. Hearst refused, claiming that the newsboys were not employees within the meaning of the law. Federal law did not specify what the term *employee* meant; it only stated that *employees* had certain labor rights.

The Supreme Court held that the National Labor Relations Board could legally conclude that newsboys were employees and that, consequently, the Hearst Corporation was guilty of an unfair labor practice in refusing to bargain collectively with them.[†] The Court thereby affected the development of national labor policy by resolving this specific dispute between several dozen sellers of newspapers and one corporation.

The point here is that judicial policy making is *inevitable*. Courts cannot limit the impact of their judgments to the parties before them. The interpretation of law changes policies and programs, sometimes altering decisions previously considered to be political or even managerial matters. How we evaluate the reality of judicial policy making is a subject of continuing controversy.

Perspectives on Judicial Policy Making

Judicial Restraint

The idea of **judicial restraint** is that courts should accept the decisions of legislative, executive, and administrative officials except when those decisions are *clearly* contrary to basic law or inconsistent with other legal guidelines. Challenges to the constitutional acceptability of a law should be evaluated according to the intentions of those who drafted the constitution or the law in question. Thus, advocates of judicial restraint argue that judges should overturn a piece of legislation *only* if it is clearly in violation of explicit constitutional provisions.

---

* The landmark case was *Goldberg v. Kelly*, 397 U.S. 254 (1970).

[†] See *National Labor Relations Board v. Hearst*, 322 U.S. 111 (1944).

Consider the welfare rights case discussed above. The drafters of the due process clause surely did not have welfare benefits in mind when they wrote it; the clause was intended to require a fair trial before a person is punished (by forfeiting life, liberty, or property) for committing a crime. Advocates of judicial restraint would therefore argue that the court "made up" law when it forced New York to provide an oral hearing to welfare recipients before termination of benefits. If policy is to be changed in this way, it is legislators, not the courts, who should make the change.

An important rationale for this position is that courts lack democratic legitimacy as policy makers. In democratic systems, legislatures and elected executives are legitimate policy makers because they were selected by the voters on the basis of their announced policy positions. If they make policy choices that the people oppose, the voters will elect different legislators or executives in the next election. Judges making policy are not subject to those critical democratic safeguards.

Other reasons have been offered in support of judicial restraint. The process of judicial decision making itself arguably makes courts poor policy-making bodies. Courts can take into account only the information brought to them, and the cases that come their way may be exceptional and unrepresentative of the broader context in which the policy change will be implemented. In contrast, legislators and executives, along with administrative agencies, can gather information extensively, and they can make policy on the basis of the typical, not the extraordinary, cases.[11]

Even in European judicial systems, where judicial review is far less prominent than in the United States, judicial policy making is controversial. Politicians and judges in Italy, France, and Germany continue to disagree about the propriety of an active judicial role. Some argue that "where a gap in the [law] exists, the judge should imagine what the legislature would do. [Others] specify that the judge should imagine what he [or she] would do if he [or she] were the legislature."[12]

Judicial Activism

One of the most common responses to the judicial restraint idea is the notion that courts have a special ability to represent minority political interests, and that these interests will never obtain adequate representation from institutions that naturally respond to majorities of voters. Proponents of **judicial activism** thus argue that some minority interests are excluded from effective participation. Judicial policy making may effectively represent those interests when the other parts of the political system are closed to them.

For example, the policy of desegregating U.S. public schools was initiated by a judicial decision (*Brown v. Board of Education of Topeka*, 347 U.S. 500, 1954). Efforts to achieve desegregation had repeatedly failed in legislative action at both the state and the federal levels. In a sense, the courts provided political representation to voices left unheeded by the other policy-making institutions of the system.* If strict doctrines of judicial restraint meant that courts could not engage in policy making, courts would not be able to enhance representation in this way.

Advocates of judicial restraint quickly point out that although judicial activism sometimes produces good policies, it is, as a process, inconsistent with democracy

---

* The idea that courts may generally represent the interests of those who are politically disadvantaged in their abilities to exert influence elsewhere in the political system is discussed in Chapter 6.

because judges (at least on the federal level) are not elected. However, at least one political scientist has recently argued that courts should be active in policy decisions even though they are not politically accountable and even though they cannot be politically neutral. According to this view, "there is nothing wrong with a political court or with political motives in constitutional adjudication."[13] The tension between advocates of activism and restraint guarantee that this issue will remain unresolved for generations. (See A Closer Look 9.4.)

A CLOSER LOOK

9.4

The Courts as Policy Makers: A Debate

The late John Hart Ely was among the most prominent legal scholars in U.S. history. His Democracy and Distrust—A Theory of Judicial Review (1980) is the most frequently cited book about law published in the 20th century. He died in 2003.

A portrait by Alonzo Chappel of Chief Justice John Marshall, who headed the U.S. Supreme Court from 1801 to 1835.

Whether or not courts should be engaged in policy making continues to be a topic of heated argument among legal scholars, political theorists, and politicians. Two well-known U.S. legal thinkers reflect opposite perspectives on the issue in striking terms.

Robert Bork, a former judge on the U.S. Court of Appeals whom the Senate refused to confirm when President Reagan nominated him for the Supreme Court in 1987, is perhaps the most famous contemporary advocate of judicial restraint. In a case involving whether the due

9.4

Former President Gerald Ford, left, introduces Supreme Court Associate Justice nominee Robert Bork, Tuesday September 15, 1987, as the Senate Judiciary Committee began confirmation hearings on the nomination on Capitol Hill. Ford praised Bork as being "uniquely qualified" for the post. At right is Sen. Robert Dole, R-KS, who also made a statement on Bork.

process clause protects the right of people to engage in homosexual conduct in private, Judge Bork described the role of the court in policy making in the following way:

> [This court is] asked to protect from regulation a form of behavior never before protected and indeed traditionally condemned. If the revolution in sexual mores that the [petitioner] proclaims is to arrive, it must arrive through the moral choices of the people and their elected representatives, not through the ukase of this court…. The Constitution creates specific rights. A court that refuses to create a new constitutional right to protect homosexual conduct does not thereby destroy established rights that are solidly based in constitutional text and history.[14]

Bork's way of thinking—one that emphasizes that judges must be careful to follow the plain meaning of the words in the Constitution and in statutes—is often termed "strict constructionism." Perhaps the first person to use this phrase in describing how judges should interpret law was Chief Justice John Marshall, in 1824:

> What do gentlemen mean by a "strict construction"? If they contend only against that enlarged construction,

which would extend words beyond their natural and obvious import, we … should not controvert the principle…. As men whose intentions require no concealment generally employ the words which most directly and aptly express the ideas they intend to convey, the enlightened patriots who framed our Constitution, and the people who adopted it, must be understood to have employed words in their natural sense, and to have intended what they have said. (*Gibbons v. Ogden,* 9 Wheat. 1, 1824).

The late John Ely, also a leading legal scholar (by one count, he is the fourth most cited legal scholar of all time), saw a broader role for judicial decision making than Marshall or Bork. Arguing that the elected institutions of government do not function perfectly to represent all of society's interests, Ely suggested that judicial policy making may fill in some important gaps:

> It is an appropriate function of the [Supreme] Court to keep the machinery of democratic government running as it should, to make sure the channels of political participation and communication are kept open. The Court should also concern itself with what majorities do to minorities, particularly [in the case of] laws "directed at" religious, national, and racial minorities and those infected by prejudice against them.[15]

Ely claimed that if courts can infuse their own ideas into the interpretation of constitutional provisions, they can make decisions that will be "representation enhancing." Thus, they would secure minority rights that would be demolished by the unchecked activities of other parts of the political system and which would be unaddressed if courts simply applied the intentions of those writing laws and constitutions in centuries gone by. To make the system work, Ely argued that courts must be able to go beyond strict constructionism, interpreting constitutional provisions not in a neutral or objective sense (which he and many others feel is impossible anyway), but by interpreting them to the advantage of groups and citizens who have little political influence in the elected branches of government.

The debate over judicial activism is a sticky problem for many political systems, but particularly for the United States, as we will see in Chapter 10.

Judicial Policy Making as a Stabilizing Force

Abrupt changes in policy can be destabilizing in any society. When legislatures create new rights or obligations, they radically affect personal, economic, and other kinds of interests. Lawmakers may attempt major transformations of policies in various areas, and although the changes may be ultimately wise, they may threaten the stability of the system. A third perspective thus approves of judicial policy making because of its potentially moderating influence on changes emerging from legislatures and executives.

Why would judicial policy making be stabilizing? In practice, it can foster more gradual changes in policy. Historians suggest, for example, that when the U.S. Supreme Court struck down numerous aspects of President Franklin Roosevelt's New Deal legislation in the 1930s, its decisions had the effect of making the greatly expanded federal regulation of the marketplace a more gradual development. If the Court had had no power to make policy, the country would have been subjected to radical shifts in economic policy literally overnight, with possibly severe impacts on political stability.

Hence, the judicial role in policy making is a mixed blessing, even in democratic systems. The necessity for judicial institutions, and their inevitable involvement in legal and constitutional interpretation, suggests that the role of courts in the political process will continue to be challenging and controversial as modern governments address contemporary problems.

◆ ◆ ◆

Key Terms and Concepts _____

adversarial system	judicial review
appellate courts	justice
basic law	Missouri Plan
civil law	natural law
common law	parliamentary supremacy
criminal law	plaintiff
defendant	positive law
grand jury	statutory interpretation
inquisitorial system	statutory law
judicial activism	trial courts
judicial restraint	

DISCUSSION QUESTIONS

1. *Why is the selection of judges often so controversial? What conflicting goals are involved?*
2. *What is natural law?*
3. *How do courts become involved in public policy making?*
4. *What is the difference between the inquisitorial and adversarial systems of justice?*
5. *Does judicial restraint mean that judges should never overturn legislation?*

Notes _____

1. Charles R. Epp. "Do Bills of Rights Matter? The Canadian Charter of Rights and Freedoms," *American Political Science Review* 90 (December 1996): p. 765.
2. Lief H. Carter, *Reason in Law* (Boston: Little, Brown, 1979), p. 110.
3. Ibid., p. 111.
4. See Sabrina Shizue McKenna, "Proposal for Judicial Reform in Japan: An Overview," *Asian-Pacific Law and Policy Journal* 2 (Spring 2001).
5. See Henry J. Abraham, *The Judicial Process*, 5th ed. (New York: Oxford University Press, 1986).
6. See Gregory A. Huber and Sanford C. Gordon, "Accountability and Coercion: Is Justice Blind When It Runs for Office?" *American Journal of Political Science* 48 (April 2004): 247–263.
7. See Gretchen Helmke, "The Logic of Strategic Defection: Court-Executive Relations in Argentina under Dictatorship and Democracy," *American Political Science Review* 96 (June 2002): 291–303; and J. Mark Ramseyer and Eric B. Rasmusen, "Why Are Japanese Judges So Conservative in Politically Charged Cases?" *American Political Science Review* 95 (June 2001): 331–344.
8. Henry J. Abraham, *The Judicial Process* (New York: Oxford University Press, 1962), p. 251.
9. See William Safran, *The French Polity* (New York: Longman, 1991), pp. 178–182.
10. K. L. Bhatia, *Judicial Review and Judicial Activism: A Comparative Study of India and Germany from an Indian Perspective* (New Delhi: Deep and Deep Publications, 1997).
11. See David Horowitz, *The Courts and Social Policy* (Washington, DC: Brookings, 1977).
12. Shapiro, *Courts*, p. 146.
13. See Terri Jennings Peretti, *In Defense of a Political Court* (Princeton, NJ: Princeton University Press, 1999), p. 73.
14. *Dronenburg v. Zech*, 741 F. 2d 1388 (1984), pp. 1396–1397. Quoted in Archibald Cox, *The Court and the Constitution* (Boston: Houghton Mifflin, 1987), p. 331.
15. John Hart Ely, *Democracy and Distrust* (Cambridge, MA: Harvard University Press, 1980), p. 76.

PART IV

POLITICS IN SELECTED NATIONS

Several of this text's earlier chapters focus on the political system's underlying functions or processes, such as political socialization or voting. Others examine critical institutions, including political parties and legislatures. In Chapters 10 through 15, we will shift our attention from particular functions or institutions to a more integrated analysis of politics in individual nations or regions. We will look at five nations to examine how the components of the political system interact in each country. In addition, Chapter 14 focuses on political and socioeconomic development in Africa, Asia, Latin America, and the Middle East. Here are some representative questions posed in this section: How has Great Britain's historical development influenced its political culture? What factors may explain why democracy is growing in Mexico and disappearing in Russia? How long will China be able to reconcile a free-market economy and an explosion in Internet use with a Leninist political system?

The countries discussed here—the United States, Great Britain, Russia (and its predecessor, the Soviet Union), China, and Mexico—represent a range of political and economic systems. Their governments share certain objectives, including the desire to protect national interests and to maintain power. But these countries also illustrate how differently governments operate, how divergent are their policy objectives, and how greatly their effectiveness varies.

Some of those differences are best explained by analyzing the issues discussed earlier in the text. For example, we can understand a great deal about a nation's political and economic systems by knowing whether it is democratic or authoritarian, Marxist or capitalist. But each country's political practices are also products of its unique culture and history. By focusing on the interplay of historical influences, social characteristics, economic forces, political beliefs and behavior, and governmental institutions within each nation, we further our understanding of politics in a changing world.

Some Critical Approaches and Issues

In the coming chapters, we revisit some of the concerns of our earlier chapters, including the influence of political culture, voting systems, political parties, interest groups, and institutional structures. But we also examine the historical forces that have shaped each country's contemporary political values, behavior, and institutions. Although a nation's history may not predetermine its present, no country can escape its past. Great Britain's tradition of gradual and peaceful change; the birth of the United States as a "land of new settlement," free of a feudal past; China's historical struggle for stability; Russia's tradition of autocratic Czarist rule; and Mexico's concentration of wealth and income have all left their indelible marks on those countries' contemporary political systems.

The wave of democracy that swept over Eastern Europe and parts of the Third World in the closing decades of the twentieth century has put to rest many doubts about democracy's viability in non-Western nations. To be sure, democracy remains too tenuous in many countries to inspire confidence that it will become firmly established. Still, the reality and the rhetoric of democracy clearly have been in the ascendancy in recent years, most notably in the recent upheavals in the Arab world. Hence, a central concern in all our case studies will be the strength of democracy or the potential for its emergence.

Finally, our case studies will focus on a critical area of contemporary government activity: economic policy. All five nations have mounted considerable debates regarding the state's proper role in the economy. In the past, Russia's and China's command economies assigned the state a dominant economic role. Great Britain and Mexico established more mixed economies, with the nature of state intervention varying considerably. Of the nations discussed here, the United States has allowed the least state economic intervention. But during the 1980s and 1990s most of the countries in our study reduced statism considerably. Time will tell how permanent a pattern that change will be and what its consequences will entail.

Great Britain and the United States: Developed Democracies

Both the United States and Great Britain are long-established industrial democracies. Both nations enjoy a high level of political freedom, a plurality of interest groups, competitive elections, and protected civil liberties. And both have advanced industrial economies guided primarily by market (capitalist) principles.

At the same time, however, important differences distinguish the two nations. Great Britain's political system has developed gradually over many centuries. Its political institutions have been emulated by other democracies and aspiring democracies throughout the world. Yet, it also maintains preindustrial traditions—a monarchy, a somewhat rigid class system—that seem inconsistent with the values of a modern democracy.

The United States, on the other hand, is still a relatively new nation whose democratic practices and public policy grew less from ancient traditions than from dramatic events such as the American Revolution, the Civil War, and the Great Depression. Its many opportunities for people of all social classes have shaped its political culture and policies. But so has its record of racial discrimination and division.

Russia and China: Past and Present Communist Giants

Until recently, the Soviet Union and China were the world's preeminent communist states. In both nations, Marxist–Leninist ideology established the political and economic agenda, and Communist Party leaders made critical political decisions with few external constraints. Their "command economies" featured state ownership and centralized planning.

Beginning in the late 1970s in China and a decade later in the USSR, however, both systems began to change. In the former Soviet Union, Mikhail Gorbachev's reforms failed to save the established political and economic systems. Instead, they contributed to the collapse of the Soviet Union and the fall of Central and Eastern European communism. In contrast, China's leaders have decentralized and privatized the economic system well beyond Gorbachev's program of *perestroika* ("restructuring"). China has established a dynamic, primarily capitalist economy, though one with a significant remaining state sector and continued state regulation. The result has been phenomenal economic growth and a continuously growing private sphere. At the same time, however, China's ruling elite has resisted pressures for democratic reform.

Our case studies reveal significant similarities and important differences between the rise and decline of Marxism–Leninism in Russia and the modification of communism in China. Despite the collapse of Soviet communism in 1991, Russia first seemed to be democratizing and subsequently regressed to authoritarianism. China's economy now emphasizes a mixture of Marxist planning and (mainly) free-market activity. But despite the country's economic boom, corruption, growing inequality, environmental degradation, and political decay are contributing to growing political protest and unrest. While not yet at a level that threatens the political system, popular discontent may do just that in the coming decades.

Mexico: A Developing Nation

Among the dozens of countries in Africa, Asia, and Latin America, none truly represents the developing world. We have focused on Mexico because it is not only a modernizing, democratizing nation but also a neighbor of the United States, one of this country's leading trading partners, and home to one of Latin America's most intriguing political histories. During the nineteenth century, Mexico suffered from severe economic inequalities, an exclusionary political system, political instability, and foreign domination. As a consequence, the country erupted in revolution in 1910, the first mass insurgency of the twentieth century. To address their country's political and economic problems, Mexico's revolutionary leaders created a more stable, more inclusive, and more effective political system. At the same time, however, the system was also authoritarian and corrupt. The 2000 Mexican presidential election brought full electoral democracy to Mexico as the PRI, the ruling party, was swept out of office after 71 years in power. Subsequent national elections have helped solidify democracy. But the bitterly disputed outcome of the 2006 presidential election demonstrates how suspicious most Mexicans are regarding the integrity of their political institutions. At the same time, the country continues to face major challenges from poverty, inequality, powerful drug cartels, and corruption.

U.S. President Barack
Obama spoke about the
home mortgage crisis at an
Arizona high school on
February 18, 2009. The
nation's financial problems
became the central chal-
lenge of his administration.

CHAPTER 10

U.S. Government: The Dilemmas of Democracy

- **The Founding Period**
- **Governmental Institutions**
- **Participation in U.S. Politics**

- **U.S. Politics: Prospects and Challenges**

The study of American government inevitably confronts a basic paradox: *Americans have extensive popular control over their governmental institutions, but the fragmented power of those institutions often makes them unresponsive to majority demands.* The system reflects the ideal of democracy in its history and in its political culture, but its constitution and institutions actually weaken the immediate influence that public preferences have over governmental decisions.

Politicians, citizens, and scholars have been divided for generations over how democratic the U.S. system is and how democratic it should be. Some argue that the system's fragmentation frustrates efforts to enact needed progressive policies. The independently elected president often vetoes decisions made in Congress, and those decisions are sometimes held unconstitutional by the Supreme Court. Presidential initiatives often fail in Congress, even when the president enjoys considerable popular backing. Fragmented power thus frustrates majority rule. Others claim that fragmented power ensures the protection of minority rights. Still others point out that the extra time it takes to get the fragmented system to act ensures that there will be time for a careful, searching analysis of policy alternatives.

As the world looks for appropriate models of democracy to guide the formation of new governments in Europe, Latin America, and elsewhere, many observers see the U.S. arrangement as a mixed bag. Although we are well aware that democracy can be undermined by tyrants and the force of arms, the U.S. experience suggests that democracy can also be compromised *by the way government institutions are designed.*

Despite a long tradition of open, competitive elections, U.S. voter turnout has often been relatively low, particularly among the poor, and some believe that the system's complexity dampens citizen interest in voting.[1] Moreover, despite notable successes, there is a widespread perception that the U.S. system has failed to achieve social and economic equality.[2] These and other problems arguably stem from the fragmented nature of the U.S. government's institutions. Citizens and leaders cannot make long-term, coordinated policies when decisions can be blocked or checked in so many ways, and voters often feel that their choices have no meaning when victorious candidates are unable to enact their platforms. The study of U.S. government thus raises fundamental questions about the nature of democracy itself.

THE FOUNDING PERIOD

Every political system reflects both its unique historical and cultural foundations *and* the political ideas that shaped its institutions. This is particularly apparent in the case of U.S. government. Things would be different if James Madison, Thomas Jefferson, Alexander Hamilton, and a few others had never lived, but the government they crafted would have been profoundly different if they had tried to apply their ideas in some other cultural setting.

Key Cultural Features at the Founding

Many Americans living in 1787 had recently emigrated from Europe, and many others were children or grandchildren of immigrants. They had vivid memories of the European experience. People recalled that in most European nations at that time, the poor did not own their own land but worked for a landlord, and business-men had to purchase permission from a guild or a government official before starting an enterprise. Most Europeans lived in the same villages in which they and their parents were born.* Recurring European wars created a continuing military presence in most of the immigrants' nations.

In contrast, even many of the poorest rural Americans owned small plots of land, and there were few restrictions on those who wanted to set up shops or factories. Early Americans were accustomed to moving around to find new opportunities and jobs, and the abundance of arable land and natural resources encouraged them to do so. Physical separation from Europe isolated them from the threats that made military authority so pervasive in the lives of ordinary French, British, or German citizens.

Those factors had a great impact on the attitudes of most Americans toward politics and government. Some of them had left Europe specifically to escape restricted opportunities, and others sought religious freedom or cheap land. Of course, some people came as slaves, and women were second-class citizens. Thus, the newly

---

*Even as late as 1870, for example, 95 percent of the people living in Bavaria had been born there. See Karl Deutsch, Jorge Dominguez, and Hugh Heclo, *Comparative Government: Politics of Industrialized and Developing Nations* (Boston: Houghton Mifflin, 1981), p. 22.

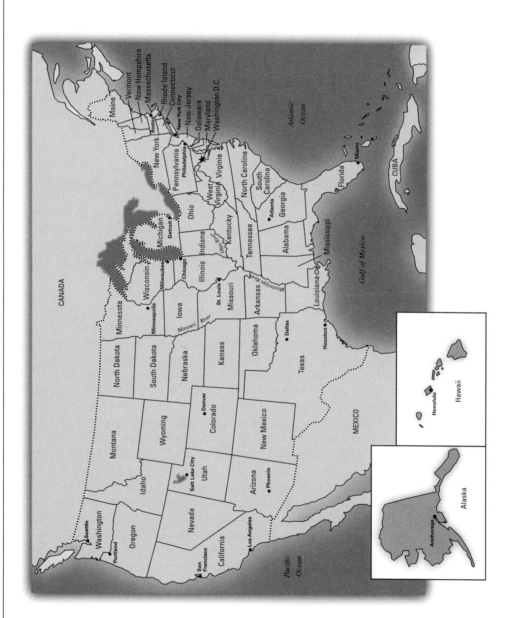

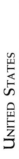

UNITED STATES

independent British colonies certainly did not constitute a fully free or democratic society. Nevertheless, the salient features of American society—poor farmers with claims to their own land, no requirements for royal licenses to start businesses, extensive geographic mobility, and the absence of a large standing army—created the beginnings of a unique political culture.

Americans developed a sense of personal initiative, a freedom to experiment, and a faith in individualism that stood in contrast to the predominant cultural outlook in Europe.[3] When they became accustomed to the lack of arbitrary official constraints on their lives, they did not want them reinstated. They consequently did not arrange their affairs around a set of governmental or social institutions, preferring instead to confront the challenges of the frontier.[4]

Early American Political Thought

The system's governmental institutions emerged in this cultural setting. But the culture did not create the system by itself. The political ideas of the founding period emerged from two main sources. The first was the events leading to the Revolutionary War and the Declaration of Independence in 1776. The second was the difficult period following independence, a time marked by events suggesting that the new democracy could become unstable. Many Americans assume that the Declaration and the Constitution were simply two parts of the same movement, but they were written more than a decade apart, and they embody very different ways of thinking. The first strengthened the democratic spirit, whereas the second gave impetus to the notion that government power would have to be checked and divided.

The Declaration of Independence proclaimed that all men were "created equal," that governmental power derives from the consent of the governed, and that people have the right to abolish government that does not answer to them. "This was a complete and sweeping repudiation of the English political system, which recognized the right of monarchy and aristocracy to thwart the will of the people."[5] The successful war effort that followed vindicated those who had faith in the ability of common citizens to work together to change society. The American Revolution affirmed the value of democracy that the Declaration of Independence pronounced.

Nevertheless, the following decade of government under the **Articles of Confederation** led many to fear democracy. Leading citizens expected that democratic government would permit the great mass of poor citizens to attack property rights. Their fears were heightened by **Shays's Rebellion** in Massachusetts in 1786. When many farmers faced foreclosures on their mortgages, Daniel Shays, a veteran of the Revolutionary War, led an assault on a Massachusetts courthouse with a mob of more than a thousand men armed with pitchforks and barrel staves. The other independent states refused to contribute money to fund a military effort to secure order, thus requiring Massachusetts to put down the insurrection with its militia. The rebellion, along with smaller incidents in other areas, had a great impact on the framers, as they pondered the design of the new Constitution:

> Shays's Rebellion, that heroic and desperate act by a handful of farmers, is surely the dominant symbol of the period and in many ways the *real source of the Constitution*. It was the

frightening, triggering event that caused a particular selection of delegates to be appointed by their legislatures, induced them to spend a hot summer at an uncertain task in Philadelphia, and provided the context for their work and its later reception.... The need to protect property and contain democracy could hardly be made more compelling.[6]

Although the Declaration of Independence and the Revolution breathed life into the idea of democracy, the unrest during the 1780s made some of the framers anxious about it. These conflicting pressures are apparent when we compare the Declaration of Independence and the Constitution: The former document is a genuine and fervent appeal to the democratic spirit, whereas the latter is cautious and fearful of popular government.

The Politics of the U.S. Constitution

The Constitution is a collection of great compromises. It reflects democratic values in its effort to accommodate broad political participation, but it includes features designed to limit the power of majority rule. Some of the framers felt that if a single legislative chamber directly representing the people could enact laws—without any check applied by a separately elected upper chamber or a separately elected chief executive—the poor (the majority) would demand laws that would destroy the liberties of the wealthy (the minority). Generations of critics have claimed that the U.S. Constitution was specifically designed to obstruct such efforts and that it is therefore profoundly undemocratic.[*]

Some are less severe in their interpretations. For example, George Carey argued that the framers put **checks and balances** into the Constitution not to frustrate the majority but to prevent arbitrary, lawless officials from abusing their powers. Although he admits that the framers *were* concerned about majority tyranny, Carey argues that they were confident that the nature of American society itself would prevent such problems. In the *Federalist Papers* (especially numbers 10 and 51), James Madison explained that the "multiplicity of interests" in the "**extended Republic**" of all 13 states would make it practically impossible for a single, narrow interest to dominate.

> In the extended Republic of the United States, and among the great variety of interests, parties, and sects which it embraces, a coalition of a majority of the whole society could seldom take place on any other principles than those of justice and the general good.[7]

According to Carey, since Madison felt that *the great diversity of interests in the society would itself moderate majority power*, it is likely that the checks and balances in the Constitution were put there simply to restrain tyrannical officials, *not* to stifle the majority. Perhaps the framers were not so undemocratic after all.[8]

---

[*] For example, consider Robert Dahl's assessment: "Madison's nicely contrived system of constitutional checks" prevented the poor from having "anything like equal control over government policy." John Manley echoed that view: "[the framers] saw inequality, heard popular demands to change it, and acted to block these demands." See Robert Dahl, *A Preface to Democratic Theory* (Chicago: University of Chicago Press, 1956); and John Manley, "Class and Pluralism in America," in Manley and Dolbeare, *The Case against the Constitution*.

The debate over the extent to which the U.S. Constitution is, or was intended to be, democratic has raged for more than two centuries, and the controversy will continue as the world moves ever closer to democratic principles. Even if we cannot resolve the ultimate question of whether the Constitution is genuinely democratic, however, it clearly was designed to create a more deliberate, more fragmented, more cumbersome governing process. Whether that is, on balance, helpful or damaging to the political system remains a basic political science question.

GOVERNMENTAL INSTITUTIONS

Both the promise and the frustrations of democracy are reflected in the structure of U.S. institutions. Imperfectly democratic, often politically inefficient, and certainly unwieldy, these institutions have been the target of much praise and much condemnation.

Congress

Although the U.S. Congress performs all the functions identified as basic to legislative institutions in Chapter 7, it remains a highly distinctive legislature.

Bicameralism Most of the world's legislatures are **bicameral** (that is, they have two houses), but upper houses are typically rather weak. In the United States, both chambers must approve legislation in identical form if it is to become law. A bill supported by the majority of the people's representatives in the House will fail if the Senate does not pass it, and—because the Senate has its infamous Rule XXII—it only takes 41 (out of 100) senators to block major pieces of legislation (See A Closer Look 10.1.)

In addition to the simple fact of having two houses, the special nature of bicameralism in the U.S. Congress makes it arguably undemocratic in other ways. Consider the *differences* between the House and the Senate. To be eligible for election to the Senate, a person must be 30 years old; the requirement is only age 25 for the House. Citizens elect senators for six-year terms; members of the House serve two-year terms. And until the Seventeenth Amendment was ratified in 1913, *state legislatures elected each state's senators*, whereas citizens elected House members in districts of roughly equal sizes.

Those differences have great political importance. Many of the framers were concerned that the House, made up of younger citizens elected directly by the people for short terms, would adopt ill-conceived, insufficiently considered legislation, driven by the whims of public opinion and the demands of the uneducated. Senators would act as a needed restraint. With six-year terms, senators could afford to make decisions that were unpopular at the moment. They would also be older, and, most important, state legislatures would elect them, making it likely that senators would be among the most educated, most accomplished citizens in each state. For those who feared that the House would reflect the demands of the unruly mob, the Senate provided reassurance: No House decisions could become law unless they were also approved by the restrained, experienced, and judicious members of the upper house.

10.1

A CLOSER LOOK

The Filibuster, Obama's Health Care Law, and Reconciliation

The filibuster is among the most notorious and most colorful features that distinguish the House and the Senate. The Senate, in keeping with its image as a grand deliberative body, has a tradition of virtually unlimited debate. The filibuster is *not* a provision of the Constitution, but a consequence of Rule XXII of the Senate's Standing Rules. The rule states that during a debate on a particular measure, 16 senators can demand a vote on a motion to end debate. Upon the submission of such a petition, the presiding officer must

> submit to the Senate by a yea-and-nay vote the question: 'Is it the sense of the Senate that the debate shall be brought to a close?' And if that question shall be decided in the affirmative by three-fifths of the Senators duly chosen and sworn … said measure, motion, or other matter pending before the Senate, shall be the unfinished business to the exclusion of all other business until disposed of.

What is the political impact of this obscure provision? Note that the rule states that the vote to end debate (actually to limit it for one final hour) must pass by a *three-fifths* vote. Consider what you could do if you were one of 43 senators opposing a proposed bill supported by the other 57. *You know that it will certainly be enacted if a vote is taken.* So, when someone makes a motion to stop debate and take a vote, your group of senators votes no, and even though your group constitutes a minority, debate must continue because the motion to stop debate was not supported by three-fifths of the Senate. The filibuster is broken when a few senators opposing the bill are persuaded to change their minds, perhaps in return for a favor on another bill or as a result of a change being made in the bill under consideration.

The filibuster thus gives power to a legislative minority. During the long Senate debate over President Obama's health care reform plan in 2009, it appeared that the filibuster would kill it. Expressing his frustration with the Senate's rule, Paul Krugman, a staunchly liberal

supporter of the bill, wrote an often-cited essay about the filibuster. According to Krugman:

> Democrats won big last year, running on a platform that put health reform front and center. In any other advanced democracy this would have given them the mandate and the ability to make major changes. But the need for 60 votes to cut off Senate debate and end a filibuster—a requirement that appears nowhere in the Constitution, but is simply a self-imposed rule—turned what should have been a straightforward piece of legislating into a nail-biter. And it gave a handful of wavering senators extraordinary power to shape the bill.[9]

When Krugman's essay was published late in 2009, both the House and Senate had passed health care reform bills, but the bills were different. It was widely expected that the Democratic Party leaders in each chamber would hammer out the differences and present a bill to the president in early 2010. However, when Massachusetts held a special election to fill the seat long held by Democrat Ted Kennedy, Republican Scott Brown won and became the 41st Republican senator. Because the Republicans were unified in opposition, the president and his allies in Congress had a problem. Rule XXII would enable the minority to block the bill in the Senate.

Perhaps not. It is important to note that the Senate had already passed a bill in December. If the House would pass the Senate's already passed version of the bill—with no changes—then the bill could be presented to the president for his signature. But the Democratic majority in the House opposed key features of the Senate version. Since a filibuster would obstruct any effort in the Senate to pass a revised version of the Senate bill, it appeared that the whole thing would die.

In a controversial move, the House passed the Senate version simultaneously with a "reconciliation" bill that addressed many of the concerns that House Democrats had with the Senate bill. The reconciliation bill process was created by the 1974 Budget Reconciliation Act to provide a streamlined procedure for making

(Continued)

A CLOSER LOOK

10.1

The Filibuster, Obama's Health Care Law, and Reconciliation
(*Continued*)

adjustments in policies so that revenue and spending levels will conform to budget levels agreed to in the annual budget resolution. A key feature of the reconciliation process is that the Senate can agree to the reconciliation measure with only a majority vote.

So, on March 21, 2010, the House fashioned a reconciliation bill that changed the health care bill that had been passed in the Senate, making the Senate bill more palatable to House Democrats. Ostensibly, they had to claim that the changes contained in the reconciliation bill were related simply to budgetary issues.

As long as they were confident that the Senate would agree to their reconciliation bill, the House Democrats could vote both for the Senate's version of health care reform *and* for the reconciliation, knowing that the final result would incorporate the changes that made the bill acceptable to them. Since the Senate had already passed the basic health care reform bill, all it had to do was to pass the House's reconciliation measure, which it could do with a simple majority. The reconciliation bill passed quickly in the Senate, and the President signed the bill into law on March 23.

The filibuster is a continually controversial feature of American politics. It is clearly undemocratic, but there are other features of the system that obstruct majority will (e.g., the fact that constitutional amendments must be passed by two-thirds majorities in both houses of Congress and then passed by three-fourths of the state legislatures, or the fact that each state has the same representation in the Senate, regardless of population). However, situations like those presented by the passage of the Obama health care reform plan make many observers especially frustrated.

Will the filibuster ever be eliminated? It is difficult to say, but it is remarkable that the senators who were so upset by its application in 2010 did not make a serious effort to change the Senate rule making filibusters possible. One explanation is that senators realize that the rule empowers each of them to demand changes in proposals when they are in the minority.

For two excellent discussions of the filibuster, see "Filibuster Abuse," by Mimi Marziani, at http://tomudall.senate.gov/files/documents/Blog/NYUBrennanCenter-FilibusterAbuse.pdf and "Should the Senate Abolish the Filibuster," by Richard Posner, at www.becker-posner-blog.com/2010/03/should-the-senate-abolish-the-filibuster-posner.html.

© AP Photo

The late Senator Strom Thurmond of South Carolina, then a Democrat, gestures while testifying before the House Judiciary Subcommittee on Capitol Hill against proposed civil rights legislation in February 1957.

As noted in Chapter 7, the other reason for the two-chamber structure of the U.S. Congress had to do with state power. If all legislative power were lodged in a single House of Representatives, with seats allocated on the basis of state population, small states would be dominated and possibly exploited by large states. But each state has two senators, *regardless of population*, giving the states equal power in that chamber. This arrangement, the **Connecticut Compromise**, was essential in obtaining the support of small states for ratification of the Constitution.

Congressional Committees   Committees perform limited functions in some legislatures, assembling information and hammering out language. British committees, for example, do not typically take it upon themselves to make basic choices about policy, and if they did, the House of Commons would not feel bound by their decisions. But much of the real deliberation that occurs in the U.S. Congress takes place in its committees. They investigate agencies, demand reports and studies, and debate major policy issues. In most instances, the whole chamber approves only bills recommended for passage by the appropriate committee.

The power of committees in the U.S. Congress is strongest when the parties are weak. When party discipline is strong, committee leaders are likely to be loyal to the party platform, and committees exert less independent influence. If party leaders in the U.S. system could deny a member the right to run for reelection under his or her party's label, and if party leaders could control most campaign spending (as they can in some other systems), committee chairs would naturally be inclined to support and oppose legislative proposals in accordance with the wishes of party leadership. But, to an extent unequaled elsewhere, candidates for the U.S. Congress are chosen in **primaries**, preliminary elections in which *voters* select each party's nominees. Primaries take away a basic power otherwise enjoyed by party leaders, enabling candidates to achieve political success without having to please party leaders.

U.S. party leaders lack those powers, and the tradition of the *seniority system* in Congress further increases the independence of committee chairs. Although it is not as strong as it once was, the seniority system is simply the practice of selecting the member of the majority party with the most consecutive years of service on each committee the committee's chair. (Nothing in the Constitution requires or even suggests the creation of a seniority system; it evolved as a way to reduce conflict. If everyone knows that the most senior member will become the committee chair, there is no need to fight about it.) But the system has a tremendous political impact.

When committee chairs know that they have their positions through seniority and *not* as a result of being loyal to their party's leaders, they are free to make decisions independently. During the 1960s, conservative Democrats from the South chaired several important committees, and they often used their positions to block civil rights legislation favored by their party. If these powerful positions had been awarded on the basis of fidelity to the majority party's platform, getting a bill "out of committee" would not be such a difficult matter.

Frustration with the independence of committee chairs led both parties to modify the seniority system, and there have been many instances in which chairmanships have been awarded to someone other than the most senior member (especially in the House). However, the tradition remains strong in the Senate, enabling legislative factions that would be outvoted on the floor to use committee leadership positions to affect policy choices. They can often "write their preferences into law" with little input from the membership outside the committee.[10]

Political Parties in Congress   Although a British citizen would find the absence of party discipline in the U.S. Congress striking, the parties do have considerable influence, and there are strong indications that party discipline increased considerably during the last two decades. From the mid-1950s through the mid-1980s, a majority of one party's members voted against a majority of the other party's members on less than half of the recorded floor votes, both in the House and in the Senate. On most votes, it was once very common for a member to disregard his or her party's "line." But things have changed dramatically.

Figure 10.1 shows the percentage of members in each house that voted with their party's majority on bills on which the parties generally disagreed. Both Democrats and Republicans in Congress have become considerably more loyal to their respective parties when voting on bills. Most Democrats in Congress are firmly committed to their party's platform, and the same is true of most Republicans. Why do members of Congress now follow their respective party lines so loyally?

One reason has to do with the realignment of voters in the South. For most of the twentieth century, the states of the former Confederacy elected Democrats to Congress, even though the South was (and is) rather more conservative than the rest of the country. The South's Democratic loyalties through most of the last century were forged during the Republican-led Civil War. Thus, for many decades, the

| FIGURE 10.1 | **Increasing Party Polarization in Congress** |

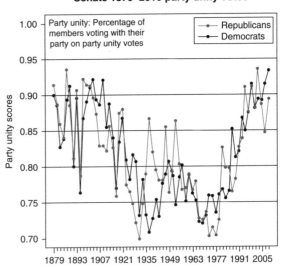

The graphs show the percentage of members that vote with their own party on "party unity votes." Party unity votes are votes in which a majority of one party votes against a majority of the other party.

Source: From McCarty, Nolan, Keith T. Poole, and Howard Rosenthal., Polarized America: The Dance of Ideology and Unequal Riches, 2 figures: House 1879-2010 Party Unity Votes, Senate 1879-2010 Party Unity Votes, © 2006 Massachusetts Institute of Technology, by permission of The MIT Press.

Democrats in Congress were made up of liberals from the other regions of the country along with conservatives from the South. This severely undermined party discipline among Democrats.

As recently as 1952, 54 percent of the Democrats in the House of Representatives were from Southern states, while only 8 percent of the Republicans were Southerners. By 1994, 33 percent of Republicans were Southerners, and in 2005 this number grew to 37.5 percent. The number of Democrats in the House who were from the South has continued to drop: Only 25 percent of House Democrats represented these states in 2005, and only 20 percent of House Democrats were from Southern states in the 112th Congress (2011–2013).

Those numbers indicate that a major partisan realignment has taken place in the South, and that it has persisted and deepened over time. Large numbers of Southern voters changed their party loyalties as the echoes of the Civil War faded. (Contemporary Southern politicians often quip, "Whenever a good old boy's great-granny passes on, he feels it's safe to become a Republican!") But political change in the Southern states is not the only factor.

Observers give three other reasons for the increasing coherence of the parties in Congress. One is that state legislatures have become more effective at drawing congressional districts to create "safe" seats for their representatives. When a district is configured so that it comprises a strong majority of voters supporting one party, the member of Congress chosen by those voters is likely to be a firmly committed partisan. With more members of Congress from such districts, it has become increasingly rare to find moderates attempting to please voters from both parties.

Another reason that the party leaders have become more effective at keeping their members in line has to do with restrictive rules. The House Rules Committee establishes rules under which bills are considered and amended. In recent years, the number of bills considered under restrictive rules has grown tremendously, and this makes it easier for the majority party to control the votes, thus producing more party-line decisions.[11]

Finally, the ideological polarization in Congress reflects an increasingly polarized electorate. For better or worse, both parties have become more coherent and unified with regard to the platforms they advocate.

Despite the influence of parties, members of Congress still stray from their parties' platforms on occasion. Campaign contributions arguably influence their votes on pending legislation. Concerns about the effect of contributions led to the enactment of the Bipartisan Campaign Reform Act of 2002, which limited so-called "soft money" and paid issue advertisements by groups in an effort to minimize the influence of money in congressional and other federal elections. (See A Closer Look 10.2.) Reformers argue that if members of Congress could be forced to adopt their respective parties' lines, campaign contributions from interest groups could not sway them, and interest groups would not try to influence elections with their money.

Recent Mid-Term Elections—A New Pattern in U.S. Politics?   "The president's party always loses seats in the House of Representatives in the mid-term election that takes place two years after his victory in the presidential election." Until 1998, political scientists and historians were confident in this statement, noting that, since the Civil War, the *only* exception was 1934. The tendency of the

A CLOSER LOOK

10.2

The Bipartisan Campaign Reform Act of 2002, the *Citizens United* Case, Corruption, and the DISCLOSE Bill

Even the appearance of corruption can create severe problems for democratic government. Citizens need to feel confident that their leaders are representing them and that the policy process is not "rigged" by interests to whom elected leaders are obligated.[12] For years, many Americans have concluded that the way campaigns are financed creates both the reality and the appearance of corruption.

In 2002, President Bush signed the Bipartisan Campaign Reform Act (BCRA) into law. The law limited "soft money" contributions to campaigns, and it restricted electioneering ads paid for by unions, corporations, and **political action committees (PACs)** *that use the names or pictures of candidates during the weeks preceding an election.* These provisions became immediately controversial because they highlighted a basic tension between the need to combat corruption and the fundamental freedom to engage in political speech.

What is soft money? During the 1980s and 1990s, this term came to mean contributions to national parties or the parties' congressional and senatorial election committees, in contrast to the "hard" money contributed directly to campaigns. The term derives from the fact that soft money contributions were exempt from the limits applying to direct contributions to campaigns because they were to be used for "party building" instead of campaigning.

However, the advocates of the BCRA argued that, in practice, soft money contributions were used almost entirely for purchasing campaign ads that merely *claimed* to be "public education" or party-building efforts. Before passage of the Act, it was not illegal for interest groups to produce and distribute ads, as long as the ads did not specifically urge the viewer to vote for or against a particular candidate. Campaign managers, having limited supplies of hard money, often contacted organizations funding soft money ads, giving them suggestions regarding the content of their ads. This coordination—often accomplished

through informal, undocumented meetings—between campaigns and soft-money contributors effectively circumvented the limits on interest group contributions to campaigns.

According to those who supported the BCRA, if coordination made it possible for campaign directors to make use of soft money contributions, candidates would presumably do things in office to please the organizations that made those contributions. Reformers argued that it was therefore not adequate to limit *hard* money contributions—*soft* money contributions also constituted a problem. The BCRA thus prohibited political parties from accepting soft money contributions after November 6, 2002. The BCRA did not ban advocacy organizations from accepting and spending soft money, however (as long as the funds did not support broadcast messages that constituted electioneering communications).

The Center for Responsive Politics compiled information on the organizations that have spent the most in recent years on federal elections. The totals include funds contributed to the parties' soft money committees (when these contributions were legal), contributions to each organization's respective political action committee, and contributions from each organization's members and their families. The five top organizations in terms of total contributions to federal elections from 1989 through 2010 were ActBlue ("the online clearinghouse for Democratic action"), $51.5 million; the American Federation of State, County, and Municipal Workers (AFSCME), $45 million; AT&T Inc., $40.8 million; the National Association of Realtors, $39.5 million; and the National Education Association, $36.2 million.[13]

The core controversy regarding restrictions on campaign contributions has to do with the Constitution's protection of free speech. Four Supreme Court cases reveal how difficult it has been to reconcile the conflicting values involved. In 1971, Congress passed

10.2

the Federal Elections Campaign Act, which restricted contributions to candidates and required the disclosure of such contributions but also limited the amount that could be spent by campaigns and candidates, even if the money came from the candidate's personal wealth. In *Buckley v. Valeo* (424 U.S. 1, 1976), the Court upheld the contribution limits, but it held that restrictions on the use of *personal* expenditures was an unconstitutional abridgement of free speech. In 1990, the Court decided *Austin* v. *Michigan Chamber of Commerce* (494 U. S. 652), concluding that it is constitutional for a state to prohibit *corporate* independent expenditures that support or oppose a candidate for state office.

Thus, when the BCRA was enacted in 2002, the law was more than a bit murky. Perhaps the most critical part of the BCRA was its provisions regarding the right of unions, corporations, and nonprofit organizations to buy issue ads within 60 days of a general election or 30 days before a primary, *if those ads refer by name to any candidate for federal office.* This issue was addressed in McConnell v. FEC (540 U.S. 93), decided in December 2003. The court majority upheld the restrictions in the BCRA, concluding that the government's interest in preventing "actual or apparent corruption of federal candidates and officeholders" justifies the contribution limits. Moreover, the BCRA's provisions that prohibit candidates and officeholders from raising soft money to promote and attack federal candidates is "a valid anti-circumvention provision," necessary to make sure that the overall objective of the Act is met. Justice Scalia wrote an emotional dissent:

> This is a sad day for the freedom of speech. Who could have imagined that the same Court which, within the past four years, has sternly disapproved of restrictions upon such inconsequential forms of expression as virtual child pornography, ... tobacco advertising, ... dissemination of illegally intercepted communications, ... and sexually explicit cable programming, ... would smile with favor upon a law that cuts to the heart of what the First Amendment is meant to protect: the right to criticize the government (*McConnell v. FEC*, Scalia, dissenting).

In January 2010, the Supreme Court issued one of its most controversial opinions in decades, *Citizens United v. Federal Election Commission* (130 S.Ct. 876), overturning important parts of both the *McConnell* and the *Austin* holdings. *Citizens United* had to do with a conservative nonprofit corporation that had released a film ("Hillary: The Movie") highly critical of Hillary Clinton, who was a senator from New York seeking the Democratic Party's nomination for president when the film was released in 2008. The group wanted to make the film available through "video-on-demand" services on several cable providers, and they wanted to advertise the film's availability.

The film and the advertisements for it mentioned Senator Clinton by name and clearly recommended that citizens not vote for her. Although the organization claimed that "Hillary: The Movie" was simply "a documentary film that examines certain historical events," the Court disagreed and concluded that it was an "electioneering communication." However, the 5–4 majority held that a blanket restriction on the film and advertisements for it was unconstitutional:

> The law before us is an outright ban, backed by criminal sanctions. [It] makes it a felony for all corporations—including nonprofit advocacy corporations—either to expressly advocate the election or defeat of candidates or to broadcast electioneering communications within 30 days of a primary election and 60 days of a general election. Thus, the following acts would all be felonies under [the Act]: The Sierra Club runs an ad, within the crucial phase of 60 days before the general election, that exhorts the public to disapprove of a Congressman who favors logging in national forests; the National Rifle Association publishes a book urging the public to vote for the challenger because the incumbent U. S. Senator supports a handgun ban; and the American Civil Liberties Union creates a Web site telling the public to vote for a Presidential candidate in light of that candidate's defense of free speech. These prohibitions are classic examples of censorship.... Speech is an essential mechanism of

(Continued)

A CLOSER LOOK

10.2

The Bipartisan Campaign Reform Act of 2002, the *Citizens United* Case, Corruption, and the DISCLOSE Bill (*Continued*)

democracy, for it is the means to hold officials accountable to the people.... The right of citizens to inquire, to hear, to speak, and to use information to reach consensus is a precondition to enlightened self-government and a necessary means to protect it. The First Amendment has its fullest and most urgent application to speech uttered during a campaign for political office.

President Obama was severely disappointed in the decision, prompting him to criticize the Supreme Court publicly during his State of the Union message several days later. In an effort to achieve some of the BCRA's objectives, Senator Charles Schumer (Democrat from New York) introduced the DISCLOSE Act ("Democracy is Strengthened by Casting Light on Spending in Elections") in July 2010. This legislation,

which failed in the Senate late in 2010, would have required organizations to disclose the sources of funding for political ads. Opponents argued that the bill included indefensible exemptions (the National Rifle Association and the American Association of Retired Persons were both exempted, for example), and that it would inhibit political speech.

The regulation of campaign finance in the United States will doubtlessly be controversial for years to come. The issue reveals the conflict between the need for fairness and transparency in elections, on one hand, and the right to engage in effective political communication, on the other. It is a safe bet that the Supreme Court will address the problem again in the near future.

---

president's party to lose House seats in mid-term elections was the single most consistent pattern observed in U.S. voting behavior.

Why has this happened so consistently? The classic explanation is known as "surge and decline," the idea that the electorate becomes larger in presidential election years and then declines in mid-term elections. The higher voter turnout during presidential elections is made up of the strong party identifiers who vote in all elections plus a large number of voters with weak party identification who vote only in presidential election years. The turnout during mid-term elections is lower because *only* the strong partisans—whose party loyalty prompts them to vote even when weaker partisans and independents lose interest—show up at the polls.

For whatever reason (economic conditions, war or other crisis, scandals), the political "winds" during a given presidential election favor one party or the other, *and it is the voters with weak partisan loyalty that are most swayed by those factors.* Many of them vote for the presidential candidate who wins with the benefit of these favorable short-term forces, and, while in the ballot box, these voters also vote for the candidate running for the House from that same party. Two years later (during the mid-term election), there is almost always less interest, and these weak partisan voters stay home, leaving the House election entirely in the hands of the strong party identifiers. Without the boost that the weak partisan voters produced when the presidential election was taking place, the president's party loses some close House seats, thus producing the "surge and decline" pattern.

However, in the mid-term election following the 1996 reelection of Bill Clinton, the Democrats gained five seats in the House and four in the Senate. *That was the first time since*

1934 that the party controlling the White House actually gained seats in the House of Representatives in a mid-term election. In 2000, the Republicans won the White House, but, contrary to the normal "coattails" effect, they suffered a net loss of three seats in the House.

In the 2002 mid-term election, the 1998 result was repeated, this time to the benefit of the Republicans. The party in the White House *again* gained seats in the House of Representatives. The Republicans gained six seats, increasing their majority to 229–205 (with one independent who votes with the Democrats), and they also gained two seats in the Senate. There was little consensus among analysts who tried to explain the result, but most observers pointed to the effectiveness of President Bush as a campaigner, the poor campaign strategies of the Democrats, and the lingering effect of the terrorist attacks on September 11, 2001.

The 2006 and 2010 mid-term elections brought back the traditional pattern on steroids. The Democrats gained 31 seats in the mid-term election following George W. Bush's 2004 reelection victory, enough to win the majority in the House. The Democrats also gained control of the Senate. As in any election, several unique factors were important in accounting for the outcome, and in this case the very low approval ratings for George W. Bush clearly had an impact. But, in 2010, in the mid-term election following Barack Obama's election, the Democrats *lost* 63 seats, the largest loss for either party since 1946, and the Republicans regained control of the House.

One explanation for this volatility is that the parties have become far more polarized ideologically in recent years, and party leaders take more extreme positions than the bulk of the electorate. When they take office, elected officials overreach, adopting programs and making decisions that many voters oppose. This opposition produces huge swings in elections (2006, 2010), but it also explains the mid-term elections in which the president's party has avoided the "normal" losses. Thus, the Democrats gained House seats in 1998 when many voters were angry with the Republicans for pursuing the impeachment of Bill Clinton, and the Republicans gained seats in 2002 when voters embraced George W. Bush's policies during the early years of the nation's reaction to the 9/11 attacks.

If nothing else, recent elections have shown us how particular events can overwhelm well-established patterns of behavior. The consistency of the "surge and decline" pattern suggests that we should still expect mid-term losses for the party holding the White House in *most* mid-term elections. But we also know that a crisis, a major policy decision, or even a scandal can produce a different outcome.

Congress: An Antique Political Institution?   For generations, critics of the U.S. Congress have argued that its decentralization of power impedes effective policy making. Congress is good at reflecting narrow, localized concerns, but it often fails to act in response to broad policy demands made by national majorities. Yet some see value in the fact that Congress represents narrow, particularistic, local interests instead of broad, national-majority preferences. Perhaps Congress—by representing interests that are overlooked in the national view taken by the president—gives voice to interests that would otherwise go unheard. Following the majority rule principle, those interests *should* be ignored, and disregarding them would certainly make it easier to enact legislation such as meaningful deficit reduction. But Congress arguably performs a helpful role by representing the diverse interests that contribute to U.S. political life, even if doing so makes the institution less efficient.

Scholars studying Congress consider those and other ideas when they grapple with the realization that the U.S. Congress is typically considered to be the world's most important legislative body, while also chronically in need of fundamental reform. Congress has more political independence from the executive than other legislatures, thus giving it more prominence than the "rubber-stamp" bodies in some democracies, but its internal divisions and the absence of consistent party responsibility make it frequently unable to act on broad majority demands. This paradox of congressional strength and weakness is why the institution remains such a fascinating subject for political research.

The Presidency

John F. Kennedy described the modern presidency in the following way:

> The American Presidency is a formidable, exposed, and somewhat mysterious institution. It is formidable because it represents the point of ultimate decision in the American political system. It is exposed because decisions cannot take place in a vacuum: the Presidency is the center of the play of pressure, interest, and idea in the nation; and the presidential office is the vortex into which all the elements of national decision are irresistibly drawn. And it is mysterious because the essence of ultimate decision remains impenetrable to the observer—often, indeed, to the decider himself.[14]

That statement captures the sense of puzzlement that strikes most observers of the presidency. The U.S. political system looks to the president for leadership, but the constitutional structure severely limits the president's power.

Presidential Powers   U.S. presidents have all the basic powers generally associated with political executives: They serve as the chief diplomat, the commander of the armed forces, the nation's symbolic leader, the leader in times of emergency and crisis, and the most important source of policy proposals. Their powers are tremendous. As discussed in Chapter 8, however, chief executives in democratic systems typically have *limited* power, and the U.S. president—sometimes called the most powerful person on earth—faces particularly severe and complex limits.

A full inventory of presidential powers includes both those with origins in the Constitution and those that have evolved through history. The Constitution at least implies that the president will conduct foreign relations, and it is explicit regarding his power to command the armed forces and serve as chief of state. Other powers derive from the essential nature of the position itself and from the way incumbents have operated within it. These include the president's leadership of his party and his role as symbolic leader of the nation.

Strong presidents use their unique political position to shape the nation's agenda: Lyndon Johnson focused national attention on the plight of the poor in the 1960s, leading to dramatic legislative enactments; in the 1980s, Ronald Reagan effectively highlighted the issues of deregulation, tax reform, and renewed military preparedness. In contrast, many observers faulted George H.W. Bush for failing to emphasize any theme or purpose during his single term (1989–1993). Bill Clinton's impeachment in 1998 was perhaps the most historically significant event during his two terms (1993–2001). The strong economy during that period, coupled with Clinton's great popularity in certain parts of the electorate, enabled him to escape conviction in the Senate. However, by most accounts, his record of legislative successes is weak.

Historians will assess George W. Bush's presidency largely on the basis of his leadership in the nation's response to the terrorist attacks of September 11, 2001, and his controversial decision to invade Iraq in 2003. As of this writing, Barack Obama's claim to being a strong president rests on his success in gaining passage of a major health care reform initiative, a goal that his party sought for generations.

By many historical accounts, the most important president was the only great president to serve but a single complete term, Abraham Lincoln.* The Civil War presented Lincoln with basic choices that would alter forever the nature and the stature of the presidency. If he had looked to Congress to set the direction of the war effort, and if he had been content to operate within the limits of his office, the presidency would have remained a relatively weak institution. Instead, Lincoln responded to the national emergency by crafting an expansive vision of leadership. He ignored Congress when he felt it necessary to do so, writing the Emancipation Proclamation without any observance of checks and balances. He ordered restrictions on the mail, blockades of ports, and other actions—all without congressional approval. Largely as a result of his choices, Lincoln's presidency established much of the foundation for the enormous powers of the modern institution.

Franklin Roosevelt assumed the presidency in 1933 during a very different kind of crisis, the Great Depression. He responded by broadening the reach of government in economic and business affairs, thus initiating the modern welfare state. He also brought the presidency into closer personal contact with citizens, forging a bond that assumed almost mythical proportions. The larger governmental role that Roosevelt demanded required changes in constitutional doctrine. Among other things, the Supreme Court eventually accepted the idea that Congress could delegate lawmaking power to administrative agencies.

Limits on the Presidency   U.S. presidents appear to be forced continually to assert their power, to struggle for the authority to act. The most important limit on their power is, of course, the fact that the president is elected independently of the Congress. Unlike British prime ministers, U.S. presidents cannot assume that the same popular vote that put them in office will ensure the passage of their legislative proposals.

Moreover, in the U.S. system, the president and the majority of Congress may be of different parties, a situation that occurred for all but 22 years between 1961 and 2012. This phenomenon of "divided government" is currently a subject of intense scrutiny by political scientists. The traditional view is that divided government produces near paralysis. Yet research reveals that many important policy innovations have been enacted during periods of divided government. Effective presidents can work with a Congress dominated by the other party about as well as they can work with a Congress led by their own party.[15]

In July 2011, the federal debt was dangerously approaching the limit established by federal statute (the debt limit had been increased in February 2010). President Barack Obama was involved in a very messy fight with Congress to increase it again. Republicans (and some Democrats) wanted him to agree to substantial spending cuts as a condition for establishing a higher debt limit, but the president wanted some tax increases coupled with somewhat smaller spending cuts. The impasse was

---

*Lincoln had begun his second term one month before he was assassinated.

protracted and frustrating. The following excerpt from a speech he gave on July 25 nicely captures the limits on the president's power:

> THE PRESIDENT: ... Now, I know some people want me to bypass Congress and change the laws on my own. (Applause.) And believe me, right now dealing with Congress –
> AUDIENCE: Yes, you can! Yes, you can! Yes, you can! Yes, you can! Yes, you can!
> THE PRESIDENT: Believe me — believe me, the idea of doing things on my own is very tempting. (Laughter.) I promise you. Not just on immigration reform. (Laughter.) But that's not how—that's not how our system works.
> AUDIENCE MEMBER: Change it!
> THE PRESIDENT: That's not how our democracy functions. That's not how our Constitution is written.[16]

Besides being limited by the nature of institutions and parties, presidential power is also limited because political conflict in the United States rarely fits a clear ideological pattern. Instead of representing one dominant majority, presidents must work to balance a large array of diverse interests. When they can command a united majority of society's political energies, they have a much freer hand, even within the checks and balances that limit their authority.

The Institutional Presidency   Analysts and politicians agreed years ago that "the president needs help," and the *institutional presidency* is the term used to describe the extensive system of supporting institutions surrounding the chief executive. Most important, the **president's cabinet**, which traditionally consists of the heads of major departments and others of similar status selected by the president to be in the group, has existed since Washington's time, and most presidents get useful advice from these individuals. But presidential cabinets rarely function as genuine policy-making bodies. Presidents typically select cabinet secretaries to please important interest groups or to repay political favors. Once in power, these officials gain independent support from important constituencies, and they usually come to identify with the goals of the departments they manage.

This tendency toward independence on the part of cabinet officials has long been recognized, as suggested by the famous remark by Charles Dawes (Calvin Coolidge's vice president) that "the members of the Cabinet are the President's natural enemies."[17] Similarly, President Lyndon Johnson complained, "When I looked out at the heads of the departments, I realized that while all had been appointed by me, not a single one was really mine. I could never fully depend on them to put my priorities first...."[18] Although hearing a diverse array of voices can be helpful to a president, the independence of many cabinet members makes the cabinet less useful than most presidents expected when they assumed office. Presidents thus usually have an informal group of close advisers, often called the "kitchen cabinet," who remain close to the president and share ideas on policies and political strategy.

The vast workings of the executive branch demand a much larger institutional establishment than the cabinet. In 1939, Franklin Roosevelt created the Executive Office of the President (EOP), an umbrella term for a group of organizations including the Office of Management and Budget, the Council of Economic Advisers, and the National Security Council. These units coordinate policy making and maintain contact between the president and dozens of administrative agencies.

The large executive establishment thus performs two somewhat contradictory functions. Some officials, especially cabinet members, are chosen to *secure political support* from interests who would otherwise oppose the administration. The units of the EOP, in contrast, are intended to *centralize presidential control.*

Presidential Character   Social scientists are often drawn to explain events by look- ing to economic and social "forces" that can be measured and predicted. However, the U.S. presidency provides an excellent context for illustrating that individuals make a difference. Although constitutional features, economic conditions, and changes in partisan alignment, among many other things, affect presidential actions and choices, it is clear that the nature of the person in the office also has great impact. This is the basis for the study of **presidential character**.[19]

The 44 men who have served as U.S. presidents constitute a varied lot. Some brought a strong ideological fervor to the office, acting aggressively to change the direction of government policies and programs, challenging Congress and the courts. Others were content to manage the status quo. Some enjoyed the office, relishing its challenges with enthusiasm, whereas others developed a siege mentality, focusing on perceived threats.

Table 10.1 lists the results of four efforts to rate the U.S. presidents based on surveys. The first three are surveys of scholars, and the fourth is a 2011 survey of U.S. citizens. Although one would expect that the political ideology of the raters would influence their choices, it is remarkable that there is so much agreement among the scholars' rankings. Washington, Lincoln, and Franklin Roosevelt are the three most highly ranked presidents in each scholarly survey, and Buchanan, Andrew Johnson, and Harding are consistently ranked very low. There is considerable dis- agreement regarding recent presidents, however: George W. Bush ranked 19th in the *Wall Street Journal study,* but 36th in the C-SPAN study.

Careful study of the U.S. presidency reveals much about the political system as a whole. Presidents are given great responsibilities and important powers, but the checks and balances of the system often deny a president the power to implement the platform that got him elected. The great presidents are those who are able to transcend those constraints, forging support in a system not inclined to grant it.

The Judicial System

If a single institution had to be selected to illustrate the distinctiveness of government in the United States, most observers would choose the judiciary. It is both powerful and politically unaccountable, and it further fragments policy-making power.

Organization   The U.S. judiciary consists of state courts (including the various municipal courts that states create) and federal courts. Each state has a system of trial and appellate courts, although each state's arrangement is unique in some respects. State courts hear cases dealing with state law (most criminal matters are issues of state law), and federal courts deal with cases pertaining to acts of Congress, administrative rules, and constitutional provisions. Each state has at least one of the 94 federal *district courts.* Appeals from the district courts and from the agencies are heard by the 13 U.S. *Courts of Appeals,* located in geographic regions known as "circuits." The single *Supreme Court* hears appeals from the appeals courts and from state supreme courts. Although the Court receives over 7,000 requests to hear cases each year, it hears oral arguments on about 80, and decides another 50 or so without hearing arguments.

TABLE 10.1	Scholarly and Public Rankings of U.S. Presidents			
	Rankings by Scholars			Public Opinion
President	Wall Street Journal (2004)	C-SPAN (2009)	USPC (2011)	Gallup Poll 2011***
Lincoln	2	1	2	2
Washington	1	2	3	5
F.D. Roosevelt	3	3	1	6
Jefferson	4	7	4	11
Jackson	10	13	9	
T. Roosevelt	5	4	5	8
Wilson	11	9	6	
Truman	7	5	7	9
Polk	9	12	16	
Eisenhower	8	8	10	13
J. Adams	13	17	12	
Kennedy	15	6	15	4
Cleveland	12	21	21	
L. Johnson	18	11	11	
Monroe	16	14	13	
McKinley	14	16	17	
Madison	17	20	14	
J.Q. Adams	25	19	20	
B. Harrison	30	30	34	
Clinton	22	15	19	3
Van Buren	27	31	27	
Taft	20	24	25	
Hayes	24	33	30	
G.H.W. Bush	21	18	22	14
Reagan	6	10	8	1
Arthur	26	32	32	
Carter	34	25	18	12
Ford	28	22	24	
Taylor	33	29	33	
Coolidge	23	26	28	
Fillmore	36	37	35	
Tyler	35	35	37	
Pierce	38	40	39	
Grant	29	23	29	
Hoover	31	34	26	
Nixon	32	27	23	
A. Johnson	37	41	36	
Buchanan	40	42	40	
Harding	39	38	38	
Garfield	*	28	*	
W.H. Harrison	*	39	*	
George W. Bush	19	36	31	10
Obama	**	**	**	7

* Garfield and W.H. Harrison were omitted from the two of the scholars' surveys because they served such short terms.

** Barack Obama was only included in the Gallup public opinion poll.

*** The Gallup poll asked the respondents the following question: "Who do you regard as the greatest United States president?" The presidents are ranked on the basis of the percentage of the sample that indicated each president as "greatest." Only 14 presidents received mentions from at least 1 percent of the sample; therefore the other presidents were not ranked in this poll, which was based on surveys in February 2011.

Source: The 2004 *Wall Street Journal* poll was based on responses from an ideologically balanced assortment of scholars in history, law, and political science. See James Taranto and Leonard Leo, eds., *Presidential Leadership: Rating the Best and the Worst in the White House* (New York: Free Press, 2004). The C-SPAN Historians Presidential Leadership Survey was completed in 2000 and again in 2009, available at http://legacy.c-span.org/PresidentialSurvey/Overall-Ranking.aspx. The USPC rankings were drawn from the opinions of a group of British historians. The project was undertaken by the United States Presidency Centre, a section of the Institute for the Study of the Americas. The results are available at http://americas.sas.ac.uk/research/survey/overall.htm. Finally, the Gallup poll was based on a survey of 1,015 U.S. adults taken in February 2011. The full study is available at www.gallup.com/poll/146183/americans-say-reagan-greatest-president.aspx.

The Evolution of Judicial Power   When it began operating in 1790, the Supreme Court had a rather limited and uncertain status. It received no important cases during its first few years, and it did not attempt to overturn presidential or congressional acts. However, the Court's power was greatly expanded as a result of ***Marbury v. Madison***, the 1803 case regarding a minor government job that became the "rib of the Constitution."[20]

President Thomas Jefferson and Secretary of State James Madison refused to grant a commission for a judgeship to William Marbury, who had been promised the job during the last days of the Adams administration. The previous secretary of state, John Marshall, had neglected to send the commission. Jefferson decided to take advantage of Marshall's oversight and give the job to a supporter of his own party. Marbury then petitioned the Supreme Court to force the president to give him his commission.

Many people expected that the Court would approve Marbury's request. (After all, the chief justice was none other than John Marshall, the former secretary of state who wanted Marbury to have the commission in the first place!) But there was a legal problem: The jurisdiction of the Supreme Court *as defined by the Constitution* did not include the power to act in response to that kind of request; instead, an act of Congress (the Judiciary Act of 1789) created that power.

There was thus a conflict between the act of Congress and the Constitution.

Marshall faced a difficult political decision. He was convinced that Marbury should have the commission. But he also knew that if he ruled that Jefferson was required to give the commission to Marbury, Jefferson might ignore him. If so, it would set a precedent establishing that the Court's rulings carry little weight.

Marshall looked at the conflict between the Act and the Constitution and held that it was *unconstitutional* for Congress to alter the jurisdiction of the Court as set forth in the Constitution.* The Court was therefore powerless to act on Marbury's petition. Although Marbury *should* get the job, he argued, the Court could not hear his petition because Congress violated the Constitution when it gave the Court jurisdiction over such matters.

Consequently, the Court did not force Jefferson to give the job to Marbury. Jefferson "won." In accepting the result in *Marbury v. Madison*, however, Jefferson helped establish what became a profoundly important principle: *The Supreme Court has the power to decide whether a law is constitutional.*[21]

U.S. voters have demonstrated their widespread acceptance of strong judicial independence on several occasions. During the 1930s, Franklin Roosevelt enjoyed tremendous support for his innovative policies both in Congress and among voters, but several features of his recovery plan were held unconstitutional by the Supreme Court in 1935 and 1936. Roosevelt criticized the "nine old men" on the Court, and then he introduced a plan to create new positions on the Court to "ease the workload" for the elderly judges—a plan that would have brought the size of the Supreme Court to 15.[22] The plan failed:

> The Court-packing plan was defeated despite the President's landslide victory at the polls only a few months earlier and despite the overwhelming popular support for New Deal legislation. Although much of the opposition was partisan, the resistance to the Court packing plan ran much deeper. At its source lay the American people's well-nigh religious attachment to constitutionalism and the Supreme Court, including their intuitive realization that packing the Court in order to reverse the course of its decisions would not only destroy its independence but erode the essence of constitutionalism....[23]

---

*The Court's jurisdiction could be changed by constitutional amendment, of course.

In the early 1970s, judicial authority was challenged in a very different way. Richard Nixon stated that he would ignore an order by a federal district court to submit tapes of conversations that had taken place in his office. The judge requested the tapes because they could show evidence that Nixon directed subordinates to obstruct an investigation of a burglary committed by members of his campaign staff (the **Watergate** affair). When the matter of the tapes first came to light, public opinion was largely on the president's side—much of the evidence that he had committed a crime was uncorroborated and ambiguous.[24] Nixon's assault on the judiciary changed things dramatically, however. Not only did he ignore the order, but he also fired a special prosecutor who would not obey him. Although Nixon changed his mind within 72 hours, his support plummeted, and eventually he was forced to resign.

The Watergate affair demonstrates the peculiar importance of the independence of the judicial system in the United States. Archibald Cox noted that a Scandinavian legal scholar was astonished by this episode: "'It is unthinkable,' he said, 'that the courts of any country should issue an order to its Chief of State.'"[25] In the United States, the idea is not at all unthinkable, and voters have shown that they will not support a president who disregards judicial power.

The Court and Policy Making   As noted in Chapter 9, judicial decisions often make public policy. Adjudication involves interpreting statutes and constitutional provisions in particular contexts, and such interpretations inevitably resolve policy issues. For example, if the Constitution prohibits "cruel and unusual" punishment, and if a court concludes that housing a prisoner without proper space or sanitary facilities is cruel and unusual, then the effect of that court's judgment is a change in state policy on prison management.

In that and many other areas, the Supreme Court has made decisions that would otherwise be made in legislative and executive institutions. Some of its policy choices simply dictate what the "political" branches of government *cannot* do (they cannot outlaw flag burning, for example), whereas others (such as the prison cases) require governments to take positive action. The status of the Constitution in U.S. society, coupled with the entrenched principle of judicial review, makes judicial involvement in policy making a fact of political life.

Of course, it is unlikely that the Supreme Court will ever steer policy in a direction that is profoundly out of step with majority opinion because elected presidents and elected senators select the justices. Presidents try to appoint justices who reflect their views (and the views of the voters electing them). Since the typical president gets to select two or three Supreme Court justices in a four-year term (along with hundreds of appointments to lower courts), the judiciary's political complexion will not remain contrary to popular demands for long periods. Nevertheless, the judiciary occasionally has tremendously important impacts on specific policy issues.

The Politics of Appointments to the Supreme Court   The Supreme Court's policy-making role makes Court appointments a very political matter. The process is quite simple: The president selects a nominee and submits the person's name to the Senate for its "advice and consent." Since 1925, nearly all nominees have

10.3

The Constitution, The Courts, and the Individual Mandate in ObamaCare

In October 2009, during the intense discussions of President Obama's health care reform plan, a reporter asked then Speaker of the House Nancy Pelosi whether or not it would be unconstitutional for Congress to force Americans to buy health insurance. She heatedly replied, "Are you serious? Are you *serious?*" Although many Americans share her apparent belief that the "individual mandate" provision's constitutionality is beyond question, many others find it to be a severe encroachment on individual liberty. As of this writing, two federal district courts have held that the provision is unconstitutional, and the issue is almost certainly headed to the Supreme Court.

The dispute over the constitutionality of the individual mandate will bring the Supreme Court into one of the most difficult and important questions it has faced in generations. Virtually all observers are convinced that the provision is essential if the health care reform is to succeed. Because preexisting conditions must be covered by all health insurance plans under the Patient Protection and Affordable Care Act, and because no one can be charged a higher premium for having such conditions, healthy people will simply wait until they suffer an illness or injury before buying insurance if they are not required to buy it. Thus, to make the system financially sustainable, the Act forces everyone to buy a qualifying health insurance plan.

The governors and/or attorneys general of 26 states, two individuals, and the National Federation of Independent Business brought the legal challenge to federal court in several districts.* In two districts, judges found that the Act is unconstitutional. The primary *legal* question is whether or not the Constitution's

commerce clause empowers Congress to compel citizens to purchase health insurance.

The commerce clause states that "The Congress shall have power to … [t]o regulate commerce with foreign nations, and among the several states, and with the Indian tribes." What does this power include? In 1995, the Supreme Court summarized the conclusions from dozens of prior cases regarding the reach of the commerce clause:

> [W]e have identified three broad categories of activity that Congress may regulate under its commerce power. First, Congress may regulate the use of the channels of interstate commerce. Second, Congress is empowered to regulate and protect the instrumentalities of interstate commerce …. Finally, Congress' commerce authority includes the power to regulate … those activities that substantially affect interstate commerce.*

The key point is that the commerce clause gives Congress the power to regulate *activities* that constitute interstate commerce or that affect interstate commerce.

A 1942 case helps to shed light on the issue. In that year, the Supreme Court held that the commerce clause gives Congress the power to restrict the amount of wheat a farmer can grow on his own land, even when he uses it for his own consumption. The case, *Wickard v. Filburn* (317 U.S. 111), upheld key provisions of the Agricultural Adjustment Act of 1938, which was intended to stabilize the prices of farm products by restricting supplies. How can it be argued that the Constitution gives the federal government the power to issue such a restriction?

The Court reasoned that, even if Mr. Filburn used the wheat for his own consumption, it would still affect interstate commerce (because it would mean that he would not have to buy wheat on the open market). Therefore, the Constitution's commerce clause gave Congress the power to penalize him for growing wheat on his own land, for his own use.

---

* As of this writing, there have been four district court decisions. The cases are *Liberty University, Inc. v. Geithner* (Virginia, Western District, 2010); *Thomas More Law Center v. Obama* (Michigan, Eastern District, 2010), *Virginia v. Sebelius* (Virginia, Eastern District, 2010), and *Florida v. U.S. Department of Health and Human Services* (Florida, Northern District, 2011). The first two cases held that the individual mandate is constitutional, and the last two found that it is not.

---

* *United States v. Lopez*, 514 U.S. 549 (1995).

(Continued)

A CLOSER LOOK

10.3

The Constitution, The Courts, and the Individual Mandate in ObamaCare
(Continued)

How does the individual mandate provision in the new health care law compare to the restriction on wheat production in the Agricultural Adjustment Act? Defenders of the Patient Protection and Affordable Care Act argue that a decision to decline to purchase health insurance affects interstate commerce because it is inevitable that everyone will need medical treatment. Deciding now to do without insurance means that you are going to impact the nation's health care system later by seeking care as an uninsured patient. Thus, declining to purchase health insurance is an activity affecting interstate commerce, and the action can therefore be regulated by the federal government under the commerce clause.

However, in *Florida v. HHS*, the judge concluded that a decision not to purchase insurance was not an activity in the sense that planting wheat was. Defenders of the new health care reform respond that states require people to buy automobile insurance, but opponents point out that this requirement only applies to persons electing to drive automobiles on public roads. The individual mandate at issue in these cases applies to everyone. The judge in *Florida v. HHS* made the following argument:

If [Congress] has the power to compel an otherwise passive individual into a commercial transaction with a third party merely by asserting—as was done in the Act—that compelling the actual transaction is itself "commercial and economic in nature, and substantially affects interstate commerce," it is not hyperbolizing to suggest that

Congress could do almost anything it wanted. It is difficult to imagine that a nation which began, at least in part, as the result of opposition to a British mandate giving the East India Company a monopoly and imposing a nominal tax on all tea sold in America would have set out to create a government with the power to force people to buy tea in the first place. If Congress can penalize a passive individual for failing to engage in commerce, the enumeration of powers in the Constitution would have been in vain for it would be "difficult to perceive any limitation on federal power …"*

Major expansions of government power have always raised questions about the Constitution's meaning. If the Supreme Court rules that the individual mandate in the Patient Protection and Affordable Care Act is unconstitutional, it will spark a major conflict among the legislative, executive, and judicial branches, and it is difficult to predict the outcome. Although public support for the new health care reforms is not currently strong, a Supreme Court decision invalidating its key provision would be deeply controversial.

If nothing else, the upcoming political struggle over health care reform will demonstrate, once again, the distinctive character of U.S. democracy and why its system of government is seen as frustrating by some and liberating by others.

* *Florida v. HHS*, Case No.: 3:10-cv-91-RV/EMT, January 2011.

testified before the Senate Judiciary Committee, answering legal questions as well as questions about their background and their positions on controversial issues. Presidents have submitted over 150 nominations, and the vast majority of them have been confirmed by the Senate.

The process reflects both the power and the constraints faced by presidents. Their choices have been accepted some 80 percent of the time, allowing them to shape the direction of the Court, often for a long time to come. However, the fact that appointments to the Court are effectively for life (justices serve "during good behavior") means that those appointed to the Court can develop views that are very different from the previously held positions that led to their nominations. After President Dwight Eisenhower appointed Chief Justice Earl Warren, who became one of the most liberal justices of the twentieth century, Eisenhower declared that his appointment was "one of the two biggest mistakes I made."[26] In his uniquely colorful way, Harry Truman complained about having appointed Tom C. Clark to the Supreme Court: "It isn't so much that he's a *bad* man, it's just that he's such a dumb son of a bitch. He's about the dumbest man I think I've ever run across."[27] Presidents have only an imperfect power to shape the Court's political orientation.

The Bureaucracy

As in all industrialized nations, bureaucracy has become a major feature of government in the United States. Nearly 18 million Americans work for administrative agencies (federal, state, or local), not counting those in the military. The U.S. bureaucracy mirrors the distinctive political traits that are apparent in the rest of the government. The same distrust of central authority that led to checks and balances within and between legislative and executive institutions has also produced a fragmented, decentralized bureaucracy.

U.S. bureaucratic institutions are deliberately arranged to maximize control by forces both inside and outside government. In countries with cultures less hostile to bureaucratic management or with strong party systems, bureaucracies are given greater latitude to make and implement policy. The majority party in such systems has the power to enact its platform, and the bureaucracy is often left free to carry it out. The U.S. bureaucracy, however, is subject to demands not only from the majority party but also from powerful individual legislators and their committees, most of whom have power to affect agency funding and authority.

Bureaucracy in the United States is thus frequently the subject of severe criticism. The idea that bureaucratic agencies are "captured" by those they serve or regulate is a familiar refrain. The bureaucracy is also criticized for being wasteful, especially when policies and programs work at cross-purposes. Many complain that the bureaucracy is "out of control," noting that bureaucrats make too many basic decisions.

Some, perhaps most, criticism of the U.S. bureaucracy reflects a generalized frustration with the intractable nature of social problems. The bureaucracy may simply be a scapegoat for problems that have little to do with the efficiency or professionalism of administrative operations. Moreover, our demands regarding how the bureaucracy should function are often contradictory. The U.S. bureaucracy is expected to behave in accordance with traditional norms of efficiency and expert management and at the same time to be open to diverse and contradictory political directions. It is ordered to plan for the future from one uncertain budget to another. The fragmented power of U.S. government produces a bureaucracy that is highly open to public involvement and scrutiny but often is unable to act in a coordinated, authoritative manner.

PARTICIPATION IN U.S. POLITICS

Political Parties and Elections

Voter turnout levels and the strength of partisan attachment have varied dramatically over the decades. These trends shape and reflect the character of modern politics in the United States.

Voter Turnout   Figure 10.2 is a graph of the percentage of voter turnout in presidential elections since 1948. Turnout was over 60 percent in the 1950s and early 1960s, but it fell substantially through the balance of the century. Voter turnout rebounded during recent elections.

Political scientists have identified several factors that explain the lower turnout during the period between 1970 and 2000. First, the dip in turnout between the 1968 and 1972 elections reflected the Twenty-Sixth Amendment's lowering of the voting age to 18 since it added a large group of citizens to the potential voting

---

FIGURE 10.2   **Turnout in Presidential Elections**

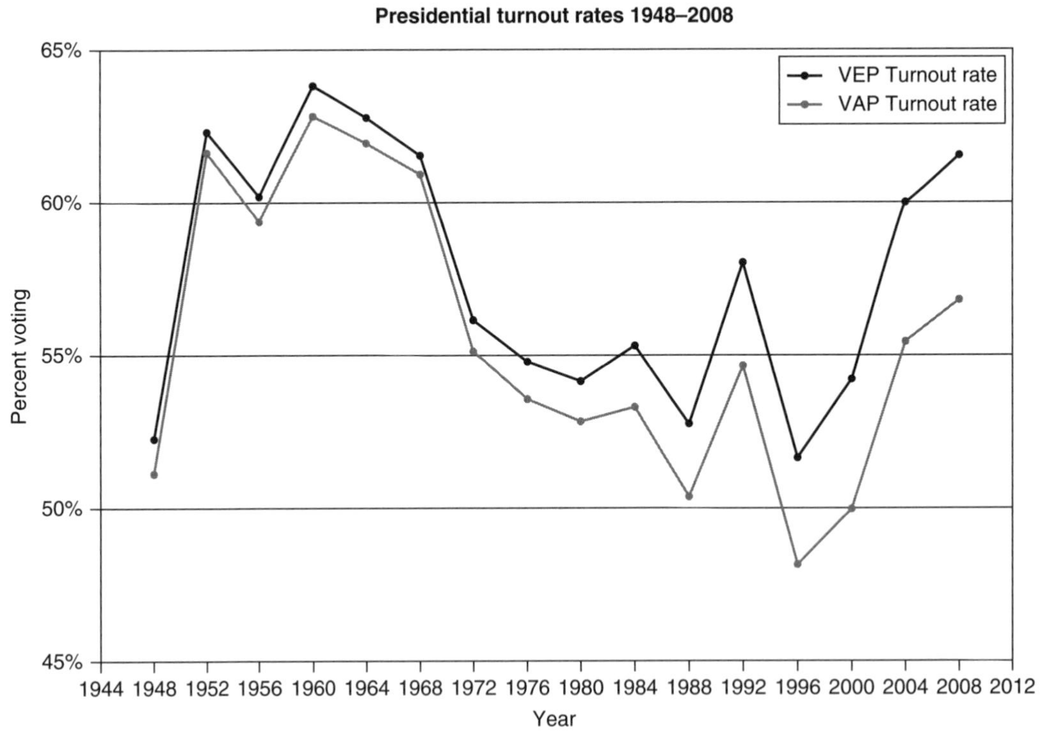

The top line (VEP turnout rate) is the percentage of *eligible voters* who actually voted; the bottom line (VAP turnout rate) is the percentage of the *voting-age population* that voted. The set of eligible voters excludes ineligible felons and noncitizens.
Source: McDonald, Michael P. Voter Participation in the 2008 Presidential Election by State. August 2011, United States Elections Project.http://elections,gmu.edu /voter_turnout.htm.

pool who do not regularly vote. Second, since the early 1960s, the proportion of voters who feel that government can effectively solve their problems has declined. The Vietnam War convinced many voters that their government could not be trusted, that it would not pursue the public interest, and that it would not always achieve its purposes. Government policies also fell short of expectations in domestic affairs. Although many citizens felt increased confidence in government as a result of experiences during the Great Depression of the 1930s, the War on Poverty initiated in the 1960s was not as successful.[28] In addition, intense media coverage of scandals made many citizens cynical about politics. Finally, declining party identification leads to lower voter turnout. One study concluded that one-fifth of the decline in turnout was caused by declining partisanship.[29]

Beginning with the tumultuous presidential election in 2000, voter turnout has increased substantially. Several factors have contributed to the growth in turnout. First, observers have noticed increasing polarization in the electorate along with stronger partisan attachment.[*] When people feel a strong attachment to a party, they are more likely to vote, even if the issues and candidates in a given election may not interest them. Without strong partisan loyalty, many voters stay home. Second, turnout also increases when election laws and procedures make it easier and less time consuming to vote, and recent innovations allow voters in some states to vote by post card and to register more easily.

Political Parties in the United States   Some 20 years ago, the authors of a leading text about U.S. political parties described U.S. political parties in the following way:

> ... [b]y the standards of the parties of the other democracies, ... the American political parties cut an unimpressive figure. They lack the hierarchical control and efficiency, the unified setting of priorities and strategy, and the central responsibility we associate with large contemporary organizations and often find in parties in other nations.[30]

That assessment echoed a famous analysis from 1950: "Alternatives between the parties are defined so badly that it is often difficult to determine what the election has decided even in the broadest terms."[31] Thus, for decades, U.S. parties were a disappointment to political scientists. They were convinced that democracy would work better, *if only the parties were better organized and more responsible.*

The two major U.S. parties still fall short of the responsible party model, but they are becoming more meaningful than they were a generation ago. Partisanship is strengthening (see Figure 10.3). Moreover, the increased partisanship of the American voter is not merely a matter of a renewed loyalty to party labels. Two political scientists recently examined the contrasting opinions of Democrats and Republicans on a number of issues.[32] They found that, on everything from foreign policy to issues involving sexual orientation, the partisan divide is deep and substantive:

> An array of economic, racial, and new social and religious values issues have become aligned more visibly to partisanship and to liberal-conservative labels and cues, producing an increasingly issue based and ideologically based partisan alignment. Self-identified

---

[*]See Nolan McCarty, Keith T. Poole, and Howard Rosenthal, *Polarized America: The Dance of Ideology and Unequal Riches* (Cambridge, MA.: MIT Press, 2006).

| FIGURE 10.3 | The Changing Strength of Partisanship among U.S. Voters |

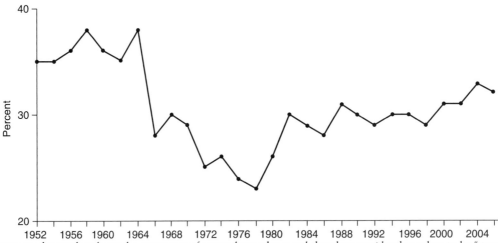

The points on the graph indicate the percentage of respondents who stated that they consider themselves to be "strong partisans."

Source: American National Elections Studies, August 2010, available at www.electionstudies.org/nesguide/graphs/g2a_3_4. htm.

Democrats or Republicans today have been as consistent partisan voters as their counterparts were in the 1950s era of party voting defined by the New Deal economic-based coalition.... [T]hese new partisan voters constitute new evidence bearing on the question of the "democratic competence" of the American voter. The critics who referred to the apparently mindless, non-ideological, non-issue driven voter that Columbia and Michigan scholars found in the 1940s and 1950s surely must change their tune.[33]

Both the weak and incoherent partisanship during the middle of the last century and the resurgence of ideologically based partisanship in this century are rooted in a number of factors. As discussed above, the Democratic Party was deeply divided for years by the fact that it contained Southern conservatives who remained with the party as a result of the lingering effects of the Republican-led Civil War. As conservatives in these states moved solidly into the Republican column, the Democratic Party became more uniformly liberal, and the Republicans became more conservative. Another reason for the resurgence of partisanship is that positions on noneconomic issues (gay rights, climate change policy, the War on Terror, and other problems) have become clearly allied with the parties.

For many years, political scientists were strong advocates for more ideologically defined differences between the major U.S. parties. Debates between party nominees would be more issue oriented and less personalized if the party labels stood for clear and contrasting positions on the problems the nation faced. Now that the U.S. parties *are* more ideological and distinct, some observers are disturbed by the decline in civility and the heated rhetoric in partisan relations. Perhaps the system is presenting voters with clearer choices, but some people would like to see a return to a period of more muted partisanship.

Interest-Group Activity   Political organizations have long been a part of U.S. politics. Perhaps surprisingly, many political scientists had a positive view of interest groups during the first half of the last century (although many others criticized their impact). Some saw interest groups as providing ways for people to register the *intensity* of their preferences (compared with voting, which indicates only the *direction* of their preferences). Most analysts now view interest groups in the United States more critically.

A basic reason for the growing concern about interest groups has to do with how they operate. As discussed earlier, the most distinctive political feature of U.S. institutions is the extent to which they fragment governmental authority. Interest groups exist in all modern democracies, and even in the developing world, but the fragmentation of power in U.S. government gives them great opportunities to affect public policy.

Interest groups in the United States take advantage of the arrangement of Congress by developing close connections with committees and committee staff and by providing campaign funds that the party leadership cannot command. In a sense, interest group power is both a cause and a consequence of weak partisanship; interest groups divert members of Congress from party platforms, and they provide a way for citizens who have lost faith in parties to express their demands. U.S. interest groups also exert considerable influence in courts, exploiting the policy-making opportunities that exist there. Interest groups that are effective in other political arenas compound their power by taking action in the judicial branch.[34]

Most observers are no longer confident that the interest group system is representative of the country as a whole. Whereas everyone has the right to vote, some people have the added benefit of effective political organizations acting on their behalf. Most citizens do not. If public policy depends to a significant degree on the balance of *organized* forces, then those who are not represented by effective organizations are at a disadvantage.

Beyond the problem of representation, others argue that the growing power of interest groups makes it increasingly difficult for Congress or the president to craft and implement coherent or comprehensive programs. Interest group influence is apparent in agriculture policy, education policy, transportation policy, and many other areas. U.S. interest groups will continue to create severe difficulties for government in the years to come; their existence reflects the openness of American society, but their influence may obstruct necessary policy making.

U.S. Politics: Prospects and Challenges

The United States currently faces profound challenges that will severely test its political system. Finding and implementing solutions will not be easy. A June 2011 Gallup poll reported that public confidence in U.S. governmental institutions continued to fall from the dismal levels of a few years earlier. The numbers in the following list are the percentages of Americans who have "a great deal" or "quite a lot" of confidence in each of these institutions:

The Military	78%
Small Business	64%
The Police	56%
The Supreme Court	37%
The Presidency	35%
Public Schools	34%
Banks	23%
Organized Labor	21%
Big Business	19%
HMOs	19%
Congress	12%

Source: "Americans Most Confident in Military, Least in Congress," Gallup Poll results, June 23, 2011, available at www.gallup.com/poll/148163/americans-confident-military-least-congress.aspx.

Each of the challenges listed below will require a sustained, committed effort from institutions already weakened by dwindling public confidence.

The Impact of International Terrorism

The attacks on the World Trade Center and the Pentagon on September 11, 2001, made U.S. citizens feel vulnerable and threatened to a degree that had not been experienced since World War II. The fact that the attacks were not from an enemy state severely complicated the nation's response in two ways. The United States had to deal with the possibility of infiltration in not only its system of airline transportation but also its systems for mail, computer communications, power plants, and other things important in everyday life. Moreover, the nature of that threat led to controversial proposals to strengthen the power of the FBI and other agencies to gather and keep information on citizens and immigrants, and to streamline judicial proceedings to prevent possibly dangerous suspects from engaging in terrorist attacks. How the nation balances its need for security with the principles of due process and individual privacy will be a major challenge for years to come. (See A Closer Look, 10.4.)

Economic Transformation and the Global Economy

The economic transformation facing the United States at the beginning of the twenty-first century presents a serious challenge to the political system. As unskilled jobs are "exported" to Mexico, Korea, and Malaysia, among many other places, the U.S. industrial base is threatened, and some jobs are lost. In recent years, General Motors, Sears, and IBM announced immediate and planned layoffs of tens of thousands of workers, devastating many communities.

10.4

The Constitution, the War on Terror, and Guantanamo Bay

In all the wars in U.S. history, the president has taken actions that arguably infringe basic Constitutional rights. On September 24, 1862, President Lincoln proclaimed that "the Writ of *Habeas Corpus* is suspended in respect to all persons arrested, or who are now, or hereafter during the rebellion shall be, imprisoned in any fort, camp, arsenal, military prison, or other place of confinement by any military authority or by the sentence of any Court Martial or Military Commission."* In †‡§§ and 918, President Woodrow Wilson signed the Espionage and Sedition Acts, which made it a federal crime to publicly criticize the draft or the president. And, during World War II, President Franklin Roosevelt ordered the internment of thousands of Japanese Americans without due process of law. The Constitutional rights violated by these actions were firmly reasserted when the wars ended.

During George W. Bush's presidency, the Supreme Court heard four controversial cases regarding the rights of those accused of being "enemy combatants," many of whom were held captive in Guantanamo Bay, Cuba. The first case, *Rasul v. Bush* (542 U.S. 466, 2004), had to do with three individuals captured after combat in Afghanistan. Although not charged with any criminal wrongdoing, they were placed in custody at Guantanamo Bay. They were given no opportunity to consult with counsel, and they were given no access to judicial proceedings. They all claimed that they were unjustly imprisoned, and the Center for Constitutional Rights (a nonprofit foundation established in 1966 by controversial lawyer William Kunstler) brought the detainees' case to federal court.

The Bush administration argued that the Supreme Court had no jurisdiction over the treatment of non-U.S. citizens in the custody of U.S. armed forces in foreign lands, using as precedent a 1950 case, *Johnson v. Eisentrager* (339 U.S. 763). This case had to

do with German prisoners held captive by U.S. forces in Europe following World War II. When a case was brought on behalf of some of these German prisoners, the Court held:

> If [the Fifth] Amendment invests enemy aliens in unlawful hostile action against us with immunity from military trial, it puts them in a more protected position than our own soldiers.... *We hold that the Constitution does not confer a right of personal security or an immunity from military trial and punishment upon an alien enemy engaged in the hostile service of a government at war with the United States.*

In the *Rasul* holding, the Supreme Court held in favor of the detainees. The Court did not overturn the *Eisentrager* case but simply argued that the precedent did not apply. Specifically, the Court noted that the detainees in question are not citizens of countries who were at war with the United States, and, unlike the German prisoners in the 1940s, the detainees denied that they had ever been involved in acts of aggression against the United States. Moreover, they had been "imprisoned in territory over which the United States exercises exclusive jurisdiction and control." Thus, the Court held that federal courts have jurisdiction to consider the rights of these detainees to challenge their detention.

In 2001, Yaser Esam Hamdi was captured on a battlefield in Afghanistan following a combat operation. Unlike the persons involved in the *Rasul* case, Hamdi was a U.S. citizen. He claimed that he was not fighting against U.S. forces and was in Afghanistan to help with relief efforts. Hamdi was taken to the U.S. base in Guantanamo Bay and held there until officials found out that he was a U.S. citizen. He was then kept in solitary confinement in a Navy brig in Charleston, South Carolina. Classified as an enemy combatant, Hamdi was held without a hearing or an opportunity to see a lawyer.

In June 2004, the U.S. Supreme Court announced its ruling in *Hamdi v. Rumsfeld* (542 U.S. 507). The government's position was that since Hamdi was captured in an active combat zone, he was properly classified as an enemy soldier taken on the field of

---

* A writ of *habeas corpus* essentially demands that a person being held in custody be brought to court so that an impartial tribunal can determine whether or not the person is being lawfully imprisoned.

(Continued)

A CLOSER LOOK 10.4

The Constitution, the War on Terror, and Guantanamo Bay (*Continued*)

battle. The Fourth Circuit Court of Appeals agreed, and concluded that "no factual inquiry or evidentiary hearing allowing Hamdi to be heard or to rebut the Government's assertions was necessary or proper."

Hamdi claimed that the Constitution guaranteed all U.S. citizens a right to due process, in particular a right to a meaningful hearing and legal representation, before they can be held in jail. If the government could disregard his due process rights merely by classifying him as an enemy combatant, the government could conceivably do this whenever it wanted to deny a citizen a right to a hearing before incarcerating him or her indefinitely.

The case presented some tremendously difficult questions, and the Supreme Court's divided opinion reflected the tension between conflicting objectives. The court majority reached a compromise: A U.S. citizen held as an enemy combatant must be given a hearing, *but* the required hearings would be less burdensome on the government than other due process hearings. First, the normal rules of evidence would not be required (the government would be allowed to rely on "hearsay," for example, in making its case against the person being imprisoned). Second, the burden of proof would be on the person charged with being an enemy combatant, not on the government.

Two very different dissents are noteworthy. Justice Clarence Thomas argued that the Court was not in a position to question the judgment of the armed forces regarding the continued imprisonment of Hamdi and those taken in similar circumstances. He concluded that the detention of Hamdi is a power that "falls squarely within the Federal Government's war powers, and [the Court] lack[s] the expertise and capacity to second-guess that decision." Justice Antonin Scalia, also dissenting, took the opposite approach:

> Where the Government accuses a citizen of waging war against it, our constitutional tradition has been to prosecute him in federal court for treason or some other crime. Where the exigencies of war prevent that, the

Constitution's Suspension Clause, Art. I, Section 9, cl. 2, allows Congress to relax the usual protections temporarily. Absent suspension, however, the Executive's assertion of military exigency has not been thought sufficient to permit detention without charge.

Scalia and Thomas both grounded their views in Constitutional provisions, but they reached completely different conclusions. Scalia explained that the Due Process clause was designed because the authors and ratifiers of the Fifth and Fourteenth Amendments did not trust the government to incarcerate only those citizens that should be incarcerated, and therefore the government must afford citizens a right to a public trial to protest their innocence. If Hamdi is dangerous and if he fought against the United States, argued Scalia, then the government should prosecute him for treason, and the ensuing trial would give Hamdi due process of law. In contrast, Thomas argued that the Constitution's grant of power to the president as commander in chief essentially authorizes him to act freely in setting policies for enemy combatants. The Court's compromise decision granted U.S. citizens taken in these circumstances a right to due process, but it made the required procedures less burdensome on the government than they would otherwise have been.

In 2006, the Court ruled on another Guantanamo Bay case, *Hamdan v. Rumsfeld* (548 U.S. 547). Hamdan, a citizen of Yemen, was charged with conspiracy "to commit crimes triable by military commission," and the commission heard his case. Hamdan claimed that the structure and procedures of the military commission violated the Uniform Code of Military Justice (an act of Congress), and the 1949 Geneva Conventions, of which the United States is a signatory. Specifically, the military commission hearing procedure did not afford the accused or his counsel the opportunity to see the evidence used against him.

10.4

A complicating factor in the case was that Congress had passed the Detainee Treatment Act in 2005. The DTA set up procedures for handling detainee cases, and it specifically stated that "no court, justice, or judge shall have jurisdiction to consider the habeas application of a Guantanamo Bay detainee." The government claimed that the courts therefore could not consider the merits of Hamdan's case. The Court disagreed, stating that since his case was pending at the time the DTA was passed, the jurisdictional limits did not apply. The Court went on to find the DTA procedures inadequate.

Finally, on June 12, 2008, the Supreme Court announced its decision in *Boumediene v. Bush*. As in *Hamdan and Rasul*, the 2008 case dealt with a non-U.S. citizen. The detainee claimed that he had a right to challenge his detention (*habeas corpus*) under the U.S. Constitution, and that the procedures afforded him through the Detainee Detention Act did not satisfy this right. The government argued that the Constitutional provision did not apply because the detainee was not being held in territory over which the U.S. claims sovereignty.

The Court rejected the government's position and extended the Constitutional grant of *habeas corpus* to the detainees at Guantanamo. While accepting that the United States does not have sovereignty over the naval base, the Court nevertheless concluded that the United States has "effective control" over the territory and that full legal sovereignty is not necessary in order for the Constitutional provision to apply.

The *Boumediene* decision was both strongly hailed and criticized. The Court's five-member majority spoke for many critics of the Bush administration:

> Although the United States has maintained complete and uninterrupted control of Guantanamo for over 100 years, the Government's view is that the Constitution has no effect there, at least as to noncitizens, because the United States disclaimed formal sovereignty in its 1903 lease with Cuba. The Nation's basic charter cannot be contracted away like this. The Constitution grants Congress and the President the power to acquire, dispose of, and govern territory, not the power to decide when and where its terms apply.

Many of those opposing the decision argued that it will vastly extend the power of the federal judiciary over activities that are vital to the prosecution of war. If the Constitution's protections now extend not only to U.S. soil and territories over which it claims sovereignty, it may be argued that persons in parts of Iraq occupied and "effectively controlled" by U.S. forces have *habeas corpus* rights under the Constitution. Concerns over this issue prompted a vigorous dissent from Chief Justice Roberts:

> Today the Court strikes down as inadequate the most generous set of procedural protections ever afforded aliens detained by this country as enemy combatants. The political branches crafted these procedures amidst an ongoing military conflict, after much careful investigation and thorough debate. The Court rejects them today out of hand, without bothering to say what due process rights the detainees possess, without explaining how the statute fails to vindicate those rights, and before a single petitioner has even attempted to avail himself of the law's operation.

The Obama administration has encountered major frustrations in dealing with the enemy combatants at Guantanamo Bay. As a presidential candidate, Senator Obama pledged to close the prison facility and to end the military tribunals that had been used to decide the fate of detainees. Both objectives proved to be unattainable. Attorney General Eric Holder announced plans for a civilian trial for Khalid Sheikh Mohammed (the person credited with operational planning for the 9/11 attacks), but the idea became increasingly unpopular because of costs and security concerns. Some detainees were released, but some returned to fight against U.S. troops. The ones remaining at Guantanamo are reportedly the most dangerous detainees held there since military operations began in 2001.

(Continued)

A CLOSER LOOK　　　　　　　　　　　　　　　10.4

The Constitution, the War on Terror, and Guantanamo Bay
(*Continued*)

Taken together, these cases and the experiences with Guantanamo Bay highlight the difficulty that American presidents encounter when attempting to balance security interests with Constitutional rights and values. Especially in the War on Terror, which will not end with a surrender ceremony and peace treaty and which does not take place on a defined theater of operations, the legal and ethical concerns are particularly difficult. On the other hand, the historical record provides a bit of comfort because it shows that even the most egregious violations of Constitutional rights did not endure after the wars that led presidents to take such steps ended.

Some observers contend that a major coordinated public response is necessary to ease the difficulties caused by these changes. Others argue that government regulations and mandates put domestic producers at a disadvantage. To keep the manufacturing activities that remain, U.S. industry must successfully compete with companies and factories with far lower labor costs. But successful competition may require investment in basic research, in urban infrastructure, and in education.

Immigration Policy

At least 12 million undocumented immigrants* are living in the United States, although some observers estimate that the actual number is considerably higher. The vast majority of these persons come to the United States in search of jobs and economic opportunity. Immigration policy has become an extremely divisive problem, touching on a great many issues and raising difficult questions:

1. Does an unsecured border with Mexico constitute a threat to national security and an opportunity for terrorists to infiltrate the United States?
2. Is it appropriate, fair, or humane to condemn illegal immigrants as felons (this was proposed in a bill introduced in Congress in March 2006) when they are simply seeking employment in jobs that U.S. citizens will not take?
3. What are the costs that taxpayers must bear to provide health, educational, and other services to illegal aliens and their families?
4. Does the presence of illegal aliens in the U.S. economy drive down the wages of U.S. workers?
5. Can the U.S. economy survive without the labor of illegal aliens?

---

* The terms *illegal alien* or *illegal immigrant* are often used to describe a foreigner who enters the United States without an entry or immigrant visa, particularly those who enter by circumventing official immigration procedures. Some are offended by the terms and prefer the phrase *undocumented immigrant*.

10.5

Arizona's Immigration Law

The state of Arizona enacted Senate Bill 1070 in July 2010, generating a great deal of controversy. Some cities and groups boycotted the state's convention facilities, and some even claimed that the law made Arizona a "police state" reminiscent of Nazi Germany. The law was quickly challenged in federal court, and its main provisions were held unconstitutional in April, 2011, by the 9th Circuit Court of Appeals.* What does the law do, and why has it been so bitterly divisive?

The stated intent of the Arizona law is as follows: "The legislature finds that there is a compelling interest in the cooperative enforcement of federal immigration laws throughout all of Arizona.... The provisions of this act are intended to work together to discourage and deter the unlawful entry and presence of aliens and economic activity by persons unlawfully present in the United States." Section 2(b) is the central provision:

> For any lawful contact made by a law enforcement official or a law enforcement agency … where reasonable suspicion exists that the person is an alien who is unlawfully present in the United States, a reasonable attempt shall be made, when practicable, to determine the immigration status of the person…. [Officials and agencies] may not solely consider race, color or national origin in implementing the requirements of this subsection except to the extent permitted by the United States or Arizona constitution….

Supporters of the law claim that it is necessary because the federal government has chosen not to enforce existing laws effectively. They argue that undocumented immigrants have been involved in

criminal activity and that they consume social and educational services that states cannot afford to provide. Opponents have focused on the idea that the law will lead to harassment of Latinos regardless of their citizenship or legal status.

The actual impact of the law, if it is ever fully implemented, is difficult to predict. Supporters claim that it only requires Arizona officials to inform federal authorities about persons whose immigration status should be investigated, and they note that federal law already requires aliens to carry a "certificate of alien registration" proving legal residency or visa status (see *US Code*, Title 8, Section 1304). But it can be argued that the law does authorize state and local officials to involve themselves in immigration policy in ways that could interfere with the activities of federal officials.

Two of the three judges who decided *U.S. v. Arizona* (9th Circuit, April 11, 2011) concluded that the Arizona law was unconstitutional because it violated the Constitution's Supremacy clause ("This Constitution, and the Laws of the United States which shall be made in pursuance thereof, … shall be the supreme law of the land...."). The majority held that "the statute is a singular entry into the foreign policy of the United States by a single state" (*US v. Arizona*, p. 4855). The dissenter argued that the Arizona law only mandated *cooperation* with federal immigration officials and that this cooperation could be seen as a problem for federal policy only if federal officials did not *want* to enforce the law.

As of this writing, several states have adopted laws similar to Arizona's. It is inevitable that immigration policy will be a hot-button issue for the next several years as the problem—and the efforts to address it—are debated.

---

* The governor of Arizona has asked the Supreme Court to overturn the 9th Circuit's decision.

Americans are bitterly divided over immigration policy (See A Closer Look, 10.5 for a discussion of Arizona's controversial immigration law). Some favor building a wall to prevent people from entering the country illegally, and an organization of private citizens has worked in several states that border Mexico to apprehend and report illegal immigrants. Others feel that a crackdown on illegal immigrants is a kind of thinly disguised prejudice against persons of Hispanic origin.

Race Relations

The status and condition of African Americans has been the most consistently diffi-cult and controversial problem faced by the U.S. government. The issue was divisive at the Constitutional Convention, when it was decided to count slaves as three-fifths of a person for the purpose of determining state population (and thus the number of seats each state would have in the House of Representatives). Slavery was, of course, a basic cause of the Civil War.

As divisive and difficult as race relations have been, the issues posed in the 1950s and 1960s were arguably less difficult for the system than the issues faced today. In the middle of the last century, the major civil rights controversies were about official restrictions on African American voting rights and laws that required African Americans to eat only at segregated restaurants. Although progress in those areas was difficult, it mainly required changing laws and providing security to protect those who would exercise their rights.

We can now say that African Americans enjoy the same legal rights to vote, travel, attend college, and pursue careers that other Americans have had for genera-tions. Nevertheless, the National Urban League issued a report in 2011 that found severe remaining inequalities. The "inequality index," a measure incorporating data on housing, wealth, education, and civic engagement, was only 71.8 percent, indicat-ing the average disparity between Blacks and Whites. Although three-fourths of White families are homeowners, less than half of all Black families own their homes. The real median household income of African Americans is only 62 percent of White median household income.[35]

It is clear that African Americans have not shared equally in the general pros-perity of American society. Not only are income levels and wealth far below aver-age levels, but African Americans also experience other problems more deeply. African Americans are much more likely to be victims of crime than other Amer-icans (murder is the leading cause of death for young African American males), and in many states more male African Americans are in prison or on parole than in college.

These problems challenge the political system profoundly. The civil rights movement of a generation ago emphasized the need to *remove discriminatory practices,* whereas current problems of race relations are more controversial. The practice of taking race into account in college admissions, awarding contracts, and hiring and promotions remains a highly divisive policy problem.

In 2003, two important Supreme Court cases addressed the use of racial factors in admissions to institutions of higher education (*Grutter v. Bollinger* and *Gratz v. Bollinger*), both arising from practices at the University of Michigan. In the *Grutter* ruling, five members of the Supreme Court upheld the affirmative action policy at the Law School, but in the *Gratz* case, six justices voted to hold the policy used by the undergraduate college unconstitutional.* The mixed signals coming from these cases will ensure that the legal status of racial preferences will remain unsettled for years.

---

* See *Gratz v. Bollinger,* 539 U.S. 244, and *Grutter v. Bollinger,* 539 U.S. 306, decided June 23, 2003.

The Status of Women

Although U.S. women are legally protected from most forms of discrimination, their status remains a major political issue. Interest groups such as the National Organization for Women (NOW) demand federal laws to establish national child care facilities and insist that employers be more flexible in accommodating workers' family responsibilities.

Thus, as with African Americans, the solutions to the concerns of women in the United States go beyond the repeal of discriminatory laws. They require decisions that confront basic moral concerns (such as abortion) and others that involve elaborate government regulation of the workplace. These problems are a major challenge for the political system, and they will not be resolved easily or quickly.

Health Care

Health care spending in the United States amounts to nearly 18 percent of the nation's gross domestic product. The Congressional Budget Office predicted that total health care spending will reach 35 percent of GDP in three decades. Both rising costs and accessibility to health care were central reasons given for passage of the Patient Protection and Affordable Care Act of 2010, also known as ObamaCare. As of this writing, opinions are divided regarding the impact of the Act, with some critics arguing that it will increase costs and lead to government rationing of care, while others insist that it will lower costs and make health care available to all. There is currently a movement to repeal the law, and the Supreme Court will almost certainly reach a judgment soon about the constitutionality of its key provision (see A Closer Look 10.3). Even if ObamaCare is a great success, managing health care will be an increasingly difficult challenge for the years to come.

Changes in the International System

The first half of the twentieth century saw the United States thrust into a leadership role in international relations. From an essentially isolationist posture that predominated in the 1800s, the United States became one of the two main forces in the bipolar world that emerged at the end of World War II. The United States devoted a large proportion of its productive capacity to fighting wars to contain the power of its major competitor, the Soviet Union, and to fostering nuclear deterrence. The Cold War shaped foreign and even domestic policies for decades.

The Cold War ended in 1991 with the official demise of the Soviet Union. East–West conflict no longer defines the international system, which is increasingly marked by more complex ethnic and cultural clashes. The problem of international terrorism thus struck at a time when the fundamental feature of the international system was no longer the bipolar competition that existed during the Cold War years. Although that change has made many nations more flexible in their diplomacy (in that they no longer have to consider how their actions and statements affect the balance of power between two hegemonic states), it has also made diplomacy more complicated. There is greater emphasis on international law and organization than in recent years. How the United States pursues its interests in international affairs in this changing environment will consume a great deal of the energies of our presidents.

The Future of American Democracy

The United States has faced enormous challenges throughout its history. Industrialization, the Civil War, foreign military threats, and the specter of nuclear holocaust presented the system with problems that required enormous and costly responses. For the most part, the challenges were met successfully. But the new challenges may actually be more threatening, possibly requiring fundamental changes in the system itself.

Still, democracy in the United States has been among the world's greatest successes, regardless of how success is measured. Even now, leaders in the fledgling democracies of Eastern Europe look to the United States—not to Great Britain, Germany, or Japan—as the model to emulate. Whether that success has resulted from the special features of U.S. government or despite them will remain an open question.

◆ ◆ ◆

Key Terms and Concepts _____

Articles of Confederation	primaries
Shays's Rebellion	political action committees (PACs)
checks and balances	president's cabinet
"extended Republic"	presidential character
bicameral	*Marbury v. Madison*
Connecticut Compromise	Watergate

DISCUSSION QUESTIONS _____

1. *In what respects was the period of the Founding ambivalent about democracy? How did that ambivalence shape the Constitution?*
2. *What is distinctive about the U.S. Congress, and how does Congress participate in policy making?*
3. *How is the power of the presidency limited in practice?*
4. *Does the Supreme Court's role in policy making make the system more or less democratic?*
5. *Why has voter participation been low in recent U.S. elections?*

Notes _____

1. According to one observer, the American poor see government as "distant, incomprehensible, and inaccessible." See Jennifer Nedelsky, *Private Property and the Limits of American Constitutionalism* (Chicago: University of Chicago Press, 1991), p. 215.
2. See, for example, John Manley, "Neo-Pluralism: A Class Analysis of Pluralism I and Pluralism II," *American Political Science Review* 77(1983): 368–383. Also see the symposium on Inequality and American Democracy in *PS: Political Science and Politics* 39 (January 2006).
3. Louis Hartz, *The Liberal Tradition in America* (New York: Harcourt, Brace, 1955).
4. Samuel P. Huntington, *Political Order in Changing Societies* (New Haven, CT: Yale University Press, 1968), pp. 125–126.

5. James A. Smith, *The Spirit of American Government*, quoted in *The Case against the Constitution*, ed. John Manley and Kenneth Dolbeare (Armonk, NY: Sharpe, 1987), p. 4.

6. Kenneth M. Dolbeare and Linda Medcalf, "The Dark Side of the Constitution," in Manley and Dolbeare, *The Case against the Constitution*, p. 127.

7. James Madison, "Federalist 51," in *The Federalist Papers* (New York: Modern Library, 1937), pp. 340–341. See the provocative discussion of this concept in George W. Carey, "Separation of Powers and the Madisonian Model: A Reply to the Critics," *American Political Science Review* 72 (March 1978): 151–164.

8. See also Pauline Maier and Lance Banning, *The Sacred Fire of Liberty: James Madison and the Founding of the Federal Republic* (Ithaca, NY: Cornell University Press, 1995). For a more recent and spirited attack on the democracy of the U.S. system, see Robert A. Dahl, *How Democratic Is the American Constitution?* (New Haven, CT: Yale University Press, 2002).

9. Paul Krugman, "A Dangerous Dysfunction," *New York Times*, December 20, 2009.

10. Ibid., p. 163.

11. See Jason M. Roberts and Steven S. Smith, "Procedural Contexts, Party Strategy, and Conditional Party Voting in the U.S. House of Representatives, 1971–2000," *American Journal of Political Science* 47(2003): 305–317.

12. See Mark Warren, "Democracy and Deceit: Regulating Appearances of Corruption," *American Journal of Political Science* 50 (January 2006): 160–174.

13. The Center for Responsive Politics compiled its "heavy hitters" list from data supplied by the Federal Elections Commission on April 25, 2011. The complete list of 100 can be viewed at the Center's website, www.opensecrets.org.

14. John F. Kennedy, foreword to *Decision-Making in the White House*, by Theodore C. Sorensen (New York: Columbia University Press, 1963).

15. See Fiorina, *Divided Government*; and David Mayhew, *Divided We Govern* (New Haven, CT: Yale University Press, 1991).

16. As reported in *The Weekly Standard*, July 25, 2011 (www.weeklystandard.com)

17. Quoted in Richard Neustadt, *Presidential Power: The Politics of Leadership from FDR to Carter* (New York: Wiley, 1980), p. 31. See also John Bibby, *Governing by Consent* (Washington, DC: CQ Press, 1992), pp. 496–500.

18. Doris Kerns, *Lyndon Johnson and the American Dream* (New York: Harper and Row, 1976), p. 253.

19. James David Barber, *The Presidential Character* (Englewood Cliffs, NJ: Prentice Hall, 1972).

20. Glendon Schubert, *Constitutional Politics* (New York: Holt, Rinehart, and Winston, 1960), p. 178.

21. Although most analysts accept this conclusion, it should be noted that some argue along other lines. For example, see Robert L. Clinton's *Marbury v. Madison and Judicial Review* (Lawrence: University of Kansas Press, 1989).

22. Archibald Cox, *The Court and the Constitution* (Boston: Houghton Mifflin, 1987), p. 149.

23. Ibid., pp. 149–150.

24. Archibald Cox, *The Role of the Supreme Court in American Government* (New York: Oxford University Press, 1976), p. 8.

25. Ibid., p. 4.

26. Elmo Richardson, *The Presidency of Dwight D. Eisenhower* (Lawrence, KS: Regent's Press, 1979), p. 108.

27. Merle Miller, *Plain Speaking: An Oral Biography of Harry S Truman* (New York: Berkeley, 1973), pp. 225–226, quoted in *The Challenge of Democracy*, 2nd ed., by Kenneth Janda, Jeffrey Berry, and Jerry Goldman (Boston: Houghton Mifflin, 1989), pp. 497–498.

28. Paul R. Abramson and John H. Aldrich, "The Decline of Electoral Participation in America," *American Political Science Review* 76 (September 1982): 502–521.

29. John Aldrich, David Rohde, Gary Miller, and Charles Ostrom, *American Government: People, Institutions, and Policies* (Boston: Houghton Mifflin, 1986), p. 290.

30. Paul Allen Beck and Frank J. Sorauf, *Party Politics in America*, 7th ed. (New York: Harper-Collins, 1992), p. 112.

31. Committee on Political Parties, American Political Science Association, "Toward a More Responsive Two-Party System," *American Political Science Review* 44(1950): 2.

32. Joseph Bafumi and Robert Y. Shapiro, "A New Partisan Voter," *Journal of Politics*, 71(2009): 1–24.

33. Ibid., 19–20.

34. See Susan Olson, "Interest Group Litigation in Federal District Court: Beyond the Political Disadvantage Theory," *Journal of Politics* 52(1990): 854–882. Also see the discussion of the "disadvantage theory" in Ch. 6.

35. See *The State of Black America 2011: Putting Urban America Back to Work*, National Urban League, available for purchase at www.nul.org/estore/content/state-black-america-2011.

CHAPTER 11

Great Britain: A Traditional Democracy

A Royal Wedding:
The marriage of Prince William and Kate Middleton brought renewed luster to the royal family.

- The Relevance of British Politics
- Contemporary British Society and Political Culture
- Political Parties and Voting
- Interest Groups
- The Structure of Government
- Public Policy and the British Economy
- Conclusion: Great Britain in the Twenty-First Century

THE RELEVANCE OF BRITISH POLITICS

Britain is intrinsically fascinating to many Americans. It is, after all, the source of many of our own cultural and political traditions. But Great Britain is also important to political scientists, since it has been a model of democracy and political stability.* Even without a written bill of rights until 1998, it has maintained considerable personal freedoms and civil liberties. British political institutions—competitive party elections, parliamentary representation, and cabinet government—have been models for democratic government worldwide. The country's record of gradual political change contrasts with the civil wars and bitter conflicts that have afflicted so many other nations. We will suggest, however, that evolutionary change and the durability of the country's historic values have also contributed to political, economic, and social rigidities.

* The country's official name is "the United Kingdom of Great Britain and Ireland" or simply "the United Kingdom (UK)." Usually, it is called "Great Britain" or "Britain," even though technically those names do not include Northern Ireland. We will use the terms interchangeably.

The Origins of British Democracy: Great Britain, a Model of Stability

From the time the so-called **Glorious Revolution** (1688) established parliamentary supremacy over the monarch, the defining features of Britain's constitutional order have remained in place. In contrast, France has had more than a dozen constitutions since its 1789 revolution, with five republics, two empires, and several monarchies.

The Slow March to Democracy

Although the growth of parliamentary power enhanced popular sovereignty, as of the beginning of the twentieth century the British political system remained far from democratic, and **Parliament** was still very unrepresentative. The House of Commons, an elected body, shared power equally with the House of Lords, whose members at that time had all inherited their seats, served for life, and, at death, passed on their seat to their male heir (women could not join Lords until 1958). Even the House of Commons was elected by a very small portion of the population (male property owners), often through corrupt electoral practices.

It was not until 1884 that **suffrage** (the right to vote or the act of voting) was extended to most adult males. Women did not receive the right to vote until 1918, and even then the franchise was limited to women older than 30 whose husbands owned property. Finally, a decade later, all women over the age of 21 received the franchise, with no property qualifications.

Similarly, only in 1911 did the Parliament Act give the House of Commons (the elected national legislature) legislative supremacy. Thereafter, the House of Lords could delay but not defeat certain types of bills passed by Commons. The number of bills proposed by the government (cabinet) that are currently rejected by the House of Lords is very limited, but varies considerably. Under Prime Minister Tony Blair (1997–2007), for example, it ranged from only two bills in 2000–2001 to 88 in 2002–2003. In all, the dominance of Commons over Lords is now so great that, although the word *Parliament* technically refers to both houses, it usually is used to mean only the House of Commons.

Constitutional reforms enacted by Blair's Labour Party government converted Lords from a body whose members primarily inherited their seats into a largely appointed body.* The recently seated coalition government (headed by the Conservatives and supported by the Liberal Democrats) has announced plans for a wholly or largely elected second chamber, whose name would possibly be changed from the House of Lords to the Senate.

The Strengths and Weaknesses of Gradual Change

In contrast to other industrial democracies, Britain's contemporary political institutions cannot be traced to a single event such as the French Revolution or the

---

* This chapter uses the British spelling of the "Labour Party" (rather than "Labor Party").

United Kingdom

England, Scotland, Wales and Northern Ireland

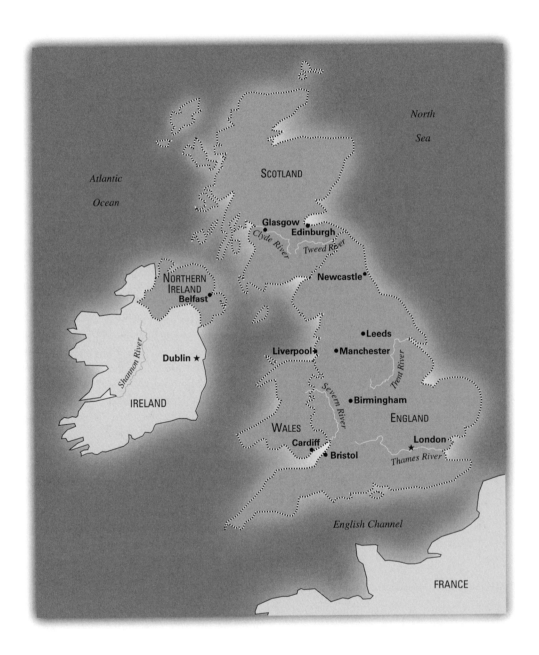

ratification of the U.S. Constitution. Instead, British democracy has been fashioned by gradual, **evolutionary change**, lacking the drama of major upheavals.

For many years, Britain was considered a model democracy. Its parliamentary form of government was copied in flourishing democracies—including Australia, Canada, and New Zealand—and was adopted less successfully in many former British colonies in Africa and Asia. The country's history of gradual change fostered an atmosphere of political openness and tolerance. It also enshrined institutions and customs—such as the monarch's coronation and the changing of the guard at Buckingham Palace—that bind the population together (and also provide the pomp and circumstance that attracts millions of foreign tourists annually).

At the same time, however, the very traditions and practices that have created national unity and stability also have frequently become barriers to progress. That is to say that although peaceful, evolutionary change has an obvious value, it some-times also has inhibited the modernization of British institutions and beliefs. For example, the country's somewhat rigid class structure has, in the recent past, restricted educational opportunities and limited upward **social mobility** (movement up the social ladder) for much of the population.

Britain was the home of the Industrial Revolution in the eighteenth and early nine-teenth centuries, but many of the aristocracy's cultural values subsequently contributed to the country's economic stagnation in the twentieth century. For example, the upper class's preference for careers in finance, law, or journalism rather than industry gave industrial entrepreneurship a diminished status. Interestingly, most of the inventors and businessmen who initiated the Industrial Revolution were not "well born." From Victorian times until quite recently, however, industrialists were often more interested in demonstrating their social standing than in improving productivity and keeping up with foreign competition. These factors contributed to the country's decline from being the world's leading economic power in the early twentieth century to second-class status today, behind the United States, Germany, Japan, France, and China.

CONTEMPORARY BRITISH SOCIETY AND POLITICAL CULTURE

In our discussion of political culture (Chapter 3), we noted that people in different countries feel differing degrees of satisfaction or dissatisfaction with their own political institutions and their fellow citizens. Whatever their complaints and grievances, the English people and, to a lesser extent, the Scots and Welsh are proud of Great Britain. A number of years ago, a Gallup poll revealed that 80 percent of all Britons were proud of being British. More recent opinion surveys have indicated that national pride is higher in Britain than in many other Western European nations.[1] In part, that pride rightly reflects the strengths of British society. It is a very safe country, with homicide and overall crime rates less than one-fourth those of the United States and a police force that normally patrols the streets unarmed. Most Britons, quite accurately, view their fellow citizens as generally trustworthy, friendly, and polite.

A part of the country's stability and political success can be attributed to its rather well-developed sense of national unity. As we noted in Chapter 3, Great Britain is often considered a model consensual political culture, most of whose citi-zens are in substantial agreement about their political goals and practices. A political consensus is more easily fostered in a society that is not deeply divided socially. When London had to endure repeated bombings during World War II, foreign observers were impressed by the sense of national purpose that united citizens of all backgrounds. Londoners seemed to exhibit a similar sense of common purpose after the city's 2005 terrorist bombings. Over time, Britain has been split by fewer ethnic, racial, religious, and geographic differences than have nations such as the United States, South Africa, Russia, and Belgium. Yet important divisions do exist within British society, and some have notable political and economic consequences.

Sources of National Unity

In our discussion of political development (Chapter 15), we will suggest that nations with many religions, languages, ethnicities, or racial groups generally have had more tumultuous political systems than have countries with more **homogeneous societies** (societies that are more uniform in social composition). That may help us to understand Britain's relatively peaceful development and the sources of its political strength.

As an island nation, its people have always felt distinct from the other European nations across the English Channel on "the Continent." At times, that distinction has contributed to a false sense of superiority. Compared with other Western European populations, the British people remain less committed to merging with the rest of Western Europe and more skeptical of the **European Union (EU)**, the 27-nation economic union (and limited political union) of European nations. Thus, for example, Britain is one of only three EU nations in Western Europe to have refused to adopt the Euro, the common European currency. Although such insular attitudes have created problems for the British in the past—for example, their economy was hurt by their initial refusal to join the European Economic Community (now the European Union)—they did contribute to a consensus within the British Isles.

Almost 85 percent of Britons come from England, with most living in southern England in close proximity to London. Furthermore, the population is overwhelmingly urban, with about two-thirds of the population of England and Wales found in seven metropolitan areas.[2] Not only does one person in six live in greater London but most of the country's political, economic, and cultural elites reside in or near the capital. In many ways, then, most Britons have similar lifestyles, read the same newspapers, and relate to the same political symbols.

Sources of Internal Division

Even though the extent of homogeneity and consensus in Great Britain is impressive, important social differences also exist.

The Role of Social Class   In the absence of rural–urban conflicts or strong ethnic, racial, or religious divisions, the greatest predictor of British political behavior and attitudes has been **social class**—defined as an individual's or group's relative rank in society as determined by wealth, income, education, occupation, status, and power. Blue-collar workers, the poor, and those with limited educations are more prone to vote for the Labour Party. White-collar workers, professionals, businesspeople, and members of the middle and upper classes are more likely to support the Conservative

Party (also known as the **Tories**). Though there is a link in most industrial democracies between class background and party preference, historically the connection was particularly strong in Britain.[3] Since the 1970s, that correlation has weakened as more British workers vote for the Conservatives and more middle-class voters support Labour. Educational reforms, the rise of a merit-oriented leadership within the Conservative Party, and other broad cultural changes have reduced the class divide somewhat and its effect on everyday life. In spite of these changes, however, social class remains the best predictor of people's electoral preference and of their children's educational achievement and occupation.

Historically, the nation's political leaders have emerged disproportionately from the upper class. Aristocratic families (those with inherited titles bestowed by the crown) dominated the political system until the twentieth century. The rise of the Liberal Party in the late nineteenth century and the Labour Party in the early twentieth opened greater opportunities for politicians of middle- and working-class backgrounds. Since the 1970s, most prime ministers have come out of the middle class.

It is within the Conservative Party that upper-class dominance has been most pronounced. Until the 1970s, all Tory prime ministers had been drawn from the aristocracy or other segments of the upper class. Since that time, access to party leadership has opened up, with Prime Ministers Heath (1970–1974), Thatcher (1979–1990), and John Major (1990–1997) coming from middle-class origins. Even so, currently most Conservative MPs (members of parliament, i.e., the House of Commons) still come from the upper or upper-middle classes. For example, the recently elected Tory Prime Minister, David Cameron, is the son of a well-to-do stockbroker. He attended Eton—Britain's most exclusive boarding school—and Oxford before marrying the daughter of a British aristocrat.

British class distinctions have been reinforced by distinct educational tracks for each class. At the top of the educational system are the country's most exclusive private boarding schools, called (confusingly for Americans) **public schools**.* The most famous of these—including Eton, Harrow, Winchester, Rugby, and Westminster— are hundreds of years old. Because of these schools' high cost and elitist orientation, their students are overwhelmingly well-to-do. Although less than 5 percent of the British population attends public schools, their graduates dominate the top ranks of the Conservative Party, the civil service, and high finance. For example, currently, 60 percent of Conservative MPs went to private high schools, with roughly half of them attending exclusive "public schools"—six times the national average.[4]

While a high proportion of the nation's upper-class and upper-middle-class families send their children to private schools of some sort (either elite "public schools" or some other type), 90 percent of Britain's entire student population attends state-run (government-run) schools, which generally serve middle- and working-class students. Within the state school system, there tend to be different educational tracks for students from those two classes. That is to say, students from middle-class families are far more likely to take academically oriented courses or attend grammar schools (academically strong government "high schools") that prepare them for possible university educations. In contrast, students from working-class backgrounds tend to take

---

* Secondary schools run by the local government have had various names (including "grammar schools," "secondary moderns," and "comprehensives"), but they are *never* called "public schools."

vocationally oriented (trade) courses, with few of them going on to university and a large portion ending their education at the age of 16. While there have been a number of reforms in the past few decades designed to reduce this disparity, the percentage of working-class students going to university remains low, and the British remain keenly aware of the class and education linkage.

Analysts agree that British class divisions are less significant today than in the past. But most of them also believe that they remain an important factor in national life. For example, when Prince William (Prince Charles and Princess Diana's son) broke up for a time with his future wife, Kate Middleton, the British news media reported that they "broke up in part because of [the royal family's distaste for] her mother Carole's so-called middle class behavior" and speech.[5] Some papers characterized her as "pushy ... and incredibly middle class" and reported that Prince William's aristocratic friends made jokes about Carole Middleton's previous employment as an airline flight attendant.

Not surprisingly, the British are highly aware of the broader role of class in their society. Moreover, unlike Americans, they believe that there are fundamental conflicts between the interests of the upper class, middle class, and working class. In a 1996 public opinion poll, Britons were asked whether "a person's social class [at birth] affects their chances in life" a lot or a little. Sixty percent of the respondents answered "a lot." And when asked in an earlier poll if there was "a class struggle in Britain" (presumably of a non-violent nature), an astonishing 81 percent of all Britons answered "yes."[6] Yet, despite the country's well-known and keenly felt class divisions, Great Britain has historically been less sharply politically divided by class *antagonisms* than countries such as France and Italy, where class divisions are less obvious but more contentious. So, whereas the communist parties in France and Italy once attracted a quarter or more of the votes (reflecting substantial working-class discontent with socioeconomic conditions and employer–labor relations), the British Communist Party has never received much support at all.

Two factors have kept British class hostilities in check. First, historically the upper class was more receptive than its counterparts elsewhere in Europe to social programs benefiting the working class and the poor. Indeed, in the late nineteenth century the Conservative Party introduced many of the country's earliest social reform programs. The Conservatives remained receptive to government welfare programs after World War II when the newly elected Labour government introduced a wide range of social programs in the welfare state (discussed later in the chapter). Although those measures were originally introduced by the Labour Party, the Tories continued to fund and support most of them after they returned to power in the 1950s. Only since the 1970s have Conservative governments (most notably Margaret Thatcher's) criticized and pared down the welfare state.

The upper classes' more conciliatory outlook contributed to a second factor that reduced class tensions over the years: the average citizens' admiration for the **aristocracy** and widespread deference to the upper classes. Even today, despite the royal family's frequent missteps reported in great detail by the mass media, the British public retains tremendous affection for the queen and, lately, Prince William.

Regional Divisions   Regional differences are another important source of political division in Britain. Despite having belonged to the United Kingdom (UK) for hundreds of years, many Scots, Welsh, and Northern Irish continue to resent English political and economic domination. In two 1997 referendums the Scots and the

Welsh voted to establish their own regional parliaments, and these were soon put in place. Scottish separatism recently surged when the Scottish National Party (SNP) triumphed in the 2011 regional parliamentary elections, emerging as the first political party to ever win a majority in that young body. The SNP plans to hold a referendum in the next two to three years on Scottish independence from the UK, and British Prime Minister Cameron has announced that his government will not block such a vote. In Wales, the nationalist **Plaid Cymru** (Party of Wales) also has attracted some electoral support. Although the majority of Scots and Welsh have so far chosen to remain within the United Kingdom, economic and cultural tensions remain.

A far more vexing challenge to the country's unity has come from Northern Ireland. Responding to clashes between Catholics and Protestants and to terrorist activities by the (Catholic) Irish Republican Army (IRA) and the (Protestant) Ulster Volunteer Force (UVF) and Ulster Defense Association (UDA), the British stationed between 10,000 and 15,000 troops in the region in an attempt to keep the peace. Between 1969 and 2001, during a conflict known as "The Troubles," about 3,500 people died, and more than 25,000 were wounded (out of a Northern Irish population of some 1.7 million). If a similar percentage of Americans had died in civil unrest, it would translate to more than 600,000 deaths. The British authorities' efforts to establish order provoked numerous violations of the residents' civil liberties, particularly those of the Catholic population. Moreover, evidence later emerged of collusion between the British authorities and UVF terrorists. Periodically, IRA terrorism extended into England, resulting in many bombings, disruptions of public transport, and several attempts on the lives of Prime Ministers Thatcher and Major.[7]

In 1998, after difficult and protracted negotiations, both sides (along with the British and Irish governments) signed the Belfast Agreement (also known as the Good Friday Agreement), creating a joint Catholic–Protestant government in the north. Shortly thereafter, the voters of both Ireland and Northern Ireland overwhelming endorsed the accord in referendums. While the Good Friday accord brought relative peace to the region, a final settlement was delayed for years by the refusal of both the IRA and the UVF to put their arms beyond reach. Finally, in 2005 the IRA began disarming, and the UVF followed suit four years later. Despite continued misgivings on both sides and substantial Protestant displeasure over having lost their former political dominance, home rule was finally established and peace seems to have finally come to the region.

Racial Divisions Until the 1950s, Britain's population was overwhelmingly White. Since then, however, there has been a large influx of immigrants from India, Pakistan, Bangladesh, the Caribbean, Hong Kong, and Africa. By 1991, the country had approximately 3.8 million immigrants, with a majority of them from former British colonies. Although non-Whites currently constitute only about 8 percent of the total population, they are concentrated in a fairly small number of urban, industrial areas. Religious differences (a majority of the immigrants are Muslim, Hindu, or Sikh), competition for jobs, and racism have contributed to ongoing social tensions, including periodic urban riots (with varying levels of racial components) since the 1980s. Most recently the extensive 2011 rioting (featuring looting and arson) in parts of London and a number of other cities started when White policemen shot and killed an unarmed Black man. The ensuing rioting began as an expression of Black resentment of the police, but soon spread into multiracial looting by Whites, Blacks, and Asians.

In recent years, the National Front (NF) and the British National Party (BNP)—two neofascist political parties expressing and fomenting racist backlash within the White working class—have received growing electoral support in a small number of localities, and their activists aggravated 2001 race riots in northern England. Both the NF and the BNP, however, have far less voter support than do comparable neofascist parties in France, Austria, and Germany. The rise of Islamic extremism among some Muslims (including the children of immigrants), most notably the 2005 terrorist attacks on London's buses and subways, has increased ethnic tensions and led to greater government surveillance of Islamic groups. Though understandable from a security perspective, this has antagonized much of Britain's large Muslim community, the vast majority of whom are law abiding and feel that they are under suspicion because of the sins of a small number of extremists in their midst.

POLITICAL PARTIES AND VOTING

Political party organizations dominate politics more thoroughly in Britain than in the United States for three important reasons. First, Britain has no primary elections. Hence, local party organizations (controlled by party activists), not the voters, select candidates for the House of Commons. Second, British voters get to vote for only one office in the national government: their representative in the House of Commons. The party with a parliamentary majority then selects its leader as prime minister. Thus, the executive branch and the legislative branch are controlled by the same party, and the electorate has no opportunity for ticket splitting. Finally, party delegations within Parliament usually vote as a unified bloc, with MPs usually voting as their party leaders urge them to. As a consequence, Conservatives, Labour, and Liberal Democrats (commonly known as the "Lib Dems") speak to the public with a more unified and more clearly defined message than do Democrats or Republicans in the United States.

A Two-and-One-Half-Party System

Great Britain has a party system dominated by two giants, but with a third party getting a significant share of the vote. Since the decline of the Liberal Party in the 1920s, most seats in Parliament have been won either by the Conservative Party or the Labour Party. But, unlike smaller parties in the United States, Britain's "third party" attracts an important share of the popular vote and wins a number of parliamentary seats. Two-party dominance peaked in the 1950s when the combined Conservative and Labour party votes accounted for as much as 97 percent of the total. In recent decades, however, that share has fallen sharply to 65 percent in 2010.

The first substantial postwar challenge to the two-party system was mounted in the 1980s, when the Liberal Party joined with the Social Democratic Party in an electoral "Alliance." Although it was able to gain about one-fourth of the popular vote in the 1983 and 1987 parliamentary elections, the Alliance ended up with less than 4 percent of the seats in Parliament. In 1988, the two Alliance partners merged into a single party later called the Liberal Democrats (Lib Dems).

The prospects for British third parties are severely hampered by the country's electoral system. Because British MPs (like U.S. congressional representatives) are elected from several hundred single-member districts (SMDs), a political party may win a substantial proportion of the nation's vote and yet have little to show for it in Parliament if it does not win many individual districts (See A Closer Look 11.2). That proved to be the downfall of the Alliance and now plagues the Liberal Democrats. Any third party that might arise in Britain, the United States, or other countries using SMD would face a similar fate. Another less common shortcoming of SMD elections is that it is possible for a party to win the most votes and not receive the most seats in Parliament. In the past 60 years that has happened twice—in 1951 and in the first of two parliamentary elections in 1974.

The Conservative Party (the Tories)

The Conservatives are Britain's oldest and most successful political party. Formally organized in the 1830s, the party began earlier as the voice of the British aristocracy and landed gentry. Over the years, however, it has become a broadly based party with electoral support from a wide range of voters.

The Conservatives continue to receive their most intense backing from upper-class and middle-class voters. Ever since universal suffrage was established in the early decades of the twentieth century, however, they have also attracted a significant segment of the working-class vote, without which they could never win at the polls. For example, Margaret Thatcher and John Major led the party to four successive electoral victories (in 1979, 1983, 1987, and 1992) by sweeping the most economically dynamic parts of the country (London and the rest of southern England) and winning over one-third of the working-class vote. Furthermore, by the time of the Conservative's 2010 victory, the percentage of British voters belonging to the working class (blue collar) had shrunk considerably as the size of the middle class had grown, benefiting the Tories.

In the past, the Tories, like conservative parties elsewhere, have often defended the status quo. In the tradition of Edmund Burke (Chapter 2), the party has insisted that change should be gradual so as not to undermine "the existing fabric of society." Whereas the Labour Party initiated bold new programs over the years, the Conservative position was more reactive until the 1980s.[8] Closely linked to the business community, the party is suspicious of big government and high taxes, at least when compared to Labour.

At the same time, however, for many years Conservative Party leaders believed that government had an obligation to protect the less privileged members of society and to protect the people's basic needs. Consequently, in the decades after World War II, various Conservative administrations accepted and supported an array of government welfare programs. Indeed, in the decades following World War II the economic policies of Conservative and Labour governments differed only modestly, as Tory leaders from the late 1940s until the 1970s supported "caring capitalism," which included the welfare state.[9]

That situation changed dramatically in the mid-1970s when Margaret Thatcher assumed the party's leadership. In her years as prime minister (1979–1990), the "Iron Lady," as she was called, launched a major assault on big government. Conservatives stridently defended free enterprise and the values of the market system.[10] In 1992, two years after Thatcher's resignation as prime minister, her successor, John Major, led the Conservatives to an unprecedented fourth consecutive victory.

Thus, by the start of the 1990s, the Conservatives seemed to have established themselves as the country's dominant political party. Soon, however, their strength evaporated. By 1997, the popularity of Major's government had sunk to record lows and Tony Blair had reinvigorated the Labour Party, producing a resounding Labour victory in the next two parliamentary elections (1997–2001) and a narrower win in

2005. For much of the period the Tories were weakened by internal conflicts between a "traditionalist" faction (which resisted gay rights, favored tighter controls on immigration, and opposed further British integration into the EU) and a "libertarian" faction that wished to modernize the party by taking a more liberal position on these issues while still wanting to reduce the government's economic role.

With Labour repositioned as Britain's middle-of-the-road party, the Conservatives seemed out of touch. After two devastating defeats at the polls, they were finally able to reduce (but not overtake) Labour's parliamentary majority considerably in 2005 (Table 11.1). Between 1997 and 2005, the Tories elected a new party leader four different times. The first three were uninspiring and unable to overturn Labour's electoral dominance. But a combination of Gordon Brown's personal unpopularity and the economic crisis of 2008 undermined Labour support. Meanwhile, Conservatives turned to David Cameron, a young, telegenic, and media-savvy party leader. During the 2010 campaign, he presented himself as a centrist, emphasizing issues previously associated with Labour— saving the environment, improving health care and the school system, and caring about the lot of society's less fortunate—though with different solutions. At the same time, his speeches generally omitted many right-wing issues and symbols—including opposition to the EU and homage to Margaret Thatcher. Ultimately, the combination of Cameron's appeal and the declining fortunes of the Labour government enabled the Tories to return to power in 2010 after 13 years in the political wilderness.

Once in office, however, Cameron introduced even bigger cuts in government spending than Thatcher had. He also announced cutbacks on Britain's extensive welfare state. These include tightening eligibility for unemployment compensation, reducing government payments to families that have children, reducing housing subsidies, and cutting educational expenditures. Given Britain's huge budget deficit and the country's enormous debt, major cuts were probably unavoidable. But a Labour government would have made those cuts more gradually.

The Labour Party

The Labour Party was founded in 1900 from an alliance of socialist organizations and labor unions. Within two decades, it had become the country's second-largest party, and in 1923 it headed a short-lived government. As its name implies, the party has been closely linked to the nation's trade-union movement and receives its most important electoral support from blue-collar workers. Unions have provided a large share of the party's financial resources and until recently played an important role in selecting its parliamentary leader. But even though many Labour MPs have entered politics from the union movement, the party's top leadership has come largely from the middle class, particularly teachers, university professors, and other professionals. Like all major British parties, Labour draws votes across class lines.

When Labour came to power in 1945, it created an extensive state welfare system and **nationalized**[*] important sectors of the economy, including the railroads, coal mines, and steel. Until the mid-1990s, the Labour Party continued to favor many socialist programs. For example, one of the most controversial sections in its charter endorsed government "ownership of the means of production" (major industries, transport, and so forth).[11]

---

[*] A process in which the government takes over companies or industries that were once privately owned (often by foreign firms) and turns them in state enterprises.

TABLE 11.1	Results of the 1983, 2001, 2005, and 2010 National Elections			
	1983	2001	2005	2010
Conservatives				
Percentage of the vote received	42.4	31.7	32.4	36.1
Percentage of seats won	61.1	24.4	30.2	47.1
Labour				
Percentage of the vote received	27.6	40.7	35.2	29.0
Percentage of seats won	32.1	60.8	55.1	39.8
Alliance (1983) or Liberal Democrats (2001, 2005, 2010)				
Percentage of the vote received	25.4	18.3	22.0	23.0
Percentage of seats won	3.5	7.6	9.6	8.8

SOURCE: Philip Norton, *The British Polity* (New York: Longman, 1994), p. 83; The British Council, britishcouncil.org/governance-expertise-election2005.htm; The UK Parliament website, http://parliament.uk/directories/hcio/stateparties.cfm; BBC (May 10, 2010).

Always controversial, government ownership of major firms had lost significant voter support by the 1970s. As the Thatcher administration **reprivatized*** British Aerospace, Jaguar, British Petroleum, the telephone system, and other enterprises, many average citizens purchased stock in those firms. Recognizing that Labour's socialist positions were hurting it at the polls, Tony Blair persuaded the party organization in the mid-1990s to end its support for extensive state ownership of important segments of the economy.

Conservative leader David Cameron, Britain's youngest Prime Minister in nearly 200 years, leads a coalition government that brought his party to power after 13 years in opposition.

* These companies, which were once privately owned, had been nationalized by various Labour governments. Now they were being reprivatized (sold back to private ownership).

Labour's other important policy objective in the postwar era was creating the **welfare state**—an array of government programs providing health care (for all citizens, regardless of income), retirement pensions, unemployment compensation, and public housing. Britain's extensive social welfare programs—including the national health system and a huge network of public housing—astounds many Americans but are fairly typical of other Western European nations. For the most part, the voters have approved of the welfare state (though they may be critical of how well it functions), and succeeding governments—Labour and Conservative alike—maintained it until it was trimmed back in the Thatcher era. Proponents of the welfare state note that it has contributed to a lower infant mortality rate, a longer life span (credited to the government-run national health program of free, universal care), and a safety net for the needy. Opponents charge that it has overtaxed the nation and stifled economic growth. Today, Labour continues to defend the remaining components of the welfare state, especially the National Health Service, but the party no longer wishes to expand it. In fact, although Labour was in office from 1997 to 2010, it restored few of the welfare programs that its Conservative (Thatcherite) predecessors had eliminated.

Blair's first budget featured a tax cut for business and differed only somewhat from John Major's. Indeed, under Blair and his successor, Gordon Brown, "**New Labour**," as the party now calls itself, abandoned most of its socialist positions and become a middle-of-the-road party. It has shed the image of a party of big government by promising not to raise taxes and to improve public services by making them more efficient rather than by increasing government spending. In doing so, it took the middle ground from the Conservatives, won considerable backing from the middle class, and won the national elections in 1997, 2001, and 2005, the party's longest stretch in office ever. A look at Gordon Brown's political career illustrates how far to the center New Labour had moved. As a young politician, he had been a committed socialist, highly critical of capitalism. By the time he became Blair's finance minister, Brown enthusiastically protected Britain's financial markets and advocated close cooperation between government and business.[12]

While accepting many of the Thatcherites' probusiness reforms, New Labour in power pursued a more pragmatic approach than either Thatcher on the right or "old Labour" on the left. Unlike Thatcherites, who were instinctively against most government programs, or the traditional Labour Party, which was instinctively for them, Blair's and Brown's position was that "what matters is what works."[13]

Although these centrist policies alienated many of the old Labour Party militants (particularly leftist ideologues and trade unionists), they proved very popular with the voting public, including the middle class. Indeed, the decision to reform the party was based on the realization that the size of the working class and the political influence of the unions (Labour's traditional voting base) were shrinking while the ranks of the middle class and white-collar workers (traditionally more likely to vote Conservative) were growing. In order to win, Blair and Brown concluded, New Labour had to become more of a "catchall party" (a broadly based party) winning support from a broad array of voters. The strategy worked. In 1997, nearly one-third of all professionals and managers and nearly one-half of all skilled white-collar workers voted for the party, a substantial gain over prior elections and the key to its victory.[14] In all, Tony Blair led Labour to three consecutive victories, something that the party had never previously accomplished. But the 2005 victory came with the party attracting only 35.5 percent of the vote, a record low for a winning party in modern times.

Weakened by his growing reputation for being "too slick," and especially by his very unpopular alliance with the United States in Iraq, Blair's personal popularity began to decline in his second term. Two years after Labour's much weaker (but still victorious) performance in the 2005 parliamentary election, Prime Minister Blair resigned. Labour selected his most powerful cabinet member and personal rival, Gordon Brown, as the party's new leader and, hence, the new prime minister. Brown governed from 2007 to 2010 when, undercut by the world's financial crisis, Britain's growing national debt, and his own abrasive personality, he failed in his bid for reelection.

The Liberal Democratic Party

Great Britain's leading "third party," the Liberal Democratic Party, was founded in 1988. Originally called the Social and Liberal Democrats, it took its present name the following year. With a policy position to the left of the Conservatives and to the right of Labour, the Liberal Democrats originally presented themselves as a centrist alternative to the two major parties, though that distinction has weakened since the 1990s when Labour moved toward the center. Indeed, in recent times the Lib Dems had supported policies to the left of Labour in areas such as public health, taxes, civil liberties, and the war in Iraq. For example, the party not only strongly opposed the war in Iraq, but was highly critical of a number of Blair's and Brown's antiterrorism measures, which it felt had unjustifiably violated civil liberties.

The foundation for this new party was laid in the 1980s through the electoral alliance between the Liberal and the Social Democratic parties. Once one of the country's two major parties (in the nineteenth and early twentieth centuries), the Liberals were passed in the 1920s by the rising Labour Party. Reduced to insignificance after World War II, the Liberals later staged a modest comeback. By the early 1970s, they

A CHALLENGING ALLIANCE   Tony Blair meets with President Bush to discuss the war in Iraq. Blair's government was the most ardent supporter of U.S. policy in the region, a position that eroded Blair's popularity at home.

A CLOSER LOOK

11.1

Hung Parliaments and Coalition Governments

Parliamentary governments, headed by a prime minister, are the norm in most European democracies and are common elsewhere, including Australia, Canada, India, and Israel. In order to govern, a prime minister normally must secure the support of a majority of representatives (over half) in the primary house of parliament (e.g., the British House of Commons). In countries with two dominant political parties—most likely to be found in parliaments with single-member districts—one of those two parties usually is able to win a parliamentary majority and thereby govern by itself. But in parliamentary democracies with multiparty representation in parliament—common in countries using proportional representation (PR)—frequently no single party is able to win a majority. In such cases, an aspiring prime minister must garner the support of two or more parties in order to form a **coalition government**. Such a coalition may include only two parties (Germany) or as many as six (Belgium) or even 13 (India).

In all British parliamentary elections held from 1931 until 2010, only one (the 1974 election) resulted in a **hung parliament**, that is, a parliament in which no single party won a majority of seats. Labour Prime Minister Harold Wilson led a minority government (with support from the Ulster Unionists) for only eight months and then called another election that year that resulted in a small Labour majority. Thus, from the end of Winston Churchill's World War II

unity coalition of Conservatives, Liberals, and Labour (1940–1945) until 2010 Britain had not had a coalition government.*

The results of the 2010 election were a surprise in several ways. Early in the campaign the Conservatives seemed to have the voter support needed for a clear majority victory. Later, when Liberal Democratic leader Nick Clegg clearly outperformed his two opponents in Britain's first televised debate between potential prime ministers, his party surged ahead of Labour into second place in the public opinion polls. In the end, however, the Liberal Democrats' share of the vote dropped back to about its 2005 level and actually netted them slightly fewer seats than they had won in the previous national election (see Table 11.1). Labour finished in second place but only attracted the party's second smallest percentage of the total popular vote (29 percent) in some 90 years. Finally, the Conservatives won the highest percentage of the 2010 vote (36.1) and the most seats in the House of Commons (47.1 percent) but failed to win an absolute majority, resulting in Britain's first hung parliament in nearly 40 years.

_____

* From 1977 to 1978 there was a "Lib-Lab" pact in which the Liberal Party agreed to support the Labour Party minority government, but the pact fell short of a full coalition agreement.

were receiving almost 20 percent of the vote. The Social Democrats, on the other hand, were not founded until 1981, when 27 Labour MPs and one Conservative defected from their respective parties, seeking a more moderate alternative. In the 1983 and 1987 general elections, the Liberals and the Social Democrats endorsed a single slate of parliamentary candidates (half from each party) called the Alliance.

Following their disappointing showing in the 1987 election, the Alliance partners decided to merge into a single party soon called the Liberal Democratic Party. In recent parliamentary elections, the Liberal Democrats have attracted around 20 percent of the vote, maintaining their position as Britain's leading third party. The party's support is greatest among middle-class professionals and managers and is somewhat weaker among blue-collar workers. As we have seen (in Table 11.1), the Lib Dems (like the Alliance and the Liberal Party before them) are unable to win a portion of parliamentary seats commensurate with their electoral strength.

11.1

Ironically, then, despite their somewhat disappointing performance, the Lib Dems emerged with the balance of power. Whichever party it threw its support to would win enough votes in parliament to head a coalition government.[†] As a left-of-center party, its ideology and policy preferences are closer to the Labour Party's than to the Tories'. Indeed, the Liberal Democrats generally differ substantially with the Conservatives on issues such as immigration, tax policy, civil liberties and integration into the EU. Ultimately, however, party leaders felt that they could not ally with Labour, a party whose government had been roundly rejected by the voters, and that it was only fair to join with the Conservative Party, which had won the largest share of the votes and MPs by a significant margin (see Table 11.1). That coalition government has been headed by Conservative Prime Minister Cameron, with Liberal Democratic leader Clegg serving as his deputy prime minister. The Lib Dems were given five Cabinet seats and more than a dozen ministerial jobs below the rank of minister.

The coalition deal did not please a number of left-leaning Liberal Democrats, nor did it satisfy right-wing Conservatives. But several factors made it possible. After years as the opposition party, Conservatives were anxious to regain control of the government

and were aware that unless they made a meaningful offer to the Liberal Democrats, that party might form a governing coalition with Labour. For the Lib Dems the alliance meant that the party would hold a significant number of ministerial and subministerial positions for the first time in over 60 years. It also might give them an opportunity to stop the Tories' most right-wing policy objectives and to push through modified versions of some of their own proposals. For example, one of the Liberal Democrats' most important goals, for obvious reasons, has been to change parliamentary and other legislative elections from a single-member-district system to PR. While the Conservatives refused to support that idea, they did agree to a national referendum in which voters would choose between the current electoral system and one called an **alternative vote** (**AV**) system. That system retains single-member districts but allows voters to rank the remaining candidates from first to last. Later, those rankings could be used to redistribute the votes of the candidates who finished last in the first or subsequent rounds of vote counting. Although using AV for parliamentary elections would not help the Liberal Democrats or smaller parties as much as PR would, it would still boost their number of MPs somewhat. Ultimately, however, when a referendum was held in May, 2011, voters chose to stick with the present system, rejecting AV by an overwhelming two-to-one margin. That outcome was not very surprising since both the Conservatives and Labour opposed the change.

[*] Actually, even if Labour had the Liberal Democrats' support, it would have needed the backing of some MPs from smaller parties in order to achieve a majority. However, it is fairly certain that it could have accomplished that.

INTEREST GROUPS

Interest groups play an important role in the British political process. Two have been particularly influential. The Trades Union Congress (TUC), roughly equivalent to the American AFL-CIO, represents 58 of the nation's largest unions (about 6.5 million workers) and is an integral part of the Labour Party. During the 1970s, the TUC and other labor unions exercised a considerable amount of political influence. Indeed, the high level of strikes and labor strife under Conservative Prime Minister Heath (1970–1974) and Labour Prime Minister Callaghan (1976–1979) helped bring their respective governments down.

But organized labor's influence declined sharply under Margaret Thatcher. Her government passed a number of bills weakening trade unions, and, in a critical confrontation, she defeated a bitter and prolonged strike by the powerful miners' union against the state-owned coal mines. During Thatcher's 11 years in office, union membership nation-wide declined from 12 million to 10 million. The shift in the country's economy away from industry and toward the service sector has further weakened the labor movement (as it has in the United States), and by 2002 union membership was down to 7.7 million. Meanwhile, the number of days lost to strikes nationwide declined by almost 90 percent from 1981 to 2000.[15] Moreover, in the mid-1990s Tony Blair's organizational reform of the Labour Party reduced the unions' political influence in the party they helped found. Yet, in March 2011 the TUC staged a massive protest march (with several hundred thousand participants) against Prime Minister Cameron's sharp budget cuts, demonstrating that the Congress still could exert some political pressure.

A second important national interest group is the Confederation of British Industry (CBI), the country's most influential business organization, representing three-fourths of its large and medium-sized manufacturers (with big business exerting the most influence). Unlike the TUC, the CBI is not officially linked to any party but has enjoyed a close relationship with the Conservatives. Unlike the TUC (which has provided major financial support for the Labour Party), the CBI itself gives no funds to the Conservatives. But many individual members of the confederation (including most of the nation's largest corporations) contribute heavily to the Tory coffers.

A CLOSER LOOK　11.2

Parties and the Electoral System

Whereas the United States and Britain have two dominant parties, most of the world's democracies have multiparty systems. In countries such as Italy and France, for example, 10 parties or more sometimes win parliamentary seats. In both countries it is unusual for a single party to hold a majority. Even in Germany, with fewer parties, the ruling party often needs the support of the smaller Free Democratic Party or the Green Party to secure a legislative majority.

Most Western European nations select their parliaments through proportional representation, an electoral system that enhances the prospects of candidates from smaller parties (Chapter 4). In place of many single-member districts (SMDs), members of Parliament are elected from larger districts having multiple representatives. Voters choose between lists of candidates presented by each party. When the votes are tallied, each party attains a percentage of seats in the Parliament proportional to its share of the total vote. Had Great Britain used PR in the four elections listed in Table 11.1 (including the three most recent), the

Alliance and its successor, the Liberal Democrats, would have won roughly 18 to 25 percent of the seats in Parliament (i.e., their proportion of the popular vote). Instead, they ended up with only 3 to 10 percent. Although Tony Blair originally promised to hold a referendum on changing Britain's electoral system to PR, his government failed to do so since such a change would inevitably cost Labour (and the Conservatives) seats in the House of Commons, seats that would be picked up by smaller parties. As we have seen, when the voters were finally given the opportunity to alter the electoral system in 2011, they rejected it.

A related distortion of SMD elections is that they usually (though not always) give a boost in seats to whichever party wins the highest percentage of the vote. For example, in the 1983 election, the Conservatives (led by Thatcher) finished first with 42 percent of the vote but ended up with 61 percent of the seats in Parliament (Table 11.1). Similarly in the 2005 parliamentary race, Labour finished first with only 35 percent of the national vote but won 55 percent of the seats.

From the early 1980s until 1997, the influence of all interest groups, including the Tories' allies in big business, declined appreciably as the Thatcher and Major Conservative governments relied less on their input.[16] Ironically, consultation between the government and the CBI increased under the New Labour governments (1997–2010) as that party sought greater business support. Still, the CBI continues to generally back the Conservatives.

In addition to lobbying, many interest groups are officially represented on government advisory and supervisory boards. But although British interest groups often have been influential at the administrative and bureaucratic level, their leverage in Parliament has been more limited. Because each party's parliamentary delegation typically votes as a fairly solid bloc, interest groups do not have the opportunity to sway individual legislators as they do in the United States. Furthermore, British campaign funding is channeled through the national political party organizations. So again, unlike the United States, it is difficult for a British interest group to win an individual legislator's support through campaign contributions. Instead, to gain their political objectives, interest groups must win the support of cabinet or other government leaders.

THE STRUCTURE OF GOVERNMENT

Britain's government structure is far more centralized—and hence more simplified—than U.S. government. There are no state governments, and the powers of local government are far more circumscribed than they are in the United States. In short, political power in Britain, as in most European democracies, is highly concentrated at the national level. Within the national government, authority is concentrated as well. There is no separation of powers and, hence, nothing comparable to the frequent struggles in the United States between Congress (or a single chamber of Congress) and the president. Under a parliamentary system (which merges the legislative and executive branches), voters also have few electoral decisions for national office. Whereas the U.S. voter selects a number of candidates for the national government—a member of the House of Representatives, two senators, and the president—British voters elect only one: their representative to the House of Commons (their MP).

Parliament

Following each general election, it is the task of the House of Commons to select a prime minister. In many ways, this is the most important function Parliament performs during its term in office. Normally, however, its choice is obvious, once the voters have spoken. Whenever one party wins a majority of the seats in the House of Commons, its leader in Commons is assured of becoming the prime minister. Only twice in the last 65 years (1974 and 2010) has no party been able to win that majority. As we have noted in the first case, Labour leader Harold Wilson, only 17 seats short of a majority, formed a minority government, which lasted only eight months. And in the second instance, the hung parliament of 2010 resulted in the current Conservative–Liberal Democratic coalition (See A Closer Look 11.1).

The prime minister's government (including the cabinet) serves only as long as it can command Parliament's confidence and support. So, any time MPs feel that the government has performed unacceptably, the House of Commons may express "no

confidence" in the prime minister by a simple majority vote. Following such an outcome, the prime minister must resign or have the monarch call a new election.
Unlike the impeachment and conviction of an American president, ousting a prime
minister requires neither a trial by the legislative branch nor the support of two-
thirds of the legislators. Moreover, a **vote of no confidence** does not require any suspicion of illegal activity or any violation of the oath of office.

On the surface, then, this process appears to place British prime ministers on
extremely thin ice, subject to the whims of Parliament. In actuality, however, they
can normally rest secure in the knowledge that they have a firm grip on power until
the next election. As long as their party has a parliamentary majority, which it almost
always has, prime ministers need only maintain the support of their own colleagues.
Because majority MPs have no incentive to force a new election, only one prime
minister in more than half a century, James Callaghan in 1979, has lost a no-
confidence vote. At the same time, however, several times in recent decades MPs
from the majority party have become so dissatisfied with the prime minister's performance that he or she has felt compelled to resign. In 1963, for example, following a
sex scandal and possible breach of national security in his cabinet, Prime Minister
Harold Macmillan resigned (though he himself was uninvolved in the scandal),
claiming ill health. More recently, Margaret Thatcher resigned in 1990 after it
became clear that she no longer had strong support among her Conservative MPs.

Besides serving as a watchdog over the prime minister and the cabinet,
Parliament's most critical function is to consider legislation. Yet its legislative powers
are startlingly limited compared with those of the U.S. Congress. The cabinet introduces all parliamentary bills of any national importance. Because the governing party
almost always has a majority in the House of Commons, and because British parties
vote largely as a bloc, rarely does a bill introduced by the cabinet meet defeat. In
recent decades, **party discipline** (voting as instructed by the party leadership) has
diminished somewhat, and more government bills than previously have been defeated
in Parliament. The number of votes lost by the prime minister (fewer than 10 percent), however, remains rather small compared with the legislative record of U.S.
presidents (including Obama, George W. Bush, and Clinton) who often face an
opposition majority in at least one House of Congress.

Unlike Congress, then, Parliament's primary function is not so much to design
legislation as to review it. Although proposed government legislation is rarely
defeated, it is sometimes altered or even withdrawn if it faces sufficient parliamentary
opposition. For example, in 2011 Prime Minister Cameron was forced to reduce his
proposed cuts to the National Health Service in the face of strong public and parliamentary opposition. Parliament also performs a watchdog function by regularly sub-
jecting the prime minister and the cabinet to intensive questioning. These obligatory
"question sessions" are closely followed by the media and force government ministers
to defend their policies before the aggressive challenge of opposition-party MPs.

The Cabinet

The cabinet is the ultimate decision-making body in British politics. Heading that
body and selecting its other members is the prime minister, the "first among [ministe-
rial] equals." The number of full ministers is normally 20 to 25. They, in turn, are

Former Prime Minister Gordon Brown addresses the House of Commons.

assisted by about 60 to 70 noncabinet and junior ministers. All ministers are chosen from either the House of Commons or, far less frequently, the House of Lords. And, whereas the U.S. Constitution prohibits individuals from simultaneously holding posts in the executive and legislative branches, British political tradition *requires* cabinet members to sit in both.

Except for the rare coalition government, such as the present one, when more than one party joins forces, ministers are selected exclusively from the prime minister's party. They usually come from that party's most respected parliamentary members and normally represent the party's major factions. Appointment to the cabinet is the crowning achievement of an MP's political career. Ministers serve at the pleasure of the prime minister, however, and he or she can remove them at any time.

The cabinet meets regularly to discuss government policy and consider potential legislation. The country's most important political decisions are made there. The prime minister sets the agenda and sums up the discussion and policy decisions at the close of each meeting. Rarely is there a formal vote. Prime ministerial styles vary greatly. Whereas most leaders try to reach a consensus, others do not hesitate to impose their policies on the cabinet, even if theirs is a minority position. It was said of Margaret Thatcher that she summed up the conclusions of the meeting even before discussion began. John Major had a far more conciliatory style and sought cabinet consensus, while Tony Blair, though not as openly aggressive as Thatcher, dominated cabinet meetings and reduced their influence on policy.

Once the prime minister has announced a decision, all cabinet members are collectively responsible for the policy and must quiet any qualms that they have. In the past, ministers who could not abide by that decision had no recourse other than to resign. Since that would undoubtedly hurt their careers as party leaders, resignations based on open policy differences have been extremely rare, though Robin Cook, a former foreign secretary and one of Labour's most influential figures, resigned from the cabinet after Tony Blair's decision to take the country into the war in Iraq. In recent times, extensive media coverage and the resulting news leaks often pierce the veil of secrecy over cabinet meetings, and internal policy differences are more easily known.

Although strong-willed prime ministers have overridden their cabinets and imposed their position, no prime minister can afford to oppose his or her colleagues consistently. Thus, Margaret Thatcher's frequent disregard of opposing views from other Conservative Party leaders and factions eventually contributed to her loss of leadership.

The Bureaucracy

The modern British civil service dates to 1854, when open competition replaced patronage as the basis for recruitment. Whereas new administrations in the United States appoint their supporters to thousands of high-ranking bureaucratic positions, British governments are much more constrained. All but the very top ministry positions are reserved for nonpartisan career civil servants. Since the highest-ranking civil servants (the "mandarins") normally have more experience and expertise in their fields than do the ministers and secretaries under whom they serve, they are in a position to exercise considerable influence. Indeed, in British popular culture (including a hit television sitcom), high-ranking mandarins are often seen as manipulating and controlling the ministers whom they serve.

In fact, the widely held notion of an "unelected dictatorship" (of bureaucrats) is exaggerated.[17] Most informed observers admire the civil service for its dedication and fairness. For the most part, it has done an admirable job of serving both Conservative and Labour governments impartially. But critics on both the left (radical Labourites) and the right (Thatcherites) have complained that entrenched civil servants often oppose policies that seriously threaten the status quo and, consequently, may drag their heels in implementing change.

Others argue that, however well motivated they may be, senior civil servants—who are drawn primarily from the upper middle class and are often educated at elite schools—are out of touch with much of society. They observe that people of working-class origins (constituting over half the nation's population) hold only 5 percent of the 3,000 senior bureaucratic positions. At the same time, a government study noted that 72 percent of those entering the civil service had attended Oxford or Cambridge universities, and 48 percent had graduated from public schools (the elitist private institutions that educate only 5 percent of the nation's population).[18]

The Judiciary

Although U.S. criminal and civil law are derived in large part from British law, the two judicial systems differ fundamentally concerning the courts' political role. As we saw in our discussion of U.S. politics (Chapter 10), the Supreme Court's political power derives from its capacity to overturn congressional legislation and executive actions by declaring them unconstitutional. The British court system has no comparable power since there is no written constitution. If the judicial branch rules that Parliament or the government has acted contrary to established constitutional norms (the country's body of legal rulings, legislation, and traditions), Parliament needs only pass a new law making its intentions explicit on the matter. Under the doctrine of parliamentary sovereignty, that new law would automatically be constitutional and not subject to reversal by the courts. But if the courts overrule an unpopular or embarrassing government practice, Parliament may be reluctant to reinstate that practice.[19]

Britain's membership in the EU—formerly the European Community (EC)—adds another level of authority to the judicial system. The 1972 European Communities Act stated that EC law takes precedence over any member nation's domestic law. Thus, for example, the EU's Court of Justice may rule that British environmental regulations conflict with rules enacted through EU treaties. That ruling would be binding on British courts, and the British law would be struck down. In 1998 the British Parliament passed the **Human Rights Act**. The bill incorporated the European [Union's] Convention on Human Rights, giving the country its first written bill of rights since the late seventeenth century. At the time, civil liberties advocates hailed this as a major step forward. However, in 2005, following the terrorist attacks and attempted attacks on the London mass transit system, Prime Minister Blair announced new security regulations, some of which appear to contradict the European Convention and his own Human Rights Act. He declared that he would ask Parliament to amend the Act if necessary. Now, David Cameron has hinted that his government may revise or repeal entirely the Human Rights Act.

PUBLIC POLICY AND THE BRITISH ECONOMY

The government first began to manage the country's economy actively in the 1930s as it attempted to counter the effects of the worldwide economic depression. World War II, which brought severe shortages and extensive German bombing of London and other British cities, inflicted further suffering. At war's end, in response to the nation's prolonged period of deprivation, the newly elected Labour Government greatly enhanced the state's role in rebuilding the economy and protecting the public's welfare. Although the Conservative opposition at that time as well as Tory governments in the following decades were more cautious than Labour about state economic intervention, they still supported an activist government working for the general good. Thus, from the late 1940s until 1979, Britain's national government (like its counterparts in most of Western Europe) intervened far more intensely in the economy and enacted more welfare measures than the U.S. government did.

The Establishment of the Welfare State (1945–1951)

The postwar Labour Government introduced an array of programs revolutionizing the state's role in society. The new national health care system offered tax-funded medical care for all. To remedy the country's severe housing shortage, the state funded a vast network of **council housing**, low-income public housing, funded by the national government but administered by local government.

The government expanded unemployment compensation and retirement pensions to create a "safety net" for the needy. In all, the Labour Government created a welfare state to provide the population with "cradle to grave" security. In addition, it nationalized a number of basic industries, including coal mining, iron, and steel—believing that those industries would better serve the national interest under state ownership.

The Postwar Settlement

When the Conservatives returned to power in 1951, they reversed some aspects of Labour's economic policy but maintained many others. For example, they reprivatized (returned to private ownership) the iron and steel industries. But during the next 28 years, Conservative and Labour governments alike retained and enlarged the national health care system and other fundamental elements of the welfare state. Public housing was greatly expanded, ultimately providing shelter for *one-third* of the country's population. Still haunted by memories of the Great Depression, Conservative and Labour administrations alike pursued full-employment policies. For example, when major private firms faced bankruptcy, the government often stepped in with loans and stock purchases, or, when necessary, took them over to keep them running.

Political scientists maintain that during that period an unofficial and unspoken compact existed (referred to as the **postwar settlement**) between the Conservative Party and the business community on one side, and the Labour Party and the trade unions on the other. Labour moderated its impulse for additional socialist reform, and the Conservatives accepted existing welfare programs that provided for the working class. That unofficial agreement remained in place until the late 1970s.[20] For much of that period, the nation enjoyed moderate economic growth, low inflation, and unemployment levels that rarely exceeded 3 percent.[21]

The Collapse of the Postwar Settlement

Thus, in the mid-1960s, the British government could truthfully tell its people that they'd "never had it so good." The nation's standard of living was higher than it had ever been before. Beneath the surface, however, serious economic problems loomed. Britain's postwar growth and industrial productivity trailed well behind Japan, the United States, and most of Western Europe. One by one, Germany, France, the Netherlands, Norway, Sweden, Denmark, and others passed the British in per capita income (GNP per capita). Britain became less competitive in the world market. Once among the world's leading producers of automobiles, motorcycles, and ships, it lost a large portion of those industries when it could no longer compete with countries such as Japan, Germany, and the United States. Burdened by budget deficits and crippling trade deficits (exporting less than it imported), the country accumulated a large foreign debt. By the 1970s, the economy had reached a crisis.

The reasons for Britain's economic slide were complex and are subject to debate. Conservative and Labour analysts offered differing explanations and conflicting solutions. As real wages (the purchasing power of people's wages) stagnated or fell, the Labour Party became more radical, and unions became more militant. At the same time, power in the Conservative Party shifted from its once-dominant centrist faction to the party's right wing. The consensus of the postwar settlement was breaking down. As inflation soared above 20 percent in the mid-1970s, labor–management conflict intensified, with both sides struggling to keep up with rising prices. During the 1970s, the country lost more days to strikes than in the preceding 25 years combined.

In the winter of 1979, six weeks of strikes cut off garbage collection, heating-oil delivery, and hospital service. That "winter of discontent," as it was called, turned public opinion against the Labour Government and helped produce a Conservative victory in the 1979 national election.

The Thatcher Revolution

When Margaret Thatcher, the newly elected Conservative prime minister, took office, she revolutionized British politics much as her friend and admirer, President Ronald Reagan, did shortly afterward in the United States. Both countries, like many industrial democracies at that time, faced stagnant economic growth, high inflation, and budget deficits.

Prime Minister Thatcher, like President Reagan, was determined to reduce the role of government in the economy and to remove what both believed were unnecessary shackles on the free-enterprise system. Thatcher's tight-fisted fiscal policies initially drove the country into a recession. Unemployment rates nearly tripled to more than 12 percent—the highest rate since the Great Depression of the 1920s and 1930s. Yet, the administration rejected a basic element of the postwar settlement. Believing that it would only lead to greater budget deficits and continued inflation, the government refused to bail out ailing industries or employ other traditional methods to combat unemployment.

Looking at the country's long-term economic slide, the administration concluded that the solution was less government rather than more. It tried to create an "enterprise culture" in which citizens would look to the free market and not government for economic solutions. Prime Ministers Thatcher and Major reprivatized a wide range of government-owned enterprises—including the telephone, electricity, natural gas, and water systems—putting their shares up for sale on the stock market. Much of the vast network of public housing was privatized as well when tenants were given the opportunity to buy their homes from the state (at favorable prices) if they wished. On the other hand, in the face of public opposition, both Thatcher and Major refrained from major assaults on state welfare plans, including dismantling the National Health Service.

How successful was **Thatcherism** (Thatcher's political policies and ideology)? The answer depends on who you ask. Conservative Party and private-sector supporters insist that she cured Britain of its excessive dependence on state-sponsored economic solutions. By reducing taxes and promoting an "enterprise culture," her government encouraged the growth of thousands of new companies, particularly in the nation's south. Supporters note that by the mid-1990s, Britain had one of the fastest-growing economies in Western Europe (although there had been sharp ups and downs under both Thatcher and Major). In many cases (though not all), privatized firms have performed more efficiently than they had under state control.

Many critics of Thatcherism in the Labour Party, the unions, and even her own party conceded a number of those accomplishments but contended that too frequently they came at an unnecessarily high cost. Although unemployment rates declined from their peaks of the mid-1980s, they remained much higher than they had been before Thatcher. Much of the north—historically Great Britain's industrial heartland—failed to share in the economic revival.

But no matter how history eventually judges the Conservative revolution, for now the champions of reduced government have won the day. In Britain, as in the United States and much of the world, the role of government has been significantly scaled back and is unlikely to return to its former level in the foreseeable future. Although many voters viewed the Thatcher revolution as too heartless or too extreme, most were more suspicious of the Labour Party's commitment to greater government intervention. Hence, the Conservatives won four consecutive national elections.

As we have seen, realizing this change in public attitudes, the Labour Party moved away from socialist or big-government solutions. New Labour governments led by Blair (1997–2007) and Gordon Brown (2007–2010) have renounced the party's previous support of government ownership of major industries, kept a lid on taxes, and left untouched most of Margaret Thatcher's major policy changes, accepting them as necessary. Much of the current Labour Party program—including improving technical and scientific education (to help private enterprise compete), lowering business taxes, and fighting crime—is quite acceptable to centrist and moderately conservative voters. Thus, the Blair and Brown governments did as much to confirm the conservative revolution as to challenge it. Now that the Tories have returned to power, state economic intervention and the welfare state are unlikely to grow and may be cut further. At the same time, Cameron's decision to reduce his planned cuts in the National Health Service indicates that public opinion will prevent him from launching a broad assault on the more popular public welfare programs.

CONCLUSION: GREAT BRITAIN IN THE TWENTY-FIRST CENTURY

Despite its impressive history of democracy and stability, Britain did not fare particularly well economically for much of the twentieth century. In recent times, the governments of Margaret Thatcher and John Major stimulated private-sector investment and opened up new opportunities for entrepreneurial talent. Progress toward improving Britain's long-sluggish economy was uneven as periods of improved growth alternated with economic downturns. But by the late 1990s the economy began to grow at an accelerated pace. For decades Britain had one of the slowest rates of economic growth in Western Europe. But by the start of the twenty-first century it had one of the fastest. Faster economic growth and higher labor productivity began under John Major's administration and continued through most of New Labour's first decade in power (1997–2008), only to be cut short by the global economic crisis (2008–2011).

Changing social attitudes and wider educational opportunities have opened up the country's confining class system. Wealthy, self-made businesspeople are more numerous and more socially accepted within the "old money" elite. Since the 1970s, a series of Conservative Party leaders have come from middle-class origins rather than the usual "old boys" network of aristocrats and other public school graduates (though that network has had a resurgence under David Cameron). The restructuring of the economy since the 1960s has diminished the size of the working class, while the middle class (particularly white-collar workers, professionals, and salaried managers) has grown. For all those reasons, there is now a weaker correlation between an individual's class origins and his or her party preference. Many workers have become homeowners, including those who bought their council flats (public housing apartments) in the 1980s. Initially at least, many of them considered themselves more middle class and were more likely to vote for the Conservative Party than when they were renters.

At the same time, however, from the late 1990s until the 2010 election, as the number of public service professionals grew substantially (including teachers, civil servants, health care professionals, and social workers), middle-class support for the Labour Party increased.[22]

Yet social class still divides society more sharply in Britain than in the United States, Japan, or most of Western Europe. Even with the social changes just mentioned, opportunities for upward social mobility remain more limited than in other industrial democracies. Indeed, a 1992 survey of top positions in business, the professions, and the arts by the *Economist*, a respected periodical, found that graduates of public schools and Oxford or Cambridge still dominated those posts and that there had been less change than previously believed.[23] More recent research (2002) by the University of Essex indicated that opportunities for upward social mobility were actually declining, after a period of greater fluidity, and that children of the working class faced the greatest obstacles.[24] Thus, young men and women whose parents can afford to send them to public schools still start life with tremendous advantages over the rest of society (once all male, many public schools now admit a small number of girls). And even with the weakened correlation between class origin and political preference, "class remains the single most important social factor underlying the vote."[25]

As it progresses in the twenty-first century, Britain will also have to decide whether it is willing to further shed its traditional insularity and become a more active, economically competitive part of Western Europe. While the European Union moves, somewhat haltingly, toward greater economic unification and a single currency, Britain has been somewhat resistant. Whereas the Labour Party once was the most suspicious of European economic unity, now it is the nationalist wing of the Conservative Party that balks at taking orders from "[foreign] EU bureaucrats in Brussels."* While Prime Minister Cameron's dependence on Liberal Democratic support make it very unlikely that he will seek a major break away from the EU, his government is likely to be less EU-friendly than its Labour predecessors were.

◆ ◆ ◆

Key Terms and Concepts _____

alternative vote (AV)	hung parliament
aristocracy	nationalized
coalition government	New Labour
council housing	Parliament
European Union (EU)	party discipline
evolutionary change	Plaid Cymru
Glorious Revolution	postwar settlement
homogeneous societies	public schools
Human Rights Act	reprivatized

* Brussels, Belgium, is the EU's administrative home, and for many Europhobic British nationals it is a symbol of the transfer of national sovereignty to the EU.

social mobility
social class
suffrage
Thatcherism

Tories
vote of no confidence
welfare state

DISCUSSION QUESTIONS

1. *In what ways has British democracy served as a model for democratic government in other parts of the world?*

2. *Discuss the effects of class divisions on British society and British politics. What is the relationship between the British educational system and its class system? Given the historically significant role that class differences have played in Britain, why have class hostilities—as expressed in political divisions—been less sharp there than in countries such as France and Italy? Over time, what has happened to the relationship between a voter's social class and his or her choice of parties in national elections?*

3. *How does the British parliamentary election system discriminate against third parties? Specifically, how have the parties in the Alliance during the 1980s and the contemporary Liberal Democrats been weakened by Britain's single-member-district parliamentary elections? What are the relative advantages and disadvantages of single-member-district elections as compared with proportional representation?*

4. *What is a hung parliament, and why does it normally lead to a coalition government? Why did the Liberal Democratic leadership decide to join a coalition government with the Conservative Party (and not with Labour) after the 2010 election, and why did that decision upset many party activists and back benchers (MPs who are not in leadership positions)?*

Notes _____

1. Philip Norton, *The British Polity*, 3rd ed. (New York: Longman, 1994), p. 32.
2. R. M. Punnett, *British Government and Politics* (Prospect Heights, IL: Waveland, 1988), pp. 4–7.
3. Robert R. Alford, *Party and Society* (Chicago: Rand McNally, 1963).
4. Tania Branigan, "Cameron Faces Elitism Claims over Grammar Schools," *The Guardian*, UK News and Analysis Section (June 2, 2007), p. 12.
5. "Why Can't the English Just Give Up That Class Folderol?" *New York Times* (April 26, 2007).
6. R. Jowell, S. Witherspoon, and L. Brook, *British Social Attitudes, the Fifth Report*, 1988–1989 ed. (London: Gower, 1988), p. 227.
7. For an accounts of the Northern Irish conflict and settlement by the British negotiator in the peace process, see Marjorie Mowlam, *The Struggle for Peace, Politics and the People* (London: Hodder & Stoughton, 2002).
8. Max Beloff and Gillian Peele, *The Government of the UK* (New York: Norton, 1985), p. 177.
9. Peter Dorey, *Policy Making in Britain* (London: Sage, 2005), p. 270.
10. For a discussion of Thatcher's enormous impact on British politics, see Peter Jenkins, *Mrs. Thatcher's Revolution* (Cambridge: Harvard University Press, 1988).
11. Beloff and Peele, *Government of the UK*, p. 185.
12. *Best for Britain? The Politics and Legacy of Gordon Brown* (Oxford, England: Oneworld, 2007).
13. Gillian Peele, *Governing the UK* (Malden, MA: Blackwell Publishing, 2004), p. 90.
14. BBC/NOP exit poll cited in Dennis Kavanagh, *British Politics: Continuities and Change*, 4th ed.

15. Peele, *Governing the UK*, pp. 349–350.
16. Neil J. Mitchell, "The Decentralization of Business in Britain," *Journal of Politics* 52, no. 2 (May 1990): 622–637.
17. Norton, *British Polity*, pp. 202–206.
18. Michael Curtis, "The Government of Great Britain," in Curtis et al., *Introduction to Comparative Politics*, p. 77.
19. Philip Norton, *The British Polity*, 2nd ed. (New York: Longman, 1991), pp. 343–345.
20. "Britain," in *European Politics in Transition*, by Mark Kesselman et al. (Lexington, MA: Heath, 1987).
21. Ian Budge, David McKay, et al., *The Changing British Political System: Into the 1990s*, 2nd ed. (New York: Longman, 1988), p. 7.
22. For an earlier discussion of this trend, see Ivor Crewe, "Parties and Electors," in *The Developing British Political System*, 3rd ed., ed. Ian Budge and David McKay (New York: Longman, 1993), pp. 101–104.
23. "The Ascent of British Man," *Economist* (December 19, 1992), p. 21.
24. Cited in Jones and Kavanagh, *British Politics Today*, pp. 19–20.
25. Crewe, "Parties and Electors," p. 102.

CHAPTER 12

Russia: From Authoritarianism to Democracy and Back

Passing the Title But Not the Power
Outgoing President Vladimir Putin celebrates the election of his hand-picked successor, Dmitri Medvedev.

- The Relevance of the Russian Experience
- The Rise and Fall of Soviet Communism
- The Birth of a New Political System
- Restructuring the Economy

- Russia in the Early Years of the Twenty-First Century: The Putin Presidency and Beyond
- The Concentration of Political Power
- Conclusion: The Transition to Democracy Derailed

THE RELEVANCE OF THE RUSSIAN EXPERIENCE

The transition from authoritarian government to democracy is always difficult and fraught with danger, particularly in countries lacking any previous democratic experience. The conversion of a command (state-controlled) economy to a free market is no less demanding. Instead of improving living standards, Russia's early transition to capitalism brought a decade of enormous suffering. Small wonder many Russians blamed capitalism and democracy for their predicament. Not surprisingly, many of them longed for the old days of communist economic stability. During the first decade of the twenty-first century until the 2008 global recession, the economy rebounded strongly. On the other hand, despite considerable, though uneven, progress toward democracy under President Boris Yeltsin (1992–1999), the country has regressed toward authoritarianism under the leadership of Vladimir Putin (2000–).

RUSSIA AND THE FORMER SOVIET REPUBLICS

Map of Russia and the former Soviet Republics, showing the Arctic Ocean, Pacific Ocean, Sea of Okhotsk, Sea of Japan, major rivers (Lena River, Yenisey River, Ob River, Irtysh River, Ural River, Volga River, Amur River), and cities including Vladivostok, Krasnoyarsk, Irkutsk, Novosibirsk, Yekaterinburg (Sverdlovsk), Chelyabinsk, Astana, Almaty, Bishkek, Tashkent, Dushanbe, Ashkhabad, Kuybyshev (Samara), Moscow, St. Petersburg (Leningrad), Volgograd (Stalingrad), Kiev, Minsk, Vilnius, Riga, Tallinn. Countries shown include RUSSIA, MONGOLIA, CHINA, KAZAKHSTAN, UZBEKISTAN, KYRGYZSTAN, TAJIKISTAN, TURKMENISTAN, AFGHANISTAN, PAKISTAN, IRAN, IRAQ, KUWAIT, SYRIA, JORDAN, ISRAEL, LEBANON, TURKEY, GEORGIA, ARMENIA, AZERBAIJAN, UKRAINE, BELARUS, MOLDOVA, ROMANIA, BULGARIA, POLAND, SLOVAKIA, LITHUANIA, LATVIA, ESTONIA, FINLAND, SWEDEN, NORWAY, NORTH KOREA, SOUTH KOREA, and JAPAN. Bodies of water include the Black Sea, Caspian Sea, and Aral Sea.

The collapse of the Soviet Union's communist dictatorship and its centrally controlled economy was years in the making. So, to understand Russia's **dual transition** from authoritarianism to democracy (and partway back) and from a command economy to a free-market economy, we must first examine the political and economic systems of the Union of Soviet Socialist Republics, (USSR, also called the Soviet Union), a country that at the close of 1991 disintegrated into 15 independent nations, including Russia (by far the largest and most influential of the 15). By exploring both Soviet communism's accomplishments and its failures we may better comprehend not only why the Soviet Union collapsed but also why many Russians have accepted or even welcomed President (and now Prime Minister) Putin's authoritarian measures. Although the Communist Party no longer draws a substantial portion of the vote, as it did in the 1990s, Putin and, to a lesser extent, Dmitri Medvedev have co-opted many communist symbols and policy positions.

Few events influenced the twentieth century as intensely as the Russian Revolution of 1917, and few affected contemporary world politics as profoundly as the 1991 disintegration of the Soviet empire. The collapse of the USSR ended the Cold War, which had dominated international relations and U.S. foreign policy in the second half of the twentieth century. At the same time, it undercut the considerable influence of Marxist-Leninist ideology in much of Africa, Asia, and Latin America. The Soviet experience demonstrates that even seemingly entrenched authoritarian systems can collapse. But subsequent developments in Russia have also highlighted the difficulty of establishing a democratic regime. As that country has slid back to authoritarianism, its relations with the United States and the West have deteriorated. Although Russia no longer poses a significant military or diplomatic threat, its vast oil and natural gas holdings, its remaining nuclear arsenal, as well as its permanent seat and veto power on the United Nations Security Council give it international leverage.

After the fall of communism, President Yeltsin's government initiated important steps toward democracy. These included greater freedom of speech, media, and religion, as well as relatively free and fair elections. But that progress was undercut by Yeltsin's chosen heir, Vladimir Putin. Today, ex-intelligence officers from the **KGB** (the much-feared Soviet secret police and spy network) and its Russian successor, the **Federal Security Service (FSB)**, along with a new class of corrupt multimillionaires and an array of organized crime syndicates, have deeply infiltrated the government and the economy.

If democracy fared far better in the 1990s than in the years that followed, the opposite has been true of the economy. The transition from a state-controlled economy to a free market created horrendous conditions for nearly a decade, with the GNP shrinking by some 40 percent and living standards falling correspondingly. Despite some recent improvement, Russian life expectancy (particularly among men) has declined significantly since 1991 as the result of a deteriorating health care system, widespread alcoholism, and high rates of infant mortality, suicide, and homicide. From 1999 to 2008, however, the soaring price of petroleum—Russia's predominant export—coupled with more stable government economic policy and improved productivity produced a dramatic economic recovery (cut short in 2008–2010 by the world economic crisis). Between 2000 and 2009 the infant mortality rate fell by over 50 percent (from over 20 per 1,000 births to about 10). But even a decade of rapid economic growth failed to erase many lingering economic and social problems. Deaths still continue to outnumber births, and in 2010 the population fell by an estimated one-half of 1 percent, one of the highest rates of decline in the world (in countries not at war). The country's population, which peaked at nearly 149 million at the time of the Soviet Union's disintegration, fell to under 142 million by 2009.[1] Although the poverty rate declined during the recent economic boom, it remains troublingly high.

These events demonstrate the difficulty of simultaneously creating a pluralist democracy in an authoritarian society and introducing capitalism into a nation long dominated by communist norms.

THE RISE AND FALL OF SOVIET COMMUNISM

An Authoritarian Political Culture

Just as we can trace the origins of British democracy to the Magna Carta and other seminal historical events, so too do the roots of Russian authoritarianism lie in the country's prerevolutionary past. More than in Western Europe, Russia had a tradition of royal **absolutism**, with total power in the hands of the monarch. Moreover, until the reign of Czar Peter the Great (1682–1725), the country had limited contact with Western Europe and was isolated from the liberalizing cultural and political influences of the Renaissance and the Protestant Reformation. Although royal despotism ended in Western Europe during the eighteenth and nineteenth centuries, the powers of Russia's czars (emperors) remained relatively unchecked.

The Fall of the Czarist Regime

The modern state in the Soviet Union, as in the United States and France, was born of revolution. During the nineteenth century, various groups challenged the repressive czarist government as a series of poorly managed military efforts undermined the regime's legitimacy. Finally, the suffering brought on by the world war and the resulting unrest toppled the system in 1917.

The moderate, provisional government that replaced Czar Nicholas was soon challenged by the **Bolsheviks** (Communists), headed by Vladimir Lenin. As in many modern revolutions, power shifted from political moderates to radicals. On October 25, 1917, Lenin, promising to end Russian involvement in the war, sparked an uprising in Petrograd and seized control of the capital and then the nation.

Lenin and Marxist-Leninist Ideology

The Bolsheviks' victory brought them to power in an unexpected setting. As we saw in Chapter 2, Marx had expected communist revolutions to take place in more industrialized societies when the oppressed **proletariat** (the Marxist term for the blue-collar working class) had developed sufficient **class consciousness** to rise up against capitalist exploitation. But Russia was among the least industrialized nations in Europe, with a comparatively small and inexperienced working class.

From Lenin's perspective, then, the Russian proletariat had yet to develop sufficient political consciousness to act in its own best interests. Consequently, he argued, the communists—who had the necessary appreciation of Marxist principles and an understanding of the mass's "true interests"—needed to organize a **vanguard party** to lead the masses and guide the revolution. Whereas Marx had called for a transitional "dictatorship of the proletariat" followed by a "withering away" of the state, Lenin stressed an all-powerful state dominated by a vanguard Communist Party. Thus, he translated Marx's utopian vision of socialist society into an authoritarian plan. By 1921, Lenin had banned all opposition parties; placed labor unions, peasant organizations, and other interest groups under Communist Party control; and forced the press, literature, and the arts to follow the party line.

Three years later Lenin died, having only begun to create a communist state. Subsequently, he assumed mythic proportions in Soviet society. During the Soviet era his bust graced all government buildings. Even after the fall of communism, many Russians still revered him for his creation of the Soviet empire and his commitment to equality.

Stalinism and the Totalitarian State

Following Lenin's death, power passed to the Communist Party's general secretary, Joseph Stalin, who established one of the world's most totalitarian governments. It was marked by extreme glorification of the national leader, state intervention in virtually every significant aspect of public life, and the regularized use of state terror against the people.

Stalin transformed private agriculture into state-dominated collective ("cooperative") farms. These large farm collectives were theoretically controlled by the peasants in the collective but in truth were run by the state. "By forced **collectivization of agriculture** [he] put the regime in control of grain, drove millions of peasants off the land and into factories, and sent to labor camps millions of ... kulaks ["richer" peasants]."[2] The resulting disruptions caused severe famine and millions of deaths. The all-powerful vanguard party and the state became the motors for rapid economic modernization, political repression, strident nationalism, and militarism.

Stalin concentrated all political power in his own hands, enforced by his dreaded secret police. At one time those internal security forces allegedly employed some 500,000 people, aided by millions of informers in all walks of life. Over the years, millions of ordinary citizens (perhaps 5 percent of the population) and many political leaders were sent to a network of slave-labor camps known as the **gulag**, where nearly a million of them perished.

From Totalitarian to Authoritarian Rule: Nikita Khrushchev and De-Stalinization

After Stalin's death (1953), his successor resolved to deny such absolute power and hero worship (a **cult of personality**) to any future leader. Although the party secretary remained the most potent figure in the political system, a new collective decision-making process required him to consult with the **Politburo** (the party's elite leadership council). Moreover, although restraints on political dissent by Soviet citizens continued, systematic repression and terror ceased being a fundamental tool of state policy.

In 1956, Nikita Khrushchev, the first secretary of the Communist Party, shocked the 20th Party Congress with a historic speech denouncing Stalin's crimes. Although the speech was officially secret, its content became widely known and symbolized the process of de-Stalinization. At the same time, the government released millions of political prisoners from the gulag and increased individual freedoms. Khrushchev's reforms were limited, and his successor rolled back a number of them. Still, he ended the worst excesses of Stalinism and opened up possibilities for subsequent change.

Leonid Brezhnev and the Period of Stagnation

Khrushchev subsequently launched several major policies that the party's **Central Committee** considered irresponsible. Consequently, that committee ousted him as party leader in 1964 (making him the first Soviet leader not to die in office). Leonid Brezhnev, who led the country for the next 18 years, succeeded him. Brezhnev's administration was far less innovative and less tolerant of dissent. The primary features of post-Stalinist politics endured: collective decision making, efforts to improve mass living standards, and increased input from scientific and technical experts. But the Brezhnev regime was obsessed with political stability and, consequently, was unwilling to risk policy innovations. As the Soviet economy began to decay in the 1970s, many government leaders recognized the need for change; but mindful of how Khrushchev's reform efforts had alienated his fellow party leaders, Brezhnev refused to rock the boat. Subsequently, the Brezhnev years came to be known as "the period of stagnation." Following his death in 1982, two elderly successors as party leader died in office relatively quickly—Yuri Andropov (1982–1984) and Konstantin Chernenko (1984–1985).

Mikhail Gorbachev and the Origins of Perestroika

When Mikhail Gorbachev assumed the leadership of the Soviet Communist Party in 1985, he was the nation's youngest and best-educated leader since Lenin. The country he led had changed substantially in the previous decades. For all its faults and brutality under Stalin, the communist system had modernized an erstwhile underdeveloped nation. Once populated primarily by scarcely educated peasants, the Soviet

Union had urbanized and industrialized considerably, with millions of high school and university graduates. The communist system also had provided Russians with the basic necessities of life: free (if mediocre) medical care, cheap (if inadequate) housing, and guaranteed employment.

By the late 1970s, however, that system had fallen victim to both its accomplishments and its failures. It had produced an educated populace with a greatly expanded middle class. But increased contacts with the West and greater intellectual freedom led many Soviet professionals and intellectuals to chafe under the limitations of Soviet life—its poor-quality consumer goods, its inefficiencies and long lines, and its lack of political freedom. Gorbachev and his colleagues understood their discontent and recognized the necessity for change. So the new leader and his team committed themselves to **glasnost** ("openness"), meaning political liberalization, greater freedom of speech and media, and more government candor about Russia's problems. This, they hoped, would facilitate restructuring and modernization of society, especially the economy (**perestroika**).

Crisis in the Soviet Command Economy

The push for perestroika was motivated principally by the need to remedy the Soviet economy's increasingly poor performance. Thus, before discussing the Gorbachev era, we turn our attention to the economy he inherited, noting both its accomplishments and its failures.

Like all communist nations, the Soviet Union had a state-controlled **command economy**. The centrally planned system maximized the Soviet government's capacity to control major economic decisions. From the 1920s until the late 1980s, virtually all the Soviet Union's factories, farms, transportation, communications, and commerce were state owned. Unlike free-market economies, government planners, rather than the market forces of supply and demand, dictated production decisions, wages, and prices.

Economic Accomplishments   Despite its more obvious weaknesses, the Soviet planned economy had a number of important accomplishments, at least in the first half-century of Communist rule (1917–1970). The government turned an underdeveloped nation into a major industrial–military power in but a few decades. "Entire industries were created, along with millions of jobs that drew peasants away from the countryside and into higher-paying jobs and higher living standards."[3] Although growth rates slowed after the 1950s, they still compared very well with those of major industrial democracies. Soviet living standards continued to improve into the early 1970s as consumers received many previously unavailable goods and services.

The planned economy did not bring the country prosperity or even the amenities that Westerners take for granted. But it did provide economic security, guaranteed employment, and a high degree of equality. Government subsidies gave consumers basic foods and other necessities at very low and very stable prices. As Soviet specialist Marshall Goldman notes, the state offered the people protection from "the three evils of capitalism": unemployment, inequality, and inflation.

In the post-Stalinist era, with terror no longer the main agent of government control, those economic benefits contributed to political stability. In effect, the government provided economic security and improved living standards, in return for which the population accepted communist political control.

Economic Weaknesses   By the early 1970s, however, the country's economic growth rate began to slow. Per capita income, which had grown at an average annual rate of 5.9 percent from 1966 to 1970, increased by only 2.1 percent annually in the five years preceding Gorbachev's administration (1980–1985).[4] Although the command economy had jump-started industrialization, it was unable to advance the country into the next stage of development. Industry and agriculture continued to use obsolete and wasteful production methods.

There were many reasons for the country's economic stagnation. In the absence of price signals, state planners could not ascertain what consumers wanted or determine how to allocate resources. Because the system rewarded factory managers primarily for meeting government production quotas regardless of production efficiency or product quality, consumer goods were usually shoddy. Furthermore, since workers enjoyed substantial job security but had little opportunity for economic advancement, the system discouraged hard work. As a popular workers' joke noted, "They pretend to pay us and we pretend to work." As long as the Soviet people had limited education and were only a generation removed from the wretched poverty of the countryside, they appreciated and supported a system that had given them secure employment, cheap food and housing, free medical care, and rising living standards. By the 1970s and 1980s, however, a far more educated population, including a larger middle class, wanted more than the basic necessities of life. Many of them desired the improved consumer goods and the freedoms that Westerners enjoyed.

At the same time, the government faced a fiscal crisis. The arms and space races with the United States, substantial foreign aid to the developing world (also in competition with the West), and the Soviet war to support Afghanistan's communist government all augmented an already huge budget deficit. Moreover, the government spent far too much on consumer subsidies designed to pacify the Soviet public. One government spokesman noted, "The state pays four rubles, eighty kopecks [cents] for a kilogram of meat and sells it [to consumers] for one ruble, eighty kopecks."[5] From the 1960s until the early 1990s, bread prices never increased. Thus, by the 1980s, the subsidized price of bread was so low that it was often cheaper for farmers to feed their livestock bread rather than grain. Total consumer subsidies rose from 4 percent of the state budget in 1965 to 20 percent in the late 1980s. Consequently, when Gorbachev took office in 1985, the national government's budget deficit was three times higher (as a percentage of GNP) than in the United States.

The Gorbachev Era: Trying to Save Communism

As we have seen, Mikhail Gorbachev's reforms had two major dimensions. Perestroika involved restructuring national institutions, with special emphasis on economic reform. Glasnost promised greater freedom of expression in the mass media, the arts, and general political discourse. Yet, beyond a vague commitment to change, Gorbachev failed to develop clearly conceived goals or a plan for getting there.

Critics used an old Russian adage to describe perestroika: "If you don't know where you are going, any road will take you there."[6]

The Flowering of Political Reform   The Soviet Union's poor economic performance since the 1970s and its evident backwardness compared to the West made a compelling case for economic reform. But the reasons why the new administration also decided to open up the political system are less clear, particularly since Gorbachev remained committed to the single-party state. Ironically, he initially conceived greater political freedom—the change that earned him the most acclaim in the West—not as an end in itself but as a vehicle for achieving economic change.

How would glasnost (political liberalization) contribute to perestroika (economic restructuring)? Jerry Hough suggested that only by offering middle-class bureaucrats, scientists, technicians, and other professionals greater freedom of expression and increased contact with the West could Gorbachev hope to win their badly needed support for economic change. Furthermore, he knew that his attempts to decentralize the economy would meet stiff resistance from the **nomenklatura**, the nation's large and powerful bureaucratic elite (discussed later), who stood to lose power and privilege. By allowing the media to expose the failures of the system, he might weaken that powerful conservative opposition.

Finally, "a bit of democracy would ... disarm the suspicions of the West, allowing him to divert resources from the Cold War and to attract foreign investment."[7] Gorbachev's top advisors had enough exposure abroad to know that Soviet economic modernization would require improved trade and communications with the capitalist world. Soviet scientists and administrators needed to be plugged more directly into the global information revolution.

But whatever were Gorbachev's original motivations, the political changes during his reign were nothing short of breathtaking. The country's most celebrated dissident, Nobel Laureate Andrei Sakharov, was released from internal exile and subsequently elected to the national parliament. Almost all political prisoners were freed. Television news programs and the press now discussed long-taboo subjects—from airplane crashes to nuclear accidents, from street crime to government corruption. In Moscow and Leningrad, independent newspapers and magazines criticized government policy. Religious freedom was restored. And, at least in the large cities, people lost their fear of freely expressing themselves to each other. In the words of one analyst, "Society ... learned to talk to itself."[8] Though the USSR was still far from democracy (for most of Gorbachev's tenure it remained a single-party state), the vestiges of authoritarianism were quickly receding.

Gorbachev's foreign policy reforms were equally dramatic. He extricated the country from its bloody war in Afghanistan, helped end the Cold War, and sharply reduced Soviet military expenditures. And when the people of Eastern Europe rose up against their communist governments in 1989, the Soviets did not intervene militarily to defend their allies. Ironically, however, as Gorbachev's popularity soared abroad, it declined at home. As the economy deteriorated (discussed below), Russians blamed him for their declining living standard and for a growing sense of chaos.

The Limits of Economic Reform   Gorbachev intended glasnost to support economic modernization. Instead, political change hurtled forward while economic reform proceeded at a snail's pace. The administration knew the economy needed repair but seemed to have few ideas of how to do it. "Behind Gorbachev's ringing call ... [for radical reform] stood a vague, incomplete set of generalities of little use in constructing actual reform legislation."[9]

Along with a series of inadequate or failed measures, one of Gorbachev's few successful economic reforms was the legalization of small private enterprise for the first time since the 1920s. Larger private firms soon emerged, some legal, others not. These included restaurants, nightclubs, taxis, banks, auto dealers, computer importers, construction firms, and black-market merchants selling smuggled goods from the West—all of them offering services that the state had not been providing adequately. By 1991, 5.6 million people earned at least a portion of their income from the slowly growing private sector.

A Worsening Economic Crisis   But, it was soon apparent that, instead of curing the nation's stagnant economy, perestroika threw it into reverse. The GNP, which had grown sluggishly in the mid-1980s, now began to plunge. By the Soviet Union's last year (1991), the economy was in a free fall, with GNP dropping some 15 percent annually and industrial production in chaos.

A fundamental problem was that a transition from a command economy to a free-market system, no matter how intelligently pursued, is inevitably terribly painful. To maintain full employment (and prevent political unrest), many state-owned firms employed more workers than they needed and continued operating even if they were losing money. As one Soviet economist had observed cynically, "Our unemployment is [really] the highest in the world. But unfortunately, all our 'unemployed' get paid."[10] Finally, as we have seen, state subsidies kept consumer prices artificially low.

When the Soviet regime collapsed in 1991, foreign economic advisors and reform-oriented Russian economists advised the new Yeltsin administration that it could only avoid bankruptcy if it phased out consumer subsidies, closed unprofitable firms, and **privatized** the economy (sold state-owned enterprises—which constituted most of the Soviet-era economy—to private-sector investors). Only by laying off unneeded workers, forcing factories to show a profit, and compelling producers to compete for customers, they insisted, would production become more efficient, profitability increase, and the quality and array of consumer goods improve. Gorbachev's only chance to save the collapsing Soviet economy in the late 1980s would have been to introduce such measures. But because these reforms would have driven prices up sharply and created unemployment in a society unaccustomed to either phenomenon, the president and his advisors were unwilling to risk the unrest that these changes would undoubtedly have produced. Furthermore, the powerful government bureaucracy (the nomenklatura) slowed or blocked many of Gorbachev's limited reforms, both because it violated their orthodox ideology and because it threatened their power and material privileges.

Ethnic Unrest and the Breakdown of Control from the Center   Together with the economy, ethnic conflict was perestroika's Achilles' heel. After all, Russians only constituted half of the Soviet population, while the rest came from more than 90 other ethnic groups, 22 of which had populations of 1 million or more—from

Ukrainians and Estonians in the west to Muslim Uzbeks and Tajiks in the south. Most had been annexed, against their will, by Russian czars or Soviet communists. The end of systematic political repression under glasnost unleashed ethnic unrest and long-suppressed calls for national independence.

The drive for secession was strongest in the Baltic States, whose citizens had been independent between the two world wars. With the USSR's highest educational levels and most advanced economies, Estonia, Latvia, and Lithuania identified more strongly with Western Europe than with the other Soviet republics. There were also strong independence movements in Moldavia, Georgia, Ukraine, and Armenia. By the late 1980s, even Russia, the predominant republic in the USSR, was demanding independence from the Soviet Union.

THE BIRTH OF A NEW POLITICAL SYSTEM

With half the Soviet Union's population, two-thirds of its area, and most of its economic and military resources, Russia dwarfed the other former republics. Now called the Russian Federation, its president and dominant political leader was Boris Yeltsin. He had made himself a popular hero when he criticized the slow pace of Gorbachev's reform and resigned from a powerful leadership position in the Soviet Communist Party. In the 1991 election for president of the Russian Republic—Russia's first free election of its leader—he easily defeated the Communist Party candidate.* Two months later, a conspiracy of hard-line generals, KGB leaders, and Communist Party officials attempted a military coup against Gorbachev. At considerable risk to himself, Yeltsin rallied troops and civilians to undermine that coup. Now with a huge popular following, he held the upper hand and forced Gorbachev to agree to the dissolution of the USSR at the close of the year. For the remainder of the 1990s, Yeltsin presided over Russia's difficult and often chaotic transition to capitalism and democracy. He showed both authoritarian and democratic tendencies. He could be strong and decisive in times of crisis, but at other times was hobbled by indecision, poor health, and alcoholism.

The Rise and Fall of Russia's Multiparty System: From Only One Party to Too Many to Too Few

Following Mikhail Gorbachev's legalization of opposition parties and the subsequent demise of the Soviet Union, Russia moved from one-party rule to a multiparty system. Although the last Soviet-era election for the Russian Republic's legislature (1990) had permitted independent candidates to enter (they won 14 percent of the seats), it did not allow political parties other than the Communists to run candidates. By the time of Russia's first postcommunist national election in 1995, however, the country had 262 legally registered parties. More than 40 of them fielded candidates for that year's parliamentary elections, of whom nearly 10 had significant support.

* The president of Russia (the largest of the Soviet Union's republics), Yeltsin, should not be confused with the president of the Soviet Union, Gorbachev.

The Russian Constitution of 1993 established a new national parliament. Initially voters cast two ballots to select the 450 deputies in the State Duma, the dominant house of parliament. One vote was for a single representative from the voter's district, one of 225 such (SMDs) nationally, and the other was for a party list of candidates. Each list that received a minimum of 5 percent of the national vote received a percentage of the 225 PR seats in the Duma roughly equivalent to its share of the national vote. Thus, for example, if the Liberal Democratic Party received approximately 20 percent of the party list votes, it would receive about 45 PR seats in the Duma. Some parties won several SMD seats but failed to win any through PR. Others won enough party-list votes to secure some seats but failed to win any single-member districts. Russia's first four contested Duma elections (from 1993 to 2003) used this two-tiered electoral system.

In 2005, however, Parliament approved President Putin's proposal to eliminate the 225 single-member districts and, instead, elect all 450 Duma members through proportional representation. In order for a party to win any seats from its list of candidates, it now needs to receive 7 percent of the vote. While such a change seems reasonable at first glance (many democracies have parliaments elected solely through proportional representation), Putin's strategic intent was clear. In the 2003 Duma election only four parties had reached the less stringent minimum (5 percent) needed to receive seats through proportional representation. Some half dozen others were able to gain seats in the Duma only through SMD elections. So, the new rules—first applied in the 2007 parliamentary election—effectively eliminated small parties from the Parliament, including Putin's most outspoken democratic critics. Other legislation has made it harder for parties to register, to form electoral coalitions, and to receive government campaign funding. Fourteen political parties tried to enter the 2007 election, but the government electoral commission accepted only 10 of them. Ultimately, only four parties won any Duma seats (Table 12.1).

TABLE 12.1	Russia's Parliamentary (Duma) Election Results, 1995–2007			
	Percentage of the Party List Votes (Total Number of Duma Seats)			
Types of Parties	**1995**	**1999**	**2003**	**2007***
Authoritarian Parties				
Communist Party	22.3% (157)	24.3% (110)	12.8% (51)	11.6% (57)
Liberal Democratic Party	11.6% (51)	6.0% (17)	11.7% (37)	8.1% (40)
United Russia			38.0% (221)	64.3% (315)
Parties of Power (formerly Center Parties)				
Unity		23.2% (74)		
Our Home Is Russia	10.1% (55)	1.2% (7)		
Democratic Reformist Parties				
Yabloko	6.9% (45)	6.0% (22)	4.4% (4)	2.6% (0)
Union of Right Forces		8.6% (29)	4.0% (3)	1.0% (0)

*In 2007 all 450 deputies were elected through proportional representation, with no single-member districts. In earlier elections, with half the Duma MPs elected from single-member districts, a party's percentage of the votes for party lists and its percent of Duma MPs often differed somewhat.

SOURCE: American Foreign Policy Council, "1999 [and 1995] Russian Duma Election Results," www.afpc.org/; Wikipedia, "Russian Legislative Election, 2007" [links to 2003 election], http://en.wikipedia.org/wiki/.

We turn now to a discussion of Russia's transition from a single-party system (until 1990) to multiparty competition and then, most recently, to single-party dominance, with opposition parties allowed to run but with little chance to win more than a token number of parliamentary seats.

The Soviet Union's Only Party A fundamental requisite of democratic government is free and fair competition between at least two political parties, each capable of winning a national election at some time. Under the Soviet Union, of course, there was no such contestation. No opposition party was permitted. From the time of the 1917 revolution until shortly before the collapse of the USSR, the Communist Party had a monopoly of power as "the leading and guiding force of Soviet society." Not only did prominent Communist Party members hold all significant government offices, but the party's Politburo (composed of some 14 to 20 of the highest-ranking party leaders), rather than the formal government leaders (the prime minister, president, cabinet, and Parliament), made all major policy decisions.

At its peak in the late 1980s, approximately 19 million people—about 9 percent of the USSR's adult population—belonged to the Communist Party. In all walks of life—in every factory, collective farm, laboratory, and university faculty—there were party members and party units. Reasons for joining the party included a mix of ideological commitment and opportunism. Membership frequently was a prerequisite for preferred employment and also enhanced a person's access to housing and scarce consumer goods. Its large and diverse membership allowed the party to penetrate virtually every aspect of Soviet life.

Communist Party power was reinforced by the nomenklatura system. This term referred to a vast list of positions within the Soviet state bureaucracy, the military, state-owned enterprises, labor unions, the media, cultural organizations, and professional groups. Appointment to all those posts required party consent. But "although *nomenklatura* implies only party approval or confirmation of personnel decisions, in fact the party often [took] the initiative in filling positions on the list."[11] In common political discourse, the name also referred to the thousands of bureaucrats who held those posts, constituting a powerful and privileged elite. Indeed, even after the collapse of communism, they have continued exerting considerable influence through Russia's state bureaucracy and its remaining state-owned enterprises. Furthermore, many former nomenklatura members managed to become important players in the country's new private sector.

Russia: From a Fragmented Multiparty System Back to Single-Party Dominance
Although democracy requires a competitive party system, it tends to function poorly when there are *too many* parties. Under those circumstances, it is difficult for any party or even a coalition of political parties to achieve a workable majority in the national parliament. During the 1990s, Russia suffered from an excess of political parties, many of them highly unstable—formed to advance the interests of a particular political figure or group and then dissolving before the following election.

Approximately 30 political parties or coalitions fielded candidates in the 2003 parliamentary elections, with about a dozen of them winning at least one seat.

As Table 12.1 indicates, in the 1995 and 1999 elections (as well as the 1993 contest, not shown) no party came close to winning a governing majority (226 seats). In 2003, however, Putin's United Russia did win almost half the Duma seats. With support from a number of other parties and deputies, Putin became the first Russian president to command a secure working majority in the Parliament. Indeed, he ultimately received the backing of two-thirds of all Duma deputies, giving him a "constitutional majority," enough votes to amend the constitution should he want to. Finally, United Russia, with 64.3 percent of the votes cast, secured an overwhelming 70 percent of the Duma seats in the 2007 election. Additional support from other parties has given Presidents Putin and Medvedev the backing of nearly 90 percent of the Duma. In short, the parliamentary opposition has been reduced to insignificance. Since the last Duma election, the only opposition to the president has come from the Communist Party. Indeed, it is only the Communist delegation in the Duma that now speaks out against the government's authoritarian behavior (an obvious irony given the party's history and its continued veneration of Joseph Stalin).

Russian parties have run the ideological gamut from communist to fascist. Other parties have been nationalist, reformist democratic, social democratic, centrist, religious, regional, and "single-issue" (including feminist, agrarian, military, and environmental). But most of the leading parties in the four parliamentary elections held since 1993 fall into one of three broad categories (Table 12.1): authoritarian parties, "parties of power" (formerly centrist parties), and democratic reformist parties.

Authoritarian (Antidemocratic) Parties   In the five parliamentary elections (over two decades) since Russia's transition to electoral democracy, between one-third and two-thirds of all votes have been cast for parties that explicitly or implicitly reject democracy. During the 1990s, most of those votes went to the far-left Communist Party or the far-right (neofascist) Liberal Democratic Party (see Table 12.1, which does not include the 1993 election). What particularly distinguishes these two parties from most others is that, while they do not admit to being authoritarian, they make few attempts to appear democratic.

Unlike several reformed communist parties in Eastern Europe that have modified their names and ideologies, the Russian Communist Party has changed neither. Since many of the party's most capable leaders and members abandoned it in the late 1980s or the early 1990s, most of the remaining leaders have been hard-liners who rejected Gorbachev's reforms but now claim to accept elements of democracy and the free market. The communists still advocate a strong role for the state in the economy (including the restoration of Soviet-era welfare measures) and a nationalistic foreign policy that is wary of the West.

With close to one-fourth of the party-list votes in the 1995 and 1999 Duma elections, the Communists were the country's leading vote-getter during Russia's first decade of democracy. Only in 2003 did United Russia pass the Communists as the largest party in the Duma. Furthermore, it has finished second in the country's four presidential elections, and its leader, Gennady Zyuganov, was a serious threat to defeat President Yeltsin in 1996, nearly matching him in the first round (Table 12.2). However, its percentage of the vote in the 2004 and 2008 presidential elections was only about half its share in the previous two elections, reflecting the party's dwindling support.

TABLE 12.2	Russia's Presidential Election Results, 1996–2008 (Leading Candidates)

1996 Presidential Elections

	First Round	Second Round
Boris Yeltsin (independent, incumbent)*	35.3%	53.8%
Gennady Zyuganov (Communist Party)	32.0%	40.3%
Alexander Lebed (independent)	14.5%	—
Grigory Yavlinsky (Yabloko)	7.3%	—
Vladimir Zhirinovsky (Liberal Democrats)	5.7%	—

2000 Presidential Election

Vladimir Putin (independent, incumbent)*	52.9%
Gennady Zyuganov (Communist Party)	29.2%
Grigory Yavlinsky (Yabloko)	5.8%

2004 Presidential Election

Vladimir Putin (United Russia, incumbent)	71.3%
Nikolai Kharitonov (Communist Party)	13.7%

2008 Presidential Election

Dmitri Medvedev (United Russia)	70.3%
Gennady Zyuganov (Communist Party)	17.7%
Vladimir Zhirinovsky (Liberal Democrats)	9.4%

*Yeltsin and Putin officially ran as independents but were backed by various political parties that had been formed largely for the express purpose of supporting them.

SOURCE: Wikipedia, "Russian Presidential Election, 2008" [links to the previous presidential elections], http://en.wikipedia.org/.

Who are the voters who have given the Communists between 12 and 40 percent of the vote in Russia's parliamentary and presidential elections*? They have come disproportionately from less-educated voters, the elderly, and the poor—the groups most devastated by the 1990s' economic crisis. Senior voters saw the value of their pensions evaporate in the 1990s due to extreme inflation, and they remain in greatest need of the economic safety net once provided by the Soviet Union. Because a disproportionate share of the party's initial voters were elderly, its support has declined over time. At the same time, the Communists have received support from Russians who wished to see the country restored to its place as a world power. In recent elections, however, many of those votes have shifted to United Russia as Putin has appealed to those same nationalistic sentiments.

The other major authoritarian party in the 1990s was the Liberal Democratic Party (the LDPR). That party is largely the personal political vehicle of its leader, Vladimir Zhirinovsky. Despite its name, it is neither liberal nor democratic but is instead authoritarian and intolerant. The LDPR came out of nowhere to win the most votes in the 1993 parliamentary elections (not shown in Table 12.1) and placed second in 1995. One of the most outrageous major political figures in contemporary Russia, Zhirinovsky at various times has advocated dropping neutron bombs on the Baltic states, waging nuclear war against Germany, and annexing former parts of the

* The party's share of votes in the second round of the 1996 presidential election was 40.3 percent.

czarist and Soviet empires, including Alaska and Finland. And his speeches have often been laced with racist and anti-Semitic slurs.

Like other extreme nationalist groups, the party appeals to Russian patriotism and to those who regret the country's loss of superpower status. Russians have historically been distrustful of the West and many now feel that their culture is being polluted by crass commercialism, from McDonald's to the limousines of the nouveau riche. Finally, the LPDR's extreme positions on law and order also attract voters. Zhirinovsky, for example, once pledged to lower the spiraling crime rate by summarily executing 100,000 criminals. Since their surprisingly strong showing in the 1993 parliamentary election, the Liberal Democrats have hovered around 10 percent of the Duma vote. But Putin's aggressive foreign policy and revived nationalism stole much of Zhirinovsky's thunder and left his party little prospect for future growth.

After the 2003 Duma elections, President Putin's United Russia emerged as the nation's dominant political party (Tables 12.1 and 12.2). Its predecessor, Unity, had been formed shortly before the 1999 Duma electoral campaign to advance the interests of government insiders, including then-President Boris Yeltsin and his prime minister, Vladimir Putin. Following that election, it merged with a former rival to become United Russia, subsequently an important arm of Putin's power. As such, both Unity and United Russia fit into the category of "parties of power," discussed below (i.e., parties whose main purpose is to serve the interests of a powerful political insider). At the same time, as Putin tightened his grip on power and crushed the opposition, United Russia has become the country's major authoritarian party.

Parties of Power   Even though the so-called parties of power trailed the authoritarian parties in the three parliamentary elections held in the 1990s (Table 12.1; again, results of the 1993 election are not shown in this table), they earned that name because of their close association with Presidents Yeltsin and Putin, as well as other powerful politicians. They have always had close links with the inner circles of the executive branch, which has been Russia's dominant branch of government since 1993. At the same time, however, these parties have been weak in terms of membership, organization, programs, and ideology. Instead, they are little more than political campaign machines for an incumbent president, presidential hopefuls, or other major politicians. As such, their fortunes have risen and fallen with those of their leaders, with most of them lasting as parties for no more than five years or so.

For example, Prime Minister Viktor Chernomyrdin founded Our Home Is Russia in 1995 to support President Yeltsin's successful reelection bid the following year. But as Yeltsin's final term wound down and his popularity plummeted, the party collapsed (Table 12.1). Subsequently, supporters of former Prime Minister Yevgeny Primakov and Moscow Mayor Yuri Luzhkov founded Fatherland All Russia in 1999 to further Primakov's presidential aspirations. Yet, after Unity won the 1999 parliamentary election and Putin swept the presidency the following year, Fatherland All Russia merged with it to form United Russia.

What distinguishes United Russia from its predecessors, most of which were short-lived, is that it will likely dominate Russian politics for years to come. With his party in firm control of the Duma and totally subservient to him, President Putin was in complete command. In 2008—when Putin was constitutionally barred from running for a third presidential term—the party ran a virtual unknown, Dmitri Medvedev, who won 70 percent of the votes, simply because he was "Putin's man."

Beyond their general, but inconsistent, support for a free-market economy, the parties of power's views have varied according to the preferences of their leaders. During Yeltsin's presidency, they generally, though inconsistently, supported democracy. That is, they favored democracy more firmly than the authoritarian parties did but less resolutely than did the democratic reformist parties, described below. Under Putin's leadership, however, United Russia has moved from the political center to authoritarianism.

Democratic Reformist Parties　These parties have most ardently and consistently supported democracy and a free-market economy. As Vladimir Putin (first as president, then as prime minister) has tightened his grip on power and curtailed the media, the democratic reformists have concentrated on defending Russia's often-threatened civil liberties. Their leaders often have enjoyed close ties to American universities and think tanks and are widely admired in the West. But most Russian voters have had little use for them. As Table 12.1 indicates, neither reformist party has received as much as 10 percent of the parliamentary vote. For one thing, most Russians have feared the fast-track transition to free enterprise that the ardent reformists favor. Furthermore, after years of political and economic turmoil, most voters have preferred Putin's enforced stability.

Democratic reformers get their greatest support from younger, more educated voters and among residents of Moscow and St. Petersburg. By the 2003 Duma elections, however, both reform parties failed to receive the required 5 percent of the party-list vote and were only able to win a few single-member seats. With the elimination of single-member districts in the most recent Duma election and a 7 percent minimum for party list seats, the democratic reform parties lost all parliamentary representation. And, under more stringent electoral laws introduced by Putin, reform parties were unable to even get on the ballot in the 2008 presidential election. Thus, for now at least, the democratic reformers are irrelevant to the electoral politics.

The Weakness of Russian Political Parties　Most Russian parties have weak organizations, small memberships, poorly articulated ideologies or programs, and limited life spans, all factors making effective governance more difficult. Only the Communist Party and, more recently, United Russia have had a substantial membership and grassroots structure. Currently, United Russia claims to have nearly 2 million members. But membership claims by all parties are notoriously exaggerated.

As we have seen, most parties, especially the parties of power, have not lasted beyond one or two elections. United Russia, dominant since 2003, has no fixed policies or ideology and simply supports whatever Putin favors. Only the Communist Party and the Liberal Democrats have been at all relevant for more than 15 years. And now, with United Russia's ascendancy, even those two have lost whatever influence they had previously exercised.

The Structure of Government: A Centralized Presidential System

The Russian constitution of 1993—approved by the voters in a national referendum—created a national government with some elements of a presidential system and some of a parliamentary system. The president is popularly elected, and if no candidate receives over 50 percent of the vote in the first round, there is a second round run-off shortly afterwards between the top two candidates. But that has only been needed in the 1996 election (see Table 12.2). Presidents serve a four-year term and are limited to two consecutive terms in office. The president appoints a prime minister subject to the approval of the Duma.

The constitution culminated a period of intense contests between the legislative and executive branches and shifted political power firmly into the hands of the president. In the years since, Presidents Boris Yeltsin and Vladimir Putin often circumvented the Parliament (sometimes in defiance of constitutional procedures) whenever it failed to support them. Since 2003, however, that has no longer been necessary since United Russia has maintained a firm grip of both branches of government. In 2008, when President Medvedev succeeded Putin and Putin became his prime minister, real power was (unofficially) transferred from the president to the prime minister, in violation of the constitution. At the same time, parliament remains powerless relative to the executive branch.

Parliament and President Yeltsin: The Executive and the Legislative Branches Battle for Power

Following the dissolution of the USSR, the Russian Republic's legislature at that time (*not* the Soviet Parliament) was automatically transformed into the parliament of the new Russian nation-state. Yeltsin and his advisors favored a broad range of reforms aimed at creating a more democratic political order and a capitalist economy. Since the members of parliament had been elected shortly *before* the collapse of Soviet communism, most were activists in the Communist Party (other parties were still prohibited at the time of that election) and opposed Yeltsin's reform plans. With the economy in a free fall, marked by huge budget deficits and rampant inflation, Yeltsin's economic team and most foreign advisors urged the government to slash spending, most notably on subsidies for food and other basic necessities. But while removing government price controls and subsidies would hopefully reduce inflation eventually, in the short run it would impose enormous price increases on Russian consumers. Seeking to present themselves as the defender of the common man, most members of parliament resisted these and other painful economic reforms.

As conflict between the two branches of government intensified over economic and political reforms, Yeltsin battled an increasingly restive parliament. In 1993, he (illegally) suspended his vice president, Alexander Rutskoi (a leader of the opposition forces), dissolved Parliament, and scheduled new legislative elections. In response, parliament (illegally) voted to remove Yeltsin from office, swore in Rutskoi as the new national president, and barricaded themselves—together with armed supporters—inside the White House, Russia's massive parliament building. When armed supporters of the rebellion tried to seize Moscow's city hall and a nearby television station, pro-Yeltsin army troops shelled the White House and captured it at a cost of almost 200 lives.

President Yeltsin had beaten back his communist and nationalist opponents, but it was hard to determine which side had more recklessly undermined the constitution and violated basic democratic principles. Yeltsin's power thereafter was considerable but not absolute, and his battles with Parliament continued, with the Duma often slowing down his reforms. On the other hand, when Putin became president, he totally dominated the legislative branch from the start of his first term. With United Russia's sweeping victories in the 2003 and 2007 Duma elections, Putin was in complete control. There seems little doubt that the 2011 parliamentary elections will have the same result.

RESTRUCTURING THE ECONOMY

> The worst is over.
>
> —Boris Yeltsin: October 1992, October 1993, April 1994, July 1997

Economic Collapse under Yeltsin

Year after year, Boris Yeltsin's economic team tried to turn around the collapsing postcommunist economy. Each time, President Yeltsin tried to reassure the public that "the worst is over" and that Russia's dizzying economic decline, which had begun in the late 1980s, would finally end. Each time, his reassurances proved false. Indeed, during the 1990s the economy shrank in every year but two, sometimes falling as much as 13 or 14 percent in a single year. Overall, from 1990 to 1998, the country's GNP declined by a total of 40 to 50 percent.

Shock Therapy and Continuing Economic Decline

At the start of 1992, Prime Minister Yegor Gaidar, the leading proponent of rapid and far-reaching economic reforms (collectively called **shock therapy** because of the pain they inflict), initiated that process by lifting government price controls on most consumer goods. With government subsidies and price controls removed, prices jumped 345 percent in the month of January alone![12] At the same time, by late 1993, the government privatized 81,000 of the country's 196,000 state enterprises, including most retail stores as well as factories that in total employed 20 percent of the industrial workforce.[13] Millions of Russians became shareholders in the largest industrial firms through a process of government vouchers. As of early 1996, some 120,000 state firms had been privatized. By then, the private sector already accounted for more than half the nation's GNP and about two-thirds of its industrial output.[14] No other former communist country has privatized the economy so rapidly.

Still, those reforms did not end the economy's free fall. Instead, things got worse. During the first years of reform, GDP and industrial production dropped more steeply than they had in the United States during the Great Depression. In 1992, the year shock therapy was introduced, *prices rose by 2,520 percent*, and for most of the 1990s inflation rates were several hundred percent annually.[15] Thus, an item that cost 100 old rubles (the Russian currency) in 1990 would cost 1,270,000 old rubles by 1998.[16] Most of the population, particularly the elderly living off pensions, saw their lifetime savings become worthless. Wages rose as well but lagged behind prices, causing the average citizen's purchasing power ("real wages") to decline by more than one half. Between 1991 and 1998, the portion of the population living below the poverty line (unable to provide adequately for themselves or their families) rose from 12 to 35 percent.[17] Thus, the transition to a market economy was far more difficult than President Yeltsin and his advisers had anticipated.

Furthermore, continuing a trend begun in the Soviet era, infant mortality rose regularly until 2002 while life expectancy declined to Third World levels. During the first half of the 1990s, life expectancy for Russian men, which had been declining slowly since the 1960s, fell astonishingly from 63.8 to 57.3 years. While recovering some ground after 1995, male life expectancy was still only 59.1 in 2007. Russian women—who have lower rates of alcoholism, smoking, and violent death (murder and suicide)—can now expect to live 14 years longer than men, the world's largest gender gap. Currently, Russia's overall life expectancy is only about 66 years, ranking it right behind India and 160th out of about 220 nations in the world.[18]

Vladimir Putin and an Economic Boom (1999–2008)

Since Russia's 1999 economic crisis, the country has finally reversed years of economic decline. The rate of inflation dropped from 86 percent in 1999 to about 12 percent in 2009.[19] Furthermore, after a decade of falling production, the Russian economy grew for 10 straight years (1999–2008), averaging close to 7 percent annually, twice the world average. During that period, the size of the middle class nearly doubled, and the country was able to pay off its large foreign debt. Most importantly, the percentage of citizens living in poverty fell from 41.5 percent (1999) to 13 percent in 2008 (only to jump back to over 19 percent in 2009 during the worldwide recession). After suffering negative growth during the world economic recession in 2009, the economy achieved modest growth in 2011.

Yet, impressive as those gains have been, many Russians have still been left behind, and many glaring socioeconomic problems remain unresolved. For one thing, the economic boom has particularly benefited Russia's two major cities—Moscow and St. Petersburg—but has been less beneficial to other cities and of little help to small towns and rural areas. Senior citizens (especially pensioners), children under the age of 16, and unskilled workers remain disproportionately poor. Indeed, the country's level of economic inequality worsened during the recent boom. This has had a particularly negative psychological effect in a country that was once proud of its comparatively high economic equality.

Furthermore, although Russia's economic surge since 1999 has been extraordinary and unexpected, it may be less impressive than it first appears. The primary impetus for the boom has been a sharp rise in the prices of natural gas and oil—Russia's predominant exports and the motors of its economy. In 2009, Russia passed Saudi Arabia as the world's largest oil exporter. The export of other commodities—timber, metals, and minerals—has also grown significantly.

But reliance on a single commodity for economic growth has long been a slender reed. Export booms for commodities inevitably are followed by a downturn, as high prices eventually drive down demand. In the past 40 years, during several oil booms, major exporters, such as Mexico and Nigeria, borrowed excessively, overestimated future petroleum prices, and were left with huge external debts that burdened their economies for years. Past surges in the price of oil have always been followed eventually by significant price rollbacks, and the most recent boom has been no exception.

At the same time, petroleum booms often induce exporting nations to concentrate economic investment in oil—an apparently quick and easy source of wealth—neglecting other sectors, such as agriculture and manufacturing. Thus, Russia's failure to invest adequately in industry has kept manufacturing productivity low. At the same time, President Putin used questionable methods to reassert state control over two of the nation's most efficient private oil and gas firms, converting them into corrupt and inefficient state enterprises. Meanwhile, Russia's richest oil fields in Siberia are beginning to run out. Oil and gas revenues currently account for one-third of the national government's budget, and declining output and productivity threaten to weaken the economy at some point down the road.

For now, however, Russia's rapid economic growth following a decade of terrible decline earned Putin astonishingly high approval ratings. It also produced his landslide reelection in 2004, United Russia's overwhelming wins in the 2003 and 2007 parliamentary elections, and Dmitri Medvedev's enormous win in the 2008 presidential race. In fact, the country's economic turnaround was largely produced by factors other than Putin's leadership and policies. The recovery actually began shortly *before* he became Yeltsin's prime minister, caused by rising oil prices and the government's 1998 devaluation of the ruble. Putin became acting president at the end of 1999 (when Boris Yeltsin resigned because of his health problems and abysmal popularity ratings), and oil prices took off soon after. Still, his administration deserves credit for ending years of weak government and vacillating policies, bringing the country political and economic stability.[20] When he took office as president, Putin was, at 48, the youngest Russian leader since Vladimir Lenin. He was a stark contrast to Yeltsin, whose poor health and alcoholism made him an unsteady and unpopular leader during his second term. Putin, a nondrinker and nonsmoker with a black belt in judo, exuded a strength and steadiness that reassured private investors and the public at large. His administration reinforced private property rights so that businessmen could concentrate less on quick profits and more on the long term. And, whereas rivalries between competing government factions had undermined Yeltsin's administration, Putin imposed central authority.

But the Russian economy still suffers from a number of fundamental flaws. The bureaucracy is too powerful and too corrupt. Control of the private sector remains in the hands of a small number of crooked multimillionaires whose monopolistic holdings exempt them from the discipline of the free market. And, as we have noted, too few Russians have benefited from the economic recovery.

Enduring Obstacles to Economic Reform: The Russian Mafia, Corruption, and More

Even the most competent Russian leaders would have encountered tremendous obstacles in transforming the economy. Eastern Europe's experience demonstrated that the transition from a command economy to a free market is very difficult anywhere. Only the Czechs and Hungarians managed the change relatively smoothly. It was particularly hard in Russia, which had experienced communist rule for a far longer period of time than its neighbors had. But Russia's privatization process was also rife with corruption, with many of the old communist nomenklatura using their positions as industrial managers to become wealthy capitalists. In a society whose adult population was raised to value equality, there has been a tremendous rise in inequality. We have noted that the number of Russians living in poverty grew sharply in the 1990s. But increased inequality, not declining GNP, accounted for most of that poverty. Today the poorest 40 percent of the population earns a substantially lower share of the national income than they did in 1991. And, while a large portion of the people struggle financially, the new super-rich financiers and speculators ostentatiously flaunt their foreign luxury cars, jewelry, and expensive, high-fashion clothing.

At the same time, corruption has become pervasive in Russian life. Much of it is linked to organized crime—powerful mafias that have filled the gap left by a declining state. As one observer noted, "The market economy in Russia is lawless, like the 'Wild West,' and organized crime controls the distribution of commodities."[21] Thus, a 1994 government report claimed that three-quarters of all Russian businesses paid 10 to 20 percent of their income to the mafia as protection money. Such payments, which still continue, drive up business costs and contribute to inflation. In the late 1990s Russia's Minister of Internal Affairs estimated that "40 percent of the country's private businesses and an even higher proportion of state enterprises [were] controlled by organized crime."[22]

© Sergey Ponomarev/AP Photo

A DIFFERENT TONY SOPRANO   Vyacheslav Ivankov and his wife head to court (2005). A Moscow jury acquitted Ivankov, an alleged Russian mafia leader, in two 1992 killings, and freed him.

As a consequence of these problems, Russia has failed to create a healthy capitalist economy. Particularly in the 1990s, many Russians longed for the time when the state offered them greater economic security. One opinion poll, for example, indicated that 72 percent of all respondents believed that the state should provide a job to anyone who needs it. Roughly 50 percent favored some state control over prices and over private business.[23] Similarly, an exit poll of more than 7,000 voters conducted during the 1996 presidential election showed that 58 percent believed that the state should own large industrial enterprises, 26 percent felt that the firms' workers should own them, and only 12 percent favored private ownership.[24]

To be sure, Russia's economic collapse had actually begun during the last years of communism (1988–1991), following a decade of economic stagnation. But that meant little to many elderly pensioners, single-parent families, farmers, and others whose living standards eroded greatly during the transition to capitalism. The country's recent economic surge has reduced nostalgia for the supposed "good old days" of communist economic security prior to Gorbachev's reforms. But rather than creating support for democracy, the economic recovery seems to have created widespread backing for Putin's brand of authoritarianism.

Russia in the Early Years of the Twenty-First Century: The Putin Presidency and Beyond

In December 1999, only months before the end of his second term and a scheduled national election to select his successor, Boris Yeltsin resigned from office and turned the presidency over to his prime minister, Vladimir Putin. Three months later, Russians elected Putin to a full presidential term, as he defeated Gennady Zyuganov—again the Communist Party challenger—by a margin of 53 to 29 percent. Thus, Putin far outperformed his mentor, Yeltsin—who had received only 35 percent of vote in the first round of the 1996 presidential election, barely edging Zyuganov. By winning over 50 percent of the vote in the first round, Putin avoided a second-round run-off.

Putin's popularity initially stemmed from his record as a resolute prime minister, especially his hard-line military policies that eventually crushed the Chechen secessionist movement in southern Russia. Many Russians are prejudiced against the culturally distinct, Muslim Chechens, and a number of bloody bombings of civilians by Chechen terrorists induced the public to support the government's brutal response. Tired of Yeltsin's alcoholism and erratic behavior, most Russians approved of Putin's strength and decisiveness. As one voter put it, "He's someone you don't have to be ashamed of. He's the first normal person to head Russia."[25] Putin's public approval rating stayed at the astounding level of 70 to 80 percent throughout his two terms as president and his first two years as prime minister. That support dropped to the still very high level of 65 percent in 2011.

© Laski Diffusion/Getty Images

REVIEWING THE TROOPS IN CHECHNYA   President Vladimir Putin stands with Russian soldiers following an awards ceremony near Grozny, Chechnya. First as Prime Minister and then as President, Putin won popularity at home and condemnation from human rights groups abroad for his policies aimed at crushing the secessionist rebellion in Chechnya at all costs.

Given Putin's very high approval rate and his government's domination of television (most Russians' major source of news), there was never any doubt that he would easily be reelected in 2004. Indeed, so many of his potential opponents had dropped out of the race that his main problem was ensuring sufficient opposition to give his reelection some legitimacy. According to rumors, some candidates were induced to stay in the race in return for favors by **the Kremlin**.* For example, Sergey Mironov, the speaker of the upper house of Parliament and the presidential candidate of the virtually unknown Party of Russia's Rebirth–Party of Life, did not sound very much like an opponent when he proclaimed during the campaign, "We all want Vladimir Putin to be the next president." Indeed, the president's reelection was so assured that he made only one official campaign speech.

There is much about Putin that has disturbed Russian human rights groups and other proponents of democracy. Following his graduation from law school, he began his career in the KGB, the Soviet Union's dreaded internal security and international espionage service. In 1998, President Yeltsin appointed him chief of Russia's post-KGB domestic security agency, the FSB. As president, Putin raised concerns about his commitment to democracy because of his closed operating style, his promotion

---

* The Kremlin is the Moscow citadel that has housed both the Soviet and Russian executive branch leaders. The name was widely used to mean the Soviet government itself (and, less frequently, the post-communist government of Russia), just as "the White House" is used to mean the U.S. president's administration.

of many former KGB and FSB colleagues to prominent posts in government, and his efforts to concentrate power in the central government, particularly in his own hands.

Continuing the policies that he began as Yeltsin's prime minister, President Putin pursued his iron-fisted policies toward the rebellion in Chechnya, grossly violating international human rights standards. Subsequently, the government took over Russia's independent television networks and harassed the other news media (discussed below). A number of journalists who had written exposés or criticisms of the government have been jailed, harassed, or, occasionally, killed. Putin later introduced several measures concentrating even greater power in his hands and increasing national government control over Russia's regional governments. Together with various forms of electoral manipulation, Putin has cut short Russia's experiment with democracy and has restored authoritarian rule, albeit in a far less repressive form than characterized communist rule before Gorbachev.

Similarly, Russia's relations with the United States since 2000 have been friendlier than they were during the Cold War but more tense than during the Yeltsin years. Following the 9/11 attacks on New York and Washington, Putin strongly backed U.S. antiterrorist policies (though not the invasion of Iraq), motivated in part by the presence of Islamic (Chechen) terrorists at home. Since that time, strains between Russia and the West (especially the United States) have increased over issues such as NATO's expansion into former Soviet satellite nations in Eastern Europe and Russian interference in the internal affairs of Ukraine, Georgia, and other former Soviet republics. Thus, while there are still areas of cooperation between Russia and the West, they are often overshadowed by tensions elsewhere.

While Russia's military no longer poses a threat to the West, its foreign policy has increasingly assumed a strongly nationalistic and sometimes hostile tone, a tone that reflects not only the Kremlin's position but the preferences of most Russians, who are upset with their country's loss of status as a major power. In 2008, relations with the West hit a low point when Russian troops invaded two break-away provinces in Georgia to protect them against the central Georgian government. At the same time, however, Putin and, especially, current President Medvedev have tried to maintain friendly ties to the West on other issues, such as a new arms-control pact named "New Start."

The Concentration of Political Power

When Vladimir Putin assumed the presidency, he inherited a powerful position anchored in Boris Yeltsin's 1993 constitution, which gave the executive branch dominance over the parliament. But Yeltsin's capacity to fully wield that power had been limited by his ill health, declining popularity (he left office with an unbelievably low 2 percent approval rating), and his frequent negotiations and compromises between different factions (clans) supporting him. Putin has none of these restraints. Consequently, he concentrated political power in his own hands in a manner unmatched since the days of the Soviet Union. As we will see, the respective powers of the president and the prime minister changed markedly in 2008, when Putin stepped down from the first job and assumed the second one.

Centralizing State Power

Soon after taking office, Putin announced his plans for a system of **vertical power** that concentrates political control and lodges the country's destiny in the hand of its supreme leader, the president.[26] At other times, he has spoken of creating a "guided democracy" and a "managed political system." Like Boris Yeltsin, Putin frequently used the president's authority to issue laws by decree, without parliamentary approval, though that became unnecessary after his United Russia Party swept the 2003 Duma election. He also expanded presidential power in a number of new ways.

One of his goals was to transfer the authority of local and regional governments to Moscow and, ultimately, the presidency. Soon after his election to a first full term (2000), Putin pushed a tax reform bill through Parliament that shifted tax revenue from local and regional governments to the federal government. At the same time, he issued a decree dividing the country into seven federal districts, each headed by a presidential envoy, which would allow him to manage the country's regional and special ethnic-minority republics. Subsequently, he had the Duma empower him to remove elected regional leaders if the courts (generally subservient to the president) decide that those officials had violated federal law. He also restructured the Federation Council—the upper house of Parliament originally created to give local officials a say in national policy—by removing regional governors from that body and making membership in the entire Council subject to presidential appointment. More importantly, the Duma passed legislation that ended popular elections of regional governors. Instead, the president, subject to the (assured) approval of Parliament, now nominates them. Legal scholars agree that the bill clearly violated the constitution, but the courts did not strike it down. With that authority, Putin removed the last independent force in national politics.[27]

Putin's critics were particularly troubled by his frequent appointment to key administrative posts of men drawn from the security services (including many former colleagues from the KGB) and the military, institutions not known for their democratic political culture. Indeed, the strongest of the factions vying for power in the Kremlin today is a group called the **siloviki** (meaning the "group with force" or the "group with power"), composed largely of current and former security—spying—agents (FSB and KGB). As of late 2003,

> Five of the seven heads of Russia's macrofederal districts [were] military or security officers, as [were] ... 25 percent of the Russian political elite as a whole, representing a six fold increase in military and security representation ... since the late Soviet period.... Two-thirds of Putin's presidential staff [had] backgrounds in the security services.[28]

Indeed, some analysts feel that the influence of the security services is greater now than in Soviet times.

Putin, the Television Media, and the Oligarchy

Another very troublesome manifestation of Putin's authoritarian tendencies was his war against independent (privately owned) television networks. After winning the 2000 election, he soon made it clear that he would not be as tolerant of media criticism or as respectful of press freedom as Yeltsin had been. Although Yeltsin had often manipulated the media and although his government sometimes intimidated journalists, for the most part he reluctantly allowed media criticisms. By contrast, in his first annual address to the Russian Parliament, Putin charged that "sometimes [the media] turn into means of mass disinformation and tools of struggle against the state."[29]

His first target was Media-MOST, the country's largest privately owned media conglomerate, and its NTV television network. Owned by **oligarch**⋆ Vladimir Gusinsky, Media-MOST had offered independent news coverage for almost a decade and was sometimes critical of the government. (See A Closer Look 12.1 for more on the Russian oligarchy.) During the first Chechen war (1994–1996), for example, its reporters had eluded Russian troops to report on their inefficiency and frequent human rights violations. To be sure, when Boris Yeltsin faced a serious challenge from the Communist Party candidate Gennady Zyuganov in the 1996 presidential race, NTV, like all the oligarchically controlled news media, blatantly slanted its news coverage in the president's favor. But Gusinsky subsequently had a falling out with Yeltsin and did not support Putin in the 2000 presidential election.

Only months after his election, Putin initiated a series of police raids of Gusinsky's businesses, with employees sometimes intimidated at gunpoint. Gusinsky himself was placed under house arrest. A month later, in return for his freedom, he agreed to sell Media-MOST to Gazprom—the national natural gas monopoly that is 40 percent government owned. Shortly afterwards, he fled the country. When the staff of NTV refused to end their criticisms of the government, Gazprom security men raided the network headquarters and ousted those journalists and employees who were not willing to toe the government's line.

Boris Berezovsky is another media oligarch driven out by President Putin. During Boris Yeltsin's presidency, Berezovsky became one of the nation's most powerful oligarchs. In addition to his private holdings—which included a major airline and much of the country's aluminum industry—he received minority ownership and operating control of ORT, the government's largest television network. Even though he supported Putin's 2000 presidential campaign, Berezovsky soon irritated the new president by criticizing his handling of a submarine disaster. With the prospect of criminal charges for fraud and money laundering hanging over him, he fled to England, where he was granted political asylum. Soon ORT, like NTV, was faithfully following the government line. Such events have a broader chilling effect, as journalists in privately owned media (including the press) increasingly engage in self-censorship to avoid angering Putin.[32]

Although these were the broadest assaults on media freedom, there have been other, more brutal, instances of intimidation. A number of journalists have been detained, some have found it prudent to leave the country, and others have been murdered. Undoubtedly the Russian mafia and other nongovernmental actors were responsible for a number of correspondents' murders. But the national government has contributed to an

---

⋆ Russian oligarchs (members of the oligarchy) are the country's richest men and, rarely, women, who were able to use political contacts to buy most of the nation's largest enterprises when the state sold them to private owners during the transition to capitalism. Under President Yeltsin, some oligarchs also wielded great political influence.

12.1

The Oligarchy—Russia's New Capitalist Tycoons

In the early years following the collapse of the USSR, President Yeltsin and his reformist advisors, such as Prime Minister Yegor Gaidar, looked for ways to quickly privatize the predominantly state-owned economy. There did not appear to be enough wealthy Russian businessmen to purchase all the major state firms, and it was politically unacceptable to sell huge chunks of the economy to multinational corporations. One solution was to distribute vouchers to workers in factories set for privatization as well as to the general public. Often, however, workers acquired only 49 percent of the stock in their company, while the former government managers received 51 percent, giving them effective control. The vouchers given to the general public could be traded for stocks in any privatized firm. Although millions of Russians did trade at least a part of their vouchers for stocks, the majority did not. Having lived their lives under communism, most had no understanding of the potential value of their vouchers, and they willingly sold them to speculators for a small fraction of their face value. Armed with these vouchers, ties to the Kremlin, and healthy bribes to government officials, these budding entrepreneurs were able to purchase state firms at perhaps 10 percent of their real value, thereby emerging as a new class of super-rich tycoons, widely known as the oligarchy.

Most oligarchs emerged from one of two groups. The first had been directors of the country's major companies during the Soviet era—members of the Communist bureaucracy who quickly jumped ship in 1992 and turned themselves into so-called nomenklatura capitalists. The second group consisted of outsiders, ranging from university professors to gangsters or businessmen who had operated in the Soviet black market before the government permitted any private enterprise. Most of the businessmen had begun quite

modestly. For example, one future billionaire (Alexander Smolensky) started his business career in pre-perestroika times by illegally selling bibles. Another (Vladimir Gusinsky) used his own car as a taxi. After President Gorbachev permitted small-scale private enterprise, aspiring capitalists began legal businesses in areas such as computer imports, auto imports, and banking. When the Russian economy was largely privatized in the 1990s, these men often used funds from their own banks to acquire control of some of Russia's largest companies (at highly discounted prices), particularly in natural resources such as oil, gas, and metals.[30] For example, in 1995, Mikhail Khodorkovsky and his associates bought oil giant Yukos for $159 million, only about 5 percent of its real worth.

All told, some estimates suggest that Russia's 10 to 30 richest oligarchs controlled almost half of Russia's gross domestic product by the late 1990s. More cautious assessments in 2004 suggested that the combined wealth of the nation's 36 richest tycoons ($110 billion at that time) equaled one-quarter of the nation's GDP. Many oligarchs lost billions in the 2008–2009 global economic crisis, but most recovered quickly. In *Forbes* magazine's 2011 listing of the world's (1,210) billionaires, 101 were Russians, the highest number in the world after the United States (413 billionaires) and China (115).[31] Moscow leaped past New York and London to become the city with the most billionaires in the world (79).

Some oligarchs established close links with President Yeltsin, and a number of them were largely responsible for his reelection in 1996 by bankrolling his campaign and giving him nearly exclusive campaign coverage on their television networks. They initially hoped to have a similar relationship with Vladimir Putin and supported his 2000 presidential campaign. But as we will see, he soon turned against many of them.

atmosphere of media intimidation and is a likely suspect in many of the most high-profile killings. Thus, Russia's most famous investigative reporter, Anna Politkovskaya, was gunned down in her apartment building in 2006. She had become famous for her articles and books on Russia's human rights violations in Chechnya. Years earlier she had apparently been poisoned while drinking tea on a flight to Chechnya and, on yet another trip to that region, she had been arrested and tortured by Russian troops. As with almost all assassinations of Russian journalists, neither the police nor the courts brought any perpetrators to justice.

Although some of the printed media have maintained their independence and journalistic integrity, 90 percent of Russians get their news from television, and the government now controls all of the stations with a national audience. As with so many of Putin's authoritarian moves, most Russians have not appeared very concerned. In a nationwide opinion poll, some 80 percent of all Russians claimed that they considered freedom of the press to be important. Yet most of those respondents were relatively indifferent to the government's assaults on NTV and other television outlets. Perhaps because the most powerful media owners ousted by Putin were members of the widely hated capitalist oligarchy, most Russians took some pleasure in their downfall and failed to view the government takeovers as a violation of press freedom.

Putin against the Oligarchy

Vladimir Putin did not limit his attacks to the leading media barons. He also did battle with oligarchs in other economic sectors, especially targeting those who wielded substantial political power under President Yeltsin, those who tried to exercise political influence during his own presidency, and those who criticized his administration "excessively." Among the most famous oligarchs—along with Berezovsky and Gusinsky—whom Putin toppled was Mikhail Khodorkovsky, at that time Russia's wealthiest man, whose estimated worth was some $15 billion. In October 2003, Khodorkovsky was arrested on charges of tax evasion, fraud, embezzlement, and theft. While he had quite likely committed a number of these infractions, those crimes were not the reason for his arrest. Nearly two years later, Khodorkovsky and his business partner were convicted and sentenced to eight-year jail terms. (See A Closer Look 12.1) He was tried again, this time on bizarre charges of having stolen from his own company, the former oil giant Yukos. He now faces five more years in jail, which, if not reduced or extended, will imprison him for a total of 13 years. Once again Putin's target had little public support, with one poll during the first trial showing that only 4 percent of all Russians considered Khodorkovsky to be innocent. A number of other tycoons have since decided to flee the country.

In truth, Putin's war on the oligarchs could be justified on a number of grounds. Almost all of the country's oligarchs acquired most of their wealth through bribery, fraud, and inside connections. They are widely despised because they amassed vast wealth during the 1990s at a time when most Russians saw their standard of living drop precipitously. Russians also resented the fact that Boris Yeltsin was so beholden to several oligarchs who had inordinate influence over government policy. Moreover, at the time that the government had great difficulty balancing the budget, oligarchs had billions of dollars in unpaid taxes. The arrest or threatened arrest of several oligarchs on charges of tax evasion under Putin produced a rapid increase in tax payments, both by oligarchically controlled firms and the private sector generally.

Yet, there is reason to suspect Putin's motives. At the outset, the new president warned the oligarchs to stay out of politics. His subsequent condemnations targeted only those who had disregarded his warnings, particularly if they dared to oppose him. For example, Mikhail Khodorkovsky—who mistakenly believed he was untouchable—had not only funded the election campaigns of many Duma deputies,

Once Russia's richest billionaire, Mikhail Khodorkovsky—shown at his trial in the cage used for defendants—dared to challenge Vladimir Putin. He was subsequently convicted of tax evasion and fraud.

who were seemingly indebted to him, but appeared set to finance a new opposition political party. But other tycoons, like Roman Abramovich, maintained excellent ties with both Yeltsin and Putin. Another oligarch, Oleg Deripaska (currently worth almost $17 billion), remained Putin's close skiing companion. And the Putin government also did not crack down on another important group of multimillionaires, the Russian mafia. Perhaps this is because many mafia tycoons were once the president's colleagues in the KGB. In their case, the government continues to tolerate "corporate looting." To be sure, current President Dmitri Medvedev frequently speaks out against government and private-sector corruption and has made some efforts to curtail it, but these generally have been ineffective.

Thus, while Putin's harsh criticisms of key oligarchs were widely applauded and bolstered his popularity, he seemed to be more interested in asserting the central government's power than in cleaning up Russian capitalism. The administration also believed that Russia's most important exports—oil and natural gas—should be controlled by the state rather than by the private sector. Consequently, to pay the billions of dollars in taxes that Yukos allegedly owed, the firm was turned over to Gazprom, the state-controlled natural gas company. Overall, the oligarchs continue to dominate the economy but have lost the enormous political power they once wielded under Yeltsin. Whereas the Yeltsin government was in many ways subservient to them, Putin reversed that power relationship.

Presidential Power after Putin's Presidency

Given his absolute control over the Duma and all sectors of Russian government, Vladimir Putin could easily have directed Parliament to change the national

A CLOSER LOOK

12.2

Who Is In Charge?

As we have seen, when Vladimir Putin was constitutionally barred from serving a third consecutive term as president, he named his protégé, Dmitri Medvedev, as United Russia's candidate—and sure winner—in the 2008 presidential election. While the Russian constitution gives the president considerably greater powers than the prime minister, it was assumed from the start that Medvedev would be simply be keeping the presidential seat warm for his long-time boss while Putin, as prime minister, would pull all the strings. Since taking office, Medvedev has almost never publically disagreed with his prime minister, nor has he ever taken any action that seemed to offend him. So nobody doubts who the boss is, and Medvedev has stated recently that he will not run for reelection in 2012 and will support Putin's candidacy. But the real questions have been, does President Medvedev have any significant policy differences with Putin and, if so, is he able to independently influence national policy?

Most political analysts within Russia and many experts in the West feel that the answer to both those questions is a careful and qualified "yes." In both politics and economic policy the president has taken a more progressive or liberal position than his mentor. In the political sphere he has called for a greater effort to stamp out government corruption (much of which is perpetrated by Putin-appointed insiders), more open political debate, and greater government responsiveness. He has championed the Internet as a vehicle for citizens to lodge complaints about police misconduct, unreported auto accidents by government officials and their families, and the like. And he has often responded to those complaints by removing dishonest and incompetent officials. In a six-month period (2008–2009), Medvedev fired more administrators than Putin had in the first five years of his presidency. These included the head of the federal prison service, the chief of Moscow police, top figures in Russia's sports establishment—all of whom had been considered "irremovable" until Medvedev fired them.[33]

Medvedev has also stated that Russia would benefit from a more competitive party system, implicitly criticizing the current dominance of United Russia (which, of course, is Medvedev's party as well).

---

constitution so as to permit him to run for a third consecutive term in office. For whatever reason, he chose not to. Instead, he selected his long-time aide, Deputy Prime Minister Dmitri Medvedev, to be United Russia's presidential candidate in 2008. Since Medvedev's political career, culminating in his nomination for president, had depended entirely on Putin, since Medvedev was virtually unknown to the Russian public before Putin tapped him, and since he had no power base in the Kremlin, almost all observers assumed that, at least at the start of his administration, the new president would largely be a figurehead while Prime Minister Putin called the shots. Indeed, shortly before Putin finished his presidential term, Parliament passed several bills transferring a number of powers from the next president to the prime minister. Nobody doubts that Putin has the final word on major policies. His current supremacy over his protégé reverses the president's prior dominance over the prime minister, which had marked the Yeltsin and Putin administrations. Yet many political analysts believe that Medvedev has managed to carve out a position for himself, which, though never openly opposed to Putin, has its own policy spin (see A Closer Look 12.2).

12.2

At the same time, Medvedev has often called for modernization of the Russian economy and has indicated that economic changes under Putin failed to stimulate any major sector except energy (mainly petroleum and natural gas). In an implicit criticism of the Putin administration, he has argued that the country must diversify from its dependence on energy exports and must reduce the role of the state in the economy. Toward that goal, Medvedev has appointed a substantial number of technocrats (technically trained bureaucrats) and reform-oriented lawyers to administrative positions, where they offer some opposition to the many former intelligence agents appointed by then-president Putin.

In foreign policy matters, whereas Putin sometimes has been confrontational toward the United States, Medvedev enjoys friendly relations with Western leaders. Recently, the Russian Prime Minister condemned the U.N. resolution supporting military intervention in Libya. Within hours, in a rare public policy clash, Medvedev issued a statement calling such comments "unacceptable" (though he did not name Putin as the target of his criticisms).

Clearly Dmitri Medvedev is in no position to challenge his prime minister (who remains very popular and controls the nation's security agencies) even if he were inclined to

do so.* And undoubtedly they coordinate their policy positions on a regular basis. But after interviewing a number of prominent political analysts, NBC correspondent Jim Maceda noted that "Very few—if any—Russian analysts buy into the idea that Medvedev is Putin's puppet." "It's much more complicated than that," said the editor of a respected Russia foreign policy magazine. "I think they respect each other much more than this simple relationship would mean."[34] At the very least the president offers a vision for Russia's future that differs somewhat from Putin's. It envisions a more open, pluralistic, and technologically oriented nation, with warmer relations with the West. Medvedev has recently agreed to step aside and support Putin, who has decided to seek the presidency in 2012. But he has begun to spell out his vision of reform—featuring more government transparency and accountability, less government interference in the economy, and more privatization of state enterprises.

* A 2007 national poll gave Putin a 81 percent approval rating, the highest of any leader in the world at that time (that same year *Time* magazine named him "Man of the Year"). As of 2011, his popularity had "plummeted" to "only" 65 percent, an approval rating that any U.S. president would die for.

CONCLUSION: THE TRANSITION TO DEMOCRACY DERAILED

Much has changed in Russia since 1990. The country has some aspects of an electoral democracy, regularly holding somewhat free (though no longer fair) competitive elections. But after halting steps toward **liberal democracy** (democracy that guarantees citizens their basic freedoms) under Boris Yeltsin, it has moved further from that goal in recent years. The country lacks adequate safeguards for civil liberties or media freedom, while public attitudes toward democracy remain ambivalent (see A Closer Look 12.3). It has established a primarily capitalist economy, but large portions of that economy are still in government hands, belong to organized crime, or are controlled by political insiders with government connections.

Major political and economic transitions are never easy, nor are their outcomes guaranteed. For example, the initial euphoria that followed the overthrow of dictators in Iran, Ethiopia, and Nicaragua during the 1970s and 1980s was soon dispelled by

A CLOSER LOOK

12.3

Russian Attitudes Toward Democracy

What are the prospects for democracy in Russia? The country's political attitudes and political culture offer some important clues. Countries, such as Russia, that had little or no prior democratic history generally have a tougher and more uncertain transition to democracy than do countries with prior experience with democracy, such as Chile or the Czech Republic. Still, there are exceptions. After World War II, Germany and Japan—both with limited democratic backgrounds—successfully democratized their political cultures through purposeful resocialization (see Chapter 3). So, what have Russian attitudes toward democracy been in the 20 years since the fall of communism?

Numerous public opinion surveys suggest a contradictory pattern. Most Russians voice general support for democracy. Despite this, many of them still vote for antidemocratic candidates and condone Putin's antidemocratic behavior. One major survey conducted early in his presidency found that 64 percent of Russians supported democracy in principle, while only 18 percent were against it. Respondents also agreed overwhelmingly (87 percent) that freedom of expression and freedom to elect their own leaders were important to them. A similar number (81 percent) said that media freedom was also essential.[35] By the end of Putin's presidency, support for democracy was down somewhat, but the percentage of Russians who supported democracy as the best form of government was still almost double those who did not.

But in spite of this generalized support for democracy *in principle*, Russians have given nondemocratic parties the largest number of votes in each of the five parliamentary elections since the fall of communism: the Liberal Democrats in 1993, the Communists in 1995 and 1999, and Putin's United Russia in 2003 and 2007. More recently, a 2010 survey indicated that 52 percent of all Russians support United Russia, while the next most popular party—the Communists—trails far behind (8 percent). At the same time, the parties most clearly committed to democracy—Yabloko and

the Union of Right Forces—have consistently finished toward the bottom in national elections, with each of them sinking to less than 3 percent of the 2007 Duma vote.

Moreover, Russians have overwhelmingly supported Vladimir Putin's leadership despite his frequent violations of democratic standards. Indeed, his approval rating has generally exceeded 70 percent during his 11 years as president and prime minister, a remarkable level rarely reached by Western democratic leaders. More perplexingly, while most Russians have professed support for democracy, they have repeatedly endorsed specific authoritarian policies. For example, by a margin of 56 to 21 percent they supported Putin's increased control over the media.

We must conclude that, even though a majority of Russians still claim that democracy is the best form of government, most do not supported liberal democracy as practiced in the West. Their definition of democracy is a form of government that serves the economic and social needs of the people, brings stability, and produces greater prosperity. So, for example, a 2006 poll asked Russians, "Which model of government has more to offer Russia—a liberal democracy, as in the United States, or a more centrally controlled government, as in China?" By a margin of 44 to 33 percent, respondents favored the Chinese model.[36] In view of Russia's enormous decline in living standards during the 1990s and the sharp rise in crime, this attitude is understandable. Yet support for democracy continued to erode even as the economy advanced sharply since 2000.

Between 2005 and 2009 the number of Russians who believed their country needed democracy dropped from 66 to 57 per cent, while the number of those who consider … democratic rule … not suitable for Russia increased from 21 to 26 per cent. These figures have deteriorated significantly in comparison with the early 1990s.[37]

the rise of new forms of authoritarianism. Much the same seems to be happening in contemporary Russia.

As we have seen, Russians endured a tremendous deterioration in their living standards in the late 1980s and the 1990s. Beginning in 1999, however, they benefited from a decade of rapid economic growth, with widespread improvements in their living standards. Yet other problems have persisted: high crime rates, rampant government corruption, and the virtual collapse of the social-welfare safety net that previously afforded citizens some protection from poverty. That there were few riots and little political turmoil (outside of Chechnya) in the 1990s is a testament to the Russian people's forbearance. Unfortunately, however, that economic crisis made many people, perhaps most of them, far more concerned about their standards of living and personal safety than about civil liberties and democracy (See A Closer Look 12.3). Consequently, their satisfaction with the recent economic boom has led them to accept a return to authoritarianism.

The Economic Challenge

The privatization of the Russian economy and the growth of the private sector have been sweeping and are seemingly irreversible. After a decade of calamitous decline, the economy enjoyed robust growth from 2000 until the 2009 world economic recession and seemed to regain its footing in 2010. But serious weaknesses and concerns remain. We have noted that Russia's recent growth is precarious in nature, as it is built primarily on soaring oil prices. But, historically, oil prices have always dropped significantly (in real terms) from their high points following an upward spike.

Income inequality, which rose substantially in the 1990s, has actually increased a bit more since 2001. As of 2002 the richest 20 percent of the population earned 40 percent of the nation's income (up from 30 percent in 1991), while the poorest 20 percent of all Russians earned only 6.4 percent of national income. Regional differences are also wide. For example, per capita income in Moscow is more than three times the national average. Although Russia's level of income inequality is not much different that the United States', it is significantly greater than in Western Europe and substantially higher than it was before the collapse of Russian communism. We have noted that life expectancy for men has declined to shocking levels, medical care has greatly deteriorated, and size of the population is declining.

The manner in which privatization took place has damaged the transition to capitalism. One of the strengths of the free market is that it fosters competition between business enterprises. In Russia, however, state monopolies were sold in their entirety to oligarchs. Just as the old state monopolies had been managed inefficiently, the new private ones, also not burdened with competition, are poorly run as well. Small wonder that, in a 2003 survey, "77 percent of Russians believed that the results of the country's privatization process should be fully or partially revised."[38] Corruption is also rife as businessmen often have to pay off organized crime groups as well as government officials. According to authoritative estimates, in 2005 Russians paid government officials $3 billion in bribes, while businesses paid as much as $316 billion—more than twice the size of the national budget. A 2005 World Bank study found that 78 percent of all Russian businesses pay bribes to government officials. That includes nearly $600 million paid to university administrators, deans, and professors by students entering university, since such bribes are virtually obligatory for admission. Others report having to pay small bribes to get the results of lab tests at hospitals.[39]

As we have noted (A Closer Look 12.2), President Medvedev sees Russian government and business corruption as an impediment to economic modernization. But he has limited powers to correct it. Since 2000, Ikea, the giant furniture and appliance chain, has opened stores and built shopping malls in a dozen Russian cities. And its multibillionaire Swedish founder, Ingvar Kamprad, has announced that the company would not pay bribes to government officials.* The result has been constant government harassment. In 2004, the opening ceremony for a new mall in Moscow was called off when, at the last minute, local authorities refused to give it needed permits, claiming that the mall's parking lot was too close to a gas pipeline. Then, shortly before the store finally did open, the city government cut off electric power to the mall (future Ikea outlets were built with their own power generators). Plans to open another mall in the city of Samara in 2007 have been delayed at least eight times by local officials. The most recent delay came when authorities said the mall was insufficiently resistant to hurricanes. This, in a city that does not have hurricanes. Finally, Ikea announced in 2009 that it was suspending all further investments in Russia. Small wonder that in 2009, Transparency International's rankings of 180 nations worldwide rated Russia as the 28th most corrupt country, tied with Zimbabwe and several other Third World countries.[40]

Political Decay: Turning Away from Democracy

As Russia closed out the twentieth century and the Yeltsin administration, its political system remained unsound. Surely Yeltsin had serious flaws. He seized excessive presidential powers and undermined the Parliament. He was far too closely connected to crooked oligarchs. His 1996 presidential victory over a Communist Party opponent was not a fair contest, as the mass media (primarily owned by the oligarchs) were totally biased in his favor and gave his opponent virtually no coverage. Still, aside from that campaign, the media could and did criticize the government. Duma elections were relatively fair and honest. In fact, opposition parties outpolled Yeltsin's supporters in every parliamentary election during the 1990s. Thus, Freedom House (a highly respected research center created to further democracy) rated Russia as "partly free." Many analysts expected further progress toward consolidated democracy, especially if the economy improved.

But although President Putin presided over an unexpectedly strong economic recovery, he turned the country away from democracy. In its 2004 report on democracy in the world, Freedom House lowered its rating of Russia from "partly free" to "not free," where it has remained ever since.[41] To be sure, despite the many authoritarian aspects of Russian politics today, the political system is still far more open and less repressive than it had been under the communist regime in the Soviet Union. Nonetheless, the resumption of authoritarian practices fell into several broad categories.

---

* Subsequently, two Ikea officials in Russia, despairing of doing business that way, did pay bribes to local officials. Ikea fired both of them.

Centralizing Federal Power   When Russia exited the Soviet Union it was a federation of over 80 federal units (republics, regions, districts, territories, and federal cities). Indeed, the country's official name is the Russian Federation. From the outset, the central government in Moscow dominated the many federal units, but a number of institutions and practices gave those units some independence. During Yeltsin's presidency, governors and other regional political bosses exercised considerable power in their own domains, and the president often needed to negotiate with them regarding his programs.

All of that changed under Vladimir Putin. First he gained control of the courts, electoral commissions, and prosecutors in those regions, allowing him to influence their selection of senators. Thus, one important component of democracy—the rule of law, including an independent judiciary—was seriously undermined. To further solidify Moscow's control, in 2004 parliament passed legislation ending the popular election of the federal units' governors. Instead, the president now appoints governors, subject to the confirmation by (compliant) regional legislatures.

State Control of the Media   During the 1990s, media freedom expanded impressively. In particular, independent newspapers, magazines, television and radio broadcasters, and book publishers offered a variety of voices, from lurid tabloids (complete with pinups and outlandish rumors) to serious analysis and independent criticisms of the government. Of courses, oligarchs owned the nation's major television networks and newspapers, and many media outlets were not very objective. Too often media moguls had too cozy a relationship with the Yeltsin administration. But at other times, even the oligarchical media outlets offered objective criticisms of government behavior.

Like so much else, this changed dramatically when Putin took office. We have already discussed the government's takeover of major television networks, often forcing their previous (oligarchical) owners to flee the country. Television news now supports the administration's line almost as slavishly as it did in the Soviet era prior to glasnost. Opposition candidates in recent presidential and Duma elections receive very little television or newspaper coverage.

There are still a number of journalists, newspapers, magazines, and book publishers that offer independent news and opinions, including criticisms of government human rights and environmental policies. Frequently, though, they are harassed or crushed by the state. Various estimates, depending on their criteria, suggest that at least 52 and as many as 200 journalists were killed in Russia from 1993 to 2010, with the government or the mafia responsible for over half of them. According to the Committee to Protect Journalists, those figures made Russia the fourth most dangerous country in the world for members of the press. Moreover, very few of the assassins are ever brought to trial, much less convicted. Examining a smaller number of such killings since 2000 for which there is strong evidence of government responsibility, the Committee concludes that Russia has one of the world's lowest percentages of convictions growing out of the journalists' murders.[42] The government has also occasionally reintroduced a method of intimidation not used since Soviet times. Through 2007, a total of almost 20 reporters had been forcibly committed to psychiatric wards. Though the number of such victims to date is relatively small (normally fewer than five per year), it only takes a few cases to intimidate many others. Other

forms of media control have not involved violence. Several hosts of popular television talk shows have recently revealed that their networks have imposed so-called
"stop lists," naming government critics who should not be invited onto their shows.
Other, "softer" intimidation techniques include tax audits of journalists who are too
critical of the government and police raids of independent publications for alleged
fire or safety code violations.

Restricting Civil Society   A healthy **civil society**—a dense network of social organizations (including unions, business organizations, religious groups, and the like)
independent of government control—is a critical component of a democracy. In the
Soviet era, civil society hardly existed as the Communist Party and the state controlled all significant organized groups: unions, professional organizations, women's
groups, youth groups, and even the Russian Orthodox Church. State control largely
disappeared after the fall of the Soviet Union as a range of independent organizations emerged, some quite critical of the government. Estimates of the number of
functioning NGOs (nongovernmental organizations) ranged from 60,000 to
350,000, and possibly even higher. Whatever the actual number, it is enormous
compared to the Soviet era, but still relatively small (on a per capita basis) compared
to the number of NGOs in the United States (the Boy Scouts, NRA, NAACP, PTA,
Little League, etc.). Even today civil society remains weak as many Russians hesitate
to join civic groups.[43]

Even so, when Putin became president his plans for a "managed democracy"
called for greater control over NGOs and civil society. A number of independent
groups were devoted to causes such as monitoring human rights, protecting the
environment, and defending women's rights, sometimes criticizing the government
or exposing government misbehavior. Some of these groups received funding from
abroad or had ties to international groups such as Greenpeace and Amnesty International. This made them particularly suspect to Putin and nationalistic siloviki in
important government positions. A 2006 bill required NGOs to register with the
government by filling out an enormous amount of paperwork. The information
demanded is so complicated and often so vague that the process affords the
authorities ample grounds for denying recognition to almost any group. NGO
activists are periodically harassed, especially those with ties to international
organizations.

Intimidating Opposition Group Activity   Despite Putin's enormous reelection
margin in 2004 and his extremely high ratings in subsequent public opinion polls,
his administration still felt compelled to intimidate and subdue remaining pockets of
opposition. Any group wishing to hold a public demonstration or rally needs official
permission, something the authorities frequently deny to opposition groups. If
groups that have been denied permits decide to hold their rallies anyway, the police
often beat them. As with the press, security officials may subject opposition groups
to bureaucratic and legal harassment ranging from burdensome tax audits to raids
on the groups' offices in which the authorities temporarily seize their computers for
some imaginary violation such as failure to pay the import tax on those computers.
Some groups have been evicted from their offices by their landlords (spurred by
government pressure) and have then found that nobody will rent space to them.

Subduing Opposition Political Parties   In the first three Duma elections held after Yeltsin's constitution (1993, 1995, 1999), between 9 and 17 political parties were able to win some parliamentary seats, as were a significant number of (non-party) independents. Never did parties supporting Yeltsin win anywhere close to a parliamentary majority, and only in 1993 did they even win the largest number of seats (tied in that year with the Liberal Democrats).

When United Russia won a working majority in the 2003 parliamentary election, the president set out to undercut many of the opposition parties. By eliminating single-member districts, changing the election of all 450 Duma members to proportional representation, increasing the number of signatures needed to get on the ballot, and raising the percentage of the vote needed to win any Duma seats from 5 to 7 percent, the government eliminated representation for nonparty candidates and shut out a number of small parties, including those most forcefully advocating liberal democracy. In fact, in the most recent Duma election, the number of parties that won seats fell to four. Other electoral changes made it far more difficult for parties to place candidates on the presidential ballot. Whereas the 1996 and 2000 presidential elections each featured 11 candidates (some with very few votes), by the 2008 race there were only four.

Both the 2007 Duma election and the 2008 presidential election showed substantial evidence of fraud at every stage. Two statistically trained bloggers examined the official figures on voter turnout and found a very improbable number of voting districts that allegedly had 100 percent turnout (everyone registered to vote did so). Not surprisingly, Dmitri Medvedev and United Russia carried all of these by huge margins. In fact, in one such district (where official tabulations claimed a 100 percent voter turnout), almost half the registered voters later signed a petition saying they had not voted. Ballot boxes throughout the country were stuffed, often with absentee ballots, which were particularly easy to fabricate or forge. The number of absentee ballot requests for the Duma election (2.4 million) was four times as high as in the 2003 parliamentary race, a jump that could only be explained by electoral fraud.[44] Evidence of fraud such as that led the UN-sponsored Electoral Observer Group of the Organization for Security and Cooperation in Europe (OSCE) to characterize the last Duma election as neither free nor fair. In the lead-up to the most recent presidential election, the Russian government placed so many restrictions on the activities of outside election-observer groups that the OSCE Observer Group decided not to monitor the vote. European observers of the 2007 parliamentary elections and the 2008 presidential election concluded that while ballots had been counted fairly, the elections were not fair because they had not been "a level field" for all contestants. That is to say, the government-controlled media had been unfairly tilted toward United Russia, and that party had an unjust advantage in resources.

What Lies Ahead?

Despite its regression to authoritarianism, Russia today remains a far cry from the Soviet system. The number of people jailed or murdered for political reasons is miniscule compared to the Stalinist era or even Brezhnev's reign. No longer do millions of secret police informants spy on their friends and relatives. Opposition political parties contest elections and sometimes win a small minority of the contests (as, for example, in the Duma). A number of independent think tanks and democratic politicians still speak out against government excesses. And while the government controls the major broadcast media, there are still independent journals, newspapers, and books that criticize government policy. Indeed, Putin's Russia is a country with fundamentally authoritarian politics coupled with some democratic elements.

In many ways it has a political system reminiscent of another country discussed in this text, Mexico (Chapter 15). From its founding in 1929 until 2000, one party (which came to be called the PRI) dominated Mexican politics. Other parties were encouraged to run, but the "official" party dominated national, state, and local politics for the last seven decades of the twentieth century. United Russia seems to be becoming (like the PRI) the nation's "official" party. In fact, most Russians today would choose United Russia in a fair and honest election, just as most Mexicans had supported the PRI for some 70 years. But in both countries the government has given the official party unfair advantages, padded its vote total, and used fraud and intimidation when necessary. Both political systems concentrated enormous power in the hands of the executive branch.

On the surface President Medvedev appears to be more open to democracy and to the West than his predecessor (see A Closer Look 12.2). Unlike so many other powerful figures in Russian politics today, including Putin, he has no prior links to the security services and he seems to favor closer links to the West. But, as we have seen, to this point his powers are dwarfed by Putin's. While Vladimir Putin is likely to wield enormous power for years to come, it remains unclear what will happen after he passes from the political scene.

◆ ◆ ◆

Key Terms and Concepts _____

absolutism	liberal democracy
Bolsheviks	nomenklatura
Central Committee	oligarch
civil society	perestroika
class consciousness	Politburo
collectivization of agriculture	privatized
command economy	proletariat
cult of personality	shock therapy
dual transition	siloviki
Federal Security Service (FSB)	the Kremlin
glasnost	vanguard party
gulag	vertical power
KGB	

DISCUSSION QUESTIONS

1. *What is a command economy? What were the major accomplishments and failures of the Soviet Union's command economy?*

2. *What factors caused Mikhail Gorbachev to introduce his policies of glasnost and perestroika? What were the major accomplishments and failures of those policies?*

3. *Discuss the changes in Russia's party system under Gorbachev, Yeltsin, and Putin. How would you characterize Russia's current political party system?*

4. *Why is there currently uncertainty regarding the roles and relative powers of the Russian president and prime minister? In what ways have Medvedev and Putin shared power, and to what extent have they taken different positions on Russia's future? Does Medvedev have any power independent of Putin?*

5. *In what ways are Russian attitudes toward democracy different from U.S. views? What are some signs that the political culture supports democracy, and what are the signs that it does not?*

6. *Discuss the ways Russia's oligarchs accumulated their wealth. Compare Putin's relationship with the oligarchy to Yeltsin's.*

Notes _____

1. ISCIP, *The ISCIP Analyst*, "Russia: Population, Immigration, and the Economy," (February 19, 2009), www.bu.edu/phpbin/news-cms/news/?dept=732&id=52411.
2. Frederick Barghoorn and Thomas Remington, *Politics in the USSR* (Boston: Little Brown, 1986), p. 16.
3. Ed A. Hewett, *Reforming the Soviet Economy: Equality versus Efficiency* (Washington, DC: Brookings, 1988), p. 38.
4. Ibid, p. 52.
5. Jerry F. Hough, *Opening Up the Soviet Economy* (Washington, DC: Brookings, 1988), p.13.
6. Jim Leitzel, *Russian Economic Reform* (New York: Routledge, 1995), p. 1.
7. *New York Times*, February 3, 1991, p. 1.
8. Ben Eklof, *Soviet Briefing* (Boulder, CO: Westview, 1989), pp. 42–45.
9. Hewett, *Reforming the Soviet Economy*, p. 304.
10. Quoted in Hedrick Smith, *The New Russians* (New York: Random House, 1990), p. 185.
11. Donald Barry and Carol Barner-Barry, *Contemporary Soviet Politics* (Englewood Cliffs, NJ: Prentice Hall, 1991), p. 137.
12. Abraham Shama, "Inside Russia's True Economy," *Foreign Policy* 103 (Summer 1996): 112.
13. *New York Times*, November 11, 1993.
14. Shama, "Inside Russia's True Economy," p. 112; *The New York Times*, January 28, 1996, and June 16, 1996.
15. Aslund, *How Russia Became a Market Economy*, p. 275; Marshall Goldman, *Lost Opportunity: Why Economic Reforms in Russia Have Not Worked* (New York: Norton, 1994), pp. 106–107, 109, claims a slightly lower rate of inflation.
16. Marshall Goldman, "Render Unto Caesar: Putin and the Oligarchs," *Current History* 102 (October 2003), pp. 320–326.
17. Yoshiko M. Herrera, "Russian Economic Reform, 1991–1999," in *Russian Politics: Challenges of Democratization*, ed. Zoltan Barany and Robert G. Moser (New York: Cambridge University Press, 2001), p. 161.
18. *The CIA World Factbook* 2010. www.cia.gov/library/publications/the-world-factbook/.
19. Ibid.
20. William Thompson, "The Russian Economy under Vladimir Putin," in *Russian Politics under Putin*, ed. Cameron Ross (Manchester, UK, and New York: Manchester University Press, 2004), pp. 114–132.
21. Leitzel, *Russian Economic Reform*, p. 41.
22. Donald D. Barry, *Russian Politics: The Post-Soviet Phase* (New York: Peter Lang, 2002), p. 1.
23. *The New York Times*, April 20, 1993.
24. Poll conducted by Mitofsky Election and Polling Research in cooperation with CESSI Ltd. and quoted in *The New York Times*, June 18, 1996.
25. "Putin's Dubious Allure: 'He's Not Making Things Worse,'" *The New York Times*, March 9, 2004.
26. Waller, *Russian Politics Today* (New York: Palgrave, 2005), p. 33.
27. Allen C. Lynch, *How Russia Is Not Ruled* (Cambridge, UK: Cambridge University Press, 2004), pp. 160–161.
28. Ibid, p. 161; Olga Kryshtanovskaya and Stephen White, "Putin's Militocracy," *Post-Soviet Affairs* 19, no. 4 (October-December, 2003): 289–306.

29. Marsha Lipman and Michael McFaul, "Putin and the Media," in *Putin's Russia: Past Imperfect, Future Uncertain*, ed. Dale R. Herspring (Lanham, MD: Rowman & Littlefield Publishers, Inc., 2003), p. 70.
30. Peter Rutland, "Putin and the Oligarchs," in *Putin's Russia*, pp. 133–152.
31. *Forbes*, "The World's Billionaires, 2011," www.forbes.com/.
32. Laura Belin, "Politics and the Mass Media under Putin," in *Russian Politics under Putin*, pp. 133–150.
33. Dmitry Babich, "Dmitry Medvedev: Russia's Hi-Tech President," *Russia Now*, March 31, 2010.
34. Jim Maceda, "Putin: Prime Minister or Puppet-Master," July 7, 2009, http://worldblog.msnbc.msn.com/archive/.
35. Timothy J. Colton and Michael McFaul, "Putin and Democratization," in *Putin's Russia*, pp. 20–22.
36. World Public Opinion, "Russians Support Putin's Renationalization of Oil, Control of Media, But See Democratic Future," www.worldpublicopinion.org.
37. Natalia Shapovalova, "Assessing Democratic Assistance: Russia," *FRIDE*, www.fride.org/download/.
38. Waller, *Russian Politics Today*, p. 208.
39. *The New York Times*, August 13, 2005.
40. Transparency International (TI), "Corruption Perceptions Index 2009," www.transparency.org/policy_research/surveys_indices/cpi/2009.
41. Arch Puddington and Aili Piano, "The 2004 Freedom House Survey," *Journal of Democracy* 16, no. 1 (January 2005): 103–108. These ratings appear annually in the January issues of this journal.
42. Committee to Protect Journalists, "Attacks on the Press in 2006: Europe and Central Asia," www.cpj.org. Russia's ranking was based on the total number of journalists killed, not the number killed per capita.
43. Lisa McIntosh Sundstrom and Laura Henry, "Russian Civil Society: Tensions and Trajectories," in *Russian Civil Society*, eds. Alfred Evans, Laura Henry, and Lisa McIntosh Sundstrom (Armonk, NY: M. E. Sharpe, 2006) pp. 305–322.
44. *RFE/RL* (Radio Free Europe/Radio Liberty) *Newsline* 12, no. 11 (January 16, 2008).

© Keren Su/China Span/Alamy Limited

CHAPTER **13**

China: Searching
for a New Vision

Shanghai's impressive skyline illustrates China's emergence as an economic superpower.

- **The Relevance of Chinese Politics**
- **The Chinese Revolution and Its Origins**
- **The Evolution of Chinese Politics and Society**

- **Reforming the Chinese Economy**
- **China's Political System**
- **Conclusion: China's Uncertain Future**

arly in 2011, China's popular prime minister, Wen Jiabao, visited (and hailed) Beijing's major "petition bureau," a state office where citizens file complaints against corrupt government officials (generally local officials) or against officials whom the petitioners charge with violating their legal rights. Unfortunately, few grievances are subsequently rectified, and petitioners are often sent home with a warning or even arrested. Consequently, Wen's comments drew considerable attention in the state-run mass media and among advocates for the rule of law.* In the first-ever trip to the bureau by a prime minister, Wen encouraged citizens to press their complaints against the government and "also instructed officials to make it easier for citizens to criticize and monitor the government."[1] At about the same time, Chinese President Hu Jintao made a state visit to Washington, D.C., in which he told President Obama that China still had a way to go in improving human rights. While groups such as Human Rights Watch welcomed Wen and Hu's statements, they continue to be understandably doubtful about how much government behavior will actually change. Thus, as China emerges as an economic superpower, questions remain as to whether it is making progress toward democracy.

---

* In China, and most of East Asia, the family name precedes the person's given name. So Hu Jintao is called President Hu and the chairman of the Communist Party, Mao Zedong, was Chairman Mao.

The Relevance of Chinese Politics

With 1.34 billion people, China contains about one-fifth of the human race, far exceeding the combined populations of the United States, Great Britain, Russia, and Mexico. This chapter will discuss the enormous capacity of Mao Zedong's totalitarian system (1949–1976) for implementing political and economic change as well as the enormous human suffering that Maoism inflicted on the Chinese people. Then we will examine the significant economic changes and more limited political change since his death. Like the Soviet Union before its collapse, China currently features an authoritarian political culture, an official Marxist ideology, and an all-powerful ruling party.

But the differences between these two communist giants, even before the fall of the USSR, are as important as their similarities. From the 1950s through the mid-1970s, China mobilized its population through a particularly hard-line brand of Marxist ideology. The Cultural Revolution (1966–1976), which elevated Mao to the level of a demigod and turned his ideology into a virtual state religion, caused enormous destruction and countless fatalities. But the moral certainty and fanaticism that characterized Mao's rule declined soon after his death. Under the leadership of Deng Xiaoping (1978–1997), Jiang Zemin (1997–2002), and Hu Jintao (2002–), China shed its Maoist economic orthodoxy and introduced far more sweeping and far more successful free-market economic reforms than anything attempted by Russian President Gorbachev's policy of perestroika.

In 2010, China surpassed Japan as the world's second-largest economy, and it is expected to pass the United States by 2050, perhaps even as early as 2030. The country's per capita income rose from only $410 in 1980 to $7,600 in 2010, a staggering 18-fold increase in 30 years.[2] China is currently the United States' second-largest trading partner (after Canada) and has become the world's largest exporter of manufactured goods. It has used much of its trade surplus to buy some $900 billion in U.S. Treasury Bills, making it the U.S. government's largest creditor. Not surprisingly, the country has become both a model for market reform in the world's remaining communist countries and the envy of developing nations.*

But economic change has not been accompanied by corresponding political reforms and freedoms, as they were in the USSR during glasnost (Chapter 12). In 1989, students from several Chinese universities staged political protests, with considerable nonstudent support, demanding a more honest and more responsive government. Week after week, they organized massive rallies in Beijing's **Tiananmen Square**, the very spot where Mao had had declared the communists' victory four decades earlier. On June 4, 1989, army tanks rolled into the square, killing several hundred student demonstrators and making Tiananmen a worldwide symbol of government tyranny. China's leaders, so recently hailed in the West for their economic reforms, were reviled for their repressive politics. Since that time, political repression has eased considerably, and individual freedoms "to buy what [people] want, enjoy private lives, speak more openly, and even to travel abroad" have

---

* But China's per capita income is still relatively low.

People's Republic of China

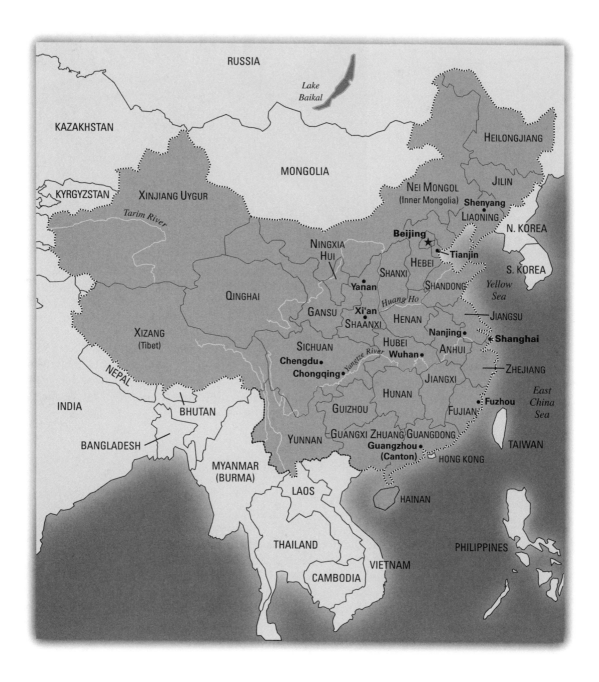

© Bullit Marquez/AP Photo

Fireworks at the Bird's Nest Stadium—2008 Beijing Olympics: China's spectacular Summer Olympic games symbolized its arrival as a major world power.

expanded substantially.[3] But the authority of the Communist Party continues to be absolute, and there are still no guarantees of basic civil liberties. In 2011 the government arrested a significant number of prominent prodemocracy activists, increased Internet censorship, and restricted foreign travel by several prominent intellectuals in one of the harshest crackdowns in recent years.

The Chinese Revolution and Its Origins

The Imperial Legacy and the Battle against Foreign Domination

Around 200 BCE the Qin dynasty first unified the country's feudal kingdoms into the Chinese empire. Over the centuries various rebellions and civil wars challenged or overthrew subsequent dynasties. Many of them took a terrible toll, including the Taiping Rebellion (1851–1864), which cost 20 million lives. That violent history explains why many Chinese still believe that authoritarian rule is necessary to avert serious disorder. Furthermore, traditional Confucian morality stressed social order and harmony, placing the group ahead of the individual.

For centuries, Chinese leaders saw their nation as the "Middle Kingdom," or the center of civilization. The country's culture and technology had filled Marco Polo and other Westerners with awe. But starting in the nineteenth century, China fell victim to Western and Japanese economic domination that weakened its political sovereignty. Its defeat in the Sino-Japanese War (1894–1895) further undermined the emperor's legitimacy. In 1911–1912, an uprising of nationalist, promodernization forces toppled the regime.

Civil War against the Warlords (1912–1928)

For nearly two decades after the empire fell, civil war raged between nationalist reformers and regional military strongmen known as **warlords**. During that time, two political parties were born that eventually dominated Chinese politics. The first, the **Kuomintang (KMT)**—the Nationalist Party—was led by a mix of Western-oriented intellectuals, military officers, businessmen, and rural landlords. Finally, in 1928, the KMT army defeated the most important warlords and established a national government.

Meanwhile, a small group of Marxist intellectuals had formed the Chinese Communist Party (CCP) in 1921. Although the Party grew to nearly 60,000 members in its first six years, its expansion was limited by its orthodox Marxist belief that only the working class could be the agent of revolution.* But in China, an overwhelmingly rural society at that time, industrial workers constituted less than 1 percent of the population. Convinced that the country was not yet ready for a communist revolution, the newborn CCP allied with the Kuomintang against the warlords. However, on the eve of the KMT's victory, Chiang Kai-shek turned against the Communists and annihilated thousands of their militants, most famously in the "Shanghai Massacre" (1927).

The Revolutionary Struggle, Japanese Occupation, and the Development of Maoist Thought (1928–1949)

Its disastrous alliance with the KMT forced the Communists to rethink their strategy. One Party faction, headed by Mao Zedong, decided to organize beyond the working class and reach out to the peasants, who made up about 85 percent of China's population. In the years that followed, Mao and his followers built a rural guerrilla army, the **People's Liberation Army (PLA)**, operating out of Communist-controlled regions.†

Soon the CCP governed some six million people in south-central China. Still no match for Chiang's more powerful army, however, the Communists retreated northward in 1934. Few of the PLA soldiers and Party militants who started that **Long March** north survived the arduous 6,000-mile trek. Despite the tremendous losses associated with it, that march and subsequent experience governing "liberated regions" in the northwest taught the Communist leadership important organizational

---

* In discussions of modern China, "the Party" always refers to the Communist Party.
† The current Chinese armed forces continue to be called the PLA.

lessons that later turned the tide in their favor. To win peasant support, they introduced greater economic and political equality in a society rife with inequalities of wealth, education, and gender. As the PLA eventually overcame great odds to defeat better-armed KMT armies, Mao became convinced that—properly organized and ideologically inspired—the masses (peasants and workers) could overcome any obstacles, no matter how daunting. That faith was reinforced by the PLA's notable resistance to Japanese occupation forces before and during World War II (1937–1945). During that time Party membership grew from 20,000 in 1935 to 1.2 million in 1945.

The Communist Victory (1945–1949) and Mao's Version of Marxist-Leninist Ideology

Following the Japanese defeat in World War II, the civil war between the Communist and Nationalist armies resumed. But having failed to defend China adequately or to win the peasants' loyalty, the KMT had lost its legitimacy. By 1949, after a series of losses, its army and other loyalists fled the mainland to the island of Taiwan. Like many other revolutionaries who achieved power after a prolonged struggle, Mao believed strongly in the power of Marxist ideology to mobilize the masses.

We have noted several features of Maoist thought: the central role of the peasantry, a strong egalitarian commitment, and a glorification of class struggle. But Mao insisted that class struggle did not end with the victory of the revolutionary forces. So even after it seizes power, he argued, a Marxist regime must be ever vigilant against the families of former capitalists and landlords still residing in China, against Western imperialism, and even against unreliable or corrupt **cadres** (Party and government officials). Citing these alleged ongoing threats, Mao justified recurring mass mobilization campaigns to maintain the people's ideological commitment. While these campaigns did inspire greater mass commitment to revolutionary goals, they also disrupted people's lives, provoked great cruelties against alleged enemies of the revolution, and weakened the economy. At their worst, as in the Great Leap Forward and the Cultural Revolution, they caused millions of fatalities. Not until the late 1970s, after Mao's passing, were Deng Xiaoping and the new CCP leadership able to moderate the role of ideology in society.

The Evolution of Chinese Politics and Society

Establishing the Basis of Communist Society (1949–1956)

The early years of Communist rule established the fundamental components of the new society. Acknowledging the peasants' essential role in the CCP victory, the government's first priority was redistribution of farmland. Before the revolution, less than 10 percent of China's rural population owned over half the agricultural land. In just a few years, those farms were taken from the landlords and distributed to more than

300 million landless peasants.[4] Economic growth—facilitated by the end of the long civil war—and more equitable income distribution improved the living standards of many poor families.

As in the USSR and other communist regimes, Communist Party authority was absolute, and perceived enemies of the revolution were brutally repressed. But for many peasants and urban poor, the new political system offered opportunities for upward mobility that were previously unimaginable. Peace, greater equality, land reform, and improved living standards all earned the new regime considerable popular support.

The Great Leap Forward (1958–1961) and the Great Debate (1959–1965)

Although the Chinese economy grew impressively during the early years of Communist rule (1949–1956), Mao feared that the Soviet-style economic development model in place was inappropriate for China's impoverished rural society. That model emphasized capital investment and the development of heavy industry. But since China had little investment capital, Mao sought to maximize Chinese self-sufficiency and to draw on the country's primary resource—the size and energy of its people. As we have noted, he believed that, if properly inspired, the Chinese masses could make tremendous progress in a short period of time.

Thus, for example, when the government launched the **Great Leap Forward** in 1958, it called on the people to gather scrap iron on their farms and streets for use in backyard steel furnaces. But the most radical changes took place in the countryside, where the state consolidated agricultural units into large, collective farms called **communes**. Peasants could no longer own private farm plots or animals, and rural life was collectivized.[5]

Although it may have promoted short-term production spurts, the longer-term effects of the Great Leap Forward were catastrophic. In the cities, production speed-ups caused machinery breakdowns, bottlenecks, and declines in output. In rural areas, however, the effects of Mao's radical policies were far more disastrous. As a result of overly centralized government planning on the communes, much of the harvest failed to reach the market, with food often rotting in the fields or being consumed by pests. From 1959 to 1962, as many as 25 million people died of malnutrition because of food shortages.[6]

Mao's failed radical campaigns generated sharp divisions among Party leaders regarding a proper strategy for reinvigorating economic development. The so-called "Great Debate" pitted more pragmatic Party leaders (whom China specialists labeled the **expert faction**) against ideologues headed by Mao (the **Red faction**). Following the failures of the Great Leap Forward, the expert faction, including the future national leader, Deng Xiaoping, forced an end to that campaign's most radical and disastrous components.

Although the expert faction helped restore economic growth, its approach troubled Mao and his radical allies. They feared it would produce the same outcome in China as it had in other communist nations—technically trained experts would take control of the state bureaucracy from dedicated revolutionaries who were committed to egalitarianism. In fact, conflict between ideologically driven leaders and pragmatic ones became an ongoing feature of Chinese politics from that time until the 1980s.

The Cultural Revolution (1966–1976)

As the pragmatists extended their influence in the CCP, Mao turned to more radical groups for support: specifically, the military and the nation's youth. In August 1966, he launched the "Great Proletarian Cultural Revolution"—or, simply, the **Cultural Revolution**—seeking to root out Party and government cadres who were allegedly subverting the revolution and to destroy all Western and capitalist influences in Chinese society. Toward that purpose, Mao exhorted Chinese youth to organize into militant units called **Red Guards** and attack cadres, teachers, artists, and intellectuals who were allegedly not sufficiently revolutionary.

Thus, the Cultural Revolution was fought at two levels. At the elite level, Red Guards attacked, humiliated, and arrested moderate Party and government leaders. More than 70 percent of the Party's Central Committee members were purged from their posts. At the mass level, the Guards ran rampant, arresting, beating, and killing hundreds of thousands of alleged reactionaries. By 1967, the nation had sunk into chaos, and Mao had to call in the armed forces to restore order. Within two years, the Red Guards were disbanded and the Cultural Revolution's worst excesses ended. But considerable thought control and intimidation continued until Mao's death in 1976.

The tragedy of the Cultural Revolution illustrates how seemingly benign objectives (keeping government officials in touch with the people and guaranteeing equality) can lead to vast human suffering when pursued fanatically in a totalitarian setting. An estimated half a million people were killed, perhaps more. Universities and other schools were shut down for long periods. Intellectuals, professionals, and technicians—the Red Guards' prime targets—were traumatized for years to come. By the early 1970s, the Red Guards themselves became the campaign's victims. Now seen by CCP leaders as a disruptive force, they were sent to the countryside for years of "reeducation."

The Death of Mao and the Struggle for Succession (1976–1981)

In 1976, a political earthquake hit China with the demise of its two most important leaders: Zhou Enlai, the nation's prime minister since 1954, and Party Chairman Mao Zedong, the revolution's "great helmsman" since the 1930s and Party chair since 1943. Although Mao's revolutionary line retained much support, the excesses of the Great Leap Forward and the Cultural Revolution had seriously weakened the regime's legitimacy.

So, only one month after Mao died, his successor, Hua Guofeng, ordered the arrest of Mao's widow, Jiang Qing, and three other leaders of the CCP's Red faction.

The members of the "Gang of Four," as they were labeled, were accused of responsibility for the worst excesses of the Cultural Revolution and were brought to trial. With those four serving as convenient scapegoats for Mao's horrors, their arrests signaled that the radical upheaval was over.

Deng Xiaoping (1978–1997), Jiang Zemin (1995–2002), Hu Jintao (2002–), and the Post-Maoist Era

Hua Guofeng was soon outmaneuvered by Deng Xiaoping in the battle for national leadership. Deng, the consummate pragmatist and political survivor, had twice come back from political purgatory to outlive or outmaneuver his radical opponents. By 1981, his supporters had ousted Hua from his positions as prime minister and Party leader. Choosing not to hold either of the top political posts himself, Deng installed two lieutenants, Zhao Ziyang and Hu Yaobang, as CCP chairman and prime minister, respectively, while he retained control of the military and dominated the Party and government from behind the scenes.

A 1981 pronouncement by the Communist Party's Central Committee called the Cultural Revolution "the most severe setback [to] ... the Party, the state, and the people since the founding of the People's Republic." With the Maoist radicals vanquished, most Party leaders agreed on the need to depart from Marxist economic dogma. Consequently, CCP policy debates during the 1980s and early 1990s often pitted those who favored more rapid market-oriented economic reform (or, less frequently, political liberalization) against those who wished to move more slowly.

During the 1980s, Deng Xiaoping's team instituted economic changes that were far more sweeping than those later introduced in the USSR by Mikhail Gorbachev. After Deng's death in 1997, Jiang Zemin and then Hu Jintao further embedded those reforms and expanded them. Unlike Gorbachev's restructuring, however, China's changes have been restricted primarily to the economic arena.

As we observed in Chapter 12, Gorbachev's most radical innovations were political: semicompetitive elections, the end to the Communist Party's monopoly on power, open debate in the legislature, and the opening of political space for public discussion. On the other hand, his economic reforms were far more limited and mostly ineffective or catastrophic. China, on the other hand, has seen far more extensive and successful economic change, while political reform has been tentative and very restricted.

REFORMING THE CHINESE ECONOMY

What prompted the Chinese leadership to introduce a major economic transformation in the 1980s? As in the Soviet Union, the early decades of Communist rule had brought rapid economic growth. From the early 1950s to the mid-70s, even with the major setbacks of the Great Leap Forward and the Cultural Revolution, the economy grew at an annual pace of 8.2 percent, one of the world's most impressive rates.[7] A combination of rapid economic growth, more equitable income distribution, better health care, and increased literacy benefited a large segment of China's peasants and laborers.

Despite such gains, however, at the start of the 1980s, China remained a very poor country, with at least half of the population still ill housed and undernourished.[8] Moreover, as in the USSR, the command economy was more effective in the earliest stages of economic growth than subsequently. By the late 1970s, the country's leaders were painfully aware that some of their capitalist neighbors were developing more rapidly than China was and were offering their citizens much higher living standards. Once praised for outpacing India and most of Asia, China now lagged behind its old adversaries Taiwan, South Korea, and Hong Kong.

In response, starting in 1978, the Chinese leadership introduced economic changes so dramatic and far-reaching that Harry Harding described them as "China's Second Revolution." Economic modernization replaced class struggle and political mobilization as the centerpiece of government policy. The People's Republic pursued economic and cultural contacts with both the West and the booming capitalist nations of East Asia that it had once scorned. Free-market mechanisms and private ownership replaced centralized state control in most sectors of the economy. We will examine the impact of those changes in three critical areas: agriculture, commerce and industry, and foreign economic relations.

The Second Revolution in Agriculture

Initially, the government's most significant reforms affected agriculture, where most of the population was employed at that time. CCP moderates had long argued that peasants are more productive when they control their own plots of land, whereas Maoist radicals favored collective agriculture. During the Great Leap Forward and again during the Cultural Revolution, private farming was prohibited, and peasants were forced into less-efficient collective farms.

In 1978 through 1980, however, the government began to give peasants control over their own family plots.[9] Within seven years, privately run family plots had largely replaced collective farm communes. Peasants were permitted to lease land, hire farm labor, and sell a portion of their crop directly to consumers at free-market prices once they had sold their crop quota to the state. Thus, farmers now had strong economic incentives, previously lacking, to boost agricultural production.

The results of "unleashing the entrepreneurial talents of China's peasants" were dramatic. From 1980 to 1984, the value of agricultural output increased by approximately 40 percent. Greater output and higher crop prices produced a remarkable 12 percent *annual* increase in rural living standards.[10] In 1985, fewer than 2 percent of all rural households had a washing machine, and less than 1 percent had a color TV. By 1998, those figures had jumped to 23 percent and 33 percent respectively.[11] Although the rate of agricultural growth has tapered off since the late 1980s, rural per capita income in 1999 was still 15 times higher than it had been in 1978.[12] Another important source of peasant income promoted by the government has been the enormous growth of rural industry, particularly those owned and run by village cooperatives known as TVEs (township and village enterprises). These not only account for a substantial portion of China's total industrial production but also improved rural incomes by allowing some family members to farm the family plot while others work for the TVE. For all those reasons, some economists credit Deng's rural reforms with the world's greatest short-term improvement ever in human living standards.

Since the late 1980s, however, rural economic growth has lagged substantially behind urban development, and the gap between urban and rural living standards is now as wide as it ever was. To be sure, rural incomes have risen during the past 20 years, but far more slowly than in the cities. And in villages, commonly located inland from the country's booming coast, without successful TVEs to supplement farm income, peasant incomes have sometimes suffered absolute, not just compara- tive, declines.[13] As peasants have become aware of that renewed inequality, as they have been burdened with high taxes, and as they have suffered the abuses of local Party bosses, rural protests have increased substantially.

Commercial and Industrial Reforms

Seeking to reduce urban unemployment and to offer consumer services not ade- quately provided by the state, government reforms in the 1980s permitted small pri- vate businesses to operate for the first time since the Cultural Revolution. As early as 1990, millions of people were employed in the urban private sector (shops, restau- rants, and the like). Although they still constituted only a small percentage of the population, this policy fostered a more consumer-oriented culture. During the 1990s, the country's urban housing stock was sold to its residents at low prices, cre- ating millions of new property owners.

Even though private businesses were at first confined to small family operations, since the 1990s, the government has allowed ever-larger manufacturing enterprises in the private sector, some employing hundreds of workers or more. By 2007 private urban firms employed some 40 million people, 14 percent of the urban work force. In addition, workers in smaller state enterprises were encouraged to assume control of their factories and manage them as cooperatives. Those cooperatives (called **collectives**), together with other newly created collective industries in China's villages, accounted for over 30 percent of the nation's industrial output. Privately owned firms contribute more than 20 percent. That has left **state-owned enterprises** (**SOEs**), which produced some 90 percent of China's industrial output in the 1980s and 50 percent in 1997, with less than 30 percent in 2007.[14] While privatization makes sense economically, it has been a delicate policy politically. In the past, large state enterprises had hired more workers than they needed in order to create jobs and keep the workers content. Typically, the SOEs also guaranteed their workers lifetime employment (barring any major infraction). With that guarantee removed, new private-sector owners (of old SOEs) usually have dismissed a portion of the previously bloated workforce. During the 1990s, most SOEs, particularly the large industrial plants, were very inefficient. About half of them lost money and needed to be subsidized by bailout loans from state banks, which often had little expectation of getting their money back. In recent years, state enterprises have become more profitable, and the government has been phasing out its bailouts of inefficient enterprises. Today the state still owns many of the country's largest industrial companies as well as almost all firms involved in national defense, transportation, public utilities, and energy. And in the past few years, partly to compensate for the loss of jobs and business during the world economic crisis (2008–2011), the state enterprises have experienced a mild resurgence as the government has tried to bolster the economy. It is believe that most of the government's $580 billion stimulus package, which successfully lifted China out of its recent economic slow-down, went to state enterprises. Indeed, in 2009 the SOEs' share of overall industrial production rose, ending a decline that had lasted more than two decades. Many experts believe that this is a temporary reversal occasioned by the global recession and that the private sector will soon resume its growth. Others are not so sure.

Foreign Economic Ties

During most of Mao's rule, China isolated itself from the outside world and denounced Western and Soviet influences. Under Deng's **open-door policy** since the 1980s, however, cultural, trade, and investment ties to the West and to the overseas Chinese communities in Asia have flourished. For example, the government opened special economic zones (SEZs) for foreign investment, primarily on China's southeast coast. It invested heavily in the infrastructure there and offered multinational companies preferred treatment to bring in advanced foreign technology and expand manufactured exports. Today, China is the world's largest exporter of manufactured goods. Deng's successor, Jiang Zemin, widened this opening to the outside world when China entered the World Trade Organization (WTO).

Between 1979 and 1991, total foreign direct investment (FDI) in China averaged only $2.16 billion annually. Since that time, FDI has exploded and reached $105 billion in 2010, making it one of the world's leading recipients of foreign investment. That investment has brought enormous prosperity to China's coastal cities and has contributed to an expanding middle class and skilled working class. But, as we have noted, living standards in the country's interior, particularly its rural villages, have lagged far behind. At the same time, China has become a major investor abroad, most notably in Asia, but in Africa, the Americas, and Europe as well. For example, the Chinese firm Lenovo purchased IBM's PC division.

The Costs of Economic Reform

Although industrial reform has been enormously successful in many ways, it has also produced several undesirable consequences—including extensive corruption, greater unemployment, environmental damage, and popular discontent. One of the most pernicious effects of economic change has been an enormous growth in corruption. While private firms are an ever-growing force in the economy, business owners must still depend on government officials to secure vital licenses, permits, and supplies. This has opened vast new opportunities for bribery, allowing many cadres or their children* to use their political positions for personal enrichment. In 2010, the independent watchdog group Transparency International ranked 178 countries throughout the world from least corrupt (Denmark, New Zealand, and Singapore) through the most (Iraq, Afghanistan, Burma, and Somalia). China ranked 78th, not a very good score, but better than Mexico (98th) and much better than Russia (154th).† Yet Chinese citizens would find little comfort in that ranking. Corruption within the state and private sector has probably done more to undermine popular support for the regime than any other factor.[15] There are several possible explanations for that resentment. Corruption in China is most intense at the village level, where many local officials exploit poor peasants (sometimes even expropriating their land) who have little enough to begin with. Furthermore, while government and private sector corruption is distressingly widespread, opinion polls indicate that the public has an exaggerated view of how common it is.

A national survey conducted by the Chinese magazine *People's Forum* revealed that 76 percent of all respondents believed that "collusion between officials and businessmen" was the "most serious factor" contributing to people's negative image of the government.[16] A government study on the causes of the country's nearly 90,000 "public order disturbances" (the police term for organized protest) in 2005 found that the foremost targets were corrupt village officials who had expropriated peasant farmland with little or no compensation and then turned it over to businessmen for a bribe.

While this growing unrest has not reached the point of threatening the country's stability, the central government has reacted with concern, periodically cracking down on corruption. In 1997, the CCP announced that during the previous five years it had investigated more than 725,000 charges of criminal conduct within its own ranks—undoubtedly only a small portion of those who were actually guilty—and, as a consequence, had expelled 121,000 members and detained 37,000 on criminal charges.[17] In 2009 and 2010, the Party launched a campaign against "corruption, gangs and violence," leading to over 256,000 arrests. For example, in 2010, a high-ranking anticorruption official for Shandong province was convicted of accepting $1 million in bribes from crooked businessmen and was sentenced to death (though that sentence is likely to be commuted to life in prison).

Faced with growing public anger, President Hu has intensified the fight against corruption. For example, in 2006 the CCDI—the Communist Party's anticorruption agency—established a website that allows whistle-blowers to report corruption by local officials without fear of retribution. Periodically, the government stages major show trials of high-ranking government officials and businesspeople, handing down harsh punishments including occasional executions. For example, the former head of the country's Food and Drug Administration was tried and executed for taking bribes to approve an unsafe antibiotic that subsequently killed at least 10 patients. In 2010 the CCDI announced the arrest of Li Qihong, the mayor of the industrial center of Zhongshan. Li, the daughter of poor peasants, had colluded with real estate speculators to amass a fortune of $293 million for her husband and other family members.

---

* These widely despised, crooked adult children are disparagingly known as **princelings**—little princes.
† The United States ranked 22nd.

A CLOSER LOOK 13.1

The Other Side of China's Economic Reforms

As we have seen, China's market reforms since the 1980s have helped produce more than two decades of breathtaking economic growth. Several hundred million people have been lifted out of poverty, a rapid and dramatic improvement in living standards that is unparalleled in all of human history. Between 1950 and 2000 the country's life expectancy rose from 43 years to 72 years. But the benefits of this surge have been unevenly distributed. Explosive growth has produced numerous winners (especially residents of China's coastal cities) but also left many behind (most notably, the country's rural population). One important component of the transformation from a state-dominated economy to one that is primarily privately owned was reducing the state welfare system created during the Maoist era.

During Mao Zedong's rule, health care was the state's responsibility. To be sure, the system was inefficient and the quality of care was generally poor. But, in line with Mao's egalitarian policies, it served millions of peasants who previously lacked any medical care at all. And in the cities, thousands of SOEs also provided workers with free health care. Because there were not nearly enough doctors to serve the country's

huge rural population, the government instituted the so-called "barefoot doctors" program.* Many thousands of villagers with some secondary school education were trained in basic medical practices for several months. Their main objective was prevention—including immunization programs, hygiene, and sanitation campaigns—along with some basic remedial care. Peasants paid only a small fee. When confronted with more serious illnesses, barefoot doctors referred patients to clinics in nearby towns with professional doctors. By the end of the 1970s, the country's rural villages had more than one million barefoot doctors. The UN's World Health Organization credited them with significantly reducing China's level of infectious diseases such as polio and smallpox.

Since the early 1980s, however, as China moved from a command to a market economy, the government has sharply reduced its expenditures on health care and shifted the burden to patients. In rural areas, the barefoot doctors program was terminated, and peasants must now pay the major share of their medical bills. In the cities, the number of people employed by SOEs has dropped

* Like their fellow peasants at that time, most health care workers could not afford shoes or sandals.

The various government campaigns (ordered from the top) appear to have had some positive effect. Corruption, which peaked in the mid-1990s, has leveled off since the end of that decade. In Transparency International's 1995 rankings, China was regarded as the fifth most corrupt country of 54 that were rated at that time. By 2005 it had improved to the middle of the countries that were rated. Still, the highest-ranking officials and their families remain immune from prosecution (unless they have fallen seriously out of favor with the CCP leadership). And corruption at the local level is still pervasive. Indeed, if the government and the CCP were to launch a full assault they would risk losing many members and potential recruits who join the Party to enrich themselves. As one high-ranking CCP official privately expressed the Party's dilemma, "fight corruption too little and [you] destroy the country; fight it too much and [you] destroy the Party."[18]

Another unpopular byproduct of rapid economic growth has been increasing inequality, particularly broad income gaps between the developed coast and the

13.1

sharply, leaving millions of workers unemployed or employed by private enterprises and cooperatives that do not provide health care coverage. At the start of the twenty-first century, China only spent 5.8 percent of its GDP on health care, less than developing countries such as India (6.1 percent) and substantially below Brazil (7.9 percent), and South Africa (8.1 percent).[20] Although low-income Chinese received some degree of coverage prior to the country's market reforms, most people are now unable to afford medical services, especially in the countryside. A 2006 government survey revealed that "49 percent of the Chinese people refuse to see a doctor when ill and 30 percent refuse to go to the hospital due to the high costs."[21]

In 2009, the average American paid 14 percent of his or her total medical costs out of pocket. By contrast, the Chinese, who are generally far less able to afford it, must pay 50 percent.[22] Furthermore, the large gap between urban and rural medical services, which had diminished under Mao, has reasserted itself. While accounting for less than 50 percent of the total national population, China's cities now receive 80 percent of government health expenditures.

Since Hu Jintao assumed power in 2002, his populist policies have aimed at redressing some of China's growing inequalities, which developed with the country's free-market reforms. The government has increased its spending on rural health care and increased funding for the country's poorer interior regions in central and western China. It has also extended state and employer medical insurance more broadly. But, as we have seen, large portions of the population remain uncovered or, if covered, unable to afford the out-of-pocket cost. Even in Beijing— where the percentage of insured citizens far exceeds the national average—many people who cannot afford legitimate medical care turn to "black clinics," the thousands of unregulated clinics where unlicensed and ill-trained personnel illegally dispense medicines and other treatments. In 2008 alone, municipal authorities closed over 3,000 such clinics, but many more continue to operate.[23]

In 2009, the government announced that it would spend $123 billion in the next two years to subsidize a "universal" health care insurance system that it hoped would cover 90 percent of the population.[24] While it will likely fall short of that goal, the program will undoubtedly expand medical care substantially. Unfortunately, the out-of-pocket costs, especially for hospitalization, will still be too costly for many citizens.

country's interior and between China's urban and rural populations. To be sure, the gap between rural and urban incomes narrowed in the early years of economic reform (1978–1984), but it has widened since, especially since the early 1990s. Whereas city residents earned only a bit over 1.5 times as much as peasants did in 1984 (China's smallest urban–rural gap ever), by 2002 they were earning more than three (3.1) times as much, one of the highest gaps in the world. At the same time, income inequality *within* both the rural and urban sectors has risen steadily since the 1980s.[19] Once a country of relative equality, China's current income inequality is greater than India's (and about the same as the United States'). That does not mean that peasant incomes have declined in recent decades. On the contrary, they have continued to improve impressively (e.g., 9 percent real growth in 2007). But urban incomes have risen more rapidly.

One consequence of the growing urban–rural income gap is the migration of millions of peasants to the cities in search of jobs and a better life. But migration has exceeded the urban areas' capacities to absorb additional labor, and many unskilled migrants have joined a new, often homeless, urban underclass. In 2010 China's "floating population" of surplus labor (as these semi-illegal migrants are called) was estimated to be 210 million people, with 3 to 6 million more added every year. When the town of Shenzhen, near Hong Kong, was declared an SEZ for industrial investment in 1979, it had a population of 20,000 people. Today its population has grown to over 12 million, of whom 7 million are migrant workers. Many live in wretched conditions. The growth of this new underclass throughout urban China has increased crime and other urban social ills. While it had been technically illegal to move to the cities without government permission, the authorities generally ignored that regulation for years. Officials have seen these migrants, who drive down urban blue-collar wages, as necessary for further economic expansion. At the same time, however, migrant workers are frequently exploited by their employers—who sometimes fail to pay their employees the wages due them—while many middle-class urban residents feel threatened by the migrants' slum neighborhoods. More recently (2011), there have been signs that official policy may be changing, as authorities have demolished or closed a number of Beijing schools that had been created in migrant neighborhoods.

Another major cost of the country's rapid economic development has been the harm to the environment. Economic growth under any circumstances causes considerable ecological damage, be it from greater use of chemicals in agriculture, damming of rivers to produce hydroelectricity, increased use of trucks and cars, new power plants, or the dumping of industrial waste. For several reasons, environmental degradation has been especially severe in China. The pace of growth has been so rapid that environmental controls have not been able to keep up. The regulation of state enterprises tends to be very lax. And pervasive corruption enables polluting private companies to pay off local government officials, who are also reluctant to restrict large enterprises that supply jobs and tax revenue to their towns.

The results have been catastrophic. Eighty percent of the country's power plants run on coal, a fuel that China has in abundance but that is a particularly "dirty" source of energy. In 2007, the World Bank reported that 20 of the world's 30 most polluted cities were in China.[25] Indeed, another World Bank study indicated that only 1 percent of the China's 560 million city dwellers breathed acceptably clean air. Air and water pollution may cause as many as 750,000 deaths annually. Until recently the national government placed such a premium on rapid economic growth that it was relatively indifferent to the accompanying ecological damage. Of late, however, several factors have committed it to greater environmental protection. For one thing, hosting the 2008 Olympics forced the government to attack Beijing's air pollution (some of the remedies were temporary, some promise to endure). As China became the world's leading generator of greenhouse gases (causing global warming), international pressures grew to reduce emissions, and China's influential scientific community has become more outspoken on the issue. Finally, growing grassroots protests have put added pressure on the government. The country has seen a rapidly growing number of urban and rural demonstrations against major environmental threats such as new power plants, nearby chemical plants, or polluted water.

As a result, the Hu administration has toughened its rhetoric and its actions against environmental destruction. But progress has been limited for several reasons. Without a free press and with tight government limits on independent political action, China lacks the large environmental lobby that exists in the United States and Europe. Second, the government continues to ignore environmental dangers if remedying them would slow economic growth. Finally and perhaps most importantly, local political officials, particularly in rural areas, depend heavily on taxes on local industries (including private firms and village cooperatives) to pay for municipal projects, particularly since the central government has reduced the amount of revenues it distributes to localities. Consequently they don't want to reduce production by imposing environmental restraints. Several leading China scholars recently noted that "local authorities have thwarted the center's environmental policy at every turn."[26]

CHINA'S POLITICAL SYSTEM

Turning our attention from China's economy to its political system, we will first examine the fundamental organisms of that nation's politics: the Communist Party and the government. Formal political institutions often have an ambiguous role in revolutionary societies. That was particularly true under Mao because of his inherent suspicion of the state and Party bureaucracies. The Cultural Revolution's assault on Party and state cadres was so savage that by the late 1960s both political institutions were on the verge of collapse.

The Communist Party

Although the constitution states that the CCP is subject to state authority, in fact the Party has always been the principal policy maker. All of the country's important government, military, and societal leaders (such as union heads) are Party members and accept strict Party discipline. The Party's leader, its general secretary—called the Party chairman under Mao—is among the country's most powerful figures. Indeed, except for the period when Deng Xiaoping ruled from behind the scenes (1978–1997), the Party secretary general (or chairman) has been the dominant force in Chinese politics.

Party Membership   As previously noted, CCP membership expanded greatly from the start of the Japanese occupation through the end of World War II and continued to grow after the PLA's victory. At the Party's Fifth Congress (1945)—the last one held before the Communists took power—national membership was 1,211,148. By the Sixth Congress (1956) it had risen to 10,734,384. As of the most recent Party Congress (2007) there were over 73 million members (the world's largest political party), constituting about 7 percent of China's adult population. For many Party members coming out of the peasantry and urban poor, membership has opened previously unimaginable opportunities. However, women are still significantly underrepresented, constituting fewer than one in five Party members.

Under Mao, Party membership was a valuable asset but also a major commitment. Members were expected to participate frequently in political activities and were required to engage in "criticism–self-criticism" sessions that probed the depths of their revolutionary commitment. Today, the terms of membership are less demanding and the level of ideological scrutiny is far lower, but members are still subjected to CCP scrutiny, and some have been expelled for corruption or lack of adequate commitment. Indeed, the Party claims to have expelled 124,000 members for corruption between 1997 and 2002. In a few cases of extensive dishonesty, sentences can be extremely harsh. For example, in 2000, the vice chairman of the National People's Congress was convicted of corruption and was executed. But these prosecutions covered only a small percentage of the perpetrators.

As in the Soviet Union, people's reasons for joining the Party into the 1980s, typically involved some mix of idealism and opportunism. Given the population's sharply diminished commitment to Marxism–Leninism in the last 25 years or so, the proportion of Party members who have joined primarily for personal advancement, contacts, or prestige has surely risen. At the same time, however, educational achievement is fast replacing Party membership as the key to securing better-paid, more prestigious jobs.[27]

Since Deng Xiaoping's ascendancy in the late 1970s, Party standards have changed appreciably. Income differences and other inequalities that Mao so abhorred are now considered acceptable and indeed are even encouraged by government policies. With the opportunities offered by an expanding private sector and with Deng's declaration that "to get rich is glorious," a new class of wealthy business entrepreneurs along with middle-class professionals has developed. Mao's exhortations to the Chinese people to sacrifice everything for the good of the whole have been forgotten as the Communist Party legitimizes itself by preaching "happiness through consumption."[28]

One of the results of China's free-market reforms was that from 1980 to 2010 the country went from one of the world's most egalitarian societies to one of the more unequal. Thus, China in recent years has had the 34th most concentrated income distribution of the 128 countries for which the United Nations has data.*

As one American journalist observed, "In practice there is little these days that is Communist about China, a country where laid-off workers hunt for jobs [and] yuppies buy stocks and houses."[29] Few people still believe in communist ideology. Indeed, one survey asked university-aged CCP *activists* whether they were proud to be Party members. A surprising 43 percent said they were not.[30] In fact, independent analysts doubt that many Party members of *any* age currently believe in Marxism–Leninism. Most of the more than 70 million Party members join out of opportunism—that is, for the material advantages and prestige it brings. In one survey of 800 graduating university students who belonged to the CCP or Communist Youth League, only 38 (under 5 percent) stated that they believed in communism.[31] Even at the higher ranks of the Party and the government, China's leaders seem to espouse communism merely for the sake of keeping themselves in power. One high-ranking Party official has even admitted—off the record—to a *New York Times*

---

* Denmark, Japan, and Sweden (in that order) had the most equal income distributions, and the African nations of Namibia, Lesotho, and Sierra Leone had the most unequal distributions. The United States was the 55th most unequal.

reporter that few of the CCP's leaders believe in Marxism either. So, as the Party has abandoned its calls for socialist equality and class struggle, it now seeks support as the protector of stability, prosperity, and nationalism.

Party Structure The CCP's structure was modeled after the Soviet Communist Party and is similarly hierarchical. Party authority is exerted from the national level down through provincial and local units. The principles of "democratic centralism" demand that Party policies initially be discussed widely at all levels, but once the Party's leaders have announced their positions, they must be obeyed without challenge. In fact, the primary purpose of local Party discussions has been to legitimize leadership policies and give the rank and file a feeling of participation.

The most important components of the Party are the National Party Congress, the Secretariat, the Central Committee, the Politburo, and the Standing Committee of the Politburo. The National Party Congress met very infrequently under Mao, coming together only twice during the Communists' first 20 years in power (in 1956 and 1969). Since the 1970s, it has met more regularly but still gathers only once every five years for a few days (meeting last in 2007). Although it is nominally the Party's supreme authority, its very brief and infrequent meetings do little more than ratify decisions made by the CCP leadership. In fact, the major function of the National Party Congress is to "elect" the Central Committee, which it also does by ratifying the choices of the Party leaders.

Between CCP congresses (i.e., most of the time), the Central Committee serves as the Party's official authority. Essentially, however, it merely endorses the choices given to its members. While its debates in recent years have been a bit livelier, it only meets once annually and, like the Party Congress, ratifies leadership decisions. Currently composed of 204 full-time members, the Central Committee represents the Party elite, including military officials and leaders of "mass organizations" representing women, youth, peasants, and workers. The number of Committee members who had graduated from college rose from 55 percent in 1982 to 98.6 percent in 2002.

At the top of China's power structure sits the CCP's Politburo (with 25 members at the present time) and particularly the Politburo Standing Committee—currently a subgroup of nine members—which carries out day-to-day operations and has the Party's most powerful figures. The general secretary leads both the Politburo and the Party itself. Until the 1980s, the Politburo was an aging group (averaging 72 years) whose members often traced their communist credentials to the early days of the Revolutionary War. Once entrenched in power, Deng Xiaoping, though himself approaching 80 at that time, pushed for a younger Party leadership. Yet while the average age of the Politburo declined, the transfer of power to a younger generation was more apparent than real until the mid-1970s. Deng and a small group of Party elders (mostly over 80 years old) retained their power from behind the scenes, even after their formal retirement, and younger Party leaders still depended on them for support.

Deng's death in 1997—after years of infirmity—finally allowed the transfer of political power from Deng's "second generation" of revolutionary leadership (after Mao's) to a "third generation" composed primarily of men in their 60s or even early 70s. Jiang Zemin, who had been selected as Deng's eventual successor eight years earlier, became China's paramount leader. Today, in addition to being younger, Politburo members are more educated than their predecessors and less likely to have come out of the military.[32] Not long after Deng's demise, the Party enforced a rule requiring its "core leaders" (those under consideration for appointment to the Politburo) to retire at the age of 70 and mandated that Politburo members already in their 70s retire at the next Party Congress (held that year and every five years thereafter). While Jiang violated that rule when he failed to step down in 1997, he did retire at the next Party Congress in 2002, at age 76. This was the first transfer of power other than through death in Communist China's history.

When Vice President Hu Jintao became CCP general secretary, he assumed the Party leadership at the relatively tender age (by Chinese standards) of 60. Similarly, the Politburo installed at that time averaged 61 years. Retirement for all Politburo members was fixed at 68. It is also understood that the Party general secretary will be limited to two (five-year) terms and should also retire by about the age of 70.[33] At the 2007 Party Congress, Hu subtly signaled that Xi Jinping would likely succeed him as CCP general secretary (hence, the paramount political leader) at the Eighteenth Party Congress (in 2012). Xi was subsequently appointed as vice chairman of the enormously powerful Central Military Commission (which controls the armed forces), a further sign that he would succeed Hu. China has become the first communist nation to establish effective term limits on its leader and a fairly orderly form of succession.

The Structure of Government

China's government primarily administers policies initiated by the CCP, but the impact of the government's vast bureaucracy on day-to-day life is enormous. The state affects vast areas of public activity, controlling a substantial (though fast declining) portion of the economy and many other functions reserved for the private sphere in pluralist democracies. Since the time of Prime Minister Zhou Enlai, those who have filled that position (now the second highest in the government) have often provided the Party's general secretary and other leaders with technical expertise, particularly in economics.

Under Deng, the influence of China's prime ministers often matched that of the Party general secretary, and both figures (along with the nation's president) were beholden to Deng, who held nominally less-powerful positions. Since that time CCP Secretaries Jiang Zemin and Hu Jintao have guided the Communist Party and the state by serving as Party general secretary and as the national president (which has surpassed the prime minister as the most powerful government office). Prime ministers have served at the President's pleasure.

The National People's Congress (NPC)   The NPC is China's legislature, whose primary function is to legitimize rather than evaluate legislation proposed by the national leadership. Since the 1980s, however, NPC sessions have sometimes featured policy debates, and congress has occasionally amended government legislative proposals. Negative votes of 20 to 30 percent on the government's draft legislation have become common. Since its members (elected every five years) include some deputies who are not Party members, the NPC offers the leaders a somewhat broader perspective on issues. In recent years a small number of its members have spoken out against government proposals, and it has exercised growing influence, sometimes even convincing the leadership to amend its policies, though in general top-down control remains in place.

The State Council and the Prime Minister   The national government's major executive body is the State Council, whose members direct the national government's ministries and commissions. Its most important concern is economic administration, but it also plays an important role in such areas as education, science, technology, and foreign affairs. In 1998, the Council was reduced in size (the number of ministers and bureaucrats was cut back), reflecting the state's diminished role in the economy. As of 2005 it had 35 members. Most ministers also sit on the CCP's Central Committee, reflecting the substantial overlap between government and Party leadership. Because of its large size, the State Council carries out most of its work in a smaller Standing Committee. Heading the State Council is the prime minister, who plays a pivotal role in policy making, especially economic policy. Usually, the prime minister is the second- or third-highest-ranking leader of the Communist Party.

Elections: The NPC and Local Officials

During the Maoist era, elections of government officials were essentially meaningless. Popular "elections" (with no choice) took place only at the village or local level for representatives to the "basic-level" People's Congress. Those representatives then elected the legislature for the administrative level immediately above them: Basic-level delegates elected their county or city congress; they, in turn, elected their provincial representatives; and finally, the various provincial congresses elected the NPC.

In 1979, the government made several very modest gestures toward greater political openness. Voters now elect township-level and county congresses directly, and most can choose between two or more opposing candidates in local races. Rural villages, townships, and counties directly select their officials in competitive elections. In many villages, very likely the majority, villagers still do not have a real choice. But in other rural communities there is genuine competition. These officials make fundamental decisions on local budgets, taxes, and village development. Sometimes they have challenged the authority of the local Party secretaries, who officially outrank them but who are not popularly elected. National and provincial legislatures are still elected indirectly, and there are still no competitive elections for urban local officials.

The Judicial System

China's court system, be it in its many criminal cases or its far smaller number of political cases, is ultimately subject to the CCP's authority and offers defendants few legal rights. For example, the defense lawyers' role has not been to defend their clients but rather to "safeguard the interests of the state."[34] To be sure, there has been some progress since the 1980s. For example, in recent years, Chinese intellectuals, dissidents, and businesspeople have even begun to bring suit against CCP organizations and government officials for defamation of character, abuse of power, and other violations. Although these plaintiffs usually lose their cases and sometimes suffer retribution, in some high-profile cases they have caused government officials to back down.

Punishment in the penal system is often harsh, and international human rights groups are still very critical of the sentences for both political and nonpolitical prisoners. Currently, 68 crimes—including rape, robbery of substantial sums, bribing government personnel, damaging state property, embezzlement, tax evasion, and distribution of pornography—are potentially punishable by death. Not only does China lead the world in official government executions, but frequently its annual total has exceeded that of the rest of the world combined. Since 2002 the number of executions has allegedly dropped by half and a judicial review process has been introduced, but human rights groups differ as to the actual number, which is a state secret. In its report *Death Sentences and Executions 2010*, Amnesty International estimates that several thousand official executions took place in China that year, far more than the combined total for the rest of the world.

A variety of legal reforms since the mid-1990s have expanded defendants' rights, allowed defense lawyers greater independence from the state, abolished the crime of counterrevolutionary activity, and, since 1996, established the principle that defendants are to be considered innocent until convicted. Despite those and other reforms in the criminal code, however, 99 percent of all criminal defendants are still found guilty.[35] Thus for now any improvement in a criminal defendant's rights must come at the pretrial stage (i.e., the decision on whether or not to bring charges). In recent years appeals courts have removed the death penalty in 10 to 15 percent of the cases that reach them.

Problems of Political Reform

Discussions of transformations in the communist world often have overstated the linkages between economic reform and political reform. Some argue that a market economy cannot develop effectively without a parallel loosening of state political controls. In theory, reducing state control over the economy and over people's lives at the workplace, creating a larger and more independent private sector, and increasing the size of the middle class should eventually create strong pressures for democratic change. Yet far-reaching economic changes in China so far have produced only a modest degree of political liberalization (discussed below).

After Deng introduced his first comprehensive economic reforms, contending factions in the CCP have debated the nature and the pace of economic and political change. During the 1980s, reformers such as Hu Yaobang (Party general secretary from 1981 to 1987) and especially Zhao Ziyang (prime minister from 1980 to 1987 and Party general secretary from 1987 to 1989) favored economic modernization and greater political freedom, although not democracy. On the other hand, influential "conservatives" (supporters of more orthodox communism) remained skeptical about far-reaching economic or political reforms.

During the decades that followed Mao's death, political repression lessened, and the Chinese people have enjoyed a more relaxed political atmosphere, particularly when compared with the terror of the Cultural Revolution. People have also been spared the constant barrage of political indoctrination that had characterized the Maoist era. At least in the cities, average citizens have expressed themselves more freely in private conversations. And the rigid, Maoist restraints on popular music, dress, and other cultural areas have largely been removed. In general, citizens who wish to avoid politics are now relatively free to select a lifestyle of their own choosing. At the same time, however, the government has severely persecuted many members of the nation's Tibetan and Muslim minorities accused of supporting secessionist movements. And in recent years, it has imprisoned thousands of members of the **Falun Gong**, a spiritual sect stressing meditation and exercises, with hundreds reportedly dying while in police custody.

Despite some progress, China has not achieved a degree of political openness comparable to that of the USSR under glasnost. Ironically, because of the great success of their economic reforms Chinese leaders were not under the same pressures as Gorbachev was to open up the political system. Nor did Deng face the major challenge from ethnic minorities that weakened the Soviet system, since 93 percent of the Chinese population is of the same ethnicity—Han. However, ethnic unrest has been a factor in the more remote regions of the country including Tibet and Muslim regions in the west.

The Chinese press, despite being somewhat more open to critical discussion than previously, is not nearly as independent as the Russian media became under Gorbachev. Indeed, censorship and periodic arrests of journalists have increased since Hu Jintao assumed power. As Nicholas Kristof has observed, "China now imprisons more journalists than any other country."[36] Obviously, the long prison terms to which some journalists have been sentenced have led their colleagues to practice self-censorship. In 2006, after the government had shut down *Freezing Point*, an influential news journal, a group of former high-ranking Party and press officials denounced the closure, indicating some division within the Party regarding censorship. Sometimes, contradictory government behavior regarding media freedom suggests that there may be differences between political leaders or factions. For example, one day in early 2010 more than a dozen big-city newspapers, regional papers, and financial publications published an identical editorial asking that the government reform residence requirements that often have denied urban migrants basic social services, including education for their children. But while these seemed to represent bold media criticism, within hours the critical editorial was removed from all of their websites. Several months later, 23 retired Communist Party officials and intellectuals (including several former executives of the state-controlled media) issued an unprecedented statement on the Internet calling for greater press (media) freedom and harshly criticizing state censorship. While this demand attracted much attention in and out of China, it was quickly blocked from the Chinese Internet, and nothing has come of it.

Similarly, at times the authorities have opened the door to complaints and criticisms from average citizens. But frequently it has backtracked when such criticisms become "excessive." One example of the government's mixed signals regarding political reform is the issue of accountability among government officials. Under President Hu's administration, Chinese citizens were encouraged to petition the national government regarding abuses by local or provincial (but not national) officials. Between 2002 and 2003 the number of such citizen complaints rose 46 percent, then another 100 percent in 2004. Yet a survey by the Chinese Academy of Social Sciences (a government research center) revealed that only 1 out of 5,000 people who had lodged complaints later felt that they had gotten any results. To be sure, some particularly corrupt local officials were disciplined or even arrested. But after a few years, the Party leadership decided to put the brakes on this process, which they felt had gotten out of hand. Consequently the national government issued new regulations that make it easier for accused local officials to punish those who lodge complaints against them. Not surprisingly, the number of complaints subsequently dropped.

To be sure, the gross excesses that characterized the Maoist era have come to an end, but the state continues to jail and torture political prisoners selectively. Despite a relaxation of repression since the early 1990s, there has been no real movement toward democracy. Instead, the government has permitted some **political liberalization**, a general (but not universal) loosening of authoritarian controls and repression. As one journalist observed:

> [The] Chinese ... increasingly live where they want to live ... [and] travel abroad in ever larger numbers. Property rights have found broader support in the courts. Within well-defined limits people enjoy the fruits of the technology revolution, from cell phones to the Internet, and can communicate or find information with an ease that has few parallels in authoritarian countries of the past.[37]

The constant indoctrination campaigns of the Maoist era are long gone. Kenneth Lieberthal, a noted expert on Chinese politics, describes the present system as "fragmented authoritarianism" (indicating that some cracks in the system have opened it up somewhat). Yet repression of individuals or groups advocating democracy, multiparty elections, and human rights are still as harsh as ever. In 2010 the Nobel Prize was awarded to Liu Xiaobo, a literary critic and prodemocracy advocate currently serving an 11-year jail sentence for "inciting subversion of state power."

Jailed Chinese Dissident and Nobel Peace Prize Laureate Liu Xiaobo

Sources of Discontent

The Problems and Limits of Economic Reform   Although China's economic transformation since the late 1970s has been nothing short of astonishing, the Western media have often exaggerated the scope of reform and underestimated the problems that it has produced. For example, some analysts have argued that Chinese leaders were moving their nation inexorably away from centralized planning toward a market economy.

In fact, even today the state continues to own important portions of the economy and to tightly regulate other parts. In the past few years, state investment has been the major engine of industrial growth. The ongoing conflict between the conservative and liberal factions of the Communist Party caused government policy under Deng Xiaoping to swing back and forth from left to right, though such divisions seem to have ended since the 1990s. Although the Western media often viewed Deng as a liberal, in truth he actually tried to balance the two factions, often siding with the conservatives on political matters (cracking down on dissidents) to win their support for liberal economic measures.

Economic policy debates continued under Jiang Zemin, but there were few policy swings. In part, that is because the conservatives have largely lost the battle and accepted the transition to a more market-driven economy. The current national president and CCP leader, Hu Jintao, has continued the process of market reforms (indeed, his daughter is married to a rich Chinese businessman) but has been far more cautious about political reform, periodically cracking down on dissent.

The West's admiration for and worry about China's economic miracle since the 1980s is quite understandable. From 1980 to 1986, the economy grew at the astonishing rate of 10.5 percent annually, the highest of any major nation in the world (only South Korea at 8.2 percent was close) and ahead of all other developing nations. After a mild slow-down in 1989 and 1990, annual GNP growth surpassed 12 percent in 1992 through 1994 and then averaged about 8 to 10 percent through 2007. In all, China's GNP quadrupled from 1978 to 2004. As we have noted, using one measure of national output (PPP), it is now the world's second-largest economy. The country's standard of living has increased correspondingly, though it is still very low by Western European or American standards outside its large cities.

This tremendous economic expansion, however, has produced numerous problems, including an explosion of government corruption. As foreign corporations and China's own private sector have rapidly expanded, private firms still depend on the state for many critical inputs. A new class of "influence peddlers" has developed, composed of people whose political influence can cut through bureaucratic red tape to secure needed licenses, credit, parts, and raw materials for the right price. As we have noted, these intermediaries are often cadres who are the children of more powerful Party and government officials. One opinion survey revealed that "corruption remains the most important source of public discontent with the regime," with 71 percent of respondents expressing dissatisfaction with the integrity of public officials and only 4 percent claiming they were satisfied.[41]

A CLOSER LOOK

The Cost of Heroism[38]

13.2

Since the death of Mao Zedong and China's transition from a totalitarian to an authoritarian political system, that nation's citizens have had greater latitude to criticize and even protest government behavior. But there are limits to such dissent, some of which are clearly defined while others remain vague and variable. Moreover, the consequences of dissent depend greatly on who is voicing the criticism and who is being criticized. Peasant or worker protests are usually repressed but occasionally provoke minor changes in government policy or even the removal of local government administrators. Widespread Internet complaints or well-crafted grievances from urban professionals sometimes elicit similar changes. But all such dissent must follow prescribed guidelines. For example, it cannot pose what the Party perceives as a threat to political stability, and it must not challenge the CCP's authority nor question the behavior of national-level officials.

The life of Dr. Jiang Yanyong, a prominent Beijing surgeon, illustrates the poorly defined possibilities and dangers of political dissent. Despite his upper-class origins, as a young man Jiang sympathized with the communists, joined the Party soon after it came to power, and enlisted as a doctor in the PLA. Eventually, he rose to chief of general surgery at a military hospital, with a rank equal to that of a major-general. As one of the country's leading surgeons, his patients included senior Party officials and their families.

During the 1989 student-led demonstrations that culminated in the Tiananmen Square bloodbath, Jiang treated a number of wounded victims. Subsequently, the CCP asked him, as a senior military officer and hospital official, to sign a document supporting the government's crackdown. When he refused, he was denied a promotion and then pressured into early retirement. However, he continued as a consultant to his old hospital and periodically performed operations. Years later (2002), he began to hear, through friends in the medical community, of a severe type of respiratory disease, which came to be known as SARS. Jiang soon learned several alarming facts about the disease: First, it could spread quickly to people in close contact with a patient, including medical

personnel; second, it had a fatality rate of nearly 10 percent; and third, health officials had ordered hospitals and doctors to keep secret the nature of the fast-spreading epidemic and had imposed a general media blackout on its dangers. That decision reflected the government's general tendency to repress bad news. Within a few months, however, it was no longer possible for the authorities to ignore the SARS outbreak as travelers spread it to Hong Kong, Vietnam, Singapore, Canada, and eventually over 30 other countries. At the same time, information on the epidemic was filtering back to China via the Internet and Hong Kong television. In response, the nation's minister of health insisted that the epidemic was under control. He also issued optimistic data on the total number of cases and fatalities, numbers which Dr. Jiang knew to be false. Such misinformation undermined efforts to control the spread of the disease.

Unable to secure the support of his medical colleagues—who were afraid to help him expose the cover-up—Jiang sent e-mails to China Central Television and to a Hong Kong television station, accusing the health minister of lying. For weeks nothing happened while the government continued to reassure foreigners that it was perfectly safe to travel to China. Eventually, however, his message was leaked to the American press and published in *Time* magazine and the *Wall Street Journal*. Swiftly, news of the extent of the SARS epidemic and the cover-up spread throughout the world. Still the Chinese government tried to hide the truth. Before inspection teams from the World Health Organization (WHO) arrived at Beijing hospitals, the staffs were told to move seriously ill SARS patients to nearby hotels or other hiding places. "At one hospital, doctors and nurses loaded patients into ambulances and rode around in circles with them until the WHO team left."[39] Dr. Jiang informed foreign media about these developments and, once again, their articles filtered back to China.

Fortunately all of this occurred while Hu Jintao was assuming power as head of the Communist Party and national president. Hu projected an image of being more responsive to the needs of the Chinese people and more responsive to grievances. Within weeks of the

13.2

publication of Jiang's sensational letter, President Hu dismissed both the national minister of health and the mayor of Beijing while at the same time releasing the government's first honest information on the extend of the outbreak. Once the cover-up had ended, health officials were able to end the epidemic within three months. Amazingly, not only was Dr. Jiang not disciplined for violating Party and military rules, but he briefly became a national hero, appearing on the cover of a popular Chinese magazine and lauded on the CCP's website. But while this turn of events probably could not have happened under earlier Party leadership, the authorities were most certainly not interested in encouraging similarly embarrassing exposés in the future. Soon the nation's media stopped mentioning Jiang and, while he remained a hero abroad, he returned to obscurity at home.

The following year, Jiang was faced with another crisis of conscience as the 15th anniversary of the Tiananmen massacre approached. Although Jiang had bravely refused to sign a document supporting the government's repression in 1989, he still felt guilty about his failure to reveal what he had witnessed that day in his surgery ward. Once again he composed a letter to the government and Party leadership describing the heartbreaking stories of some of the victims whom he had seen die.

Still a Party member, Dr. Jiang followed CCP rules—as he had in his message on SARS—by first sending his letter to top-ranking Party and government officials rather than to media outlets abroad while also distributing copies to politically connected medical colleagues. As before, he received no response. And as before, somebody leaked his statement to the foreign press, which then wound its way back into China via the Internet. But while China's new political leaders had been receptive to Jiang's message on SARS, his latest criticism hit a raw nerve. From the start, CCP and government leaders have always considered the 1989 democracy movement to be a fundamental challenge to the authority of the communist regime, which had to be crushed for the sake of political stability. At the same time, reacting to the tremendous amount of international criticism leveled against them, China's leaders had always insisted that nobody was killed at Tiananmen.

At first a series of medical and military officials came to Jiang's home and office to convince him to repudiate his letter. When he refused, he was detained at an empty ward of another military hospital and was told that he was being held for an indefinite period until he "changed his thinking." In the weeks that followed he was subjected to repeated indoctrination sessions in which he was asked to repudiate his letter. Finally, wishing to go home to see his wife, Dr. Jiang wrote a long letter to Party officials stating that while the loss of lives at Tiananmen was a tragedy, he could now understand why CCP leaders felt their actions were necessary to maintain stability. Probably feeling that this was the most they could get out of him, the authorities allowed him to go home after seven weeks of detention. He was kept under house arrest for eight more months until the government dropped all charges against him.

Jiang Yanyong's long struggle to unveil the truth clearly reveals China's restraints on free speech and the unwillingness of the CCP to accept serious criticism. At the same time, his story illustrates other interesting features of Chinese politics today. First, as a longstanding Party member and high-ranking military officer, Jiang made great efforts to pursue his causes within the system and to follow CCP and government rules. He initially sent his letters to Party leaders and through proper channels in his hospital rather than to foreign news outlets. And while charging the government with deceit, he never challenged the Party's right to rule. These factors and Jiang's international fame (as a result of his SARS exposé) may have contributed to his comparatively light punishment for his letter on the Tiananmen massacre. He was never tortured or even physically mistreated. In contrast, for example, Wang Wanxing staged a one-man prodemocracy protest at Tiananmen Square on the third anniversary of the massacre. The authorities confined him to a police-run hospital for the criminally insane, where he spent 13 years. For five of those years Wang was placed in a ward for "severely psychotically-disturbed inmates, most of whom had committed murder."[40] At the time of his release in 2005, he was one of an estimated 3,000 political prisoners being held in China's mental hospitals. Unlike jailed prisoners, they are committed for indefinite periods of time.

The Causes of the Student Democracy Movement   Discontent over several issues—some limited to the students' own lives, some more generalized—helped spawn the country's most powerful protest movement since the revolution, the 1989 student democracy movement. Ultimately, the breadth of that movement and its eventual brutal repression dramatically altered China's image in the world and has influenced Chinese political attitudes until today. In some ways, it is quite surprising that a major protest movement of that nature erupted when it did. During the preceding decade, China's standard of living had doubled, agricultural production had soared, and consumer goods had become far more available. At the same time, political regimentation had eased since Mao's death.

The government's open-door policy to the outside world had been designed to bring the country into the modern technological age. But as Chinese governments had discovered as far back as the nineteenth century, it is generally impossible to import foreign technology and expertise without also exposing the population to new cultural and political values, some of which may be threatening to the ruling elite. As thousands of young Chinese studied in Western universities, as foreign tourists and businesspeople poured into China, and as foreign literature and radio broadcasts became more widely available, inevitably Chinese students, professionals, entrepreneurs, and intellectuals were influenced by new ideas. Many students were impressed by Western-style democracy while others looked enviously at Mikhail Gorbachev's policies of glasnost and perestroika in the Soviet Union.

Though not necessarily favoring liberal democracy, student leaders and their supporters desired a more open society—including greater freedom of speech, more independent mass media, and reduced political repression. Interviews of student activists suggested that most of them were primarily interested in reforming the system from within rather than overturning it. Some political leaders, most notably CCP General Secretary Zhao Ziyang, favored dialogue with the students and sympathized with some of their goals.

But government hard-liners were increasingly anxious as they saw student demonstrators joined by large numbers of workers, government bureaucrats, and intellectuals. Protests spread to dozens of Chinese cities, and demands widened. As the base of dissent grew, marches in Beijing drew as many as one million people, many of them moved by resentment over nonideological issues such as inflation and government corruption.

When Deng finally threw his support to the hard-liners, martial law was declared, and troops were brought to the capital to clear Tiananmen Square and break up the demonstration. On June 4, 1989, the PLA brutally ended the democracy movement, killing hundreds, perhaps thousands, of young people who were encamped in the square.*

The Aftermath of the Democracy Movement   The crushing of the democracy movement led to a broader crackdown on political dissent and the purge of several high-ranking Party and government reformers. Zhao was stripped of power, replaced as Party general secretary by Jiang Zemin, and placed under house arrest for the

---

* Hundreds of protestors were also killed outside of Beijing. The Chinese government still insists that nobody died at Tiananmen.

remaining 15 years of his life. Throughout society, political controls were tightened. Several thousand students and worker activists were arrested in the months following the massacre, many of them were sentenced to long jail terms. In short, much of the progress away from totalitarian politics during the 1980s was rolled back.

But the post-Tiananmen crackdown was relatively short lived. Since 1992, many freedoms have been restored, and individual rights, at least outside the political arena, are now more respected than they had been before the student democracy movement. Today, young Chinese can surf the Internet (subject to extensive government censorship), listen to Western rock or their favorite Taiwanese singers, and aspire to be rich businesspeople. At the same time, however, most of them now consciously avoid politics and hence pose no challenge to the system.

Rural Unrest Although rural protests have remained localized and as of yet pose no threat to the government, they are becoming more frequent. In the last decade, peasants have often demonstrated—sometimes violently—against corrupt and arbitrary local officials, high taxes, pollution by power plants, harsh population-control policies, and, most significantly, confiscation of their land. Indeed, local Party officials frequently appropriate farmers' land and then sell it to private developers for their personal profit or to raise revenues for local government, with peasants often receiving as little as 5 to 10 percent of the sale price. Farmers who resist these seizures face police intimidation. From 1990 to 2002 alone, over 66 million farmers had some of their land confiscated, often illegally and with little compensation. Not surprisingly, these seizures have spawned many of the recent peasant protests.

Until the early 2000s, the primary cause of farmer protests and petitions was taxes, which, on average, were higher than urban rates, even though rural incomes are substantially lower. Sometimes local officials imposed illegal taxes (bound for their own pockets), stolen other tax revenues, and refused to distribute tax refunds. Protesters sometimes succeed in removing such officials or in getting some financial satisfaction. In the early 2000s, responding to rural discontent, the national government reduced rural tax rates significantly. Since then there have been fewer peasant demonstrations caused by arbitrary taxes, and most protests are now related to land seizures.

Occasionally, local Party officials have even been put on trial for police violence committed against demonstrators. But, in general, the protesters' complaints have not been satisfied. A 2005 protest in the village of Dongzhou sought to prevent the construction of a new coal-fired electric power plant. There, as in many other instances, farmers' land had been confiscated with little compensation. Police opened fire on several hundred villagers, many of them armed with homemade bombs, killing about 30 protesters.

Ethnic Conflict The Chinese government officially recognizes 55 ethnic minorities (non-Han), residing primarily along the country's northern, western, and southern borders. The Zhuang, the largest of these, have a population of some 17 million. Although many ethnicities accept their status, some do not. Earlier in this chapter we noted the Tibetans' long struggle for autonomy or even independence. In the western region of Xinjiang there are over 8 million Uighurs, who speak a Turkic language and practice Islam. For years several separatist groups have carried out occasional bombings and other violent acts. The Chinese government's response (as in

A CLOSER LOOK

13.3

China's Communist (Red) Capitalists

Political scientists and other scholars have long sub-scribed to the view that an emerging business class (the bourgeoisie), associated with the rise of capital-ism, is critical in the development of democracy. In a widely quoted statement from his seminal study of the origins of democracy and dictatorship, Barrington Moore stated "no bourgeoisie, no democracy."[42] Con-sequently, many analysts expected that China's emerg-ing capitalists would be a strong force for democratic reform. Not only has that not happened, but much of the new business elite has instead forged close links with the Communist Party.

During the Cultural Revolution the last vestiges of private enterprise were eliminated. Since the 1980s, however, the government has promoted the free market. In an astonishing reversal of Maoism, the economy is now primarily privately owned. From the early 1990s to 2000 alone the total value of private enterprises rose from $1.5 billion to $150 billion. China not only has an army of business entrepreneurs, but it is currently home to the second largest number of billionaires in the world (115), trailing only the United States.[43] Private firms cur-rently account for about 95 percent of all industrial companies and employ some 80 percent of all indus-trial workers. Despite their enormous economic strength, why haven't businessmen been a force for democratization?

The answer lies in the origins of China's business class and in its relationship with the state. Many observers were startled by Jiang Zemin's 2001 decision to welcome capi-talists into the Communist Party, thereby creating a new group of so-called "red-hat businessmen,"* or **Red capital-ists** (i.e., communist capitalists), an apparent contradic-tion in terms. As it turned out, however, most businessmen who belong to the CCP were Party mem-bers *first* and entrepreneurs later, not the other way around. Many of the private sector's larger industrial firms today started life as SOEs. When the government began to privatize them, they were often sold to the firms' state managers, or to well-connected Party officials or their relatives for a small fraction of their true value. The state also dismantled other SOEs that were too inef-ficient to be sold, stripped them of their assets (worth billions of dollars in total), and transferred them to priva-tized companies owned by Party officials or their families. From *98 to 2005, in both rural and urban areas, 22 per-cent of all the government's land expropriations (involv-ing over a million landholdings) were grabbed illegally. Most were turned over to politically connected business-men for construction of new plants. Near the city of Dingzhou, "hundreds of hired thugs forced villagers to evacuate their homes because the government wanted to build a factory. When [many] residents refused, six

* Actually about 20 percent of Chinese "businessmen" are women.

Tibet) has been to encourage Han Chinese to migrate to the area. This in turn has led to tensions between Uighurs and immigrant Hans, who hold most positions of political and economic power in the region. In 2009, armed clashes between mobs of Uighur and Han youth led to nearly 200 deaths in the regional capital of Urumqi. Despite a government crackdown, Uighur separatist groups have continued to set off bombs occasionally in the area. Occasional violence has also erupted between Hans and other minorities such as the Mongolians. That violence is discon-certing to CCP leaders, but since all of China's ethnic minorities combined total less than 10 percent of the country's population and since they are geographically sepa-rated and politically unattached to each other, ethnic conflict seems does not seem to pose a threat to China's stability.

13.3

were killed and over 50 were hurt."[44] Small wonder that illegal expropriations are the primary source of peasant protest in China today.

According to a study by two government research centers, "90 percent of China's richest people [worth at least $12 million] are the children of senior officials."[45] Those include President Hu Jintao's son (whose firm sells the government 90 percent of all airport security scanners), his son-in-law (the former head of one of China's largest Internet firms), Prime Minister Wen Jiabao's son (who received $900 million in shares in a major insurance firm just before its stocks were sold to the public), and Wen's son-in-law (once ranked as China's 15th richest person). The privatization of most of the smaller firms has been controlled by local officials who sell or give them to friends and relatives or unrelated entrepreneurs who bribe them. Some large capitalists have made it to the top on the basis of their own abilities with no prior Party or government ties. However, they are greatly outnumbered by "crony [Red] capitalists" in all sectors but high technology.

Once in operation, private business owners frequently bribe local and national officials, Party cadres, or their adult children in return for special favors such as government loans, sweetheart contracts, or confiscated land. Frequently, business owners bribe local officials to ignore violations of government safety and other regulations. For example, China's mining industry (especially coal) has by far the largest number

of accidental deaths for any country in the world. Most of those fatalities are in privately owned mines. Given this symbiotic relationship, neither capitalists nor government or Party officials have any desire to weaken the other. And businessmen have increasingly been joining the CCP. In 1988 during the early growth of the private sector an estimated 15 percent of all business entrepreneurs were Party members. By 2006 that figure reached 38 percent and was rising (compared to about 5 percent Party membership for China's population as a whole). Surveys showed that many more businessmen would like to join the Party if they could get in.[46] Capitalists frequently see joining the Party as a good business decision because it allows them to network with powerful government officials. Some businessmen have actually been selected for government offices. A number of them currently serve in government legislatures from the local level through the National People' Congress.

Unlike Russia, where the creation of a private sector was equally corrupt and also tilted towards party or KGB insiders, China's new rich are more diverse and diffuse. So, unlike Russia, there is no small group of oligarchs who dominate the new economy. Even if the new capitalist entrepreneurs wanted to push for democracy, as they have done elsewhere, they are too unorganized and dispersed to challenge the political system. But, given their cozy relationship with the Party and the government, they also have shown no interest in mounting such a challenge.

CONCLUSION: CHINA'S UNCERTAIN FUTURE

For more than 20 years experts on China have debated that nation's future. In 1989, as communist governments were tottering in Eastern Europe and Mikhail Gorbachev was opening up the Soviet political system, many analysts believed that China's mass, student-led demonstrations for democracy would soon bring down its authoritarian political system. Instead, the Chinese regime has proven to be far more resilient than the crumbling communist governments of the Soviet Union and Eastern Europe. The CCP crushed the democracy movement and has managed to control unrest since then.

Since the Tiananmen democracy movement there has been no massive protests that compare to those demonstrations. At the same time, living standards have improved impressively, many personal freedoms have been expanded, much of the population has become more knowledgeable (through the Internet, foreign travel, or study abroad) of alternative ideas from the outside world, and educational levels have risen. As Bruce Dickson has observed, "For the vast majority of Chinese, the political atmosphere is more relaxed and less obtrusive than in the Maoist period."[47]

Yet in the past decades the number of peasant, worker, and middle-class protest demonstrations, strikes, and riots has grown substantially. Several years ago one analyst put the number of riots, strikes, demonstrations, and other types of collective protest at about 90,000 annually.[48] Thus, political scientists continue to debate two basic issues regarding Chinese politics: First, how stable is the government, and how much of a challenge to stability does the growing number of citizen protests constitute? Second, if the coming years do bring important political changes to the country, are they likely to move China toward greater democracy or to reinforce authoritarianism?

The Growth of Citizen Protests

Since the early 1990s, government controls and restrictions on citizens have been considerably relaxed. As we have noted, few Chinese, not even CCP members, believe in Marxism any more, much less its radical Maoist version. Instead the Party has staked its legitimacy on nationalism, stability, and rising living standards. Against those pillars, the regime faces a substantial amount of popular disillusionment and frequent protest.

Peasant villagers, who comprised 80 percent of China's inhabitants at the time of Mao's death, still constitute about half of the country's population. They were the backbone of Mao's revolution, and for several decades continued to be the communist government's most reliable supporters. Since the 1990s, however, there has been a surge in rural unrest despite the general improvement in the peasantry's standard of living. In 1997 approximately 900,000 peasants in nine of China's 22 provinces took part in either group demonstrations or collective petition drives, mostly directed against local officials. That number spiked at 5 million farmers in 1999 and then fell back somewhat to two million in 2003. Since 2005, the Chinese government has stopped publishing statistics on the number of protests.[49] Although most of these protests have been small and peaceful, a growing number involve hundreds of demonstrators— sometimes thousands—and many erupt into violence, with the worst riots resulting in the deaths of 100 or more protesters and up to 20 policemen.

Even though the issue has not been the focus of organized protests, many peasants deeply resent the government's population control strategy, known as the one-child policy. It limits families in China's cities to one child, a number that coincides with the preferences of most young urban couples, who generally don't feel they can afford a second. In the countryside, however, farmers usually wish to have more children to work the land, and they are especially anxious to have sons. For that reason, the government has allowed many villagers to have a second child, but only under certain circumstances. If a rural family's first child is female, they are permitted to have a second one.* An unknown but significant number of peasants, who know (through ultrasound or other tests) that the second child is also going to be a girl, have abortions. Many others have the child but abandon her to orphanages (whose children are almost entirely girls) or, sometimes, commit infanticide.

The urban working class is theoretically the core constituency of the CCP (and all communist parties), and they trailed only the peasantry in their initial support for the Party. In recent years, however, several issues have sparked labor unrest. Undoubtedly the greatest cause of worker dissatisfaction is the many layoffs that take place when industries shifted from state- to private-sector ownership. Like many state-owned industries (including the Soviet Union's and Mexico's), SOEs often had bloated payrolls in order to create extra employment and solidify worker support for the ruling party. Because of such inefficiencies, most state enterprises regularly lose money. For years, state banks lent excessively to money-losing SOEs with little expectation of getting their money back. Two things have changed. First, many SOEs have been transferred to private owners who trim their payrolls. Second, because state banks could no longer afford to subsidize insolvent state enterprises, SOEs have been forced to become more efficient, partly by firing unneeded workers. From 1995 to 2003 alone, 55 million workers were laid off in a country that had previously guaranteed them lifetime employment (known as "the iron rice bowl"). Although a lot of them found new jobs, many others were unable to find work or had to settle for jobs with lower wages and benefits. As of 2000, *official* urban unemployment stood at 20 million workers, a figure that surely underestimated the real total. More recently the actual number of unemployed may have been as high as 100 million during the current global recession.

In the past decade or so, there have been a growing number of worker strikes—all of them illegal—protesting layoffs or complaining about the size of severance payments. Some of these have been very large, and some have become violent. For example, in 2002, tens of thousands of laid-off workers protested in the city of Daqing when a state-owned petroleum company failed to pay them their promised severance pay. Protests by terminated workers have spread, particularly in the northeast, home to some of the country's most outdated industrial plants. In 2008 the government introduced a new labor law designed to give workers expanded rights, greater job security, and guaranteed severance pay. More recently, strikes by employed workers seeking higher wages and better working conditions have broken out at a number of foreign-owned firms, most notably at companies supplying parts for Honda and Toyota assembly plants. At the giant electronics firm Foxconn—whose 300,000 workers manufacture iPhones, iPods, and Hewlett-Packard computers, among other products—10 worker suicides in the first five months of 2010 convinced the company to offer a 66 percent performance-based wage hike. The coastal city of Guangdong had 36 strikes in 48 days, all aimed at foreign firms. Striking workers are also using technology to garner public support. In a recent strike of 1,700 workers at the Honda Lock auto parts factory, strikers sent out cell-phone photos of security guards roughing up employees, texted strikers with coordinating instructions that bypassed government censors, and sent photos and text messages to the general public and to striking workers elsewhere.[50]

---

* If their first child is a boy, a rural family is allowed to have a second child only if they wait five years.

The Resilience of Communist Rule

The worker and peasant protests just described are but two of the problems facing China's current leadership. Other difficulties include the exploitation and poverty of the country's migrant workers and the rising urban crime rate widely blamed on those migrants; resistance from ethnic minorities; alternative faiths and religious sects such as the repressed Falun Gong, whose millions of followers reject government authority; and the urban middle class and university students, who have lost faith in Marxist ideology.

Small wonder that for years many specialists have predicted that China would soon move to a more democratic political system or that the communist regime would collapse into a chaotic and uncertain future. Neither of those two scenarios now seems likely in the foreseeable future. Why has Communist Party rule been so resilient?

More than anything else Party leaders since Deng Xiaoping have legitimized their power, based on rapid economic growth and enormous improvements in most people's living standards. With per capita income now more than 18 times higher than it was in 1980, greater availability of coveted consumer products, and much longer life expectancy, few Chinese are willing to risk those gains for the unknown risks of a major political transformation. Indeed, the emerging capitalist class and members of the middle class, historically the lead actors in democratic transitions, either are Red capitalists, who depend on the CCP and the government for their newfound wealth, or they have too much to lose in any transformation and fear government repression too much to challenge the regime. As we have seen, a large portion of China's richest businessmen today were Communist Party activists before going into business. The crushing of the 1989 democracy movement and the years of oppression that followed caused university students and young professionals to withdraw from politics and political protest. Today, young adults generally seem more interested in making money than in campaigning for political reform.

At the same time, after years of civil war followed by the instability of the Maoist era (including the Great Leap Forward and the Cultural Revolution) and the political repression and aftermath of Tiananmen Square, most Chinese credit the current CCP leadership with the comparative tranquility of the past 20 years. Finally, China's transformation from one of the world's poorer nations to a global economic powerhouse has been a source of enormous national pride as symbolized by Beijing's extremely successful 2008 summer Olympics. For all these things most Chinese credit the CCP and are wary of major political change.

Indeed, an international poll taken six months before the 2008 Olympics found that 86 percent of Chinese respondents said the country was headed in the right direction (up from 48 percent in 2002), by far the highest percentage of the 24 countries where the survey was conducted. Australia was a distant second, with 61 percent believing that their country was headed in the right direction, while in the United States the number was only 23 percent. Similarly, the Chinese had the highest rate of satisfaction with their economy (82 percent, up from 52 percent in 2002).[51]

While those results were surely influenced by the fact that the Chinese media usually report mostly good news about the country and by higher national pride generated by the Olympics, it seems clear that the country's economic boom had bought substantial popular satisfaction and that the government uses that satisfaction to support its own legitimacy.

Another important element that has allowed the CCP to maintain control is its impressive flexibility, in contrast to many fallen authoritarian regimes that lacked such adaptability. Perhaps the greatest innovations came after the death of Mao Zedong under the leadership of Deng Xiaoping. Faced with a population that was exhausted from the Cultural Revolution and the previous mass political campaigns, Deng and his successors moved away from the constant political propaganda and the frequent mobilizations that had so intruded into Chinese life. As long as they did not challenge the authority of the Party, people were freer to choose their own lifestyle, to travel, and to enjoy music and dress styles from abroad. At the same time, Deng rejected numerous Marxist dictates and started the economy on a path toward the free market. Unlike Gorbachev's failed economic initiatives in the Soviet Union, Chinese economic reform succeeded spectacularly (although with some negative consequences noted previously).

One of the greatest challenges (and sources of discontent) the country's present leaders—Party General Secretary (and President) Hu Jintao and Prime Minister Wen Jiabao—have had to deal with is the growing economic inequality brought about by China's market reforms. From the early stages of their administration, the two have called for "harmonious socialist development," meaning growth that improves the lot of those who have gained the least from China's economic boom: the peasantry, urban migrants, and residents of the country's less-developed interior (central and western) regions. Often Hu's and Wen's rhetoric has outstripped their accomplishment, but they have introduced some important changes designed to assist the poor. Perhaps the most important reform has been reducing the burdensome taxes that peasants have to pay. Many villagers have benefitted from state subsidies. At the same time, the government has increased its spending on rural health care, allocated greater funds for the less developed interior regions in China's central and western regions, and funded recent medical-school graduates who are willing to serve one or two years in those regions. It has also extended state and employer medical insurance more broadly.

In 2005, the regime announced new, long-term policies for agriculture designed to raise rural incomes. These included "funding for agricultural research and technology, protecting farmland against illegal confiscation, supporting irrigation and environmental projects, and directing more investment and credit toward the countryside."[52] Authorities also declared expanded programs of rural benefits in the areas of education, health care, and welfare. Earlier we noted that the government issued plans in 2009 to spend $123 billion over the next two years to expand to build a health insurance system that would cover 90 percent of the population and promised to build 700,000 new rural health clinics. But perhaps the most potentially significant rural reform related to control over farmland. Under Deng Xiaoping's sweeping reform, farming was decollectivized as the former agricultural cooperatives were parceled out to family-controlled plots. While the peasant recipients have had effective control of their farms, they could not own them. Instead the land was leased from the cooperative for 30 years, and the farmers could not sell or release their land. Under the country's 2008 agricultural reform law, peasants, for the first time, were granted the right to lease their land use rights to other farmers or corporations. They may now also swap part or all of their leased land with other farmers. If this reform is widely implemented, peasants will be close to having the full rights of land owners (though they still only control the land for a 30-year period) and will more fully be integrated into the market economy. Hopefully, this would also reduce the level of control and exploitation by local CCP officials.

Influenced by Hu's populist rhetoric and his reform measures, peasant protest leaders tend to see the national government and CCP as their patrons. Thus, if they are discontent with the political system, and many are, they blame their woes on *local* CCP and government officials. Consequently, rural protests are almost always confined to one, or occasionally a few, villages, and currently pose no threat to the national political system. In the cities, the government has responded to the current global economic crisis and the layoffs of millions of blue-collar workers by expanding the number of jobs in state-owned enterprises for the first time in many years.

The State's Capacity for Repression

Although the CCP, under Hu Jintao's leadership, has tried to redress some of the inequalities in Chinese society, has been more tolerant of rural protests and urban strikes, and has been more responsive to citizen complaints, it still has set strict limits on protest and dissent. The authorities often allow peasant protests, workers' strikes, and middle-class demonstrations as long as they focus on economic issues or decry corruption by local Party or government officials. In recent years there have been a growing number of protests against factories, power plants, mines, and other sources of environmental pollution that have exposed the surrounding population to serious health hazards. In a limited number of such economic and environmental campaigns, protestors have actually gained some of their objectives.

But should the authorities view the protests as essentially political—that is, threatening political instability, challenging the national CCP or government, or questioning the absolute power of the Party—they are crushed ruthlessly. Indeed, in these situations the Hu government has probably been more repressive than its predecessors.

So although China's overall level of personal freedom remains higher than it was prior to 1990, at times Hu has imposed some of the strictest limits on the press and independent political analysis in recent memory. For example, in a 2004 speech to the Communist Party Central Committee, he warned that "hostile forces" were trying to undermine the Party by "using the banner of political reform to promote Western bourgeois parliamentary democracy, human rights, and freedom of the press." Noting that openness had led to the collapse of Soviet communism, Hu insisted that the media cannot "provide a channel for incorrect ideological points of view."

And the state's capacity to repress protests or other forms of dissent is enormous. As Minxin Pei has observed:

> The regime maintains the People's Armed Police, a well-trained and well-equipped anti-riot force of 250,000. In addition, China's secret police are among the most capable in the world and are augmented by a vast network of informers.[53]

In short, the prospects for meaningful democratic reform in the next decade or two seem remote. Predictions beyond that time frame are difficult for any country, even more so in countries such as China with secretive governments and muzzled mass media. Few analysts forecast the fall of Soviet communism before it happened. There are, however, a number of important hazards that could weaken or topple the Chinese regime. Perhaps the biggest challenge facing the CCP leadership is maintaining the dynamic economic growth which has been the cornerstone of its support. Unlike strong democracies, which have multiple sources of legitimacy, including the very fact that they are accountable to the public, most authoritarian regimes rely on performance-based legitimacy—that is, popular support depends on their performing well, particularly in the economic sphere. According to some estimates, China's economy must grow nearly 10 percent annually if it is to provide enough jobs for the millions of workers, including rural-to-urban migrants, entering the urban work force each year. Since 1979, the economy has been able to grow on average by 9 to 10 percent annually. It is not certain that China can continue that remarkable record in the coming decades. Should the impressive growth in living standards over the past 30 years level off or should real income actually decline for a period of time, we might expect increased working-class and migrant unrest and greater middle-class alienation from the political system.

But ironically, while some analysts believe that slower economic growth would pose the greatest threat to continued CCP dominance, others believe that in the long run *sustained* economic growth is likely to eventually erode the authoritarian communist regime and open the way to a peaceful democratic transition. In Europe, East Asian countries such as South Korea and Taiwan, and Latin American nations such as Brazil and Mexico, democracy has usually emerged in countries with comparatively higher per capita income and literacy rates. Economic development normally increases the size and political influence of the bourgeoisie, the middle class, and organized labor, all of whom have historically been associated with democratic change. Thus, George Gilboy and Benjamin Read argue that

> Time is on the side of all ... who wish to see greater freedom and more enlightened government [in China]. A trend toward liberalization is likely to continue gaining strength because the drivers of reform, a robust society interacting with an adaptive CCP, are likely to strengthen.[54]

An explosion in the number of **NGOs** (several hundred thousand of them) has opened up new avenues for expressing citizens' opinions. Many current civil society activities were unthinkable before the 1990s. For example, the independent Institute of Public and Environmental Affairs operates a website that has "named and shamed" thousands of private and state-owned polluting companies. In response to public pressures, state environmental regulators turned down over $90 billion of proposed factories and other projects in 2007 alone.

◆ ◆ ◆

Key Terms and Concepts _____

cadres	open-door policy
collectives	People's Liberation Army (PLA)
communes	political liberalization
Cultural Revolution	princelings
expert faction	Red capitalists
Falun Gong	Red faction
Great Leap Forward	Red Guards
Kuomintang (KMT)	state-owned enterprises (SOEs)
Long March	Tiananmen Square
NGO	warlords

DISCUSSION QUESTIONS

1. *What was new and distinct about Mao Zedong's interpretation and application of Marxism–Leninism (communism) in China? How has China's application of communist principles changed since the death of Mao?*

2. *What have been the major accomplishments of the economic reforms instituted under the leadership of Deng Xiaoping and his successors? What are some of the major social and political problems that arose out of those reforms?*

3. *China seems to be the first communist nation to produce an orderly process for changing the country's top political leaders. What changes have been introduced to guide that process?*

4. *Since the end of the 1970s, China has moved from a communist (command) economy to a largely free-market (capitalist) one. Describe the main features of that conversion. What are the potential political consequences of that change?*

5. *China stands today as the last major nation with a political system dominated by its Communist Party. What developments in recent years suggest that it has started a slow transition to democracy? What evidence suggests that there will be no such transition in the coming decades?*

6. *What is a communist capitalist in China? What does the existence of such businessmen tell us about the current nature of Chinese politics?*

Notes

1. David Barboza, "China Leader Encourages Criticism of Government," *The New York Times* (January 26, 2011), www.nytimes.com/2011/01/27/world/asia/27china.html?_r=1&emc=eta1/.
2. World Bank, "Gross National Income Per Capita," World Development Indicators database, July 1, 2010; CIA, *The World Factbook* (online publication, updated July 5, 2011). Per capita income is calculated to reflect purchasing power (PPP).
3. Orville Shell quoted in *China's Transition*, by Andrew J. Nathan (New York: Columbia University Press, 1997), p. 227.
4. James Wang, *Contemporary Chinese Politics* (Englewood Cliffs, NJ: Prentice Hall, 1989), p. 13.
5. Roderick MacFarquhar, *The Origins of the Cultural Revolution*, vol. 2, *The Great Leap Forward (1958–60)* (New York: Columbia University Press, 1983).
6. Harry Harding, *China's Second Revolution* (Washington, DC: Brookings 1987), p. 12.
7. Harding, *China's Second Revolution*, pp. 30–31.
8. Research at the World Bank, "Fighting Poverty: Findings and Lessons from China's Success" (2005), http://econ.worldbank.org/WBSITE/EXTERNAL/EXTDEC/EXTRESEARCH/.
9. Nicholas Lardy, "Agricultural Reforms in China," *Journal of International Affairs* (Winter 1986): 91–104.
10. Harding, *China's Second Revolution*, p. 106; Marc Blecher, "The Reorganization of the Countryside," in *Reforming the Revolution*, ed. Robert Benewick and Paul Wingrove (Chicago: Dorsey, 1988), p. 100.
11. Teressa Wright, "Tenuous Tolerance in China's Countryside," in *Chinese Politics: State, Society and the Market*, eds. Peter Hays Gries and Stanley Rosen (New York: Routledge, 2010), p. 115.
12. The World Bank Group, *Transition Newsletter* (February–March 2001), pp. 13–14. http://worldbank.org/transitionnewsletter/febmarch2001/pgs13–14.htm.
13. Wright, "Tenuous Tolerance," p. 115.
14. George J. Gilboy and Benjamin L. Read, "Political and Social Reform in China: Alive and Walking," *The Washington Quarterly* 33, no. 3 (Summer 2008), p. 149.
15. Mixin Pei, *Corruption Threatens China's Future* (Washington, DC: Carnegie Endowment for International Peace, Policy Brief 55, October 2007).
16. Russell Hsiao, "Red Cadres and Red-Hat Businessmen," *Asia Times Online* (June 26, 2010), www.atimes.com.
17. Richard Baum, "Jiang Takes Command: The Fifteenth National Party Congress and Beyond," in *China under Jiang Zemin*, eds. Hung-mao Tien and Yun-han Chu (Bolder, CO: Lynne Rienner Publishers, 2000), p. 30, fn. 20.

18. C. Fred Bergsten, et. al., *China's Rise: Challenges and Opportunities* (Washington, DC: Peterson Institute for International Economics and the Center for Strategic and International Studies, 2008), p. 98.
19. Carl Riskin, Zhao Renwei, and Li Shi, eds., *China's Retreat from Equality* (Armonk, NY: Sharpe, 2001), chaps. 1 and 2.
20. World Health Org, *Core Health Indicators*, 2002, http://apps.who.int/whosis/database/core/core_select.cfm.
21. Yanzhong Huang and Mixin Pei, "China's Health Reform: Not Just a Policy Failure" Lecture presented to the Carnegie Endowment for International Peace, Washington, D.C., April 24, 2007.
22. All of the statistics in this paragraph not otherwise credited come from Chee Hew, *Health Care in China* (IBM Institute for Business Value, 2006), www-05.ibm.com/de/healthcare/downloads/health care_china.pdf.
23. Michael Bristow, "Beijing's Poor Visit Illegal Clinics, *BBC Website* (November 19, 2009), http://news.bbc.co.uk/2/hi/health/8358301.stm.
24. Edward Wong, "China Plans Universal Health Care," *The New York Times* (January 22, 2009); Drew Thompson, "China's Health-Care Challenge," *Wall Street Journal Asia* (April 16, 2009).
25. World Bank, "China Facts" (2007), www.worldbank.org/.
26. Bergsten et. al., *China's Rise*, p. 80
27. Bruce J. Dickson and Maria Rost Rublee, "Membership Has Its Privileges," *Comparative Political Studies* 33, no. 1(2000), 87–112.
28. Jeffrey N. Wasserstrom, "China's Brave New World," *Current History* 102, no. 665 (September 2003): 267.
29. *The New York Times*, May 2, 2002.
30. Yiu-chung Wong, *From Deng Xiaoping to Jiang Zemin* (Lanham, MD: University Press of America, 2005), p. 273.
31. Peter Hays Gries and Stanley Rosen, eds., *State and Society in Twenty-First Century China* (New York and London: Routledge Curzon, 2004), p. 242
32. Ellis Joffe, "The People's Liberation Army and Politics: After the Fifteenth Party Congress," in *China under Jiang Zemin*, pp. 88–89.
33. Yongnian Zheng, "The 16th National Congress of the Communist Party," and Gang Lin, "Leadership Transition, Intra-Party Democracy and Institution Building in China," in *Leadership in a Changing China*, ed. Weixing Chen and Yang Zhong (New York: Palgrave Macmillan, 2005), pp. 16–17 and 38–70.
34. Wang, *Contemporary Chinese Politics*, pp. 137.
35. June Teufel Dreyer, *China's Political System*, 6th edition (New York: Longman Publishing Group, 2008), pp. 179–184.
36. Nicholas Kristof, "A Clampdown in China," *The New York Times* (May 17, 2005).
37. Howard W. French, "Despite Flaws, Rights in China Have Expanded," *The New York Times* (August 2, 2008). That assessment is still valid today.
38. This box is drawn primarily from Philip P. Pan, *Out of Mao's Shadow* (New York: Simon & Schuster, 2008), pp. 199–234.
39. Ibid, p. 216.
40. Human Rights Watch, "China: Political Prisoner Exposes Brutality in Police-Run Mental Hospital," www.hrw.org/en/news/2005/10/31/china-political-prisoner-exposes-brutality-police-run-mental-hospital.
41. Mixin Pei,"Racing against Time: Institutional Decay and Renewal in China," in *China Briefing: The Contradictions of Change*, ed. William A. Joseph (Armonk, NY: Sharpe, 1997), p. 18.
42. Barrington Moore Jr., *Social Origins of Dictatorship and Democracy* (Boston: Beacon Press, 1967).
43. "The World's Billionaires, 2011," *Forbes*, www.forbes.com/.
44. Bruce J. Dickson, *Wealth into Power* (New York: Cambridge University Press, 2008), p. 208.
45. Ibid, p. 220.
46. Jing Yang "Red Capitalist: The Rising Chinese Private Entrepreneurs," in *China in an Era of Transition*, eds. Reza Hasmath and Jennifer Hsu (NY: Palgrave Macmillan, 2009), p. 176.
47. Bruce J. Dickson, "Dilemmas of Party Adaptation: The CCP's Strategy for Survival," in *Chinese Politics*, eds. Gries and Rosen, p. 23.
48. Michael Bonnin, "Perspectives on Social Stability after the Fifteenth Congress," in *China under Jiang Zemin*, p. 155.
49. Timothy Weston, "The Iron Man Weeps," in Gries and Rosen, *State and Society*, pp. 67–86.
50. "In China, Labor Movement Enabled by New Technology," *The New York Times* (June 17, 2010).
51. Pew Global Attitudes Project data reported in "Economy Helps Make Chinese the Leaders in Optimism, 24 Nation Survey Finds," *The New York Times* (July 23, 2008).
52. Manfred Elstrom, "The Meaning of China's New Agricultural Policy," China Elections and Governance website (April 2005), www.chinaelections.org.
53. Mixin Pei, "Will the Chinese Communist Party Survive the Crisis?" www.carnegieendowment.org/publications/?fa=view&id=22847.
54. Gilboy and Read, "Political and Social…," p. 159.

CHAPTER 14

The Politics of Developing Nations

Hundreds of Thousands of Egyptian pro-democracy protestors gather in Cairo's Tahrir Square in one of the ongoing demonstrations that led to the ouster of longtime dictator, Hosni Mubarak. These protests were a crucial part of the wave of anti-dictatorial revolts that swept across the Arab world, which came to be known as the Arab Spring.

- **The Meaning of Underdevelopment**
- **Theories of Under-development and Development**
- **Sources of Political Conflict**
- **Problems of Political Participation**

- **Women in Third World Society and Politics**
- **Third World Political Institutions**
- **Conclusion: Recent Developments and Future Trends**

Even in the most modern and affluent nations, politics often evokes passionate conflict as, for example, in the last U.S. presidential election. Such conflicts tend to be more intense in the world's less-developed countries—sometimes called the **Third World**—where the scarcity of government resources may provoke bitter struggles between different political parties, regions, religions, and ethnic groups.*

For example, in recent decades Somalia has become a **failed state** where government is unable to provide many of the basic functions of a sovereign state (protecting national borders, maintaining public safety, and providing basic services such as education and sanitation). Currently the "national government" controls only a few blocks of Mogadishu, the country's capital. Militias tied to al-Qaeda currently rule much of the country and periodically bomb strategic targets. Libya appears to have recently ended a deadly civil war in which a large portion of the population rose up and overthrew a 40-year tyranny, at the cost of thousands of lives. And Mexico, a relatively more advanced Third World country, has been virtually paralyzed by a

---

* The term *Third World* refers to the politically and economically less-developed nations of Africa, Asia, Latin America, and the Middle East. The term was coined to differentiate them from the world's industrial democracies (the First World) and from Soviet-bloc countries (the Second World). Although the origins of this title are now dated because of the collapse of the Second World, the term is still commonly used interchangeably with *developing world* and *less-developed countries* (LDCs).

bloody and seemingly endless war against its drug-trafficking cartels. Throughout the developing world, many millions of people live on less than $2 per day.

Yet there are also signs of progress and reasons for optimism. The world's two most populous nations, China and India—whose combined population of 2.5 billion constitutes more than one-third of the world's total—have enjoyed rapid economic growth for a number of years. China has reduced the number of people living in extreme poverty by 300 to 400 million since 1990. In the past decade more than 100 million Indians have escaped poverty and entered the middle class. Other Third World economies—including Brazil, South Korea, Turkey, and Vietnam—have also grown impressively and have escaped the recent global economic crisis more success-fully than have the developed Western nations. In the political arena, countries such as Indonesia, Mexico, and South Africa have successfully made the transition from authoritarian government to democracy. In Egypt, Tunisia, and Syria hundreds of thousands of people have taken to the streets and risked their lives in their struggles for democracy (See A Closer Look 14.2). And countries such as Chile, Cuba, and Mongolia have raised their literacy rates to 97 percent or more.

THE MEANING OF UNDERDEVELOPMENT

Still, the list of difficulties and challenges in the developing world remains immense. In recent times there have been: famines in various countries including North Korea, Ethiopia, Burma, and Chad (most of them worsened by government policy); extended rebellions and civil wars in El Salvador, Lebanon, Libya, Sudan, and the Congo; growing economic inequalities in Mexico and much of Latin America; war-fare between Sunni and Shi'ite Muslims in Iraq; and continuing political repression in countries such as Burma, Syria, and Iran. To many Westerners, these nations seem to be constantly in crisis. But developing nations have made important political and economic progress in a number of significant areas that are unlikely to attract much Western media attention. Democracy has spread broadly in Latin America, Asia, and parts of Africa. The number of ethnic conflicts in Africa and Asia, though still sizeable, has decreased over time. The percentage of the Third World's popula-tion living in extreme poverty has declined, while literacy rates and life expectancy have grown. Efforts by governments and nongovernmental organizations (NGOs) promise to reduce the worldwide rate of malaria, meningitis, polio, and other fre-quently fatal diseases.

The more than 150 nations that compose the developing world are a disparate group. An elite few, including Singapore and Hong Kong, have per capita incomes that equal or exceed those of developed nations such as France or Italy.[1] Others, including Trinidad-Tobago and Costa Rica, are economically well off and have polit-ical systems that are relatively stable and effective. But all of them, even the most sta-ble and affluent, share some important elements of social, economic, or political underdevelopment, be it substantial illiteracy, great vulnerability to world commodity prices, sharp social and economic inequalities, political corruption, or authoritarian government. In many **less-developed countries (LDCs)**, several factors, such as poverty, illiteracy, ethnic conflict, foreign intervention, and sharp class divisions, combine to produce political instability, government repression, or both.

Africa, Asia, Latin America, Caribbean, Middle East

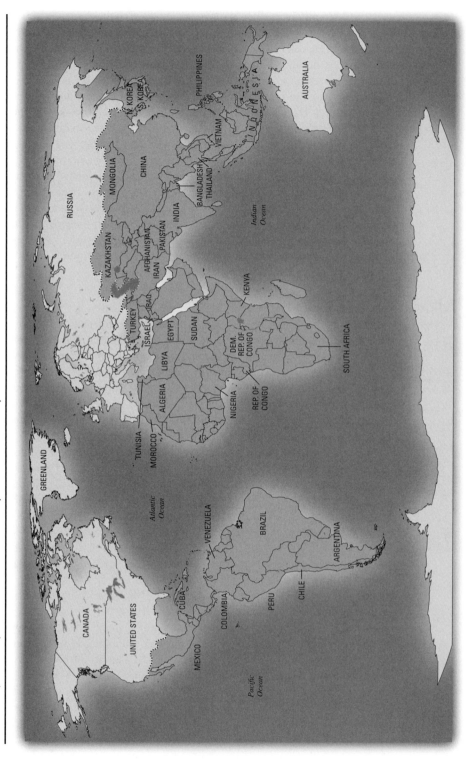

What accounts for the Third World's political and economic underdevelopment? No single answer suffices. This chapter will evaluate the nature of political and socioeconomic development in Africa, Asia, Latin America, and the Middle East. To begin our analysis, we define and examine two distinct but closely related phenomena: socioeconomic underdevelopment and political underdevelopment.

Economic and Social Underdevelopment

Upon first visiting many LDCs, outsiders are often shocked by the widespread poverty: people living in shacks, beggars in the street, and inadequate infrastructure, to name a few visible signs. Using categories established by the World Bank, Table 14.1 presents basic economic indicators for two highly developed nations (the United States and Norway); two upper-income Asian countries (South Korea and Singapore); two upper-middle-income Latin American nations (Mexico and Colombia); an upper-middle-income African country (South Africa); a lower-middle-income, highly industrialized Asian giant (China); and a low-income African country (Ethiopia).

Column 1 indicates each country's per capita income, adjusted for purchasing power (**parity purchasing power, or PPP**). Clearly, there are broad differences between developing economies. South Korea and Singapore are **newly industrialized countries (NICs)** whose per capita incomes are comparable to those of advanced industrialized nations but which continue to demonstrate aspects of political and social underdevelopment, such as high inequality (Singapore) or substantial political corruption (South Korea). More typically, however, LDCs have annual incomes that are somewhere between one-fourth (Mexico) and one-60th (Ethiopia) the level of the United States or Norway.

A country's average income gives us some measure of its standard of living, but the way in which that income is distributed is equally important. If two countries have the same average income, but income in one of them is more concentrated in a few hands, that nation will have more people living in poverty.

Columns 2 and 3 of Table 14.1 indicate whether each nation's total income is more concentrated or more equally distributed. Column 2 presents each country's

TABLE 14.1	Measures of Economic Development		
Country	**Per Capita Income (PPP)**	**Distribution of Family Income (Gini Index)**	**Percent of National Income Earned by the Richest 20%**
Norway	$57,400	25.0	36%
United States	$46,000	45.0	46%
Singapore	$52,200	48.1	50–55%*
South Korea	$28,100	31.3	39%
Mexico	$13,200	48.2	57%
South Africa	$10,300	65.0	65%
Colombia	$ 9,200	58.5	61%
China	$ 6,600	41.5	47%
Ethiopia	$ 900	30.0	48%

*Estimate

SOURCE: CIA, *World Factbook 2010* (Cols. 1–2); World Bank, *World Development Indicators 2010* (Col. 3).

Gini index. Based on income data, each country is assigned a score, which, theoretically, can range from 0.0 (if a country has total equality) to 100.0 (the highest possible inequality). In the real world, Gini indices currently run from about 25.0 (Norway and Sweden) to 70.7 (Namibia). The U.S. index is 45.0, ranking it as one of the most unequal highly industrialized nations. Although developed nations generally have more equal income distribution than poorer countries do—the Nordic countries, Japan, and Germany are amongst the world's most equal nations—this is not always true. For example, as measured by the Gini index, income is more equally distributed in India, Pakistan, and Yemen than in the United States or Britain. Table 14.1 also reveals considerable variation *among* developing countries. While income is fairly concentrated in South Africa, Colombia, Mexico and Singapore, it is relatively evenly distributed in Ethiopia and South Korea.

The last column in Table 14.1 offers a more graphic gauge of income distribution. It indicates the portion of each country's national income earned by the wealthiest 20 percent of the population (the "upper class"). Thus, in the United States the richest 20 percent of the population earns almost half (46 percent) of the national income, a substantially higher share than in Norway (36 percent) or South Korea (39 percent), but much lower than Colombia (61 percent) or South Africa (65 percent).

Several factors underlie the high rates of inequality in many developing countries. On the one hand, per capita incomes in the more economically developed cities tend to be as much as four or five times greater than in rural areas. Within the countryside itself, particularly in most of Latin America and parts of Africa, land ownership is usually highly concentrated, making peasants the poorest group of all. This commonly stimulates substantial migration from countryside to city. As some Third World cities have doubled their populations in little more than a decade, sprawling slum neighborhoods have developed, lacking adequate sanitation or water facilities. This creates further layers of inequality—between the urban population as a whole and the rural poor and, within the cities, between the middle class and unskilled workers.

Even though economic growth and modernization usually lead to greater inequality initially, government policies can alter that relationship significantly. Nations such as Taiwan, South Korea, Costa Rica, and Cuba, with very different economic and political systems, have achieved more equitable income distributions through redistribution of farmland from landlords to peasants, mass education, and public welfare programs. More typically, countries such as Brazil and Mexico have achieved strong economic growth but have poor income distribution, while others, such as Cuba, have accomplished more equitable economic distribution but only slow growth. Unfortunately, some countries—including Zimbabwe and Bolivia—have produced both weak growth and high inequality. Only a few—such as Indonesia, South Korea, and Taiwan—have achieved both high growth and relative income equality.

While per capita income and income distribution data are important indicators of a country's economic level, they do not tell us all we need to know about the population's well-being. Not surprisingly, more affluent countries tend to have better health care and educational systems. Yet Table 14.2 indicates that countries that make concerted efforts in those areas may achieve better social conditions for their citizens than do some countries that are better-off but less committed. The **Human Development Index (HDI)**—column 1—is probably the best measure of a population's quality of life. It is a

TABLE 14.2	**Indicators of Social Development**			
	HDI (Rank)	**Life Expectancy (Years)**	**Adult Literacy (Percent)**	**National Income Per Capita Rank Minus HDI Rank**
Norway	.938 (1)	81.0	99.0	+2
United States	.902 (4)	79.6	99.0	+5
South Korea	.877 (12)	79.8	99.0	+16
Chile	.783 (45)	78.8	96.5	+11
Saudi Arabia	.752 (55)	73.3	85.0	−20
Brazil	.699 (73)	72.9	90.0	−3
China	.663 (89)	73.5	93.3	−4
Egypt	.620 (101)	70.5	66.4	−8
India	.519 (119)	64.4	66.0	−6
Nigeria	.423 (142)	48.4	72.0	−12
Ethiopia	.328 (157)	56.1	35.9	−2

SOURCE: United Nations Development Programme (UNDP), *Human Development Report, 2009 and 2010*, http://hdr.undp.org/en/.

composite index combining a country's per capita income, average life expectancy, and educational level. That index theoretically can range from a high of 1.000 (the best possible score) to a low of 0.000. The table lists countries in the order of their HDI scores, from a high of .938 in Norway to a low of .328 in Ethiopia (column 1). The number in parentheses following each score indicates where that country ranks in the world compared to 168 other nations. Thus, Norway has the world's highest HDI score while Ethiopia ranks 157th. Columns 2 and 3, respectively, indicate each country's life expectancy at birth and its adult literacy rate.

During the past half century, many developing nations have realized important gains in life expectancy and adult literacy. Once it was common to encounter LDCs with life expectancies below 60 years and literacy rates under 50 percent. Table 14.2 reveals that today countries such as South Korea and Chile match the most developed nations in these dimensions. But Egypt, India, Nigeria, and Ethiopia clearly lag far behind. Other LDCs not shown in the table have even lower life expectancies, such as Zimbabwe (47 years) and Afghanistan (45 years). Similarly, some countries have lower literacy rates than Ethiopia, including Mali (26 percent) and Niger (29 percent).

Finally, the last column may have the most interesting statistic in this table. It compares a country's ranking in per capita income with its HDI ranking. Since HDI scores generally correlate with per capita income (i.e., richer countries tend to have the highest HDI scores), we would expect a wealthy country such as Norway to invest heavily in education and health care, thereby producing a high-ranking HDI. On the other hand, very poor countries, such as Ethiopia, have few resources to invest and so tend to have low HDI scores.

But other factors besides wealth influence how strong a country's HDI ranking is. Some LDCs, including some of the poorest nations and others that are better off, are particularly committed to improving their citizens' health care and education. Therefore, they devote a substantial portion of government expenditures to those areas, even if they have limited resources. Consequently, their global ranking on the HDI

A Picture of Poverty   Children play near their meager home in a Calcutta, India, slum.

is better than their per capita income would have predicted. In column 4, each country's HDI ranking is subtracted from its per capita income ranking. For example, in our table, Chile, which has the world's 56th highest per capita income (not shown in the table), manages to rank 45th in its HDI. So, when we subtract Chile's HDI ranking from its income ranking ($56 - 45 = 11$) we come up with a *positive* score for the last column of +11. Thus, Chile was an "overachiever" in that it has a better quality of life than its per capita income ranking would lead us to expect, presumably because the government has placed special emphasis on public health and education. Conversely, Nigeria ranks 130th in the world for per capita income but fares even worse on HDI (142nd), giving it a *negative* score of -12 (see the table's last column). Countries in the table with negative scores (most notably Saudi Arabia, Nigeria, and Egypt), are underachievers.

Why do some countries underachieve—that is, why do they fail to use their income effectively to improve their life expectancy, educational level, and per capita income? In Nigeria (-12), extensive corruption siphons off the country's oil income from beneficial government programs. Indeed, developing nations whose state funding comes heavily from oil exports tend to have negative scores. These include Venezuela (-9), Saudi Arabia (-20), and the United Arab Emirates (-28). Misuse of oil revenues is particularly severe if countries have repressive dictators who direct much of their nations' oil income to themselves and their inner circles. Finally, some countries have poor HDIs relative to their income partly because they do not provide women with adequate health care and educational opportunities. This is often true of Muslim nations such as Afghanistan and Morocco but holds for a number of non-Muslim African countries as well.[2]

Over the past 40 years or so, much of the developing world has achieved impressive gains in health and education, but serious shortfalls remain, and in some regions there has been backsliding. On the one hand, between the early 1970s and the end of the twentieth century, Third World infant mortality rates—the proportion of infants who die in the first year of life—fell by an impressive 40 percent. That decline and other health improvements lifted life expectancy from 53.4 years in 1960 to 66 years in 2007.[3] At the same time, however, since 1990 the AIDS pandemic in sub-Saharan Africa has reduced life expectancy dramatically in a dozen countries, including Botswana and South Africa.[4] Throughout the LDCs, even with lowered infant mortality, each *hour* an average of 1,200 children die, yielding an annual mortality toll that is 36 times greater than the 300,000 people killed in the Asian tsunami of 2004. And while the proportion of people living in extreme poverty (i.e., on less than $1.25 per day) has fallen substantially since 1981, that group still accounts for some 25 percent of the LDCs' population (down from 50 percent in 1981) and twice that figure in sub-Saharan Africa and South Asia.[5]

Political Underdevelopment and Development

Of course, underdevelopment also has a political component. Defining it, however, has been elusive at times, and some leading scholars have questioned the value of the term **political underdevelopment** itself.[6] With that caveat in mind, let us consider some definitions and characteristics of political underdevelopment and development.

Fundamental Definitions Nations suffering from low political development—most notably in Africa, Asia, and the Middle East—often have created their current government institutions—such as parliament or the bureaucracy—relatively recently compared to Western nations that have had their major institutions for centuries. Consequently, Third World institutions have not been around long enough to acquire their own traditions, while much of the population has yet to develop respect for them. If they perform poorly or are corrupt, their **legitimacy** is weakened even further.

Second, in developed countries, most political participation takes place "within the system"—that is, within regularized and legal channels such as elections or lobbying. In contrast, much of the political activity in many LDCs is illegal and sometimes violent. For example, the conflicting needs and interests of different ethnic groups may be solved peacefully through existing political institutions or may erupt into violence. More politically advanced Third World countries, such as Costa Rica and the Bahamas, have made progress relatively peacefully through interest group politics, negotiation, and legislation. By contrast, where within-system solutions have failed—as in Egypt, Indonesia, and Zimbabwe—political tensions have often provoked bloody conflict.

Finally, LDCs often lack the capacity to govern effectively. They may have great difficulty collecting necessary taxes, responding effectively to emergencies, or maintaining order. For example, during the 1970s, Nigeria and Mexico, major petroleum exporters, accumulated considerable wealth from their oil exports and appeared on the verge of an economic takeoff. But excessive external borrowing, wasteful spending, ineffective administration, and corruption all caused their governments to squander their opportunities and to plunge their countries into extended economic declines.

Democracy and Development   Before the late 1980s, most political scientists stressed two goals of political development: achieving political stability and establishing effective governments. More important, many of them suggested that achieving stability was the first priority, and other goals—such as democracy, social justice, and equity—would have to follow later. Some observers questioned whether democracy was yet attainable in Third World settings or even desirable at that time. In recent years, however, troubled by the numerous instances of government repression in the developing world, a growing number of analysts have concluded that democracy and social equity must be integral parts of political development.[7]

Beyond the prima facie moral argument that *all* societies, no matter how poor, should be protected from state repression and should be free to choose their own political leaders, most experts now agree that although democracy does not guarantee political stability or efficiency, in the long run those goals may be unattainable without it. Amartya Sen, a winner of a Nobel Prize in economics, has provided one additional advantage of democracy. He notes that among the many famines that have occurred in LDCs, none have taken place in a democratic country with a free press. Even when democracies such as India and Botswana have suffered droughts or floods, domestic and foreign public opinion (informed by a free press) have ensured that their governments take appropriate actions to avert famine. On the other hand, dictatorships in countries such as Ethiopia and Sudan have frequently ignored or covered up famines, or even enhanced them, when they have affected people in "enemy" regions or ethnicities. For example, the Nigerian military government used famine as a method of subduing the Ibo break-away state of Biafra (in the 1960s), while the Sudanese regime has limited foreign food aid to Darfur, where several rebel groups operate. Following Burma's recent, devastating cyclone, the military dictatorship first delayed foreign assistance and then permitted only limited external aid. It was less concerned about saving lives than in proving it could handle the situation itself and in limiting contacts between its people and foreign relief workers.

Other Manifestations of Political Underdevelopment   Let us now turn our attention to several political conditions that do not *define* political underdevelopment but are common characteristics of less-developed countries. Like economic resources, political influence in the developing world tends to be unequally distributed. Power is often concentrated in the hands of particular ethnic minorities or with economic and political elites (See A Closer Look 14.1). Furthermore, government policies frequently favor the urban upper and middle classes and, to a lesser extent, unionized blue-collar workers at the expense of the rural poor and unorganized urban workers, who together usually constitute the majority of the population.

The number of Third World **electoral democracies** (countries with free and fair contested elections, but which may violate the basic freedoms of their citizens) has grown substantially since the 1970s. But most developing nations still lack the fundamental standards of **liberal democracy**—free and fair elections and a government that respects its citizens' civil liberties. Despite gains in recent decades, most Third World

14.1

Kenya's Struggle for Development

When Kenya achieved independence from Britain in 1963, it was widely believed to have one of Africa's greatest potentials for political and economic development. Nearly half a century later, it has lived up to some of those expectations—for example, it has avoided the military takeovers that have bedeviled so much of the region, and has moved from one-party rule to multiparty electoral competition. Until recently, it was considered one of the most stable countries in the continent. But in other respects it has fallen far short of its promise, as it has endured periodic ethnic violence, rampant government corruption, and sporadic political repression. Thus, in many ways, it is emblematic of the mixed record of many Third World countries.

Kenyans are divided into more than 40 ethnic groups (tribes), with none accounting for as much as one-fourth of the country's total population. The Kikuyus are the largest ethnicity, with some 22 percent of the population. Prior to British colonization (1895–1963), Kenya had not suffered the violent ethnic clashes common to many other African countries. During the colonial era, however, the British pursued "divide-and-rule" strategies designed to pit one tribe against the other as a means of weakening anticolonial opposition.[11] For example, starting in 1915 they drove much of the Kalenjin and Masai population out of Kenya's best farmland—in the Rift Valley province—so that British settlers and plantation companies could grow cash crops such as coffee and tea. At the same time they invited in Kikuyus and others to work as tenant farmers and workers. After independence the Rift Valley was to become the focal point of ethnic conflict.

Unfortunately, Kenya's political leaders after independence exacerbated ethnic tensions. Jomo Kenyatta, the foremost figure in the independence struggle and Kenya's political leader from independence until his death (1963–1978), was a Kikuyu, a tribe prominent in the struggle against the British. His political party KANU (Kenya African National Union), which controlled national politics for nearly 40 years (1963–2002), was initially dominated by the Kikuyus but also drew support from the Luos and other ethnic groups. Like a number of other developing countries, Kenya's economy depends very heavily on the public sector, which employs about one-fifth of the nonagricultural workforce. Consequently, government patronage jobs are a key source of employment. Predictably, KANU supporters, especially Kikuyus, were the primary beneficiaries under Kenyatta, causing resentment among other tribes.

Furthermore, several ethnic groups also objected to the government's program resettling farmers in the fertile Rift Valley on land that the British had sized from its traditional owners and turned over to White settlers. As we have noted, prior to the colonial era that region had been populated primarily by Kalenjins. But after independence, when most of the colonial settlers left the country, the government transferred much of their farmland to Kikuyus, many of whose fellow tribesmen had worked for the White farmers after the Kalenjins had been expelled. When Kenyatta died, he was succeeded by his vice president, Daniel arap Moi, also a KANU leader but a Kalenjin. Moi, a cunning and repressive leader, governed for the next 24 years (1978–2002) as state patronage and land ownership policy in the Rift Valley shifted somewhat in favor of his tribe.

The formal structure of Kenyan government during the last four decades of the twentieth century also aggravated ethnic tensions. At that time, the nation's constitution and its political practice concentrated tremendous authority in the hands of the president. So even when the country opened up to multiparty elections in 1992, opposition parties in parliament were unable to check presidential power.[*] Consequently, presidential races have been fiercely contested. Given that office's grip on power, the major political parties and ethnic groups logically have viewed presidential elections after 1992 as "winner-takes-all" competitions. Small wonder that the greatest surges in ethnic violence have coincided with those contests.

---

[*] Following Kenyan independence, KANU dominated electoral politics, and in 1982 the Constitution was amended to make the country a one-party state. That amendment was repealed in 1992 in advance of the national elections.

(Continued)

A CLOSER LOOK

14.1

Kenya's Struggle for Development
(*Continued*)

When Moi's final term ended in 2002, his choice as the KANU presidential candidate was resoundingly defeated by Mwai Kibaki, the leader of the National Rainbow Coalition (NARC), ending 40 years of KANU dominance. NARC benefitted from public disaffection with the corruption and heavy-handedness of Moi's long reign. After serving as Moi's vice president and as a long-time KANU leader, Kibaki had quit that party and joined the opposition when Kenya abandoned one-party rule. With his victory, once again a Kikuyu assumed the presidency. In office, President Kibaki introduced a number of progressive reforms. But his government was as corrupt as its predecessors and failed to live up to its campaign promises. Most importantly, his administration reneged on a 2002 agreement to limit the president's power by reinstating the office of prime minister, which would share executive power.

Kibaki's primary challenger in the 2007 election was Raila Odinga, formerly a close political ally. But when Kibaki broke his pledge to support the creation of a prime minister and instead proposed a constitution that actually strengthened the president's already considerable powers, Odinga broke with him in 2005 and led a successful campaign against that proposed constitution in a national referendum.

Soon Odinga left NARC and created another breakaway coalition called the Orange Democratic Movement (ODM). When he challenged Kibaki in the 2007 presidential election, most opinion surveys showed him in the lead, as did early election results. But, after an unexplained delay in the vote count, the official electoral commission declared Kibaki the winner. Odinga and his followers believed (and most international observers agreed) that they had cheated out of victory by fraud. As protests grew violent, ethnic warfare pitted Kikuyus (largely pro-Kibaki) against Luos (Odinga's tribe) and other ethnic groups. Conflict was most intense in the Rift Valley, where thousands of Kikuyu villagers were driven out of the region, their homes often set afire. Elsewhere in the province, Kikuyus drove out Luo farmers as a process of ethnic cleansing drove hundreds of thousands, on both

sides, back to their ancestral homelands. As in other ethnic conflicts, many villagers turned on their neighbors and friends from competing ethnic groups. By the time peace had been restored an estimated 1,000 people had been killed and perhaps 600,000 had been forced to flee, as the country became more ethnically segregated.

While many foreign observers portrayed the violence as an expression of traditional ethnic tensions, in fact political leaders on both sides had instigated the tribal bloodshed. Several Kikuyu and Luo political leaders had organized mob action and provided arms. In 2011, six of them (including the country's deputy prime minister and former cabinet members) were summoned by the International Criminal Court (ICC) in the Netherlands on charges of crimes against humanity.* While Kenya had seen other violent ethnic clashes during its nearly 50 years of independence, the intensity of this violence, along with international pressures for a change in Kenya's political institutions, brought Kibaki and Odinga to negotiations led by former UN Secretary General Kofi Anan. First, the two sides agreed on a power-sharing arrangement in which Kibaki would hold the presidency and Odinga would serve as prime minister (finally reestablishing that office). Subsequently, the two leaders endorsed a new constitution, a "grand compromise" supported by most of the country's political leaders.

"In an alliance unimaginable six months [earlier, during the ethnic upheavals], Kibaki and Odinga barnstormed the country together to support the passage of the new constitution" in a national referendum.[12] Voters approved the document by a margin of better than two to one. It addressed a number of flaws in Kenya's political system. While the president is still the chief executive, he lost his prior ability to unilaterally appoint people to the most important positions in the judiciary and the executive branch, a power that

---

* For years the Kenyan government had stalled an ICC investigation by promising to set up its own special tribunal to investigate these men's alleged responsibility for the massacres, but it never did so.

14.1

had enabled previous presidents to dominate the political system and reward their supporters with patronage jobs. The new constitution subjects all of these appointments to parliamentary approval. The election commission, which had certified Kibaki's questionable victory in the 2007 election, will now be outside the president's control. Beyond that, the new constitution strengthens the previously weak parliament relative to the president. Finally, the legislature acquired the power to impeach the president.

In an equally important reform, the new constitution devolves tax revenues and political power away from the national government toward elected county governments. By returning revenue to tribal constituencies, it more equitably divides resources among ethnic groups and allows the smaller tribes a greater share of state funds. Kenya has one of the most concentrated distributions of income of any country in the world, with larger tribes, especially the Kikuyus, enjoying a higher standard of living than the smaller ones. This new devolution of funds promises to reduce that inequality while giving the smaller ethnic groups a greater sense of empowerment.

Kenya's political progression illustrates both the accomplishments and failures found of many developing political systems. The 2008 massacre and other ethnic clashes (resulting in nearly 7,000 deaths between 1991 and 2010) notwithstanding, the country has avoided the kinds of massive tribal bloodshed experienced in countries such as Congo, Rwanda, Sudan, and Indonesia that have resulted in hundreds of thousands or even millions of deaths. Kenya has a highly educated middle class and, despite occasional turmoil, is still considered one of Africa's most stable nations. Its literacy rate

(85 percent) is one of the highest in Africa. Its life expectancy is only 59 years but is still higher than in 32 other African countries. Still, clearly it has not lived up to the high expectations that many analysts had at the time of independence.

Several aspects of the nation's political system have held back its social and economic development. First, the excessive concentration of power in the president's hands enabled him to deliver economic resources, government positions (including many white-collar jobs), and land to his own tribe and other supportive ethnic groups. Second, political leaders have manipulated tensions, even fomented violence, between the country's many ethnic groups. Finally, government corruption has put an enormous economic burden on all ethnic groups. In its most recent rankings, Transparency International, a respected watchdog group, rated Kenya as the 20th most corrupt country (tied with several others) among 178 of the world's nations.[13]

By transferring substantial revenue from the central government to more local, ethnically based regions and by strengthening the parliament relative to the president, the new constitution will hopefully reduce tribal anxieties and interethnic violence over presidential elections. The fact that the constitution was vigorously championed by the country's two most powerful political leaders, men who had previously been bitter rivals, greatly improves the likelihood of that document reducing tribal confrontations. So too does the fact that it was endorsed by over two-thirds of the voters in a national referendum. What these reforms do not do is check rampant political corruption.

governments (even some freely elected ones) still violate the rights of free speech, media freedom, freedom of association, or other constitutional liberties. In the Middle East, much of Africa, and parts of Asia, military or single-party rule is still the norm. Elsewhere, in such countries as El Salvador and Guatemala, even when contested elections do take place, the military, security forces, or armed vigilantes often intimidate targeted candidates, parties, or organized groups. Few nations in

Africa, Asia, or the Middle East enjoy a free press, as their governments generally control the airwaves. Prominent human rights monitoring groups, including Amnesty International and Human Rights Watch, have cited countries as diverse as Syria, Sudan, North Korea, and Colombia in the recent past for their imprisonment and torture of political dissidents and for their murder of alleged government opponents.

During the 1970s, as many as 30,000 young Argentinians died or disappeared in the military government's "dirty war" against the left. The fanatically leftist Khmer Rouge regime was responsible for the deaths of more than one million Cambodians. Since the 1980s, human rights conditions have improved dramatically in Latin America and in parts of Asia. There has also been some progress in Africa, but a considerable number of nations on that continent, in the Middle East, and in Asia are still the victims of political repression.[8] In its 2011 annual report on freedom in the world, Freedom House notes that global political-rights and civil-liberties conditions worsened for the fifth consecutive year (though they remain significantly better than they were 15 to 25 years ago).[9]

In parts of India, corruption is so pervasive that poor mothers in run-down maternity wards often have to bribe the nurse and doctor—handing over as much as one week's wages—to be permitted to see or hold their own babies.[10] Despite years of U.S. pressure on the Afghan government to reduce corruption, the United Nations recently estimated that Afghan citizens paid $2.5 billion in bribes last year, an amount equal to about one-fourth of the country's entire GDP. A U.S. congressional committee recently concluded that about one-sixth of the total American military and civilian aid sent to Afghanistan and Iraq was stolen by government officials or by private contractors (both local and foreign), a total of $60 billion lost to corruption.

Given the unrepresentative and repressive quality of many Third World governments, it is easy to understand why so many lack legitimacy. Citizens may view their government with apathy or hostility. In a number of LDCs, popular unrest has challenged the government, often at great risk to the protestors, including protests by Buddhist monks against government tyranny in Burma and Tibet as well as mass demonstrations against government corruption and repression in Syria, Yemen, Egypt, and Tunisia (resulting in the overthrow of the last two governments). The most intense forms of popular discontent have led to revolutionary movements or civil war in nations such as Sudan, Nicaragua, Vietnam, and Pakistan.

The types of grievances that lead to violence are varied. Latin America's guerrilla struggles have been rooted in class conflict. Revolutionary movements in Cuba, Nicaragua, El Salvador, Peru, and Colombia have brought disenchanted students and intellectuals together with peasants and the urban poor. The primary sources of their discontent have been inequitable land and income distribution, poverty, rising prices, state corruption, and government repression. Violent conflict in Africa and parts of Asia, on the other hand, is more frequently tied to ethnic or regional hostilities, with class divisions playing a secondary role. Secessionist movements in Eritrea and Tigre fought for decades before gaining independence or greater autonomy from Ethiopia.

The toll from these conflicts has been staggering. From 1981 to 1991, some 75,000 people died in El Salvador. In the Congo, over five million have perished since 1998 from the fighting itself, war-related starvation, and disease. While the intensity of fighting has diminished somewhat mass slaughters and mass rapes continue. In Nigeria, Ethiopia, Sudan, Mozambique, Guatemala, Indonesia, India, Cambodia, and Lebanon, staggering numbers of citizens have died directly and indirectly from ethnic or class conflict. Recently, attacks by progovernment militia in Sudan and government interference with food shipments have caused between 200,000 and 400,000 deaths in the Darfur region, many from starvation.

Because governments in the developing world so frequently lack legitimacy or effective links to the people, many of them are extremely vulnerable. Often, the armed forces seize power with one or more of the following goals: defeating a rebel movement or other perceived subversion; establishing political stability; replacing an ineffective or corrupt leader; promoting economic development; or simply promoting the military's own institutional interests. In most cases, however, these military regimes have turned out to be more corrupt, more repressive, and less efficient than the civilian governments they had replaced.

Before examining manifestations of political underdevelopment in greater detail, we will consider the ways in which social scientists have tried to explain the *causes* of underdevelopment and the pathways that they have prescribed for change.

THEORIES OF UNDERDEVELOPMENT AND DEVELOPMENT

Having described the differences between developed nations and LDCs, we must now ask why it is that some countries have improved their political and economic systems, while others are still struggling. Over the years, analysts have offered two distinct explanations. The first insists that political and economic development are each driven primarily by *internal* factors within the Third World, most notably changes in the country's cultural values. The second approach emphasizes the effects of international trade and investment, suggesting that *external* exploitation is the primary cause of underdevelopment. These approaches are called, respectively, *modernization theory* and *dependency theory*.

Modernization Theory and the Importance of Cultural Values

In the decades after World War II, as the demise of European colonialism produced a host of newly independent nations in Africa and Asia, Western social scientists formulated an understanding of underdevelopment known as **modernization theory**.[14] Despite the tremendous array of problems facing less-developed countries, modernization theorists were initially relatively optimistic about their prospects for development. They expected that most developing nations could follow a path of economic and political modernization roughly parallel to that which had earlier been traveled by Western industrial democracies. The LDCs merely needed to promote modern cultural values and to create appropriate economic and political institutions. Transforming the culture of developing nations was considered the key to modernization.

Drawing on the theories of Max Weber and Talcott Parsons, the theory distinguished between clusters of traditional versus modern values. Modern societies, it claimed, were more prone than traditional ones to judge people by universal standards (that is, to evaluate them according to their own ability rather than their family, race, or ethnic origins); to believe in the possibility and desirability of change; to be concerned with social and political issues beyond the scope of family, village, or neighborhood; and to believe that citizens should try to influence the political system.

But how can a society with traditional values acquire modern ones? In large part, the argument ran, modern values emerge as a natural byproduct of socioeconomic change, particularly urbanization, greater literacy, and industrialization. When people leave their farms for jobs in the cities, they commonly become literate, are more exposed to the mass media, and encounter new ideas and social situations. All of these influences are believed to create and transmit modern values and behavior.

Thus, modernization theory focused on the *diffusion* of modern ideas both from the developed world to the developing world and, within the Third World, from city to countryside. Western foreign aid, trade, and institutions such as the Peace Corps may help speed the process since modern values are generally associated with the West. Along with modern values, modernizationists argue that LDCs need to develop more specialized and complex political and economic institutions. This includes creating more skilled, professionally trained, and honest bureaucracies; developing a modern legal system that operates fairly and honestly; and establishing political parties that effectively channel citizens' demands and aspirations to the government.

Eventually, many of the early assumptions of modernization theory had to be modified. Initially, it had been too optimistic in its view of political and socioeconomic change, assuming that modernizing countries could simultaneously and relatively smoothly achieve economic growth, greater equality, democracy, stability, and greater national autonomy. Yet in countries such as Iran, Mexico, and Vietnam, early modernization shattered the traditional societies before new ones could be constructed, resulting in social unrest, religious fundamentalism, or revolution. Elsewhere, as greater urbanization and increased literacy produced higher political participation, political institutions such as political parties were often unable to handle the rising number of demands from the public. In due course, a more pessimistic version of modernization theory emerged, asserting that change is often a painful and disruptive process involving difficult choices. Indeed, as Samuel Huntington observed, although modern nations tend to be more politically stable, the difficult transition from a **traditional society** to a modern society is often profoundly destabilizing.[15]

Dependency Theory

In time, a number of social scientists, primarily in Latin America and the United States, challenged modernization theory itself. Under the banner of **dependency theory**, they objected to many of its fundamental assumptions. First, they denied that LDCs could follow the same path to development as Western nations had. For one thing, Britain and other early industrial powers faced no external competition in the eighteenth and nineteenth centuries. In today's world, nations trying to industrialize have to compete against well-established economic giants. Furthermore, most of them still rely on the United States, Japan, Germany, and other advanced industrial economies ("the core") for credit, investment capital, sophisticated machinery, and advanced technology. That supposedly leaves developing countries ("the periphery") dependent on the core.

Whereas most modernization theorists felt Western influence in the Third World was beneficial, *dependentistas* (dependency theorists) insisted that Western colonialism had turned Africa and Asia into poorly paid sources of cheap food and raw materials for the colonial powers. So, long after developing nations had achieved political independence, they remained economically and politically dependent.

In political terms, dependency theorists argued that Third World economic elites, backed by the economic and military power of core nations such as the United States or France, maintained a political system that benefited the few at the expense of the majority. Dependency theory was obviously an attractive model for Third World scholars, suggesting that underdevelopment was not the LDCs' fault but, rather, the result of foreign exploitation. But in American universities as well, dependency theory challenged modernization theory as the major scholarly explanation of underdevelopment.

Yet just as early modernization theory had been overly optimistic about the prospects for simultaneous economic and political development, early dependency theory was excessively pessimistic. Despite the theory's bleak prognosis, nations such as Brazil and Taiwan began to see substantial industrial growth. In a more advanced version of dependency theory, Fernando Henrique Cardoso rejected the contention that all countries in the periphery were condemned to underdevelopment. Drawing from the experience of his native Brazil, Cardoso contended that a combination of Third World government intervention and links between domestic firms and multinational corporations allowed some LDCs to industrialize and enjoy economic growth. He referred to this process as "associated-dependent development."[16]

Nevertheless, he considered that type of development undesirable. It promoted highly mechanized companies that hired too few local workers and produced more expensive goods that benefited middle- and upper-class consumers but were beyond the reach of the masses. So, instead of reducing poverty, dependent development had contributed to growing income concentration. At the same time, the alliance of Third World elites with multinational corporations supported unrepresentative regimes.

Modernization Theory and Dependency Theory Compared

Dependency theory offered a useful correction to modernization theory in several ways. It highlighted an important influence on Third World societies that previously had been largely neglected—the role of international trade, finance, and investment. Further, whereas initially modernization theorists had concentrated almost exclusively on internal causes of underdevelopment, its proponents came to recognize that development required more than adopting new values or changing domestic political structures.

Dependency theorists also helped redefine the concept of economic development. While earlier research had stressed the significance of economic growth, *dependentistas* pointed to the importance of economic distribution. When rapid economic growth produces increased concentration of wealth and income, as has frequently happened, the poor may even end up worse off. Influenced by dependency theory and similar critiques, even establishment groups such as the World Bank reoriented their goals toward "redistribution with growth."[17]

But just as modernization theorists tended to overemphasize the internal causes of underdevelopment, early *dependentistas* erroneously attributed virtually all Third World problems to external economic forces. LDCs were often portrayed as nearly helpless pawns with little hope for development. Cardoso refined the theory by insisting that developing nations had options within the broad limits of dependency. With the proper government policies and the appropriate relationships between social classes, less-developed nations could achieve associated-dependent development.

But even this refinement fails to explain East Asia's spectacular development record since the 1960s. Those economies have been tremendously dependent—that is, very closely tied to the developed world through trade, credits, investment, and technology transfers. Indeed, they are far more integrated into the world economy than most developing nations. But contrary to what Cardoso and others had predicted, highly globalized economies in East and Southeast Asia have been the economic stars of the Third World, coupling astonishing economic growth with comparatively equitable economic distribution. Similarly, rather than supporting entrenched dictatorships in that region, greater economic growth and dependency in countries such as South Korea, Taiwan, and Indonesia opened the way to democratic transitions. Although East Asia's economic expansion does not prove that greater economic interdependence would have similar success in Africa, Latin America, or the Middle East, at the least it does indicate that one must look for factors beyond economic dependency to explain underdevelopment.

In fact, the evidence regarding foreign economic penetration is mixed. Although many developing nations such as India and Chile have benefited from increased international trade and foreign investment, greater economic integration and **globalization** of the world economy also introduces important risks. As developing countries become more heavily dependent on exports and financial links to the developed world, they become more vulnerable to global economic and financial crises. In the late 1990s some of the most dynamic economies in East Asia suffered severe setbacks when the collapse of Thailand's currency caused foreign investors to panic and dump a number of East Asian currencies. While many developing nations have survived the 2008–2010 global financial crisis fairly well, several types of fallout slowed their rates of growth: Recessions in the United States, Europe, and Japan reduced demand for many Third World exports (though their increased export of raw materials to China and India helped mitigate that effect); when stock markets in the United States and Europe fell sharply, markets in countries such as Brazil, China, India, and South Africa reacted with abrupt drops of their own; as a result of their own economic downturns, some advanced nations reduced their investment and loans to shakier economies in the developing world; and as many immigrants from the LDCs lost their jobs in the West, they sent fewer funds (remittances) back to their families at home. This was particularly damaging to countries such as Mexico and Tunisia, whose economies depend heavily on remittances (from the United States and France, respectively).[18] What this means is that developing countries that benefit from globalization during periods of world economic growth need to be on guard against the downturns that periodically beset the global economy.

Today, many political scientists agree that a full understanding of development must draw on the strengths of both modernization and dependency theories while recognizing the limits of each. In the sections that follow, we turn from general development theories to an examination of specific challenges and obstacles to development facing Third World nations today.

SOURCES OF POLITICAL CONFLICT

Viewers of the evening news might understandably believe that developing counties are in a constant state of upheaval. News stories stress revolutions, civil wars, riots, and military coups (takeovers) in such countries as Egypt, Iraq, Libya, Pakistan, Congo, and Sri Lanka. Although many Third World nations are peaceful, sharp internal divisions plague many others. Two particularly vexing sources of tension have been class conflict and ethnic conflict.

Class Conflict

In all nations, modern and developing alike, some people are wealthier than others. Invariably, that inequality causes some degree of political division. In more harmonious societies, class differences may merely influence the voters' electoral preferences. For example, blue-collar workers tend to vote for the Socialist Party in France and Spain, while well-to-do businesspeople tend to support the British Conservatives and the German Christian Democrats. Because wealth and income in the developing world are often more concentrated in a few hands, and because the political battle for scarce economic resources is often more heated, class conflict there is frequently more intense and even violent.

As we have noted, the initial stages of economic modernization often heighten class tensions as income gaps between the "haves" and "have-nots" widen. In the cities, industrialization often expands the size of the middle class and creates a "labor elite" of skilled, unionized factory workers, while many unskilled and underemployed workers are left behind in the slums. In the countryside, as large commercial farms expand their operations to take advantage of new export opportunities, they often evict neighboring peasant cultivators from their small family plots.

Early economic modernization not only tends to sharpen class tensions but also increases the political capacity of previously powerless groups. For example, as the gap between rural and urban living standards widens, increased rural migration to the cities raises the literacy rate of those former peasants and exposes them to more political information from the mass media. Consequently, the newly arrived urban poor tend to be better informed and more politically active than they had been in the countryside. Eventually, some of these urban migrants may return to the countryside and mobilize their fellow villagers. Peasants being forced off their land by the expansion of large, commercial farms also may be radicalized. Industrialization also generates labor unions, giving workers an important vehicle for political mobilization. The growing middle class—particularly university students, professionals, and intellectuals—provides leadership for antiestablishment political parties, labor unions, or even revolutionary groups in some nations.[19]

For all those reasons, the earlier periods of economic development—when a country moves out of socioeconomic backwardness toward greater modernity—often witness heightened class tensions. That conflict may express itself peacefully at the ballot box and through union activity. In Chile, for example, organized labor formed the backbone of Popular Unity (the UP), a Marxist coalition that elected Salvador Allende to the presidency in 1970. Ultimately, however, political tensions pitting the

UP government and its labor and peasant supporters against opposition parties, business groups, and parts of the middle class precipitated a brutal military coup against Allende in 1973. More recently, disgruntled peasants and the urban poor have helped elect leftist presidents such as Hugo Chávez in Venezuela and Evo Morales in Bolivia.

But the most acute class conflict in the developing world has often pitted the rural poor against local landlords and the national government. At the bottom of the political and economic hierarchy and often unable to assert their demands within the political system, peasants sometimes turn to violence. Vietnam and China, for example, had peasant-based, communist revolutions. Peasants also played important roles in the Mexican, Cuban, and Nicaraguan insurrections. Recently, they have formed the backbone of guerrilla movements in Colombia and Nepal, and not long ago were the core of revolutionary movements in El Salvador and Vietnam.[20] Thus, although Karl Marx, the father of modern revolutionary theory, had expected class conflict to manifest itself in the tensions between urban capitalists and blue-collar workers, twentieth- and twenty-first-century revolutionary struggles in the LDCs have more frequently been waged in the countryside. No matter how appalling living conditions for many Third World industrial workers may be, those workers are generally better off economically and politically than peasants and, hence, are less prone to join armed rebellions. Although urban labor unions may be quite militant and often support radical political parties, most of them still work within the framework of legal and peaceful political action.

With the fall of the Soviet communist bloc, China's embrace of capitalist economic policies, and the decline of the communist model, class conflict seems to be declining as a source of political polarization in the developing world, only to be replaced by increased ethnic conflict.

Ethnic Conflict

No type of political division has brought Third World nations more protracted and bitter conflict than **ethnicity** has. In many less developed countries, people have been drawn into opposing camps based on language, culture, religion, and race with an intensity that frequently exceeds conflicts between socioeconomic classes.

Of course, ethnic conflicts have not been limited to the Third World. They have flared up fairly recently in such disparate places as Serbia, Northern Ireland, the former Soviet Union, and Canada. But they are often particularly bitter in the LDCs because of the intense competition for scarce economic resources. So, although American urban politics has sometimes featured competition between African Americans, Anglo-Saxons, Hispanics, Irish, Italians, or Jews, the stakes of American ethnic competition are not as high as in India, Sri Lanka, or Syria. In those countries, contending ethnic groups frequently feel that their very survival depends on how the state distributes public-sector jobs, schools, and development projects.

Ethnic tensions have been most intense in Africa and parts of Asia, where colonial powers frequently drew national boundaries that threw conflicting ethnic groups into a single country. In India, the struggle for independence highlighted deep divisions between Muslims and the Hindu majority. Ultimately, it resulted in the establishment of two nations: India (primarily Hindu) and Pakistan, a separate Muslim state carved out of colonial India. In the months leading up to and following independence, communal violence between Hindus and Muslims led to some two million deaths and uprooted 12 million refugees.[21] Today, periodic, religiously based strife continues in the Indian state of Kashmir, where Islamic rebels seek independence or unification with Pakistan, and in Punjab, where the Indian military and Sikh separatists have waged a bloody conflict.

In Africa, tribally based civil wars have afflicted the continent for decades, producing widespread destruction and vast numbers of fatalities in countries such as Sudan, Ethiopia, and Congo. Interethnic violence has also torn apart Sri Lanka, Indonesia, Lebanon, Syria (where the Alawite Muslim minority dominates the Sunni majority), and other Asian and Middle Eastern nations. Ethnicity and race relations are not as volatile in Latin America, but in the recent past rural guerrilla movements in Guatemala and Peru drew support from indigenous peoples (native Indians) resentful of White domination. Currently, tensions between Bolivian Indians supporting President Morales versus his White opponents have occasionally burst into violence.

Not all ethnic divisions have led to violent conflict, however. Although nearly all African nations have multitribal populations, many have reached accommodations between ethnic groups. Elsewhere, in countries such as Malaysia, ethnic violence has seemingly been brought under control. Worldwide, after 50 years of steadily rising conflict, the level of ethnic protests and rebellion within nations began falling in the early 1990s.[22] Still, ethnic conflict is likely to remain among the Third World's greatest challenges for years to come. These tensions not only can endure for generations but also may resurface after a long period of apparent calm.

Religious Conflict

For many years political scientists had believed that the socioeconomic modernization of traditional societies would lead to reduced religiosity—that is, as LDCs became more literate and urban, fewer people were likely to be devoutly religious, and those who remained religious would become more tolerant of nonbelievers or believers in other religions. But, in much of the Third World that has not happened. Indeed, religious beliefs are among the most firmly held, and they have sometimes been the source of bitter political conflict. This is not entirely unique to the developing world. For example, Northern Ireland was torn for many years by armed conflict between Catholics and Protestants.

PROBLEMS OF POLITICAL PARTICIPATION

The intense political and economic tensions that divide many LDCs present them with a difficult dilemma. In many ethnically divided nations, large portions of the population have been denied full political participation. In Iraq, for example, Saddam Hussein and his ruling elite were drawn primarily from the country's Sunni minority, denying representation to both the Shi'ite majority and the large population of Kurds. Today, following the toppling of Saddam's regime, it is the Sunnis who fear exclusion from political power. As previously noted, in Bahrain antigovernment demonstrators were primarily from the majority Shi'ite population while the ruling royal family and the economic elite are Sunnis. Ethnic conflicts also divide a large number of African and Asian nations, while in some Latin American countries (including Ecuador, Guatemala, and Peru) the large Native American populations have long suffered discrimination.

In other LDCs, military and single-party governments deny the entire population the right to participate in meaningful elections. Even in the growing number of nations with contested elections, the peasantry and the urban poor often lack the resources, political skills, or connections to receive a fair hearing from government policy makers. The failure of their political systems to allow representation for so many citizens means that many Third World governments are not held accountable for their actions, corruption flourishes, and inadequately represented groups, such as the rural poor, do not get their fair share of government resources. For all those reasons, political development requires additional channels for mass political participation.

On the other hand, there is also a danger that political participation may expand faster than the nation's political institutions can accommodate. Years ago, Samuel Huntington warned that developing countries may confront an explosion of demands on the political system as formerly nonpoliticized people move to urban areas, attain higher educational levels, and otherwise increase their political awareness.[25] Unless more sophisticated political institutions can be created to channel those rising demands, he argued, political disorder and decay lie in waiting.

Huntington looked to long-term solutions through the creation of political institutions that could effectively aggregate and channel citizens' demands. Developing strong and effectual political parties, he argued, is the key to orderly political participation, bringing together diverse groups in society and translating a wide array of conflicting demands into workable political alternatives. Other institutions also need improvement. Government bureaucracies, for example, must become more competent and honest so that they can better implement state policies and satisfy their citizens' needs.

Ultimately, then, there is a delicate balance between the need for increased political participation and the dangers of an excessively rapid escalation in participation. Since the 1970s there has been an explosion of democratic government throughout the world, including both former communist nations and LDCs. The change has been most dramatic in Latin America, a region previously governed almost exclusively by authoritarian regimes and now composed almost entirely of democracies. Mexico completed that transformation in 2000 when the PRI was ousted from office after 71 years as the ruling party (see Chapter 15). Although democracy has advanced far more haltingly in Africa, the number of electoral democracies on that continent has also grown impressively. And in Asia, authoritarian governments have given way to democratic ones in South Korea, Taiwan, Indonesia, the Philippines, and seemingly in Thailand. For years the glaring exception to that trend was the Arab world, where, until the recent "Arab Spring," authoritarianism seemed well entrenched (See A Closer Look 14.2).

Although the developing world's new democratic governments have not always performed well (many are corrupt, incompetent, and even occasionally repressive), on the whole they have opened up new avenues of participation to their citizens without the resulting unrest that Huntington feared. What has caused this flurry of democratic transitions in what has been the most widespread democratic revolution in world history?

14.2

The Arab Spring—Democratic Upheaval in the Arab World

On December 17, 2010, Mohamed Bouazizi, a young fruit vender in the Tunisian town of Sidi Bouzid, could no longer take his repeated harassment by local police who had levied severe fines on his stall and prevented him from earning a living. Taking matters into his own hands, he doused himself with paint thinner in front of a town government building and set himself on fire, dying a few weeks later. In earlier times the death of a poor, provincial vendor would have attracted little attention. But in an era of the Internet, Twitter, and Facebook (even in developing countries), information and news can spread enormously quickly and widely. A cell-phone picture of Bouazizi's suicide soon went viral. Although Tunisia had been considered North Africa' most stable nation, this act of desperation struck a chord with millions of citizens, many of whom suffered from unemployment, and most of whom had tired of the 30-year dictatorship of Zine el-Abidine Ben Ali (a former military officer). Protest demonstrations in Bouazizi's home town quickly spread throughout the country, bringing out a broad cross-section of the population. After three weeks of massive demonstrations in Tunis (the nation's capital) and other cities—during which government security forces killed more than 200 protestors—Ben Ali fled to Saudi Arabia.

When a wave of democracy had swept over much of the developing world (and the communist bloc) in the closing decades of the twentieth century, one group of nations withstood that trend—the Arab world. Throughout the Middle East and North Africa, power still remained in the hands of military strongmen, military-led political parties, or traditional monarchs. Many analysts believed that some aspects of Arab culture blocked democratic values. Others noted the distorting effects of excessive economic dependence on oil exports (the "oil curse"), which has obstructed democracy in countries such as Iraq, Saudi Arabia, Russia, and Venezuela.[23] Yet other observers noted that some Arab despots—including Libya's Muammar Qaddafi and Syria's Hafez al-Assad (father of the current president, Bashar al-Assad)—appealed to nationalism, resentment toward Israel, anti-Western grievances, and sympathy

for the Palestinians to deflect attention from their own regime's repression and corruption. Whatever the causes of the region's "democracy gap," recent dictators—including Bashar al-Assad, Egypt's Hosni Mubarak, and Iraq's Saddam Hussein—maintained power through the iron fists of their police and armed forces. But Ben Ali's fall in Tunisia persuaded people throughout the Arab world that toppling a long-standing dictatorship was possible. Suddenly, many of them were willing to risk their lives for a more democratic society (and, hopefully, a better standard of living).

Within weeks of the triumph of Tunisia's "Jasmine Revolution" (named after the national flower), protestors in neighboring Egypt began sit-ins at Cairo's Tahrir (Liberation) Square, aimed at ending Hosni Mubarak's 30-year-old dictatorship. Like Ben Ali, Mubarak was a former military officer who had led a pro-Western government characterized by political repression, enormous corruption, and failure to alleviate the country's extensive poverty. But Egypt's uprising was far more significant than Tunisia's. With a population of some 80 million, Egypt is 10 times larger than Tunisia and almost twice the size of any other Arab state. Strategically, it has been the United States' most important Arab ally, Israel's crucial peace partner, and the Arab world's most important cultural and religious voice. As time went by, antigovernment demonstrations spread to Alexandria, Suez, and other Egyptian cities. When organizers called on the people to fill Tahrir Square, crowds swelled to the hundreds of thousands.

With the eyes of the world focused on Cairo, other Arab dictators were alarmed while, at the same time, Israel feared that a new Egyptian government might renounce their peace treaty, so vital to Israeli security. The West's major concern was that Mubarak's overthrow might bring to power the Muslim Brotherhood, an Islamic fundamentalist group that had been banned and persecuted for decades, but which had survived to become the country's largest, most committed, and most well-organized opposition group.

For a time, outside observers believed the mass protests were spontaneous and leaderless. It soon

(Continued)

A CLOSER LOOK

14.2

The Arab Spring—Democratic Upheaval in the Arab World
(Continued)

emerged, however, that there had been considerable planning behind the scenes. A critical group of leaders consisted of 15 young professionals—mostly doctors and lawyers—many of whom had known each other as university students. In many ways they were astonishingly diverse, representing demographic and ideological groups known for their hostility toward each other—liberals, leftists, a Google marketing executive, a leader of the Muslim Brotherhood Youth, and a 32-year-old feminist, improbably named Sally Moore (a Coptic Christian psychiatrist of Irish and Egyptian descent).

> Yet they brought a sophistication and professionalism to their cause—exploiting the anonymity of the Internet to elude the secret police, planting false rumors to fool police spies, staging "field tests" in Cairo slums before [organizing real demonstrations], then planning a weekly protest schedule to save their firepower.[24]

Dr. Moore helped enlist the support of the Arab Doctors Union (many of whose leaders are in the Muslim Brotherhood), which set up a series of clinics to treat anyone hurt in the demonstrations. Earlier, Wael Ghonim, the Google executive, had anonymously created a human-rights Facebook page entitled "We are all Khaled Said." Established in mid-2010 in honor of Said, an Alexandria businessman who had been beaten to death by the police, the page drew thousands of viewers, and its title became a major slogan of the democracy movement. Slowly but surely, key elements of Mubarak's regime withdrew their support, most importantly the armed forces, which adopted a policy of neutrality and refused to use force against the demonstrators. On February 11, 2011—after a series of minor or meaningless government concessions that failed to satisfy the protestors and only 18 days after prodemocracy demonstrations began—President Mubarak resigned from office and the military named a caretaker government.

Several common characteristics of the two "democratic revolutions" stand out. In both countries long-term dictatorships had failed to address widespread unemployment and poverty. Extensive government corruption at the top made that poverty all the more infuriating. Earlier opposition from either pro-democracy or Islamist political groups had been repressed in both nations. Young people, who have suffered some of the world's highest unemployment rates, formed the backbone of both protest movements in countries where 29 percent of the population is between 15 and 29 years of age (compared to only 21 percent in the United States). Young professionals, making innovative use of information technology, found ways of outwitting the security forces in order to mobilize and organize protest activities. In both countries demonstrators were remarkably disciplined and nonviolent (even in the face of bloody attacks by the police or government-hired thugs), and in each the military's decision not to use force against the protestors was critical to the movements' success.

Soon the torrent of democratic protests spread across the Arab world—to Bahrain, Yemen, Syria and, in a very different form, to Libya. Some of the opposition to the government was linked to ethnic grievances. In Bahrain, demonstrators came from the country's Shi'ite Muslim majority (70 percent of the population), which had long been the victim of discrimination at the hands of the country's Sunni monarchy and power elite. Hostility toward the Libyan government was strongest in the nation's east, whose tribal groups had been excluded from Qaddafi's ruling circle. There, protests against Qaddafi's particularly brutal dictatorship turned into civil war as the government introduced massive force. Eastern cities took up arms, bolstered by segments of the armed forces who defected to the rebel army and by NATO air support. Other regimes—Bahrain and Yemen—when unable to win over the protestors with promises of limited reform, also turned to force. In Bahrain—a tiny, oil-rich, island state, which hosts the United States' Fifth Fleet—the king invited in troops from neighboring Saudi Arabia to help crush the protests.

14.2

How likely is this democratic surge to succeed in other Arab countries such as Syria and Yemen? In both Tunisia and Egypt, the military has been a respected and popular institution. Anxious to maintain that respect, the generals refused to attack the demonstrators even though both Ben Ali and Mubarak had originally seized power as high-ranking, career military officers. In Bahrain, Syria, and Yemen, the armed forces and police have not felt that reluctance (though some troops did defect to the opposition). Several other factors have bolstered other governments in the region. First, some Arab states have monarchs who enjoy considerable legitimacy and support, particularly those who have introduced some progressive reforms. These include the kings of Morocco and Jordan and the sultan of Oman. Second, other regimes have such a repressive grip on society that it is hard for opposition movements to succeed (Syria) or even to get off the ground (Saudi Arabia).

Moreover, it is too early to tell if even Egypt's or Tunisia's revolts will actually pave the way for a liberal democracy in those two countries. For now, both upheavals have resulted in transitional military rule, led by the same commanders who were the pillars of the previous regimes. The currently ruling generals, particularly in Egypt, are making their political

decisions secretly, with little or no outside scrutiny and limited public input. Furthermore, the civilian leaders that the generals originally selected (e.g., cabinet ministers) for the transitional governments included a number of holdovers from the previous, dictatorial regimes. While the level of government repression is down dramatically, the Egyptian transitional military regimes continues to arrest and torture some dissidents. At the same time, however, ongoing demonstrations have forced both military-led governments to remove some of those holdover officials and to pass a number of reforms. For example, one month after Mubarak's fall, heavy popular pressure (including large street demonstrations) persuaded Egypt's ruling military council to dissolve the state security organization, a widely hated body that had spied on the civilian population and had harassed, jailed, and tortured Mubarak's opponents. While the military rulers in both countries have promised to transfer power to a democratically elected civilian government, it is uncertain how much behind-the-scenes power either the armed forces or others associated with the old regimes will have. In Libya, where the revolutionaries' ruling council has been quite open and closely allied with the West, tribal conflicts and Islamist movements may still derail democracy.

There are many reasons, but we will highlight two. The first factor involves contagion—the tendency of certain political trends or forces to spread from one country to another. From the late 1940s to the 1960s, as the former European colonies in Africa, Asia, and the Middle East gained independence, many new national leaders were attracted to Marxism because it promised a path to rapid economic development and reduced dependency on the former colonial rulers. In countries such as Ghana, Egypt, and Indonesia, authoritarian governments offered a host of arguments (mostly self-serving) claiming that open electoral competition would be too divisive in ethnically and economically divided countries such as theirs. At the same time, in Latin America right-wing military dictatorships took power in countries such as Argentina, Brazil, and Chile to avert an alleged communist threat. Beginning in the 1970s, however, as the weaknesses of military and single-party rule became increasingly apparent, democracy acquired new legitimacy. By the start of the 1990s, as communism collapsed in the Soviet Union and Eastern Europe, authoritarian government of any kind "fell out of style" and democracy became more fashionable. Democracy was now contagious. For example, when South Korean students—watching the local news or CNN—witnessed their counterparts in the Philippines overthrow the Marcos dictatorship, they began to think more seriously of toppling their own authoritarian government, which they later did.

The second important factor is that, over time, socioeconomic modernization in many developing nations has produced a more hospitable environment for democratic government. Despite serious setbacks in certain cases, LDCs as a whole have significantly raised their educational levels in the past three or four decades and have often improved their per capita incomes as well. Those two developments have important political implications since there is substantial evidence that nations with higher levels of income and literacy are more likely to sustain democracy. For example, at least until recently, few countries with literacy rates below 50 percent have been able to sustain democratic government (though there are notable exceptions, such as India before the 1990s), whereas countries above that point are likely to be democracies.[26] At the same time, countries that are better off economically are much more capable of sustaining democratic government. In a study of how well democracy endured in 135 countries over a 40-year period (1950–1990), the authors found that it is most fragile in poor countries (with per capita incomes below $1,000) and becomes more sustainable as national income rises. "Above $6,000 [per-capita income]," they note, "democracies are impregnable and can be expected to live forever; no democratic system has ever fallen in a country where per capita income exceeds $6,055 [Argentina's income level when a military dictatorship took over in 1976]."[27]

WOMEN IN THIRD WORLD SOCIETY AND POLITICS

In most of the developing world, women have found it difficult to secure full political and economic participation. In fact, they are often the victims of social and economic deprivation and exploitation. For example, in parts of Asia and Africa, millions of young girls—often as young as nine or ten—have been sold by their impoverished parents into arranged marriages while many thousands of others live in virtual slavery. Fundamentalist Islamist societies, such as Afghanistan, Iran, and Saudi Arabia, severely restrict women's lifestyles, including the types of jobs that they may hold and the kinds of apparel they may wear.

Women's Economic and Social Status

In recent decades, Third World women have narrowed the gender gap in many areas, most notably in education and literacy.[28] But in much of the developing world they continue to have fewer educational opportunities than males, shorter life expectancies, and fewer occupational opportunities in both government and the private sector. Thus, as Table 14.3 makes clear, women continue to trail men in the major indicators of economic, social and political development.

TABLE 14.3	The Status of Women in the Developing World		
	Adult Male Literacy Rate (percent)	Adult Female Literacy Rate (percent)	Rank on Gender Inequality Index	Rank on Gender Empowerment Index
United States*	99	99	37	18
South Korea	99	99	20	61
China	96	88	38	72
Mexico	89	85	68	39
Namibia	87	84	75	43
Brazil	88	89	80	82
Egypt	83	80	108	107
India	73	48	122	–
Yemen	71	30	138	109
Afghanistan	43	13	134	–

*The UNDP does not provide literacy data for more-developed countries such as the United States and South Korea. However, since the combined adult literacy rates are above 99 percent, we can assume that rate for each sex.

SOURCE: United Nations Development Programme (UNDP), *Human Development Report 2009 and 2010*; CIA, *World Factbook 2010*.

The table's first two columns compare male and female adult literacy rates in the United States and in a sample of African, Asian, Latin American, and Middle Eastern nations. In several countries (including South Korea, Namibia, Mexico, Brazil, and Egypt) women's literacy rates are about equal to men's. Yet in India, Yemen, and Afghanistan, their literacy rates trail far behind (with female literacy in Afghanistan less than one-third the men's rate). During the past two to three decades, many developing nations—most notably in Latin America and the Caribbean—have narrowed the educational gap between the sexes considerably. But in much of Africa, South Asia, and the Middle East, educational opportunities for women remain far more limited. Currently, there are close to 900 million illiterate adults in the Third World, and about two-thirds of them are women. Raising female literacy rates obviously opens many opportunities for women and girls. It also has a number of other important benefits. For example, it is one of the most effective means of lowering fertility rates, thereby facilitating improvements in the population's standard of living.

Column 3 presents each country's ranking on the **Gender Inequality Index (GII)**. The GII is an index of women's status in society that combines data on health, education, performance in the labor market, and political advancement. Measuring and combining these factors, each country was assigned a GII score, and the 138 countries with available data were ranked from 1 (the country with the least gender inequality, the Netherlands) to 138 (the country with the greatest inequality, Yemen). Finally, the last column compares each country's **Gender Empowerment Measure (GEM)** and again ranks them from first to last on this dimension. The GEM is a composite index of how women compare to men on four dimensions: the degree of economic participation and decision making, the degree of political participation and decision making, the proportion of academic and technical positions in the workforce, and estimated income. Thus, it is an indication of women's power in the economic and political system. Unfortunately, only half of the world's countries (109 out of some 200 nations) have calculated GEMs, and most of the world's poorest countries have not done so.

Even so, several patterns emerge when we examine the GII and GEM rankings. As expected, wealthier Western nations tend to have the highest rankings on both measures, especially Northern European countries (not shown in the table). More affluent developing nations, such as South Korea (and Singapore, not shown here), tend to have high GII rankings but not necessarily strong GEM rankings. Very poor countries tend to rank poorly on both indices (India, Egypt, Yemen, and Afghanistan).

But religious and cultural factors are also important. For example, the level of gender inequality is high and female empowerment is low in most Muslim countries, even in more wealthy countries such as Saudi Arabia and Turkey (not shown). And while women in East Asian countries such as China and South Korea (as well as Japan, not shown) tend to have a relatively good ranking on the GII (indicating standards of female health care and education that are close to men's), they are much weaker on the GEM. This seems to indicate that those countries have cultural barriers hindering women from assuming positions of authority. It is also interesting to note that the United States has a lower GEM ranking and a much lower GII ranking (indicating a surprisingly wide gender gap) than we would expect from one of the world's most wealthy and developed nations. The data indicate that European countries (which are not shown in the table but have most of the highest rankings) have a higher commitment to gender equality than the United States does.

Women as Political Leaders

If we turn our focus from the socioeconomic and political status of Third World women generally to women's opportunities for high-level political leadership, we find a mixed picture. A surprising number of women have risen to the pinnacle of their political system, serving as prime ministers or presidents. Thus, for example, while the United States has never had a woman president, the Muslim countries of Turkey, Bangladesh, and Pakistan have all been governed by women prime ministers. So too have non-Muslim countries such as Liberia, Brazil, Chile, India, Sri Lanka, and Thailand, while Argentina and the Philippines have each had two women presidents. Yet on the other hand, as we will see, those women have usually made it to the top as heirs to political dynasties begun by male relatives.

The list of past and current women government leaders includes Indian Prime Minister Indira Gandhi, Argentine Presidents Isabel Perón and Cristina Fernández, Nicaraguan President Violeta Chamorro, Filipino Presidents Corazon Aquino and Gloria Macapagal Arroyo, Pakistani Prime Minister Benazir Bhutto, Bangladeshi Prime Ministers Begum Khaleda Zia and Sheik Hasina Wazed, Sri Lankan Prime Minister Sirimavo Bandaranaike and President Chandrika Kumaratunga, Panamanian President Mireya Elisa Moscoso Rodríguez, Indonesian President Megawati Sukurnoputri, and about a dozen lesser-known leaders. In recent years, Ellen Johnson-Sirleaf—a Harvard-trained banker—has been president of Liberia, Africa's first elected female head of state. At about the same time, Michelle Bachelet—a doctor, former defense minister, and former political prisoner—was elected as Chile's first woman president. And in 2011, Dilma Rouseff, an economist, became the first woman president of Brazil, Latin America's largest nation.

In 2010, Dilma Rousseff—a one-time revolutionary guerrilla turned moderate—was elected as Brazil's first woman president.

While this list is impressive, it may give an exaggerated picture of the opportunities open to women. Most of the women just named assumed the leadership of their country as the widows or daughters of former male prime ministers, presidents, or opposition leaders, many of them national heroes. For example, Indira Gandhi was the daughter of India's revered first prime minister, Jawaharlal Nehru. Bangladesh's two most recent prime ministers have been, respectively, the widow and daughter of assassinated presidents. The Philippines' Corazon Aquino and Nicaragua's Violeta Chamorro were elected president following the assassination of their husbands, who had been leading figures in the opposition to their countries' dictators. Former Prime Minister Benazir Bhutto was the daughter of a prime minister who had been executed by the military. Argentina's Isabel Perón was the widow of legendary President Juan Perón, while that country's current president, Cristina Fernández de Kirchner, succeeded her husband in that post. Indonesia's former president, Megawati Sukarnoputri, was the daughter of

Sukarno, the country's founding father and first president. Some of these women proved to be very qualified. Others did not. But what brought them to the top of the political ladder was primarily their lineage. On the other hand, more recently Chile's Bachelet, Liberia's Johnson-Sirleaf, and Brazil's Rousseff were elected on their own (without the benefit of inherited power) and may presage a new trend.

Almost all female heads of government have come from elite families, making them very unrepresentative of other women in their country. For example, former Pakistani Prime Minister Bhutto and Philippine ex-president Aquino were born to wealthy land-owning families, and Bhutto was educated at Harvard and Oxford. Similarly, Burmese opposition leader Aung San Suu Kyi, the winner of the 1991 Nobel Peace Prize, is the daughter of the country's most revered founding father and also earned two degrees from Oxford. For women who are not born to the nation's elite and, more significantly, are not the daughters or widows of prominent national leaders, opportunities for political leadership remain limited. Nor does the election of a female president or prime minister necessarily lead to improvements in the lives of the average woman in their country. Nations such as Bangladesh, India, Indonesia, Sri Lanka, and Turkey, all of which have had female government leaders, still have relatively poor GEMs and GIIs. For example, while Bangladesh has been led most of the time since 1991 by one of two women prime ministers, it currently ranks next to last among the 109 countries that report GEM scores and 116th out of 138 nations on the GII.

Third World Political Institutions

Often the weaknesses of Third World political institutions, especially political parties, compound the problems of inadequate political participation and ineffective government representation. Political parties are most productive when they reach out to a large segment of the population, incorporate their supporters into the political system, socialize them into the prevailing political culture, build coalitions, and forge compromises among contending groups in society.

In the developing world, however, parties often fail to provide badly needed representation to women, urban migrants, peasants, and disadvantaged minorities. All too frequently, they represent the interests of economic elites or those of a single ethnic group, religion, or region. Consider the example of Iraq, where the major political parties represent the primary religious or ethnic groups—Shi'ites, Sunnis, and Kurds—and where politicians have generally been unwilling or unable to bridge the gap between those three antagonists. In a number of other countries, political parties are built around a single charismatic leader with no clearly defined political program. Once in power, such parties usually are unable to govern effectively. The Third World's democratic surge since the 1970s has restored or given birth to more effective political parties in a number of countries. But in many LDCs, parties—as well as other key political institutions—remain relatively weak.

Although many governments in the Third World have structures that resemble Western Europe's or America's, those institutions tend to operate quite differently. Congresses and parliaments are frequently subservient to the executive branch. Their legal powers are often limited, and many regularly rubber-stamp the chief executive's policies. The judicial branch is usually weaker still, rarely challenging the executive's authority.

Military Intervention

One of the most persistent and troublesome characteristics of Third World politics, at least until recently, has been the frequent intervention of the armed forces. Between the 1930s and the 1960s, more than half of all developing nations suffered at least one military **coup** attempt. During the 1970s and early 1980s, the number of military takeovers and the frequency of extended military rule peaked, with most of Latin America and about half of Africa governed by the armed forces. But the tide began to turn toward the end of that period. Since 1980, there have been fewer new coups and a growing number of military regimes have turned power over to elected, civilian governments.

Of course, coups are but the most comprehensive form of armed forces intervention. But even elected, civilian governments may be controlled by the military. El Salvador's army effectively dominated the political system for decades under the cover of carefully controlled elections. Until recently, elected civilian governments in nations such as Guatemala, Turkey, and Thailand have been subject to the military's veto power in important policy areas.

What accounts for the frequency of armed intervention? The answer lies less in the nature of Third World militaries than in the weakness of civilian governments and their political institutions. The armed forces are more likely to seize power when civilian governments are inept or corrupt, when elected officials have little legitimacy or popular support, when there is internal political disorder or an economic crisis, or when there is a perceived likelihood of revolution. Studies of Africa, for example, show that military coups are far more likely to succeed against authoritarian civilian regimes than against democratic ones. For the most part, then, the more legitimate a civilian government is, the more it is backed by a strong political party, and the more effectively it governs, the lower the likelihood of a military coup.

The goals of military governments are as varied as the circumstances that produce them. In the most underdeveloped political systems, military officers tend to have little professional training. Consequently, the armed forces in such countries generally have no developmental goals and seize power simply to further their own interests. These types of coups often revolve around the personal ambitions of a single leader seeking power and wealth. So-called **personal coups** (led by a dominant, charismatic figure) were once common in Central America and other parts of Latin America but have largely ended there as those societies and the military's training have modernized. In recent decades, Africa has experienced a number of personal coups by ambitious officers, including Uganda's Idi Amin, Liberia's Sergeant Samuel Doe, and the Congo's General Mobutu Sese Seko. Most of those regimes governed disastrously. The Central African Republic's General Jean Bokassa, for example, killed and tortured thousands of his people, including schoolchildren. Declaring himself emperor, Bokassa spent millions of dollars on his coronation while his subjects suffered from one of the world's lowest standards of living. Idi Amin's government in Uganda killed up to half a million people.

In the more-developed Third World nations, where the officers' corps normally has greater professional training, military governments generally represent the armed forces as an institution rather than a single officer, and they tend to have broader objectives. For example, in 1973 the armed forces of Latin America's two most long-standing democracies, Chile and Uruguay, seized power for the purpose of reordering their nations' political and economic systems. Each coup sought to crush unions and leftist political parties and create a healthy environment for business investment.

Elsewhere as well, many **institutional coups** (carried out by the armed forces as an institution rather than led by a single charismatic leader) have attacked or harassed radical mass movements (guerrilla groups, militant unions, mass demonstrations, and the like); however, their strategies have varied. For example, conservative military regimes in Argentina, Chile, and Indonesia imprisoned, tortured, or killed union militants and leftist political party activists. In contrast, the left-nationalist Peruvian military government tried to outflank revolutionary movements by implementing its own radical reforms—instituting one of Latin America's most sweeping land reforms, organizing the poor into government-directed unions, and introducing limited worker ownership of urban businesses. For the most part, though, military rule in Latin America and East Asia has been conservative, whereas in Africa and the Middle East (e.g., Ethiopia, Libya, and Sudan) it often has been leftist.

Whether left-wing or right-wing, whether acting in their self-interest or for perceived national objectives, most military regimes have had poor human rights records. In the most appalling cases, they have killed many thousands (Argentina, Uganda). Elsewhere (Peru, Ecuador) they have been relatively benign but still have harassed political opponents and the media. Ultimately, all of them, no matter how well intentioned, inhibit the spread of political participation and the development of badly needed political institutions. Although some military regimes have succeeded in specific areas—agrarian reform in Peru and Ecuador, industrialization in Brazil, rapid economic growth in Indonesia and South Korea—military rule in most countries has been incompetent, corrupt, and repressive. For example, in Nigeria, a low-income nation, the former military ruler, General Sani Abacha, stole over $3 billion from government coffers (1993–1998).

As democracy has spread across Latin America and parts of Africa and Asia, the number of military governments has declined substantially, and new military takeovers are less common. In countries such as Argentina, Brazil, Chile, Indonesia, and South Korea where the military was once politically dominant, the armed forces seem committed to removing themselves from the front lines of politics. But there continue to be a significant number of attempted coups (and some successful ones) in Africa. Furthermore, since the start of the twenty-first century, the armed forces have still toppled governments in a dozen developing nations and threatened others, including Ecuador, Haiti, and Thailand.

Strong States, Weak States

In a number of Third World countries, governments are incapable of carrying out even their most basic functions: controlling their national territory, maintaining law and order, defending national sovereignty, and providing essential public services (such as schools and public health programs) to their citizens. In some cases, the state has collapsed. Journalists, academics, and diplomats often refer to such countries as failed states. Since 2005, the Fund for Peace (a research center) and the journal *Foreign Policy* have produced a Failed States Index, which ranks the strength or weakness of all United Nations member states based on 12 criteria, including economic stability and growth, human rights, number of fleeing refugees, and provision of public services. Failed states are those that perform most poorly on these dimensions. According to their 2011 index, seven of the world's 10 most badly failed states are in Africa, topped by Somalia, Chad, Sudan, and the Congo. Two of the remaining "top 10" countries—Afghanistan and Iraq—are countries where the United States has recently been involved in wars. Pakistan is not far behind with the 12th worst score. Most of the top 20 on the list are extremely poor countries such as Haiti, Ethiopia, Burma, and Yemen. About half of them have been torn apart by ethnically related or religious conflicts.[29]

Of course, most Third World states have not failed, but they have often taken on responsibilities that exceed their capabilities. Either because the private sector appeared incapable of dealing with important economic objectives or because of the government's political ideology, Third World nations frequently turned to the state (governmental authority) for solutions. For example, because it is not sufficiently profitable for private developers to build housing for the urban poor, many LDCs have created public housing agencies to address shortages in that area.

In the past, a number of Latin American governments, backed by populist political coalitions representing the middle and working classes, used government resources to promote industrial growth and expand education. Following World War II, the governments of newly independent countries in Africa and Asia were particularly inclined to intervene in the economy. Some of their earliest leaders shared a socialist vision acquired during their studies in Europe. They believed that a powerful state could promote economic development in countries with inadequate private capital. Government, they argued, could also achieve greater economic and social equality and could provide better education and health care for their impoverished populations.

But leftists were not the only ones who favored a powerful state. During the 1960s and 1970s, several right-wing military regimes in South America, most notably Brazil, increased state power in order to control radical labor unions and to stimulate industrialization. Even in the Far East, where conservative political leaders revered the free-enterprise system, the governments of Taiwan, South Korea, and Singapore helped plan and direct industrial growth.

Thus, throughout the Third World, the size and the formal power of the state expanded substantially from the 1940s to the 1980s. Large government bureaucracies were created to promote education, health care, and economic development. State enterprises often dominated banking, transportation, communications, electric power, mining, and the marketing of agricultural products. On both the left and the right, proponents of broad government intervention felt that a powerful state was the solution to a range of socioeconomic and political problems.

At the same time, despite the enormous expansion of state activities and the proliferation of government agencies, many Third World states that have appeared to be strong actually have been weak. As Lynne Hammergren has noted, "constitutions and legislation often accord enormous powers of control to central governments, but … the limited success of … governments in enforcing their own legislation suggests that the extent of this control is not great."[30] Extensive governmental programs that look impressive on paper often are far more limited in their application.

The reasons for that gap vary. In some countries, powerful, vested-interest groups such as agribusiness or bankers are able to block government initiatives that threaten their well-being. Elsewhere, governments lack the financial and technical resources to satisfactorily implement programs in areas such as public health, education, and transportation. In still other instances, government agencies simply lack the trained personnel needed to implement approved legislation. So, since the 1980s, critics have blamed excessive state intervention for many of the developing world's political and economic ills, and various governments have reduced the state's economic role.

In general, governments seem to be least successful when they manage large firms such as railroads, telephone companies, and steel mills. Frequently, such enterprises face no competition, leaving them little incentive to be efficient. All too often, the size of their payroll spirals out of control as they hire loyal supporters of the government or the ruling party for patronage jobs. Finally, many of these companies lose money by design because their products are sold at a subsidized price determined by political pressures rather than by the market. Not surprisingly, consumers soon view benefits such as cheap utility and transportation prices as their right. Consequently, few governments are prepared to alienate voters by ending those subsidies.

As government spending for subsidies and other programs spiraled without commensurate tax revenues, central governments often covered their deficits by borrowing abroad. By the 1980s, many LDCs found themselves deeply in debt to foreign banks and had alarming government budget deficits and high rates of inflation. As a consequence, there has been a strong trend in recent decades toward reducing state economic involvement. Many governments—from India and Pakistan to Argentina and Mexico (see Chapter 15)—have reduced state economic regulation and embarked on privatization programs (the sale of state enterprises to the private sector). Although some state enterprises had been successful, others had clearly been inefficient. As large government deficits and escalating foreign debt forced many developing nations to reduce state economic involvement, they often borrowed conservative economic models (referred to as neoliberal reforms) from the West. The aggressively conservative economic policies of Great Britain's Prime Minister Thatcher (Chapter 11) and American President Reagan influenced many Third World governments. Finally, the collapse of the communist Soviet bloc further discredited state-centered economies.

It is probably too early to evaluate fully the effects of privatization and government downsizing. Plagued by budgetary deficits and rampant inflation, many governments had no choice but to reduce state subsidies for basic consumer items. Undoubtedly, many privatized enterprises are now run more efficiently and make healthier profits. Yet there are also social costs to these changes. Since government subsidies were removed, already-malnourished urban families have been forced to pay higher (sometimes far higher) prices for necessities such as bread, milk, and rice. Newly privatized companies have fired thousands of workers in nations already burdened with high unemployment.

In countries such as Mexico and Pakistan, high-ranking government officials have used their inside information and influence to make fortunes in the sale of state firms. Thus, policy makers must balance the uncertain promise of longer-term economic gains with the more immediate economic and political costs of transforming their economies.

Although most analysts agree that the size of Third World governments had gotten out of hand, some worry that the pendulum has swung too far in the other direction. They argue that the state can have a positive economic influence if it channels its activities prudently. For example, working closely with the private sector, East Asian state planners have played an important role in promoting the area's economic boom. Similarly, Taiwan and South Korea achieved relatively low levels of income inequality through government intervention in the form of agrarian reform and education policy. Conversely, unfettered private enterprise may intensify already existing sharp economic inequalities in many LDCs. It remains to be seen how well governments will be able to balance the need for economic efficiency with demands for social justice and greater economic equality.

CONCLUSION: RECENT DEVELOPMENTS AND FUTURE TRENDS

The road to development has been more difficult to travel than many Third World leaders and outside analysts had originally imagined. Africa remains the most impoverished region in the developing world—devastated by civil war, dictatorship, and corruption. Famine, the result of war and government policy as much as of natural disasters, continues to afflict parts of countries such as Somalia, Malawi, and Sudan. Since the 1990s there have been some signs of improvement in both economic and political development. South Africa has created a vibrant multiracial democracy, which, whatever its limitations and current problems, has impressively reduced racial antagonisms. Between 1988 and 1994 alone, the number of electoral democracies on the African continent rose from five to 21.[31] In its most recent (2011) rankings, Freedom House rated nine sub-Saharan African nations as "Free," 22 as "Partly Free," and 17 as "Not Free" (a major improvement over the 1990s but a slight regression from the most recent annual ratings).[32] At the same time, with some notable exceptions, African economies have enjoyed one of their longest periods of sustained growth. The continent's annual economic growth rate, which averaged 2.7 percent in the 1990s, has jumped to about 4 percent since 2000.[33] Still, with populations growing at annual rates of 3 percent or more in countries such as Madagascar, Congo, Uganda, and Liberia, economic growth rates are struggling to keep up. Moreover, most African economies remain heavily dependent on a few commodity exports (such as petroleum, coffee, cocoa, copper, and sugar). Commodity prices have generally boomed in recent years, contributing heavily to the region's economic surge. But these prices have always been cyclical in the past and may very well come down in the future.

The 1980s debt crisis brought Latin America the most intense economic decline since the global depression of the 1930s. Per capita GNP diminished, unemployment rose sharply, and high rates of inflation badly eroded consumers' purchasing power.

Since that time, the severe inflation that had afflicted countries such as Argentina, Brazil, Mexico, Peru, and Nicaragua has been brought under control, and much of the region has experienced economic growth. But that growth has been rather erratic, and some countries have suffered sharp reverses. Thus, although Argentina was growing at a very rapid clip in the early 1990s, it suffered from a severe economic crisis at the start of this century, sending living standards plunging. After 2002 the economy resumed growth, but the rate of poverty has only fallen slowly from its record highs. And even in countries that have benefited from more sustained economic growth, that growth often has not translated into greater employment or improved living standards for the poor.

Ironically, at the very time Latin America's economies were at their worst, the region was making impressive progress toward more democratic and responsible government. In the mid-1970s, most of Latin America was ruled by military dictatorships, some benign and others quite ruthless. By the start of the 1990s, however, democratically or semidemocratically elected governments had been installed in nearly every country in the region. Human rights and personal liberties have improved considerably in such countries as Argentina, Brazil, Chile, El Salvador, and Uruguay, though other governments, such as Colombia's and Haiti's, still frequently violate their citizens' fundamental rights.

The Far East and parts of Southeast Asia have enjoyed the Third World's greatest economic success in recent decades. The economies of South Korea, Taiwan, Singapore, Hong Kong, China, Thailand, Malaysia, and Indonesia all grew at annual rates of 7 to 10 percent or more from the 1980s into the late 1990s and resumed that rate in the twenty-first century. As we noted earlier (Chapter 13), China now has the second-largest economy in the world. Moreover, countries such as South Korea, Taiwan, Singapore, and Indonesia have achieved extraordinary growth rates while maintaining relatively equitable distributions of income. The impressive success of the Far Eastern economic model suggests the value of balanced development strategies, increased industrial exports, and a cooperative relationship between government planners and private enterprise. To be sure, East Asia's 1997–1999 financial crisis threw millions of people out of work in Thailand, Malaysia, Indonesia, South Korea, and Singapore, indicating that the region's heavy dependence on the international economy has some risks. But those economies have since recovered.

Politically, however, the region has made slower progress toward democracy and the protection of human rights than Latin America has. Until relatively recently, NICs such as Taiwan and South Korea retained nondemocratic governments long past the thresholds of economic development and literacy that enabled other countries to turn to democracy, though they have now made that democratic transition. Singapore and Malaysia, two of the most economically developed LDCs, have yet to achieve even electoral democracy. Indonesia now has had fair and honest national elections but still suffers from continuing human rights abuses, especially in its treatment of rebellious ethnic minorities. And nations such as Bangladesh, Vietnam, and Zimbabwe have made little progress toward any kind of democracy. In the Middle East and North Africa, revolts in Tunisia, Egypt, and Libya will hopefully usher in an era of greater democracy and lower corruption, but those outcomes are by no means assured.

All of that suggests the enormous difficulty of trying to achieve economic growth, equitable income distribution, political stability, democratic government, and national autonomy simultaneously. Although many of the world's LDCs hope to become "another Hong Kong" or "another South Korea," (i.e., very economically developed) it is uncertain how many will have the internal capabilities or external possibilities that will permit them to do so.

Since the nineteenth century, there have been three important worldwide waves of democratization (1828–1926, 1943–1962, and 1974–present). The first two advances were followed by more limited reverse waves back to authoritarianism. So, although there is considerable worldwide pressure for Third World governments to join the current wave of democratization in the LDCs and former communist nations, it is difficult to know how effective or how permanent those pressures will be. As we have noted, Freedom House's 2011 evaluations of democracy in the world report that average scores for political rights and civil liberties have declined somewhat in each of the past five years. In the Arab world, democracy still faces an uncertain future. The paths of political and economic development are challenging, complex, and sometimes difficult to predict. So far, there has been only a slight reverse wave (a retreat from democracy) in the developing world. It remains to be seen whether or not the recent Arab Spring will set off a new wave of democratization in other developing countries.

◆ ◆ ◆

Key Terms and Concepts _____

coup	institutional coups
dependency theory	legitimacy
electoral democracies	less-developed countries (LDCs)
ethnicity	liberal democracy
failed state	modernization theory
Gender Inequality Index (GII)	newly industrialized countries (NICs)
Gender Empowerment Measure (GEM)	parity purchasing power, or PPP
	personal coups
Gini index	political underdevelopment
globalization	Third World
Human Development Index (HDI)	traditional society

DISCUSSION QUESTIONS

1. *Why has the Arab world been the slowest region to democratize in the third wave of democratization? What factors set off the 2010–2011 Arab Spring (the wave of mass prodemocracy protests), and what are the remaining obstacles for democracy in that region?*

2. *Compare the explanations for underdevelopment offered by modernization theory with those offered by dependency theory. What are the strengths and the weaknesses of each theory?*

3. *What are the major economic and political problems that particularly confront women in the developing world? How well represented are women in important political offices? How have women managed to make it to the top of the political system in a number of Asian countries?*

4. *What factors account for the wave of democratic change that has swept over much of the developing world since the mid-1970s?*

5. *What accounted for the traditionally high number of military takeovers in the politics of Third World nations? Why has military intervention been declining?*

6. *What lessons might Kenya's political leaders learn from a careful study of their country's past ethnic conflicts?*

Notes _____

1. World Bank, "GNIC Per Capita, 2010." http://data.worldbank.org/indicator/.
2. Like Table 14.1, all the data contained in the preceding discussion of the table come from the UNDP's *Human Development Report 2010*, or in the few cases where 2010 data were not available, from the 2009 report.
3. United Nations Development Programme (UNDP), *Human Development Report*, 1997 (New York: Oxford University Press, 1997), pp. 24–26; Population Reference Bureau, 2007 *World Population Data Sheet*, www.prb.org/pdf07/07WPDS_Eng.pdf.
4. UNDP, *Human Development Report*, 1997 (New York: Oxford University Press, 1997), pp. 24–26; *Human Development Report*, 2007 (New York: Oxford University Press, 2007).
5. World Bank Group, *World Development Indicators* (2005); http://devdata.worldbank.org/wdi2005/Section1_1_1.htm.
6. Samuel P. Huntington, "The Goals of Development," in *Understanding Political Development*, ed. Myron Weiner and Samuel Huntington (Boston: Little, Brown, 1986), p. 3.
7. Guillermo O'Donnell and Philippe Schmitter, *Transitions from Authoritarian Rule: Tentative Conclusions about Uncertain Democracies* (Baltimore: Johns Hopkins University Press, 1986).
8. See data by Freedom House published each year in the January issue of the *Journal of Democracy*.
9. Freedom House, *Freedom in the World 2011*.
10. *The New York Times*, "Where a Cuddle with Your Baby Requires a Bribe," August 30, 2005.
11. John O. Oucho, *Undercurrents of Ethnic Conflict in Kenya* (Boston: Brill, 2002).
12. Joel Barkan and Makau Matua, "Turning the Corner in Kenya: A New Constitution for Nairobi," *Foreign Affairs* (August 10, 2010), www.foreignaffairs.com/search/turning%20the%20corner%20in%20Kenya.
13. Transparency International, *Corruption Perceptions Index 2010*, www.transparency.org/.
14. The most important modernization literature includes Huntington, *Political Order in Changing Societies*, and Gabriel Almond and James Coleman, eds., *The Politics of Developing Areas* (Princeton, NJ: Princeton University Press, 1960).
15. Huntington, *Political Order in Changing Societies*.
16. Fernando Henrique Cardoso and Enzo Faletto, *Dependency and Development in Latin America* (Berkeley and Los Angeles: University of California Press, 1979).
17. Hollis Chenery et al., *Redistribution with Growth* (London: Oxford University Press with the World Bank and the University of Sussex, 1974).
18. Dirk Willem te Velde, *The Global Financial Crisis and Developing Countries* (Overseas Development Institute, October 2008). www.odi.org.uk/resources/download/2462.pdf.
19. See, for example. Jeffrey Page, *Agrarian Revolution* (New York: Free Press, 1975) and Theda Skocpol, *States and Revolutions* (Cambridge, UK: Cambridge University Press, 1979).
20. Eric Wolf, *Peasant Wars in the Twentieth Century* (New York: Harper and Row, 1969).
21. Crawford Young, *The Politics of Cultural Pluralism* (Madison: University of Wisconsin Press, 1976), p. 301.
22. Ted Robert Gurr, "Preface" and "Long War, Short Peace: The Rise and Decline of Ethnopolitical Conflict at the End of the Cold War," in *Peoples versus States: Minorities at Risk in the New Century*, ed. T. Gurr (Washington, DC: United States Institute of Peace Press, 2000), pp. xiii, 27–56.

23. Michael Ross, "Does Oil Hinder Democracy?" *World Politics* 53 (April 2001): 328–356.

24. David Kirkpatrick, "Wired and Shrewd, Young Egyptians Guide Revolt," *The New York Times* (February 9, 2011).

25. Huntington, *Political Order*.

26. Mitchell A. Seligson, "Democratization in Latin America: The Current Cycle," in *Authoritarians and Democrats: Regime Transition in Latin America*, ed. James M. Malloy and Mitchell A. Seligson (Pittsburgh: University of Pittsburgh Press, 1987), pp. 7–9.

27. Adam Przeworski et al., "What Makes Democracies Endure," in *Consolidating Third Wave Democracies*, ed. Larry Diamond et al. (Baltimore: Johns Hopkins University Press, 1997), p. 297. The dollar amounts quoted here are in constant dollars—that is, the effect of inflation over the years has been statistically factored out.

28. Population Reference Bureau, "Taking Stock of Women's Progress," www.prb.org.

29. "The Failed State Index, 2011," *Foreign Policy* www.foreignpolicy.com/failedstates.

30. Linn A. Hammergren, "Corporatism in Latin American Politics: A Reexamination of the 'Unique' Tradition," *Comparative Politics* (July 1977): 449.

31. Michael Bratton and Nicolas van de Walle, *Democratic Experiments in Africa: Regime Transitions in Comparative Perspective* (New York: Cambridge University Press, 1997), p. 120.

32. Freedom House, *Freedom in the World 2011*.

33. Frans Cronje, "SAIRR Today: African Growth—20th June 2008," www.sairr.org.za/sairr-today/sairr-today-african-growth-20-june-2008.html/. The regional growth rate dropped to 2 percent in 2009 and rebounded to 4 percent in 2010, according to IMF data.

CHAPTER 15

Mexico: The Birth Pangs of Democracy

As the power (and firepower) of the Mexican drug cartels has grown to new heights, President Felipe Calderón has turned to the armed forces, shown here, to supplement or replace often-corrupt police anti-drug units.

- The Relevance of Mexican Politics
- Mexico's Formative Years and the Legacy of the Mexican Revolution
- The Postrevolutionary Order
- The Making of a Modern Economy
- The Struggle for Political Development
- Conclusion: A Developing Democracy

2010 was a year of celebrations in Mexico. The nation commemorated both the 200th anniversary of the start of its war of independence against Spain and the 100th anniversary of its revolution, which created a modern nation-state. But for many Mexicans, just emerging from a decade of economic stagnation, facing a rising homicide rate, and increasingly cynical about the government's bloody war on drugs, there was little to celebrate. Across the border from El Paso, Texas, Ciudad Juárez and several other cities at the center of drug-war violence canceled their celebrations out of concern for public safety. Coincidentally, 2010 was also the 10th anniversary of the country's transition to democracy. For the last 71 years of the twentieth century, Mexico had been governed by the **Institutional Revolutionary Party (PRI)**.* During the decade following the collapse of Soviet communism, the PRI was the world's longest-standing, continuously ruling political party.† But on July 2, 2000, Vicente Fox—candidate of the **National Action Party (PAN)**—became the first fully democratically elected president in the nation's history. It was an outcome that few Mexicans would have predicted and that many, including the winners, initially found hard to believe. Six years later, Mexicans consolidated their country's

---

* Mexico's three leading political parties—the Institutional Revolutionary Party, the National Action Party, and the Party of the Democratic Revolution—are known respectively by their Spanish acronyms (PRI, PAN, and PRD).

† The party had two other names before changing its name in 1946 to the PRI. To simplify matters, we will call it the PRI even when referring to events that occurred before it took that name.

democratic transition by electing the PAN's presidential candidate, Felipe Calderón. The once all-powerful PRI not only suffered its second consecutive presidential election defeat but actually finished a distant third.

For most of the twentieth century, Mexican political and economic development was structured by the country's 1910 revolution and by the "official party" that emerged from that struggle. The revolution unleashed a period of chaos and devastation, but ultimately it also laid the foundation for the nation's political and economic modernization. It spawned a ruling party that governed Mexico from 1929 to 2000, established political stability, improved political representation, and produced 50 years of rapid economic growth. Presidents wielded enormous power but were limited to one term in office. Unlike most of its Latin American neighbors, military coups were (and still are) unknown. At the same time, however, the revolution and the PRI also created authoritarian rule, rampant corruption, and severe economic inequality. Because of both its accomplishments and its willingness to win at any cost, the PRI won all elections of any importance until the 1980s and continued to hold Mexico's all-powerful presidency until 2000. The country continues to face serious political, social, and economic problems. But it has taken the first giant steps toward creating a more democratic and responsive political system.[1]

THE RELEVANCE OF MEXICAN POLITICS

As America's neighbor, one of its largest trading partners, a major supplier of petroleum, and the point of origin for substantial legal and illegal immigration, Mexico's importance to the United States is profound. Its impressive record of growth and industrialization until the early 1980s seemed to offer valuable lessons for other developing nations. During the late 1980s and the 1990s, the country reversed its long-standing, state-centered, protectionist economic model and became a leader in neoliberal reform (the process of opening up the country to greater foreign trade and investment while reducing government's role in the economy).

More recently, however, the flaws in Mexico's economic and political development models have become more apparent. Economic crises in 1982 and 1995 highlighted both the continuing poverty that afflicts about half the Mexican population and the inefficiencies of the country's economy. Although there has been slow economic growth since 1996, it has been inconsistent, with a substantial decline during the 2009 world economic crisis. And while the neoliberal reforms of the 1990s were likely necessary, they also caused great suffering among the nation's poor.

At the same time, the combination of extensive political corruption, periodic government repression, and growing political opposition under the PRI revealed that Mexico was not "a peculiar democracy" (as it had once been labeled) but rather an authoritarian system in need of reform. The slow but steady erosion of PRI dominance since the 1980s and the emergence of two major opposition parties reflected mounting discontent with the old political order. That progress culminated with Vicente Fox's 2000 presidential victory. In 2006 the PAN once again won the presidential election. But although Mexico has achieved the primary prerequisite of democratic government—fair and competitive elections—it still retains some of its old authoritarian characteristics.

MEXICO

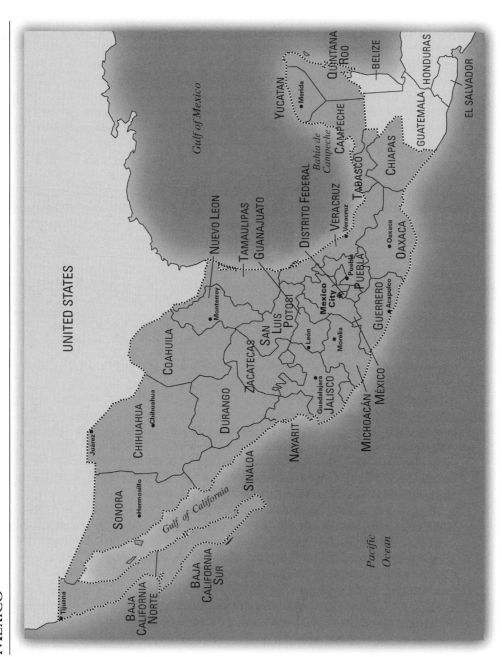

Before looking at Mexico's current political system, however, we must first examine the country's past. Its colonial heritage of sharp class divisions (reinforcing racial distinctions), its weak political system in the nineteenth century, and its twentieth-century efforts—starting with the Mexican Revolution—to create a strong nation-state and a more equitable society have all left indelible marks on the contemporary political scene.

MEXICO'S FORMATIVE YEARS AND THE LEGACY OF THE MEXICAN REVOLUTION

Like many developing nations, Mexico achieved independence with few of the prerequisites for a successful nation-state. During much of the nineteenth century, the central government was unable to control the country's regional military–political bosses. Thus, during Mexico's first 40 years of independence, some 50 presidents (including some repeats) governed the country. Internal strife and government instability left the country vulnerable to foreign intervention. Consequently, Texas's secession and the subsequent war with the United States (1848) stripped the nation of nearly half its territory.[2]

In addition, Mexican society was sharply divided along ethnic and class lines. The Spanish colonial conquest had imposed European culture and religion on a large Native American population, with power concentrated in the hands of the Spanish authorities and a small upper class of Whites born in the New World (*criollos*). At the same time, the largest segment of the population consisted of poor Indian or *mestizo* peasants,* who were often forced into virtual serfdom on White-owned agricultural and ranching estates. Independence failed to temper those racial and class cleavages. And even when subsequent modernization reduced racial divisions, class-based barriers to social mobility remained strong.

In 1876, General Porfirio Díaz established himself as the country's supreme military strongman. He was the first Mexican national leader to exercise firm control over the regional *caciques* (political bosses) and ruled with an iron fist until 1911. Attracted by Mexico's newfound stability, its favorable climate for investment, and its restrictive labor laws, foreign investors built Mexico's railroad, electrical power, and telephone networks while further developing manufacturing, mining, agriculture, and ranching. Although those investments contributed to economic growth, they also provoked a nationalist backlash. Díaz himself allegedly exclaimed, "Poor Mexico, so far from God and so close to the United States!"

The economic modernization that Díaz fostered carried within it the seeds of his regime's destruction. The expansion of plantation agriculture in the south and ranching in the north further encroached on the small farms of the beleaguered peasantry. The development of mining, petroleum, railroads, and limited manufacturing created an incipient working class that lacked the fundamental right to unionize or strike.

---

* In Latin America, the term *mestizo* generally refers to Indians who have been integrated, either voluntarily or forcefully, into the dominant White (Spanish) culture. While some mestizos have Indian and White parentage, most do not. Thus, the term usually refers to a cultural, rather than a biological, union.

In the cities, economic growth produced a small but influential middle class. With political and economic power in the hands of foreign corporations and the tiny Mexican elite, this emerging group of professionals and small businesspeople had few opportunities for upward mobility and, consequently, had their own grievances.

In 1910, Francisco Madero, a wealthy political reformer who had just lost to Díaz in a fraudulent presidential election, appealed to the Mexican population, particularly the middle class, to overthrow the government. Although Madero's goals were largely modest political reforms, his call for revolt provoked the twentieth century's first mass-based revolution. In the cities, workers mobilized to fight for trade-union rights. In various parts of the countryside, peasants and cowboys organized to regain their lands under the leadership of men such as Emiliano Zapata and Pancho Villa (Shown in the photo below). For the next decade, the revolutionary struggle convulsed the nation. Before the fighting ended with a revolutionary victory, it killed more than 1 million people (out of a total population of 14.5 million) and wiped some 8,000 villages off the map.[3] Unlike many other twentieth-century revolutions, however, the Mexican insurrection lacked a unifying political party, ideology, or charismatic leader. Peasants, workers, land owners, the middle class, and military leaders all fought for different political and socioeconomic goals. Counterrevolutionary forces soon assassinated Madero. Eventually, many other revolutionary leaders—including Zapata, Villa, and revolutionary president Venustiano Carranza—lost their lives in the struggle.

ZAPATA AND HIS MEN   Despite his limited education and political experience, Emiliano Zapata was one of the most important regional military leaders of the Mexican Revolution. Shown here (center, with a large hat in his lap), Zapata is joined by Pancho Villa (to his right, in uniform). Both revolutionary chiefs are flanked by their men. A man of great personal integrity, Zapata remains today perhaps the most revered revolutionary hero. The Zapatista rebel movement that shook Mexico in the 1990s was, of course, named after him.

As an indication of Mexico's newly competitive political system, presidential candidates now regularly confront each other in nationally televised debates. Here we see the second televised debate of the most recent (2006) campaign. Felipe Calderón (PAN), the eventual winner, is the second candidate from the right. His leading opponent, Andrés Manuel López Obrado (PRD), is on the far right of the photo.

Although numerically superior, the peasants and workers lacked the leadership, the funds, and the organization to carry the revolution's radical wing to victory. It was the centrist forces—led by middle-class (or upper-class) military men—that emerged triumphant. Although the constitution of 1917 called for limits on foreign investment, pledged land to the peasants, and offered union rights to the workers, it would be almost two decades before Mexico's government seriously addressed most of those more radical promises.

THE POSTREVOLUTIONARY ORDER

Political Consolidation (1920–1946)

Political turmoil and bloodshed carried into the next decade. In 1929, seeking to end the perpetual conflicts between regional strongmen and to stabilize the political system, Mexico's political leaders created the National Revolutionary Party (PNR), a coalition of the winning factions in the revolutionary upheaval. The party brought together various regional parties, military and civilian strongmen, and organized sectors of the civilian population. "From the beginning the PNR was envisioned as a dominant, governing party."[4] Its function was to represent and control significant sectors of the population: the peasantry, labor, the middle class, and the military. Other parties ran candidates, but for more than half a century they hardly ever won at any level. In the late 1930s, the party strengthened its labor and peasant wings and soon thereafter ended party representation of the military. In 1946, its name was changed (for the second time) to the Institutional Revolutionary Party, or PRI.

The Cárdenas Era of Social and Economic Reform (1934–1940)

Having established political stability, Mexico's leaders turned their attention to the revolution's still unfulfilled social and economic promises. President Lázaro Cárdenas's election in 1934 was a victory for the more progressive wing of the ruling (official) party. Cárdenas initiated Latin America's most far-reaching land reform, distributing some 29 million acres to the nation's peasantry.* He also expanded the country's labor movement substantially and incorporated previously excluded radical unions into the PRI. Finally, Cárdenas implemented many of the revolution's nationalist objectives. Recall that widespread resentment of foreign economic dominance was a major cause of the revolutionary struggle. But the postrevolutionary regime did little to address that issue until Cárdenas's administration nationalized Mexico's petroleum industry and railroads. In the following decades, the government also took control of the electrical power, telephone–telegraph, and banking sectors and established substantial footholds in steel and in agricultural marketing. Although most of the economy remained in private hands, the state became Mexico's largest economic player by controlling most of the country's infrastructure (transportation, telecommunications, and energy—most notably petroleum and electric power) and many of its largest corporations in a mixture of state-controlled and private market economies known as **state capitalism**.

Government economic activity expanded further in the 1970s and early 1980s. But by the late 1980s and 1990s, a large portion of the once-substantial public sector was privatized (sold to the private sector) as part of a package of neoliberal (free-market) reforms.

THE MAKING OF A MODERN ECONOMY

The Mexican "Economic Miracle"

Cárdenas's radical reforms (particularly those designed to redistribute resources to the poor) proved to be a short-lived deviation from the otherwise centrist path of the revolution. From the 1940s onward, state economic policy was designed to stimulate growth, with little concern for how that affected the distribution of income and resources. Agricultural credits and state irrigation projects that Cárdenas had directed toward the peasant communities were instead channeled toward agribusiness. From the 1940s until the 1980s, Mexico's government, like its counterparts in most of Latin America, supported private-sector industrialization through government subsidies, tax credits, and restrictions on competing imports. At the same time, government control over the nation's labor unions restricted labor unrest and kept wages down in order to attract greater business investment.

Those policies led to what many scholars have called the **Mexican economic miracle**. The country's GDP grew at an average annual rate of more than 6 percent during those decades of state intervention (see Table 15.1), a more prolonged period of high growth than either the United States or Japan had enjoyed during their primary economic expansions.[5] As a consequence, within several decades Mexico changed from a predominantly rural, agricultural country to a largely urban nation with a

---

* In fact, he distributed more land to the peasantry than the combined total of all previous presidents since the 1910 revolution. The agrarian reform reduced peasant unrest and rural poverty somewhat.

TABLE 15.1	Mexico's Average Annual Growth, 1940–1980 (Average Percentage Growth per Year)			
	1940–1950	**1950–1960**	**1960–1970**	**1970–1980**
Population	2.8	3.1	3.8	3.6
GDP	6.9	5.6	7.0	5.5
Agriculture	5.1	4.6	3.7	2.4
Industry	8.1	6.5	8.8	6.7
Service	7.0	5.6	6.8	5.2

SOURCE: An Overview of the Mexican Economy in *Economic Policy Making in Mexico*, Robert Looney, pp. 5–27 (use of Table 1.2). Copyright, 1985, Duke University Press. All rights reserved. Reprinted by permission of the publisher. www.dukeupress.edu

workforce primarily employed in the service and manufacturing sectors.* Education expanded apace. Whereas only 10 percent of the population had been literate at the time of the Mexican Revolution, more than 90 percent were literate by the end of the century.

The Other Side of the Miracle

Despite the country's dramatic record of modernization and growth, critics insisted that the economic miracle left too many people behind. Peasants and workers had fought and died in the revolution hoping to improve their living conditions. Champions of economic redistribution, such as Emiliano Zapata, became national folk heroes. Yet it had clearly been the poor, especially the peasantry, who gained least from the revolution and its aftermath.

The economic boom that began during World War II expanded the size of the urban middle class and created a significant number of better-paid industrial jobs for skilled workers. But government policies placed a higher priority on economic growth than on equitable income distribution. Table 15.2 indicates that during Mexico's extended economic expansion (1940 to 1982), the richest 20 percent of the population earned between 54 and 64 percent of the nation's income, by world standards a very high concentration of wealth in the hands of a few.[6] Although income concentration diminished somewhat in the 1970s, the gaps have widened again since the 1980s, leaving the country with a high level of inequality (Table 15.2).[7] The CIA's World Factbook 2011 indicated that, of 136 countries for which income distribution data (Gini indices) are currently available, Mexico is the 27th most unequal.[8]

In the decades following World War II, the government's preferential treatment toward large-scale, mechanized farming undermined peasant producers and contributed to rural poverty. Many peasants who could not compete with larger farms

---

* In 1940, some 65 percent of Mexico's economically active population worked in agriculture. Consequently, agrarian reform was a major issue. By 2000, however, only about 5 percent of the country's GDP (though perhaps two to three times that proportion of the workforce) came from agriculture, 69 percent came from the service sector, and 27 percent came from industry (see the *Economist* Intelligence Unit, April 19, 2001).

TABLE 15.2	Income Distribution in Mexico, 1950–2000		
	Percentage of National Income		
Year	Poorest 50 Percent	Middle 30 Percent	Richest 20 Percent
1950	17.4	23.7	58.9
1969	15.0	21.0	64.0
1992	18.4	27.4	54.1
2000	15.6*	26.2*	58.2*

*The 2000 data are extrapolated from the World Bank, *World Development Report, 2000/2001*, which breaks down the population slightly differently for the 40th to 50th percentiles of the population.

Source: Daniel Levy and Gabriel Székely, *Mexico: Paradoxes of Stability and Change* (Boulder, CO: Westview, 1983), p. 144; Daniel C. Levy and Kathleen Bruhn, "Mexico: Sustained Civilian Rule without Democracy," *in Politics in Developing Countries: Comparing Experiences with Democracy*, eds. Larry Diamond, Juan J. Linz, and Seymour Martin Lipset (Boulder, CO: Lynne Rienner Publishers, 1995), p. 195; and World Bank, *World Development Report, 2000/2001: Attacking Poverty* (New York: Oxford University Press, 2001), pp. 282–283.

instead had to work as poorly paid agricultural laborers or migrate to the cities. Today, Mexico's rural poor are still more likely to be malnourished than their urban counterparts and are less well-paid, less educated, and less likely to enjoy amenities such as electricity or clean drinking water.

As a consequence of that gap, Mexico, like many developing nations, has experienced substantial rural-to-urban migration. Between 1940 and 1981, despite higher birth rates in the countryside, urban centers grew from 22 percent of the nation's population to 55 percent.[9] But because industrial development has been capital-intensive rather than labor-intensive, the cities have failed to produce sufficient employment to meet the needs of their burgeoning workforce. Consequently, even at the height of Mexico's economic boom, some 35 percent of the economically active population lacked full-time employment.[10] As a consequence of the economic crises in the 1980s and 1990s and slow growth since, that figure has increased.

Excessive migration to cities has produced other problems as well. Mexico City's metropolitan area currently houses close to 20 million people, making it one of the world's largest urban centers. Moreover, each year an additional 500,000 people migrate to the capital. Because resources have not matched that enormous growth, it has become one of the world's most polluted and most traffic-congested cities.* Millions of inhabitants live in shantytowns and slums, where they suffer from unsanitary conditions, crime, and inadequate social services. For many others who feel that neither the countryside nor the cities offer sufficient opportunities, the United States has always beckoned. Although illegal immigration obviously creates problems for U.S. policy makers, it does provide Mexico with an important pressure valve for its social and political tensions.

* In recent decades the government has reduced air pollution in the capital by restricting auto traffic, introducing taxis and buses with lower emissions, and moving industry out of the city. Still, pollution remains a problem, as do poor sewage and other environmental health hazards.

A number of government programs since the 1970s, under PRI and PAN presidents alike, have sought to improve living conditions and incomes for the poor. At various times, these plans have included irrigation projects for poor farmers, potable water and sewage services for low-income urban neighborhoods, construction of schools and medical clinics, employment programs, and, most recently, a program granting subsidies to poor families whose children stay in school. But the benefits from these programs have failed to compensate for declining living standards during the country's repeated economic crises since 1982. Nor, as we have seen, have they reduced Mexico's great income inequality.

Since the 1980s: From Boom to Bust to Slow Recovery to Renewed Crisis

During the 1970s, economic growth in Mexico, as in most of Latin America, was fueled by a large infusion of loans from international banks and lending agencies. When President Luis Echeverría took office in 1970, support for the regime was at a low point in the wake of a government massacre of as many as 300 student protestors shortly before Mexico City hosted the 1968 Summer Olympics. He tried to rebuild the government's support by introducing a number of welfare programs and business subsidies. As spending increased and revenues failed to rise correspondingly, the government turned to external borrowing.

Fiscal deficits and external borrowing increased further under Echeverría's successor, José López Portillo (1976–1982). Unfortunately, the state petroleum corporation's discovery of vast new oilfields in the mid-1970s gave the government an exaggerated sense of the country's projected oil-export revenues in the coming years. As a consequence, the government accelerated its spending far faster than its short-term revenues grew in order to satisfy the population's increasing demands for services and benefits. Mexico's private sector shared the government's optimism about future economic growth as corporations also accelerated their borrowing from abroad. Both the Mexican government and foreign lenders (U.S., Japanese, and European banks) believed that the sharp rise in oil prices in the early 1970s would continue into the foreseeable future, guaranteeing Mexico sufficient funds to repay its debt. From 1970 to 1981, the government's foreign debt grew from $4.3 billion to $53 billion and private-sector external debt jumped from $1.8 billion to $20.3 billion. Other Latin American countries, including those without oil, became similarly indebted, but Mexico and Brazil led the way. When the price of oil dropped sharply in 1981, Mexico's economic boom unraveled.

President José López Portillo's 1982 announcement that Mexico was no longer able to make payments on its debt put a brake on further loans to all of Latin America and precipitated the region's debt crisis, which lasted throughout the decade. For one thing, it became more difficult to receive international loans. To deal with the crisis, the Mexican government was forced to introduce **economic austerity**—belt-tightening measures including cutbacks on government spending, ongoing devaluation of the nation's currency, and policies that prevented wages from keeping pace with inflation.

From 1982 to 1988, the country experienced almost no economic growth (the GNP actually declined in three of those years), whereas the population increased by approximately 15 percent. Inflation rose sharply, peaking at an annual rate of 160 percent in 1987, but wages failed to keep pace. As a consequence, the average worker's real income (actual purchasing power) declined by 40 to 50 percent in the 1980s, wiping out many of the gains achieved during the oil boom. A United Nations study conducted at the end of that decade revealed that over half the population was at least somewhat malnourished.

By the end of the decade, the government had brought inflation under control, but living standards had not recovered.[11] Not surprisingly, support for the PRI and the government—which had been bolstered by the earlier economic boom—eroded. Finally, soon after the country resumed modest economic growth in the early 1990s, a renewed fiscal crisis in 1995 sent it into another severe depression. GDP fell by 6.9 percent that year, the worst decline since the Mexican Revolution, and unemployment increased by two million as many companies went bankrupt.[12] Although economic growth resumed in 1996 and per capita income has returned to 1994 levels, this growth has been very slow and erratic—averaging less than 1 percent since 2005— and a large portion of the nation's poor have yet to benefit from the recent recovery. Moreover, that modest recovery was cut short by the world economic crisis in 2009 as the country's GDP declined by 6.8 percent, the steepest drop in years.* Because Mexico's state petroleum monopoly (Pemex) is now so inefficient and so badly strapped for investment funds, oil production and exports (in volume) have stagnated in recent years. Consequently, the country has not benefited nearly as much as it should have from soaring oil prices during the past decade.

THE STRUGGLE FOR POLITICAL DEVELOPMENT

Creating a Powerful State

As we have seen, in the years from the end of its revolution (1920) until the early 1980s, Mexico experienced substantial growth in state power over the economy and society. By the 1970s, as the task of managing the economy became more complex, a growing number of key government decisions were being made by a new elite of highly trained government bureaucrats—often with graduate degrees in economics, public administration, or planning from leading American universities—rather than by elected politicians.[13] Since Mexican political institutions are often less than they seem—the Congress, for example, exercised very little independent power until the late 1990s—the discussion of Mexican politics that follows focuses less on political institutions and more on the role of the state in mediating conflicts in society over income distribution, economic growth, political rights and freedoms, and other issues fundamental to developing nations. We will also be examining the proper role and size of the state itself. And finally, we will look at Mexico's recent transition to democratic government and discuss future prospects for Mexican democracy.

---

* Moreover, during the first half of the decade (2000–2005) when most economies were doing well, World Bank data showed that Latin America had the slowest annual rate of economic growth of any world region (2.3%, about half of Africa's rate and a bit over one-fourth of East Asia's). And Mexico's average annual growth rate of 1.9% during that period was among the lowest in Latin America.

Nominally, Mexico is a federal republic modeled after the United States. Like the United States, it features a division of federal powers between the president, Congress, and the courts. In practice, however, Mexican politics has featured a tremendous concentration of power. State governments depend on the federal government for revenues, and until recently presidents could remove state governors from office when dissatisfied with their performance (although formally it was Congress that declared the post vacant). Within the national government itself, the president exercised extraordinary power, though that had begun to change after 1997 when Ernesto Zedillo (1994–2000) became the first Mexican president in some 70 years to lack a congressional majority. His successors, Vicente Fox (2000–2006) and Felipe Calderón (2006–2012), also lacked majority support in Congress. Furthermore, Zedillo and Fox voluntarily restricted some of their presidential authority and also transferred some power from the central government to state and local authorities.

The Executive Branch and the Bureaucracy

Before the revolution, Mexico alternated between rule by *caudillos* (military strongmen), such as Porfirio Díaz, and periods of great instability. The chaos of the revolution and the spate of political assassinations that continued through the 1920s convinced the revolutionary elite that the country had to invest great power in the presidency. Consequently, the president, no matter who held the office, dominated the political system until quite recently. Before the 1980s, even newspapers and opposition political parties hesitated to criticize the chief executive directly, focusing instead on his advisers or his policies. But, at the same time, to prevent the return of an extended dictatorship like Díaz's, the 1917 constitution limited the president (as well as all other elected officials) to a single term in office. Subsequently, the length of that term was fixed at six years. Until 1997, "Congress ... [was] a rubber stamp, passing nearly all laws proposed by the president without effecting major modifications; the judicial branch of government ... exhibited only a slightly greater degree of autonomy."[14]

But even before the recent transition to democracy, one person could not rule a nation as large and complex as Mexico. Hence, a vast bureaucratic network developed within the executive branch, whose members constituted a new ruling class of administrators. At the pinnacle of that administrative elite has been the cabinet. The president has given cabinet ministers—particularly those holding such posts as finance minister and interior minister—extensive powers (subject, of course, to his approval). Under PRI governments, the cabinet also served as a stepping-stone to the presidency.

Until the election of Vicente Fox (a former governor with extensive prior experience as a business executive), presidents in recent decades had emerged from that bureaucratic elite. Typically, a modern PRI president started his career by attaching himself to a patron in a powerful ministry, following him up the rungs of the administrative ladder. If his patron eventually reached the presidency, the new chief executive named his most talented government aids to his cabinet, and in the last months of his presidency he picked one of them to be the next PRI presidential candidate (in an election which, until 2000, he was assured of winning).

For most presidents from the 1970s through the 1990s, their own presidential campaign was their first race for any elected office. That pattern of political advancement through a bureaucratic, patron–client network (called a *camarilla*) has now seemingly come to an end. In the 2000 presidential election, the PRI presidential candidate was elected in a party primary, a far cry from the past practice of the outgoing president handpicking his own successor. Fox, the candidate of a party (PAN) that had never previously won a presidential election, took a different route to that office. He first established himself as a rancher and a Coca-Cola executive in Mexico and was then elected governor of his home state of Guanajuato. In fact, in a reversal of recent patterns, all three major presidential candidates in both the 2000 and 2006 elections had previously been elected to important government offices.

Presidentialism (presidential political supremacy), although undemocratic, fulfilled several important functions. Symbolically, the head of state was the bearer of the revolutionary tradition and a source of unity for a geographically and socio-economically diverse nation.[15] Ironically, when President Zedillo tried to promote greater democracy by limiting the "imperial presidency"—including renouncing his own right to handpick the next PRI presidential candidate—much of the Mexican public dismissed him as weak, so widely accepted had the idea of an all-powerful presidency become. President Fox faced some of the same criticisms. But with Mexico's Congress now divided between three major parties (and a handful of smaller ones), no president has commanded a majority in the national legislature for over 10 years, nor does it seem likely that anyone will in the near future. Without guaranteed congressional support, which was a given for 68 years of PRI presidents in the twentieth century, the president's powers have been significantly cut. While Congress eventually passed most of Fox's and Calderón's proposed legislation (and both men had a higher success rate than most U.S. presidents), many important bills were significantly amended or watered down before they were approved.

Congress

Mexico's Congress is composed of two branches, the Senate and the Chamber of Deputies. Because the Chamber of Deputies controls fiscal appropriations and the budget, it is the stronger house as regards domestic policy. But the Senate has primary responsibility for foreign policy. Between 1929 and 1985, only one senator was elected who did not belong to the PRI. In response to public pressure for greater representation of other parties, the size of the Senate has been enlarged and the method for electing senators has been changed several times since 1993. Currently, 128 senators are elected from the 31 states and the Federal District (Mexico City) through a complicated mix of single-member districts, proportional representation (PR), and allocation of a seat to second-place finishers.

Elections for the Chamber of Deputies have also become more complex. Historically, deputies were elected from single-member districts. Beginning in the 1960s, however, a small number of seats in the chamber were available to the opposition through the addition of deputies who are elected through PR. The number of PR seats was raised several times over the years in response to demands for greater democratization. Currently, 300 deputies are elected from single-member districts. Until 1988, opposition parties had never won more than a handful of those races. In addition, 200 congressmen are now elected through proportional representation.

TABLE 15.3	Results of Chamber of Deputies Elections: Percentage of Seats Won*		
Year	PRI	PAN	PRD
1976	80.1	8.5	—
1988	50.4	18.0	10.5**
1997	39.1	26.6	25.7
2000	42.2	44.2	13.6
2003	48.2	29.8	19.4
2006	24.6	41.2	31.4
2009	51.6	29.4	14.4

*The percentage of seats listed for each of the three major parties includes those won by small, closely allied parties. For example, the PRI percentage in 2009 includes a small number of seats won by the Green Party.
**Seats won by the Democratic National Front (FDN), an electoral coalition of small parties, most of whom later merged into the PRD.

SOURCE: Mexican Federal Electoral Institute (IFE); Howard Handelman, *Mexican Politics* (New York: St. Martin's, 1997), p. 75; David Shirk, *Mexico's New Politics* (Boulder, CO: Lynne Rienner Publishers, 2005), p. 217.

The formulas governing the allocation of those seats have changed several times, but they always have enabled opposition parties to enlarge the number of seats that they were able to win in single-member districts.

Given the PRI's dominance of Congress until the late 1990s and the president's domination of the PRI at that time, it is not surprising that the national legislature rather routinely passed the president's proposed legislation. Thus, for example, between 1934 and the mid-1990s, the Chamber of Deputies approved at least 95 percent of executive-sponsored bills, and in some years that figure reached 100 percent. Almost all of those bills passed the Congress without amendment.[16] In 1997, in what proved to be a precursor of their loss of the presidency three years later, the PRI lost its absolute majority in the Chamber of Deputies for the first time since its founding, though it remained the largest party in the chamber (see Table 15.3). Therefore, during the second half of his presidency, Ernesto Zedillo (PRI) could no longer demand the congressional subservience to presidential desires that all his predecessors had enjoyed, nor did he use his powers as party leader to pressure PRI deputies to the extent that his predecessors had. Consequently, the success rate of executive-sponsored bills dropped from 97 percent to "only" 90 percent.

Congress has become even more independent of presidential control since 2000. During the 2000–2003 congressional sessions, President Fox's party, PAN, held two-fifths of the seats in the Chamber of Deputies but was unable to form a majority coalition with other parties on many key votes. Consequently, in that period Congress passed only 86 percent of his proposed legislation, significantly lower than his predecessors' success rate. While 86 percent may still seem like a high success rate, "nearly every single bill [proposed by the executive branch] that could [legally] be amended was modified."[17] In the 2003 congressional elections PAN's representation in the Chamber of Deputies declined further, and while it reemerged as the largest congressional bloc in the 2006 elections, President Calderón's party was still short of a majority. In the 2009 national election, the PRI staged a major comeback, winning slightly more than half the seats (Table 15.3). This gave that party the power to defeat or significantly revise any of President Calderón's proposed legislation.

Another way of measuring the extent to which presidential control over the Congress has declined during the past decade is to look at the origin of bills that *are* passed. During the 56th congressional session (1994–1997), three-fourths (74 percent) of all bills passed by Congress were originally proposed by the executive branch. But in the first two years of the 59th Congress (2003–2005), under Fox, only one-eighth (12 percent) of the approved legislation had been introduced by the executive branch, while 62 percent originated with the deputies themselves.[18] And although the percentage of the president's proposed legislation that passed may seem high, most of the bills were routine and uncontroversial. On the other hand, Congress rejected many of the president's key legislative proposals or modified them substantially, sometimes to the point of gutting them.

For example, when President Fox took office, one of his key priorities was settling a long-term stand-off between the government and the **Zapatista** rebels— officially the Zapatista Army of National Liberation (the EZLN)—in the impoverished southern state of Chiapas. The rebels—consisting of 600 to 1,000 lightly armed peasants led by their charismatic spokesperson, "Subcommander" Marcos (a former university professor)—had gained enormous national and international attention during their brief armed seizure of four towns in 1994 on behalf of the state's oppressed Indian population. Initially at least, the Zapatistas attracted considerable public support, especially among Mexican intellectuals and professionals. In the years that followed, EZLN leaders—always appearing in ski masks so as to hide their identities—articulated the grievances of the Chiapas Indians and, more generally, the nation's rural poor.[19]

In time, the government and the Zapatistas called a truce, and they sporadically pursued negotiations aimed at a peace treaty for years, though direct negotiations had been stalled since 1996. Soon after taking office, President Fox agreed to terms of a settlement with the rebels that had eluded his predecessors. He proposed a number of constitutional amendments to improve indigenous (Indian) human rights, proposals that the EZLN found acceptable. But when the Congress stripped key provisions from Fox's proposed settlement, the Zapatistas rejected the package as inadequate. In this case, as with a number of his other reform proposals, the president was unable to count on the support even of many of his own party's congressmen.

Of course, Congress's newfound ability to say no to the president and to reject his legislative proposals promotes the separation of powers and greater democracy (since Congress is no longer the president's lapdog). On the other hand, particularly under Fox and Calderón, opposition congressmen have often used their votes to stymie presidential initiatives for purely partisan motives, sometimes blocking needed reforms.* Given the three-party system that has emerged, future presidents will

---

* We are not suggesting that all the president's legislative initiatives should have been passed. Furthermore, a person's evaluation of any particular bill will depend on his or her own political leanings. We are merely indicating that some meritorious presidential proposals have been rejected for purely partisan reasons.

probably lack a congressional majority for most (or all) of the coming decades and will have to confront that reality. During Felipe Calderón's first three years in office, he enjoyed a healthy plurality (the largest number of seats, but short of a majority) in both houses of Congress (something Fox never had), but he still needed some PRI (or, less frequently, PRD) votes to pass his proposed legislation. Now that the PRI holds a working majority (together with a small allied party) in both houses of Congress, the president is further weakened and has to negotiate with the PRI on all of his legislative proposals.

Fox's experience did not bode well for cooperation between parties and between branches of government. It suggested that unless a president's party had a congressional majority, the national government would often be bogged down in stalemate. In the first half of Calderón's term, he worked more harmoniously with Congress and managed to gain approval of several important bills. Calderón is a more skilled negotiator than his predecessor. Whereas Fox had been a businessman most of his life and had limited political experience prior to becoming president (he remained something of an outsider in his own party), Calderón, the son of one of the PAN's founders, has been a political insider since his 20s, when he was elected president of the party's youth wing, and has served in a variety of important political posts since then. That experience gave him political skills that Fox lacked. Even so, many of his proposals were watered down or otherwise revised by the congressional opposition. Since the end of 2009, when the PRI achieved a virtual congressional majority, the president's negotiating position has been weakened considerably.

The Judiciary

As in the United States, the Mexican judiciary has local, state, and federal components. Unfortunately, the level of professionalism is generally low in local and state courts, many of which are riddled with corruption. Moreover, that problem has worsened in the past decade or two as narcotics dealers have exercised growing influence over the courts. Until the 1990s, the Mexican judiciary exercised little political influence and was normally subservient to the executive branch. Judges who showed independence could face severe retribution. In 1995, for example, the government's desire to prosecute several union leaders was stymied when Superior Court Judge Abraham Polo ruled that there was insufficient evidence to issue an arrest warrant against them. Subsequently, the judge publicly charged the chief justice of his own court with having pressured him to change his decision. Polo, though a longtime PRI activist, refused to back down. Several months later an unknown assailant gunned him down.

To be sure, the Supreme Court has had the constitutional power to address the complaints of individuals claiming that the government has violated their rights. If the court finds in favor of that complaint, it may issue writs that command the government to cease a particular act or undertake a remedy. But traditionally the courts used these writs exclusively for nonpolitical cases and, unlike the U.S. Supreme Court—which periodically overruled decisions by Congress or the president—it has carefully refrained from challenging the president's political power. Furthermore, while the Mexican Supreme Court could remedy a particular government action, it could not rule on the constitutionality of government behavior. "In other words, the decision would only affect the appealing party, not any other citizen."[20]

Presidents Zedillo, Fox, and Calderón all pledged to introduce judicial reform as an important component of democratization. Zedillo introduced constitutional initiatives designed to increase the independence and the integrity of the judicial system. Perhaps the most important of these empowered the Supreme Court to declare laws unconstitutional under certain circumstances. Subsequently, the high court gave circuit courts the power to rule on the constitutionality of local laws.

The Fox administration attacked corruption in law enforcement and had some limited success in its efforts to clean up antinarcotics units. But it failed to pass significant court reforms. At the same time, however, the Supreme Court itself assumed a more activist role following the end of PRI dominance. For example, during the *six* years of the Zedillo administration (the last PRI government) the Court ruled on issues of constitutionality 27 times. But during the first *three* years of the Fox government alone, it ruled on such cases 44 times.[21] In recent years, the higher courts have shown much greater independence from the executive branch. For example, the Supreme Court has rejected the Zedillo administration's position by upholding the legality of three controversial laws passed in the Federal District (Mexico City): the unconditional right of a woman to have an abortion up to the 12th week of pregnancy, the legalization of gay marriage, and the right of gay couples to adopt children. These rulings applied only to the nation's capital (home to nearly 10 percent of the nation's population), but also allowed nonresidents to travel to the Federal District for an abortion. Not only could nonresident gay couples also travel to Mexico City to marry, but the court required all other states to recognize such marriages.

In 2008, Congress passed several Calderón proposals on legislative and constitutional changes aimed at reforming the judicial system. Whereas criminal trials were previously based on a presentation of legal briefs by both sides, the reforms introduce oral arguments and adversarial procedures that include the cross-examination of witnesses. That strengthens the due process rights of criminal defendants, who are now considered innocent until proven guilty. At the same time, however, the reforms also include tougher police and judicial powers to battle organized crime, some parts of which trouble civil libertarians.[22]

In short, since the end of PRI dominance, higher-level courts have been more assertive and independent. But while there has been progress toward establishing a more independent and trustworthy Supreme Court, there is considerable distance to go at the lower levels. As in most of Latin America, judicial reform has progressed quite slowly, and establishing the rule of law has been one of the greatest challenges in the transition to democracy. Although important reforms have taken place at the top of the judicial system, law enforcement by the local courts and police remains enormously corrupt. This, in turn, promotes gang violence, particularly by groups involved in the narcotics trade. As a result Mexicans still have little confidence in the police or the judicial system. It is estimated that only about 25 percent of all crimes are even reported to the police since most victims or their relatives have little confidence that the perpetrators will ever be brought to trial. And, in fact, only 2 percent of all crimes are ever prosecuted.[23] Meanwhile, Human Rights Watch has reported that 40 percent of all prisoners in Mexican jails have never been convicted of crimes but are languishing there awaiting trial by Mexico's very slow court system.

Political Parties

Until the late 1980s, most political scientists described Mexico as a "modified one-party authoritarian state."[24] To be sure, other parties beyond the PRI existed, but they served a purely symbolic role. As one observer of Mexican politics during that period noted, "Without formal opposition, elections would be meaningless. And without elections the system would lose its mask of democratic legitimacy."[25] But PRI electoral dominance eroded considerably during the deep recessions of the 1980s. Once able to attract more than 90 percent of the seats in the Chamber of Deputies, PRI dropped below 50 percent for the first time in 1997, and in 2000 it was surpassed as the leading congressional party by the PAN-led Alliance for Change (Table 15.3). After a comeback in the 2003 congressional elections, the PRI finished a distant third in 2006 (with less than one-fourth of the seats), an unimaginable outcome just 10 years earlier. Most significantly, Vicente Fox's 2000 presidential victory ended the PRI's 71-year chokehold on political power. Thus, Mexico has become a truly competitive multiparty system, currently dominated by three major political parties.

The Institutional Revolutionary Party (PRI)   Mexico's once-dominant party was created in 1929 (with a different name) and was designed both to be the ruling party and to give official representation to the groups that had been part of the victorious revolutionary coalition—the middle class, white-collar workers, unionized blue-collar workers, and peasants.

As we have seen, drawing especially on peasant, blue-collar, and white-collar votes, the PRI (and its predecessors) dominated the electoral system for nearly 60 years. During that time, PRI candidates illegally received government funding and programs to outflank the opposition. The party could also count on biased television news coverage in favor of its candidates. Until 2000, the PRI presidential candidates received three or four times as much air time as their opponents. Compliant unions endorsed government economic policies even when they damaged their rank-and-file membership. Meanwhile, poor peasants and slum dwellers understood that producing a strong PRI vote in their village or neighborhood was the best way to secure government aid (such as irrigation projects, potable water, and electricity). In the rare case where PRI candidates, despite all their advantages, were not certain of victory, the party resorted to electoral fraud. The party's strongest electoral support has come from poorer, less-educated, and older voters. Ironically, when it was in power the PRI's most dependable source of votes was poor peasants, who were the most impoverished, least educated group in Mexican society and, thus, the group that had benefited least from PRI rule. Yet, because they were so weak and marginal, they were especially dependent on government assistance and hence, prior to 2000, were more likely than any other group to vote for the PRI in hopes of receiving aid.

Unlike many other ruling parties, such as the Chinese and Cuban Communists, the PRI never offered a clearly articulated ideology, nor was it responsible for formulating government policy. Instead, the official party was the national president's instrument, whose primary purpose was to co-opt important interest groups and to mobilize support for the government and for PRI candidates. In the 1990s President

Zedillo fought against his party's bosses as he tried to democratize the PRI. In his most significant reform, he ended the long-standing practice of having the outgoing national president pick the PRI's next presidential candidate, which until 2000 was tantamount to naming his own successor. Since the 2000 election, the party's presidential nominees have been chosen in a primary election.

The party's historic defeat in the 2000 presidential election has forced the PRI to compete for the first time in a democratic setting without the benefit of government financial support. While many political analysts had predicted that, stripped of government patronage and state financial resources, the PRI would wither away, so far it has been more resilient than they expected. Since 2000, its electoral support has oscillated but, in general, it has done well other than in the presidential races. As Tables 15.3 indicates, after its 2000 defeat, the party staged a mild recovery in the 2003 congressional election, performed terribly in both the 2006 presidential and congressional elections, but then bounced back impressively in 2009 to double its share of seats in the Chamber of Deputies and win control of that body with the support of the small Green Party. As of 2010, the party held the governor's seat in 19 of Mexico's 31 states plus the Federal District. Currently, the PRI is considered the frontrunner for the 2012 presidential election.

Several factors help explain the PRI's impressive recent comeback. For one thing, it still has a large and effective party organization that, under the right circumstances, can get out the vote. Second, unlike the PAN, whose electoral strength is concentrated in the more developed northern region of the country, or the PRD, which draws most of its votes from Mexico City and the poorer southern states, the PRI is the only party that can compete in all parts of the country.

The National Action Party (PAN) The PAN originated in 1939 as the voice of conservative Catholics and disgruntled businessmen who opposed the government's growing intervention in the economy and its anticlericism (opposition to the Church hierarchy) at that time. For nearly four decades, the party offered the only significant electoral opposition to the PRI. As relations between church and state have improved, the party has deemphasized religious issues in its campaigns and focused on other concerns. At the same time, however, it continues to draw disproportionate support from observant Catholics. Not coincidentally, the current president, Felipe Calderón of the PAN, is a devout Catholic who opposes abortion (except under very limited circumstances), gay marriage, and euthanasia.* The party has considerable support within the business community (particularly smaller businesses) and within the middle-class more generally. Its probusiness faction (called *neopanistas*) is more pragmatic, focusing on what it takes to win elections and less ideologically committed than the party's Catholic bloc is.

Since the 1980s, as the neopanistas have gained strength, the party has campaigned more heavily on principles of free enterprise and reduced government intervention in the economy. But it has also received support from outside the ranks of economic conservatives by presenting itself as the party of honest government. During the closing decades of the twentieth century, it staked its claim to office by

---

* This was less true of Vicente Fox, who had divorced before becoming president and remarried while in office.

opposing one-party dominance and official corruption. That reformist image was enhanced by the comparative efficiency and honesty of PAN mayors and governors elected in the 1990s, when the political system began to open up (though there certainly were some corrupt *panista* office holders). The party receives its greatest electoral support in Mexico's more prosperous northern states such as Coahuila and Chihuahua, and in some devoutly Catholic western states, particularly in urban areas. In the most recent presidential race, the PAN candidate, Felipe Calderón, won 14 of the 17 northern states while winning only two of 15 southern states. At the same time, however, the party has broadened its support somewhat in recent years and won several gubernatorial races in states outside the north. Similarly, although its core support remains the urban middle class and the business community, of late it has also picked up many urban working-class votes.

Ironically, the PAN began mounting its successful challenge to PRI dominance in the 1990s, not long after the PRI government enacted neoliberal economic reforms that mirrored the PAN's position. When the party did finally win the presidency, Vicente Fox stressed his commitment to honest government and human rights more than his conservative economic policies (though he still favored those policies). The administration's commitment to honest government, protecting civil liberties, and exposing past government repression of left-wing activists during the 1960s through the 1980s initially earned it praise from many moderate leftists. At the same time, Fox's independence from his own party's party structure, his eclectic ideology, and his appointment of several moderate leftists as cabinet ministers and key advisers alienated many PAN leaders. Thus, though the party is usually characterized as being conservative or right-of-center, under both Fox and, to a lesser extent, Calderón it has governed from the center. The party remains quite conservative on social issues such as abortion and gay marriage.

In the 2000 national elections, the PAN won the presidency, a plurality of the seats (44 percent) in the Chamber of Deputies (Table 15.3), and 38 percent of the Senate. Since then its fortunes, like those of all three major parties, have fluctuated sharply in successive congressional elections. Three years after its breakthrough victory, the party suffered substantial losses in the Chamber of Deputies, in part because of Fox's failure to deliver on many of his overly optimistic promises. That defeat obviously made it even more difficult for Fox to get his legislative initiatives passed. Still, the PAN rebounded strongly in the 2006 election, winning the presidency once again (though barely) and, for the first time ever, gaining a plurality in each house of Congress (Table 15.3). Yet in the 2009 congressional elections it was trounced by the PRI, losing almost one-third its seats in the Chamber of Deputies as the economy was hit by the global economic crisis.

Because of the PRI's dramatic comeback in that election, party leaders in both the left-of-center PRD and the right-center PAN feared further PRI surges in the dozen 2010 gubernatorial races and in subsequent elections. To prevent that outcome, they formed a perplexing alliance in five gubernatorial races. That pact seemed unlikely for a number of reasons. First, it brought together two parties considered to be on opposite sides of Mexico's ideological spectrum—the center-right PAN and the leftist PRD. Indeed, during the 2006 campaign, PRD candidates had sometimes referred to the PAN as "the rich tyrants that oppress the people." Second, PRD leaders believed that Calderón and the PAN had stolen the 2006 presidential election and that the PRD had really won (See A Closer Look 15.1).

A CLOSER LOOK

15.1

A Hotly Disputed Election

As we have noted, for most of its 70 years in power, the PRI stuffed ballot boxes and otherwise manipulated the vote count in order to inflate its margin of electoral victories (only rarely did they need to cheat in order to prevent an opposition-party victory). Understandably, most Mexicans were skeptical about the integrity of the electoral process. In the 1988 presidential election, supporters of left-center candidate, Cuauhtémoc Cárdenas, were convinced that he had been defrauded of his rightful victory. Although election procedures became more transparent and honest in the 1990s, when results were announced for the 2006 presidential election, once again PRD adherents believed that their candidate, this time Andrés Manuel López Obrador, had been cheated out of victory.

When the Federal Election Institute finally issued its results, four days after the July 2 election, it declared that conservative PAN candidate, Felipe Calderón, had defeated López Obrador by less than 1 percent of the total vote, with the PRI candidate a relatively distant third. Claiming he had been victimized by ballot stuffing in the (pro-PAN) north and by arithmetical errors in over half of the nation's 130,000 polling stations, AMLO refused to accept the results

and demanded a recount of *all* ballots cast. Subsequently the Federal Election Tribunal ruled that such a complete recount was unfeasible and unwarranted. Instead it ordered a partial recount covering those polling stations where it believed there were solid grounds for a challenge (about 9 percent of all stations). Ultimately it ruled that, although there had been some irregularities, the recount only reduced Calderón's margin of victory by a minuscule amount (from 0.58% to 0.56%), leaving the PAN candidate as the winner. By law, that decision was final and could not be appealed.

López Obrador and his supporters rejected that outcome, insisting that he was the legitimate president-elect. That was not an isolated reaction. Public opinion polls indicated that 35 to 40 percent of all Mexicans (and about 60 percent of Mexico City residents) believed that the results were bogus. Hundreds of thousands of his supporters camped out in tents in the heart of the city, blocking streets leading to the Zócalo, the city's central square since pre-Colonial times. Observing the events, an American journalist noted that, "the blockade look[ed] more like a fair than a protest. City workers and party members ... erected enormous circus-like tents the

But politics makes for strange bedfellows, and state leaders in both the PAN and PRD had concluded that beating the PRI (which both parties consider corrupt and authoritarian) was more important than any ideological differences or past grievances that they might have. In the end, the alliance elected three governors in states that previously had been PRI strongholds for over 70 years.

The Party of the Democratic Revolution (PRD) For decades, an array of small parties, each with its own ideological slant, challenged the PRI from the left. Whereas the PAN at that time attacked PRI governments for excessive state intervention in the economy (prior to the PRI's conversion to neoliberal economics in the 1980s), the independent Marxist parties criticized it for failing to fulfill its revolutionary promises of reduced poverty and greater economic independence from the United States. In other words, whereas the PAN rejected much of the PRI's revolutionary ideology, the independent left chided it for failing to live up to that party's revolutionary rhetoric.

15.1

length of the avenue. There [were also] stages where musicians entertain[ed] the protesters...."[27] The sit-in lasted for weeks, punctuated by huge marches and rallies featuring speeches by AMLO to crowds of more than one million people. Other protestors briefly occupied government buildings and seized a number of tollbooths on roads leading into the city, allowing motorists to pass through free of charge for several hours.

Subsequently, a week before Fox's term drew to an end, López Obrador was unofficially "sworn in" as president of Mexico in a symbolic ceremony held before 100,000 supporters. Finally, in a bizarre twist, the PRD congressional delegation announced that it would block the halls of Congress, where the presidential inauguration is normally held, and would not allow Calderón's ceremony to take place. In a preemptive move, PAN deputies seized the Congress's main floor three days before the scheduled inauguration. This was followed by several days of verbal taunts and fist fighting between PAN and PRD deputies. Finally, in a surprising and unprecedented move, outgoing President Fox appeared with Calderón on national television shortly before midnight on the eve of inauguration day and turned over presidential power to him. The next morning, accompanied by the Presidential

Guard, Calderón was sworn in on the floor of Congress, punctuated by shouts of support from PAN Congressmen and catcalls from the PRD. The new president stayed for less than five minutes and then left.

Ultimately, while the mass street demonstrations energized many PRD supporters, it also weakened López Obrador's national standing. Even though most voters in Mexico had supported AMLO for mayor and subsequently for president, many of them were put off by the continued demonstrations. Although they believed that the PRD had valid grievances, they felt that this did not justify a month-long occupation of the city center, causing great inconvenience for many and financial hardships for businessmen and street vendors in the Zócalo area. Others believed that the continued demonstrations, the seizure of government buildings, and the fist fights on the floor of Congress indicated that AMLO and the PRD did not respect legal procedures. A number of eminent leftist intellectuals, and even some PRD leaders who had supported his candidacy, criticized his postelection tactics. At the same time, however, the election count and the demonstrations reinforced many Mexicans' distrust of their electoral process.

But although many Mexican intellectuals and student activists have been attracted to Marxism over the years, leftist candidates had not mounted a serious electoral challenge until the 1980s. In fact, the combined vote of some half-dozen leftist parties in national elections had never exceeded 10 percent. In the late 1980s, however, the major left-of-center parties finally overcame their internal conflicts and united behind the candidacy of Cuauhtémoc Cárdenas, the son of modern Mexico's most revered president, Lázaro Cárdenas. The younger Cárdenas had been elected governor of Michoacán on the PRI ticket. But in 1987, he and several other leaders of the PRI's progressive wing were expelled from the party in the wake of their unsuccessful campaign for internal (party) democratic reforms. Cárdenas's 1988 presidential candidacy won the support of dissidents (such as himself) who had left the PRI and of several small Marxist parties, forming a coalition called the National Democratic Front (FDN).

TABLE 15.4	Results of Recent Presidential Elections				
Party	**1976**	**1988**	**1994**	**2000**	**2006**
PRI*	92.3	50.7	53.4	36.1	22.3
PAN*	—**	16.8	28.6	42.5	35.9
PRD*	—	32.5***	18.0	18.9	35.3
Other	7.6	15.8	—	3.7	6.53

*In at least one of the past two presidential elections, the three major parties have allied with much smaller parties to form coalitions with names other than their own.
**The PAN boycotted the 1976 presidential election.
***In 1988, Cárdenas actually ran as the candidate of the FDN, the PRD's predecessor.
SOURCE: The CFE (Federal Electoral Commission) and the IFE (Federal Electoral Institute).

The left's unification behind the son of the PRI's most popular president could not have come at a worse time for the then-ruling party. The economic crisis of the 1980s—bringing higher unemployment and declining living standards—had weakened PRI control over the peasantry and the urban working class. Cárdenas's campaign called for greater democratization and a rollback of President Miguel de la Madrid's painful economic austerity policies (1982–1988). Whereas the PAN's demand for less government appealed to many middle-class voters and the more prosperous regions of the north, Cárdenas's call for antipoverty programs, public works, and a suspension of international debt payments won him considerable support among the nation's poor and segments of the middle class. The official 1988 presidential vote count showed Cárdenas surging past the PAN to take 32 percent of the vote while the PAN candidate received only 17 percent. Carlos Salinas, the PRI candidate, finished first, but he barely achieved 50 percent in the official tally, reaching that level only through electoral fraud. Many Mexicans believed that Cárdenas had really won the election and had been robbed of his victory. Independent analysis, however, indicated that while Salinas's vote had been inflated he had actually finished first.

Not long after the 1988 elections, the FDN dissolved, and many of the parties in that coalition formed the **Party of the Democratic Revolution (PRD)**. Because it was born out of a coalition of disparate leftist parties and former PRI leaders, the new party has been plagued from the start by internal battles between leaders and factions with differing ideological and strategic beliefs. Running as the party's presidential candidate in 1994 and 2000, Cárdenas received only about half the share of the vote than he had garnered in 1988 (Table 15.4). Although outgoing President Salinas's disgraceful exit in 1994 (he and his brother were exposed for engaging in massive corruption) and an extremely severe economic crisis in 1994–1996 opened new opportunities for opposition parties, the PRD was weakened by internal squabbles and political ineptitude. Instead, the PAN reemerged as the primary challenger to the PRI in the 1994 presidential contest and went on to win the 2000 and 2006 elections, thereby decisively ending the PRI's dominance.

The PRD's foremost stronghold is in Mexico City, DF (Federal District), the country's capital, with about 9 million people.* From the time that the citizens of

---

* The greater metropolitan area of Mexico City has a population of over 21 million, making it one of the world's largest urban areas.

Mexico City first received the right to elect their own mayor in 1997 until today, the PRD has continuously held that post, considered the nation's second-most-powerful elected position.* Beyond its base in the Federal District (the most wealthy part of the country), the party's greatest support has come from the south, home to the country's poorest states.[26] In the most recent presidential race, the PRD candidate, López Obrador, won 13 of the 15 southern states along with the Federal District while taking only two of 14 northern states. At the individual level, PRD is strongest among lower-income voters, but has considerable middle-class support. Like the PRI and the PAN, its support in national elections has fluctuated significantly.

In the 1997 election, the party won nearly 26 percent of the seats in the Chamber of Deputies, placing it almost even with the PAN (Table 15.3). Three years later, however, it lost almost half of those seats and finished a very weak third in the presidential race (Table 15.4). Yet in the 2006 elections it captured almost one-third of the Chamber of Deputies (its best showing ever) and nearly won the presidency. But, again following its electoral rollercoaster, it lost over half its seats in that Chamber in the 2009 election.

When the PRI was still in power, the PRD often sided with the PAN on issues of political reform and human rights while sometimes siding with the PRI on economic policies. Since 2000 it has occasionally supported bills proposed by Fox and Calderón that it considers progressive. As President Fox's popularity declined in the final years of his presidency and the PRI's reputation remained tarnished, the PRD optimistically approached the 2006 national elections. Rejecting the candidacy of Lázaro Cárdenas, who had lost the past three presidential elections, they turned to Andrés Manuel López Obrador (widely known by his initials, AMLO), the popular, charismatic, and controversial former mayor of Mexico City. Through most of 2005 and the early months of 2006, most public opinion polls indicated that AMLO led the race. In the final months of the campaign, however, the PAN candidate, Felipe Calderón—aided by a business-funded media campaign that depicted López Obrador as an authoritarian, left-wing extremist—erased that lead. And when Calderón officially won the July 2 election by a razor-thin margin (0.56%), the PRD insisted that it had been denied victory by a falsified vote count (see A Closer Look 15.1).

From its inception, the PRD (formed out of a coalition of parties) has suffered from factional and leadership divisions, conflicts that have often weakened its electoral appeal. As of 2008, in the aftermath of its severe setbacks in the previous presidential election, the party has been split between leftist and more centrist blocs. The leading militant faction (called the United Left), led by López Obrador, favors a more confrontational stance again the PAN government. The second, more centrist party bloc (called the **New Left**), now dominates the PRD and supports a more pragmatic approach, which would include reaching out more to the middle class and even some of the business community. While the New Left faction now recognizes Calderón as Mexico's legitimate president, the United Left still does not. The 2010 electoral alliance with the PAN drove a further wedge between López Obrador, who strongly opposed that alliance, and party leaders from the New Left, who

---

* Before 1997 the president appointed Mexico City's mayor. Officially, the mayor is now the governor of the DF, with a status equivalent to the governors of Mexico's 31 states.

favored it. Currently, while López Obrador continues to attract the largest number of devoted supporters, many PRD leaders have concluded that he is too radical and strident to attract the additional votes from outside the party that they need to achieve a presidential victory or even a congressional plurality. While the PRD has a long history of factional fighting and has had several leaders leave the party, this battle is particularly intense. Should the New Left continue to control the party and determine its 2012 presidential nominee, many experts believe that AMLO will lead his supporters out of the party.

A Changing Political Culture

Even though Mexico remained an authoritarian political system after the 1910 revolution, opportunities for political participation expanded greatly.[28] Throughout the world, an individual's or group's degree of political participation is closely related to their educational level. Since the Mexican population was overwhelmingly illiterate at the time of the revolution—and since alternative sources of political information, such as radio or television, did not yet exist—the country's degree of political involvement was predictably low.

During the first decades of the twentieth century, many Mexicans belonged to what political scientists call a "parochial political culture."[29] That is, they generally lacked sufficient political knowledge to appreciate the impact of government policies on their lives and, consequently, tended to abstain from active political participation even when they had the opportunity. But over the span of the century, as the country's literacy rate climbed past 90 percent, as mass media exposure spread, and as the country became more urbanized, political involvement grew.

Still, even today many Mexicans have received fewer than six years of formal education and do not actively follow politics. When compared to the United States, Mexicans are still more skeptical of their political institutions—political parties, the Congress, the police, and the judiciary.[30] For most of the twentieth century, memories of the widespread violence and chaos of the Mexican Revolution—recollections passed on to succeeding generations—contributed to a political culture in which many citizens feared radical change and cherished political stability, even at the cost of greater democracy.[31] That anxiety helped solidify the PRI's grip on power into the 1990s.

As the urban middle class has expanded over the years and more people have graduated from high school and university, more Mexicans have become involved with politics and seek to influence the political system. But negative mass attitudes persist. Shortly before the 1988 presidential elections, a national poll revealed that over half of all citizens did not expect that their votes would be counted honestly. Less than one-fourth of those polled expected an honest count (another fourth was unsure). The voters' general wariness was well grounded. As we have seen, the PRI candidate's official tally was almost certainly inflated by a dishonest vote count. In fact, the country had a long history of ballot stuffing. However, with the introduction of effective electoral safeguards over the next decade and the rise of effective opposition parties over the next 12 years, culminating in Vicente Fox's (PAN) landmark presidential victory in 2000, voter confidence increased considerably. By 2005, fully three-quarters of Mexicans polled (75 percent) felt that their votes were honestly counted. Still, nearly one-fourth believed that they were not tallied honestly, and trust in the integrity of national elections remains fragile. As A Closer Look 15.1 indicates, only one year later the highly polarized 2006 presidential election caused nearly 40 percent of Mexicans to believe that Felipe Calderón's (PAN) extremely close victory was a sham. In another poll conducted at about that time, "only 59 percent of Mexicans rated democracy as preferable to other kinds of government."[32]

Voting and the Changing Electoral System

Although only a few generations ago voting was extremely restricted, Mexican citizens have come to view it as an important right, which they have exercised in substantial numbers even when the PRI candidates faced no serious opposition. In the presidential election of 1917, only 5 percent of the total population voted, but by the 1970s that figure approached 30 percent of the total population and a much higher percentage of adults.[33] Until 1988, the PRI's electoral dominance meant that presidential elections in Mexico served a different purpose than their role in more democratic nations. They were vehicles for introducing the PRI presidential candidate (who usually had never run for public office before) to the population and a means of legitimizing his authority when he later took office. In the 1982 race, for example, the PRI's Miguel de la Madrid made more than 1,800 campaign speeches, although he faced little serious opposition and eventually won more than 74 percent of the vote (his leading opponent received only 16 percent). The new, competitive electoral scene since 2000 has added actual urgency to the major parties' campaigns.

The lack of a viable electoral opposition to the PRI for much of twentieth century limited both the election's impact on government policy and the population's incentive to vote. Increased voter cynicism caused abstention rates (registered voters who do not actually vote) to rise from between 30 and 35 percent in the 1960s to nearly 50 percent in the 1985 congressional election.

Still, after the 1970s, the PRI government responded to growing pressures from the increasingly educated population by introducing electoral reforms that made it easier for opposition parties to run candidates and to gain office. As noted earlier, one of the most important of these was the eventual creation of 200 seats of the Chamber of Deputies that are elected through proportional representation. These deputies join with the 300 others that are elected in single-member districts. As a consequence of these reforms and a changing electorate, the PRI's share of seats in the Chamber declined from more than 80 percent in 1972 to 24 percent in 2006 (though it rebounded in 2009). Thus, the once-dominant "official party" has now lost the presidency, its absolute majority in the Chamber of Deputies (until 2009), and a significant number of state governors and municipal mayors.

Interest Groups

Recognized Interest Groups   Between elections, Mexican citizens engage in a range of interest group activities. Indeed, for a less-developed country, Mexico is surprisingly highly organized. But until 2000, the government and the PRI controlled most politically significant interest groups. As the ruling party developed, it organized itself on a corporatist model. **Corporatism** involves the organization of the population into government-sanctioned interest groups based on occupation or other socioeconomic characteristics. These organizations have a direct communication channel to the government and in some countries they are the only legally sanctioned representatives of that sector of society.[34] Thus, as we have seen, most Mexican labor unions, the giant peasant confederation (CNC), and a large array of professional and small-business associations have been represented in the PRI. When that party controlled the political system, their relationship gave those groups a voice within the government that their counterparts elsewhere in Latin America often lacked. At the same time, however, corporatism provided the party, and thus the government, considerable control over those sectors.

Most of Mexico's blue-collar labor unions belong to the Congress of Labor (CT). Within the CT, the most powerful force is the Mexican Confederation of Labor (CTM), once representing some six million workers. Because of its links to the PRI, the CTM used to exercise considerable political clout, but three important developments have undercut that influence. First, the multiple economic crises that have befallen Mexico in the past 30 years—including extended periods of slow economic growth (1980–1995, 2000–2010) and occasional periods of high inflation (peaking at an annual rate of 160 percent in 1987)—put most workers in a precarious financial position and weakened their unions' bargaining power. Second, privatization of many state industries in the 1980s and 1990s (i.e., the sale of state-owned industries to private owners) led to the firing of many workers and reduced the government's ability to reward loyal unions. Since the PRI lost the 2000 presidential election, CTM unions no longer have the access to government leaders that they previously enjoyed. Given the PAN's probusiness orientation, it is not surprising that union political influence has declined further under the Fox and Calderón administrations.

But even when organized labor had enjoyed direct links to PRI governments, unions did not necessarily serve their rank-and-files' interests well, much less the interests of workers more generally. For decades, Mexico's powerful unions have generally been led by corrupt labor bosses who use strong-arm tactics to stay in power and who have been more concerned with amassing wealth and power for themselves than in effectively representing their members. Moreover, Mexican unions tend to represent only the more skilled and more highly paid workers employed in modern industries such as petroleum, steel, automobiles, and electric power. Thus, as in the United States, most of Mexico's workforce is not organized into unions, especially the poorest, unskilled workers, who are in most need of help.

As the PRI's strength has declined since the 1990s, the number of independent (non-CTM) unions has risen. The independent National Workers Union (UNT)—consisting of unions that had broken with the CTM and the PRI—was born in 1997 and within five years claimed to represent more than 100 unions with some two million members. Another influential union federation committed to union democracy is the Authentic Workers' Front (FAT). The old CTM labor bosses suffered a further blow in 2001 when the Mexican Supreme Court overturned portions of the Federal Labor Law that had favored the PRI's corporatist unions over independent challengers. At the same time, the Court ruled that employers could no longer fire workers for leaving a union that has a collective bargaining contract with the company. This reduced the employers' opportunities to sign sweetheart contracts with undemocratic unions and reduced the corrupt labor bosses' abilities to intimidate their rank-and-file.

While the CTM has made some efforts to work with the PAN governments, relations between the more radical, independent unions and the Calderón government have been strained. All major unions, CTM and independent alike (as well as the PRI and PRD), opposed the president's attempts to revise Mexican labor laws. While the administration argued that the proposal would strengthen the rights of individual workers, opponents countered that would make it harder for unions to unionize firms and would restrict the right to strike. Calderón failed to pass the bill in 2009, when the PAN held a congressional plurality, and its chances probably collapsed when the election that year produced a PRI majority.

If independent unions gain further strength, it will probably have both positive and negative consequences for organized labor. On the one hand, many of the emerging independent unions are more democratic and more responsive to their members' desires. On the other hand, they have less influence on government policy than the PRI-affiliated CTM unions once had and may have again.[35]

Under the PRI regime, businesses above a certain size were legally required to belong to one of two government-sanctioned business federations: the Chamber of Industry or the national Chamber of Commerce. Mexican law "grant[ed] semiofficial status to the chambers ... and allow[ed] the state to intervene in various facets of the chambers' operation, although state interference in business groups [was] usually low."[36] So, like labor unions, businesses were incorporated into a corporatist structure (in which government only dealt with the sanctioned chambers), but in this case the structure lay *outside* the PRI. Rather than serve as a hindrance, the exclusion of business organizations from the PRI allowed them a greater degree of independence than peasant and labor groups enjoyed. A 1996 Supreme Court decision eroded the corporatist relationship by ending mandatory membership in the chambers, thereby opening the door to independent business groups. Some private-sector interest groups have long maintained close ties to the government, particularly those representing economic sectors originally established with government support. Others had more conflictual relationships with the government under the PRI but now have much closer ties to the PAN administration. At the same time, Mexico's richest and most powerful businessmen have long maintained informal contact with the president and his advisors. Sometimes a group of them will meet with the chief executive as a semisecret big-business council. Business contacts have become more frequent and more important since the PAN took office.

Through much of Mexico's "economic miracle," powerful business interest groups (represented informally by major conglomerates, known as *grupos*) had close links to the government and the PRI. While business leaders differed with the PRI government on many issues, they pragmatically chose to work with a ruling party that for decades was invincible. Beginning in the early 1970s, however, the private sector turned more hostile toward the government, as Presidents Luis Echeverría (1970–1976) and López Portillo (1976–1982) expanded the state's role in the economy. For the first time, some powerful *grupos*, particularly those located in the industrial capital of Monterrey, allied themselves with the PAN. In the following years, however, neoliberal reforms by President de la Madrid (1982–1988) and, especially, President Salinas (1988–1994) won back much of the business community's support. A number of the country's richest businessmen contributed large sums to Salinas, which gave them insider access to purchasing the state enterprises that his administration privatized. But never were the bonds between big business and the government so strong as they have been under Presidents Fox (himself a wealthy former businessman) and Calderón, whose party (PAN) has long been linked to business. During the years of PRI dominance, business leaders kept a low profile in politics and relied on behind-the-scene contacts with the government to lodge any grievances or requests. Since the 1990s, however, many business organizations have openly supported and contributed to the PAN.

"Outsider" Interest Groups: The Politics of Protest   For those representing the nation's poor—nonunionized and unskilled workers, peasants, and other "outsiders" who lack the political clout or resources to participate in the normal interplay of Mexican interest-group politics—the political system increasingly has permitted an alternative form of pressure-group activity—political protest. Like the U.S. civil rights movement in the 1960s, many of Mexico's university students, peasants, and urban poor organize sit-ins, protest marches, and the like. To succeed, protests by political outsiders must attract media attention and some degree of sympathy and support from the public, especially the middle class.

Protestors must walk a fine line, however. To be effective, they need to demonstrate their capacity to disrupt daily life or to arouse popular support. Yet they must be wary not to threaten the stability of the political system or to question its fundamental legitimacy. In 1968, when huge student protests threatened to disrupt the Summer Olympics (hosted by Mexico) and embarrass the government, the authorities brutally suppressed them, killing hundreds of people. By contrast, Mexico's most-noted recent rebel group—Chiapas's Zapatista guerrillas—while initially appearing as an armed revolutionary movement, has, in fact, evolved into a political group working peacefully within the system. Under Fox, and to a somewhat lesser extent Calderón, the federal government has given protestors more room to operate.

But state and local officials often take a harder line against protestors. In 2006, in the southern city of Oaxaca (capital of the state with the same name), the PRI governor sent 1,000 state police to evict striking teachers who had occupied the city center. The protesting teachers, whose list of demands included the resignation of the state's governor, were later joined by radical students, indigenous peasant groups, and other local organizations. During their months-long confrontation with state police and later federal police, a number of demonstrators were shot dead, and the protests were eventually vanquished.

CONCLUSION: A DEVELOPING DEMOCRACY

As a consequence of PAN's 2000 and 2006 presidential victories Mexican politics will never be the same. Now that the Mexican people have seen that they can vote out the party in power without negative consequences, single-party domination is extremely unlikely to return. Elections for president, Congress, state governors, and mayors are now competitive in substantial parts of the country. An official network of citizen electoral monitors, instituted in the 1990s, and other related reforms now seem to have produced an honest vote count, although the PRD did claim fraud in the 2006 presidential election. As we have seen, the number of seats each of the major parties has won in the last four congressional elections has fluctuated wildly. Many state and local elections in Mexico's economically developed north now feature real competition between the PAN and PRI candidates. Meanwhile, the PRD and the PRI field viable candidates in the poor southern states. In some areas, there is intense competition among all three major parties. In short, the phenomenon of competitive elections is now firmly established. To succeed politically, candidates and elected officials from all three parties will need to be more responsive to the needs of individual voters and interest groups.

In Mexico, as in many developing nations in transition to full democracy, there continue to be government human rights abuses of journalists, political protestors, indigenous peoples, and those suspected of common criminal behavior. In its 2010 annual report on Mexico, Amnesty International reported that:

> Reports increased of serious human rights violations committed by members of the military carrying out law enforcement activities. Federal, state and municipal police forces also continued to commit serious human rights violations in several states. Women experienced high levels of gender-based violence with little access to justice.... Several journalists and human rights defenders were killed, harassed or faced fabricated criminal charges. Marginalized communities whose lands were sought for economic development were at risk of harassment, forced eviction or denial of their right to adequate information and consultation.[37]

Still, while serious problems persist at the state and local level, the national government's human rights record has improved significantly in the past decade. President Fox released long-secret government documents detailing the national security forces' murder of hundreds of alleged subversives in the late 1960s and 1970s. The national government has seemingly ended such abuses, with the notable exception of some army behavior in the war on drugs.

At the same time, the Fox government was more even-handed than prior administrations were in dealing with political protests by marginal groups (outsiders). For example, he softened the government's negotiating stand with the Zapatista rebels in Chiapas and offered a peace settlement that the EZLN accepted until Congress altered it. And when peasants protested the planned expansion of Mexico City's international airport (which would have encroached on their land), the Fox administration did not use force to crush the demonstrators (which had been the norm under previous presidents) and moved the location of the new runways. Thus, in a variety of ways—from the ballot box to protest demonstrations—the appeals and demands of many Mexican citizens are increasingly being heard.

But the struggle for full democracy is far from over. The high end of the judicial system operates more honestly and fairly today. The Supreme Court, in particular, has been quite vigilant in protecting civil liberties. But below the top, the court system continues to be inefficient and corrupt. Many government bureaucrats and politicians continue to demand bribes for their services. According to one estimate, during the last years leading up to Fox's victory, Mexicans paid $2.5 billion in bribes to government functionaries *annually*, averaging $100 per family.[38] That "corruption tax" has probably diminished since then, but it is still considerable.

Indeed, political corruption and misbehavior continue to pose a fundamental challenge to Mexico's new democracy. Misconduct has crossed party lines. In the

2004 mayoral election in Tijuana, the PRI used intimidation, vote-buying, and patronage to secure victory for its candidate, Jorge Hank Rhon. Hank, the son of a notorious party boss, had previously been convicted of smuggling. He is widely believed to have links to Tijuana's **drug cartel**, and two of his bodyguards have been jailed on charges of assassinating an investigative journalist. But the PRI had no monopoly on corruption. A senator from the Green (ecology) Party, formerly allied with Fox but now tied to the PRI, was videotaped taking a bribe from a businessman who wanted to build a hotel in a protected nature preserve. Within the PRD, several high-ranking Mexico City officials have been taped taking bribes, and the city's director of public finance was caught gambling in Las Vegas with public funds.[39] And in the current PAN administration, Calderón's Interior Minister, one of the party's rising stars, was implicated in an influence-peddling scandal.

President Calderón's record on human rights and civil liberties has been weaker than Fox's. Critics charge that in his first two years in office, dozens of leftists, including members of a guerrilla group, have been kidnapped by government forces and have subsequently disappeared. Because the drug cartels have corrupted so many police officers, Calderón has sent the military and special police units into a number of their strongholds where the local or state police appear incapable of containing them (see A Closer Look 15.2). But the drug war has been associated with many human rights violations against both drug cartel members and innocent civilians. According to Amnesty International, Mexican law enforcement agents continue to torture many criminal suspects.[40] Calderón's overhaul of the justice system extended some civil liberties to police suspects (including the presumption of innocence) but also offered police some questionable new powers.

Meanwhile, the country's drug bosses have lashed back against the military's offensive and battled among themselves to replace dead or jailed colleagues, creating a virtual street war in several cities between cartel gunmen and with government forces. Thousands have died, including drug cartel gunmen, police, soldiers, and innocent bystanders.

Another important political challenge for Mexico's new democratic order is the relationship between the branches of government. Although Congress's new independence from presidential dominance is an important step forward, all too frequently the legislature has replaced blind obedience (before 1997) with indiscriminate opposition. Calderón has worked more effectively with Congress than Fox had. But whenever any president lacks a congressional majority (likely to be the norm), there is a danger of gridlock between the branches of government.[51] Hopefully all three parties will learn the art of political compromise. At the same time, while the judiciary, especially the Supreme Court, is far more independent from the executive branch than it used to be, there needs to be further progress in that area.

In the economic sphere, Mexico's major challenge—achieving greater economic justice and equity—has become even more elusive as the repeated economic crises between 1982 and 2009 have widened the gap between rich and poor. Presidents Fox and Calderón have proposed a number of targeted programs designed to help Mexico's poor, but the basic structural obstacles to greater equality remain in place and in some respects have grown because of changes in economic policy. The two PAN presidents have been even more committed to neoliberal reforms than the previous PRI governments. Those policies—which focus on increased competition

15.2

Mexico's War on Drugs

Mexico's nearly 2,000-mile border with the United States makes it a prime location for feeding America's huge appetite for illicit drugs. Aside from being a transit point for South American cocaine, Mexico also produces substantial quantities of marijuana and, more recently, methamphetamines. Mexican drug trafficking into the United States dates back at least a century but has exploded in the last 20 to 30 years. Currently, that country's drug cartels account for about two-thirds of all narcotics flowing into the United States, including about 90 percent of the cocaine trade.[*]

Beginning in the 1960s and 1970s, as cocaine replaced heroin as America's drug of choice, the hub of drug trafficking to the United States relocated to Colombia, where labs processed coca leaves that had been grown primarily in Bolivia and Peru. Some of that cocaine was shipped to Mexico, where local cartels smuggled it into the United States. During the 1990s, as Colombian authorities, aided by the United States, broke up the famed Medellin and Cali cartels, Mexican drug networks took over most cocaine transportation to the United States. Since the profits generated by trafficking narcotics far exceed earnings from producing it, Mexico's drug lords soon became enormously wealthy. While it is impossible to measure precisely the monetary value of illegal activities such as these, informed estimates of Mexican cartel profits run from $14 billion to $48 billion annually.[41] That tremendous income gives them enough money to buy advanced armaments such as assault rifles, light antitank rockets, missiles, grenades, and fragmentation grenade launchers. It also provides them with substantial funds to bribe police officers, judges, and other members of the law-enforcement system as well as many politicians and soldiers. The reach of the narcotics cartels into Mexico's economy is enormous. For example, "the U.S. intelligence community estimates that some 450,000 people work in one or more facets of Mexico's drug sector."[42] Some analysts argue that the 1994 free trade agreement (NAFTA) between the United States,

Mexico, and Canada—reducing trade barriers between those three countries—has unwittingly contributed to the drug trade. For one thing, increased trade across the Mexican–American border made it somewhat easier to smuggle drugs north to the large U.S. market and to send guns southward from the United States to the Mexican cartels. At the same, by reducing trade restrictions on cheap American food crops entering Mexico, NAFTA drove thousands of poor farmers, who were unable to compete, into bankruptcy. Many of those peasants turned to working for the cartels out of financial desperation.[43]

The Mexican narcotics trade has been controlled by seven to nine large cartels headquartered in specific states or cities but operating in far more extensive regions of the country.[*] These include the Gulf Cartel, the Sinaloa Cartel, the Juárez Cartel, and Los Zetas. During the past two decades, a number of once-influential cartels have declined, new ones have emerged, others have splintered, and most have periodically fought each other in bloody battles for a larger share of the narcotics trade. On occasion cartels have formed alliances and at other times those agreements have broken down. These turf wars have cost thousands of lives, including many innocent bystanders. Much of the violence has been horrendously brutal. Some cartels have deposited severed heads in town squares or hung bodies from bridges to serve as a warning against collaborating with the police or with other cartels. Others have executed groups of patients in drug-treatment centers located in the territory of rival gangs.[44] Over the years, the drug lords have also murdered many law-enforcement officers, a number of mayors, and the front-running candidate for governor of the state of Tamaulipas.

Beyond the violence it has spawned, drug trafficking has taken an enormous toll on Mexico's political institutions and on the government's legitimacy. With hundreds of millions of dollars at their disposal, the drug lords have been able to bribe numerous judges, police officials, and military officers. In 2008 the Gulf

---

[*] Extensive drug trafficking organizations are commonly referred to as cartels. In economic analysis, a cartel (unrelated to the drug trade) refers to a group of companies or countries that collude to fix prices. That meaning does not apply to drug cartels.

[*] Most analysts name seven important cartels, though some list up to nine. The number has changed over time as old cartels fall and new ones arise.

(Continued)

A CLOSER LOOK

15.2

Mexico's War on Drugs
(Continued)

Cartel hung banners in the border city of Nuevo Laredo "promising good pay, free cars and better food to army soldiers who join the cartel's elite band of hit men." Weeks before they had distributed fliers in the city of Reynosa that read "Former soldiers sought to form armed group; good pay..."[45] Because the cartels pay salaries and benefits that far exceed military incomes, hundreds of soldiers have jumped at the opportunity. In fact, the most brutal of the cartels, Los Zetas, was founded in the 1990s as a private army for the Gulf Cartel (with whom they later split and battled). The group's founders were deserting officers from the Mexican army's Special Forces Airmobile Group, one of the military's most elite units. Most of its command structure still consists of former military and police officers. Many police officials, politicians, and judges who did not initially want to collaborate with the narco-traffickers have been faced with a terrible choice. They can increase their income considerably by collaborating with the drug gangs or, if they refuse, they and their family can risk being murdered. That choice is referred to as *plata o plomo*—meaning "silver" (taking bribes) or "lead" (being shot).

In August 2010, the Deputy Police Chief of Mexico City announced that his force was firing 3,200 policemen, 10 percent of the federal police force that serves the nation's capital. Another 500 were fired in Ciudad Juarez, Mexico's murder capital. It is widely understood that most were dismissed for corruption. Optimists viewed these dismissals as a sign that the Calderón administration was taking a tougher stand against corruption. Pessimists argued that the flood of dismissals was an indicator of how widely police corruption has spread. Unfortunately, rampant police and judicial corruption has delegitimized the criminal justice system. So too has the government's inability to provide its citizens with a feeling of safety and well-being, particularly in the northern regions of the country bordering on the United States.

Upon taking office in 2006, President Felipe Calderón declared an all-out war on drug trafficking. Since then, he has dispatched 45,000 soldiers and

5,000 federal police into the 18 states most heavily involved in the narcotics trade. The president's policies were initially supported by most Mexicans because they resent drug-related violence and corruption and have much greater respect for the military than for the local police. Since it started the war on drugs, government forces have been able to kill or capture several cartel leaders along with many lower-ranking bosses. Because some drug lords had previously been able to bribe their way out of jail, Mexico has extradited several hundred captured bosses to the United States, where they face charges. A substantial number of marijuana fields have been eradicated and meth labs destroyed. Additionally, thousands of cartel "foot soldiers" have been jailed or killed, and the government claims to have seized almost $400 million in drug money.

By some estimates, the volume of cocaine shipment across the Mexico–U.S. border fell by 16 percent from 2006 to 2009, but it is hard to know how much of that apparent decline was caused by the attacks on the cartels. In fact, cocaine shipments to the United States had already been falling in 2005, *prior to* Calderón's war on drugs. At the same time, from 2006 to 2009 cross-border shipments of narcotics other than cocaine—most notably marijuana, methamphetamines, and heroin—increased. Furthermore, data from the United Nations Office on Drugs and Crime (UNODC) indicate that the percentage of American drug consumers using cocaine primarily declined from 42 percent in the late 1990s to 31 percent in 2008.[46] In short, it appears that the drop in cocaine trafficking may stem principally from falling U.S. demand rather than from Mexico's war on drugs, as many cocaine users have apparently switched to other narcotics.

While most analysts feel that the gains from the drug war have been limited, nobody doubts that the cost to Mexican society has been great. While the killing and capture of high-level drug lords are victories in many respects, unfortunately they have ushered in bloody succession struggles among cartel factions and leaders wishing to take the place of those who

15.2

have fallen. As the government has tried to restrict the narcotics trade, the cartels have diversified into contract killings, kidnappings, extortion, and other brutal crimes. As of mid-2011 as many as 40,000 people may have been killed in drug-related violence during the nearly five years since Calderón started the war on drugs. More troubling, in the six months from November 2009 to May 2010, the *monthly* toll of people killed doubled—from 500 to 1,000—by far the largest number since Calderón took office.[47] Overall, the largest number of deaths (70 percent or more) has occurred within the cartels—men killed by rival gangs or by the military and police. The next highest death toll has been among law enforcement officials and the military. But over 1,000 innocent civilians have also been victims, including a sizable number of journalists, antidrug politicians, women, and children. Although the drug cartels are responsible for most of the civilian deaths, some of them have been killed by the army or the police. Since the start of the war on drugs began, more than 40 journalists have been killed or have disappeared, a number exceeded only by Iraq during that period. As a consequence, "several news organizations have resorted to not reporting on drug-related crime and corruption for fear of running afoul of drug kingpins, who have planted operatives in newsrooms and corrupted some journalists."[48] Equally troubling, Amnesty International and other human-rights groups have reported a rising number of abuses by government forces, including the torture of narcotics suspects. In 2010, the U.S. government announced that it was withholding $26 million in promised aid to the war on drugs because of the Mexican government's failure to adequately protect its citizens from military and police mistreatment.

In mid-2010, the authorities discovered 72 bodies of Central and South American migrants (who had intended to cross into the United States) in a mass grave some 90 miles from the Texas border. The victims were apparently killed by the Zetas cartel, which was either trying to move into the lucrative human-trafficking business or, according to one of

the only survivors of the bloodbath, were trying to force these (and other illegal migrants) to work for them. The day after the bodies were discovered, the government prosecutor leading the investigation and a policeman who was with him disappeared. Their bodies were discovered several weeks later. At the same time, the mayor of the nearby town was assassinated while driving his car. His four-year-old daughter was wounded. Within the space of a month three other mayors were also assassinated in northeastern Mexico. In fact, in the first nine months of 2010 alone, 11 mayors were murdered nationwide. At least one of them was killed by members of his own police force who had links to Los Zetas. Ciudad Juarez, a city of some 1.6 million people bordering on El Paso, Texas, is now believed to have the world's highest murder rate, with a per capita homicide rate more than 20 times higher than in New York City. The brutality of many of those murders and the many cartel victims left in the streets with signs of torture—some with severed heads, hands, or feet—worsens their psychological impact.

To be sure, the drug-related homicides are largely limited to northern cities near the U.S. border, such as Juarez and Tijuana. Mexico City and most of the rest of the country are much safer. Still the magnitude and brutality of drug-related violence has not only terrified northern Mexicans (many of whom are afraid to leave their houses at night) but has left much of the rest of the country on edge as they see narco-violence spreading south. Furthermore, the criminal justice system's low rate of apprehending and convicting cartel gunmen, coupled with the evidence of substantial police and judicial corruption, has reduced the government's legitimacy. Surprisingly, public opinion polls in late 2010 indicated that over 80 percent of all Mexicans continued to support the war on drugs, but the percentage of the population that believed that the government was making progress had fallen substantially to only 55 percent.[49]

Whether they support the war on drugs or not, most Mexicans agree that their country is being asked to

(Continued)

A CLOSER LOOK   15.2

Mexico's War on Drugs
(*Continued*)

shoulder most of its cost in human lives and financial expenditures. Although the U.S. government does provide financial aid, it is a relatively small fraction of what the Mexican government spends on the drug war. But the overwhelming majority of drug buyers are Americans. Thus, Mexicans insist that the only way of winning the war on drugs is to sharply reduce the American appetite for narcotics. Without that decline in demand, some experts argue, even if it were possible for Mexico to crush its traffickers, much of the drug trade would simply move elsewhere (for example, to Central America and the Caribbean), just as it had moved from Colombia to Mexico when the Colombian cartels were under intensive attack. Mexicans also complain that the United States must do more to control cross-border smuggling of arms since most of the cartels' weapons, especially the most deadly ones, can be traced back to U.S. dealers. In fact, officials of America's Bureau of Alcohol, Tobacco, Firearms, and Explosives (ATF) have estimated that 90 percent of the pistols and rifles recovered from Mexican drug dealers originated from U.S. dealers, mostly in Arizona and Texas.[50]

between firms, reduced government subsidies for producers, lower government regulations of business, and the consolidation of farmland into larger commercial units—are all designed to make the Mexican economy more efficient and competitive. When applied in various developing nations, these reforms have frequently stimulated economic growth (less so in Mexico), lowered inflation rates, and reduced government budget deficits. But often they have also widened economic inequalities, at least initially, and removed government safety nets for the poor. The needs of Mexico's poor are now sufficiently evident and well-articulated that conservative politicians such as Felipe Calderón, populist PRI politicians, and leftist PRD politicians all find it politically necessary to propose poverty-alleviation programs.

While Mexico has seemingly recovered from the deep economic downturn of 2009, almost half the population remains below the poverty line, making less than $2 per day. Most poor Mexicans, particularly those from rural areas, still lack an adequate diet, satisfactory health care, and an education for their children that will enable them to compete in the twenty-first century. These are great challenges that the nation will continue to face for decades.

Another fundamental problem is that the Mexican government has long depended financially on revenues from the state-owned petroleum industry, making it vulnerable to sharp fluctuations in the world price of oil. Moreover, Pemex, the state petroleum monopoly, is extremely inefficient, and oil production has stagnated in recent times. Furthermore, even in good years, the government lacks sufficient revenues because the country has one of the lowest rates of tax collection in Latin America. For example, compared to Brazil, it collects only one-third as much in tax revenues relative to gross domestic product.[52] As a consequence, the government lacks sufficient financial resources to pay for needed investments in education, infrastructure (including roads and electric power), and antipoverty programs. President

Calderón did push through a tax reform bill that, among other things, raises corporate taxes. But most analysts feel that the new tax revenues will be insufficient to meet the country's needs.

And despite substantial democratic gains in recent years, many Mexicans remain suspicious of government institutions. Polls indicate that they have little faith in the police, the courts, and most elected officials. Government corruption compounds that distrust. Even though President Calderón has achieved and maintained a fairly high approval rating, more than one-third of all Mexicans believe that he owed his 2006 electoral victory to fraud and, in that respect, holds office illegitimately.

◆ ◆ ◆

Key Terms and Concepts _____

caciques
corporatism
drug cartel
economic austerity
Institutional Revolutionary
  Party (PRI)
Mexican economic miracle

National Action Party (PAN)
New Left
Party of the Democratic Revolution (PRD)
presidentialism
state capitalism
Party of the Democratic Revolution (PRD)
Zapatista

DISCUSSION QUESTIONS

1. *The Mexican Revolution of 1910 dramatically changed that country's political and socioeconomic systems for the remainder of the twentieth century. Discuss the major positive and negative political and socioeconomic effects of that revolution.*

2. *Given Mexico's recent economic difficulties and growing concerns about violence and crime, PRD activists expected that the party's strength would grow. But instead the party and the left in general have lost support. Why has this happened?*

3. *Discuss the relationship between Congress and the president under the PRI presidencies. Who had the upper hand, and why? How has that relationship changed since the late 1990s?*

4. *Why has Mexico's current balance of strength among the major political parties created obstacles for effective government, and why is it likely to do so in the near future?*

5. *What factors led to the gradual decline of PRI political dominance after the late 1970s, leading to the 2000 presidential victory of PAN candidate Vicente Fox? What factors help explain PRI's recent comeback?*

6. *How would you argue that Mexico's current war on drugs is necessary in order to **preserve** the nation's democracy? In what ways does the war on drugs **undermine** the government's legitimacy, and how might that war undermine Mexican democracy?*

Notes _____

1. See Emily Edmonds-Poli and David A. Shirk, *Contemporary Mexican Politics* (Lanham, MD: Rowman and Littlefield, 2009); Jorge Domínguez, Chappell Lawson, Alejandro Moreno, eds. *Consolidating Mexico's Democracy.* (Baltimore, MD: The Johns Hopkins University Press, 2009); Jorge Castañeda, *Mañana Forever?*(New York: Alfred A. Knopf, 2011).

2. See Michael C. Meyer, William L. Sherman, and Susan Deeds, *The Course of Mexican History*, 9th ed. (New York: Oxford University Press, 2010).

3. See Anita Brenner, *The Wind That Swept Mexico* (New York: Harper and Bros., 1947); and Judith Adler Hellman, *Mexico in Crisis*, 2nd ed. (New York: Holmes and Meier, 1988).

4. Dale Story, *The Mexican Ruling Party* (New York: Praeger, 1986), p. 21.

5. Martin Needler, *Mexican Politics: The Containment of Conflict* (New York: Praeger, 1982), p. 108; see also Miguel Ramírez, "The Social and Economic Consequences of the National Austerity Program in Mexico," in *Paying the Costs of Austerity in Latin America*, eds. Howard Handelman and Werner Baer (Boulder, CO: Westview, 1989).

6. See also R. M. Sundrum, *Income Distribution in Less Developed Countries* (New York: Routledge, 1990), p. 77; and United Nations Development Program, *Human Development Report 2000* (New York and Oxford: Oxford University Press, 2002), p. 195.

7. Manuel Pastor and Carol Wise, "The Fox Administration and the Politics of Economic Transition," in *Mexico's Democracy at Work*, eds. Russell Crandall, Guadalupe Paz, and Riordan Roett (Boulder, CO: Lynne Rienner Publishers, 2005), pp. 98–99.

8. CIA, *World Factbook* www.cia.gov/library/publications/the-world-factbook/rankorder/2172rank.html. Country comparisons such as this are not fully precise since the years in which the data were collected in each country vary somewhat.

9. Peter Ward, *Welfare Politics in Mexico* (Boston: Allen and Unwin, 1986), p. 17.

10. Daniel Levy and Gabriel Székely, *Mexico: Paradoxes of Stability and Change* (Boulder, CO: Westview, 1987), p. 147. Most of those had part-time employment or were self employed.

11. Nora Lustig, *Mexico: The Remaking of an Economy* (Washington, DC: Brookings, 1992).

12. Sidney Weintraub, "Detour on the Way to the Promised Land," *Hemisfile* 7, no. 3 (May–June 1996): 6–7.

13. Miguel Angel Centeno, *Democracy Within Reason: The Technocratic Revolution in Mexico*, 2nd ed. (University Park: Pennsylvania State University Press, 1997).

14. Centeno, *Democracy Within Reason*, p. 49.

15. See Carlos Monsiváis, "'En virtud de las facultades que me han sido otorgadas, . . .' Notas sobre el presidencialismo a partir de 1968," in *La transición interrumpida: México 1968–1988* (México: Nueva Imagen, 1993), pp. 113–125.

16. Jeffrey A. Weldon, "Changing Patterns of Executive-Legislative Relations in Mexico," p. 137, and Kevin J. Middlebrook, "Mexico's Democratic Transitions," in *Dilemmas of Political Change in Mexico*, ed. Kevin J. Middlebrook (London, England: Institute of Latin American Studies of the University of London, 2004), p. 24.

17. Weldon, ibid, p. 165.

18. Wayne Cornelius and Jeffrey Weldon, "Politics in Mexico," in *Comparative Politics Today* (New York: Pearson Longman, 2006), ed. Gabriel Almond et al., p. 486.

19. The Mexican journal *Proceso* is the best Spanish-language source on the Zapatista movement. Among the many books on the Zapatistas are Philip L. Russell, *The Chiapas Rebellion* (Austin, TX: Mexico Resource Center, 1995); and Neil Harvey, *The Chiapas Rebellion: The Struggle for Land and Democracy*. (Durham, NC: Duke University Press, 1998).

20. Roderic Ai Camp, *Politics in Mexico* (New York: Oxford University Press, 2007), p. 190.

21. Ibid, p. 191.

22. Human Rights Watch, "Mexico-2008," www.hrw.org/en/node/79216.

23. David Shirk, director of the University of San Diego's Trans-Border Institute, as quoted in the *Arizona Daily Star* (September 27, 2010).

24. Samuel P. Huntington, "Social and Institutional Dynamics of One-Party Systems," in *Authoritarian Politics in Modern Society: The Dynamics of One-Party Systems*, eds. S. Huntington and C. Moore (New York: Basic Books, 1970), p. 5.

25. Alan Riding, *Distant Neighbors* (New York: Vintage, 1986), p. 135.

26. Andrew Gelman and Geronimo Cortina, "Income and Voter Choice in the 2000 [and 2006] Presidential Election[s]" (July 13, 2006), pp. 4 and 9. Available at SSRN: http://ssrn.com/abstract=1010104.

27. "Leftist's Blockade Divides City and His Supporters," *New York Times* (August 6, 2006).

28. Excellent survey data on the period leading up to the 2000 election can be found in Jorge Domín-guez and Alejandro Poiré, eds., *Toward Mexico's Democratization: Parties, Campaigns, Elections, and Public Opinion* (New York and London: Routledge, 1999).

29. For a discussion of political culture and types of subcultures, see G. Almond and G. B. Powell, *Comparative Politics: A Developmental Approach* (Boston: Little, Brown, 1966), pp. 27–30; and Gabriel Almond, "The Intellectual History of the Civic Culture Concept," in *The Civic Culture Revisited*, eds. G. Almond and S. Verba (Boston: Little, Brown, 1980).

30. Camp, *Politics in Mexico*, 4th ed. (2003), pp. 54–74.

31. Linda Stevenson and Mitchell Seligson, "Fading Memories of the Revolution: Is Stability Eroding in Mexico?" in *Polling for Democracy: Public Opinion and Political Liberalization in Mexico*, ed. Roderic Ai Camp (Wilmington, DE: Scholarly Resources, 1996), 59–80.

32. Roderic Ai Camp, *Politics in Mexico*, 5th ed. (2007), pp. 62–68, 73.

33. Needler, *Mexican Politics*, p. 5. Increased voting over time resulted primarily from higher educational levels, extending the vote to women, and lowering the voting age from 21 to 18.

34. While corporatism is often associated with European fascism, governments throughout Latin America and even many Western democracies have corporatist features. See Howard Wiarda, *Corporatism and National Development in Latin America* (Boulder, CO: Westview, 1981).

35. Katrina Burgess, "Mexican Labor at the Crossroads," in *Mexican Politics and Society*, eds. Tulchin and Selee (Boulder, CO: Lynne Rienner Publishers, 2003), p. 100.

36. Dale Story, *Industry, the State and Public Policy* (Austin: University of Texas Press, 1986), p. 82.

37. Amnesty International, "2010 Annual Report for Mexico," www.amnestyusa.org/annualreport.php?id=ar&yr=2010&c=MEX.

38. Martin Needler, "The Government of Mexico," in *Introduction to Comparative Government* (New York: Pearson Longman, 2006), p. 617.

39. Denise Dresser, "Fox's Mexico: Democracy Paralyzed," *Current History* 104, no. 679 (February 2005): 64–68.

40. Open letter from Amnesty International to Mexican President Felipe Calderón (February 7, 2008), www.amnestyusa.org/countries/mexico/coxtocalderonenglish.pdf.

41. Colleen W. Cook, "CRS Report to Congress: Mexico's Drug Cartels" (Congressional Research Service, 2007 http://fas.org/sgp/crs/row/RL34215.pdf; Department of State Bureau of International Narcotics and Law Enforcement Affairs, *International Narcotics Control Strategy Report 2008*, state.gov/p/inl/rls/nrcrpt/2008/index.htm; Department of State Bureau of International Narcotics and Law Enforcement Affairs, *International Narcotics Control Strategy Report 2008*, Edmonds-Poli and Shirk, *Contemporary Mexican Politics*, pp. 309–315, 320–322. Some analysts argue that annual profits actually exceed $50 billion.

42. George W. Grayson, *Mexico: Narco-Violence and a Failed State?* (New Brunswick, NJ: Transaction Publishers, 2010), p. 254.

43. Elizabeth Sahner et. al. "Mexican President Comes to Washington: What Will Become of President Calderón's Visit to Washington?" Council on Hemispheric Affairs (May 19, 2010), www.coha.org/.

44. "19 Patients Killed at Mexican Drug Rehab Facility," CNN.com (June 11, 2010).

45. Chris Hawley, "Mexican Cartels Post 'Help Wanted' Ads," *USA Today* (April 24, 2008), USAToday.com.

46. UNODC, *World Drug Report 2010* http://unodc.org/unodc/en/data-and-analysis/WDR-2010.html.

47. "Drugs and Violence: Mexico's Addiction," BBC (September 3, 2010), www.bbc.co.uk/news/world-latin-america-11174174.

48. "Mexico Reporters Fall Victim to Crackdown on Drug Trafficking," World Briefing, *New York Times* (September 8, 2010).

49. Richard Wike, "Mexicans Continue to Support Drug War: But Sense of Progress and Support for U.S. Involvement Declines" (Pew Research Center, Global Attitudes Project, August 12, 2010), http://pewresearch.org/pubs/.

50. James McKinley, "U.S. Stymied as Guns Flow to Mexican Cartels," *New York Times* (April 14, 2009), nytimes.com. The NRA and other opponents of government gun regulation dispute this figure.

51. Chappell Lawson, "Fox's Mexico at Midterm," *Journal of Democracy*, 15.1(2004), 139–153.

52. Reuters, "Factbox: Key Facts about Mexico's Tax Reform," www.reuters.com/article/idUSN1419707820070915.

PART V

INTERNATIONAL RELATIONS

Up to this point, we have focused primarily on the domestic aspects of politics—how political behavior, institutions, and ideologies function within the boundaries of the nation-state. In Part V, we turn our attention to another important field within political science: the international relations between nation-states. In truth, domestic politics and international relations are frequently intertwined. A country's decision to go to war may be motivated by domestic politics. A nation's environmental policy may affect the purity of the air or water in neighboring states. But, in the absence of some form of regional or world government, the rules and norms of political and economic relations between sovereign states are distinct from those of domestic politics.

Chapter 16 deals with approaches to the study of the causes of war, nuclear weapons, foreign policy decision making, international political economy, international organization, and international law. Chapter 17 examines important contemporary issues in international relations such as world trade, human rights, and international terrorism.

CHAPTER

16

Approaches to International Relations

French soldiers fire a 120mm mortar during Operation "Glued Finger 2" in the village of Dwakoleh in Afghanistan in September 2010. These soldiers were part of a NATO force fighting the Taliban.

- **International Relations versus Domestic Politics**
- **Idealists and Realists**
- **War and International Relations**
- **Foreign Policy Decision Making**
- **International Political Economy**

- **International Law and Organization**
- **Ethics and International Relations**
- **Conclusion: War, Trade, Foreign Policy, and the Stakes of International Politics**

The decade following the terrorist attacks on September 11, 2001, saw a number of terrorist attacks in Britain, Spain, and Indonesia, among other places, and major armed conflicts in Iraq and Afghanistan. Especially in recent years, few people doubt that international events have substantial impacts on commerce, policy, and well-being.

Many citizens immediately think of the possibility of armed conflict when they consider international relations, and indeed, wars are among the most important events in human history. Even the preparation for war transforms the allocation of economic resources and influences how nations treat their citizens. But international relations are also important when wars are not raging. Economic relations among countries dramatically change domestic conditions everywhere. Modern advances in transportation, communications, and weapons systems have created a world of complex interdependence among nations in which economic progress and national security increasingly require attention to conditions and policies in other countries.

Although international relations is basic to the study of politics and government, approaches to this field are fundamentally different from those encountered in the study of domestic politics. For example, we cannot apply the concepts of political participation through voting, interest group membership, and party identification in explaining international relations in the same ways that we employ these concepts in analyzing domestic politics. In this chapter, we discuss the most important approaches to studying international relations, and we devote Chapter 17 to a discussion of contemporary issues.

International Relations versus Domestic Politics

International relations is the study of how wars are fought, their causes, the complex issue of deterrence, the effects of shifts in the balance of power, strategy and tactics, the political impact of nuclear weapons, and even the ethical questions suggested by the idea of a "just war." We are sometimes tempted to assume that international relations is distinguished from domestic politics *entirely* by its emphasis on violence and war.

Yet the problem of conflict, even violent conflict, is a part of both domestic *and* international politics. The difference is not in the *existence* of conflict but in *how conflict is managed*. Kenneth Waltz, a leading theorist, explains the point in this way:

> The threat of violence and the recurrent use of force are said to distinguish international from national affairs. But in the history of the world surely most rulers have had to bear in mind that their subjects might use force to resist or overthrow them. If the absence of government is associated with the threat of violence, so also is its presence.... To discover ... differences between internal and external affairs one must look for a criterion other than the occurrence of violence.... *The difference between national and international politics lies not in the use of force but in the different modes of organization for doing something about it.*[1]

Domestic politics usually takes place within a context of a generally settled order, whereas international politics takes place in a state of relative anarchy. In domestic affairs, the state assumes a "monopoly on the *legitimate* use of force, [meaning] that public agents are organized to prevent and to counter the private use of force."[2] Because such a monopoly on the use of legitimate force does not exist in international relations, Waltz describes the international arena as one in which nations engage in **self-help**; each nation must look to its own security because there is no higher authority that can consistently and effectively perform that function. Of course, forces of stability and order do exist in the international system, such as shared cultures and ideologies, and international law and organization—and they are effective in preventing and managing some conflicts. The difference between domestic and international politics lies in the extent to which a given actor is on its own with respect to protecting its security. Although both citizens and individual nations can be threatened with adversaries, and although both may work to defend themselves, the *primary* approach to security in domestic politics is reliance on a higher authority (for example, the police), whereas the *primary* approach to security in international politics is self-help.

Idealists and Realists

Historians and philosophers have been analyzing international relations since the time of ancient Greece. Among the earliest works in the field was *The Peloponnesian War*, written in the fifth century BCE by the Greek historian Thucydides.[3] Other ancient studies include Sun Tzu's *The Art of War* and Kautilya's *Arthasastra*.[4] These works continue to suggest insights to modern scholars. The unprecedented destruction and complex origins of World War I, however, led to rapid growth in academic study of the field, producing two sharply opposing perspectives: idealism and realism.

Idealism*

Idealists assume that war and international tensions can be prevented by establishing international law, by creating effective international organizations, by asserting rights and obligations in international affairs, and by educating citizens and leaders regarding the wastefulness of war. **Idealism** thus advocates a set of normative principles—it tells us what we *should* do. Yet idealism also contains implicit explanations of national behavior, thus approaching the status of an empirical theory.

Idealists suggest that the causes of war can be found in ill-conceived ideologies, in excesses of nationalism, and in the underdevelopment of law. If we want to know why a given war was started, we should look to those factors. On a positive note, idealism reflects the belief that effective political management can help prevent wars that otherwise appear unavoidable: People can be brought to understand the wrongfulness of belligerent ideologies or aggressive forms of national pride, and they can be persuaded to accept a workable code of international law. Wars need not be fought.

U.S. President Woodrow Wilson (1913–1921) was a key proponent of idealism. Following World War I, his support for the creation of the ill-fated League of Nations (an international organization intended to maintain international security) was a moral mission, one that reflected a sincere belief that war could become obsolete if nations had a forum in which they could solve their differences without recourse to armed conflict. Wilson believed that war is something that humankind can "grow out of," much as adults can emerge from a rocky adolescence to become cooperative, productive citizens.

Realism

Although many people share the goals of idealism, few analysts of international relations fully accept its assumptions about the underlying forces governing international affairs. **Realism** holds that the actual motivations for national behavior are often quite different from what is implied in the public rhetoric of leaders: A national leader may *claim* to act in accordance with moral, religious, or even legal principles, but his or her real purpose is almost always the pursuit of security and power. Realists claim that because idealism is flawed as a way to explain the origins of war, it cannot serve as a blueprint for preventing war. It is necessary to identify the forces that lead to war, and then leaders can make policies that make war less likely.

---

* Some analysts prefer the term *liberalism* or *liberal idealism* in this context. For example, a text by Charles W. Kegley, Jr., and Eugene R. Wittkopf, *World Politics, Trend and Transformation* (New York: St. Martin's, 1997), used *liberal idealism*, which the authors defined as the assumption that "people are not by nature sinful or wicked but that harmful behavior was the result of structural arrangements motivating individuals to act in their own self-interest" (p. 19). We prefer to use the term *idealism* here to avoid confusion with the rather separate set of ideas associated with the term *liberalism* in social and economic domestic policy (as discussed in Chapter 2), and because *liberalism* is synonymous with advocacy of free trade in the subfield of international political economy, as we discuss later in this chapter.

A CLOSER LOOK

16.1

Idealism, Realism, and U.S. Military Action in Iraq, Afghanistan, and Libya

Compare these two statements:

President George W. Bush, September 2004: In this young century, our world needs a new definition of security. Our security is not merely found in spheres of influence, or some balance of power. *The security of our world is found in the advancing rights of mankind.* These rights are advancing across the world—and across the world, the enemies of human rights are responding with violence. Terrorists and their allies believe the Universal Declaration of Human Rights and the American Bill of Rights, and every charter of liberty ever written, are lies, to be burned … and forgotten…. [We see] how the terrorists measure their success—in the death of the innocent, and in the pain of grieving families. [Our] nation is grateful to the soldiers of many nations who have helped to deliver the Iraqi people from an outlaw dictator.[7]

President Barack Obama, March 2011: At this point, the United States and the world faced a choice. Gaddafi declared that he would show "no mercy" to his own people. He compared them to rats, and threatened to go door to door to inflict punishment. In the past, we had seen him hang civilians in the streets, and kill over a thousand people in a single day. Now, we saw regime forces on the outskirts of the city. We knew that if we waited one more day, Benghazi—a city nearly the size of Charlotte—could suffer a massacre that would have reverberated across the region and stained the conscience of the world. [S]ome question why America should intervene at all—even in limited ways—in this distant land. They argue that there are many places in the world where innocent civilians face brutal violence at the hands of their government, and America should not be expected to police the world, particularly when we have so many pressing concerns here at home. It is true that America cannot use our military wherever repression occurs…. But that cannot be an argument for never acting on behalf of what's right. In this particular country—Libya; at this particular moment, we were faced with the prospect of violence on a horrific scale. We had a unique ability to stop that violence….[8]

Both statements, the first by President George W. Bush in 2004, and the second by President Barack Obama in 2011, embody idealism, and analysts from

Hans J. Morgenthau, an important twentieth-century realist, described realism as the assumption that "politics … is governed by objective laws" and that "the main signpost that helps political realism to find its way through the landscape of international politics is the concept of interest defined in terms of power."[5] If we want to understand the behavior of nations in international affairs, according to realist thinking, we must begin with the assumption that everything of importance that nations do is driven by their interests in maximizing their power and security.

By emphasizing *power* and *security*, realists minimize the place of ideals as a motivating force in international relations. Proponents of realist theory have probably produced the most influential research in the field of international relations. Beginning with the assumption that "states, … at a minimum, seek their own preservation and, at a maximum, drive for universal domination," realism is the foundation for a wide range of useful predictions about international behavior.[6] (See A Closer Look 16.1.)

16.1

the realist perspective criticized both leaders. Realists have long argued that national security and national interest should be the primary objectives of foreign policy, and that it is dangerous and futile to use military power for other purposes. Many critics of the war in Iraq argued that overthrowing Saddam Hussein would not enhance U.S. security, and critics of the U.S.-led airstrikes in Libya in 2011 stated similarly that the uprising there was "not our business." Referring to a far larger operation, many realist observers insist that the U.S. war in Afghanistan does not serve national interests. Especially following the death of Osama bin Laden on May 1, 2011, critics of the war contend that the United States has no real security interests in Afghanistan and that it is only pursuing a futile humanitarian effort to build democracy.

It is remarkable that these two otherwise very different presidents would justify their policies with such similar idealist rhetoric. But it is important to note that both Bush and Obama claimed that their actions were also justified on realist grounds. In these and many other speeches, both presidents argued that combating terrorism and tyranny is *necessary to protect the U.S. national interest*. Both claimed that the unsettled and undemocratic character of the regimes in Iraq, Afghanistan, and Libya undermines stability and breeds terrorism. Thus, while they both offered moral justifications for military action that echoed Woodrow Wilson's idealism, they both argued that addressing the humanitarian tragedies was in the national interest.

The contrast between idealism and realism is reasonably clear in the abstract, but it is often murky when we apply these concepts to actual cases. It is particularly difficult to determine whether idealism or realism was the primary motivation for a particular decision when we attempt to find the answer in public speeches. Voters often respond very strongly to reports of atrocities and terrible violations of human rights, and political leaders try to inspire citizens with the idea that the idealists' peaceful world is within reach. But voters also want to be assured that costly military efforts are in the national interest.

The U.S. actions in Iraq, Afghanistan, and Libya during the first decade of the century were supported by liberals and conservatives, Democrats and Republicans, but they were also heatedly opposed. In part, the divergent opinions reflect the fact that the decisions involved could be debated from the perspective of idealism ("we can bring peace and reduce suffering by overthrowing dictators and fighting terrorists"), *and* from the perspective of realism ("our national security requires regime change and the elimination of terrorist breeding grounds"). An honest accounting by the decision-makers involved would almost certainly reveal that both perspectives figured in the choices they made.

For example, whereas idealists would see the outbreak of World War II as caused by the fanatical ideology of fascism, realists feel that Hitler's or Mussolini's totalitarian ideologies were less instrumental in producing the war than was the imbalance of power that developed between the two world wars. Since nations will *always* seek power and domination (regardless of the ideologically charged statements in stump speeches and editorials), realists contend that the more basic "cause" of the war was the military weakness of Great Britain, France, and the United States, which presented Germany (and perhaps Japan) with the opportunity to pursue expansionist plans.

Realists thus criticized British Prime Minister Neville Chamberlain (the prime minister who preceded Winston Churchill) for his actions during the months preceding World War II. Chamberlain sought to appease Hitler as Germany moved its armies into Austria and Czechoslovakia. He refused to accelerate British defense spending in the face of the rising German military threat because he thought that

Hitler would see this as provocative. Hitler exploited the opening created by British weakness, and World War II began. Realists employ this example to support their contention that preventing wars requires a consistent recognition that all nations seek power and security, and that military weakness in critical areas will present opportunities that aggressors will exploit. The positive element in realism is the idea that the behavior of most states is predictable.

Criticisms of Idealism and Realism

Critics of idealism argue that an approach based on national interest and the assumption that nations will always pursue security and power provides a better foundation for explaining conflict and war. Skillful politicians may engage in florid rhetoric to persuade their citizens to sacrifice for a "moral" cause, but the objectives they most often pursue are their more concrete concerns for power, security, and self-interest.

On the other hand, critics of realism contend that realists read history too narrowly. Edward Hallett Carr, whose analysis of idealism and realism remains an influential statement, pointed out that realist thinking is excessively cynical. Although he admitted that moralizing speeches do sometimes serve simply as a cover for the pursuit of self-interest, it does not follow that the behavior of nations is as simple or predictable as realists claim.[9] Moreover, the concept of a nation having "a" national interest is more applicable to nations that are governed by a single monarch or ruling elite (whose precise and explicit interests can be identified and acted on) than to democratic nations, whose citizens and groups have multiple and usually conflicting interests. Realism is thus an oversimplification of the motivations involved in foreign policy.

NATO military intervention in Bosnia (1992–1995), the U.S. military action in Somalia (1992–1993), and U.S. bombing in Libya (2011) are policy choices that cannot be easily explained by realist assumptions. The United States has no strategic interests in those areas. The relief efforts placed some military personnel in real danger and cost billions of dollars. Similarly, some claim that the policies former British Prime Minister Tony Blair adopted in 2002 and 2003 supporting the U.S.-led invasions of Afghanistan and Iraq cannot be explained through realism. In fact, it can be argued that British security from terrorist attacks would have been enhanced if he had taken a more neutral position during this period.

The idea that nations pursue foreign policies *entirely* on the basis of a simple concern for self-interest is becoming increasingly difficult to defend. An important study by a leading analyst concluded that the existence of a "security community," defined as "a group of countries among which war is unthinkable," can influence policy. He claims that a security community has developed among the United States, Western Europe, and Japan. A shared conviction among these countries—the conviction that war would be absurdly costly, whereas peace produces important gains—exerts real force over their policy choices.[10] Something larger than a nation's individual interests may shape foreign policy, and idealists would point to that observation as support for the idea that peace may be maintained or strengthened by building on these larger, collective influences.

Debates over the usefulness of realism and idealism in international relations will not be resolved soon. Realists have always noted that the political rhetoric used to justify states' foreign policy choices usually makes it *appear* that idealistic motivations are involved; the *actual* motivations are power and security even when domestic politics requires speeches implying a higher purpose. Empirical research is unlikely to yield definitive answers to this debate partly because of the difficulty of ascertaining the motives of national leaders.

WAR AND INTERNATIONAL RELATIONS

The possibility of armed conflict often influences behavior even when other issues dominate relations among nations. A country's ability to attack its enemies or to defend itself in war represents a critical factor in its interactions with other nations. Thus, a great deal of scholarly attention is rightly devoted to the study of war. In this section, we consider the most widely known approaches to understanding the causes of war, and then we focus on two special issues: the balance-of-power concept and the problem of nuclear weapons.

The Causes of War: Waltz's "Images"

War is a horribly wasteful but seemingly inescapable part of life. This paradox has led philosophers and politicians to devote a great deal of attention to discovering its ultimate causes. Kenneth Waltz's classic book, *Man, the State, and War*, synthesized much of the prevailing scholarly thinking about the subject into a three-way classification of "images."[11] (In terms of the discussion in the previous section, Waltz would say that the Third Image is most closely associated with realism and that the First Image is most closely tied to idealism.)

The First Image: Human Nature and the Causes of War   Waltz described the "First Image" of the causes of war as follows: "The locus of the important causes of war is found in the nature and behavior of man. Wars result from selfishness, from misdirected aggressive impulses, from stupidity."[12] To find out why World War II occurred, for example, we study Adolf Hitler's personality, his foolish ideology, and his tragic power to inspire millions of followers. Quoting Confucius, Waltz summed up the First Image: "There is deceit and cunning and from these wars arise."

There are both optimistic and pessimistic versions of this First Image. If the cause of war is found in human nature, then war can be ended if education and experience can correct human failings. Perhaps people can be brought to see war as wrong and avoidable. Others, who believe that war is an inherent part of human nature, imply that wars can never be fully prevented. The "laws" of human nature, they argue, are no more malleable than are the laws of physics.

Although the importance of human nature cannot be easily dismissed, it becomes quickly limited as a basis for generally understanding international conflict. If human nature were all that mattered in the origin of wars, *then we have no way of understanding why there are periods of peace*. Since nations are not always at war (or peace), human nature cannot be the exclusive source of war. "The causes that in fact explain differences in behavior must be sought somewhere other than in human nature itself."[13]

The Second Image: The Nature of States   An alternative explanation of the cause of war focuses on the nature of states. Even if people could control their aggressive impulses, the nature of the states that govern them may create conditions leading to war. The Second Image implies that we can explain war by looking at the ways in which different *kinds* of states increase or diminish the likelihood of war.

There are two excellent illustrations of the Second Image approach: the concept of the **democratic peace** and the Marxist–Leninist view on international conflict. Proponents of the former argue that it is largely nondemocratic governments that are prone to war (see A Closer Look 16.2). Such states need to repress dissent, and it is easier to do so if the citizens are unified and loyal. The leader of a nondemocratic government thus may start a war in order to make citizens focus on a common external threat. By some interpretations, there has never been a major war between two genuinely democratic nations—an idea that seems to confirm this connection between the nature of a state's political system and its tendencies toward war.

The conventional Marxist–Leninist interpretation of international affairs also accounts for conflict by focusing on the nature of states. One of Lenin's contributions to Marxist thinking was the idea that capitalist states engage in aggression because their inevitably failing economic systems force them to do so in order to gain more wealth. States with socialist systems (or very primitive states) do not go to war because they are not forced to do so by the consequences of capitalist economics.

The "democratic peace" concept and Lenin's theory of imperialism share the idea that some kinds of political systems are more likely to be involved in wars than others. The limitation of the Second Image is its assumption that the warlike (or peaceful) nature of states is entirely determined by domestic factors. Waltz points out that just as individual behavior cannot be understood apart from the societies in which individuals live, the behavior of individual *states* cannot be understood apart from the world in which they operate. Many actions taken by states reflect the nature of the international system as much as they reflect their own internal structure and domestic political needs.

The Third Image: The International System   Waltz's Third Image emphasizes that understanding international relations requires an appreciation of the nature of the system in which states operate. The key feature of that system is *anarchy*, as noted earlier. For Waltz, the fact that the system is anarchic creates a situation in which each state is *always* threatened, and most of the important actions of states are driven by pervasive concerns for security. Wars are not the consequence of human nature, or even of the nature of political systems, but of the way in which the anarchy of international relations creates insecurity.

As alternative approaches to understanding the causes of war, all three images can be coherent and persuasive. Biologists and psychologists may convince us that human nature is innately aggressive, but we see that some states prevent such alleged tendencies from leading to war. Switzerland, for example, has managed to avoid direct involvement in armed conflicts for centuries. And although the anarchic nature of the international system may create widespread insecurity, nations are sometimes able to conduct themselves in ways that avoid turning insecurity into armed conflict. Along with most mainstream experts in the field, Waltz places the greatest

16.2

A CLOSER LOOK

The "Democratic Peace"?[14]

The democratic peace concept has gathered momentum among specialists in international relations during the last few decades. In simple terms, its proponents argue that the more democratic a nation is, the less likely it is to be involved in a war with another democracy. There is considerable empirical support for this proposition, although it is not well established that democracies are *generally* less involved in wars—the point is that they rarely fight other democracies.[15]

Why should this be so? Although the matter is far from settled among political scientists and diplomats, a few themes consistently appear in discussions of the "democratic peace" phenomenon. Perhaps the root of the idea can be traced to a 1795 essay by philosopher Immanuel Kant, entitled "Perpetual Peace: A Philosophical Sketch," in which he concluded that governments that act in "responsible" ways would be reluctant to go to war. The most obvious explanation is that, in democratic systems, the people will force their leaders to avoid war because they know that they will bear its terrible costs. Dictators, not being similarly constrained by public opinion, will initiate wars much more often.

While this makes intuitive sense, it only tells part of the story. One recent study found that, when faced with war, leaders in democratic systems are more likely to allocate a greater share of national resources to military efforts than leaders in authoritarian regimes. Voters in democratic systems dislike military defeats even more than they dislike war. Consequently, nations of all kinds are less likely to attack democratic systems, bringing them into war less often. Moreover, democratic leaders try to avoid defeat by being very selective about the countries they would make war upon. Because they are less reckless about engaging in war, and because would-be aggressors fear the all-out effort that democracies would make in response, the historical record indicates that democracies are less likely than nondemocracies to be involved in war.[16]

A newer refinement to the democratic peace theory is a distinction between established democracies and newer democracies. Why would the maturity of a democracy matter? A country that has taken the first steps toward democracy has probably not yet established institutions that create real accountability (such as a civilian-controlled military, a genuinely free press, and a strongly independent judiciary). In such countries, political leaders may be particularly motivated to take their countries to war. They realize that engaging in aggression can generate domestic support because they can "sell" the resulting war to their citizens as a response to a past injustice at the hands of the invaded country, for example. Not being restrained by well-institutionalized legislative or judicial bodies, or by a competitive party system, *emerging* democracies may actually be more belligerent than dictatorships.[17]

One of the most troubling questions raised by this research has to do with the future of Iraq. Will Iraq be torn by an intractable civil war? Will it return to a dictatorship just as horrific as Saddam Hussein's? Even if Iraq continues on its path toward democracy, it may be just as likely to go to war against its neighbors as it was when it had a fascist dictatorship. The Iraqi case raises important questions about the democratic peace idea, even if the historical record generally supports it.

---

importance on the Third Image, but the complexity of the origins of war makes it likely that all three approaches will continue to find able advocates.

The Balance of Power

At its core, the concept of the **balance of power** says that the *relative* power levels among competing states is the main determinant of stability in international relations and that "the behavior of individual states is explained in terms of the state of the whole system."[18] Where power is balanced, some wars will be prevented; imbalanced power invites aggression by the superior power or prompts the formation of alliances among weaker states to restore balance.

Most analysts agree that the balance-of-power concept worked best as a way to understand the European "multipolar system" as it existed between 1648 and 1945. One of the clearest statements about the balance-of-power idea was made by Winston Churchill, who stated that "for four hundred years the foreign policy of England has been to oppose the strongest, most aggressive, most dominating power on the Continent." At least until World War II, the shifting balance of power in Europe prevented any one nation from dominating the world.[19]

As Waltz explains, nations that do not preserve their own security "will fail to prosper [and] will lay themselves open to danger, [and thus] ... fear of such unwanted consequences stimulates states to behave in ways that tend toward the creation of balances of power."[20] If one state begins to threaten another state (as Germany threatened the Soviet Union and Great Britain in the 1930s), the threatened state will normally attempt to augment its power, perhaps by forming alliances (as did those two nations during that period). The aggressor's threatening posture will prompt others to make similar alliances.

The balance-of-power concept is a Third Image approach because it focuses on what states do *in response to the essential anarchy of the international system*. It is also an application of realist principles because it explains war and the avoidance of war without reference to the idealist notions that wars occur because of misguided ideologies and that they can be prevented by nurturing the love of peace. The idea is one of the oldest concepts in political science. Writing in 1742, David Hume argued that "the maxim of preserving the balance of power is founded so much on common sense and obvious reasoning, that it is impossible it could altogether have escaped antiquity...."[21]

A major source of confusion regarding the balance of power is that the idea is sometimes presented as an *empirical* statement (states *do* act in ways that preserve or restore a balance of power) and sometimes as a *normative* statement (states *should* act in such ways). In fact, a fundamental but common misunderstanding of the balance-of-power concept is the idea that balanced power and efforts to maintain balanced power always *prevent war*. As stated by Edward Vose Gulick in 1955, "The basic aim of the balance of power was to ensure the survival of independent states. This ... should be distinguished from those goals, such as 'peace' and (to a lesser degree) the 'status quo,' which were incidental to it."[22] To maintain their security, states will seek to keep power between states balanced. Sometimes power can be brought back into balance by engaging in war (perhaps to weaken an enemy); on other occasions, balancing power may require that established alliances be dismantled. The ultimate effect of the balance of power is to preserve state survival, not to secure peace.

While still useful, the balance of power is less useful in the modern world than it was a few centuries ago. The concept assumes that leaders are free to respond, quickly and with subtle precision, to a continuously changing power calculus. If an alliance with an evil tyrant or with a former enemy would improve the balance of power, such an alliance will and should be made. But modern states often find that their policy choices are constrained by economic forces, by culture, or by domestic politics. Whereas Germany's Bismarck or France's Napoleon could craft foreign policy decisions with considerable secrecy and latitude, their modern descendants are forced to carry out diplomacy in a more constrained, more public, and more complex environment. The balance-of-power idea cannot produce useful predictions of state behavior when that behavior is subject to the political demands inherent in today's democracies.

The Politics of Nuclear Weapons

Many analysts believe that the development of nuclear weapons has fundamentally changed the nature of international relations. Before the nuclear age, the military force available to major nations was a small fraction of what it is now. The largest bombs dropped in World War II before the atomic bombs that leveled Hiroshima and Nagasaki were capable of destroying no more than a city block. By contrast, a 10-megaton nuclear device, yielding the destructive power of 10 million tons of TNT, is incredibly more devastating. Such a bomb would collapse all but the strongest buildings within a radius of more than 12 miles; it would inflict immediate second-degree burns on anyone within 24 miles of the blast; it would engulf a whole city in a raging firestorm; and, under "ideal" conditions, it would produce severely destructive radioactive fallout over an area of some 100,000 square miles (roughly the size of New York, New Jersey, and Pennsylvania combined).

The availability of this kind of power not only has made war more appalling but it has changed the way nations conduct their foreign policies. In earlier eras, war was an instrument of policy through which one nation dissuaded another from doing something it opposed. Nuclear weapons have reduced the extent to which the threat of war can serve as a policy tool. A state holds nuclear missiles and bombs so that a potential aggressor will be convinced that aggression will be unacceptably costly. For that reason, it is often pointed out that—in a statement attributed to former U.S. Defense Secretary Robert McNamara—nuclear weapons are not weapons at all; they are only deterrents. The certainty of large-scale retaliation undercuts the credibility of most threats to start a nuclear war. Moreover, since the possibility exists that a nuclear power will use its nuclear weapons to retaliate for even a conventional (nonnuclear) attack, these weapons may serve as a deterrent to *any* direct aggression.

The idea of *mutually assured destruction* (MAD) thus suggests that the overwhelming destructiveness of nuclear war prevents armed conflict among nuclear powers as long as a balance of *nuclear* power is maintained. The logic is simple, as described here in a hypothetical statement from the leader of one nuclear power to another:

> We both know that the outcome of a nuclear exchange is incalculable in advance, because if such an exchange occurs, we shall probably prove incapable of limiting the damage, whether we consider ourselves under those circumstances to be rational or irrational. For on one side or the other or both there will be "rationalists" who will say that to stop now is to accept defeat. They will be joined by the irrationalists who are primarily driven by the desire for excitement, revenge, or suicide, or something else. Thus we both face the danger of escalation to mutual extinction, simply because we shall exercise all the advantages of war once we are in it.[23]

Both sides thus choose alternatives to war. In Winston Churchill's memorable words, "Peace is the sturdy child of **nuclear terror**."[24] In fact, many analysts argue that the existence of nuclear weapons accounts for the fact that the major powers of the world have not fought each other in more than half a century. There has never been a longer period of peace among the most powerful nations on earth in all of recorded history. Wars have been avoided, but "reckless" behavior among the superpowers has also been reduced. If we count the 1962 Cuban missile crisis as the last time there was a superpower conflict that brought the world to the brink of nuclear war, it has been 50 years since anyone came close to "pushing the button."[25]

The idea that nuclear weapons reduce the usefulness of war and the threat of war as tools of foreign policy rests on basic calculations of costs and benefits. According to Robert Jervis, fighting is rational if a country expects to be better off after the fighting than before *or* if it would be better off by fighting than by granting the concessions needed to avoid war.[26] He notes that engaging in war was rational in that sense for some countries in World War II: "Although Britain and France did not improve their positions by fighting, they were better off than they would have been had the Nazis succeeded. Thus it made sense for them to fight even though, as they feared at the outset, they would not profit from the conflict."[27] But no country would improve its position by fighting in a nuclear war.

However, the assumption that nuclear weapons will continue to make war less likely has at least two major problems. First, it assumes that the nuclear weapons of the world are controlled by a small number of major powers, each having a sufficiently developed society so that large-scale retaliation would be costly. Although 189 countries have signed the Non-Proliferation Treaty, committing them to refrain from producing or transferring nuclear weapons, most observers now know or suspect that several unstable or potentially aggressive nations possess nuclear weapons. North Korea announced in October 2002 that it had a weapons program, and it withdrew from the Non-Proliferation Treaty in 2003. Iraq had a substantial program in the past, and Iran is almost certainly working on one now. Some other states, including Israel, India, and Pakistan, never signed the treaty and have demonstrated tests of nuclear weapons.

Second, some analysts reject the idea that nuclear weapons have ever been an influence for peace. John Mueller argues that the absence of a major war since 1945 is the result of several factors that have nothing to do with nuclear weapons. The **superpowers** that emerged from World War II—the United States and the Soviet Union—were relatively content with their clear dominance in world affairs, in great contrast to the unsettled situation persisting after World War I. The Soviet Union's ideology, moreover, stressed revolution rather than armed conquest. Finally, World War II demonstrated that armed conflict can escalate far beyond initial expectations, making leaders arguably more cautious about starting wars. In short, the major players in international relations may have simply become either satisfied with their situations or ideologically driven to alternatives to war while sharing a realization that war is too costly. Mueller argues that those factors, *not the distinctiveness of nuclear weapons*, prevented war.[28]

Waltz also contends that the effect of nuclear weapons on international politics is often overstated. For example, some analysts expected that nuclear weapons would essentially equalize state power (since any one of many nations could conceivably start a war that would bring doomsday). According to Waltz, nuclear weapons did not accomplish that: "Gunpowder did not blur the distinction between the great powers and the others, however, nor have nuclear weapons done so. Nuclear weapons are not the great equalizers they were sometimes thought to be."[29]

Contemporary international relations seem to confirm Waltz's idea regarding the primacy of economic power. Although many factors are certainly important, the far superior economic base of the United States relative to that of the former Soviet Union was one reason for the latter state's inability to "keep up" in the arms race. The demise of the Soviet Union adds support for the view that the economic bases of a nation's power, if fundamentally weak, cannot be offset by the possession of nuclear weapons. Conversely, even without nuclear weapons, Japan and Germany have emerged as two of the most powerful players in the post–Cold War era.

FOREIGN POLICY DECISION MAKING

In recent decades, the *process* of making foreign policy has become an increasingly important area of inquiry. Politics and government in the modern era make the decision-making process itself more complex and less predictable than in earlier times. Analysts once spoke of "France" taking some step or of "Washington" or "Tokyo" preferring some alternative. Such statements implied that a single actor decided foreign policy or, at least, that a highly unified governing elite framed and implemented policies to further a single vision of the national interest. Drawing on insights derived from studies of organizations, psychology, and even economics, contemporary international relations analysts now stress that foreign policy decision making involves a wide range of often conflicting interests and actors, making it more difficult to predict and more important to understand.

Rationality and Foreign Policy Making

When we want to understand why someone made a particular choice, we generally begin by assuming that the decision maker was *rational*. We assume his or her actions were driven by an effort to achieve the objective furthered by those actions. In foreign policy, the rationality assumption means that, for example, when a nation increases or decreases defense spending, abrogates a treaty, or invades a neighbor, we consider what purpose may have been behind the actions taken. We then infer what the nation was trying to accomplish.

This assumption of rationality is often valid and useful. Many foreign policy actions do reflect a clear policy goal. But much of the work on foreign policy decision making has been devoted to discovering the ways in which foreign policy decisions are *not* rational. For several reasons, actual foreign policy decisions may be shaped by something other than a straightforward effort to attain a clearly defined goal.

First, foreign policy decisions may be constrained or influenced by the force of *organizational routines* in the institutions involved in a nation's foreign policy system. Whereas rationality assumes that a single decision maker is free to shape his or her choices purely on the basis of a clear policy objective, the actual decision-making process requires the cooperation of an array of institutions (for example, the Ministry of Defense, the State Department, congressional committees). Even when those institutions share the same overall goals, their established routines or traditional ways of operating may affect their contributions to the decision-making process, leading to a result that deviates from the ultimate objective.

Graham Allison's study of the 1962 Cuban missile crisis demonstrated how a decision regarding the positioning of U.S. naval forces in a blockade of Cuba reflected, in part, the organizational routines (standard operating procedures, or SOPs) of the navy. The force of those routines was a factor that could have influenced policy actions. When the Navy was instructed to carry out President Kennedy's decision, high naval officials wanted to use the Navy's SOPs to implement the president's plan. According to the Navy's standard procedures, the U.S. ships were supposed to be many miles from Cuba (which would have reduced the amount of time that would elapse before the arriving Soviet ships encountered them), and the U.S. forces would insist on boarding any ships approaching the blockade. If the Navy's insistence on its routines had not been overcome, the naval confrontation would have taken place sooner, and U.S. sailors would have tried to board the Soviet vessels. Seeing these actions as part of a rational plan, the Soviets would conclude that the *apparent* policy of the United States was to threaten them and that President Kennedy *wanted to provoke war*. In other words, the policy as actually implemented could have been rather different from the policy the president intended. Although the Navy was forced to depart from its standard procedures in that case, the influence of those procedures was a real factor that had to be overcome.[30]

Second, foreign policy decisions may not amount to a rational plan to achieve a leader's clear objectives because of conflicting political influences that affect those policies. Especially in modern democracies, the actual foreign policies of nations often deviate from the policies that pure rationality would predict because the process involves interest groups and other participants with conflicting goals. The ideal condition for rational decision making is a single leader acting in isolation, free from demands by interest groups, parties, and campaign contributors. Yet such influences exert significant power over foreign policy choices, particularly in democratic systems.

Finally, limits on information and on time for careful deliberation can produce irrational decisions. A leader may fail to choose the best option because he or she did not know about it or because there was not time to consider all options. Intelligence failures have influenced policy choices in many cases, including the U.S. failure to take action to prevent the Pearl Harbor attack in 1941. In such instances, it would be inaccurate to assume that policy actions were fully informed, coherent choices in pursuit of clear objectives.

Public Opinion, Mass Media, and the Foreign Policy Process

Chief executives generally have a much freer hand in making foreign policy than in making domestic policy, in part because the public is less informed about foreign policy than about domestic affairs. Popular influences on foreign policy can be significant, however, particularly in democracies.

The idea that the public's "mood" affects decisions is a well-known axiom in the study of foreign policy.[31] The public's mood takes the form of, for example, greater or lesser support for an active role in world affairs. In the United States, the public mood has changed significantly, strongly supporting an activist foreign policy during the years following World War II and then becoming more isolationist in the 1990s. After the attacks of September 11, 2001, many U.S. citizens became increasingly aggressive in their support of military activities. And, after years of daily reports of U.S. military deaths in sectarian violence in Iraq, the public's mood turned against the idea of an indefinite presence of U.S. troops there. The prevailing mood affects the range of choices that a leader can consider.

Foreign policy leaders in the United States (and in most other countries) do not follow the public's opinions very closely on many matters. However, leaders in modern democracies cannot ignore public sentiments, and, with the influence of the contemporary mass media, public attitudes are becoming increasingly important. Before the 1950s, newspapers and radio had minimal impact since they primarily reported information received from official military sources. Today, modern technology has enabled journalists to get information quickly and independently and to communicate with citizens almost instantly. Television coverage of civilian casualties is a powerful force, and some leaders actually choose tactics that will lead to particularly disturbing pictures to influence public opinion.

Some critics contend that, beyond the impact of violent images, the U.S. press was actively biased in its coverage of the Vietnam War, undermining public support for U.S. military involvement. In a famous broadcast in early 1968, Walter Cronkite (then the CBS News television anchor) stated that, despite heavy losses, no real progress was being made in the war effort. His announcement reportedly had a great impact on President Lyndon Johnson, who halted some bombing operations shortly thereafter.[32] Cronkite made his pessimistic statement during the Tet Offensive, a large-scale Viet Cong military effort in January 1968 (named after the Vietnamese lunar New Year). According to most historians, the Tet Offensive was a significant military setback for the Viet Cong and North Vietnamese; they suffered heavy casualties and took no new territory. Nevertheless, U.S. media coverage created the widespread perception that the enemy was about to overrun U.S. and South Vietnamese forces.[33] Although historians disagree about the ultimate significance of media coverage in influencing policy choices, the influence of newspaper and television on U.S. public opinion during the Vietnam War was certainly a factor considered in the decision-making process.

The media can also be a useful *tool* of foreign policy in addition to being an influence on it. According to K. J. Holsti, most Poles learned about the Solidarity Movement in the 1980s from British radio broadcasts and from broadcasts on Radio Free Europe and the Voice of America, two pro-U.S. radio networks. North Korea broadcasts "commentaries" intended for an audience in South Korea; the content of those broadcasts depicts South Korea as a fascist state propped up by U.S. imperialists.[34] Radio is a cheap and generally effective way of reaching a target domestic population, even in areas where illiteracy limits the effectiveness of print media.

In short, leaders usually are forced to take public views into account as they make foreign policy decisions, and the mass media are playing an increasingly important role in developing a supportive or an opposing public. Whether that is a positive development remains an open question. On the one hand, an independent, inquisitive press and an informed public may act as a restraining force, preventing leaders from taking their countries into disastrous military involvements. Perhaps the greatest impact of the heightened importance of the media and public opinion in foreign policy (especially in democracies) is that it makes leaders emphasize quick, low-casualty military options when military responses are necessary. If costly military steps are necessary to maintain national security, and if the pressure of the media and public opinion inhibits appropriate action, the country may suffer. On the other hand, political leaders may be actually tempted to take certain military steps in order to produce the "rally 'round the flag" support that the inevitable media coverage often generates.

Foreign policy decision making is not a simple process of a unified, well-informed leadership choosing the optimum alternative to achieve a definite objective. If the process was ever that simple, it is certainly more complex now. In the modern world, the foreign policy process involves a wide range of organizational and political influences and requires access to accurate information about a staggering array of factors. Understanding the influences affecting that process, and how the process can be improved or degraded, is thus a central problem in the study of foreign policy.

International Political Economy

The nature of economic relations among states has been an important subject of study for hundreds of years. In fact, until the terrorist attacks of September 11, 2001, economics had surpassed security concerns in foreign policy debates. Modern advances in communications and transportation make multinational corporations a common form of business organization, and their activities significantly affect prices, wages, and even economic security in many nations. The strategic value of petroleum, coupled with the geographic concentration of oil fields in a few areas, creates a volatile situation. The persistent economic underdevelopment of much of the world challenges the industrialized states that rely on them for labor and raw materials. Growing interdependence makes international political economy an increasingly important issue.

As with military affairs, in economic matters states can relate to one another in antagonistic or cooperative ways. The character of those relations depends on many things, including the nature of each country's domestic economy, its ideology and culture, and its other (noneconomic) foreign policy objectives. Although a great range of factors affects international economic relations, specialists have outlined three general approaches designed to explain them.[35]

Liberalism (or Economic Internationalism)

Employing the term *liberal* differently from its usage in common parlance, Robert Gilpin defined **liberalism** (sometimes termed **economic internationalism**) in this context as the international counterpart to free-market economics. Derived from the ideas of Adam Smith (1723–1790), the architect of classical economics, liberal political economy suggests that states should naturally become cooperative in economic affairs. The concept of **comparative advantage** is basic to the approach. If one state is able to produce a particular good or service cheaply and efficiently, it is said to have a comparative advantage in that area. The principles of liberal political economy imply that *as long as governments do not interfere with economic affairs*, nations will ultimately produce goods or services for which they have (for whatever reason) a comparative advantage.

Liberal political economy assumes that most, if not all, states enjoy a comparative advantage with respect to *some* goods or services. If governments do not get in the way, the production of all goods and services worldwide will naturally gravitate to the state or states that can produce them with the highest quality and the lowest costs. A state that tries to produce something for which it has no comparative advantage will quickly find that it cannot produce it at competitive prices, and, because the countries that *do* have comparative advantages with respect to this good or service will capture the world market, such a state will eventually devote its resources to producing other things.

Thus, goods and services will end up being produced where they can be made most efficiently. However, if a government restricts imports into its country so that a comparatively *inefficient* domestic industry is protected from competition, the good or service will be produced, but inefficiently, consuming more of the world's resources to produce them than would be consumed if countries with a comparative advantage produced them.

According to liberal political economy, the *total productivity* of the world economy will increase as free trade allows goods and services to be produced where comparative advantages exist. The world would suffer a net loss in output if, for example, a country that is unable to produce steel very efficiently still allocates significant resources to steel production (motivated perhaps by the prestige of producing steel). The resources of such a country could produce a more valuable output in a different usage.

Since the world economy grows indefinitely as goods and services are produced in accordance with comparative advantage, liberal political economy assumes that economic relations will normally be cooperative. Every state will be better off if all states act in accordance with the principle of comparative advantage.

In regard to policy, liberal political economy advocates free trade (eliminating import restrictions and tariffs). Of course, governments are often under severe domestic pressure to restrict imports. For example, textile and clothing manufacturers in Thailand, Korea, Taiwan, Sri Lanka, and Malaysia have recently developed a comparative advantage over U.S. producers. Although U.S. consumers benefit from the importation of cheaper clothing, U.S. textile workers and many U.S. companies have demanded protective tariffs to restrict Asian imports. As you will recall from our discussion of interest groups in Chapter 6, it is likely that the domestic *producers* will be more influential politically than domestic *consumers*, and thus governments often enact import restrictions. In the light of those political realities, liberal political economy remains more a prescription for good policy than a description of how nations actually behave in economic terms.

The ratification by the U.S. Congress of the North American Free Trade Agreement (NAFTA) and the Central American Free Trade Agreement (CAFTA), in 1993 and 2004, respectively, were major steps toward free trade in the Western Hemisphere. As of this writing, important free trade agreements between the United States and South Korea and between the United States and Colombia are under consideration. Such treaties are controversial because, at least in the short run, they may jeopardize some jobs and lead to the production of goods and services in areas with the lowest costs, which may be a result of lax environmental or safety standards.

Economic Structuralism

Unlike those who advocate the liberal approach, some analysts and many Third World leaders argue that international political competition does not take place on a level playing field. Generally speaking, this perspective focuses on the fact that Japan, North America, and Europe have advanced industrial states, whereas most states in Africa and Latin America are, on average, less advanced, and that this difference in development makes free trade unavoidably unfair.

In regard to international political economy, **economic structuralism** (closely identified with Marxist–Leninist thinking) sees states' economic relations as simply one component of the capitalist oppression that dominates all political life. Whereas liberalism claims that advancing productivity and cooperation are at least possible, economic structuralism implies that increasing conflict and exploitation will characterize international relations.*

The North–South conflict in international political economy is often interpreted from this perspective. (The term comes from the observation that, generally, the Northern Hemisphere contains countries that are wealthier than those in the Southern Hemisphere.) Those who reject liberalism because of the persistent disparities in North–South development generally oppose free-trade agreements. According to their way of thinking, such agreements make it impossible for the poorer countries to gain a foothold in the international economy since they will always be undersold by the more advanced nations in anything they produce.

Economic structuralists thus argue for strict state controls on imports and exports, or state ownership of all industry. In accordance with Marxist principles, they contend that public control of commerce will end exploitation of the poor, both at home and abroad, creating a system of fair compensation for workers, environmental protection, and general world prosperity.

Economic Nationalism (Mercantilism)

Ironically, both liberal (free-market) and Marxist–Leninist ideas about international political economy assume that economic relations are the primary force behind politics. For liberals, economics determines where comparative advantage exists, and economic structuralists claim that economics explains the inevitability of capitalist exploitation. In contrast, **economic nationalism**, sometimes termed **mercantilism**, sees *politics* as the primary force in international economic relations. It emphasizes the importance of state interests in national security, power, and industrial development, and it claims that states naturally pursue economic policies that promote those foreign policy goals.

For example, mercantilists argue that governments have a clear national interest in protecting their domestic industries from foreign competition, and that this

---

* See the discussion of *dependency theory* in Chapter 14.

interest may outweigh the purely economic advantages associated with free trade. Even if such restrictions mean that consumers have to pay higher prices for less efficiently produced local goods and services, the state may have a legitimate reason to act contrary to the principles of liberal political economy.

Some analysts argue that a policy of free trade for the steel industry may endanger a country's ability to maintain a steel production capacity, something that is essential for national defense. If other countries can make steel more cheaply, domestic plants will eventually shut down, and they cannot be reconstructed quickly. This could leave a country militarily weak because abundant steel is needed for military hardware.

As we discuss in Chapter 17, the growth of international trade during the second half of the last century has had many important consequences. Those favoring economic nationalism argue that one of those consequences is a reduction in the autonomy and power of nation-states. Whether for good or for ill, many analysts agree that the globalization of finance has "undermined the capacity of states to determine their own future."[36] The advancing global economy thus brings political and economic concerns into conflict in several ways, ensuring that this will be a challenge for governments for decades to come.

Each of the three main approaches to international political economy provides persuasive explanations for certain patterns or events in international affairs. The concept of comparative advantage describes an arrangement that produces an efficient allocation of productive resources, but sometimes other objectives naturally dominate a nation's foreign policy. Some analysts find Marxist–Leninist ideas helpful in explaining

© Andrew Toos/www.CartoonStock.com

"Yep, first the gold run out, then the microchip manufacturing went overseas."

HARD TIMES Economic changes created by free trade often lead to demands for government intervention.

the economic underdevelopment of much of the Third World. Economic nationalism helps explain the motivation for seemingly inefficient economic policies based on national security needs. As economic relations become increasingly critical in international relations, the connections among domestic politics, foreign policy, and economic productivity will command increasing attention from analysts and policy makers.

International Law and Organization

Although anarchy is the essential characteristic of the international system, the presence of international law and international organization suggests that the anarchy of the international system is not absolute. International law and organization reflect efforts to create order and stability in international relations.

International Law

International law consists primarily of traditionally recognized treaties and rights and duties. Treaties can be *bilateral* (between two countries) or *general* (ratified by a large number of countries). Some treaties are highly specific, such as a treaty in which the United States and Canada cooperate with respect to usage of the Great Lakes; some treaties apply to a broad range of related matters, such as the General Agreement on Tariffs and Trade (GATT). Other "laws" are simply traditions, such as long-accepted ideas regarding self-defense and the size of the area that each country claims as national waters.

Law is an attempt to constrain behavior. For law to be effective, there must be some way to interpret when a given action runs afoul of the law and to enforce the requirements of the law. In those respects, international law is much weaker than domestic law (in well-established political systems). The International Court of Justice (ICJ, or World Court), established as part of the United Nations, has broad jurisdiction to hear disputes about international law, but it has been ignored in many cases, thus reducing its status and influence. For example, in 1979, Iranian students took over the U.S. embassy in Tehran, holding more than a hundred U.S. citizens hostage. The Iranian government essentially supported the students' effort and refused to recognize the jurisdiction of the ICJ to adjudicate the dispute leading to the hostage-taking. In the 1980s, the United States engaged in military activities against Nicaragua (mining harbors and funding an insurgent movement) when the country was governed by the Sandinistas, a Marxist party. When the ICJ concluded that it had jurisdiction to hear a Nicaraguan complaint that the United States had violated international law with those actions, the United States refused to participate in the judicial process. When the court eventually found that the United States was in violation, the court's influence was severely weakened by U.S. disregard for it in this matter.

The International Criminal Court (see A Closer Look 16.3) was established through a treaty (the "Rome Statute"), which became effective on July 1, 2002.*

---

* The home page of the International Criminal Court contains the Rome Statute and other information, including a complete, updated list of the countries that have ratified the ICC. www.icc-cpi.int/Menus/ICC/Home.

Over 100 nations have joined in supporting the ICC, although the United States, Russia, China, Israel, and several other countries have not. In the case of the United States, refusal to sign the agreement was based on concerns that the ICC would engage in "politically motivated" investigations and prosecutions of military personnel.

In a 2011 study, three political scientists reported the results of an extensive examination of territorial disputes from 1945 through 2000. Their research was designed to determine if the behavior of leaders in such disputes could be explained *wholly* on the basis of national interest (i.e., the realist assumption). The findings demonstrated that foreign policy actions are more complicated. International law exerts a strong, independent influence: "when the legal principles relevant to the dispute are unambiguous and clearly favor one side," negotiations often focus on a legal point, generally facilitating a settlement.[43]

Moreover, even when international law does not produce a settlement, it may still serve as a basis for communication. "To present one's claims in legal terms means to signal to one's partner or opponent which [norms] one considers relevant or essential, and to indicate which procedures one intends to follow and would like the other side to follow."[44] Law can also be a source of *prestige* since nations that can claim to abide by legal requirements enjoy greater legitimacy both in domestic politics and in foreign capitals.[45] In some circumstances, international law can be used as a *tool of policy*, strengthening a position and mobilizing domestic and allied support.

Still, international law has its liabilities. Once a state uses a provision of international law to legitimize an action, it may experience a loss of flexibility in future policy choices. Although leaders are often selective in observing international law, repeatedly using it as a legitimizing tool may make it difficult or costly to disregard international law when the national interest requires it.[46]

If democracy becomes more widespread, international law may become increasingly influential. With the end of the Cold War and the growing international dominance of the United States, Western Europe, and Japan, states such as North Korea and Iran may find it increasingly difficult to violate international law. Since superpower conflict is no longer the dominant fact in international affairs, a state that openly violates international law cannot depend on prestigious support from a superpower sponsor, who previously would have advocated the position of its client state and protected it from sanctions. The fact that the most powerful states are less divided by profound ideological conflicts increases the potential that international law will be a significant force.

International Organization

Although the individual nation-state remains the most important kind of actor in international relations, the fastest-growing force in international affairs is the **international organization** (often termed an *intergovernmental organization*, or IGO). These bodies include general-purpose organizations such as the United Nations and, with narrower memberships, the Organization of American States or the Organization of African Unity. Other IGOs are functional units with a more specific purpose, such as the Central American Common Market or the Association of South East Asian Nations.

A CLOSER LOOK

16.3

The Law of War and The International Criminal Court

Most citizens consistently comply with established laws in developed democracies. As noted above, however, the realm of international relations is distinguished from domestic politics by the absence of a settled order and the resulting inability to rely on institutional enforcement of law as a method for managing conflict. Nevertheless, international law exists, and most specialists in international relations agree that it has important effects.

Researchers and theorists generally can be classified as "realists," "liberals," or "constructivists" on the issue of how international treaties affect the behavior of states. As discussed earlier in this chapter, realists assume that leaders make foreign policy on the basis of what is good for the national interest (defined in terms of power and security), and thus they will only comply with treaties and international law when they would have acted the same way in the absence of the treaties or laws. Liberals argue that treaties and international law can create some stability and order in the international system and that leaders take their value into account when making decisions. Clearly, leaders occasionally violate treaties, but violations are less frequent when they are enforced by a principle of reciprocity. Finally, "constructivists" contend that treaties and international laws create "shared understandings of proper conduct" and that these

understandings actually structure the conduct of foreign affairs.

In a remarkable study of compliance with the laws of war from the Boxer Rebellion (1899–1901) through the Gulf War (1990–1991), political scientist James D. Morrow looked for patterns of compliance and noncompliance among the dozens of nations and wars contained in the data.[37] He found that several factors help to explain when compliance with the laws of war are more likely:

- Compliance is more probable when both sides have a "legal obligation through joint ratification."
- The degree of legal clarity in the law in question increases the probability of compliance, but clarity has no real effect when both sides have ratified it.
- Democracies comply more often and more completely than nondemocracies if they have ratified the treaty or law in question.
- Democracies commit more violations than nondemocracies if they have not ratified the treaty or law in question.
- Joint ratification (i.e., both countries involved signed the treaty in question) produces higher rates of compliance.
- The issue addressed by the treaty or law in question affects the degree of compliance.

Whereas the number of states has more than doubled since 1950 (primarily as a result of colonies gaining independence), the number of IGOs has nearly quadrupled.

As a force in world affairs, international organization is often discussed in regard to its limitations. Many analysts felt that the failure of the League of Nations to prevent World War II demonstrated that nations will not sacrifice much of their sovereignty to an international organization. Similarly, critics note that the United Nations has been allowed to survive only because five major powers have been able to veto any significant proposed action. In other words, the UN's existence has depended on the fact that those nations did not have to sacrifice any real sovereignty in order to join it. Moreover, the United Nations has not prevented numerous "small" wars (in Vietnam and in the Persian Gulf region).

16.3

- Chemical and biological weapons treaties have the strongest record of compliance, followed by armistice or cease fire agreements, treaties relating to conduct on the high seas, and those regulating aerial bombardment. Laws relating to the treatment of civilians have the worst record of compliance.

The data provide some support for the realist perspective in that *reciprocity* is a key factor in explaining compliance—the fact that leaders take the likely behavior of other states into account when deciding whether or not to comply is an indication that state actors are following their national interests and not simply complying with the law in making decisions. The data also lend some support for the constructivist view by revealing the increased effect that ratification has on democracies. If realism provided a complete explanation, the ratification status of a law would have no significant impact on behavior.[38]

Morrow's research sheds some light on recent controversies regarding the treatment of detainees captured by U.S. and coalition forces in Afghanistan and Iraq. "Faced with non-state opponents who do not recognize the laws of war and adopt atrocity as their central strategy, the willingness of the Bush administration to stretch and perhaps break the standards of humane treatment to which the U.S. is legally committed is not surprising in light of the results reported here."[39] The absence of reciprocity may undermine compliance, even by democracies.

In another article in the same issue of the *American Political Science Review*, political scientist Judith Kelley assembled and analyzed data on the decisions of states regarding a U.S. request that they refuse to surrender Americans to the **International Criminal Court** **(ICC)**.[40] The U.S. government claimed that its soldiers and others would not receive fair treatment from the ICC and thus asked other states to sign bilateral agreements not to surrender Americans to the Court. Some countries signed these agreements and others did not; Kelley wanted to know the factors that accounted for the differences in behavior.

One of her key conclusions is that "some states refused [to sign] nonsurrender agreements because they valued the ICC highly, defending it on moral and normative grounds.... Some states prize adherence to commitment for its own sake."[41] Kelley's findings provide strong support for the idea that international commitments are not irrelevant or that they only serve as "cover" for actions taken for other reasons. A 2010 study confirmed Kelley's idea that a state's commitment to the rule of law makes it reluctant to sign bilateral agreements that undercut the ICC, but it also found that the degree to which a state is dependent on the United States has an impact on whether it signs such agreements.[42] These findings make a strong case for the idea that the degree to which a state values the rule of law and its own treaty commitments has a real impact on its foreign policy choices.

Nevertheless, the United Nations remains an important feature of the international system, and its prominence is likely to increase. Since 1945, nearly one-fourth of the international and civil conflicts that have erupted have been submitted either to the UN or to regional organizations. According to Holsti, those organizations handled 291 cases during that time, many of which were "high-intensity" conflicts. Until 1985, only one-fourth of the submitted cases were handled successfully, but between 1985 and 1990 the success rate increased to more than one in three.[47]

As with international law, the United Nations provides a context for communication, and its approval and disapproval can provide nonviolent support for foreign policy choices. Moreover, there are signs that in the 1990s the United Nations may have approached the ability to "maintain or restore international peace and security," as called for in its charter. Bruce Russett and James Sutterlin point out that the United Nations has traditionally used force often for "peacekeeping": standing between hostile forces, maintaining stability in an unsettled region, and even monitoring elections.[48]

Although it did not prevent the war, the United Nations arguably functioned to enforce "the will of the council on a state that has broken the peace" in the 1991 Gulf War. Russett and Sutterlin point out that "the Gulf action became possible because the permanent members of the Security Council cooperated on a matter of peace and security in the way originally foreseen when the UN was founded."[49] The UN has handled scores of smaller conflicts, and the demise of East–West conflict as the centerpiece of international affairs will probably make the organization even more important in the future.[50] Recently, with varying degrees of success, the United Nations has involved itself in peacekeeping operations in El Salvador, Cambodia, the states of the former Yugoslavia, Somalia, and Afghanistan (see Figure 16.1).

ETHICS AND INTERNATIONAL RELATIONS

Most discussions of international affairs deal with explanations of state *behavior*, just as the study of domestic politics normally focuses on explaining the observable behavior of citizens, parties, and institutions. Nevertheless, the ethical dimensions of international relations have long been a subject of inquiry by politicians, philosophers, and others.

The oldest ethical perspective relevant to international affairs is pacifism. Pacifists contend that war is simply and inherently *wrong* and that any alternative (including submitting to domination by a foreign power) is morally superior to fighting. Although there have always been many individuals and religious movements that support pacifist principles, most leaders and citizens reject pacifism as an absolute guide for policy.

A much more widely accepted ethical concept is the idea of the **just war**. Richard Miller explains that the just war tradition shares with the pacifist tradition a conclusion that war is evil and should be avoided; but whereas pacifists claim that war should *always* be avoided, advocates of the just war concept feel that war can be justified under certain special circumstances.[51]

Just war theory has two components, the first pertaining to *when war is justified* and the second addressing *how wars are conducted*. War is justified when necessary to defend against outside threats, when innocent lives would otherwise be lost, when basic human rights are severely deprived, or when the future of the world community is at stake. The idea of the just war requires that war be a last resort, that only competent authorities make war (no "private" wars are just), that no "futile" fighting in defense of a cause be undertaken, and that there be no intentional attacks on civilians.[52]

The ethical issues related to war offer moral philosophers fertile ground for discussion. If the basic concepts of the just war become widely accepted, those ideas may assume some moral force, thus limiting the incidence of war. Just-war principles are obviously subject to varying interpretations, however: What appears to be a just war to one side is naked aggression to the other. However, ethical concerns have widespread impact in other foreign policy issues, notably in matters involving human rights and humanitarian assistance.

FIGURE 16.1 United Nations Peacekeeping Operations since 1948

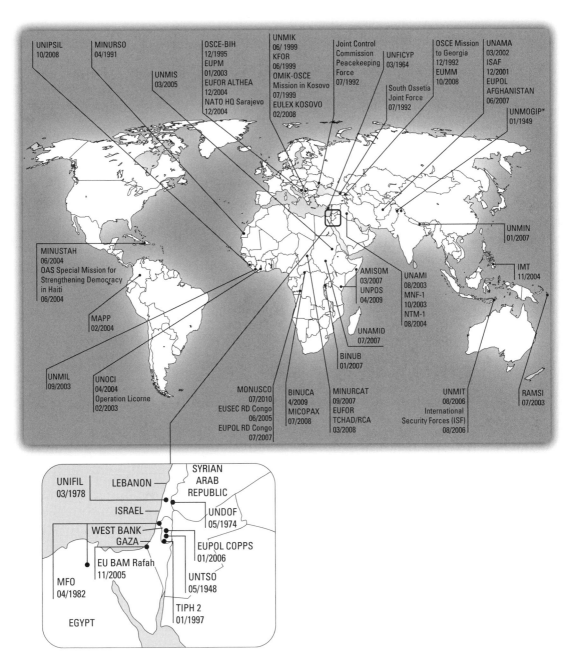

Source: United Nations Peacekeeping Fact Sheet, October 31, 2011, at http://www.un.org/en/peace keeping/documents/bnote010101.pdf. Please see this website for the full names of each of the peace-keeping operations shown in the figure.

CONCLUSION: WAR, TRADE, FOREIGN POLICY, AND THE STAKES OF INTERNATIONAL POLITICS

The same interests and motivations that characterize domestic politics—economics, moral disputes, ethnic and racial divisions, and political power—are also basic to the relations among states. Nevertheless, the virtual absence of effective central authority in international relations creates a different kind of political system from that which prevails in domestic affairs. The approaches discussed in this chapter represent different and useful ways of interpreting and predicting the behavior of states.

As we noted with respect to domestic politics, international relations is currently undergoing fundamental change. The demise of communism in most of the world, increasing economic interdependence, and contemporary concerns about nuclear proliferation and the global environment are but a few of the issues that will make international relations more complex and more critical. International organizations and law exert more force now than in previous eras in which national sovereignty was unchallenged. Chapter 17 addresses the most important of these issues in an effort to identify and evaluate the central problems in modern international relations.

◆ ◆ ◆

Key Terms and Concepts _____

balance of power	International law
comparative advantage	international organization
democratic peace	just war
economic internationalism	liberalism
economic nationalism	mercantilism
economic structuralism	nuclear terror
idealism	realism
International Criminal Court (ICC)	self-help
	superpowers

DISCUSSION QUESTIONS

1. *How is the existence of violence different in domestic and international relations?*
2. *Compare the three "images" regarding the causes of war. Which do you find most persuasive in explaining the cause of the War on Terror?*
3. *What factors can lead a nation to adopt foreign policies that do not amount to a rational effort to pursue a clear objective?*
4. *What is a "just war"?*
5. *Explain how wars can be prevented by international law and international organization.*

Notes _____

1. Kenneth Waltz, *Theory of International Politics* (New York: McGraw-Hill, 1979), pp. 102–103; italics added.
2. Ibid., p. 104.
3. Thucydides, *The Peloponnesian War*, trans. Crawley (New York: Modern Library, 1951).
4. Sun Tzu (sixth century BCE), *The Art of War*, trans. Samuel B. Griffith (Oxford, UK: Clarendon Press, 1963); and Kautilya, *Arthasastra*, trans. R. Shamasastry (Mysore, India: Mysore Printing and Publishing, 1967).
5. Hans J. Morganthau, *Politics among Nations*, 5th ed. (New York: Knopf, 1973), pp. 4–5.
6. Waltz, *Theory of International Politics*, p. 118.
7. President George W. Bush, Speech to the United Nations General Assembly, September 21, 2004. Available at www.globalsecurity.org/military/library/news/2004/09/mil-040921-whitehouse01.htm, accessed May 18, 2011.
8. President Barack Obama, televised speech on March 28, 2011.
9. Edward Hallett Carr, *The Twenty Years' Crisis, 1919–1939: An Introduction to the Study of International Relations* (London: Macmillan, 1939).
10. Robert Jervis, "Theories of War in an Era of Leading-Power Peace," *American Political Science Review* 96 (March 2002): 1–14.
11. Kenneth Waltz, *Man, the State, and War* (New York: Columbia University Press, 1959).
12. Ibid., p. 16.
13. Ibid., p. 33.
14. Some of the most important writings on the democratic peace are Erich Weede, "Democracy and War Involvement," *Journal of Conflict Resolution* 28 (December 1984): 649–664; T. Clifton Morgan and Sally Howard Campbell, "Domestic Structure, Decisional Constraints, and War," *Journal of Conflict Resolution* 35 (June 1991): 187–211; Alex Mintz and Nehemia Geva, "Why Don't Democracies Fight Each Other?" *Journal of Conflict Resolution* 37 (September 1993): 484–503; Michael E. Brown, Sean E. Lynn-Jones, and Steven E. Miller, *Debating the Democratic Peace* (Cambridge, MA: MIT University Press, 1996), and Bruce Russett, *Hegemony and Democracy* (New York: Routledge, 2011).
15. See Bruce Bueno De Mesquita, James D. Morrow, Randolf M. Siverson, and Alastair Smith, "An Institutional Explanation of the Democratic Peace," *American Political Science Review* 93 (December 1999): 791–807.
16. See Edward D. Mansfield and Jack Snyder, *Electing to Fight: Why Emerging Democracies Go to War* (Cambridge, MA: MIT Press, 2005).
17. Ibid., p. 159.
18. Holsti, K. J., *International Politics*, 7th ed. (Englewood Cliffs, NJ: Prentice Hall, 1995), p. 17.
19. John T. Rourke, *International Politics on the World Stage*, 9th ed. (Guilford, CT: Dushkin, 2002), p. 34.
20. Waltz, *Theory of International Politics*, p. 118.
21. David Hume, *Essays and Treatises on Several Subjects*, vol. 1 (Edinburgh, Scotland: Bell and Bradfute, and W. Blackwood, 1825), pp. 331–339, quoted in *Contending Theories of International Relations* by James E. Dougherty and Robert L. Pfaltzgraff, Jr. (Philadelphia: Lippincott, 1971), p. 30; Edward D. Mansfield and Jack Snyder, *Electing to Fight: Why Emerging Democracies Go to War* (Cambridge, MA: MIT Press, 2005).
22. Edward Vose Gulick, *Europe's Classical Balance of Power* (New York: Norton, 1955), p. 30.
23. Dougherty and Pfaltzgraff, *Contending Theories*, p. 265.
24. Quoted in John Mueller, "The Obsolescence of War in the Modern Industrialized World," in *International Politics*, 3rd ed., ed. Robert J. Art and Robert Jervis (New York: HarperCollins, 1992), p. 188.
25. Robert Jervis, "The Utility of Nuclear Deterrence," in Art and Jervis, eds., *International Politics*, p. 202.
26. Ibid., p. 204.
27. Ibid.
28. Mueller, "Obsolescence of War," pp. 188–189.
29. Waltz, *Man, the State, and War*, pp. 180–181.
30. Graham Allison, "Conceptual Models and the Cuban Missile Crisis," *American Political Science Review* 63(1969): 689–718. Also see Allison and Philip Zelikow, *Essence of Decision: Explaining the Cuban Missile Crisis*, 2nd ed. (New York: Addison-Wesley, 1999).
31. See Jack E. Holmes, *The Mood/Interest Theory of American Foreign Policy* (Lexington: University Press of Kentucky, 1985).
32. As a *New York Times* reporter noted, "It was the first time in history that a war had been declared over by an anchorman." See David Halberstam, *The Powers That Be* (New York: Knopf, 1979), p. 514; see also Austin Ranney, *Channels of Power: The Impact of Television on American Politics* (New York: Basic Books, 1983).

33. See Peter Braestrup, *Big Story* (New York: Anchor Books, 1978). For a different view, see Daniel Hallin, *The "Uncensored War": The Media and Vietnam* (New York: Oxford University Press, 1986).

34. Holsti, *International Politics*, p. 160.

35. Much of the text discussion is drawn from Robert Gilpin, "The Nature of Political Economy," in Art and Jervis, eds., *International Politics*, pp. 237–253.

36. Charles W. Kegley, Jr., and Eugene R. Wittkopf, *World Politics: Trend and Transformation*, (New York: St. Martin's, 1997), p. 257.

37. James D. Morrow. "When Do States Follow the Laws of War?" *American Political Science Review* 101 (August 2007): 559–572.

38. Ibid., p. 568.

39. Ibid., p. 571.

40. Judith Kelley. "Who Keeps International Commitments and Why? The International Criminal Court and Bilateral Surrender Agreements," *American Political Science Review* 101 (August 2007): 573–589.

41. Ibid, p. 573.

42. Irfan Nooruddin and Autumn Lockwood Payton, "Dynamics of Influence in International Politics: The ICC, Bias, and Economic Sanctions," *Journal of Peace Research* 47 (2010)L: 711–721.

43. Paul K. Huth, Sarah E. Croco, and Benjamin J. Appel, "Does International Law Promote the Peaceful Settlement of International Disputes? Evidence from the Study of Territorial Conflicts since 1945," *American Political Science Review* 105 (May 2011): 415.

44. Stanley Hoffmann, "The Uses and Limits of International Law," in Art and Jervis, eds., *International Politics*, pp. 90–91.

45. Holsti, *International Politics*, p. 301.

46. Ibid., p. 92.

47. Ibid., p. 354.

48. Bruce Russett and James Sutterlin, "The U.N. in a New World Order," in Art and Jervis, eds., *International Politics*, pp. 102–103.

49. Ibid., p. 106.

50. Ernst B. Haas, "Collective Conflict Management: Evidence for a New World Order?" in *Collective Security in a Changing World*, ed. Thomas G. Weiss (Boulder, CO: Lynne Rienner Publishers, 1993), pp. 63–120.

51. Richard B. Miller, *Interpretations of Conflict: Ethics, Pacifism, and the Just-War Tradition* (Chicago: University of Chicago Press, 1991), p. 106. Also see John F. Coverdale, "An Introduction to the Just War Tradition," *Pace International Law Review* 16 (2004): 221–277, available at http://digitalcommons.pace.edu/pilr/vol16/iss2/1.

52. Miller, *Interpretations of Conflict*, pp. 13–14.

CHAPTER 17

A Changing World Order

Oil spill workers clean the beach of Naval Air Station Pensacola, FL as oil washes ashore from the BP spill on June 10, 2010.

- From the End of the Cold War to the Beginnings of an Uncertain Future
- Policing Trouble Spots: A New World Order or a World without Order?
- The Changing Nature of the International Arms Race
- Current Trends in World Trade: Economic Unification and Beyond

- North–South Relations
- Protecting the Environment
- Human Rights
- Women's Rights
- International Terrorism
- Conclusion: The Changing Face of International Relations

As each new year approaches, many mass media outlets list the major international news events of the preceding year. It seems that every year brings major challenges, unforeseen developments, new threats to regional or world peace, and in some years, reason for hope. But international developments during the past two to three decades have been particularly dramatic, featuring: the fall of Soviet and Eastern European communist regimes; the spread of democracy to those countries and much of the developing world; China's rise as an economic superpower; India's emergence as a major world economic actor; the growth of international terrorism as a major threat to world security; and perhaps the worst recession in the industrial democracies since the Great Depression of the 1920s and 1930s. The title of this text, *Politics in a Changing World*, reflects the authors' keen awareness that in an era of mounting environmental concerns, rapid technological breakthroughs, widening political participation, and constantly redefined ideologies, political behavior and beliefs in the twenty-first century are being played out against a background of constant change. Nowhere has that been more apparent than in the realm of international relations—the interaction between nation-states, multinational alliances (economic, military, and political), **nongovernmental organizations (NGOs)**, multinational corporations, and armed nongovernmental militias and armies (especially terrorists and cross-national rebels). In many ways, economic development, technological innovation, intensified human migration, and changing lifestyles have increased international interdependence. Problems such as the growing pressures on the world's natural resources (including oil, arable land, and water), illegal immigration, Third World government debt, debt crises in several European Union (EU) members, international trade competition, environmental decay, and drug trafficking cannot be resolved exclusively at the national level.

From the End of the Cold War to the Beginnings of an Uncertain Future

From the end of World War II (1945) to the late 1980s, the **Cold War** was the defining element of the international system: a protracted confrontation pitting the United States and its allies in the **North Atlantic Treaty Organization (NATO)** against the Soviet Union and other nations of the Warsaw Pact (the Soviet-dominated Eastern European military alliance). Tensions between the two superpowers rose and fell periodically, but for each, the underlying factor shaping its foreign policy was fear of the other one.[1] Throughout the Cold War, each side maintained a negative "mirror image" of its opponent.[2]

The United States and the USSR had been allies in World War II. But relations turned hostile in the war's aftermath as the Soviet army overran Eastern Europe. The Truman Doctrine (1947) established the U.S. policy of "containment": The United States, President Harry Truman declared, would resist Soviet armed aggression and the spread of communist insurgencies.[3] At the same time, the Russians felt threatened by Western "capitalist imperialism." As most of the former European colonies in Africa, Asia, and the Middle East gained independence in the decades after World War II, both superpowers perceived the problems of the developing world through the lens of East–West conflict. Each side extended foreign aid to developing nations primarily to counter the influence of its rival rather than to serve the recipients' needs. For example, American aid to Pakistan rose sharply when the United States needed to funnel arms to anti-Soviet guerrillas (including Jihadist groups) in neighboring Afghanistan, and then subsequently surged again after 9/11 to pursue the War on Terror in both of those countries. In neither period was the boost in U.S. assistance caused by a rise in Pakistan's internal needs.

As recently as 1988, Europe was divided between Western democracies (mostly allied with the United States.) and the communist Central and Eastern European bloc of countries tied politically, militarily, and economically to the Soviet Union. Only in the late 1980s was the so-called balance of terror—the mutually assured destruction (MAD) awaiting both sides if they went to war—replaced with greater mutual understanding and negotiations for arms reduction.

By the start of the twenty-first century, so much had changed. The fall of communism in Eastern Europe (symbolized dramatically by the collapse of the Berlin Wall), the subsequent disintegration of Soviet communism and the decline of Russian military might, the growth of the **European Union (EU)** as a major economic and political actor, and the continued spread of democracy into developing nations all seemed to promise a more tranquil and peaceful world. The United States had become the world's dominant economic, military, and diplomatic power, with no other nation capable of challenging it. To be sure, Russia retains a formidable arsenal of nuclear weapons, and its renewed nationalism and suspicion of the West have worsened its relationship with the United States. But with its reduced economy and a greatly weakened military, that country is no longer in a position to challenge the West as forcefully as the USSR had.

That is not to say that the world felt trouble free. Far from it! The problems of poverty, financial crises, overpopulation, environmental degradation, ethnic warfare, and political repression, just to name a few, remained enormous concerns. As the expanding economic reach of vast **multinational corporations (MNCs)** created far-flung industrial and financial empires that showed little concern for national boundaries and as a globalized economy promised (or threatened) to weaken the importance of the nation-state, many observers worried about such a concentration of economic power and saw it as a challenge to national sovereignty. Debt and other monetary crises were once associated with Third World economies such as Brazil, Indonesia, Mexico, and Thailand, but currently the financial crises in Iceland, Ireland, Greece, Italy, and other developed nations threaten the world economy.

Furthermore, the West's sense of post–Cold War security ended with the al-Qaeda terrorist attacks of September 11, 2001. Suddenly, the War on Terror became the centerpiece of American foreign policy and a central concern of governments from Europe to the Philippines. Fear of even worse assaults heightened public anxieties—visions of nerve-gas attacks, biological terrorism, or a nuclear attack delivered not by missiles but in a backpack. At the same time, the War on Terror has had important implications for domestic policy as well. As the United States and other nations search for the right balance between counterterrorist surveillance and the protection of civil liberties, many voices have weighed in on different sides of the issue, including politicians, intelligence agencies, journalists, and scholars. The Bush administration often held that the United States was effectively in a state of war and that the dangers of another 9/11-type terrorist attack meant that certain strong counterterrorism measures were necessary tools in the War on Terror—including warrantless wiretaps of U.S. citizens, indefinite imprisonment of suspected foreign terrorists without trial, and the use of "enhanced coercive interrogation techniques" (which many outsiders considered torture) on prisoners suspected of terrorism. Civil libertarians argued that these methods were unconstitutional and often ineffective. They further maintained that it was wrong (and illegal) to give the government powers that were not needed to fight terrorism and that posed a threat to individual freedoms. Osama bin Laden's death and the killing of a number of al-Qaeda commanders by U.S. drone attacks has seemingly reduced the terrorist threat, but one major terrorist attack against the West could change all that.

While the end of the Cold War greatly reduced the dangers of a full-scale nuclear war between the world's powers, a new concern has taken center stage—the proliferation of nuclear weapons to nations such as Israel, India, Pakistan, and North

Korea and quite possibly soon to Iran, another so-called "rogue state," in the near future.* When the Soviet Union was still a world power it had been a major source of military and economic assistance to those states. Not wishing to be drawn into a war with the West by these sometimes irrational allies, the Soviets restrained them from developing their own nuclear weapons. Now, with the Soviet Union's demise, ironically, that constraint has been removed. Moreover, Russia itself and several other former Soviet republics have been awash with nuclear weapons that often lack adequate security. To be sure, the danger of an all-out nuclear war—an event that would dwarf the worst terrorist attack—has all but disappeared, at least for now. Still, great challenges remain, with terrorism being the most newsworthy but possibly not the most dangerous. If these are to be successfully resolved, it will require a greater degree of international cooperation and purpose than we have seen to date. This chapter examines several critical issues that will hold center stage in the twenty-first century. The topics discussed are obviously not exhaustive, but they do illustrate the opportunities and the problems facing our ever-shrinking world.

Policing Trouble Spots: A New World Order or a World without Order?

In the aftermath of the 1991 Gulf War, President George H. W. Bush envisioned a **new world order (NWO)**. The NWO would entail the rule of international law and close cooperation among all the world's major powers to deter future aggression and maintain international stability. Furthermore, it seemed to include a commitment to defending and spreading democracy and free-market economics throughout the world.

Clearly, international politics has not proceeded as smoothly as the elder Bush envisioned. Subsequent wars in Afghanistan, Lebanon, Iraq, and Yugoslavia have demonstrated how elusive world peace still is. Indeed, in some respects we may be facing a more unstable world today since the old East–West balance of terror no longer inhibits regional conflicts. The rise of international terrorism also presents a particular problem. With no defined home territory and an ideology that enshrines martyrdom, terrorist organizations such as al-Qaeda cannot be contained by the prospect of nuclear or conventional retaliation.

The collapse of the Soviet bloc unleashed old ethnic hostilities in Bosnia, Macedonia, Armenia, Tajikistan, and elsewhere. Observing those events in the early 1990s, former Secretary of Defense and CIA chief James Schlesinger warned, quite prophetically, that "although the world after the Cold War is likely to be a far less dangerous place because of reduced risks of a cataclysmic clash, it is likely to be more unstable rather than less."[4] In fact, some observers point to events since the end of the Cold War—including internal wars in the former Yugoslavia, Russia, Sudan, and Libya; continued conflict in the Middle East; and the September 11

---

* *Rogue state* is a term used mainly by the United States to characterize governments that do not respect international law or the rights of other states and which are authoritarian. The label has been applied at various times to Iran, North Korea, Libya, Sudan, Syria, and others.

assaults and the rising menace of terrorist organizations as evidence of a "new world disorder."

During the 1990s, some Washington foreign-policy planners favored working with United Nations peacekeeping operations in selected world trouble spots. That was the framework for the 1991 Gulf War intervention that freed Kuwait from an Iraqi invasion. But poorly conceived UN interventions in Somalia and Bosnia raised doubts about how well that body functions as a peacekeeper in difficult situations. Repeated UN condemnations of the massacre of tribesmen in the Sudanese region of Darfur have lacked teeth as member states have not been willing to commit substantial military forces to that region. At the same time, many in the U.S. Congress, particularly conservatives, feel that the United States should stay clear of UN-sponsored peacekeeping missions because the United Nations should never be in a position to dictate or even influence U.S. foreign policy.

In the coming years, ethnic hostilities and, possibly, prodemocracy uprisings will likely precipitate civil or international wars in Africa and Asia. Most of the world's trouble spots in the post–Cold War era have included some level of ethnic hostility: Somalia, Iraq, Sudan, Kashmir (India and Pakistan), and Yugoslavia come to mind. In addition, a renewed upsurge in Islamic fundamentalism could provoke civil conflict in the Middle East and North Africa. When these conflicts occur with a single nation-state, they raise difficult new challenges for the international community and its most powerful member, the United States. Should the United Nations, NATO, the African Union (AU), or the United States send peacekeeping forces to contain civil wars in countries such as Bosnia, Libya, or Sudan? The United States and other Western powers generally have been reluctant to intervene in ethnic or other internal conflicts, even when hundreds of thousands (Rwanda, Sudan, Indonesia) or even millions (Congo/Zaire) of people have been slaughtered. While there may seem to be a moral imperative to intervene, they argue, the international community should not violate a nation's sovereignty by interceding militarily. China and Russia have been particularly insistent that neither the United Nations nor its individual members should ever violate national sovereignty no matter what the reason. For example, both have used their veto powers in the United Nations Security Council to limit the role of UN peacekeeping troops in Sudan's Darfur region. African leaders, many of whom face ethnic tensions in their own countries, have generally been reluctant to criticize governments that allow or encourage ethnic massacres.

In Washington, "realist" critics of intervention insist that these ethnic conflicts rarely pose a threat to U.S. national security. Absent that threat, the United States was unwilling to put American ground troops in harm's way in Bosnia and limited its defense of Kosovo's Albanian population (against the Serbian government) to the use of air power. European nations have been even more reluctant to send their troops into potentially dangerous trouble spots. Thus, for example, the United States, France, Belgium, and the United Nations stood by while Rwanda's Hutu population massacred perhaps 500,000 to 800,000 Tutsis. While protesting the Syrian government's assaults on its own population, Western nations have rejected intervening militarily. In a parallel situation in Libya, NATO gave air support to the rebels but did not use ground troops.

To be sure, the United States *has* been willing to involve itself militarily when the president and his advisors believe its national interests are at stake—as in

Afghanistan and Iraq. But many of the internal wars and ethnic conflicts in the Third World and Eastern Europe do not particularly affect the national interests of the United States or other major powers. Consequently, neither the United States, NATO, nor other powerful actors have been willing to send peacekeeping forces to end horrendous civil wars in Rwanda, Liberia, Mozambique, Congo, and the Sudan even though those conflicts have collectively killed millions of people.

Proponents of international peacekeeping missions and other interventions to halt or contain ethnic conflicts argue that many internal ethnic quarrels spill across national borders and may create international conflicts that could threaten American national interests and international stability. For example, when as many as two million Hutus fled Rwanda, mainly to the Congo (then called Zaire), troops from Rwanda and Uganda crossed the border—along with smaller forces from four other African nations—and joined the Congo's own civil war in what has been called "Africa's First World War." As that war dragged on for years (despite multiple peace treaties), more than 5 million people (primarily civilians) have died from war, starvation, and disease. Furthermore, an estimated 1.8 million women (12 percent of all Congolese women) have been raped during the war (mainly by various militias), a rate of 48 rapes per hour according to a recent comprehensive study.[5] Yet there has been no third-party, international intervention to limit the violence.

A second argument for peacekeeping interventions is that if the United States is to maintain its status as a world leader, it cannot succumb to isolationism and must take some responsibility as the "world's policeman." Proponents of that position note that the United States lost status in Western Europe when it initially failed to assume leadership during the Bosnian crisis. Yet this is a position that President Obama specifically rejected when he turned over American air operations in Libya to NATO.

Finally, some who favor international intervention into internal ethnic conflicts and massacres raise a moral challenge. When the international community sits back and allows mass starvation in Somalia, tribal genocide in Rwanda and Burundi, or death camps in Bosnia, they argue, it is as morally bankrupt as those who did nothing to help Jews escape Hitler's genocide.

Despite such moral arguments, however, foreign governments are understandably reluctant to risk the lives of their nations' soldiers to save the lives of civilians in far-off nations. Nor is it realistic to expect external intervention every time there is a human rights crisis. Therefore, the question of where and when to intervene will continue to be a major issue facing the United Nations, NATO, and the United States, among others.

An obvious case in which major powers did intervene in an internal war was the NATO bombardments of Muammar Qaddafi's government forces and command centers in Libya. NATO agreed to get involved only after intervention was endorsed, at least in part, by the United Nations, the AU, and the Arab League. Several factors explain why NATO decided to intercede in this case but not in Syria or many other civil conflicts. President Muammar Qaddafi had personally offended a number of Arab and African leaders, making them more willing to support sanctions against him than they were with more brutal dictators such as Sudan's President Bashir. Second, and more importantly, Libya is an important source of oil for Western Europe and is home to major European investments (particularly from Italy), and the West was concerned about the prospects of a prolonged civil war. Third, because Libya is located on the Mediterranean and is a relatively short boat ride from Italian soil, its civil war had driven a huge number of refugees, both Libyans and foreign workers who had been employed there, to set off for the small Italian island of **Lampedusa**. Once granted asylum in Italy, they could easily travel to other EU nations. Thus, NATO leaders hoped their military intervention would drive out Qaddafi before Europe was flooded with unwanted refugees. Finally, the UN's mandate only allowed NATO to conduct aerial attacks on Qaddafi's forces (and, officially, only to protect civilian lives, but NATO commanders have interpreted that mandate very broadly). So there would be no "boots on the ground" and, once Libya's air defense system had been quickly destroyed, no danger of American or European soldiers coming home in body bags. Obviously, such a combination of special circumstances is very unlikely to exist elsewhere.*

THE CHANGING NATURE OF THE INTERNATIONAL ARMS RACE

East–West Disarmament

President Mikhail Gorbachev's political and economic reforms in the Soviet Union and the USSR's collapse (see Chapter 12) both contributed to a series of agreements between the world's two greatest military powers, reducing their nuclear arsenals and, in turn, the likelihood of nuclear war. In 1988, the two nations signed the Intermediate-Range Nuclear Force (INF) Treaty calling for the destruction of more than 2,500 missiles between them. That treaty constituted "the first formal agreement that actually reduced the number of nuclear weapons in existence rather than just slowing down the rate of increase...."[6]

Three years later, following the demise of the Soviet Union, Russia and the United States signed START I (the Strategic Arms Reduction Treaty), committing each of them to reducing the number of deployed strategic nuclear warheads to 6,000 on a total of 1,600 intercontinental ballistic missiles (ICBMs), bombers, and submarine ballistic missiles. On December 1, 2001, both Russia and the United States announced that they were in compliance with those terms. Soon afterwards, Russian President Boris Yeltsin declared that Russia would no longer target its missiles to hit U.S. cities. START II, signed in 1993 (but not ratified by the U.S. Senate until 1996 nor by the Russian Duma until 2000), mandated further cutbacks of strategic nuclear weapons to 3,000 or 3,500 for each country and banned multiple-warhead MIRV ICBMs.

Finally, in a rather unexpected move, Presidents George W. Bush and Vladimir Putin announced in May 2002 that their countries would reduce the number of their strategic nuclear warheads to 1,700 to 2,200 by the close of 2012 (the Strategic Offensive Reductions Treaty, SORT). Critics of that agreement note that the decommissioned warheads were to be placed in storage but not destroyed and warn that there are no provisions for verifying compliance. Indeed, there are potential flaws in

---

* NATO also conducted air strikes against Serbia in 1999 to protect the breakaway region of Kosovo from potential atrocities by Serbian forces. Here again, intervention took the form of an air war only.

A CLOSER LOOK   17.1

Nuclear Weapons Proliferation and "Rogue States"

Currently, the two most worrisome examples or potential examples of nuclear proliferation are North Korea and Iran, the former because of its unpredictable and belligerent behavior, the latter because of its association with Islamic extremism and terrorism. The North Korean weapons program dates back to the 1960s or 1970s. Generally reclusive and paranoiac, its communist regime felt particularly threatened by American deployment of nuclear weapons in South Korea in 1958 (weapons that were removed by 1991). Despite later signing the Nuclear Non-Proliferation Treaty and an additional pact with the United States promising to dismantle its plutonium program, North Korea continued its clandestine weapons program. In early 2003 it became the first nation to ever withdraw from the Non-Proliferation Treaty. Later that year it reactivated a reactor at its main nuclear complex and announced a joint program with Iran to develop long-range ballistic missiles with nuclear warheads. In 2005, the North Koreans claimed to have produced nuclear weapons, one of which they allegedly tested in 2006. Equally ominously, they have been testing missiles capable of delivering such weapons.

Six-party talks (involving both North and South Korea, the United States, China, Russia, and Japan) designed to dismantle North Korea's program have crawled on (and off) since 2003, with few significant accomplishments to date. North Korea has not provided information on whether it is trying to produce nuclear weapons in a uranium-enrichment program, where any weapons are stored, and whether it had helped Syria develop a nuclear weapons program (subsequently destroyed by Israeli bombers). Since North Korea has stalled and withheld information for the past years of negotiation, there is no certainty that the negotiations will reach a successful ending, though there are some clear benefits for the Koreans if they do (badly needed food assistance, among other things).

Iran's nuclear energy program dates to the late 1960s when it was governed by the Shah, Mohammad Reza Pahlavi, a close ally of the West. Hence its (non-weapons) program received assistance during the following decade from the United States and West Germany. Its purpose was to produce energy for internal consumption, allowing Iran to export more of the petroleum it produced. As a signatory to the NPT, Iran allowed inspection by the IAEA. Following the 1979 Islamic Revolution overthrowing the Shah, the program was frozen, and during the Iran–Iraq War of 1980–1988 the entire nuclear program was suspended. Iran resumed nuclear energy development in the 1990s, and in 2002 the United States accused it of seeking to develop nuclear weapons at secret plants. However a few months later, the IAEA stated that its

several of these bilateral agreements. One of the limitations is that either county has the right to opt out of these or previous accords. So, for example, in June 2002 the United States withdrew from the 1967 Anti-Ballistic Missile Treaty. That treaty had limited its signatories' ability to build antimissile defense systems, which presumably would reduce the chances that either side would launch an offensive attack. In all, however, both superpowers have appreciably reduced their nuclear arsenals, and the likelihood of massive nuclear war has declined substantially.

The Dangers of Nuclear Proliferation

Ironically, at the very time that prospects for global nuclear war have receded, actual and potential **nuclear proliferation** to the Third World has intensified, as has the possibility of regional nuclear conflicts. In fact, the very collapse of the Soviet

17.1

inspectors had found no evidence to support the American charge.

Still, in 2004, that agency's director general, Mohamed ElBaradei, accused Iran of not fully cooperating with inspectors. As with the North Korean case, the United States has taken a harder line on this issue than its allies. Britain, France, and Germany have held periodic talks with Iran in which the European nations have offered to give Iran assistance for its nuclear energy program if it would agree to stop uranium enrichment.

Experts agree that Iran is moving toward the capability to produce nuclear weapons, but they disagree about how long that might take and what, if anything, it would take to stop them or persuade them to stop. Recalling the United States' mistaken belief that Saddam Hussein's Iraq had weapons of mass destruction, some analysts suggest that Iran may not even intend to build a bomb. In fact, the November 2007 U.S. National Intelligence Estimate concluded that Iran had, in fact, halted its nuclear weapons program in 2003, but it resumed the program in 2005 and was "keeping open the option to develop nuclear weapons."[8] Since 2005, the EU has been engaged in slow and halting negotiations with Iran with the intention of giving that country assurances and assistance in return for international inspection that could verify its claim that its nuclear program is solely designed for peaceful purposes. Like North Korea's behavior in the

six-nation talks, Iran has used repeated stalling techniques. The Bush administration, which had taken a tougher stance toward Iran, somewhat changed course in 2008 and joined the negotiations. Liberal critics of administration policy argue that the United States has been too unbending and not sufficiently committed to negotiations. Conservative critics, such as former UN Ambassador John Bolton, faulted the Bush administration with entering into negotiations that were doomed to failure.

Although there is uncertainty over the current status of Iran's program and over where it is headed, the prospects are worrisome. Not only does that nation have links with Middle Eastern terrorist groups, but it is very hostile toward Israel, having expressed a desire to destroy it. At the same time, the Iranians have announced that they have successfully tested nuclear-capable missiles able to reach Israel (and other potential enemies). In fact, Israel has hinted that if it becomes convinced that Iran is close to developing a nuclear weapon, it might launch a preemptive air attack on Iranian nuclear facilities just as it did to an Iraqi reactor in 1981 and to a suspected Syrian nuclear facility in 2007. However, the Iranian facilities present a far greater challenge. They have built a very widely dispersed system of centrifuges, many (or most) of them hard to locate. Thus, many military experts feel that it may be impossible for Israel (or the United States) to destroy the program.

Union created another possible source of proliferation. Because Russian professionals, including nuclear scientists and technicians, now drew very low salaries, some might be hired by Third World nations seeking to develop their weapons programs. There was also concern that nuclear weapons or components would be sold abroad by Russian military officers wishing to enrich themselves. While those fears now have receded, other developments have been troublesome. Currently, two Asian rivals—India and Pakistan—have tested nuclear weapons. Israel undoubtedly has them as well. And in 2006 North Korea announced it had tested its first nuclear device.

Several factors make Third World proliferation particularly worrisome. First, two potential nuclear powers—Iran and North Korea (Libya, formerly in that category, terminated its nuclear program under Qaddafi)—are considered rogue states with records of belligerence that do not inspire confidence (see A Closer Look 17.1). Others—India, Pakistan, and Israel—with nuclear capabilities are embroiled in bitter regional conflicts with each other or with nonnuclear nations. Finally, even if all new nuclear powers were to act responsibly, the chances of war by miscalculation increase greatly as the world's nuclear club grows.

The Nuclear Non-Proliferation Treaty (NPT) came into effect in 1970 and currently has 189 national signatories. The treaty's purpose was to prevent the spread of nuclear weapons beyond the hands of the five countries (the United States, the Soviet Union, Britain, France, and China) that possessed them at that time. The treaty prohibited countries with nuclear weapons from giving or selling them to nonnuclear countries and from sharing weapons technology with them (though China and France did not become signatories until 1992). One difficulty with the treaty is that it allows countries without nuclear weapons to develop nuclear energy for peaceful purposes even though such uranium-enrichment programs can be converted to weapons production. Enforcement depends on inspections by the International Atomic Energy Agency (IAEA), an arm of the United Nations.

So far, the NPT has been fairly effective but not totally so. For one thing, India, Israel, and Pakistan (all nuclear powers) have never signed the treaty. India and Pakistan have announced that they have nuclear weapons, and Israel probably has 100 to 300 warheads (though it officially refuses to confirm that it has any). North Korea has withdrawn from the NPT while still others have evaded inspection. South Africa secretly developed some nuclear weapons in the 1980s but dismantled its program and its weapons in 1990 and signed the NPT the following year.[7] Iraq apparently had a nuclear weapons program for a number of years but seems to have abandoned it in the early 1990s, years in advance of the U.S. invasion. As new countries have developed nuclear weapons, the risk of further proliferation increases. Israel is believed to have assisted the South African program. Pakistan has admitted that the father of its nuclear weapons program, Abdul Qadeer Khan, sold Libya and North Korea technology and equipment for building nuclear weapons (Libya has since abandoned its program and agreed to IAEA inspection).

The post–Cold War world will be hard-pressed to contain the Third World nuclear arms race and possible regional nuclear wars. As nuclear expertise spreads and as it becomes easier to deliver nuclear weapons in small packages, the possibility that a group such as al-Qaeda may acquire nuclear capability, though currently unlikely, remains chilling. This is one of the reasons that the West is so concerned about Iran developing nuclear weapons, given its ties to Islamist terrorist groups (though not al-Qaeda). Not only might some rogue state give a terrorist group nuclear technology, but an individual high-level scientist might do it independently, as illustrated by the case of Pakistan's Abdul Qadeer Khan.

Current Trends in World Trade: Economic Unification and Beyond

Globalization (economic, cultural, and political) is a very different type of international concern. Unlike other issues discussed in this chapter, globalization presents both benefits and disadvantages. As a trip to any American shopping mall quickly reveals, the world is becoming more interconnected. Labels on clothing indicate that they were made in an array of developing countries such as Honduras, Guatemala, Turkey, Sri Lanka, and Indonesia. An enormous range of household items—from toys to dishware and home tools—are manufactured in China. Electronic goods such as clock radios often come from Malaysia and Thailand, while computer keyboards and computers come from Mexico, Brazil, South Korea, and Taiwan. In the shopping malls of Los Angeles, Chicago, Boston, and Miami, many of the goods for sale, as well as many of the customers and sales staff, originated in dozens of foreign nations.

Perhaps the most widely discussed and analyzed economic and political phenomenon of the early twenty-first century, **globalization** involves the rapid spread of economic activity, political interactions, migration, culture, and ideas across national borders, often in de facto defiance of national sovereignty. Through the World Wide Web, e-mail, cell phones, films, and the mass media, the quantity of international communications and cross-cultural contacts are growing enormously. For example, Hollywood movies are now among America's leading exports. And more than one billion people worldwide have access to CNN news broadcasts.[9] Some view globalization as a positive development, promising economic growth, greater cross-cultural understanding and cooperation, and even the spread of democracy. For others in the United States and Europe, it is a suspect force that frequently causes plant closings, the loss of jobs to countries with cheap labor, and a flood of undocumented immigrants. Finally, many Third World political activists and analysts believe that globalization spreads American imperial dominance, exploits factory

© Vahid Salemi/AP Photo

IRAN: A NUCLEAR THREAT?   An Iranian security official, dressed in protective clothing, walks inside that country's uranium conversion facility. Iran's 2005 decision to restart uranium conversion and exclude international inspectors raised Western fears that the country was planning to build nuclear weapons.

workers in the less-developed countries (LDCs), and destroys cultural diversity. Thus, Benjamin Barber warns that globalization could force "nations into one homogeneous global theme park, one McWorld, tied together by communications, information, entertainment, and commerce."[10]

Perhaps nowhere has the growth of international economic links been more impressive and important than in the realm of world trade. As Figure 17.1 indicates, on the eve of World War I (1913) the total value of world trade was a mere $20 billion annually. During the next 50 years, it grew gradually to an annual rate of $154 billion in 1963. At that point, international trade began to spiral rapidly upward, increasing by about 700 percent from 1973 to 1993 and then nearly doubling again in the following eight years (1993–2001). The volume of world trade grew by nearly 9 percent annually from 2004 to 2007. The recent world recession saw trade volume increase by only 3 percent in 2008, then *decline* by 13 percent in 2009 and rebound somewhat in 2010.[11]

That unprecedented growth was stimulated by a number of factors, including improved transportation technology; the dramatic growth of the world economy from the late 1940s to the 1990s; the creation of multinational economic unions and free-trade agreements such as the North American Free Trade Agreement (NAFTA), the EU, the Asia Free Trade Zone, and the Southern Common Market (MERCOSUR, an association of four South American nations promoting free trade); worldwide free-trade agreements and enforcement mechanisms through the General Agreement on Tariffs

---

FIGURE 17.1 | **Growth in the World Trade, 1913–2001**

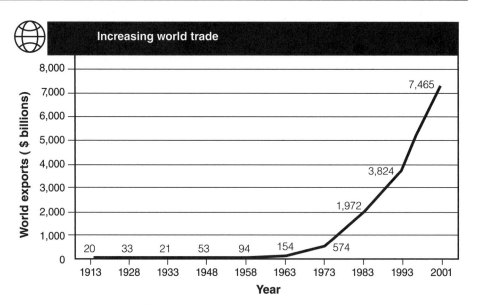

Source: IMF, *World Economic Outlook*, May 2002, on the Web at http://www.imf.org/. As presented in John T. Rourke, *International Politics on the World Stage*, 9th ed. (Guilford, CT: McGraw-Hill-Dushkin, 2003), p. 410.

and Trade (GATT) and its successor, the World Trade Organization (WTO); a sharp drop in the rates of tariffs on imports; and the explosion of exports by **newly industrialized countries (NICs)**, particularly from East Asia.* For example, today about 40 percent of Taiwan's, South Korea's, Singapore's, and Hong Kong's respective GNPs are devoted to exports. The volume of trade varies according to the rate of global economic growth, picking up during high growth periods such as the 1980s to 1990s and slowing during periods of slow growth or recession, such as 2007 through 2009. But the size of international trade has grown at a far greater pace than the world's economy has. For example, from 1990 to 2005 the volume of world trade grew at twice the rate of the world's GDP.

While experts differ as to exactly when economic globalization took off, many trace its origins to the early years after World War II. In 1947, seeking to rebuild the world economy after the devastations of the war, the United States and 22 other nations signed the GATT, designed to remove barriers to international trade.[12] By early 2011, its successor, the WTO, had 157 member nations (with 10 to 20 other countries negotiating for admission). Between them, they conduct more than 90 percent of world trade.[13] With the recent addition of China to its membership rolls in 1995, the WTO is continuing the process of opening up most of the world's markets to **free trade** (international trade that is relatively unrestrained by quotas, tariffs, or other government-imposed barriers).

The newly emerging economic order has several important features that will influence interstate relations and economic conditions worldwide in the twenty-first century. First, the international division of industrial production has shifted. During the 1960s and 1970s, the first East Asian NICs—South Korea, Taiwan, Hong Kong, and Singapore—enormously expanded their exports of low-cost, labor-intensive consumer goods such as garments, footwear, textiles, and inexpensive consumer electronics.

Taking advantage of their low wages, they were able to undersell Western producers. In the 1980s and 1990s, these "East Asian tigers" emerged from underdevelopment and, as local wages rose substantially, they shifted to production of more expensive, technology-intensive products such as computers, computer software, automobiles, and steel, whose prices are less dependent on labor costs.[14] In Latin America, more industrially developed countries, particularly Brazil, Mexico, and to a lesser extent Argentina, have also increased exports of sophisticated industrial products. At the same time, production of components, lower-end industrial exports, and apparel has moved to East Asian countries with lower labor costs (including China, Malaysia, and Thailand) and to Latin America's more recent export manufacturers, such as Honduras and Costa Rica.

In all, a significant share of the world's industrial production and exports (especially labor-intensive manufacturing) has shifted from the developed to the developing world. The NICs can no longer be ignored as trade competitors. Not only have many former textile- and shoe-manufacturing towns in the American South and New

---

* The term *NIC* refers to countries (and the city of Hong Kong) in East Asia (especially South Korea, Taiwan, Singapore, and Hong Kong) and in Latin America (especially Argentina, Brazil, and Mexico) that have recently developed substantial industrial manufacturing and export capacities. More recently, countries such as Thailand and Malaysia have joined that club, and China obviously should be included.

England seen their plants and jobs shift to East Asia and Latin America, but many steel companies in Germany, France, and the United States are also unable to compete with more modern mills in Brazil, Mexico, and South Korea.

Developing nations are now not only major exporters of manufactured goods to the United States but are also major importers of American products—making them both trading partners and competitors. Currently, China is the United States' largest trade partner, and Mexico is third (Canada is second). The United States absorbs about 80 percent of Mexico's exports. At the same time, Third World NICs and other developing economies are major consumers of U.S. products. Thus, for example, between 2000 and 2010 the value of U.S. exports to China rose from $16 billion to nearly $92 billion, an increase of some 500 percent. Almost 10 percent of the value of all U.S. exports now goes to Brazil, India, and China alone. So while Americans often complain about the manufacturing jobs being lost to developing nations (especially Asian countries), they tend to ignore the rising number of jobs being created by companies that export to the Third World.

A second important trend in world trade is the growing importance of services as an exportable commodity, particularly from the United States. As a portion of the world's industrial production has moved to Asia and Latin America in recent years, the service sector (banking, insurance, computer services, social services, education, health care, entertainment, and the like) has accounted for a growing portion of America's GNP and exports. Currently, over one-third of the value of world trade is in services, with the United States playing a major role. At the same time, an increasing number of U.S. firms are outsourcing services to India and elsewhere, including computer and software consulting and booking airline tickets.

Finally, a third major development has been the emergence of regional trading blocs and investment zones. We have already referred to the most important of those, the EU and NAFTA. Starting with the European Coal and Steel Community (1952) and the creation of the European Economic Community (1958), Western Europe has moved steadily toward a fully integrated economy. Today, a tourist or a businesswoman traveling to any significant Western European nation except Switzerland, Norway, and Great Britain—or a U.S. firm investing in the region—only needs to work with a single currency, the Euro, which has replaced the French franc, the German deutschmark, and 15 other national currencies. The single currency capped a half-century of steadily growing economic integration in most of Western and Southern Europe. A number of new EU members from Eastern Europe may adopt the Euro in the near future. The combined GNP of all EU members had already exceeded that of the United States prior to the Union's expansion into Eastern and Central Europe.

Unlike other regional trading blocs, the EU has gone beyond trade and fiscal unification, moving toward growing political unity as well. For example, the European Court of Justice has the authority to overturn decisions made by the national courts of EU member states, thereby somewhat limiting national sovereignty.[15] The popularly elected European Parliament passes laws in a number of policy areas that are binding on all members. Moreover, pan-European linkages may override national identification as a determinant of parliamentary behavior. For example, rather than organizing themselves by country, members of the European Parliament organize according to their political ideologies: Conservatives, Christian Democrats, Social Democrats, Greens (environmentalist parties), and the like. Very slowly (sometimes haltingly), the EU has been moving toward a loose political union, a process recently slowed by nationalistic backlashes in countries such as France, Denmark, and the Netherlands.

In East Asia, less-formal economic zones have developed based on trade and investment. As China has opened its doors to foreign investment, Hong Kong and Taiwanese businessmen have moved in to forge strong economic ties. Since June 1997, China has administered Hong Kong (a former British colony), producing even closer economic bonds between the two. At the same time, Japan has established important trade and investment links with Thailand, Malaysia, and Indonesia. Those ties, however, are bilateral (between two countries) rather than the multinational arrangements found within the EU.

Finally, in North America, the United States, Mexico, and Canada have created NAFTA, which, at the time it took effect (1994), became the world's largest free-trade zone. Initially subject to bitter opposition in the United States from many labor unions and from independent presidential candidates Ross Perot and Ralph Nader, NAFTA for the most part merely cemented the already-growing economic ties among the three nations.[16] While the agreement has not stimulated as much economic growth as its champions predicted, it has bolstered trade and has not brought the disastrous effects that its opponents warned of. Still, it has hurt some workers and farmers on both sides of the border, particularly in Mexico, For example, many small farmers in Mexico, particularly producers of corn and other grains, have been unable to compete with imports from the United States.

These changes mark a dramatic shift away from the economic nationalism that had previously characterized Latin American trade policy. Supporters of free trade argue that it will force the region's formerly protected companies to become more competitive and will allow Latin America to emulate East Asia's rapid, export-based economic growth. But critics of the new "outward looking" development model worry that, at least in the short run, the relatively unrestricted entry of American, East Asian, and European goods will drive less competitive local firms and farmers out of business and create substantial unemployment. Both sides of the debate, however, recognize that one way or another, Latin America must inevitably join North America, Europe, and Asia in an increasingly interdependent world economy.

Issues such as these often pit the interests of developed nations against those of less-developed countries. (See "North–South Relations," below.) Thus, in July of 2008, seven years of trade negotiation between WTO members (the "Doha Round") collapsed when the United States and the EU were unable to come to terms with India and other developing nations over trade tariffs and export subsidies on agricultural and manufactured goods. Since that time, negotiations have resumed. A number of world leaders have insisted that it is critical for the WTO to reach agreement by the end of 2011, but it is unclear whether they will reach that goal.

NORTH–SOUTH RELATIONS

One type of international economic–political relationship that has been particularly sensitive over the years is the one between the world's highly industrialized nations (referred to as "the North") and the less developed, Third World countries ("the South"). The demise of Western colonialism from the 1940s through the

1960s produced a steadily growing number of sovereign Third World nations. The United Nations General Assembly became a forum in which developing nations expressed their views and aired their grievances. Many of them, subscribing to theories of dependency and Western imperialism (see Chapter 14), blamed the capitalist nations of North America and Europe for their regions' economic difficulties. Others held the United States and the Soviet Union equally culpable for spending billions on the arms race while ignoring the needs of the world's poor. Unhappy with international trade patterns and desiring more foreign assistance, they demanded that the major economic and military powers pay more attention to **North–South relations** and less to the East–West conflict between the West and the Soviet bloc.

Yet ironically, the end of the Soviet–U.S. conflict has had several negative consequences for less-developed countries. Whereas the Soviet Union once provided significant economic and military aid to countries such as Cuba, India, Syria, and Iraq, contemporary Russia, particularly during its economic crisis of the 1990s, is no longer in a position to provide significant foreign aid to the Third World. At the same time, developing nations have far less leverage over the United States, which, during the Cold War, often gave them foreign assistance to keep them from falling into the Soviet sphere of influence. Similarly, Third World governments (including a number of corrupt and repressive ones) could count on American assistance if they were threatened by a communist insurgency. However, since the end of the Cold War in the early 1990s, foreign aid has represented a dwindling percentage of the U.S. federal budget. In fact, the share of the U.S. federal budget devoted to foreign aid in 1965 (4.5 percent) was more than four times higher than the current portion (1 percent).[*]

Still, as a consequence of growing economic interdependence, increased trade, and the United States' standing as the world's only military and diplomatic superpower, developing nations have fallen more deeply into the American sphere of influence. In years past, many Third World leaders complained that the Western industrial powers had victimized Africa, Asia, Latin America, and the Middle East, first through colonialism and then through unjust postcolonial economic relations. Consequently, they once argued, the West had a moral obligation to aid Third World development. But following the demise of the Soviet bloc and the failure of their alternative development strategies, most LDCs had no alternative other than seeking closer economic ties to the United States and other First World industrial powers. Most of them now look to foreign aid and, particularly, improved trade relations with the North to help them escape poverty.

Trade and Investment

Although most developing nations now see increased North–South trade as both inevitable and desirable, the *terms* of that trade remain controversial. As we saw in Chapter 14, Third World analysts have maintained that, over time, international

---

[*] Opinion polls consistently show that Americans believe that 20 to 25 percent of the federal budget goes to foreign aid. When asked what the proper share should be, they respond, on average, that it should be 10 percent, 10 times the actual figure. When told what the United States really spends on foreign aid, a majority of respondents reverse their position and say that is still too much. In fact, the United States allocates one of the lowest percentages of it GNP to foreign aid of any of the world's 34 most industrialized countries.

"terms of trade" have deteriorated for developing countries that depended on the export of commodities. In other words, they argued that, in the long run, the prices of the commodities that most of them export—including bauxite, copper, cotton, coffee, fruits, and sugar—have increased more slowly than have the prices of their manufactured imports such as tractors, autos, or refrigerators. Consequently, over the years, they contended, countries such as Costa Rica and Guatemala have needed to export more and more bananas and coffee to pay for the same number of imported televisions and trucks. Years ago, economists at the United Nations Economic Commission for Latin America (ECLA) produced extensive statistics on Latin American trade that supported that assertion. More recent economic data, however, show no consistent pattern in the comparative prices of Third World commodity exports and their manufactured imports. Commodity prices, it seems, can rise or fall sharply in a rather short period of time. Therefore, Third World commodity exporters are at a disadvantage in some years and benefit in others. Of course, petroleum exporters such as Saudi Arabia, Mexico, Venezuela, and Nigeria have reaped huge comparative price advantages in recent years. But even oil has oscillated greatly since the first price spikes of the early 1970s, and economies that have relied excessively on oil income (such as Ecuador and Nigeria) have stagnated. Most recently, the world price of crude oil per barrel, controlled for inflation, soared from $30 in September 2003 to $147 in July 2008, fell to $30 by the end of that year, then rose to $81 per barrel in early 2010.

This suggests a different kind of obstacle to economic development. Since commodity prices tend to fluctuate wildly over time, it is difficult for LDCs to anticipate their future export revenues. How, for example, can countries such as Kenya make long-term development investments absent some idea of their anticipated income from coffee, one of its major exports, over the next five to ten years? In an attempt to remedy that problem, from the 1970s into the 1990s many commodity exporters tried to create international cartels of banana-, coffee-, or cacao-growing nations, which could limit supply when the price of a crop or mineral export dropped excessively, thereby restoring prices to an acceptable level.

Industrialized nations have viewed commodity cartels as an unreasonable restraint on free trade. Ultimately, with the obvious exception of the Organization of Petroleum Exporting Countries (OPEC), most cartels have been short-lived and have failed to protect their members from declines in world prices. Their effectiveness depends on the cartel members' willingness to limit their exports of, say bananas, when the price drops too low (in an effort to drive up the price). But that is precisely the time when banana-producing nations are most desperate for export revenues and therefore are most tempted to break ranks and export more bananas.

In recent decades, the principles of free trade have become widely accepted internationally. Indeed, when the World Bank, the International Monetary Fund (IMF), or the United States extends economic assistance to developing nations, they often insist that the recipient remove its barriers to trade. Moreover, as increasing numbers of Asian and Latin American countries have diversified their exports, adding manufactured goods to their traditional exports of crops and minerals, they too have often benefited from free trade. Whereas Brazil may have once favored a coffee cartel to control that crop's volatile price, today it is more concerned with reducing trade barriers to its exports of airplanes, weapons, and shoes. In fact, aircraft are now one of Brazil's leading exports.

Yet while the world's industrialized nations have pressed developing nations to accept free trade, they have sometimes violated its basic doctrines themselves. For example, the United States, EU, and Japan provide their own farmers some $300 billion annually in subsidies. That gives, say, American, French, or Japanese producers an unfair competitive advantage over Third World farmers. In 2003, the G20 alliance of "Southern" nations (later expanded to 22), led by Brazil, China, and India, challenged the industrialized nations in WTO negotiations over a new treaty, demanding that the North end its agricultural subsidies. The following year, in the Doha round of negotiations, a general agreement in principle was reached calling for the North to reduce its agricultural subsidies and the South to lower tariff barriers to manufactured goods. But, as we have seen, participants have subsequently been unable to reach final agreement on a new WTO treaty.

Foreign investment has also generated North–South friction. Lacking sufficient investment capital and technological expertise, developing nations have long solicited foreign investment. But often they did so warily. For one thing, some MNCs have meddled in the domestic politics of their host countries, bribing local officials or even trying to topple unfriendly governments. In one of the most noted examples, International Telephone and Telegraph encouraged the CIA to destabilize Salvador Allende's democratically elected, leftist government in Chile. Even when MNCs act responsibly, many LDCs were uncomfortable having their leading exports controlled by foreign corporations, as the United Fruit Company did in Guatemala and in other banana-exporting countries.

More recently, however, as free-market ideals have triumphed in the international community, attitudes toward foreign investment have changed. Countries that were once wary of foreign investment now yearn for more. For example, China, once the most forceful voice against "capitalist imperialism," is now the Third World's largest recipient of foreign direct investment. Fernando Henrique Cardoso, once the most articulate, academic exponent of dependency theory (and its suspicion of foreign investment), later vigorously courted MNC investments during his two terms as Brazil's president. His successors, leftist Presidents Luiz Inácio Lula da Silva and Dilma Rousseff (who was in a Marxist guerrilla group in her youth), have established good relations with both the U.S. government and Wall Street.

The Debt Crisis

A final issue dividing North and South has been the Third World's foreign debt. Starting in the 1970s, many developing nations, particularly in Latin America, incurred substantial external debts in order to invest in economic development projects, compensate for international trade deficits, or cover budget deficits. Western and Japanese commercial banks extended credit to LDCs that they felt were reasonable risks. When OPEC raised petroleum prices sharply in the 1970s, American, Japanese, and European banks accumulated billions of "petrodollars" (money deposited by oil-exporting nations), much of which they in turn lent to countries such as Argentina, Brazil, Mexico, South Korea, Indonesia, and Nigeria.

As of the early 1980s, the developing world (excluding the Middle East's petroleum-exporting nations) had accumulated a total foreign debt somewhat over $700 billion.[17] By the end of the twentieth century, Third World debt had climbed to $2.06 trillion ($2,060 billion) and then to $3.35 trillion in 2007.[18] Some of those loans were invested wisely in roads, schools, or factories, helping to stimulate economic growth. But a lot went to less productive uses: covering short-term budget deficits, making payments for imported consumer goods, or purchasing armaments. Too often, a substantial amount of money was wasted because of corruption and poorly designed economic policies. Furthermore, Latin American nations, the largest Third World debtors, borrowed most of their money at variable interest rates, as did many African countries (Asian debtors generally locked into fixed rates). As interest rates shot up at the end of the late 1970s, these countries were often unable to keep up with their payments. By the 1980s, then, many LDCs were burdened with debts that were taking up large, and growing, portions of their export earnings and their GDPs.

In 1982, when Mexico—the developing world's second-largest debtor—announced that it was unable to pay the interest on its external obligations, the international banking system faced a serious crisis. Loans to Latin America constituted up to two-thirds of the net corporate assets of some international banks. Unwilling to take any further risks in the wake of Mexico's partial default, they curtailed additional loans to the developing world. The consequences for Latin American and African economies were disastrous since they had depended on a steady inflow of new credit to maintain any economic growth. Both regions suffered a steep economic decline that lasted until the 1990s.

In time, most debtors received additional funding. To secure that additional credit, however, countries such as Argentina, Brazil, Mexico, and Nigeria had to agree to stringent economic austerity programs, often designed by the IMF. These programs required debtor nations to slash government spending, privatize state-owned enterprises, and devalue their currencies in order to reduce their budgetary and trade deficits. While these measures were necessary to restore their financial health (though many analysts feel that the programs should have been less drastic), their immediate effects were devastating. In order to cut huge budget deficits, debtor nations needed to decrease social services such as health care and education, reduce consumer food subsidies (thereby sharply increasing the price of basic foods), and lay off government employees. Privatization allowed governments to sell major state firms (including telephone companies, railroads, and steel mills) whose bloated payrolls and inefficiencies kept them permanently in red ink. But when private sector firms purchased them, the new owners frequently slashed their workforce by firing many employees. Finally, currency devaluations improved a country's balance of trade by stimulating its exports and reducing imports. However, since so many consumer items and factory inputs had been imported, this further drove up the cost of living. Throughout Africa and Latin America, economies plummeted and living standards dropped as much as 40 percent.

As their economies staggered under the weight of these measures, many LDCs, especially the poorest ones, complained that they would never recover unless they were granted some form of debt relief. By the mid-1990s, the worst of the **debt crisis** seemed to have passed. After a decade of stagnation, a number of countries resumed economic growth. Still, despite the considerable debt relief or forgiveness extended in recent years to the LDCs by the World Bank and the world's most developed nations, debt payments remain a tremendous burden. Total debt services (the amount paid annually in interest and principal) accounted for 2.8 percent of GDP in 1980 and grew during the debt crisis to 6.9 percent in 1999 before declining to

5.2 percent in 2006 (as a result of stronger GDP growth in the Third World and debt relief). Still, even with that improvement in recent years, this meant that for every 20 dollars these economies produce annually, they still had to pay more than one dollar to service their debt. In fact, the LDCs' annual debt service far exceeds the amount of foreign assistance they receive from the developed world. So in Africa, the most impoverished region of the developing world, debt payments often soak up funds badly needed to improve the economy and to fight malnutrition and diseases such as AIDS. These problems have led to a worldwide movement of concerned citizens seeking to persuade their governments to forgive the debts of the most poverty-stricken nations (see A Closer Look 17.2).

A CLOSER LOOK

17.2

Rocking the Debt: Bono Makes Africa's External Debt a Hot Issue

At first glance, few topics seem drier and less hip than Third World debt. Not surprisingly, the issues of foreign exchange rates, balance of trade, commodity prices, and variable interest rates do not normally attract the interest of rock stars. But the huge external debt that so many Third World nations accrued during the 1960s and 1970s took a terrible toll, the effects of which are still being felt, especially in sub-Saharan Africa.

At the close of the twentieth century, Africa was home to 16 of the 17 poorest nations in the world (as measured by per capita income).[19] Although the total size of that continent's debt is actually much smaller than Latin America's, it constitutes a much higher percentage of its foreign export revenues and GDP. Currently, in some African nations, annual debt repayments account for as much as 60 percent of the country's export earnings.[20] That means that those LDCs must allocate most of the income that they receive for, say, cacao, coffee, or copper exports to interest payments rather than to roads, schools, factories, or electric power plants. And because most of the debt is owed by the region's governments (rather than the private sector), debt payments consume a major portion of the national budget, taking away funds that would otherwise be used to fulfill critical needs in areas such as education and health care. To take one extreme example, between 1972 and 1986 allocations for education in Congo, one of Africa's largest countries, fell from 15.2 percent of the national budget to 0.8 percent.[21] And for most of Africa, the debt burden continues to take its toll. In a number of countries, including those ravaged by AIDS, the cost of debt payments dwarfs government expenditures on health care.

In the past decade, a number of grassroots NGOs have tried to put a human face on the suffering that lies beneath the dry statistics on the foreign debt. One such group, Jubilee 2000, has pressured the world's wealthiest nations to forgive the debts of Africa's poorest nations. Although nobody doubts that corrupt and ineffective African governments bear much of the responsibility for their own countries' debt crises, various NGOs argue that it is unfair to make starving villagers and AIDS victims pay the costs.

Africa's debt has become a trendier topic in recent years since the rock star Bono, of the famed Irish group U2, became Jubilee's most prominent spokesman. Like other famous music and film stars who have campaigned for political or social causes—including Sting, Angelina Jolie, and George Clooney—he has given much wider visibility to what might otherwise have been an obscure issue. Jeffrey Sacks, perhaps the most influential American economist analyzing debt issues, joined with Bono in a series of visits to the finance ministers of the world's eight largest economic powers, arguing for debt relief. And indeed, at their 1999 summit in Cologne, Germany, the Group of Seven (G7)—the group of leaders from the world's major economies—promised to cancel up to $100 billion of Africa's $300 billion debt. Although the amount of subsequent assistance fell well short of that total, Cologne still provided helpful relief. It is true that many other actors and factors beyond Bono and Jubilee 2000 influenced that decision, but we should not discount the importance of star power in these changes.

ROCKING THE DEBT   Irish rock star Bono has become perhaps the leading spokesperson for a campaign to convince Western governments to cancel the foreign debt of Africa's most impoverished nations. Here he is joined by Irish singer Bob Geldof and Italian singer Jovanotti at a news conference in Italy.

Interestingly, during the most recent global economic crisis (2008–2011), the LDCs have held their own in terms of their ability to pay their national debt. Instead, the crisis this time has involved the excessive budgetary deficits and debt in European countries such as Iceland, Ireland, Greece, and perhaps Italy, Spain, and Portugal.

Responding to calls for debt relief, in 1996 the World Bank initiated a program called the Heavily Indebted Poor Countries (HIPC) initiative, which enabled a number of very poor nations to reduce their loan payments to the bank if they agreed to channel those savings into education, health care, and other vital social services. Critics have argued that any financial "bailout"—be it for African nations or for U.S. financial institutions currently threatened by the crisis in the housing market—creates a "moral hazard," that is, it may encourage borrowers (or lenders) to make questionable loans in the future, expecting that they will be bailed out if the loan can't be repaid. The Bush administration was initially skeptical of debt cancellation but came to support the idea of some relief. Interestingly, the United States' overthrow of the Saddam Hussein regime in Iraq played some role. Following its occupation of that country, the United States cancelled its share of Iraqi debt and pressured other nations to do the same, arguing, in part, that the Iraqi people should not have to pay the debt accrued by a corrupt dictator. Debt relief advocates argued that countries such as Congo (formerly Zaire) and Nigeria—also indebted by corrupt dictators—should get the same consideration. While some analysts remain concerned about the "moral hazard," many supporters of debt relief argue that the world's richest nations have not done enough. They note that developed nations give their own farmers many billions of dollars yearly in subsidies, a contradiction in free trade principles. These subsidies give U.S. and European farmers a tremendous advantage when competing with Third World growers in the international market.[22]

Beginning in 2000, as economic growth in the LDCs accelerated and as the world's developed nations forgave some of the debt of the world's poorest countries, the debt burden on the developing world began to decline. Thus, in 2000, the LDCs' total foreign debt amounted to 38 percent of their combined gross national incomes (GNIs, roughly equivalent to the GDP). By 2008, that figure had been reduced to 21 percent. Improvement was greatest in sub-Saharan Africa, the major beneficiary of debt forgiveness, where debt fell from 62 percent to 21 percent of GNI during that same period. But the developing world remains vulnerable to changes in the world economy. Consequently, when the 2009 world recession reduced LDC exports to the developed world, the external debt as a percentage of Third World GNI rose somewhat, and it grew even more as a percentage of Third World exports.[23]

PROTECTING THE ENVIRONMENT

Worldwide concern for the environment has grown steadily since the birth of the ecology movement in the 1960s. In the United States, it has expressed itself through celebrations of Earth Day and other consciousness-raising events; the growth of environmental groups such as Greenpeace and the Sierra Club; and a spate of congressional legislation designed to clean the air, water, and soil. In many Western European nations, environmentalists have become an electoral force. **Green Party** candidates, for example, have won seats in the EU parliament and in the national parliaments of several member states.

The ecology movement originally focused on domestic remedies such as the America's Clean Air Act of 1970. But environmentalists soon realized that many important ecological problems cross national borders and are only amenable to international solutions. For example, pollutants from American power plants have created acid rain, some of which fell on Canada, killing fish and vegetation. Industrial pollution on the Rhine River flows across the borders of Switzerland, France, Germany, and the Netherlands. The smoke and ash from fires intentionally set to clear jungles in Indonesia pose a health threat to neighboring Malaysia and Singapore. And the deforestation of the Amazon basin reduces the world's oxygen supply. Preserving the ozone layer, slowing global warming, and protecting endangered sea life are but a few of the environmental concerns that can only be addressed through international cooperation.

Frequently, however, these issues pit environmental needs against national sovereignty. For example, European and North American environmentalists are extremely concerned about the rapid decimation of the Third World's tropical rain forests. Possible consequences include reduction of the world's oxygen supply, intensification of global warming, destruction of endangered species, and loss of potential medical cures from jungle plants. But nations such as Brazil, Indonesia, and Malaysia view their forests as a valuable source of exportable timber, potential locations for commercial plantations and cattle ranches, and areas for resettling poor, land-hungry peasants.

Because they badly need foreign exchange—particularly when carrying huge external debts—these countries frequently are reluctant to accept environmental regulations that would reduce their export capacities. With some justification, they complain that the industrialized nations now pointing an accusatory finger at the Third World have already depleted their own forests at an earlier stage of development and continue to be the major sources of air and water pollution as well as the depletion of other resources (see A Closer Look 17.3). For example, as of 1990, industrialized countries—with only 25 percent of the world's population—consumed 75 percent of its energy and 85 percent of its forest products. They were also responsible for 75 percent of global warming.[24] Since that time, the developed nations' contribution to global warming has fallen to about 57 percent of the world's total, largely because emissions from industrializing Asian countries, most notably China and India, have grown so dramatically.[25] Still, in many ways industrialized nations cause more ecological damage than developing countries do. For example, carbon emissions *per capita* in the United States are roughly 20 times as high as in India.*

In recent decades, as the world has recognized the magnitude of worldwide ecological damage—particularly global warming—there have been a growing number of international treaties and agreements aimed at preserving the environment.† In 1997, during negotiation of the Kyoto Climate Change Protocol (an international agreement aimed at reducing global warming), the United States resisted European pressures for stronger emissions restrictions. Eventually, a treaty emerged requiring signatories to reduce their emissions of carbon dioxide and other greenhouse gases (gases that contribute to global warming) back to 1990 levels by the year 2010. Although some progress has been made, especially in Europe, toward reducing emissions, the signatories badly missed that goal.

Moreover, no matter how much progress the Kyoto signatories may make, a major limitation is that the United States (currently the world's second-largest source of greenhouse gases, after China) decided in 2001 not to sign the protocol, much to the chagrin of its Western European allies.

Opponents of mandatory emission controls believe that the dangers of global warning are still unproved and exaggerated, while the most certain effect of emission limitations would be to slow down the economy. Although the Obama administration has been more sympathetic to environmental concerns than the Bush administration, it has failed to push its proposed carbon emission caps through Congress. At the same time, for some 10 years, the signatories to the Kyoto Protocol have failed to agree on new targets for greenhouse gas emissions. A fundamental obstacle has been a continuing rift between developed and developing countries over what share of the cutbacks each group should have to make.

---

* Of course, with its much larger population, India's *total* emissions are actually about one-fifth of America's.

† A number of scientists still deny that we are experiencing long-term global warming or question how much of global warming is due to human activity. However, the America's National Academy of Sciences, the American Association for the Advancement of Science, the United Nations' panel on climate change, and many other scientific bodies have all concluded that there is a broad, though not universal, consensus in the scientific community about the existence and danger of climate change.

A CLOSER LOOK

17.3

Economic Development and Ecological Concerns

Like industrialized nations, Third World countries face difficult trade-offs between economic needs and ecological considerations. Often, the poor recognize the dangers of industrial waste and other environmental hazards but must accept them to survive. One extreme example of such a calculation occurred in an impoverished village outside Bahia de Salvador, Brazil. Villagers there catch and eat fish containing dangerously high levels of mercury emitted from nearby industrial plants. Well aware that the mercury will eventually kill or paralyze many of them, they continue to fish. "What is better," asked one poor villager, "to die of starvation now or to die from the mercury later?" Like many U.S. politicians, Third World political leaders and

bureaucrats often give the immediate needs of economic development precedence over long-term ecological concerns. When one of this text's authors questioned the environmental consequences of a Jamaican development project he was visiting, he received a frosty reply from a government economist: "You Americans raped your environment in order to become a wealthy industrialized nation," he said. "We Jamaicans insist on the right to do the same." Still, environmental movements have begun expanding in many Third World nations. In the long term, environmentally harmful development may actually be counterproductive for the economy. But companies and governments often fail to think about the long term.

Many political scientists note that solutions to problems such as protecting natural resources and cleaning up the environment need to confront "the tragedy of the commons" and must better protect collective goods. A collective good is a product or service to which members of a particular community (e.g., the worldwide community of nations) has ready access, such as ocean fishing waters beyond national boundaries. The tragedy of the commons describes a "situation in which [actors] have an incentive to increase their consumption of a collective good even though their consumption will [eventually] significantly reduce either the quality or the supply of that good."[26] Thus, every country bordering on an ocean has access to international fishing waters (the collective good). For each vessel and each nation's fleet, its immediate interests (making money) lie in catching as many fish as it can. Of course in the long term, if all the boats maximize their catch, they will deplete the supply of valued fish such as salmon and cod, to the detriment of all. But absent some enforceable international agreement, no boat or country will reduce its catch while its competitors do not. Similarly, although it is obviously in the collective interest of all nations to protect the world's ozone layer, each country seeks to maximize economic growth (even at the expense of the collective good) while hoping that the other nations make the necessary sacrifices.

The challenge, then, is to reconcile a country's economic interests and its environmental concerns. On the one hand, as we have seen, many LDCs were hard-pressed to repay their large debts to Western banks. So debtors, like Indonesia, that were home to large jungle or forest regions found it hard to resist payments from lumber or agribusiness companies (in this case, mostly Japanese) planning to exploit those resources. On the other hand, international environmental groups such as the World Wildlife Federation, hoping to avert such commercial deals, have arranged a number of "debt for nature swaps" in which they have purchased external debt notes of countries such as Ecuador and Bolivia at highly discounted prices.* They have then canceled those debts in return for a commitment from the debtor government to protect an agreed-upon area of forest from exploitation. In countries such as Costa Rica, the rain forest and other environmentally threatened resources have been preserved and transformed into an economic resource through "eco-tourism." In most cases, however, international environmental efforts will have to confront difficult trade-offs. First, as we have seen, each country (including developed ones) will have to weigh environmental protection against pressures for economic growth; second, international regulations will have to balance the sovereignty of independent nations with the need for international cooperation.

HUMAN RIGHTS

Even more than environmental issues, human rights concerns frequently confront fundamental conflicts between the emerging values of the global community and the sovereignty of individual states. Recent world history is replete with massive human rights violations. Not long ago, the world recoiled in horror when the Khmer Rouge government murdered one million Cambodians and when Hutus in Rwanda massacred an estimated 500,000 to 800,000 people, most of them ethnic Tutsis. More typically, governments in Burma, Syria, Iran, China, Sudan, and Colombia, among others, at times have imprisoned, tortured, or killed suspected political opponents.

International NGOs devoted to protecting human rights, such as Amnesty International and Human Rights Watch, have raised public consciousness about political repression. The media have brought some of these horrors into our living rooms, and a number of entertainment celebrities have involved themselves in global campaigns for human rights. Although particular governments, international agencies, and NGOs often employ different standards, there is a growing consensus that three fundamental types of human rights violations are unacceptable: the execution, imprisonment, or torture of individuals because of their political beliefs; repression based on race, religion, ethnicity, or gender; and the use of cruel and unusual punishment such as torture or excessive punishment for nonviolent crimes. For example, in China criminals convicted of such nonviolent crimes as tax evasion, embezzlement, and accepting bribes are sometimes (legally) executed.

Human rights concerns have played a particularly important role in the foreign policies of countries such as Sweden, Norway, Canada, and the Netherlands. As a superpower with a complex network of alliances, the United States has found it harder to take a consistent position on this issue. On the one hand, as a leader of the "free world," Washington has spoken forcefully against political repression and discrimination. At the same time, however, administrations of both political parties

---

* Since the banks were pessimistic about recouping anywhere near the full value of their loans, many of them sold their debt notes—for as little as 10 percent of their face value—to purchasers who were willing to assume the risk. Consequently, an environmental protection organization such as the World Wildlife Fund could purchase (and retire) $100 million of the Bolivian debt notes for as little as $10 million.

have violated those norms for strategic purposes. During the Cold War, for example, the United States provided aid and support for a number of regimes that flagrantly abused human rights but were considered needed allies in containing communism. These included the Shah's government in Iran (overthrown by the 1979 Islamic Revolution), various military governments in South Korea from the 1960s to 1980s, and the Suharto dictatorship in Indonesia. Supporters of American policy argued that this double standard was necessitated by the requirements of realpolitik.* Furthermore, they pointed to Iran as evidence that when unsavory allies such as the Shah are toppled, they are sometimes replaced with more oppressive governments. Human rights activists countered that it was not only immoral to ally with repressive governments but that it often proved counterproductive. They argued that when American-backed dictators in countries such as Cuba, Iran, and Nicaragua were eventually overthrown, their peoples held the United States culpable for having backed those dictatorships.

The end of the Cold War largely freed the U.S. foreign policy of this dilemma, at least temporarily. Congress and the State Department turned critical of governments such as the Pinochet dictatorship in Chile, which Washington supported during the Cold War. But the War on Terror following the 9/11 attacks once again caused the West to court allies, some of whom had poor human rights records. The United States bestowed huge amounts of foreign aid on the military government in Pakistan and the Mubarak dictatorship in Egypt (both governments were subsequently overthrown by popular unrest). The West also supported the 33-year dictatorship of Yemeni President Ali Abdullah Saleh (now also facing a mass uprising) as a key ally in the war against al-Qaeda.

The War on Terror also raised another human rights dilemma. The issue was, "What tactics are necessary or acceptable in order to keep the United States and Western Europe safe from terrorist attacks?" Because terrorist networks are secret and have no territorial base, many Bush administration policy makers (including then Vice President Richard Cheney) and intelligence officials felt it was necessary to extract information from captured operatives even if that meant using extreme methods. As a consequence the United States used a program of "extraordinary rendition" in which suspected terrorists from nations such as Egypt, Afghanistan, and Pakistan were secretly sent back to their home countries so that they could be tortured for information in a manner that would not have been permitted in the United States. Other terrorist suspects were sent to the U.S. military base in Guantanamo Bay, Cuba, where, for a period of time, some were subjected to waterboarding.[†] Proponents of these techniques argued that they were justified if they could save innocent civilians from dying at the hands of terrorist bombers. Critics of torture techniques, including 2008 Republican presidential candidate John McCain, argue that torture is illegal and immoral and that it puts American soldiers at risk of suffering similar treatment if they become prisoners of war. Furthermore, they maintain

---

Realpolitik means political policies that are based on realism and power rather than on ideology or idealism. The term is frequently applied to particular foreign policy decisions.

[†] Waterboarding is a form of interrogation in which large quantities of water are repeatedly forced into the prisoner's pharynx and trachea, inducing choking and gagging, a feeling of drowning, and resulting panic.

that it is not an effective means of securing reliable information and that it is some-times used on suspects who turn out to be innocent.

Today torture is widely condemned, and virtually no country admits using it. Ethnic massacres (such as in Darfur) and other mass human rights violations are also widely condemned. But no matter what their moral concerns or outrage, countries have rarely intervened individually or collectively in the internal affairs of even the worst human rights violators. There are several reasons for that reluctance. Some-times they feel that intervention would have little effect. For example, many experts felt that Western democracies could do little in the short run to reduce Chinese political repression in the wake of the 1989 Tiananmen Square massacre and argued that foreign pressure would actually be counterproductive. Human rights groups have generally disagreed. In other instances, as we have noted, geopolitical considerations have led world powers to overlook human rights violations by their own allies. Thus, the West long overlooked the Mubarak government's human rights violations.

Ultimately, however, the main reason that the international community rarely intervenes to avert or stop human rights abuses is that such intervention breaches a basic tenet of international law, national sovereignty. The principle of noninterven-tion is "the most important embodiment of the modern idea that states should be treated as autonomous entities."[27] The primary function of international organizations such as the United Nations and the Organization of American States has been to deter international aggression, not domestic repression. Even in the 1990s, when the United Nations determined that human rights violators in Bosnia should be brought to trial before the International Court of Justice in The Hague (the Netherlands), American and European peacekeeping troops were reluctant to arrest well-known Serbian war criminals for fear of upsetting Bosnia's fragile peace.

As the international community's focus on human rights has intensified, some actors have overstepped the traditional limits on intervention imposed by norms of national sovereignty. In 1998, when former Chilean dictator General Augusto Pino-chet was in London for medical treatment, the Spanish government asked Britain to extradite him to Spain so that he could be tried for the murder of Spanish citizens residing in Chile. Two factors made this request significant. First, it challenged the international norm of head-of-state immunity, which holds that a head of state (or a former head) cannot be prosecuted for behavior committed while he or she was in office. Second, the Spanish court asked for extradition for a crime that had not occurred on Spanish soil and had not been committed by a Spanish citizen. After extended legal proceedings, the British courts ruled that Pinochet could legally be extradited to Spain to face the charge of torture. Ultimately, however, the British government decided not to extradite him because, at his advanced age, he suffered from diminished capacity and allegedly would not be able to understand the charges against him. He returned to Chile, where he subsequently spent time under house arrest and faced charges of human rights violations in Chilean courts. No matter the particulars of the case, the British courts' decision that former President Pinochet could be extradited and tried by a non-Chilean court on charges of torture set an important precedent in international law. In other important cases, the former presi-dent of Serbia, Slobodan Milosevic, the former Bosnian Serb President Radovan Kar-adzic, and former Liberian President Charles Taylor all were apprehended and brought before the UN's International Criminal Court (ICC), which was set up in

2002 to try people accused of war crimes and crimes against humanity.[28] In 2008 the ICC issued an arrest warrant for Sudanese President Omar al-Bashir, charging him with war crimes in Darfur. He was the first sitting head of state to be charged by that court and the first to be charged with genocide. Yet because there is no chance of Bashir's own government executing the warrant and because he can still travel to a large number of countries that refuse to honor it (including China, Russia, and all of the countries in Africa), the warrant has so far had no effect. In mid-2011 the court issued an arrest warrant for Libya's Muammar Qaddafi, another sitting head of state. Subsequently, Qaddafi was overthrown and killed by rebel forces.

In 1993, Belgium issued a more far-reaching challenge to the principle of sovereignty when it passed the War Crimes Law, giving Belgian courts "universal jurisdiction" over persons suspected of "crimes against humanity." That is, Belgium gave itself the right to try anyone accused of committing war crimes regardless of their nationality or that of their victim and no matter where the crime was committed. In 2001, a Belgian court convicted four Rwandans (including two Catholic nuns and a university professor) of war crimes for their participation in the 1994 massacre of Hutus in their homeland. Several international human rights groups hailed the law and the convictions as positive contributions to international law.

But while various Belgian prosecutors filed charges against an array of alleged war criminals—many of them famous, others little-known—the Rwandan convictions turned out to be the only ones secured under that country's War Crimes Law. The law faced two serious problems—one practical and the other legal. The practical problem was that suspected war criminals could only be brought to trial if they were extradited to Belgium (something no countries were willing to do) or if they set foot in Belgium. The four convicted Rwandans had taken refuge in Belgium and were recognized by Tutsis from their town. The second, more important, problem was that the law enabled prosecutors to file charges against a huge array of political leaders, including Israeli Prime Minister Ariel Sharon, Cuba's Fidel Castro, Palestinian leader Yasser Arafat, President George Bush, and British Prime Minister Tony Blair. These charges were clearly unenforceable and generally considered legally questionable. Ultimately, the Belgian government and courts threw out many of the indictments and many of the law's provisions until that law was finally scrapped and replaced with much narrower legislation.

At times, individual nations and international organizations have reacted to human rights violators by means short of direct intervention. For example, the United States, the British Commonwealth, the EU, and much of the Third World invoked trade and cultural-exchange sanctions against South Africa when its minority-controlled (White) government pursued apartheid policies of racial segregation and repression. In the 1980s, the United States suspended military assistance to Uruguay, Chile, and Guatemala because of their human rights violations. Today, most Western countries have suspended aid to Burma for the same reason.

Although many scholars and diplomats laud the growing world concern for human rights, the question of international enforcement remains controversial. For example, many Third World nations fear that human rights issues could be used as a wedge for Western intervention in their internal affairs. There is also a problem of consistency. If international sanctions are invoked to protect democratic rights in Burma or Sudan, shouldn't they also have been used to protect Catholics in Northern

Ireland or Native Americans in South Dakota? The international system has yet to settle on universal standards for answering such questions. But, in spite of these obstacles, a growing number of nations and international organizations seem inclined to incorporate human rights concerns in formulating their foreign policies as shown by the strong international condemnation of the Syrian military's killings of pro-democracy protesters.

WOMEN'S RIGHTS

Both cross-national statistics and case studies make it clear that in many parts of the world women have fewer economic opportunities than men, suffer disproportionately from poverty, exercise less political power, and are more often the victims of exploitation. As with many other concerns discussed in the chapter, we find that governments, NGOs, and scholars disagree over which of these women's issues are the proper subject of international action. For example, in some countries religious custom may mandate the veiling of women or offer them fewer rights of inheritance than men. Elsewhere, local custom may permit or encourage practices such as arranged marriages, child brides, or educational limitations for girls. Unfair as such practices may seem, they are generally protected by the rules of national sovereignty. There is no international compact, for example, that would force Saudi Arabia to let women vote and drive or that would end bridal dowries in India. But international concern has grown in recent decades over acts of violence and brutality routinely inflicted on women in some nations.

For years human rights groups focused primarily on assisting "prisoners of conscience," people who had been imprisoned, tortured, or executed because of their political or religious beliefs. In time, rights activists turned their attention to genocide and other abuses perpetrated by some governments against particular ethnic groups or religions. With the rise of the women's rights movement and the human rights community, the world now pays greater attention to systematic violations of women's rights, such as compulsory female circumcision, forced marriages, and enslavement in the international sex trade. In all, these violations and a host of others probably make women the largest group of victims of rights abuse.

International attention on women's rights issues intensified in the 1970s, prompted by the growth of the feminist movement in many Western industrialized nations. Declaring 1975 to be International Women's Year, the United Nations staged its first conference on the status of women, with 133 member states attending. After that, the UN held three additional World Conferences on Women at five-year intervals, designed to develop strategies for improving women's status worldwide. At the same time, a wide range of NGOs has emerged dedicated to addressing issues such as violence against women and female poverty.

Forced labor generates over $30 billion annually, half of that produced in the United States and Europe. Much of that total comes from the sexual exploitation of women (forced prostitution). A substantial portion of the women involved come from Eastern Europe and the developing world. By one recent estimate, two million women and children are sold into the sex trade annually, either within their own country or across national borders. In India alone, perhaps as many as 200,000 girls from neighboring Nepal, many under the age of 14, work as sex slaves.[29] Since 1996, the EU has promoted greater international cooperation in combating human trafficking. And in 2000, the U.S. Congress passed the Victims of Trafficking and Violence Protection Act, which enhanced a victims' ability to bring suit or testify against international traffickers. For example, it allows such women to stay in the United States for a longer period of time and offers legal assistance. But these efforts have failed to make a serious dent in this trade, as many LDCs have not been responsive to the problem and Western industrialized nations have not always given the issue the priority it deserves.

Other abuses of women grow out of traditional Third World customs and values. In some countries (mostly, but not exclusively, Muslim) women are sometimes victims of "crimes of honor." **Honor killings** are defined as punitive murders of women whose families feel they have shamed them by acting immorally. The victims usually are women who have allegedly committed one of the following offenses: adultery, refusing to participate in a marriage arranged by their parents, or acting immodestly. Typically they are murdered by their brother(s), father, or uncle. Even if a woman is merely *accused* of having premarital or extramarital sex they are considered to have brought dishonor on their family. In some instances they are banished. But in other cases they are murdered. In Pakistan, which appears to have the world's largest number of honor killings, a substantial portion of them are committed by Pashtun tribal communities, some 40 million people living on both sides of the Pakistani–Afghan border. In both countries, civil and religious courts treat these crimes very differently than other homicides. Perpetrators generally receive a much lighter sentence or quite frequently go unpunished. Indeed, of the thousand or more honor killings committed in Pakistan every year, only about 10 percent ever go to trial. At the same time, hundreds of Indian and Pakistani woman are set on fire and then reported as the victims of accidental kitchen fires.

Many women are murdered by their families for rejecting an arranged marriage or for seeking a divorce. Even more shockingly, husbands, fathers, or brothers sometimes punish, or even execute, a woman who has been raped because she (the victim) has brought dishonor on her family. In other cases, relatives have killed women merely because they are suspected of having an unacceptable relationship with a man. In one documented case in a Pakistani village, two brothers killed a man who had disobeyed their orders not to walk past their house to talk with their sister. Then they murdered the sister. As one human rights worker told Amnesty International, "the distinction between a woman being guilty and a woman being *alleged* to be guilty of illicit sex is irrelevant. What impacts on the man's honor is the public perception, the belief in her infidelity. It is this which blackens honor and for which she is killed.… It is not the truth that honor … is about, but [rather] public perception of honor."[30] With accurate statistics hard to come by, estimates by experts in this area place the annual number of honor killings worldwide anywhere between 5,000 and 20,000. But these generally receive little media attention at home or abroad. Nor are they an issue easily addressed by international actors, be they foreign governments or NGOs. Still, local and international NGOs have often helped victims and focused attention on the most grievous examples. In some cases international pressure has forced some changes, as when Pakistan shifted jurisdiction for honor killings from religious to civil courts. But substantial improvement will only come when traditional values begin to change.

INTERNATIONAL TERRORISM

The use of terrorism as a political tactic is not new. During the nineteenth century, for example, anarchist revolutionaries in Russia, Italy, Spain, and other parts of Europe perpetrated bombings and assassinations designed to destroy organized government and capitalism. But the September 11, 2001, attacks on the World Trade Center and the Pentagon brought death and destruction to the heart of American society on a scale never previously experienced. Suddenly, in spite of its vast military and economic power, the United States seemed vulnerable.

Although 9/11 was the most horrendous attack of its kind, it was not the first terrorist action against the United States and other Western nations by Islamic fundamentalist groups. Al-Qaeda or similar groups had previously bombed U.S. military housing in Saudi Arabia (1996), American embassies in Kenya and Tanzania (1998), and the naval ship USS Cole off the coast of Aden (2000). Since the September 11 assault on the World Trade Center and the Pentagon, some of the bloodiest terrorist attacks have included a bombing that killed 202 people (mostly foreign tourists) in a Bali, Indonesia, night club (2002); a series of bombs on several Madrid commuter trains, which killed nearly 200 commuters and wounded over 1,700 people (2004); and bombs on three London underground trains and a transit bus, which killed over 50 passengers and wounded some 700 more (2005). More recently, terrorist attacks have killed thousands of Iraqi and Afghan civilians in their respective civil wars.[31] But Islamic extremists have no monopoly on terrorism. As we have seen, terrorist activity in Europe, Latin America, and Asia predates today's Islamists. And even in recent decades there have been many deadly non-Islamic terrorist groups, including the Irish Republican Army (IRA) in Northern Ireland and England, Tamil extremists in Sri Lanka, and paramilitary armies in Colombia.

Yet despite its frequency, there is still no broad consensus on what constitutes terrorist activity. Some analysts have questioned why only violence perpetrated by nongovernmental actors is considered terrorism. Why, they ask, are Palestinian suicide bombings and the Bali assault called terrorist acts whereas Russia's purposeful bombing of Chechen civilians, Israel's retaliations against Palestinian civilians, and the Guatemalan army's massacre of more than 100,000 Indian villagers are not similarly labeled? Another debate pits those who support the causes of alleged terrorists against those who oppose them. As more than one observer has noted, "Your terrorist is my freedom fighter." Many Catholic Irish Americans took that position when they contributed substantial funds to the IRA, whose gunmen were seen as heroes by some and terrorists by others.

The U.S. Department of Defense defines terrorism as, "The calculated use of violence or the threat of violence to inculcate fear; intended to coerce or to intimidate governments or societies in the pursuit of goals that are generally political, religious, or ideological."[32] For our purposes, we will further define a terrorist act as an act of violence carried out by nongovernmental actors against civilians or against soldiers who are not engaged in war. This does not mean that intentional slaughters of civilians by the military (as in Chechnya, Guatemala, and Bosnia) are any less immoral or reprehensible than bombings by terrorists. It is simply that those atrocities fall in a separate category, sometimes labeled "state terrorism." Ironically, economic and cultural globalization in recent decades has unwittingly contributed to the surge in international terrorism. The spread of capitalism, Western values, and Western culture—including democracy, McDonald's, and R-rated Hollywood movies, among many other things—has led many in the Third World, most notably Islamic fundamentalists, to believe that they are being engulfed and spiritually polluted by Westernization. Living in societies that have little military power and limited international influence, some of them see terrorism as their only means of defending themselves and preserving their religious and ideological values.

So, precisely at a time when wars between nations have become less common and war between major military powers is almost unimaginable, terror has become perhaps the leading cause of anxiety in international relations. Because terrorist groups such as al-Qaeda operate in the shadows and cannot be targeted as easily as a nation-state and because their behavior is so hard to predict, they evoke intense fear.

Another feature of terrorist organizations is their capacity to create carnage and chaos with very limited resources. The only weapons held by the men who killed some 3,000 people on September 11, 2001, were box cutters. Thus, even with al-Qaeda currently weakened, the terrorist threat is not likely to go away for many years to come.

Conclusion: The Changing Face of International Relations

Political trends are hard to predict, especially in the area of international relations, where so many uncontrolled forces are at play. Few analysts or policy makers anticipated the end of the Cold War only five or six years before it happened. Before the September 11 terrorist attacks not many experts could have predicted the magnitude of that attack or how it would change the nature of domestic and international politics. The firestorm of prodemocracy protests that swept across the Arab world this past year surprised scholars of that region. Today, as U.S. and NATO forces face an uncertain future in Iraq and Afghanistan, as scientists still warn of possible worldwide pandemics killing millions of people, and as others debate the dangers of global warming, we do not know what other major developments will unfold in the next five to ten years.

However, some issues seem likely to endure. While there may be little likelihood of a new arms race between world powers, nuclear proliferation will remain an ongoing danger in Iran, North Korea, and elsewhere. Should most of the democratic gains made since the 1970s in the developing world and Central Europe consolidate, it would bode well for the prospects of world peace. Until now, at least, democratic nations have never waged war against one another (or virtually never, depending on how each scholar defines democracies).[33]

Small wars will continue to rage in the Third World. Some conflicts—such as Middle East hostilities and ethnic violence in Africa—seem more intractable than even pessimists had imagined. The Russian conflict with Georgia indicates that some East–West tensions remain and are likely to flare up periodically. But competition among the world's major powers seems likely to be primarily economic rather than military or ideological. That conflict will pit the United States against Japan, China, and the EU, with rapidly industrialized countries such as India, South Korea, Taiwan, and Brazil likely to play increasingly important roles. Third World poverty, protecting the environment, ethnic conflict, and human rights are likely to demand increasing attention. Solving these problems will be extremely difficult and may require new levels of international cooperation.

◆ ◆ ◆

Key Terms and Concepts _____

Cold War	nongovernmental organizations (NGOs)
debt crisis	multinational corporations (MNCs)
European Union (EU)	new world order (NWO)
free trade	newly industrialized countries (NICs)
globalization	North Atlantic Treaty Organization (NATO)
Green Party	North–South relations
honor killings	nuclear proliferation

DISCUSSION QUESTIONS

1. *Since the end of the Cold War, how has the prospect of nuclear war decreased in some respects, and how has that prospect increased in other ways?*
2. *In what ways has protection of the environment become an international issue? Why must solutions to some environmental problems transcend national boundaries?*
3. *What are the principal arguments in favor of substantial external debt cancellations for the poorest developing nations? What are the major arguments against cancellation?*
4. *Discuss how international efforts to protect human rights (including prosecution of leaders who violate those rights) may come into conflict with the doctrine of national sovereignty. In what ways has the international community begun to change the balance between human rights principles and principles of national sovereignty?*
5. *In what ways are Third World women particularly victimized by human rights abuses and, therefore, in need of special protection?*
6. *What progress, if any, has there been in talks with Iran and North Korea aimed at getting them to halt their apparent nuclear weapons programs? Why are their programs of particular concern?*

Notes _____

1. For a picture of how each nation saw the world during the Cold War, see Walter S. Jones, *The Logic of International Relations* (New York: Harper Collins, 1991).
2. Urie Bronfenbrenner, "The Mirror Image in Soviet-American Relations," in *Analyzing International Relations*, eds. William Coplin and Charles Kegley, Jr. (New York: Praeger, 1975), pp. 161–166.
3. The concept of containment was first developed by diplomat George Kennan, writing under a pseudonym. See "X," "The Sources of Soviet Conduct," *Foreign Affairs* (July 1947): 566–582. Later, Kennan charged that foreign policy makers had misinterpreted his arguments.

4. James Schlesinger, "New Instabilities, New Priorities," *Foreign Policy* (Winter 1991–1992): 4.

5. Jo Adjentuni, "Forty-eight Women Raped Every Hour in Congo, Study Finds," *The Guardian* (May 2011), www.guardian.co.uk.

6. James Lee Ray, *Global Politics* (Boston: Houghton Mifflin, 1990), p. 375; see also Marshall Shulman, "The Superpowers: Dance of the Dinosaurs," *Foreign Affairs* (Winter 1987–1988).

7. Wikipedia, "Nuclear Non-Proliferation Treaty," retrieved on August 39, 2005, from http://en.wikipedia.org/wiki/Nuclear_Non-Proliferation_Treaty. South Africa is the only country to have produced a nuclear weapon and then destroy it and close its program.

8. Quoted in Greg Bruno, "Backgrounder: Iran's Nuclear Program," *Council on Foreign Relations* Web site (July 17, 2008), www.cfr.org/bios/13554/greg_bruno.html?groupby=0&hide=1&id=13554&filter=397.

9. John T. Rourke, *International Politics on the World Stage* (New York: McGraw-Hill-Dushkin, 2002), p. 42. Rourke cites a figure of one billion, and the numbers have obviously grown since 2002.

10. James Barber, *Jihad vs. McWorld: How Globalism and Tribalism are Reshaping the World* (New York: Ballantine, 1996), p. 4.

11. United Nations Department of Economic and Social Affairs, *Report on International Trade 2011*.

12. Jack Finlayson and Mark Zacher, "The GATT and the Regulation of Trade Barriers: Regime Dynamics and Functions," *International Organization* (Autumn 1981): 561–602.

13. World Trade Organization website, available at www.wto.org; Uri Dadush and Julia Nielson, "Governing Global Trade," *Finance and Development (IMF)* 44, no. 4 (December 2007), www.imf.org/external/pubs/ft/fandd/2007/12/dadush.htm.

14. Gary Gereffi, "Rethinking Development Theory: Insights from East Asia and Latin America," *Sociological Forum* (Fall 1989).

15. Geoffrey Garrett, R. Daniel Kelemen, and Heiner Schultz, "The European Court of Justice, National Governments, and Legal Integration in the European Union," *International Organization* 52(1998): 149–176.

16. Robert Pastor, *Integration with Mexico* (New York: Twentieth Century Fund Press, 1993), pp. 14–15, 42–50.

17. For a summary of the debt crisis and its consequences see Howard Handelman, "Consequences of Economic Austerity: Latin America and the Less Developed World," *Britannica Book of the Year: 1990* (Chicago: Encyclopaedia Britannica, 1990), pp. 192–193.

18. World Bank data; World Bank, *Global Development Finance*: Volume 2, Summary Debt Data, www.undp.org/publications/annualreport2008/downloads.shtml.

19. United Nations Development Program, *Human Development Report 1999* (New York: UNDP and Oxford University Press, 1999), pp. 136–137.

20. Nikoi Kote-Nikoi, *Beyond the New Orthodoxy* (Brookfield, VT: Avebury, 1996), p. 15.

21. Bill Turnbull, "The African Debt Situation," available at www.thewhitefathers.org.uk/302dt.html.

22. "Can Africa Get Out of Debt?" *Time Europe* (October 3, 2004), www.time.com/time/magazine/article/0,9171,708965,00.html; "Debt Forgiveness Gathers Steam," *Christian Science Monitor* (September 30, 2004).

23. World Bank, *Global Development Finance 2011: External Debt of Developing Countries*, http://issuu.com/world.bank.publications/docs/9780821386736.

24. "Women, Population and the Environment," in *Great Decisions: 1991* (New York: Foreign Policy Association, 1991), p. 65.

25. International Energy Agency, *World Energy Outlook 2002*. www.iea.org/textbase/nppdf/free/2000/weo2002.pdf.

26. Alan Lamborn and Joseph Lepgold, *World Politics in the Twentieth Century* (Upper Saddle River, NJ: Prentice Hall, 2003), p. 418.

27. Charles Beitz, *Political Theory and International Relations* (Princeton, NJ: Princeton University Press, 1979), p. 71; quoted in Ray, *Global Politics*, p. 497.

28. Bruce Broomhall, *International Justice and the International Criminal Court: Between Sovereignty and the Rule of Law* (New York: Oxford University Press, 2004).

29. "Sex trade's reliance on forced labour," BBC News (May 12, 2005), http://news.bbc.co.uk/2/hi/business/4532617.stm: Jan Jindy Pettman, "Gender Issues," in *The Globalization of World Politics*, 3rd ed., eds. Jon Baylis and Steve Smith (New York: Oxford University Press, 2005), p. 678; "Sex Slavery: The Growing Trade," CNN archive website (March 8, 2001), http://archives.cnn.com/2001/WORLD/europe/03/08/women.trafficking/index.html.

30. "Pakistan: Cost of a Lie," in *Le Monde Diplomatique*, English version (May 2001), http://mondediplo.com/2001/05/13pakistan.

31. However, more Iraqis currently die from sectarian violence (Shi'a versus Sunni) than from terrorist bombings.

32. Available at http://terrorism.about.com/od/whatisterrorisi/ss/DefineTerrorism_4.htm.

33. Jack S. Levy, "Domestic Politics and War," *Journal of Interdisciplinary History* 18, no. 4 (Spring 1988): 653–673. Some scholars challenge these findings.

GLOSSARY

Absolutism The concentration of tremendous political power in a single source, such as an absolute monarch. (Ch. 12)

Adversarial Democracy The kind of democratic politics created by the use of a single-member district electoral system. Since the winning party receives all of the representation from each district, there is usually no need to form a coalition with minority parties. *See also* Consensual Democracy. (Ch. 4)

Adversarial System A legal system in which an independent judge (sometimes with a jury) hears arguments presented by two opposing sides before rendering a decision. (Ch. 9)

Agents of Political Socialization Individuals, groups, and institutions—such as the family, schools, churches, or labor unions—that transmit political values to each generation. (Ch. 3)

Allocation of Resources The distribution of a society's wealth among its members. Resources may be allocated authoritatively, by government action, or by the workings of a free market system. (Ch. 1)

Alternative Vote (AV) This system retains the single-member district system now used to elect members of the British House of Commons and the U.S. House of Representatives. However, rather than simply selecting their preferred candidate, voters are also asked to rank all the other candidates from most to least preferred. In districts in which no candidate secures a majority of the votes cast (over half the votes), the candidate with the most votes (a plurality) does not automatically or necessarily win. Instead, the lowest candidate is eliminated and his/her votes are reassigned to the persons ranked next highest on those ballots. AV is also known as "Instant Runoff Voting." (Ch. 11)

Anarchism The opposition to government in all forms. The advocates of this ideology believe that government is unnecessary and inevitably harmful and divisive, and that people would coexist peacefully without it. (Ch. 2)

Appellate Courts Courts that hear appeals from decisions made by trial courts. Normally, appellate courts do not hear new evidence, but instead respond to claims that a trial court misinterpreted the law or made a procedural error. (Ch. 9)

Arab Spring The 2011 upsurge of democratic protest movements, some of which toppled long-term dictatorships (in Tunisia, Egypt, and Libya). Pro-democracy protests continue in Syria and Yemen. (Chs. 3, 14)

Aristocracy The most prestigious echelon of a stratified society. In Great Britain, aristocratic families have a royal title, often dating back to centuries. (Ch. 11)

Articles of Confederation The basic agreement among the former British colonies in America ("states") that governed the relations among them and the powers of the national congress until the Constitution was ratified in 1789. (Ch. 10)

Authoritarian Systems Non-democratic (dictatorial) government that exercises extensive control or authority over society. (Chs. 1, 5, 12, 13)

Balance of Power The relative levels of military strength among potential adversaries. Many "realist" theorists of international relations feel that the balance of power is the most important factor in explaining the outbreak of war. (Ch. 16)

Basic Law A body of law that supersedes other laws; for example, the U.S. Constitution is basic law in that statutes that contradict it are invalid. (Ch. 9)

Behavioralism An approach to political research that emphasizes observation of individual political behavior, as contrasted with approaches that focus on political documents and laws. (Ch. 1)

Bicameralism The division of the legislature into two chambers, or "houses." (Chs. 7, 10)

Bolsheviks The Marxist faction in the Russian Revolution headed by Vladimir Lenin. The Bolsheviks evolved into the Soviet Communist Party. (Ch. 12)

Budget Formulation The process of forming a proposal for a government's budget, including plans for both revenues and expenditures. (Ch. 8)

Bureaucracy The government organizations, usually staffed with officials selected on the basis of expertise and experience, that implement (and sometimes make) public policy. (Ch. 8)

Bureaucrat A person working for the public sector who is appointed on the basis of training and experience; usually applied to an official with a specified realm of authority. (Ch. 8)

Caciques Mexico's regional political bosses or strongmen. (Ch. 15)

Cadre In China, the term means a public official holding a full time, responsible position in the Communist Party or the government. (Ch. 13)

Candidate Evaluation The personal appeal of an electoral candidate. Candidate evaluation may be positive or negative, and where it is a strong factor, it may exert greater influence on vote choices than party identification or voters' opinions about issues. (Ch. 4)

Capitalism An ideology advocating private property and minimal government. Also, the third stage of "prehistory" in Marxist ideology; in this stage, ownership of capital becomes the basis for political power and industrial workers are exploited by those who own factories. (Ch. 2)

Central Committee In countries ruled by the Communist Party—including China and the Soviet Union—the Party's Central Committee is officially its governing body between Party congresses (i.e., most of the time). In actuality the Committee takes its lead from the Party's Politburo. (Chs. 12, 13)

Charismatic Authority The ability to evoke allegiance and loyalty from citizens or subordinates by virtue of image, speaking skills, and the generation of emotional responses. (Ch. 8)

Checks and Balances The principle, associated most prominently with U.S. government, holding that arbitrary, irresponsible government power is best prevented by establishing a system in which each part of the government can check the actions of the others. (Ch. 10)

Chief Administrator An individual who manages and coordinates the implementation of programs through administrative agencies; one of the primary roles of modern chief executives. (Ch. 8)

Christian Democrats Political parties and their supporters who profess a political doctrine usually linked to the Catholic Church. Important in Latin America and Europe, these parties range from right of center to left of center ideologically. (Ch. 5)

Citizen Participation The practice of involving citizens in the bureaucratic decision-making process. (Ch. 8)

Civil Law The body of law pertaining to efforts by private parties to gain compensation for injuries inflicted by other private parties; for example, one person suing another for damages arising from libelous statements is a civil law matter. (Ch. 9)

Civil Society The network of groups such as labor unions, business associations, church groups, and the like that can influence the political system but are independent of government control. (Ch. 12)

Class Consciousness A Marxist term used to describe a given socioeconomic class's awareness of its common self-interest. A socioeconomic class, most particularly the working class, needs class consciousness if it is to act cohesively to pursue its interests. (Chs. 2, 12)

Classical Political Philosophy A body of political philosophy based on the ideas of Plato (427–347 BCE) and his student Aristotle (384–322 BCE), associated with a distrust of democracy and efforts to envision the just state. (Ch. 1)

Coalition Government A government formed, usually when no single party has a majority in Parliament, from a coalition of parties. In countries such as India and Israel, where frequently no single party wins a majority in Parliament, national elections are followed by negotiations between possible coalition partners since the prime minister must have the backing of a parliamentary majority. (Chs. 5, 11)

Coercive Authority The authority that a leader enjoys by virtue of possessing the power to force compliance with his or her demands. (Ch. 8)

Cold War The period of tensions and confrontation between the world's major military powers, the United States and the Soviet Union, lasting from the mid-1940s until the collapse of the Soviet Union. (Ch. 17)

Collective Agriculture (Collectivization of Agriculture) Farming on land that is allegedly collectively controlled by the families living on it. The governments of communist nations such as China and the Soviet Union induced or forced family farms to merge into these cooperatives. While the people on the collectives supposedly ran and owned the collective; in fact, they actually were controlled by the government. (Chs. 12, 13)

Collectives A term used in China to describe cooperatively owned factories and other enterprises. These are neither state-owned nor private enterprises. (Ch. 13)

Command Economy A highly centralized, communist economy in which key decisions on production, employment, and the like are made by a powerful state and party bureaucracy. (Ch. 12)

Committee System The way in which committees are empowered in a legislature. Committees in some systems are quite powerful, independently determining which bill becomes law, whereas in other systems committees normally have little influence. (Ch. 7)

Common Law A set of principles first developed centuries ago by British courts in efforts to establish a basic code of fairness for situations in which no statutory law applied. (Ch. 9)

Communes Highly collectivized agricultural units that were introduced to China in the late 1950s and subsequent decades. Because the commune system involved enormous state intrusion in their lives, the peasantry generally resented them. (Ch. 13)

Communism The stage in Marxist ideology in which "true" human history begins; in this stage, technological development has advanced to the point at which scarcity of resources no longer exists, and there is no class conflict or exploitation. (**Ch. 2**)

Comparative Advantage In international political economy, the idea that virtually all countries have an advantage over most other nations with respect to how efficiently they can manufacture or provide some good or service. When international trade is not restricted, a given good or service will be produced in those countries that have a comparative advantage in producing it. (**Ch. 16**)

Conflictual and Consensual Political Cultures In consensual political cultures, citizens tend to agree on basic political procedures as well as the values and general goals of the political system. Conversely, conflictual political cultures are highly polarized by fundamental differences over those issues. (**Ch. 3**)

Connecticut Compromise The decision made, in drafting the U.S. Constitution, to divide the legislative power into two chambers, with the upper chamber designed so that each state would have two members in it regardless of population. Smaller states had been reluctant to support the Constitution if all legislative power were to be placed in a single chamber with districts allotted to states on the basis of population. (**Ch. 10**)

Consensual Democracy The kind of democratic politics created by the use of proportional representation electoral systems. Since a party does not have to win a majority of the votes in any state or district to gain parliamentary representation, this arrangement is said to force several parties to form an inclusive coalition and to govern in a more consensual manner. *See also* Adversarial Democracy. (**Ch. 4**)

Conservatism An approach to political life that sees traditional values as important in solving social problems. Edmund Burke (1729–1797) produced a landmark statement of conservatism in his criticism of the French Revolution, arguing that it destroyed aristocratic and religious traditions and would destabilize and coarsen French society. (**Ch. 2**)

Constituent Service Activities by legislators to obtain information, favors, and exceptions to regulations for their constituents, normally by making requests of administrative officials. (**Ch. 7**)

(The) Core *See* Dependency Theory

Corporatism A political system in which citizens are represented in government by major interest groups. In its most advanced form, it involves the organization of the population into officially sanctioned interest groups based on occupational or other socioeconomic lines. (**Ch. 15**)

Council Housing Public housing built for the poor by the local government council. (**Ch. 11**)

Coup d'État (or **Coup**). An irregular, unconstitutional removal of a head of state by a small group. A rapid takeover of the government, usually by the military (**Chs. 8, 14**)

Criminal Law The body of law pertaining to the prosecution and punishment of those accused of crimes. (**Ch. 9**)

Cult of Personality An effort, commonly encountered in totalitarian political systems, such as Stalin's Soviet Russia or Nazi Germany, to glorify a political leader and develop a cult following behind him. Cults of personality developed around Joseph Stalin, Mao Zedong and Hitler, for example. (**Ch. 12**)

Cultural Revolution Mao Zedong's effort (1966–1976) to revitalize China's revolutionary spirit and to cleanse the nation of real or alleged antirevolutionary cultural aspects. It involved a reign of terror in which hundreds of thousands, perhaps millions, were killed. (**Ch. 13**)

Debt Crisis The severe economic downturn suffered in the 1980s by nations in Latin America and Africa, arising from their inability to repay outstanding international debts. (**Chs. 15, 17**)

Declaration of Independence The formal statement, written primarily by Thomas Jefferson and adopted by the Second Continental Congress on July 4, 1776, that the 13 American colonies were independent of British control. (**Ch. 10**)

Defendant The person accused of a crime or sued by a plaintiff in a civil action. (**Ch. 9**)

Delegate Model An approach to representation in which the representative acts in accordance with the expressed preferences of the constituency that elected him or her. (**Ch. 7**)

Democracy A system of government in which government is ultimately accountable to the citizens. Although democracy literally means "government by the people," in practice it normally means that the people can select and remove those that govern them. (**Ch. 1**)

Democratic Peace The idea that something about the nature of democratic government makes it very unlikely that democratic states will go to war with other democracies. (**Ch. 16**)

Dependency Theory A theory once supported by many scholars that suggested that the Third World's underprivileged position was attributable to the control that powerful capitalist nations held over them. Dependency involves a measure of economic and political control by developed nations (the core) over the less developed ones (the periphery). (**Ch. 14**)

Diplomacy The communications and negotiations among national leaders regarding matters of foreign policy. (Ch. 8)

Disadvantage Theory The idea that the organized interests that use litigation as a strategy of influence do so because they are disadvantaged relative to other interests when trying to influence legislative and executive institutions. The classic example used to illustrate disadvantage theory was the successful effort of the groups working in the U.S. to stop racial segregation in public schools: facing virtually no chance of changing policy by lobbying state legislatures, these groups brought suit in federal court to change policy. (Ch. 6)

Drug Cartels Extensive drug-trafficking organizations that usually control a defined area of the country and violently defend it against competitors. The most widely known cartels are located in Mexico and Colombia. (Ch. 15)

Dual Democratic Legitimacy A characteristic of presidential systems; the fact that the chief executive and the legislature are separately elected means that both institutions can claim to represent the people, and when these institutions disagree over policy, gridlock can ensue. In parliamentary systems, only the Parliament can claim definitive democratic legitimacy, and the chief executive (prime minister) is elected from that body. (Ch. 7)

Dual Transition A simultaneous transition from a command economy to a free market and from a communist political system to democracy. (Ch. 12)

Economic Austerity A set of government economic policies, often imposed as the result of pressure from the international financial community, designed to reduce inflation, trade deficits, and budget deficits, and to facilitate repayment of the country's external debt. Such policies, at least in the short run, generally lead to reduced living standards, especially for the poor. At the same time, they may be necessary to restore a nation's economic health. Hence, the precise form that they take is subject to heated debate. (Ch. 15)

Economic Determinism The idea that economic forces govern changes in the nature of societies; largely, but not exclusively, associated with Marxism. (Ch. 2)

Economic Internationalism (Liberalism) An approach to international political economy that emphasizes the benefits of free trade among nations. It is associated with classical liberal economics; often termed "liberalism" in this context. (Ch. 16)

Economic Nationalism An approach to international political economy that focuses on the importance of national interest and national power, holding these to be more important than the economic efficiency gains that may be obtained through free trade. *See also* Mercantilism. (Ch. 16)

Economic Structuralism An approach to international political economy associated with Marxist-Leninist thinking; it emphasizes the persistent economic inequalities separating poor and rich countries, and focuses on how state economic systems produce a structure of dependency and inequality. (Ch. 16)

Electoral Democracy A political system that features competitive (free and fair) government elections but may not respect fundamental civil liberties. *See also* Liberal Democracy. (Ch. 14)

Elite Theory The idea that a single, generally unified, elite dominates society; typically contrasted with pluralism. (Ch. 6)

Emergency Leadership The effort by a chief executive to initiate, coordinate, and energize governmental activities in time of crisis. (Ch. 8)

Environmentalism An ideology holding that the issues pertaining to the state of the physical environment, and policies directed toward it, are of primary importance. The most intense advocates of this ideology argue that environmental problems sometimes supersede other issues, such as economic development, poverty, and international relations. (Ch. 2)

Ethnicity A type of group identification in which individuals identify with people like themselves (and set themselves apart from other people) on the basis of race, religion, culture, language, nationality, and the like. Examples of ethnicities in the United States include Irish-Americans, Afro-Americans, Catholics, Italian-Americans, Jews, and Gypsies. (Ch. 14)

European Union (EU) The Western European trade and economic organization that binds together 27 of the region's nations. It is the successor to the European Community (EC) but involves a more intensive and geographically extensive union. (Chs. 11, 17)

Evolutionary Change A process of gradual, interrelated change, as distinguished from more rapid, and often disruptive, revolutionary change. (Ch. 11)

Expert Faction That faction of Chinese Communist Party leadership in the 1960s and 1970s that favored assigning management positions to trained experts even when they were not the most ideologically "correct" citizens. (Ch. 13)

Extended Republic The idea, associated with James Madison, that political disputes would be less violent and destabilizing if the political system were extended to comprise all the states (rather than continuing to resolve most political disputes independently in each of the states). (Ch. 10)

Failed State A country whose government is unable to carry out even its most fundamental functions such as maintaining law and order or enforcing basic health standards. (**Ch. 14**)

Falun Gong A Chinese spiritual sect stressing meditation and exercises. The government has repressed the movement, with hundreds of members allegedly dying while in police custody. (**Ch. 13**)

Fascism An ideology that emphasizes extreme appeals to national unity, hatred of foreigners and ethnic minorities, and complete obedience to the state. (**Ch. 2**)

Feminism An ideology that advocates equal rights for females. Some versions of feminism also identify specific feminine traits, such as compassion and sharing, that proponents claim will improve society as women achieve more leadership positions. (**Ch. 2**)

Feudalism The second stage of "prehistory" in Marxist ideology; in this stage, land ownership becomes the basis for political power and farm workers are exploited by those who own the land. (**Ch. 2**)

Fixed Jurisdictions The bureaucratic principle holding that agency officials should have clearly established areas of activity or specialization, making it possible to determine who is responsible for any given decision or program. (**Ch. 8**)

Folkways The norms and traditions observed in a legislature pertaining to the way members treat one another and expect to be treated. (**Ch. 7**)

Formal-Legal Analysis An approach to political science that emphasizes the study of laws, constitutions, and official institutions. (**Ch. 1**)

Free-Rider An individual who enjoys the benefits of a collective effort without contributing to it. (**Ch. 6**)

Free Trade A trade system in which the export and import of goods and services internationally is relatively unimpeded by tariffs, quotas, or other government-created barriers. (**Chs. 16, 17**)

FSB The Federal Security Service of the Russian Federation. The primary successor to the Soviet KGB, the FSB is primarily concerned with internal security operations. Its first director was Vladimir Putin, who then moved on to be Prime Minister, then President, and then Prime Minister again. While not as feared or repressive as the KGB, it may be a more powerful force in Russian politics than its predecessor was in Soviet politics. (**Ch. 12**)

Functionalism An approach to comparing and analyzing political systems. It begins with the idea that all healthy political systems must perform certain basic functions, although the institutions that perform them may be very different. (**Ch. 1**)

Gender Empowerment Measure (GEM) A statistical measure of how much gender equality or inequality exists in a country or set of countries in terms of economic and political power. (**Ch. 14**)

Gender Gap A significant difference between men as a group and women as a group with respect to some specific criterion, such as support for a given political party. (**Ch. 4**)

Gender Inequality Index (GII) An index of women's status in society that combines data on women's health, educational and political advancement, and performance in the labor market. It includes measures of female educational achievement; the proportion of women in the parliament and in the general workforce; the maternal mortality rate; and the teenage pregnancy rate. (**Ch. 14**)

Generation Y The generation of young people who were born in the last two decades of the twentieth century (in the United States and other affluent democracies) and have or will come of age politically in the early decades of the twenty-first century. (**Ch. 3**)

Gini Index (Gini Coefficient) In order to compare how equally or unequally income is distributed in different nations, economists periodically use individual income data to construct a Gini coefficient (or index) for each country. The highest index number a country can have is 100, meaning all of that country's income goes to one person (perfect inequality). The lowest index number a nation can achieve is 0.0, meaning every person has the same income (perfect equality). Of course, no country in the world has a score at either of these extremes. (**Ch. 14**)

Glasnost The opening up of Soviet politics under Mikhail Gorbachev's government. *Glasnost* allowed greater media freedom and freedom of speech in an attempt to remedy the faults of Soviet communism through more honest discussion. (**Ch. 12**)

Globalization The spread of economic activity, political interactions, mass culture, and ideas across national borders, often in de facto defiance of national sovereignty. (**Chs. 14, 17**)

Glorious Revolution The removal of King James II by the British Parliament in 1688, firmly establishing parliamentary dominance over the monarch at a time when royalty elsewhere in Europe still based their authority on divine right. (**Ch. 11**)

Government The people or organizations that make, enforce, and implement political decisions for a society. (**Ch. 1**)

Government Functions The basic tasks that governments perform in healthy, developed political systems. *See also* Functionalism. (**Ch. 1**)

Grand Jury A group of citizens who determine whether there is sufficient evidence to charge (or indict) a person or persons with a crime. **(Ch. 9)**

Great Leap Forward China's ultimately disastrous effort (1958–1961) to rapidly accelerate industrial and agricultural production through the use of mass mobilization and other radical techniques. **(Ch. 13)**

Green Party A party with a platform primarily devoted to protecting the environment. Taking a strong stand on ecological issues such as global warming and pollution, these parties have been most successful in Western Europe but exist in other regions as well. **(Ch. 17)**

Gulag The extensive network of prison camps to which millions of Soviet citizens were sent under Stalin. **(Ch. 12)**

Hierarchical Political or social system in which people have clearly understood ranks, from a governing elite down to the lowest ranks of society. **(Ch. 5)**

Hierarchy The bureaucratic principle holding that clear lines of super- and subordinate status should exist in organizations. **(Ch. 8)**

Homogeneous Societies Societies that lack sharp class, racial, regional, or ethnic divisions. **(Ch. 11)**

Honor Killings Murders committed by male family members against female relatives who have allegedly dishonored the family. The women are accused of committing adultery, engaging in extramarital sex, marrying someone who is unacceptable to her family, rejecting an arranged marriage, or even being the victim of rape. As many as 7,000 women are murdered annually in honor killings, mostly in the developing world. Many of them had not even committed the "sins" of which they are accused. **(Ch. 17)**

Human Development Index (HDI) A composite measure of life expectancy, school enrollment, literacy rate, and per capita income used to evaluate living standards. **(Ch. 14)**

Human Rights The principle that all people, regardless of their culture, their level of economic development, or the type of political system in which they live, are entitled to certain fundamental freedoms and privileges. **(Ch. 1)**

Human Rights Act Legislation passed by Parliament in 1998 that gave Britain its first written Bill of Rights drawn from the European Union's Convention on Human Rights. **(Ch. 11)**

Hung Parliament A parliamentary election result in which more than two parties win seats in the legislature and none of them has gained a parliamentary majority. This commonly happens in parliamentary elections using proportional representation. **(Ch. 11)**

ICT *See* Information and Communications Technology. **(Ch. 3)**

Idealism An approach to international relations holding that wars are caused by evil and ignorance and that they can be avoided by nurturing a spirit of international community and justice. **(Ch. 16)**

Ideology A fairly coherent system of political thinking. A vision of society as it should be. **(Ch. 2)**

Income Inequality A measure of how the wealth of a society is shared among its members. A highly equal income distribution is one in which the difference in income between the poorest and the richest segments of the population is not great. *See also* Gini Index. **(Chs. 2, 4)**

Individualism A way of thinking that emphasizes individual interests, needs, and rights in contrast to social or communal interests, needs, and rights. **(Ch. 2)**

Industrial Democracies Highly industrialized and economically advanced countries with a democratic political system. **(Chs. 5, 11)**

Information and Communications Technology (ICT) The wide array of new, electronic information and communications innovations, including the Internet, podcasts, text messaging and the like. These are particularly important to young adults as sources of political information and opinion. **(Ch. 3)**

Inquisitorial System A system of criminal law in which the judge acts as a representative of the state, seeking information from the person or persons accused of a crime in an effort to determine guilt or innocence. **(Ch. 9)**

Institutional Coups Military takeovers carried out by the armed forces as a unified institution rather than a coup led by a single military strongman. Such coups tend to have some motivating ideology or plan of action. **(Ch. 14)**

Institutional Revolutionary Party (PRI) The party that ruled Mexico continuously from that party's formation in 1929 until 2000. **(Ch. 15)**

Interest Articulation The process of expressing concerns and problems as demands for governmental action. **(Ch. 1)**

Interest Group An organization that attempts to influence public policy in a specific area of importance to its members. **(Ch. 6)**

International Criminal Court (ICC) Established in 2002, the International Criminal Court draws its authority from a treaty (the "Rome Statute") ratified by 106 nations. The U.S., Russia, China, and Israel are not among the ratifying nations, however. The countries that ratified the ICC agreed to allow it to prosecute persons "accused of the most serious crimes of international concern, namely genocide, crimes against humanity and war crimes." (**Ch. 16**)

International Law The body of law consisting of treaties (both bilateral and general) and traditionally recognized rights and duties pertaining to the relations among states. (**Ch. 16**)

International Organization An organization whose members are individual nation-states. Such organizations may be general, dealing with a wide range of issues, or they may be designed to address only a single set of problems. (**Ch. 16**)

Iron Triangles The idea that interest groups, legislative committees, and bureaucratic agencies in a given policy area engage in continuing interaction, and that they act together to perpetuate policies and programs, resisting change and control. (**Ch 8**)

Islamic Fundamentalism An extremely devout movement within the Islamic religion whose members believe in a traditional and literal interpretation of the Quran, the Muslim holy book. They reject many aspects of modern life and reject such Western cultural influences as Hollywood movies, rock music, and "immodest dress" as corrupt threats to traditional, conservative Islamic values. Some fundamentalist Muslims support the use of violence to advance their cause; others do not. (**Chs. 2, 3, 14**)

Judicial Activism The principle holding that judges should follow their own values in deciding how to interpret statutes and provisions of basic law. (**Ch. 9**)

Judicial Restraint The principle holding that judges should be reluctant to overturn legislative or executive laws and decisions, doing so only when absolutely necessary. (**Ch. 9**)

Judicial Review The power of courts to overturn or void actions or laws that they feel are unlawful or inconsistent with basic law. (**Chs. 9, 10**)

Justice The quality of being righteous, fair, and deserved. (**Ch. 9**)

Just War The philosophical tradition that attempts to define the conditions under which war is just and those under which it is not. (**Ch. 16**)

KGB The Committee for State Security (KGB) was the last of a series of Soviet security agencies dating back to 1917 (the end of the Russian Revolution). It combined overseas espionage activities (like those of the American CIA), internal security operations, combating crime, maintaining internal security (like the FBI), and extensive spying on Soviet citizens. Its ruthless repression of real or suspected dissent made it greatly feared. It was dissolved in 1991 and replaced by Russia's FSB. (**Ch. 12**)

The Kremlin A historic fortified complex in Moscow, which has served as the seat of (and symbol of) national political power under both the Soviet Union and the Russian Federation. The term "the Kremlin" was used to mean the Soviet government and is now often used to represent the Russian government as well, just as "the White House" is used to mean the U.S. government. (**Ch. 12**)

Kuomintang (Guomindang) (KMT) The Chinese nationalist party that toppled the imperial government but, following a prolonged civil war, was overthrown nearly forty years later by the Chinese Communists. (**Ch. 13**)

Law of 1/n An idea, drawn from rational choice theory, predicting that legislatures with a larger number of legislators will spend more on public policies than legislatures with fewer legislators. A given legislator's constituents will only have to pay $1/n$ of the tax revenue for a given project (where "n" is the number of legislative districts), although they will receive the majority of the benefits from any policies or programs targeted for that district. Since all legislators face the same situation, they all have an incentive to favor decisions that are wasteful for the country as a whole, because they are still a net benefit to their constituents. The "law" suggests that this incentive is more potent in larger legislatures. (**Ch. 7**)

LDCs *See* Less Developed Countries.

Leadership Recruitment The process through which a political system attracts its leadership. In most countries, political parties play a critical role in this process. (**Ch. 5**)

Leftist (Left-Wing) Political Parties, Unions Political parties (and other groups and individuals) that support substantial reform of the existing political and economic systems. They often support active government involvement in the economy, which they believe will benefit the less fortunate members of society (the poor, the lower-middle class, racial minorities etc). Conversely, right-wing political parties tend to support the status quo and defend values such as the traditional family, religion, and patriotism.

Legal quotas are mandated by the government either in the constitution or through election laws. They are binding on all political parties and, in turn, include two subtypes. One subtype reserves a certain percentage of all parliamentary seats for women (i.e., only women may run for or be appointed to those seats). The second, more common, subtype does not assign specific seats to women, but rather mandates that a certain percentage of parliamentary candidates for each party must be women. (**Ch. 5**)

Legitimacy A government's or a state's basis for claiming authenticity, the right to rule. (**Ch. 14**)

Leninist (Party or Ideology) V. I. Lenin, the leader of the 1917 communist revolution in Russia, argued that in a revolutionary society, the Communist Party must have absolute power and that strict Party discipline within the Party must commit its members to support all the leadership's decisions. At least until 1989, all ruling Communist parties adhered to these principles, and even most Communist parties that were not in power enforced Leninist unity within the party itself. (**Chs. 5, 12, 13**)

Less-Developed Countries (LDCs) Countries in Africa, Asia, Latin America, and the Middle East that have less-developed economic and political systems including greater poverty and more conflictual politics. (**Ch. 14**)

Liberal Democracy A political system characterized by both free and fair elections (electoral democracy) *and* respect for civil liberties, including a free press (media), free speech, and freedom of religion. (**Chs. 12, 14**)

Liberalism (1) A political ideology stressing tolerance for diverse lifestyles and opinions and demanding public assistance for those in need. (2) An approach to international political economy holding that trade barriers are counterproductive and wasteful. Synonymous with "economic internationalism" in this context. (**Chs. 2, 16**)

Libertarianism An ideology advocating minimum government and maximum individual liberty. (**Ch. 2**)

Lobbying Efforts by groups or individuals to influence public officials through formal and informal contacts with them. (**Ch. 6**)

Long March The PLA's difficult 6,000-mile trek fleeing the KMT army in 1934–1935. Though they suffered enormous losses in the march, the Chinese Communists planted the seeds of their eventual victory by organizing villagers along the march's path. (**Ch. 13**)

Majority Rule A decision-making principle that holds that when individuals disagree about which alternative is best, the choice taken will be that which the larger number of individuals prefer. (**Ch. 1**)

Malapportionment A condition in which legislative districts are of very different sizes, making the vote of a citizen in a district with a large population effectively less influential than the vote of a citizen in a district with a small population. (In the United States, the Supreme Court required states to correct malapportionment in the 1962 *Baker v. Carr* decision.) (**Ch. 4**)

Marbury v. Madison The U.S. Supreme Court case from 1803 that, for the first time, held an act of Congress unconstitutional. Most historians believe that the opinion in this case established much of the power of the Supreme Court. (**Ch. 10**)

Marxism A comprehensive political and economic ideology based heavily on the writings of Karl Marx (1818–1883). It offers an explanatory theory of historical development and calls for class struggle (political struggle, either peaceful or violent) between the working class and the capitalists. Marxist thought is the basis of communist and radical socialist ideology. (**Ch. 2**)

Mass Parties Parties growing out of the working class movement, usually with a socialist orientation. (**Ch. 5**)

Mercantilism An approach to international political economy holding that states pursue their national interests in making international economic policies, especially those pertaining to trade. *See also* Economic Nationalism. (**Ch. 16**)

Mexican Economic Miracle The period of dramatic economic growth and industrialization from the 1940s until the 1982 debt crisis and the country's subsequent deep recession. (**Ch. 15**)

Missouri Plan An approach for selecting judges. Adopted by Missouri in 1940, the plan allows the governor to select judges from a list of candidates compiled by a nominating commission made up of legal experts and citizens. (**Ch. 9**)

Modernization Theory A popular academic theory that attributes a country's political and socioeconomic underdevelopment to the Third World's traditional cultural values and weak political and economic institutions. To modernize, the theory suggests, LDCs must borrow (and possibly adapt) Western values and institutions. Modern values are transmitted through urbanization, increased education and literacy, as well as through greater exposure to the mass media. (**Ch. 14**)

Modern Political Philosophy A body of political philosophy associated with Machiavelli (1469–1527), Hobbes (1588–1679), Locke (1632–1704), and others. In contrast to "classical" political philosophy, modern political philosophy places greater emphasis on individualism and on pragmatic concerns about how government works. (**Ch. 1**)

National Action Party (PAN) One of Mexico's major parties (along with the PRI and PRD), it now holds the presidency. It is a conservative, pro-Catholic party with close links to the business community. Its strong stance against government corruption and in favor of democratic reform helped it gain power. (**Ch. 15**)

Nationalize (Nationalization) The process whereby the government takes control of an economic enterprise, as when Great Britain nationalized the country's railroads and steel mills after World War II. (Ch. 11)

Natural Law A moral or ethical standard grounded in some concept of nature or divinity. (Ch. 9)

Neofascist Parties Political parties that support a modified, and usually toned down, form of fascism with an emphasis on supernationalism, ethnic prejudice, and, in Europe, a commitment to limiting or ending further immigration. (Ch. 5)

New Labour The title that Prime Minister Tony Blair and his supporters gave the Labour Party after it largely abandoned socialism and converted to a more centrist political ideology. (Ch. 11)

The New Left The recently organized, more moderate and pragmatic wing of the Mexico's PRD party. (Ch 15)

Newly Industrialized Country (NIC) Countries in East Asia and Latin America—including Taiwan, South Korea, Hong Kong, Mexico, and Brazil—that have expanded their industrial capacities dramatically in recent decades and have become important international economic actors. (Chs. 14, 17)

New World Order (NWO) A concept proposed by President George Bush following the end of the cold war and the Allied victory over Iraq in the 1991 Gulf War. As envisioned by its proponents, it would entail close cooperation among the world's major powers to deter future aggression and would maintain international stability based on the rule of law and collective security. The vision has largely faded since it was of little utility during the conflicts in Bosnia and Iraq. In the 21st century, America's European allies have often differed with Washington over many international issues, including the best way to combat terrorism, the invasion of Iraq, policies toward Iran, and global warming. (Ch. 17)

NICs *See* Newly Industrialized Country.

Nomenklatura The list of positions (some one million) within the Soviet Communist Party, the government bureaucracy, the military, state-owned business enterprises, labor unions, the media, cultural organizations, and professional groups for which appointment required party approval. The term more commonly referred to the hundreds of thousands who held important posts, constituting a tremendously powerful and privileged elite. (Ch. 12)

Nongovernmental Organizations (NGOs) Organizations that are active and often influential in areas such as education, health care, the environment, and promoting the needs of the poor, but have no formal links to government. They can be very influential in developing nations. (Chs. 16, 17)

No-Party Regimes Political systems in which there are no organized political parties, often because the government has banned them. (Ch. 5)

North Atlantic Treaty Organization (NATO) A defense community established by the United States and many of its Western European allies during the cold war. Its purpose was to defend Europe against a possible attack by the Soviet Union and its Eastern European allies in the Warsaw Pact. It has survived the end of the Cold War. (Ch. 17)

North–South Relations Economic and political relations between the more economically developed nations of the world (the North) and the developing nations of the South. (Ch. 17)

Nuclear Proliferation The spread of nuclear weapons or of the capacity to produce nuclear weapons to additional countries, most notably in the developing world. (Ch. 17)

Nuclear Terror The idea that the prospects of nuclear war are so horrible that leaders take steps to avoid it, even when their national interests would have led to war in the absence of nuclear weapons (Ch. 16)

Oligarchy The relatively small group of multi-millionaire or billionaire businessmen in Russia who often gained their wealth illicitly after the fall of communism and who now control most of the economy. Individually they are known as oligarchs, and collectively they are called the oligarchy. (Ch. 12)

Ombudsman A person who attempts (or an office that attempts) to resolve the problems that individual citizens have with administrative agencies and programs. (Ch. 7)

Open-Door Policy Deng Xiaoping's policy of opening up China to economic, trade, and cultural exchange with the West and, later, Japan, Hong Kong, and Taiwan. (Ch. 13)

PAN *See* National Action Party.

Parliament The entire British national legislature consisting of the elected House of Commons and the House of Lords (with inherited or appointed seats). In common usage, however, *Parliament* refers only to the far more influential House of Commons. (Ch. 11)

Parliamentary Supremacy The idea that the Parliament enjoys sovereign power, and that no court or executive can abrogate its decisions. (Ch. 9)

Parliamentary System A system of executive–legislative relations in which the legislature elects the chief executive. (Ch. 7)

Party Discipline The capacity of a party to have its legislative representatives vote as a unified bloc. (Ch. 5, 11)

Party Identification A citizen's sense of attachment to a political party. (Ch. 4)

Party of the Democratic Revolution (PRD) A coalition of Mexico's leftist, nationalist parties originally headed by Cuauhtémoc Cárdenas, the son of the legendary former president, Lázaro Cárdenas. In 1988, heading a predecessor coalition to the PRD, Cárdenas mounted a formidable challenge to the ruling PRI. In a symbolically important election, the PRD gained control of Mexico City in 1997, led by Cuauhtémoc Cárdenas, who became the first popularly elected mayor of the giant metropolis in more than 70 years. The PRD is one of Mexico's two major opposition parties (along with the PRI) that now control the Chamber of Deputies. It expresses the unhappiness felt by many of Mexico's poor over their country's severe economic setbacks in recent years. (Ch. 15)

Party Platform The set of policy orientations officially held by a political party. (Ch. 5)

Patronage The practice of selecting bureaucratic officials on the basis of their political support for the elected official with the power to appoint them; contrasted with appointment on the basis of neutral competence or expertise. (Ch. 8)

Patron-Client Relations Relations between a politically or economically powerful figure (the patron) and a less powerful individual, often a fairly dependent person such as a Third World peasant (the client). The patron (such as a local political party boss) gives the client services or goods that he or she needs (a job in the civil service, financial credit, or a welfare payment, for example) and, in return, the client agrees to vote for or even campaign for the patron's political party. (Ch. 5)

People's Liberation Army (PLA) China's Red army, which, under Mao Zedong's leadership, carried out the communist revolution. After the communists came to power, China's national armed forces continued to be called the PLA (Ch. 13)

Perestroika The restructuring of Soviet political and, especially, economic institutions introduced by Communist Party Secretary Mikhail Gorbachev. The goal was to make communism more humane and more efficient. (Ch. 12) This term is also used to designate a movement created by a group of contemporary political scientists who oppose what they see as the domination of the discipline by rational choice theory and quantification. (Ch. 1)

Personal Coups Coups led by a single military strongman, such as Somoza in Nicaragua, with little in the way of long-term goals other than increasing the power and wealth of the leader. (Ch. 14)

Personalistic Party A political party whose primary purpose is to further the political career of one person, the party leader. Sometimes the party is actually named or nicknamed after that leader, as, for example, the Peronist party in Argentina (nicknamed after its founding leader, Juan Perón). (Ch. 5)

PLA See People's Liberation Army.

Plaid Cymru A Welsh nationalist political party. (Ch. 11)

Plaintiff The person who brings a legal action against another person for damages in a civil suit; the "complaining party." (Ch. 9)

Pluralism The idea that there are many centers of political power in society (typically contrasted with elite theory or other views holding that a single class or group dominates society). Also, the condition of having many centers of power in a society. (Ch. 6)

Policy Initiation The first steps taken to make or change policy. Executives and administrators have increasingly taken over this function in industrial democracies. (Ch. 7)

Politburo The highest-ranking decision-making body of the now-defunct Soviet Communist Party. Its roughly 12 to 16 members represented the power elite of the party and made most key political and economic decisions until it was stripped of much of its power shortly before the fall of the Soviet Union. Other ruling communist parties (such as China, Vietnam, and Cuba) also had politburos at their helms. (Ch. 12)

Political Action Committees (PACs) Organizations established to gather and disburse campaign contributions to candidates in the United States. (Ch. 10)

Political Aggregation The process through which a political system reduces the multitude of conflicting societal demands to a manageable number of alternatives. Frequently this is done through programmatically oriented political parties. (Ch. 5)

Political Culture The pattern of individual attitudes and orientations toward politics among the members of a political system. (Ch. 3)

Political Development The idea that nations become modern by acquiring certain capacities and capabilities. The term is sometimes considered controversial because it implies that traditional (or "underdeveloped") nations will change along a known path to become similar to the Western industrial democracies. (Chs. 1, 14)

Political Economy The study of the impact of government on economic conditions, including analysis of alternative public policies and different systems of government. (**Ch. 1**)

Political Liberalization The process of loosening authoritarian controls over society and allowing a higher degree of political freedom. But it falls well short of a transition to democracy. (**Ch. 13**)

Political Party An organization that unites people in an effort to win government office and thereby influence or control government policies. (**Ch. 5**)

Political Resocialization The active effort by government to transform society's political culture. Political resocialization is common during radical revolutions (such as Maoist China's) or after a mobilized country has suffered a defeat in war (as in the postwar de-Nazification efforts in Germany). (**Ch. 3**)

Political Socialization The process of creating a shared political culture among the members of a political system, typically from one generation to another. It may also entail changes over time that lead to a gradual transformation of the culture. (**Chs. 1, 3**)

Political Subcultures The distinct political orientations of a region, a class, an ethnicity, or a race found within a larger political culture. (**Ch. 3**)

Political Underdevelopment A condition marked by lack of state and national autonomy, weak government institutions, weak political parties, limited opportunities for popular political participation and articulation, and instability. (**Ch. 14**)

Politico Model An approach to representation in which the legislator alternately represents constituents in accordance with the delegate model and the trustee model (see definitions), depending on the nature of the issue and the degree of public concern about it. (**Ch. 7**)

Politics The process of making collective decisions in a community, society, or group through the application of influence and power. (**Ch. 1**)

Popular Consultation A regularized process through which citizens can make known their preferences regarding governmental policies and decisions: a key component of democracy. (**Ch. 1**)

Populist (Parties) Political parties that try to build a broad electoral coalition of working-class, middle-class, and, sometimes, business-community voters, often by promising a wide range of government programs that would benefit each sector of that coalition. (**Ch. 5**)

Positive Law Laws made by governments; normally contrasted with "natural" law. (**Ch. 9**)

Postmaterialism A somewhat distinctive set of political orientations common to many individuals in industrial democracies who were politically socialized during the era of postwar affluence. Postmaterialists tend to be somewhat less concerned with ideology and with economic issues and more concerned with issues such as civil liberties, grassroots political participation, the environment, and civil liberties. (**Ch. 3**)

Postmodernism Advocates of postmodernism can be found in many disciplines. In political science, postmodernism is a reaction to what its advocates see as excessive faith in the certainty and objectivity of scientific method. Believing that all researchers "construct" their own reality as they analyze data, postmodernists argue that scientific methods can only rarely generate useful findings. (**Ch. 1**)

Postwar Settlement An unspoken agreement between Europe's labor or socialist parties and allied labor unions, on the one hand, and conservative parties and the business community, on the other. The right agreed to accept a welfare state in return for the left's agreement to abide by the ground rules of the free-market system. (**Ch. 11**)

Power Elite The name given to the set of forces that, in C. Wright Mills's interpretation, dominates American society; it consists of the leaders of the military, corporate, and political establishments. (**Ch. 6**)

PRD *See* Party of the Democratic Revolution.

Presidential "Character" Developed in the study of the U.S. presidency, the idea that the behavior of individual presidents is largely determined by basic elements of their personalities and character. (**Ch. 10**)

Presidentialism Concentration of political power in the hands of the national president. (**Ch. 15**)

Presidential System A system of executive–legislative relations in which the chief executive is elected independently of the members of the legislature. (**Ch. 7**)

President's Cabinet The secretaries of the cabinet-level departments in the executive branch of the U.S. government. (**Ch. 10**)

PPP (Parity Purchasing Power) A calculation of each country's Gross Domestic Product, computed by converting the GDP into purchasing power parity (PPP), that is by calculating what that GDP could buy in that country. This method is considered a more accurate measure of a country's economic size and its per capita income than the traditional calculation based on currency exchange rates. (**Ch. 14**)

PR *See* Proportional Representation.

PRI *See* Institutional Revolutionary Party.

Primitive Communism The first stage of "pre-history" in Marxist theory. According to Marx, in the most primitive settings, there was no ownership of land or class oppression, because the productivity was too low to allow anyone enough time to manage slaves or defend land. (Ch. 2)

Primaries Elections held to select candidates for a general election. (Ch. 10)

Princelings Children of high-ranking Chinese government and Communist Party officials who use their connections and privileged position to enrich themselves and gain power in the growing private sector. (Ch. 13)

Privatize (Privatization) Selling state-owned enterprises (such as petroleum companies or electric power) to the private sector through the sale of stock. *See also* Reprivatize. (Chs. 11, 12)

Proletariat The Marxist word used to describe the working class. The proletariat were viewed by Karl Marx as the greatest victims of capitalist exploitation and, hence, the ones who would bring the communist revolution to fruition. (Ch. 12)

Proportional Representation (PR) An electoral system in which parties receive seats in the legislature in proportion to the share of the popular vote they receive. Voters choose between party lists in larger, multi-member districts, rather than choosing a particular candidate. (Chs. 4, 11)

Public Opinion Polls Data on the opinions, demographic characteristics, and vote choices of citizens; nearly always estimated by gathering information about a sample of the larger population of citizens. (Ch. 4)

Public Schools The term used to describe Great Britain's most elite private schools (pre-university). The meaning of term *public* here is totally different from its meaning in reference to U.S. schools. (Ch. 11)

Rational Choice An approach to political theory distinguished by its application of economic principles, particularly the assumption that individuals seek their own interests in making political decisions. (Chs. 1, 6)

Rational-Legal Authority The authority that a leader enjoys when his or her actions are consistent with established legal principles. (Ch. 8)

Realism An approach to international relations that emphasizes the role of national interest in explaining the causes of war and conflict. (Ch. 16)

Red Capitalists Chinese business-people that belong to the Communist Party (CCP). Many of them used their Party membership as a tool for acquiring a privatized business or for gaining economic favors from the government. They are also referred to as "Red-Hat businessmen." (Ch. 13)

Red Faction That faction of Chinese Communist Party leadership in the 1960s and 1970s that favored

assigning all leadership and management positions in society to those individuals who proved themselves most committed to Maoist, communist ideology. (Ch. 13)

Red Guards Young people who became the shock troops of China's Cultural Revolution and helped enforce its terror. (Ch. 13)

Red-Hat Businessmen *See* Red Capitalists.

Redistricting The process of redrawing the boundaries of legislative districts; necessary to avoid malapportionment as populations grow at different rates in different areas. (Ch. 4)

Representative Authority The authority that a leader enjoys when it is perceived that he or she is representative of the "people" or the "majority." (Ch. 8)

Reprivatize To take a firm or industry that had once been privately owned, then nationalized by the state, and resell it back to the private sector. *See also* Privatize. (Ch. 11)

Responsible Parties Parties that can demand discipline from members elected to a legislature, who almost always vote in accordance with the party's stance. (Ch. 7)

Right-Wing (Rightist) *See* Leftist (Left-Wing) Political Parties, Unions. **Roe v. Wade** A landmark U.S. Supreme Court decision in 1973 establishing that it is unconstitutional for states to make abortion illegal. A reversal of *Roe v. Wade* would permit states to criminalize abortion services, but it would not require such legislation. (Ch. 2)

Routines Patterns of bureaucratic activity that become established. (Ch. 8)

Rule Adjudication The process of applying governmental rules to individual cases. (Ch. 1)

Rule Execution The process of implementing or carrying out policy decisions. (Ch. 1)

Rule Making The process of establishing laws, orders, edicts, regulations, and other authoritative acts by government. (Ch. 1)

Self-Help The idea that in the international system, states cannot rely on protection provided by a higher power (as citizens can rely on government to protect them from criminals). (Ch. 16)

Shays's Rebellion An uprising in Massachusetts in 1786–1787 challenging the foreclosures of farm mortgages and demanding government action to improve the position of debtors. (Ch. 10)

Siloviki This group is widely considered the most powerful of several contending factions within the Kremlin's inner circle. Composed primarily of former officers from the KGB, the FSB (the KGB's successor), and the military, many of its leaders were colleagues of

Vladimir Putin in the KGB and/or come from Putin's home city of St. Petersburg. (**Ch.** 12)

Shock Therapy Drastic government measures designed to reduce rampant inflation, large budget deficits, and troublesome trade deficits. Typically, shock treatment involves currency devaluation, slashes in public spending, layoffs of public employees, restraints on wages, and other painful measures that, at least in the short run, reduce popular living standards. (**Ch.** 12)

Single-Member Districts An electoral system in which each electoral district has one representative in the legislature; sometimes called "winner-take-all" because, in contrast to proportional representation systems, parties receiving fewer votes than the winner get no representation from that district. (**Ch.** 4)

Social Capital The density of associational involvement (belonging to groups ranging from church choirs to the League of Women Voters) in a town, region, or country, and the norms and social trust that these group activities produce. (**Ch.** 3)

Social Class *See* Socioeconomic Status.

Social Democrats Political parties and their supporters who adhere to a non-Marxist, moderate form of socialism. (**Ch.** 5)

Social Mobility Movement by individuals or families up or down a society's social class ladder. The level of "upward social mobility" in a country indicates how easy or difficult it is for a lower-class or middle-class person or family to move up to a higher class status by virtue of education, professional advancement or the like. (**Ch.** 11)

Socialism The fourth and final stage of "prehistory" in Marxist ideology; in this stage, following a revolution by the workers exploited under capitalism, the state is governed in the interests of the workers; also an ideology advocating social equality, public ownership of industry, and a lesser role for private property. In the non-communist world (especially Europe) socialism has a different, more moderate meaning. *See* Socialist (Party) and Social Democrats. (**Ch.** 2)

Socialist (Parties) In Western Europe where socialist parties are most influential and often govern, the terms *socialist* and *socialism* have shed the Marxist meaning found in the previous definition of socialism. Instead, they have become left-of-center, democratic parties that favor working class and middle-class economic interests and a somewhat more active state. Often used interchangeably with the label *social democratic.* (**Ch.** 5)

Socioeconomic Status (SES) A person's position in society, with regard to income, educational attainment, and occupational status. (**Ch.** 4)

SOE (State-Owned Enterprise) A firm, primarily in industrial manufacturing, still owned by the communist government. The term is used especially regarding Chinese firms of this kind. (**Ch.** 13)

State Capitalism An economic system in which most of the economy is owned and managed by private enterprise but the state controls important segments (such as Mexico's giant petroleum industry) and uses its economic wealth and political power to help direct the economy. (**Ch.** 15)

Statutory Interpretation The process of deciding how statutes apply to particular contexts; normally a task of courts. (**Ch.** 9)

Statutory Law The body of law created by acts of the legislature; distinct from provisions in constitutional law, law made by judges, and administrative regulations. (**Ch.** 9)

Suffrage The right to vote or the exercise of that right. (**Ch.** 11)

Superpowers States whose military strength is of a higher order than that of all but the other superpowers. (**Ch.** 16)

Symbolic Leader One who serves as the unifying symbol of the nation; a key function of modern chief executives. (**Ch.** 8)

Technical Responsibility The idea that bureaucrats may be controlled by their own sense of professional standards, even when public control is weak or absent. (**Ch.** 8)

Techno-Enthusiasts Analysts who believe that the ICT revolution (the Internet, text messaging, YouTube etc.) has had a beneficial effect on the political socialization of young adults in the United States and other advanced democracies. The term is also used to describe people who are enthusiastic about other new technologies. (**Ch.** 3)

Thatcherism The philosophy of the British Conservative Party's right wing as espoused by former Prime Minister Margaret Thatcher. Thatcherites rejected much of the welfare state and sought substantial reductions of state intervention in the free market. (**Ch.** 11)

Third Wave of Democracy The most recent world-wide surge of transitions to democracy (1974-the present). Earlier waves rook place in 1828–1926 and 1943–1962.

Third World A category of nations in Africa, Asia, Latin America, and the Middle East that share two primary characteristics: they are politically and/or economically less developed; and they are neither industrialized democracies (the First World) nor former members of the Soviet–Eastern European bloc of communist nations (the Second World). The term "Third World" is used interchangeably with "developing nations" and "less-developed countries" (LDCs). (Ch. 14)

Tiananmen Square Located near Beijing's imperial Heavenly City, it has been the locale of major political gatherings in communist China. In 1989 it was the center of student pro-democracy demonstrations, and the June 4 massacre there made it a symbol of China's ongoing political repression. (Ch. 13)

Tories Members or supporters of the British Conservative Party. (Ch. 11)

Totalitarian Government (System, Regime) A form of authoritarian (non-democratic) government in which the government exercises near-total control over all forms of political activity and organized societal activity. Such extreme control is very rare and perhaps only Nazi Germany, the USSR under Stalin, and China under Mao exercised it. (Chs. 1, 5, 12, 13)

Traditional Authority The authority that derives from a leader's embodiment of long-standing, widely accepted social and political traditions. (Ch. 8)

Traditional Society A society that tends to stress long-standing beliefs; evaluations of individuals based on their ethnicity, class, or other innate qualities rather than on their abilities; and other pre-modern social values. (Ch. 14)

Trial Courts The lower of the two basic levels of courts in most judicial systems. The evidence pertaining to a case is presented in trial courts, whereas appellate courts normally rule on claims that trial courts made errors of law or procedure. *See also* Appellate Courts. (Ch. 9)

Trustee Model An approach to representation in which the representative acts in accordance with his or her independent judgment, regardless of the wishes of the constituency that elected him or her. (Ch. 7)

Two-and-One-Half-Party System A national party system in which two parties are predominant but a third party presents a significant challenge, as in Great Britain. (Ch. 5)

Two-Party Systems A national party system in which the same two parties regularly receive a total of at least 75 percent of the votes (but neither of them receives as much as 65 percent). (Ch. 5)

Vanguard Party A term used by Vladimir Lenin to describe the Communist Party as an enlightened elite acting in the best interests of the working class. (Ch. 12)

Voluntary Quotas Quotas that are not legally required but rather are introduced voluntarily by individual political parties. (Ch. 5)

Vertical Power Russian President Vladimir Putin's efforts to concentrate political power in the hands of the federal government and, in turn, in his own hands. (Ch. 12)

Vote of No Confidence A vote by the Parliament expressing its unwillingness to support the prime minister and his or her cabinet. (Ch. 11)

Voter Turnout A measure of how many eligible voters actually vote in a given election. (Ch. 4)

Warlords Regional military leaders who exercised much of the local power in the Chinese imperial era and later resisted the KMT's nationalist revolution. (Ch. 13)

Watergate Refers to the wide-ranging patterns of illegal and abusive activities of the Nixon administration during 1972–1974. The Watergate is the name of an office and apartment building in Washington, DC, in which a burglary associated with the Nixon reelection effort took place. (Ch. 10)

Welfare State The arrangement of public services, regulations, and programs of income redistribution that are established to provide a basic standard of living to all members of society. (Chs. 2, 11)

Zapatista A member of the contemporary revolutionary group in the Mexican state of Chiapas known as the EZLN (Zapatista Army of National Liberation). They were named after the legendary hero of the Mexican Revolution (1910-1920), Emiliano Zapata. (Ch. 15)

Zipper-Style Quota An electoral system for a legislature or parliament that is based on proportional representation and the introduction of quotas for women or other underrepresented groups. Women candidates are given a guaranteed share (often 30 percent) of candidates on the party list and are alternated from the top of the list (those who are most likely to win seats) to the bottom in accordance with that quota. *See also* Proportional Representation. (Ch. 5)

INDEX